THE Boundary Waters *wilderness*

ECOSYSTEM

The University of Minnesota Press

gratefully acknowledges the generous financial support

of the Boundary Waters Wilderness Foundation,

Kenneth O. Johnson,

Donald L. Spotts,

and the Heinselman family.

Miron Heinselman

THE Boundary Waters *wilderness* ECOSYSTEM

University of Minnesota Press

Minneapolis & London

Published by the University of Minnesota Press
III Third Avenue South, Suite 290
Minneapolis, MN 55401–2520

First paperback printing, 1999

Printed in the United States of America on acid-free paper
Book and cover design by Diane Gleba Hall

LIBRARY OF CONGRESS CATALOGING-IN-PUBLICATION DATA

Heinselman, Miron L.
    The Boundary Waters Wilderness ecosystem / Miron Heinselman.
        p.   cm.
    Includes bibliographical references (p.   ) and index.
    ISBN 0-8166-2804-1 (hc)   ISBN 0-8166-2805-X (pbk)
    1. Natural history—Minnesota—Boundary Waters Canoe Area.
    2. Ecology—Minnesota—Boundary Waters Canoe Area.
    3. Boundary Waters Canoe Area (Minn.)   I. Title.
    QH105.M55H43   1996   95-50347
    508.776'7—dc20

The University of Minnesota is an equal-opportunity educator and employer.

Contents

Foreword

H. E. Wright Jr.

M. L. Heinselman had two passions, which he pursued with equal vigor during the last four decades of his life. The first was to gain a full understanding of the intricacies of the natural conifer forest ecosystem as represented by the Boundary Waters Canoe Area Wilderness (BWCAW) of northeastern Minnesota. As a field ecologist with the North Central Forest Experiment Station of the U.S. Forest Service, he cut his teeth on black spruce ecology and then on the vast patterned peatlands of northern Minnesota, where black spruce thrives. Working with a completely pristine system, he was able to develop a picture of peatland development that has led to modern concepts of how such a blanket peatland is controlled in its patterns by gradual water movements.

The peatland studies led Heinselman to a greater challenge—deciphering the ecological forces that control the composition of the upland forest of northeastern Minnesota, where water movement plays a minor role compared to such factors as soil, topography, aspect, and especially fire. Fire can radically change the mosaic of the forest composition through burning old stands and allowing new growth to emerge, and it was clear that the fire suppression since 1910 was having an unnatural effect. This perception encouraged him to map all the forest stands of the uncut portions of the Boundary Waters area, with the aid of aerial photographs, and to determine the dates of fires by tree ring counts on fire scars. Many summers of field work, accompanied by his wife or other assistants, opened his eyes to the many other intricacies of the natural ecosystem of northern forests and led to his ambition to write it all down.

Heinselman's second passion was to promote the protection of the Boundary Waters so that others might enjoy it the way he had. Although the area had been incorporated in the Wilderness Act of 1964, an ambiguous clause had been inserted that was interpreted by the Forest Service to permit logging and motorized travel, although these activities would seem to be incompatible with the principles loftily stated in the preamble of the Wilderness Act. When the Environmental Policy Act was passed in 1972, the opportunity came to challenge the renewal of timber sales in the Boundary Waters. This led to injunctions against logging until the Congress could clarify the ambiguities of the Wilderness Act. Here is where Heinselman shifted his considerable energies from forest ecology to wilderness advocacy. With the help of many others, he built a national advocacy group, and legislation was passed in 1978 that has since protected the BWCAW from logging, mining, and most motorized travel.

Heinselman has succeeded in expressing his two passions in this book, which he completed just before his death. It has the scientific prose that characterizes his several widely respected ecological articles and reviews, and at the same time, it has the easy flow of writing suitable for the more casual reader. Throughout the pages, one senses the sincerity of the message, and one develops a picture of the interaction of the complex biological and physical processes by which natural ecosystems have functioned over time—including the recognition of fire as a major force in shaping the nature of the forest ecosystem. He would be pleased to learn that Forest Service managers are slowly recognizing the natural role of fire and are helping to educate the public. This book will provide them with insights that are soundly based and clearly expressed.

Editing of the lengthy manuscript was a labor of love for me, for I was pleased to absorb more of the knowledge and lore of the BWCAW. Deleting or reducing many paragraphs of elegant or informative prose was an unpleasant task, but necessary to sharpen the message or simplify it for the less dedicated. I was aided by several specialists who reviewed particular chapters, notably Donald Baker on climate, Lewis Ohmann and John Pastor on forest composition, Peter Jordan on mammals, Janet Green on birds, James Underhill on fishes, Guy Gibbon on prehistoric peoples, and David Lime and Kevin Proescholdt on visitor usage. The entire manuscript was read by David Foster, William Baker, Charles Wick, and Janet Green, and special efforts were made in organizing the illustrations and tables by Frances Heinselman, Ann Stolee, and Russell Heinselman. All of the colored photographs were provided from the collections of J. Arnold Bolz. Barbara Coffin aided in the early stages of text preparation, and Mary Keirstead in later. Completion of the book is a tribute to the dedication of the Heinselman family and to bequests from the Friends of the Boundary Waters Wilderness.

Preface

The Boundary Waters, the Quetico-Superior Country, the Canoe Country, the Voyageurs' Highway, the Boundary Waters Canoe Area Wilderness! These names evoke visions of serene lakes, thundering rapids, endless ranges of ancient bedrock hills, dark forests of pine, fir, and spruce, the eerie cry of the loon echoing among the islands, the distant howl of timber wolves on a far-off ridge, campfires, friendships, and the vast solitude of the northern wilderness.

The Boundary Waters Canoe Area Wilderness is a million-acre unit of the National Wilderness Preservation System administered by the U.S. Forest Service. It stretches 115 miles along the Minnesota-Ontario border north of Lake Superior and is adjoined on the north by Ontario's Quetico Provincial Park and at its western tip almost by Voyageurs National Park. Together these three areas encompass nearly 2.5 million acres of incomparable forested lake land. This book focuses on the Boundary Waters Canoe Area Wilderness, but because of their proximity and similar environments, much of the information applies in principle to Quetico and Voyageurs as well.

More than 1,000 island-studded lakes, interconnected by hundreds of miles of streams and portages, are present within the Boundary Waters Canoe Area Wilderness. The wilderness contains the largest contiguous areas of virgin forest remaining in the eastern United States—half of its forested landscape has never been logged. The animal part of the ecosystem is also remarkably intact with most of the natural prey and predator species, making for remarkably complete food chains. Many of the mammals, birds, and fish that are present here are absent, rare, or endangered elsewhere in the contiguous 48 states. Yet half of the forested landscape has been logged, some of it very recently. Fire suppression has drastically changed the natural disturbance regime. Fish species have been introduced in many lakes, and the woodland caribou was extirpated about 1925, although individuals still wander into the region from Canada.

I fell in love with the north woods as a child in Duluth, Minnesota. It was a love fostered by many family camping, fishing, and hunting trips and by countless days roaming the wild range of cliffs overlooking Lake Superior near Duluth. I was fascinated by the many kinds of mammals, birds, fish, and insects, by the variety of trees, shrubs, flowers, mosses, and lichens, each with its characteristic habitat. I mused over the meaning of fire scars on the trunks of ancient pines. Babbling brooks, silent rivers, thundering rapids, waterfalls, and shimmering lakes cast their spell over me. I was awed by such things as the silent arrival of winter's first snowfall and the sparkling brilliance and numbing cold of a long clear winter night.

I was also struck by the great blackened pine stumps that dotted many a northern pasture, by abandoned farms and crumbling log cabins, and by the vast young forests of aspen and birch that clothed the new stump lands along the sand trails of the north. At age 11 I took my first long trip into the Boundary Waters, to Lac La Croix. Here we camped in a grove of ancient red and white pines, and I began to appreciate the changes Western peoples had wrought on most of the north. Later I bought a canoe, an Old Town 15-foot lightweight, and in 1939, 1940, and 1941 George Collier and I took long canoe trips in the Superior-Quetico wilderness.

These experiences ultimately shaped my career. After World War II, I returned to the University of Minnesota to take a degree in forestry. Then came 26 years of research with the U.S. Forest Service's North Central Forest Experiment Station, mostly in northern Minnesota. Over the years I actually pursued several questions posed by childhood observation. Finally, from 1966 to 1974, I mapped the remaining virgin forests of the Boundary Waters Canoe Area Wilderness, studied their origin, mapped their fire history, and conducted a field-mapping project and historical study of logged areas within the wilderness.

My wife, Fran, also loves the wilderness, and together with our two children we explored the north from one end of the continent to the other. We took our first Boundary Waters canoe trip soon after we were married, and later canoed parts of the Canadian north, even a remote region west of Hudson Bay not far south of the arctic tree line. But like our departed friend Sig Olson, we still sense a charm in the Boundary Waters matched nowhere else. Now we have a small home near Ely and spend as much time in the north as our activities allow. Canoe trips, fall hikes in the woods, and snowshoeing treks in winter are experiences we look forward to each passing year.

In the 1950s my concern over renewed logging and road building and the spread of motorized recreation in the Superior roadless areas (as they were then designated) made me realize that if the Boundary Waters was such a major force in my life, it also deserved political support. I became involved in endless efforts to protect the Superior-Quetico wilderness, an experience that brought me into contact with thousands of wonderful Boundary Waters devotees. That story is too long to tell here. But one of the most pleasant discoveries was the realization that my insatiable curiosity about the Boundary Waters ecosystem was shared

by most Boundary Waters adventurers! Now, because of the encouragement of many friends and the editors of the University of Minnesota Press, this book is my effort to share what I have learned along the way.

My hope is that the book will prove an accurate and fairly detailed source of information about the total Boundary Waters wilderness ecosystem—its history, landscape, climate, forests, bogs, lakes, wildlife, and fish—and also a reliable and usable field guide to locating and understanding some of its fascinating natural features and historic sites. The text is not purely descriptive. Several chapters delve into the workings of various natural processes and into the historical and evolutionary roots of the present landscape and its plant and animal communities. The word ecosystem implies a unified, holistic view of both the physical environment and all of its living organisms. This is the viewpoint I have tried to project, because one cannot really understand any part of the web of life by itself.

I have attempted to make the book useful to Boundary Waters visitors with a deep interest in nature, as well as to present and future managers, staff people, and seasonal employees of the Superior National Forest, Quetico Provincial Park, and Voyageurs National Park, to scientists and graduate students engaged in research in the area or in similar ecosystems, and to educators and their students who may be using the Boundary Waters as a field laboratory. To communicate with such a diverse audience, I have avoided most of the technical jargon of ecology. Where important concepts or terms must be included, explanations or definitions are given. Common names are used for plants and animals except for certain important plants that have no well-known colloquial names. References are cited by author and date where credit should be acknowledged, or where sources might be helpful to readers. A complete listing of cited sources is in the literature cited. An index is included to help those seeking information on specific places, subjects, plants, animals, and so forth. For professionals already familiar with many aspects of the region, the chapters on the fire and logging history and on the role of fire in the ecosystem and the maps of fire and logging history and stand origins may prove most useful.

If I can help you see a bit more of the fascinating diversity, complexity, and beauty of the natural systems of the Boundary Waters, and increase your understanding of the changes we have already imposed on this remarkable region, then some of my goals will have been achieved. For the professional, if portions of this book or its maps are useful in the administration of an area or in research or teaching, then another goal will have been met. Greater knowledge also tends to increase our respect for the intricate relationships of natural systems, and I hope such knowledge will strengthen your resolve to cherish and protect the Boundary Waters ecosystem. Public understanding, loving care, and eternal vigilance are needed to safeguard this remarkable ecosystem from the rising pressures of our technological world, and to help restore as best we can those areas and ecosystem elements already damaged or lost through past actions.

January 1993
M. L. Heinselman

Acknowledgments

Although Miron (Bud) Heinselman had finished the manuscript for this book at the time of his death in 1993, the process of publication had not been started. We have labored to ensure that his original content has been preserved to as great an extent as possible. We have edited only for form and readability. The pictures and maps are, to the best of our knowledge, ones that Bud intended to accompany his manuscript. We are grateful to the publisher for providing reviewers and a copy editor. We offer special mention to Dr. H. E. Wright Jr. for his comprehensive editing of the manuscript. To all of those who reviewed the manuscript for Bud—we know that he valued your efforts, and we offer our thanks on his behalf. We are grateful to the family of J. Arnold Bolz for the privilege of including his photos. To the readers—treasure this book. It is a labor of love.

Frances Heinselman
Russell Heinselman
Ann Heinselman Stolee

Introduction

Three contiguous legally protected wilderness units lie along the Minnesota-Ontario border north of Lake Superior (figure 1.1). The Boundary Waters Canoe Area Wilderness (BWCAW) is administered by the U.S. Forest Service as a unit of the National Wilderness Preservation System. Voyageurs National Park, which almost adjoins the BWCAW at its western tip, is administered by the U.S. Department of the Interior. Quetico Provincial Park is a unit of the Parks Branch, Ontario Ministry of Natural Resources. This book focuses heavily on the BWCAW because that is where my ecological research was concentrated, but much of my discussion of the BWCAW applies in principle to Quetico and Voyageurs even where they are not specifically mentioned.

The vastness of this wilderness region is difficult to grasp unless you have traversed its length and breadth. The two legally protected adjoining ecosystems on the Minnesota side of the international boundary extend for 150 airline miles or about 220 miles of waterway. The width of this protected region in Minnesota ranges from a few miles to 28 miles. On the Ontario side, Quetico adjoins the BWCAW for about 80 miles of waterway and stretches northward more than 40 miles. The total international wilderness is more than 60 miles south to north at its widest point. The combined protected area of these three reserves is 3,859 square miles—an area larger than Yellowstone National Park (table 1.1).

The BWCAW contains more than 1,000 lakes over 10 acres in area, hundreds of small ponds, many miles of streams, about 1,300 miles of canoe routes (lakes, streams, and portages), and thousands of miles of shoreline. Voyageurs contains three of the largest border lakes—Rainy, Namakan, and Kabetogama—plus dozens of smaller interior and border lakes. Quetico contains even more lakes, streams, and canoe routes than the BWCAW. The total international wilderness contains nearly 3,000 lakes. Hundreds of miles of hiking and cross-country skiing trails also exist in the BWCAW and Voyageurs. The BWCAW has about 2,000 established campsites, each with a fire grate and pit toilet. Voyageurs also has established campsites. In Quetico visitors are not required to use established campsites.

The ecosystems of these three wilderness units are as remarkable in character as in their vastness. They contain large areas of landscapes and vegetation with little human disturbance, as well as a nearly full complement of native prey and predator species among the mammal, bird, and fish populations. They also have extensive areas of varied terrestrial, aquatic, and peatland environments and a climate marked by large seasonal variations in temperature, radiation, precipitation, and storminess.

About half the land of the BWCAW and Quetico still supports unlogged virgin forest, covering about 1,000,000 acres (1,560 square miles) in several large contiguous areas.

Figure 1.1 / Three contiguous protected wilderness units on the Minnesota-Ontario border. (Map by Stephen Lime, Department of Forest Resources, University of Minnesota.)

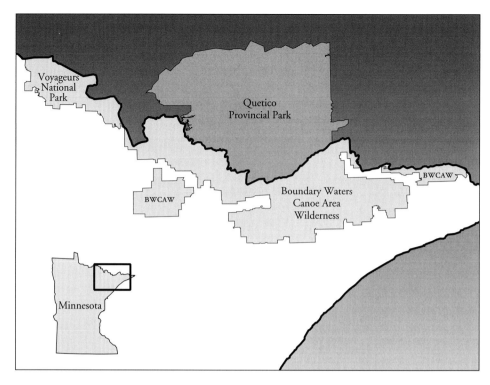

Those in the BWCAW comprise the largest tracts of virgin forest in the eastern United States. A vast display of forest age classes and vegetation types reflects centuries of interplay among forest, environment, and fire. Ancient red and white pines still keep their lonely vigil over the very waterways that were home to countless generations of Native Americans and saw the canoe brigades of the voyageurs two centuries ago. The logged areas are quite different, but they too have their own interesting histories. The contrasts between logged and virgin areas hold many lessons for plant and animal ecologists.

Table 1.1 / Total protected ecosystem area in the Boundary Waters region

Unit	Acres	Square miles	Square kilometers
Quetico Provincial Park	1,183,141	1,849	4,788
BWCA Wilderness	1,084,000	1,694	4,387
Voyageurs National Park	218,035	341	882
Total area of all 3 units	2,485,176	3,884	10,057

Herbivores such as moose, white-tailed deer, black bear, beaver, porcupine, snowshoe hare, red squirrel, chipmunk, and several other small rodents occur along with a nearly full complement of their native mammalian predators: the gray wolf, black bear, red fox, lynx, fisher, pine marten, mink, otter, weasel, and others. The year-round resident bird population includes raven, pileated woodpecker, gray jay, chickadee, ruffed and spruce grouse, and the great horned owl. Summer residents include several species of warblers, white-throated sparrow, red-eyed vireo, cedar waxwing, bald eagle, common loon, merganser, black duck, and osprey. The fish population includes lake trout, walleye, northern pike, smallmouth bass, largemouth bass, perch, crappie, whitefish, sucker, sturgeon, burbot, and many species of minnows.

Major scientific and educational values exist in a natural ecosystem of such vast scale. We still have much to learn about the evolution and workings of natural systems, and the Boundary Waters has already been the focus of major research in plant and animal ecology, animal behavior, paleoecology, geology, fire history, and limnology. Many colleges, youth camps, and related groups use the region for natural-history education each year. A region such as this is a storehouse of genetic resources—germ plasm—where we should maintain as much as possible of the natural diversity that existed in this part of the world before settlement by European people began little more than a century ago.

All of these attractions have drawn increasing numbers of recreational users in recent decades. Each year the BWCAW hosts some 200,000 visitors, who spend over 1.5 million visitor days in the area. The numbers for Quetico are lower but still large. In the last decade most visitors have traveled by canoe, on foot, or on skis or snowshoes. Motorized visitor travel is prohibited in Quetico, and motorboats are allowed on only a few lakes in the BWCAW. In Voyageurs all the big lakes are open to motorboat and snowmobile use, but these lakes are large enough that reasonable isolation is still possible in many areas. In Quetico and the BWCAW, real solitude is still achievable for those who penetrate far into the interior, especially in fall and winter.

Protecting the Boundary Waters region from commercial development and mechanized recreation did not come quickly or easily. The Boundary Waters region as we know it today arose out of an 80-year struggle to protect its natural features and wilderness recreation potential.

The Climate of the Boundary Waters

The climate of the Boundary Waters region is a product of its location near the center of North America, with long cold winters, short warm summers, moderate precipitation, and strong seasonal changes. The highly variable weather can be attributed to frequent excursions of the continental polar air mass into the area, especially in winter, invasions of warm moist Gulf air from the southeast, especially in summer, fall, and early winter, and invasions of dry Pacific air.

Temperature

Average and extreme temperature records for the Boundary Waters area are shown in figure 2.1. The greatest annual range (152°F) is at International Falls, which also has the greatest monthly range (114°F for March). Temperature changes of 50 to 60°F within a few days occur in most years. Even summer temperature variations of 40 to 50°F within two or three days occur in many years. March and November have the most extreme short-term temperature changes.

A lack of reliable long-term climatic data for the eastern BWCAW obscures important differences caused by proximity to Lake Superior. Gunflint Lake is the only available inland eastern station, and its data are too recent and sporadic to tell us much. Gunflint is also farther from Lake Superior than much of the eastern BWCAW. The effect of the lake on temperatures varies seasonally (Baker, Kuehnast, and Zandlo 1985). In November, December, and January the average monthly maximum is several degrees warmer at Gunflint Lake than at International Falls (figure 2.2), because Lake Superior almost never freezes over entirely, and warms the air above it. This effect is even stronger along the North Shore, where, at Grand Marais winter minimums are often 10 to 15°F higher than inland. In summer the effect is reversed, as the icy waters of Lake Superior cool nearby inland areas. Summer temperatures also drop off northeastward toward Hudson Bay, making average July temperatures near Pickerel and French lakes in Quetico about 2°F cooler than in Voyageurs and the Lac La Croix region of the BWCAW (Ontario Ministry of Natural Resources 1977).

Winter in the Boundary Waters is a succession of long periods of clear, dry, cold arctic-air-mass weather, interrupted usually by shorter periods of cloudy, warmer, and often snowy weather as storms track through the region. Thaws may occur in any winter month, sometimes with clear, mild Pacific air. The coldest weather often comes on the heels of major winter storms, when the mercury may plummet to -30 or -45°F after a mild day, and subzero cold may persist for several days or weeks. During these arctic outbreaks the temperature may not rise above zero even at midday. Occasionally it fails to rise above -20° or even -25°F.

Figure 2.1 / *(right)* Regional extreme temperatures for the Boundary Waters region. The greatest annual range is at International Falls in the west. (Data from Baker, Kuehnast, and Zandlo 1985.)

Figure 2.2 / *(below, right)* Average monthly temperatures for three stations in the Boundary Waters region. Note the higher winter temperatures in the east (Gunflint Lake) as compared to in the west (International Falls), caused by the lake effect.

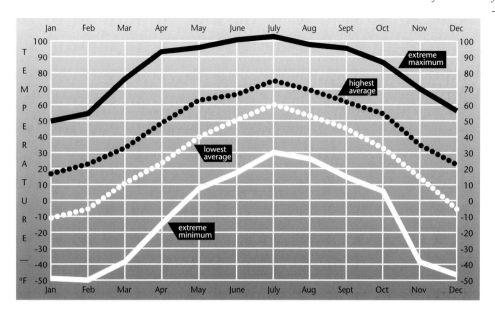

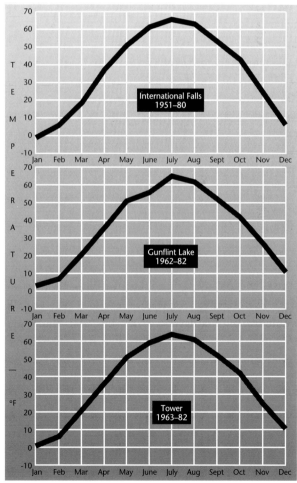

Summer is a succession of hot and often humid days when Gulf air masses persist over the region, broken by frequent episodes of clear, dry, and cool arctic air. During hot spells, especially in July and August, the daytime temperature may reach 85 to 90°F, and rarely, 95 to 100°F. At night during hot spells the mercury may fall no lower than 65 to 75°F. Even in midsummer, a stretch of cold, drizzly days or clear, cool days may have daytime temperatures of 50 to 60°F. Nighttime temperatures of 40 to 45°F are not uncommon, and temperatures near or below freezing occasionally occur even in July and August.

The growing season for most native trees, shrubs, herbs, and mosses is not strictly limited to the frost-free period, shown in figure 2.3 for three localities in the Boundary Waters region. Late-spring frosts can severely reduce the successful flowering and fruiting of numerous species. Plants, such as blueberries, that flower in May and early June are especially vulnerable. Frosts at this time of year are strongly influenced by local environments. On cold, clear nights killing frosts may occur in low or open areas, while ridgetops, south-facing slopes, forested areas, lakeshores, and islands may escape.

Fall freeze-up of lakes usually begins in late October on small ponds on cold nights when the temperature drops into the 20s (Baker and Strub 1965). Large and deep lakes usually freeze over one to three weeks later than small and

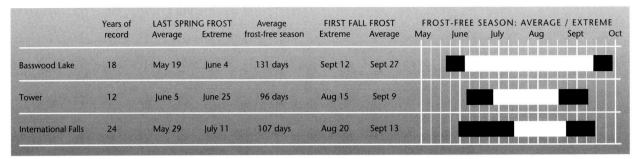

	Years of record	LAST SPRING FROST Average	LAST SPRING FROST Extreme	Average frost-free season	FIRST FALL FROST Extreme	FIRST FALL FROST Average
Basswood Lake	18	May 19	June 4	131 days	Sept 12	Sept 27
Tower	12	June 5	June 25	96 days	Aug 15	Sept 9
International Falls	24	May 29	July 11	107 days	Aug 20	Sept 13

Figure 2.3 / Average dates of latest killing frost in spring and earliest killing frost in fall, length of frost-free season, and dates of latest and earliest frost on record

shallow lakes. In most winters, permanent ice cover is established on virtually all lakes and streams by late November, but occasionally the largest and deepest lakes do not freeze over completely until early December. Freeze-up is a dramatic event, often accompanied by awesome booming, creaking, and groaning of the expanding ice, especially on the first subzero nights and days after a full ice cover is established. These sounds are one of the most impressive natural phenomena of the northern lake country.

Once ice cover is established, its thickness depends on winter temperatures and on the timing and amount of insulating snow cover. Late-winter ice thickness commonly ranges between 15 and 30 inches, except on fast-moving streams and in channels and upwelling areas of lakes. If deep snow accumulates on lake ice, its weight may push the ice below water level. Water then rises above the ice through cracks and may form a slush layer several inches thick beneath the snow. The slush creates havoc for snowshoers and skiers.

Table 2.1 / Ice-out dates for Boundary Waters region lakes

Lake	Earliest	Average	Latest
Crane	—	May 5	—
Vermilion	April 10, 1945	May 2	May 23, 1950
Fall	April 10, 1945	April 29	May 18, 1950
Mitawan	April 18, 1958	May 1	May 20, 1950
Gunflint	April 25, 1963	May 9	May 26, 1966

Sources Minneapolis *Star Tribune*, February 12, 1987; the Minnesota Weather Guide calendar, 1985; and Kuehnast, Baker, and Zandlo (1982).

Spring breakup of lakes and streams may come anytime from mid-April to late May. By early April the snow cover melts, and the ice turns dark and porous. After a narrow belt of open water appears along shorelines and islands, on a warm, windy day, the ice shifts along great rifts, which widen under the stress of winds. The average date for ice-out is near May 1 in the western Boundary Waters region and about May 5 to 10 in the east and for the larger lakes of Quetico (table 2.1).

Precipitation

In the Boundary Waters precipitation has characteristic seasonal patterns, yet with strong variations. Total annual precipitation (rain plus snowfall water equivalent) aver-

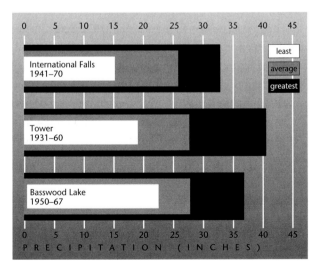

Figure 2.4 / Annual total precipitation statistics for three stations in the Boundary Waters region

ages about 27 inches in the central and eastern BWCAW, about 2 inches more than at International Falls (figure 2.4). A pronounced summer peak enhances forest growth (figure 2.5). Most snowfalls occur at temperatures well below freezing, and the water content is small. Late-winter snowpacks usually measure between 18 and 36 inches and have a water content of 4 to 6 inches. In very snowy winters snow depths might reach 40 to 50 inches, but even then the water content is only 8 or 9 inches.

The major sources of precipitation in the Boundary Waters are the Gulf air masses. Continental polar air masses are usually clear, cold, and dry. Snow and rain in the eastern Boundary Waters may be enhanced by moisture brought by winds blowing off Lake Superior. In winter, alternations of air masses are associated with the movement of low-pressure systems along characteristic paths. Large temperature drops, high winds, and blizzard conditions may accompany or follow such storms. A frequent winter storm pattern is the Alberta Clipper. These storms start as low-pressure areas along the eastern front of the Rocky Mountains in Colorado or Alberta and generate a clash of arctic and Gulf air, with resulting snow, sleet, or rain (Baker, Haines, and Strub 1967; Baker and Kuehnast 1978). In the Boundary Waters these storms often produce significant snow.

A common springtime weather phenomenon is the persistence of Hudson Bay weather. Especially in April and May, a vast area of cool, dry air may build up over the regions west and southwest of Hudson Bay, including the Boundary Waters. If the air mass is stable enough, it may block the invasion of Gulf or Pacific air masses for many days, resulting in long periods of clear, dry weather. At first the Hudson Bay air is cold, especially at night, but as the high persists, the days may become warmer, until the high finally breaks down. Humidities may be very low. Such episodes often set the stage for forest fires in May or early June.

Most prolonged heavy summer rains are generated by combinations of frontal and convective activity (Baker, Haines, and Strub 1967). If an unstable moisture-laden Gulf air mass is present, the result can be strong shifting winds, heavy rain, hail, and much dangerous lightning.

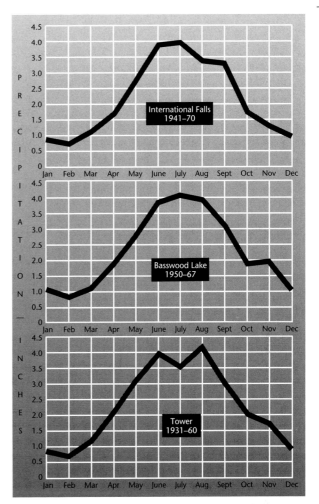

Figure 2.5 / Average monthly precipitation records for three stations in the Boundary Waters region

Such storms are often relatively local events, contributing to the usually spotty nature of summer rainfall. On average there are about 27 thunderstorms annually at some point in the Boundary Waters region (U.S. Dept. of Agriculture 1941). Spring and fall rains are more often of frontal origin, longer duration, and lower intensity, with cold drizzles marked by east, northeast, or southeast winds, sometimes lasting 24 to 36 hours. Lightning occurs mostly from mid-May to mid-September.

The degree to which total annual precipitation falls in the growing season is important biologically. In the Boundary Waters region about 41 percent of total precipitation falls in June, July, and August (Baker, Haines, and Strub

8 1967), and about 64 percent in the five months May through September (Basswood Lake data, Ahlgren 1969). The spring snowmelt usually releases 3 to 6 inches of water, mostly in April. Although much of this snowmelt runs off into lakes and streams, it normally saturates soils to a considerable depth, so the growing season begins with high soil moisture.

Snowfall and Snow Depth

Normal annual snowfall ranges from about 55 to 70 inches across the Boundary Waters region but is highly variable (figure 2.6). The lowest amounts occur in the western end of Voyageurs and in the Lake Vermilion-Trout Lake region. The highest amounts occur in the highlands of the eastern Gunflint Trail region (Baker, Haines, and Strub 1967; Kuehnast, Baker, and Zandlo 1982). Most snowfalls are light, but occasional heavy storms contribute much to the snowpack, cause significant biological effects, and create safety problems for unwary visitors. Snowstorm data for Babbitt, located south of Ely, give a picture of snowfall frequencies (Baker, Haines, and Strub 1967). From 1931 to 1960, the average annual number of snowfalls of 1 inch or more was 19. Of these storms, 83 percent resulted in falls of only 1 to 4 inches (figure 2.7).

The heaviest snowfall recorded in northeastern Minnesota for a single season through 1966 was 147.5 inches

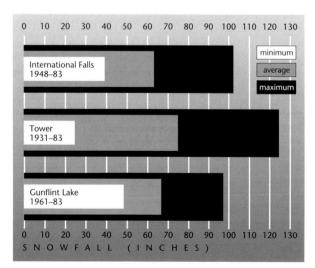

Figure 2.6 / Annual total snowfall for three stations in the Boundary Waters region

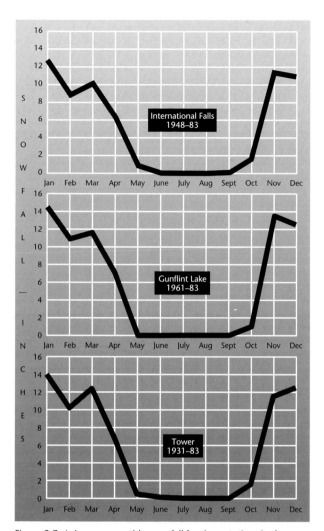

Figure 2.7 / Average monthly snowfall for three stations in the Boundary Waters region

at Pigeon River in the 1936–37 winter. The heaviest snowfall for a 24-hour period, also at Pigeon River, was 28 inches on April 4 and 5, 1933 (Baker, Haines, and Strub 1967). The Pigeon River station is in the Lake Superior snowbelt and is not typical of most of the Boundary Waters region. The great Armistice Day blizzard of November 11, 1940, produced 22 inches of snow at Orr (just south of Voyageurs) in two days (Watson 1974). Early in November 1983 approximately 24 inches of snow fell in the Crane Lake region of Voyageurs and the BWCAW. It was not a typical blizzard—the snow was wet and heavy, there was not much wind, and there was no immediate outbreak of arctic air.

Table 2.2 / Mean number of snow cover days for indicated depths and the first and last dates of 1-inch snow cover, October 1959 to May 1979 in the Boundary Waters region

Station	Average number of seasonal snow cover days					Average date of first 1-in snow cover	Average date of last 1-in snow cover
	1 in	3 in	6 in	12 in	24 in		
International Falls	145	131	113	75	13	Nov. 6	April 17
Crane Lake	150	138	121	90	25	Oct. 30	April 19
Babbitt	144	132	114	72	17	Nov. 15	April 21
Gunflint Lake	151	150	127	91	25	Nov. 7	April 20
Gunflint Trail crest	175	170	160	150	100	Nov. 1 (e)	May 5 (e)

Note e = estimated.

Source Kuehnast, Baker, and Zandlo (1982).

In fact, it thawed two days after the storm. Subzero temperatures arrived a few days later.

In most years the first measurable snowfall occurs by late October, and the last snowfall occurs in late April or early May. Permanent snow cover is usually established by mid-November, and nearly continuous snow cover remains until mid-April. The average number of days with 1 inch or more of snow cover is about 145 days in the western end of the Boundary Waters region and up to 175 days in the eastern end (table 2.2). On average, maximum snow depth occurs about March 10. Thereafter the spring snowmelt usually begins to reduce the snowpack, even though sig-

nificant snowfalls may occur much later (figure 2.8). The average late-winter snowpack is only half as deep in the western end of Voyageurs as on the highlands of the eastern BWCAW.

Humidity, Cloudiness, Evapotranspiration, and Runoff

Humidity is strongly related to the particular air mass present at any given time, and to time of day. The average relative humidity in the Boundary Waters at noon in July is about 62 percent (U.S. Dept. of Agriculture 1941), but

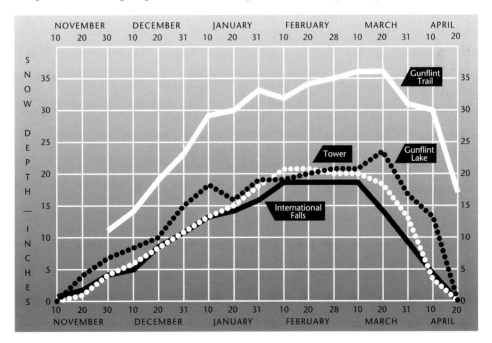

Figure 2.8 / Median snow depth in inches at 10-day intervals in the Boundary Waters region

few days represent the average. When cool, clear Canadian air masses are present in summer, the relative humidity is usually in the range of 20 to 40 percent by early afternoon. With hot, humid Gulf air, the humidity is often 65 to 95 percent even in the afternoon. Early-morning and late-evening humidities are higher in both cases.

On average about 110 clear days and about 130 cloudy days occur annually in the Boundary Waters region. In summer the area receives about 65 percent of possible sunshine. July and August have the clearest weather. Clear weather in January and February is often the coldest. The cloudiest month is often November. On average about 20 days annually have dense fog (U.S. Dept. of Agriculture 1941); foggy weather occurs especially in September and October but can occur in any season.

The amount of water running off the soil surface into lakes and streams and leaving the region as net runoff is a function of precipitation and of evaporation from living plants, soil and bedrock surfaces, and water bodies. In a forested region such as the Boundary Waters, much of this evaporation occurs as transpiration from trees, shrubs, herbs, and mosses. The total of all forms of evaporation in a region is called evapotranspiration. Recent estimates put the average annual evapotranspiration loss in the Boundary Waters at about 19 to 20 inches in the Gunflint Trail region and up to 20 to 22 inches in Voyageurs (Baker, Nelson, and Kuehnast 1979). Snowmelt runoff averages about 1 to 4 inches, and total annual runoff averages about 8 to 14 inches, with the highest amounts in the Gunflint Trail region.

Drought

For the ecosystem, one of the most crucial characteristics of the Boundary Waters climate is the periodic occurrence of severe drought. Drought can cause the death of trees and other plants, failure of berry crops, drastic lowering of stream flows and lake levels, and many other more or less direct effects. Perhaps the most significant effect historically has been indirect—forest fires. One or two months with little or no precipitation in spring or midsummer can set the stage for forest fires and cause berry crop failures of importance to wildlife. Prolonged drought extending over many months or even years can trigger major forest fires and cause widespread death of sensitive plants and animals and changes in water tables and lake levels. The great drought of the 1930s is the best documented example of prolonged drought. At most stations in northern Minnesota, total annual precipitation was below normal for most years from 1929 through 1936. The summer of 1936 saw prolonged record-breaking hot weather as well as below-normal precipitation most of the summer. The result was widespread forest fires. The years 1894 and 1976 are prime examples of severe short-term droughts that also resulted in major forest fires. In 1894, July and August were catastrophically dry, but at most stations the year as a whole ended with near- or above-normal precipitation. Virginia, for example, received only 1.67 inches of rain in July and only 0.94 inch in August, yet the annual total was 34.73 inches—bolstered by heavy rains in September and October that came too late to prevent major fires.

Origin of the Lakes and Landforms

General Physiography of the Region

The Boundary Waters region is a low plateau of modest relief, broken by a labyrinth of lakes and streams and locally by steep cliffs and endless rocky ridges. A major continental divide cuts across the eastern end of the area, separating the Hudson Bay watershed, which drains all of Quetico and Voyageurs and most of the BWCAW via the Rainy and Nelson rivers, from the Lake Superior watershed, which drains the Sawbill-Brule-Winchell region of the BWCAW via the Temperance, Cascade, and Brule rivers and the region east of South Lake via the Pigeon River.

The plateau rises quite abruptly from Lake Superior to a crest about 1,600 to 1,900 feet above sea level along the divide area from Sawbill Lake northeastward through Brule and Winchell lakes to South, Rose, Clearwater, and Mountain lakes. Here numerous ridges exceed 2,000 feet in elevation. The highest point in the entire Boundary Waters region is Eagle Mountain, located just inside the BWCAW 4 miles south of Brule Lake. Its elevation, 2,301 feet above sea level, is the highest point in Minnesota. West of the divide the plateau slopes gently westward toward Voyageurs, where Rainy Lake is only 1,107 feet above sea level. In most of the region the ridges rise only 50 to 100 feet above the lakes and streams, but in the most rugged areas of the Brule-Winchell-Gunflint Trail region, and in Quetico along the Man Lakes chain and near Kahshahpiwi Lake,

nearly vertical cliffs rise 200 to 400 feet above the lakes. Elsewhere the landscape is certainly not flat, and many bedrock ridges break off in sheer drops of 10 to 50 feet, but the skyline is nearly level.

Origins of the Preglacial Landscape

Some of the rock outcrops of the Boundary Waters are among the oldest on our planet—more than 2.7 billion years old. But the present landscape is the result of erosion, several volcanic events, and finally the work of the great continental glaciers of the Pleistocene, which retreated from the area about 10,000 years ago and whose last remnants melted away in northern Labrador only 6,000 years ago. The bedrock of the Boundary Waters is part of the vast Canadian Shield that covers northeastern North America. These rocks are all Precambrian in age, the earliest period in Earth's history, encompassing a time from about 4,500 million to 600 million years ago.

THE EARLY PRECAMBRIAN ROCKS

In the BWCAW Early Precambrian bedrock is exposed at the surface from Ely eastward to Sea Gull and Saganaga lakes, and in the vast ranges of granitic hills from Basswood Lake westward through Lac La Croix to Voyageurs and south to Vermilion and Burntside lakes. Most of the Early Precambrian rocks in the belt between Ely and Saganaga Lake belong to the steeply tilted, layered, and heavily fractured graywacke, argillite, phyllite, gneiss, and schist of the Knife Lake Group (plate 1). Most of the lakes are long, narrow, and deep and trend northeast; examples are Moose, Newfound, Knife, and Cypress. In the east around Saganaga, Sea Gull, and Alpine lakes, the granite of the Saganaga Batholith forms a more gently rolling landscape, with many shorelines featuring rock shelves.

The largest area of Early Precambrian terrane in the BWCAW is the massive Vermilion Batholith, which occupies most of the area from Basswood Lake to Lake Vermilion and north and northwestward far into Quetico and Voyageurs. Many shorelines, islands, and ridgetops show rounded exposures of the typically massive, homogeneous, pinkish gray Vermilion Granite, as along the Moose and Little Indian Sioux rivers.

In Voyageurs Park the southern third is crossed by the Vermilion Granite. Most of the Kabetogama Peninsula consists of gray biotite schist with occasional granitic zones. The far northwestern corner of the park north of Black Bay displays a belt of metamorphosed volcanic and sedimentary rocks (Ojakangas and Matsch 1982).

Most of the bedrock of Quetico is also Early Precambrian. The oldest is the Wawa Greenstone Belt, a Canadian extension of the Ely Greenstone and related rocks, found mainly in a northeast-trending belt from Birch Lake through the Man Lakes to Saganagons and Saganaga lakes. They have been radiometrically dated at more than 2.7 billion years old. These rocks are steeply tilted and folded metamorphosed sedimentaries that produce a rugged topography with long, narrow lakes, steep cliffs, and plunging shorelines.

The most abundant rocks exposed in the interior of Quetico are granite, syenite, and related rocks coextensive with the Vermilion Batholith in the BWCAW. Much of the terrain here is a maze of low rolling hills and irregular to roundish lakes and bogs, but in some areas the lakes lie in deep north-trending troughs, as in the Kahshahpiwi-Keefer chain and the Agnes, Louisa, and Silence areas. The rocks of this region are thought to have intruded the older rocks during the Kenoran Orogeny, dated at about 2.6 billion years ago.

Rocks of the Quetico Gneiss Belt are an extension of the metasedimentary schist and gneiss of Voyageurs and locally produce a landscape of low rounded ridges, although steep slopes may occur along faults. Waterways in the gneiss belt include the Maligne River, Beaverhouse, Wolseley, and Minn lakes, and the north shore of Lac La Croix. Two narrow northeast-trending belts of iron formation also occur along the Man Lakes, comprised of hematite and magnetite interbedded with chert and jasper.

THE MIDDLE PRECAMBRIAN ROCKS

The end of Early Precambrian time in the BWCAW is marked by an ancient erosion surface, overlain by a cherty and locally magnetic rock unit called the Gunflint Iron Formation, exposed near the east end of the Kekekabic Trail and along the shores of Gunflint and North lakes. Radiometric dating puts the age of this formation at about 2 billion years (Morey 1969). Thick tilted beds of slaty argillite and graywacke known as the Rove Formation lie above the iron formation. These rocks are exposed in the BWCAW east of the Gunflint Trail along the shorelines of the many long, narrow lakes of the Caribou Unit, where they are in part responsible for the steep topography of that area. Their age is about 1.7 billion years.

THE LATE PRECAMBRIAN ROCKS

In Late Precambrian time an igneous intrusion forced gabbroic magma into the layered sedimentary beds of the Rove Formation, creating siltlike layers and dikelike plugs of diabase. These rocks, called the Logan intrusives, were emplaced more than 1.1 billion years ago and were subsequently uplifted and tilted with the Rove Formation. A long period of differential erosion then eventually produced the present sawtooth topography. Today this region has the most rugged relief in the BWCAW. The lakes lie in deep east-west troughs where the softer Rove Formation has been eroded out, first by streams and then by the ice sheet, whereas steep to nearly vertical cliffs formed of the harder Logan intrusives rise 200 to 500 feet along their south shores (Zumberge 1952).

The massive Duluth Complex cuts across the southeast half of the BWCAW from Gabbro Lake northeastward. This great arcuate body of dark gray gabbro, and locally in the southeast of reddish syenitic rocks, was emplaced some 1.1 billion years ago near the close of the Precambrian Era (Southwick and Weiblen 1971). West of Sawbill and Cherokee lakes the landscape on the Duluth Complex is a maze of low rolling bedrock ridges interspersed with many irregular shallow basins, some now occupied by lakes, others by bogs. Most of the lakes and streams have brownish tea-colored water because of drainage from peatlands. Toward the east the relief increases, until around Winchell and Misquah lakes and Eagle Mountain the highest elevations in Minnesota are attained amidst high ridges and steep cliffs. Among the best known waterways on the Duluth Complex are the Kawishiwi, Isabella, and Temperance rivers. Copper and nickel sulfide mineralization occurs along the northern rim of the Duluth Gabbro in contact with the older rocks to the north. The South Kawishiwi River and Howard Lake areas have been scenes of conflict over the possible mining of these deposits.

The Great Ice Age Shapes the Landscape

In most of the Boundary Waters region, Precambrian time was followed by eons of weathering and erosion. If any later rocks were ever laid down over the Precambrian surface, they have been eroded away. Thus a landscape of generally low relief already existed when the Great Ice Age (Pleistocene) began some 2 million years ago. Since then, vast continental glaciers repeatedly pushed southward across the border area from centers in the Hudson Bay–Labrador region. Glaciers of the last major period of the Pleistocene, called the Wisconsin, removed virtually all evidence of earlier glaciation. Grooves and striae on the exposed bedrock in the Boundary Waters region show that the last glacial advances came from the northeast and north (Zoltai 1965; Wright 1972; Ontario Ministry of Natural Resources 1977). The Boundary Waters was primarily an area of glacial erosion; thus glacial deposits are generally thin except for a few areas where the ice margin remained stationary for a time during its retreat. The main effect of the ice was to grind down or pluck away the old weathered

and fractured rock, deepen already existing valleys and lowlands, and round off ridges. The last ice to advance across most of the BWCAW was the Rainy Lobe, which built the lengthy Vermilion Moraine just south of the BWCAW about 16,000 years ago (Wright 1972). Then, as the ice slowly wasted away, it deposited a generally thin and patchy layer of glacial till, which is the parent material for the thin, rocky soils that now mantle most of the region's bedrock. Some drumlins (oval ridges of till oriented parallel to ice movement) were also built by the ice in a belt from Snowbank and Ima lakes through the Gabbro-Bald Eagle lakes area, and from Kelso Lake and Kelso Mountain southwest through the Perent Lake area (Hobbs and Goebel 1982). Ice wastage apparently was slow because active glaciers still remained nearby in the Lake Superior basin and to the west until after 12,000 years ago (Wright 1972), and the retreating ice built the Steep Rock and Eagle-Finlayson moraines across northeastern Quetico only 11,000 years ago (Zoltai 1961, 1965; Ontario Ministry of Natural Resources 1977). The front of the retreating ice sheet was still positioned 260 miles northeast of Quetico only 8,000 years ago (Bryson et al. 1969). The last ice melted on the Quebec-Labrador plateau about 6,000 years ago.

Another significant event in shaping the modern landscape was the ponding of glacial meltwaters in front of the wasting ice sheet to form Glacial Lake Agassiz about 11,500 years ago. This vast lake developed in northwestern Minnesota and adjacent North Dakota and Manitoba when the melting continental ice sheet retreated north of the divide between the Gulf of Mexico and the Hudson Bay drainages, and northward drainage was still blocked by the ice sheet. Meltwaters rose until they overflowed southward via the present valleys of the Minnesota and Mississippi rivers. The early high-water stages of Lake Agassiz expanded eastward into Quetico and Voyageurs at least as far as French, McKenzie, Kawnipi, and Basswood lakes and along the Canadian border also into the BWCAW as far east as Basswood Lake. The lake did not exist very long in the Boundary Waters, but it left patchy deposits of gray clay over lower areas of much of Quetico, Voyageurs, and the northwestern quarter of the BWCAW. Some of these clays, which locally show annual layers (varves), may have been deposited by a smaller, higher, and slightly earlier meltwater lake in the northwestern BWCAW. The maximum elevation at which such clays occur is about 1,400 feet in the southeast near Ely and 1,300 or 1,250 feet in Voyageurs and southwestern Quetico. The level of Lake Agassiz lowered in stages as the melting ice uncovered eastern and northern outlets in Ontario, exposing even the lowest terrain in western Quetico by 8,000 years ago (Zoltai 1965; Ontario Ministry of Natural Resources 1977). Most of the higher ground occupied by Lake Agassiz in the BWCAW and south-central Quetico was probably drained by 11,000 years ago.

The Soils

The key to understanding soils and their productivity in the Boundary Waters region lies in knowing the bedrock geology and glacial history in the area of interest. For example, soil texture, the relative percentage of sand, silt, and clay in the various soil layers, is strongly dependent on the bedrock source of the soil materials and the type of glacial deposit on which the soil develops.

All the mineral soils owe their origin to glacial deposition by one mode or another. Most soils were formed from glacial till, a heterogeneous mix of sand, silt, and stones laid down by glaciers as the ice melted. Till varies in texture and fertility depending on its bedrock sources. In general, granitic bedrock produces coarse-textured stony soils low in water-holding capacity, low in fertility, poorly buffered, and acidic. Granitic soils are found chiefly over granitic bedrock or a short distance to the south or southwest of granitic rock, because a glacier usually transported most of its load only short distances. Soils derived from metamorphosed sedimentary rocks and greenstones are finer-textured, less droughty, higher in nutrients, somewhat better buffered, and moderately acidic. Many are sandy loams to silt loams, often with less rock content. The till derived from gabbroic rocks of the Duluth Complex produces soils that tend to be intermediate in texture, water-retaining capacity, fertility, and acidity. The most fertile soils in the region are those formed on the calcareous clays deposited by Glacial Lake Agassiz. These soils are very fine-textured, usually contain few stones, are high in water-holding capacity and nutrients, well buffered with bases, and often neutral or slightly alkaline in reaction (Ontario Ministry of Natural Resources 1977).

Thickness of the soil and its parent glacial materials over bedrock varies with the mode of glacial deposition and local topography. Till in this region ranges from a few inches thick on ridgetops to 5 to 10 feet or more at the bases of slopes and in depressions. Some ridgetops are bald, either because a glacier scraped them clean or because erosion has moved all the finer soil materials downslope, leaving only perched boulders. Bald ridgetops are frequent on the Vermilion Granite. Lake-deposited clays can vary from only a foot or two to many feet in thickness. Locally, eskers and other outwash deposits of sand and gravel may be many feet thick, but these are not extensive in the Boundary Waters. Terminal moraines may be more than 100 feet high. Except for the Steep Rock Moraine, which extends from Pickerel to Cache and Lindsay lakes in Quetico, few significant ridges of this type occur in the region (Wright 1972; Ontario Ministry of Natural Resources 1977).

Depth to the groundwater table and the presence of percolating subsurface waters are also important factors influencing plant growth. Local bedrock depressions, valleys, streamsides, lakeshores, and bog or swamp margins are common situations where water tables may occur in the mineral soil at a slight depth below the surface. Percolating soil water is seasonally frequent on lower bedrock slopes, along streams, and in valleys, making dramatic differences in apparent soil productivity.

Lake and Stream Origins

Virtually all lakes and streams in the Boundary Waters region owe their origin to factors controlled by the preglacial bedrock landscape and by glacial erosion and deposition. The following circumstances were probably the most common ones that produced the lakes in the region today:

- Preglacial stream erosion created a lengthy lowland, often along an old bedrock fault line or along an exposure of softer rock.
- Glaciers moved across the landscape from the north-

east and deepened the old lowland by gouging out easily fractured rock.

- As the last ice melted, the glacier may have deposited sand, silt, and gravel in some portions of the new trough more than in others, thus enclosing a series of deep basins.
- These basins then filled with water and established drainageways from one basin to the next down the old lowland, creating a chain of lakes interconnected by small streams (Zumberge 1952).

Another common form of lake origin is the classic ice-block lake. In this case huge masses of stagnant ice became buried in glacial debris being deposited by the glacier. Then, when the glacier receded, the buried ice slowly melted out from beneath its covering, leaving a large depression to fill with water to form a lake (Zumberge 1952). This mode of origin is not as common in the Boundary Waters region as in areas with more glacial deposits.

In a few cases lake basins are separated partially or entirely by eskers, ridges of sand or gravel built by subglacial streams. Wave-built bars and spits built of glacial sands in postglacial time by the present lake are also found on a few lakes but are uncommon because of the greater prevalence of bedrock and boulders compared to sandy shorelines.

Origin of Bogs, Swamps, and Muskeg

No description of landscape origins in the Boundary Waters region would be complete without considering the ever-present organic soils. Peatlands consist of undecomposed and partially decomposed organic matter, here mostly mosses, sedges, grasses, aquatic plants, twigs from shrubs, and wood from trees. Peat forms when the rate of accumulation of plant and animal matter exceeds the rate of decay in the cold, waterlogged, anaerobic (oxygen-poor), and often acid environments.

In the Boundary Waters region there are three reasonably distinct peatland-forming processes: (1) the classic lake-filling succession, (2) the swamping (or paludification)

process, and (3) beaver-assisted swamping. Intergrades and combinations of these processes are common.

Lake-filling is clearly the dominant mode of peatland formation on the Laurentian Shield in Minnesota. This process usually involves four or five intergrading stages:

- Aquatic lake muds, derived from algae and other aquatic microorganisms, remains of submerged and floating-leaf aquatic plants, and silt and clay washed in or blown in from adjacent land areas, first accumulate on the lake bottom, especially in quiet bays and deep basins.
- Emergent aquatic plants may also begin to grow in shallow bays, contributing to the accumulating organic matter.
- After these processes have built up the floor in the quiet waters of the bay, a floating mat of sedges, mosses, herbs, and shrubs may begin to extend out from the lakeshore.
- Eventually this floating sedge-moss mat becomes sufficiently consolidated and grounded to support the growth of small black spruce or tamarack trees.
- Gradually the sedge-moss mat extends across the lake, and a bog forest of black spruce may occupy the entire original lake basin.

The paludification or swamping process, in contrast, is capable of building up a peat layer on cold, wet mineral soils or bedrock without an initial aquatic stage. In the Boundary Waters region paludification often builds thin layers of sphagnum moss peat near the bases of north-facing slopes, especially on granitic bedrock or sandy, gravelly, or rocky soils derived from granite or other sterile acidic rocks. Thin sphagnum peat layers are also often found well up on elevated granitic landforms on flats, slight north slopes, and in shallow depressions. These types of paludified land are usually occupied by black spruce forest.

The third mode of peatland formation is a combination of lake-filling and paludification assisted by the dam-building activities of beaver. Beaver dams may raise the level of lakes or streams substantially, and over centuries they may cause adjacent peatlands to expand well above and beyond the original water level.

The Forest Communities

The forests of the Boundary Waters region contain the last large remnants of the old "north woods" of the upper Great Lakes area. An idealized view of the original north woods pictures unbroken forests of giant white and red pine, mixed here and there with spruce, balsam, jack pine, aspen, and birch. Such forests did cover large areas in Minnesota, Wisconsin, Michigan, and Ontario. These "pineries"—the stands of mature white and red pine—were the primary target of the early timber industry. A realistic picture of the original or virgin forests includes a much wider range of forest communities than the mature big-pine types. The U.S. General Land Office Survey records and other reliable early data clearly show that only about a quarter of the forests of northeastern Minnesota consisted of mature white and red pine at the time of European settlement (Marschner 1930). The composition of the forests of both today and yesterday has a diversity important to wildlife and to an aesthetic and factual understanding of the modern and the prehistoric landscape.

A Continental Perspective

The vegetation of the Boundary Waters is transitional between that of the Boreal Forest Region, which crosses the continent from Newfoundland to Alaska, and the Great Lakes–St. Lawrence Forest Region (Rowe 1972). All of the principal tree species of the central Canadian boreal forest are abundant in the Boundary Waters (black and white spruce, jack pine, balsam fir, tamarack, northern white cedar, quaking aspen, paper birch, and balsam poplar), and they often form extensive forests lacking a significant component of white or red pine. There are also many areas within the virgin forests where white and red pine are abundant, and even some where red maple, red oak, and black ash are common, all typical species of the Great Lakes forests. Yellow birch, basswood, red oak, northern pin oak, bur oak, large-toothed aspen, and red maple also occur, and they all reach their northern limits within or just north of Quetico. A similar situation exists with the shrubs and herbs: many boreal species are abundant within the Boundary Waters region, and some Great Lakes forest and eastern deciduous forest species reach their northern limits within the area. Kuchler (1966) recognizes this transitional situation in his map of the "Potential Natural Vegetation of the United States" by mapping the forests of northeastern Minnesota as a complex of Great Lakes pine forest, Great Lakes spruce-fir forest, and conifer bog.

Rowe (1972) maps the Quetico region of Ontario as Great Lakes–St. Lawrence forest, thus placing the BWCAW and Voyageurs within that region as well. The nearly boreal character of the Boundary Waters forests is underscored, however, by the complete absence of sugar maple, beech, and eastern hemlock and the scarcity of yellow birch, the principal dominant trees of much of the Great Lakes–St.

Lawrence region. The regional affinities of the shrubs, herbs, grasses, sedges, lichens, and mosses of the Boundary Waters also reflect the nearly boreal character of the vegetation. Some prairie elements within the flora toward the western ends of the BWCAW and Quetico and in Voyageurs also suggest the transitional nature of the vegetation.

The vegetation of the Boundary Waters region is thus part of a grand continuum of plant distributions that exhibit a gradual shift in species composition and abundance within plant communities from the deciduous forests of southeastern Minnesota and southern Wisconsin through the Great Lakes region to the true boreal forests of northwestern Ontario. The lines on vegetation maps are artificial, drawn to help us understand how plant distributions have adjusted to climate and soil. Seen in this light, the forests of the Boundary Waters clearly reflect a strongly northern aspect when compared to the forests of most of the northeastern United States, and many patches of essentially boreal forest occur.

Classification of Plant Communities

Plant communities are distinct assemblages of plants that grow in particular regions and often in a specific habitat or range of habitats. They are, of course, artificial constructs made to facilitate our understanding of nature. A complete classification of the plant communities of the Boundary Waters region is still not available, but a sound basis is provided by the classification of most of the upland vegetation of the Boundary Waters by Ohmann and Ream (1971) and Grigal and Ohmann (1975), using statistical random sampling in the field and quantitative computerized classification procedures. A similar classification was developed for Voyageurs by Kurmis, Merriam, and co-workers (1978). For Quetico, Walshe's (1980) excellent flora was used to apply the Ohmann/Grigal classification.

For peatland and other wetland vegetation types, my classification of the plant communities of the Lake Agassiz Peatlands Natural Area (Heinselman 1970) is here modified to apply to Boundary Waters peatlands on the basis of local research in the area (Heinselman 1961; Dean 1971).

A classification is particularly useful if the units can be readily mapped from air photos, although important differences in understory species cannot be easily detected using the types of air photos or satellite imagery available. Ground mapping in a large wilderness is prohibitively slow and costly. Although good plant-community maps are still not available, major differences in the species composition and size of overstory trees in forests are visible on air photos and have been mapped in the BWCAW by the Superior National Forest. Such maps, usually called cover-type maps, are very useful in forestry but less well adapted to applied ecological work concerned with plant communities and their relation to bird and mammal populations. The only cover-type maps that include the entire BWCAW were made from 1948 air photos. They were very helpful to me in mapping fire and logging history, but they are not a substitute for plant-community maps.

The area estimates for BWCAW upland communities (table 4.1) are based on the percentage of plots in each logging-history class assigned to each plant community by Grigal and Ohmann (1975). Lowland plant-community areas are based on cover-type area data from the 1964 to 1974 Superior National Forest timber management plan for the "Extensive Management Zone" (that part of the BWCAW [then called the BWCA] open to logging in 1964). At that time the Extensive Zone included about 479,000 acres of federal land, more than half of the present BWCAW. The land and water areas and plant-community areas in table 4.1 have been updated from Heinselman (1973) to include the 1978 additions to the wilderness and changes in virgin forest and logged areas due to logging between 1973 and 1979.

No satisfactory data exist for the many and varied plant communities on the uplands logged since 1940, so these areas are simply listed as "unclassified logged upland" in table 4.1. There also are no figures for the areas of the virgin forest communities within the 400-foot-wide lakeshore and streamside no-cutting reserves specified by the Shipstead-Newton-Nolan Act in areas logged after 1940, nor for the many smaller patches of virgin forest within generally cutover areas. Thus the actual area of virgin forest is greater than shown, and the area of logged land is correspondingly smaller.

Table 4.1 / Area of the Boundary Waters Canoe Area Wilderness classified by plant communities, water areas, and logging history

Plant community[a]	Virgin areas[b]		Logged 1895 to 1940		Logged 1941 to 1978		Total BWCAW	
	Acres	%	Acres	%	Acres	%	Acres	%
UPLAND TYPES								
Lichen	21,400	4.7	5,300	2.3	6,700	3.0	33,400	3.7
Jack pine–oak	21,400	4.7	2,600	1.2	—	—	24,000	2.7
Red pine	17,700	3.9	2,600	1.2	—	—	20,300	2.2
Jack pine–black spruce	50,900	11.2	7,900	3.5	—	—	58,800	6.5
Jack pine–fir	28,700	6.3	5,300	2.3	—	—	34,000	3.8
Black spruce–feathermoss	28,700	6.3	34,200	15.1	—	—	62,900	7.0
Maple-oak	—	—	13,100	5.8	—	—	13,100	1.4
Aspen-birch	28,700	6.3	7,900	3.5	—	—	36,600	4.0
Aspen-birch-white pine	21,400	4.7	26,300	11.6	—	—	47,700	5.3
Maple-aspen-birch	32,300	7.1	28,900	12.8	—	—	61,200	6.8
Maple-aspen-birch-fir	28,700	6.3	28,900	12.8	—	—	57,600	6.4
Fir-birch	72,800	16.0	7,900	3.5	—	—	80,700	8.9
White cedar	17,700	3.9	13,100	5.8	—	—	30,800	3.4
Unclassified logged upland	—	—	—	—	174,800	78.4	174,800	19.3
Total upland types	370,400	81.4	184,000	81.4	181,500	81.4	735,900	81.4
LOWLAND TYPES								
Mixed conifer swamp forest	2,300	0.5	1,100	0.5	1,100	0.5	4,500	0.5
Black spruce bog forest	33,200	7.3	16,500	7.3	16,300	7.3	66,000	7.3
Tamarack bog forest	500	0.1	200	0.1	200	0.1	900	0.1
Sphagnum–black spruce bog	9,500	2.1	4,800	2.1	4,700	2.1	19,000	2.1
Ash-elm-swamp forest	500	0.1	200	0.1	200	0.1	900	0.1
Alder-willow wetland	11,400	2.5	5,700	2.5	5,600	2.5	22,700	2.5
Marsh and open muskeg	20,000	4.4	9,900	4.4	9,800	4.4	39,700	4.4
Open water communities	7,200	1.6	3,600	1.6	3,600	1.6	14,400	1.6
Total lowland types	84,600	18.6	42,000	18.6	41,500	18.6	168,100	18.6
Total all communities	455,000	100.0	226,000	100.0	223,000	100.0	904,000	100.0
Lakes and streams	90,000		73,000		17,000		180,000	
TOTAL AREAS	545,000		299,000		240,000		1,084,000	

Note Upland type areas were obtained by applying Grigal and Ohmann's (1975) sample-plot percentage distributions to land areas within each logging-history category. Virgin and logged areas were obtained by dot counts on maps prepared by M. L. Heinselman. Area counts and calculations were made by M. L. Heinselman, Feb. 16, 1973, updated July 6, 1989, for additions to the BWCAW by Public Law 95-495 and for the final status of logging in 1979 when all logging ceased. Lake and stream areas are based on lake-by-lake classification to logging-history category from Appendix Table 2, U.S. Forest Service BWCA *Handbook* (1969), updated for additions to BWCAW by P.L. 95-495. Type areas are rounded to the nearest 100 acres; BWCAW total areas are rounded to the nearest 1,000 acres.

[a] Upland plant communities and area percentages from Grigal and Ohmann (1975). Lowland types adapted from Superior National Forest Timber Management Plan July 1, 1964–July 1, 1974 for Extensive Management Zone BWCA.

[b] Virgin areas are those never logged, cleared, roaded, etc. Nearly all areas have burned within the past 400 years. Only solid contiguous forests within generally uncut regions are included. The lakeshore reserves within logged regions specified by the Shipstead-Newton-Nolan Act and small tracts of virgin forest within generally cutover areas are *not* included in virgin areas even though such areas do contain significant areas of virgin forest in total.

Description of Plant Communities

THE UPLAND FORESTS

Plant communities are described by showing in some quantitative way the presence, abundance, and size of the many species that give them their character. These kinds of data are available for the uplands. Data for the most characteristic and abundant plants of the 13 upland plant communities are defined by Grigal and Ohmann (1975). A description of each community rounds out the picture (Grigal and Ohmann 1975; Ohmann and Ream 1971; Kurmis, Hansen, et al. 1978; Walshe 1980).

Lichen

The nearly treeless lichen-dominated community characteristically occurs along the crests and upper slopes of bald bedrock ridges in forest openings with much exposed bedrock. It may occur as openings within the jack pine–oak communities. The type is most common on ridges that were last burned by forest fires 50 to 150 years ago. It is probably most abundant in the west along the ridgetops of the Vermilion Granite, from Basswood Lake west into Voyageurs and north into Quetico.

Lichens, especially the so-called reindeer mosses (*Cladonia*), give this community its most striking aspect, a ground layer of greenish gray to greenish yellow primitive plants that often covers more than half of the otherwise barren bedrock. Lichens are complex combinations of fungi (their body) and algae (their green photosynthesizing elements). Four species of ground lichens are common in the Boundary Waters region. The tiny red-capped British soldiers lichens cover little area but locally add interest and color to the ground lichens.

About 30 percent of the landscape in this community is usually bare rock. Clumps of lowbush blueberry (see appendix C for scientific names) often occur along fractures in the bedrock and on pockets of thin soil that occupy depressions. Bearberry is sometimes present. Bush-honeysuckle, juneberry, and willow are often the only shrubs. Among the few and usually sparse herbs are pale corydalis, bristly sarsaparilla, white cinquefoil, wild lily-of-the-valley, large-leaved aster, cow-wheat, wood anemone, false Solo-

mon's-seal, starflower, everlasting, pearly everlasting, and bluebell. Grasses, sedges, mosses, and lichens other than *Cladonia* comprise most of the remaining ground layer.

Jack Pine–Oak

An often clumpy overstory of jack pine with an understory of stunted and very limby red oak and/or northern pin oak and red maple gives this community its characteristic appearance. The oak and maple frequently occur in gaps between patches of jack pine, and the shrub and herb layers are typically sparse, giving the community an open aspect. The type commonly occurs on the upper slopes and crests of bedrock ridges with a thin and discontinuous soil cover. Northern pin oak is most common on the driest ridgetops of the Vermilion Granite from Ely westward. Overstory trees are nearly even-aged and not usually very old, dating from forest fires in virgin forests or fires in logging slash from 1864 to 1920. In the BWCAW bur oak occasionally takes the place of or mingles with red oak and/or pin oak, as along the portage between Ensign and Vera lakes east of Ely. This community is most common in the western BWCAW and Voyageurs on the Vermilion Granite and on the granitic terrain of southwestern Quetico near the border lakes. Both red oak and northern pin oak are rare elsewhere in Quetico and are probably small and stunted both because of adverse site conditions and because they are so near their climatic limits.

The shrubs, herbs, and ground-layer vegetation indicate dry conditions. The most abundant tall shrubs are juneberry, beaked hazelnut, willow, and green alder, with lesser cover of common juniper, fly-honeysuckle, and pincherry. Common low shrubs and herbs include lowbush blueberry, wintergreen, bush-honeysuckle, sweet fern, and creeping snowberry. Trailing arbutus is a rare but lovely spring flower. Other frequent herbs include wild lily-of-the-valley, grasses, large-leaved aster, cow-wheat, wild sarsaparilla, bracken, starflower, bunchberry, and twinflower. Rare herbs include the dwarf rattlesnake-plantain orchid and the stemless lady-slipper orchid (moccasin flower). The ground layer consists mostly of mosses and lichens, especially *Dicranum* moss, Schreber's feathermoss, haircap moss, the reindeer mosses, and clubmosses.

Red Pine

Stately groves of tall old red pine, often with some mature white pine as well, usually give this community instant recognition. Some examples have a main canopy of mostly younger trees, however, and on some sites poor growing conditions result in smaller tree sizes; thus not all stands feature large trees. Typically the sapling understory and shrub and herb layers are sparse, giving most examples an open aspect. Many red pine stands occur near lakeshores, along streams, or on islands, perhaps because such sites provide some protection from severe fires. Many examples occur on south- or west-facing slopes and on dry gravelly or rocky soils, but other stands are on ridges or flats, so no generalizations hold for all cases. Soil depth is usually moderate (20 to 36 inches) but varies greatly. Red pine communities often consist of groves of nearly even-aged pines that became established after a forest fire that may have occurred 70 to more than 300 years ago. Many such groves also include survivors from their parent age class and younger groups of pines that date from fires that burned through the grove without killing many trees.

Red pine forests were heavily logged from 1895 to about 1940 in many areas of the BWCAW and Quetico and in most of Voyageurs. Some were cut as late as the 1970s. Thus good examples of this community are confined largely to the remaining virgin forests of the BWCAW and Quetico. Some good younger examples occur in certain areas logged between about 1895 and 1925. The community is now most common in the virgin forests of the western BWCAW, particularly in the Lac La Croix region and southward on the Vermilion Granite, and in the virgin forests of the western Hunter Island region of Quetico on granitic landforms. Good examples exist farther east as well, notably in the Saganaga–Sea Gull lakes region on the Saganaga Granite.

Along with red and white pine, the canopy layer may include some paper birch, jack pine, red maple, red oak, balsam fir, black spruce, and northern white cedar. The usually sparse understory often includes white pine seedlings and saplings, as well as some black spruce, paper birch, red pine, red maple, and balsam fir. Tall shrubs are usually not abundant, but juneberry and beaked hazelnut are the most common, and green alder, sweet fern, common juni-

per, and willow are often present. Blueberries, bush-honeysuckle, and wintergreen are the most common low shrubs, and bearberry and pipsissewa are among the more unusual members of the community. The ground layer is typically sparse. More than half of the ground surface is usually covered with litter, often mostly pine needles. Mosses and lichens usually cover more area than herbs. *Dicranum* moss, Schreber's feathermoss, and hair-cap moss are the most abundant mosses, and reindeer mosses are the most common lichens. Wild lily-of-the-valley, large-leaved aster, cow-wheat, wild sarsaparilla, and bunchberry are the most common herbs. Grasses and sedges also usually cover a little area. Bracken, twisted-stalk, twinflower, bluebead-lily, greater rattlesnake-plantain orchid, stemless lady-slipper orchid, starflower, and clubmosses may be present as well.

Jack Pine–Black Spruce

Pole-sized stands of jack pine with a full canopy typify this community, along with an understory of black spruce, sparse shrub and herb layers, and moss ground cover. Black spruce outnumber pine in the codominant and intermediate canopy positions and in the sapling and seedling size classes. The type occurs on both upper and lower slopes but usually not on ridgetops or valley bottoms. Many stands are on south or southwest-facing exposures, often farther from lakes or streams than the red pine type. Depth to bedrock is usually 2 to 3 feet. Bedrock outcrops are uncommon, but surface boulders are usually abundant.

This community is the second largest in area within the virgin forests of the BWCAW, and it also occurs to some extent in logged areas. In the virgin forests jack pine–black spruce stands have nearly even-aged overstories that originated after forest fires in 1863–64, 1875, 1894, 1903, 1910, 1918, and a few other fire years. Many of the smaller spruce in the intermediate and sapling size classes are almost as old as the overstory trees. These relationships certainly hold for the extensive virgin forests of Quetico. In many examples of this community much of the black spruce died following the severe drought of 1976. The jack pine–black spruce type is probably most common in granitic bedrock area such as the western BWCAW, southwestern Quetico, and the Saganaga Batholith region, but it occurs to some extent on the Duluth Gabbro and elsewhere.

Along with jack pine and black spruce, the canopy layer may contain a few quaking aspen, large-toothed aspen, paper birch, white pine, red pine, balsam fir, white spruce, and red maple. Juneberry and beaked hazelnut are the only tall shrubs worth noting, and they rarely cover much area. The rather sparse low-shrub layer is composed mostly of bush-honeysuckle, lowbush blueberry, and wintergreen. Wild lily-of-the-valley, large-leaved aster, twinflower, bunchberry, wild sarsaparilla, grasses, and dwarf rattlesnake-plantain orchid are the most common herbs. Other noteworthy but much less abundant herbs and low shrubs include clubmosses, trailing arbutus, pipsissewa, and the stemless lady-slipper orchid. The most abundant true mosses are the three feathermosses (*Pleurozium schreberi, Hypnum crista-castrensis, Hylocomium splendens*), *Dicranum* moss, and hair-cap moss. Together these mosses cover more than half of the ground surface in typical examples of this community. Reindeer mosses are present but usually not abundant, because the overstory does not admit enough light.

Jack Pine–Fir

Typical examples of this community have an overstory of large pole-sized jack pine, with some large quaking aspen and lesser numbers of balsam fir, black spruce, paper birch, and white spruce. They have a sapling and seedling layer dominated by balsam and birch, a well-developed shrub layer, a fairly rich herb layer, and sparse moss ground cover. The type occurs frequently on mid to lower slopes as well as occasionally on upper slopes and ridgetops, and often on north or northeast-facing slopes. Depth to bedrock is generally 20 to more than 40 inches, and the soils usually contain a higher percentage of silt and clay than do those in other jack pine types. There is little bedrock outcrop, but boulders are abundant. Soil moisture is generally higher than in the other jack pine types. The overstory trees are even-aged, dating from forest fires that in most cases occurred between 1854 and 1925. The type occurs on several landforms where deeper and more fertile soils are found and is therefore widespread geographically. The crucial factor in its location seems to be fire history, not landforms per se.

The sapling layer often contains at least as many black spruce as balsam, but the balsam are often larger, and balsam seedlings far outnumber black spruce. Because balsam is more shade-tolerant than black spruce, the balsam understory will eventually occupy much of the overstory unless fire, wind, or insects intervene. Some paper birch saplings also have the potential to move into the overstory. The prominent tall-shrub layer is dominated by beaked hazelnut and mountain-maple, but juneberry, round-leaved dogwood, and fly-honeysuckle are also common. Bush-honeysuckle, both blueberries, and wild rose are the most common members of the rather sparse low-shrub layer. Wintergreen and creeping snowberry are rarer but of interest.

The herb layer is rich in species and significant in cover. Large-leaved aster is by far the most important, followed by wild lily-of-the-valley, bunchberry, twinflower, grasses, wild sarsaparilla, bluebead-lily, starflower, running clubmoss, goldthread, violets, ground-pine clubmoss, pale pea, three-parted bedstraw, sedges, and bracken. Rarer herbs of special interest include shinleaf, trailing arbutus, and stemless lady-slipper orchid. The well-developed herb layer precludes much moss or lichen cover. Schreber's feathermoss is the most common.

Black Spruce–Feathermoss

This community is an upland black spruce forest with almost no shrub or herb understory vegetation and a striking nearly continuous carpet of feathermosses. Some jack pine, balsam, and quaking aspen are usually present in the overstory along with the spruce, but black spruce strongly dominates both the overstory and sapling layers. The type may occur on gentle slopes with any compass orientation, on rocky flats, on some ridgetops with a thin soil cover, and sometimes on fairly steep north-facing slopes. Depth to bedrock is variable but mostly 18 to 24 inches. Bedrock outcrops are uncommon. The community may be more common on granitic bedrock such as the Vermilion Granite, Saganaga Batholith, and the granitic terrain of southwestern Quetico, but it occurs on other rocks as well.

Overstory trees are even-aged, dating from forest fires usually between 1854 and 1925. Most intermediate and sapling-sized black spruce are nearly as old as the overstory dominants, often having seeded in after the same fire as the dominant trees. In virgin forests most present stands undoubtedly resulted from fires that burned previous black spruce–feathermoss forests. In logged areas some stands apparently seeded in after fires in logging debris (slash), but others may have developed from the residual stands left after scattered big pines were cut in the locality.

Along with black spruce, the canopy layer often has a few jack pine, quaking aspen, balsam fir, paper birch, or white spruce trees in dominant, codominant, or intermediate crown positions. Some of these species may appear in the sapling layer, particularly balsam and birch, which also are abundant as seedlings. Tall shrubs are not abundant; beaked hazelnut and mountain-maple are the most common. A scant low-shrub layer usually consists of scattered bush-honeysuckle and blueberries. Herbs are very sparse, the most likely being wild lily-of-the-valley, twinflower, bunch-berry, large-leaved aster, wild sarsaparilla, grasses, and run-ning clubmoss. The stemless lady-slipper orchid and trailing arbutus are occasionally found. The ground layer is usually a carpet of feathermosses and other mosses, especially Schre-ber's feathermoss, *Dicranum* mosses, and hair-cap moss.

Maple-Oak

A heterogeneous mixture of red maple, red oak, quaking aspen, balsam fir, red pine, paper birch, and white pine in both the tree and sapling layers distinguishes this com-munity. Red maple, red oak, and balsam, in that order, are the most common. It is found only in areas logged in the early big-pine logging era, chiefly on dry former red pine sites that burned after cutting. Red pine stumps are often still present. Except for its canopy composition, it is similar to the jack pine–oak and red pine types. The type occurs chiefly on ridgetops and upper slopes with shallow soils and considerable exposed bedrock. Most examples are on sites that were logged between 1895 and 1930, and the age of overstory trees usually reflects origins between about 1900 and 1936, depending on when the logging and slash fires occurred. It occupies the smallest area of all the upland forest communities defined by Grigal and Ohmann (1975).

Abundant seedlings of maple, balsam, and oak suggest that the type will persist. The most abundant shrubs are characteristic of dry sites: juneberry, beaked hazelnut, bebb willow, sweet fern, blueberries, and wintergreen. The rather sparse herb layer also indicates dry conditions. Wild lily-of-the-valley and large-leaved aster, which often occur on moist sites, do not cover much area in this type. Grasses, sedges, cow-wheat, and bracken are common and more typical of dry sites. The scant mosses and lichens, particu-larly *Dicranum* mosses, hair-cap moss, and reindeer mosses, also suggest dry conditions.

Aspen-Birch

An overstory chiefly of mature quaking aspen and paper birch, often with a few intermingled balsam fir, black and white spruce, and jack pine, is the first visual impression one gets of this community. The birch tend to be smaller than the aspen and mostly in codominant, intermediate, and suppressed canopy positions. Birch is also important in the sapling layer. The type occurs on all slope positions, but compared to the jack pine communities, it is more likely to be found on lower slopes and in valleys. Depth to bedrock is generally great for this region, often 36 to 40 inches. Soil moisture and fertility are often better than average. This is a common community in the virgin forests, but it also occurs in areas cut in the early logging era. In virgin areas most stands originated after fires in 1864, 1875, 1894, or 1910. In logged areas most examples date from logging and slash fires between 1895 and 1930. It is common throughout the region and does not seem to be confined to particular geologic landforms. It is generally lacking on the more prominent bedrock ridges of the Vermilion Gran-ite and related Quetico landforms, although it does often occur on lower terrain within that region, especially where soils contain some clay derived from Glacial Lake Agassiz deposits.

Because it is shade-tolerant and can eventually replace aspen, balsam fir is important in the seedling and sapling layer. Tall shrubs are abundant; beaked hazelnut, juneberry, green alder, round-leaved dogwood, and mountain-maple are most important. Bush-honeysuckle is the most promi-nent low shrub. Thimbleberry, a disjunct Pacific North-west shrub, occurs in the eastern BWCAW and Quetico as far west as Prairie Portage (Walshe 1980) and rarely as far west as Lake Kabetogama in Voyageurs. The herb layer is conspicuous and often rich in species. Large-leaved aster is by far the most important. Other common herbs with less cover are grasses, wild lily-of-the-valley, wild sarsaparilla, strawberry, bracken, bunchberry, bluebead-lily, sweet bedstraw, sedges, starflower, pale pea, and twinflower.

Aspen-Birch-White Pine
(Including Old-Growth White Pine Stands)

This community includes two subgroups. In virgin forests it is usually seen as a grove of mature white pine with a few red pine, balsam, paper birch, quaking aspen, and perhaps white or black spruce, jack pine, or red maple in the understory or canopy—a classic old-growth white pine forest. In areas cut for pine in the early logging era, it can vary from a chiefly white pine forest similar to the one just described to stands with an overstory largely of aspen, paper birch, and a few white pine, usually with a balsam understory. Combining these groups into one community results from the quantitative classification methods of Grigal and Ohmann (1975), which group together stands with similar species composition, considering all stand elements (trees, shrubs, herbs, and mosses). These two outwardly quite different groups are very similar: the logged and burned stands are simply white pine forests that have lost most of their white pine trees, whereas the understory, shrub, herb, and ground-layer vegetation remains much the same. On average, white pine is the most important tree because of its greater size, even though aspen and birch often outnumber it in the overstory. Balsam is consistently present but is smaller and less important in numbers in the tree layer.

The community occurs on a wide range of slope positions and aspects. Depth to bedrock may be 24 to more than 40 inches. The type is not confined to particular geologic landforms or bedrock types but seems to be more common near lakes and streams. In the virgin forests the overstory white pines originated following fires as long ago as 1610 or 1681, or as late as 1864, 1875, or 1894. In logged areas the main stand usually dates from about 1895 to 1930. Some white pines survived the logging and thus date from 1800 or earlier. There is often a considerable spread in pine

ages, sometimes with two or more distinct age classes present. In many stands there are several standing dead white pines, recently killed by white pine blister rust (*Cronartium ribicola*). The type occurs here and there throughout the BWCAW, Quetico, and Voyageurs.

Balsam fir, paper birch, white pine, and red maple are the most important seedlings. Beaked hazelnut, juneberry, fly-honeysuckle, and mountain-maple are common tall shrubs. The scant low-shrub layer usually includes bush-honeysuckle, blueberries, and dewberry. Large-leaved aster is the herb with the highest cover value, followed by wild sarsaparilla, bracken, wild lily-of-the-valley, grasses, bunchberry, and twinflower. Mosses are the most significant ground-layer plants but usually cover little area. Where the overstory contains many white pines, their needles cover much of the ground.

Maple-Aspen-Birch

An overstory of aspen and paper birch with a strong red maple element in both the tree and sapling layers is the key feature of this community. Most red maple trees are likely to occupy codominant or intermediate canopy positions, but the abundance of this shade-tolerant species in the sapling and seedling layers suggests its increasing importance in many stands without fire. Both quaking and large-toothed aspen are often present. A variant of this community is present in the west, particularly in Voyageurs, where bur oak, basswood, green ash, and ironwood are often present along with the dominant trees identified earlier. The type occurs in valleys and on upper slopes as well as in intermediate positions. It is one of the most common types in valleys. Depth to bedrock is usually 20 to 40 inches, and some low-elevation stands west of Basswood Lake in the BWCAW, Quetico, and Voyageurs are on relatively deep Lake Agassiz glacial clays. Such sites are very moist and fertile. The type is not confined to particular landforms or bedrock regions but is less frequent on granitic ridges.

Maple-aspen-birch communities occur in both virgin and logged areas. Most stands in BWCAW virgin forests originated after fires in 1863–64 or 1894, some in areas that may not have burned since 1784 or even 1759. In logged areas most stands followed cutting and/or slash fires between 1895 and 1930. Most logged areas probably were cut for white pine. Similar histories undoubtedly apply to Quetico and Voyageurs. The type occurs throughout the region.

Besides aspen, birch, and red maple, the tree layer usually includes balsam fir, a few jack pine, white pine, or spruce, occasionally black ash, and in Voyageurs often also bur oak, basswood, and green ash. Paper birch, red maple, and balsam are the important saplings, and red maple and balsam are the seedlings with the most potential to develop. The tall-shrub layer is usually well developed, with beaked hazelnut most prominent, followed by mountain-maple, juneberry, green alder, round-leaved dogwood, and fly-honeysuckle. Low shrubs are less abundant; bush-honeysuckle, lowbush blueberry, and dewberry are present in most stands. The herb layer is often prominent and rich in species. Large-leaved aster is the most important, covering on average 19 percent of the herb layer. Other abundant herbs are wild lily-of-the-valley, wild sarsaparilla, bluebead-lily, grasses, starflower, ground-pine clubmoss, bunchberry, twisted-stalk, bracken, violets, and sedges. Jewelweed, pyrolas, horsetails, and interrupted fern are less frequent but indicate good soil moisture and fertility. Many moss species are typically present in the ground layer, but they usually cover little area.

Maple-Aspen-Birch-Fir

In appearance this type differs from maple-aspen-birch chiefly in the greater importance of balsam fir in the tree and sapling layers. Quaking aspen is still the dominant overstory tree, but balsam and paper birch are about equal as codominants. Red maple is important as a small tree and abundant as a seedling. White and black spruce are also more important, but large-toothed aspen is lacking, suggesting that many stands have even better soil moisture than do maple-aspen-birch sites. The range of landforms, slopes, and aspects on which this type occurs is apparently similar to that for the maple-aspen-birch type, although Grigal and Ohmann (1975) are not specific. It may be quite common on flats as well as in valleys. The type is common in both virgin and logged areas through-

out the region. The logging and fire history and range of stand ages of this type are probably similar to those of the maple-aspen-birch type, with which it integrates.

The tall-shrub layer is prominent, with mountain-maple sharing dominance with beaked hazelnut. Blueberries and dewberry are the only low shrubs of significance, and they are not very abundant. Again the herb layer is rich in species and relatively high in cover. Large-leaved aster has the highest cover, but wild lily-of-the-valley has greater numbers and is thus of equal importance. Other herbs usually present are bunchberry, bluebead-lily, grasses, wild sarsaparilla, starflower, ground-pine clubmoss, violets, twisted-stalk, bracken, running clubmoss, twinflower, bristly clubmoss, goldthread, sweet bedstraw, and sedges. The ground layer usually has a patchy and somewhat more extensive moss cover than the other broadleaf communities. Schreber's feathermoss is the most common.

Fir-Birch

Balsam fir and paper birch share overstory dominance in this community, the single most extensive type in the upland virgin forests of the BWCAW. Balsam and birch also dominate the sapling and seedling layers, although balsam is by far the more abundant seedling. Other common trees in both the overstory and understory include black spruce, white cedar, white spruce, and quaking aspen. This community has been in a constant state of flux for decades because of repeated outbreaks of the spruce budworm, a native needle-eating insect that periodically kills much of the balsam and some of the white spruce in the entire region.

The community is most often found on lower slopes and flats but sometimes also on middle or upper slopes at low elevations. Depth to bedrock is normally 20 to 40 inches or more. In more cases than with any other type the stands occur near lakeshores, streams, or wetlands such as marshes or beaver ponds. It is common throughout the region and not confined to specific geologic landforms, but it rarely occurs on granitic ridges except on lower slopes, particularly where the soils are formed on glacial clays. In virgin forests most stands have not been burned for more than 100 years. In logged areas the cutting usually occurred between 1895 and 1930, and in many cases the area either did not burn or was burned lightly. Often the logged area was formerly a white pine site.

The tall-shrub layer is usually well developed and strongly dominated by mountain-maple. Beaked hazelnut is typically second but much less abundant. The low-shrub layer is poorly developed. Only bush-honeysuckle and dewberry are often present. Herbs are not abundant either, probably because of heavy shading by the overstory and/or mountain-maple. Bunchberry is the most frequent, followed by wild lily-of-the-valley, large-leaved aster, twinflower, bluebead-lily, wild sarsaparilla, violets, grasses, starflower, twisted-stalk, ground-pine clubmoss, and sweet bedstraw. Mosses dominate the ground layer, and although patchy, they usually cover about a quarter of the surface. The moss flora is often rich in species, with Schreber's feathermoss and species of *Dicranum* most abundant.

Where the balsam component of the overstory has been heavily defoliated or partially killed by the spruce budworm, the lower branches of living balsam and spruce and the entire crowns of dead balsam are usually draped with old man's beard tree lichens (*Usnea*) and hairy tree lichens (*Bryoria*).

White Cedar

White cedar is often thought of as primarily a swamp forest tree, but this community is an upland community dominated by cedar. The principal trees associated with upland white cedar in the tree, sapling, and seedling layers are balsam fir, paper birch, and white spruce. The type occurs most frequently on lower slopes, flats, or in valleys, often along lakeshores, streams, wetlands, near waterfalls, or on islands, all sites where forest fires were less frequent or intense before European settlement. It often covers only small areas but occurs in both virgin and logged areas. Most stands have escaped significant fire for a very long time, and in logged areas the site usually did not burn after cutting.

White cedar tends to be more abundant on lime-rich soils, or at least on sites that are not strongly acidic. Cedar is very easily eliminated by fire. These factors in combination have made the environment more favorable for

cedar in the eastern BWCAW and eastern Quetico than in the western parts, except locally in lowlands where Glacial Lake Agassiz calcareous clay soils meet some of these needs. Thus this community is more common in the eastern half of the region, away from the dry, acidic, fire-prone ridges of the Vermilion Granite and the related bedrock of southwestern Quetico.

Mountain-maple is the dominant tall shrub and is often quite abundant. Red osier dogwood and, rarely, American yew may also be present. Low shrubs are usually very sparse; only dewberry is consistently present, but thimbleberry occurs on some lime-rich sites in the eastern BWCAW and Quetico. The herb layer is often rich in species but not very high in total cover. In descending order the most abundant species are bishop's-cap, starflower, bunchberry, wild lily-of-the-valley, violets, wild sarsaparilla, bluebead-lily, sweet bedstraw, large-leaved aster, twisted-stalk, twinflower, sedges, goldthread, one-sided pyrola, one-flowered pyrola, and clubmosses. The ground usually has a patchy, species-rich moss cover. All three feathermosses and *Dicranum* are usually present, but several additional species make up most of the cover.

THE LOWLAND PLANT COMMUNITIES

This section describes the eight lowland communities I define for the BWCAW, adapted from types used by the U.S. Forest Service in mapping the Superior National Forest and from the combined cover types used in the 1964–74 timber management plan for the BWCAW. An estimate of the area of each type in the BWCAW for the virgin and logged areas is given in table 4.1. These descriptions are based on my earlier research in peatlands (Heinselman 1961, 1963, 1970), on the data and descriptions for Voyageurs (Kurmis, Merriam, et al. 1978), on Walshe's (1980) notes for Quetico, on Dean's (1971) data for peatlands in the eastern BWCAW, and on the cover type definitions used in the 1948–52 Forest Service type-mapping project.

Mixed Conifer Swamp Forest

This is a species-rich peatland community in which white cedar is often the most abundant tree, with black spruce and/or tamarack the usual associates. It includes some stands of nearly pure cedar and is close to my rich swamp forest (Heinselman 1970). Relatively species-rich shrub, herb, and moss layers are typical.

Peat near the surface is usually dark, relatively fertile, and not very acid, consisting of a matrix of well-decomposed plant remains and partially decayed wood. Peat depth to mineral soil ranges from 1 to 10 feet or more. The type generally occurs either near the mineral soil edge of the peatland or downslope in the path of moving ground and surface waters. The peat surface is typically a complex of irregular hummocks and fairly deep hollows. Water flows very gently in most hollows except during prolonged dry periods. Surface waters are nearly neutral or only slightly acid (pH 6.0–7.0) and relatively high in calcium, magnesium, and other plant nutrients. The key site factor is location in the path of moving water that issues from or has percolated across reasonably fertile mineral soils.

The type is not extensive but apparently is most common in the eastern BWCAW and Quetico. In Voyageurs, the western BWCAW, and western Quetico it may occur chiefly on lowlands with mineral soils having surface layers of base-rich Glacial Lake Agassiz clays. Cedar is easily killed by fire and often is slow to repopulate burned swamps. Most examples of this type have not burned for many decades, often not since 1864 or earlier. Where stands were logged, they were usually cut only for the larger cedar, spruce, or tamarack before 1930 and did not burn after cutting.

Besides cedar, black spruce, and tamarack, the tree layer may contain a few balsam fir, paper birch, and black ash. The principal saplings are usually white cedar, balsam fir, or paper birch, and the sapling layer is often sparse, in part due to past deer browsing of cedar. The most important tree seedlings are cedar, balsam, and black spruce. The principal tall shrub is speckled alder, with red osier dogwood common in many stands and juneberry and/or willow often present but less abundant. Occasionally there may be a few clumps of American yew. If the tree layer is poorly stocked, tall shrubs may be dense, but if the overstory is heavy, and especially if there are many cedars, then tall shrubs are sparse. Low shrubs are typically sparse. Dew-

berry, creeping snowberry, velvet-leaf blueberry, and Labrador-tea are seen most often. The herb layer is often quite rich in species but usually low in cover. The most common species in decreasing order of abundance are starflower, bunchberry, bog false Solomon's-seal, bluebead-lily, jewelweed, clubmosses, wild lily-of-the-valley, goldthread, ferns, sedges, horsetails, bishop's-cap, and violets. Other less common but interesting herbs are marsh-marigold, blue flag, pyrolas, bedstraws, asters, marsh cinquefoil, and rarely club-spur orchid and blunt-leaf orchid. The ground is partially carpeted by a profusion of mosses. Most common are several sphagnum mosses, all three feathermosses, *Dicranum* mosses, hair-cap mosses, ribbed bog moss, *Mnium*, and *Thuidium*.

Black Spruce Bog Forest

This community is generally a species-poor peatland forest on acid but moderately productive bog sites. It is a deliberately broad type that encompasses stands with a tree layer dominated by relatively fast-growing black spruce, including both stands with a feathermoss ground layer and some with a richer flora that includes speckled alder in the shrub layer. It is most closely related to my black spruce–feathermoss forest (Heinselman 1970).

The type occurs on peats usually over 2 feet and sometimes more than 20 feet deep that are moderately decomposed below the fresh moss and litter. Partially decomposed wood, mosses, and charcoal are often found in the spruce rooting zone. The bog surface is an undulating complex of raised moss cushions and damp or wet sedge and sphagnum moss hollows, and the general contour of the bog surface as a whole is often slightly convex in cross section. The water table usually stands just below the peat surface during the growing season, and there is little standing water except in spring or after heavy rains. Bog waters are quite acid (pH 3.7 to 5.0).

In virgin forests many stands are even-aged and postdate forest fires that swept the locality in 1863–64, 1875, 1894, or 1910. Often the bog spruce is the same age as stands of jack pine–black spruce or aspen-birch on adjacent uplands. In some areas black spruce was extensively logged for pulpwood between 1940 and 1978 and usually clearcut. Here the stands postdate the logging. Some stands have a multiaged structure.

This community is the most extensive lowland type and occurs throughout the region. It is not confined to particular geologic landforms or bedrock regions but occurs on peatlands in poorly drained depressions and old lake basins wherever the groundwater is not so mobile or fertile as to favor white cedar. Many bogs of this type adjoin existing lakes or streams along portions of their perimeter. The type probably occupies a higher percentage of the landscape on the Vermilion Granite, on the related bedrocks of Quetico, and on the Duluth Gabbro than in other regions simply because there is more terrain suitable for peatland development there. In large peatlands it often occurs in a band of varying width inward from the bog margin, merging toward the center with the sphagnum–black spruce bog type. It sometimes also integrates with or adjoins mixed conifer swamp forest.

The tree and sapling layers are usually pure black spruce, although occasional jack pine or tamarack may occur. In most stands the tall-shrub layer is absent, and where shrubs are present speckled alder is virtually the only species. Labrador-tea is the most abundant low shrub, but where the spruce canopy is dense, this layer too may be almost lacking. Creeping snowberry, both blueberries, small cranberry, leather-leaf, bog-rosemary, and bog-laurel are often present but cover little area. The herb layer is scanty; the most common species are bog false Solomon's-seal, sedges, cotton-grass, cinnamon fern, pitcher-plant, bunchberry, bristly clubmoss, Indian pipe, bluebead-lily, starflower, and rarely dwarf rattlesnake-plantain orchid and stemless lady-slipper orchid. A continuous ground carpet of mosses is a hallmark of this community. All three feathermosses are often present, but Schreber's moss is by far the most abundant, often covering about 30 to 50 percent of the peat surface. Several species of sphagnum mosses also cover large areas. *Sphagnum magellanicum, S. angustifolium*, and *S. fuscum* are among the more common species (Janssens 1992). *Dicranum* and hair-cap mosses cover less area. Reindeer mosses often occur in small openings but cover little area.

Tamarack Bog Forest

This peatland community is uncommon in the Boundary Waters area but widespread to the west in the Big Bog region of Minnesota. The principal tree is tamarack, which occurs on slightly less acid and more fertile sites than it does in the black spruce bog forest. The peat surface is hummocky, and water usually stands in the bog hollows. Peats may be deep, and they are often decomposed, mucky, and difficult to walk on. Many examples occur along sluggish boggy streams, inland from the nearly treeless open muskeg that often borders such streams.

Most stands are even-aged, usually postdating a larch sawfly outbreak that killed the previous forest. Some stands date from past fires. Tamarack is potentially a large tree, but in the Boundary Waters most stands have been repeatedly killed by the sawfly since about 1900.

Often the tree layer is virtually pure tamarack, but black spruce is the most frequent associate. Saplings of other species are black spruce and/or cedar. Tall shrubs are often abundant, the most common being speckled alder. Bog-birch, willow, and red osier dogwood may also occur. Low shrubs may include Labrador-tea, leather-leaf, bog-laurel, bog-rosemary, creeping snowberry, dewberry, and small cranberry. Herbs include bunchberry, violets, bedstraws, blue flag, asters, bog false Solomon's-seal, pitcher-plant, clubmosses, ferns, horsetails, marsh cinquefoil, cotton-grass, other grasses, cattail, sedges, and rarely orchids. Mosses dominate the ground layer. Most common are several sphagnum mosses, hair-cap moss, and Schreber's feathermoss (Janssens 1992).

Sphagnum–Black Spruce

This community is the familiar open, stunted black spruce bog type so characteristic of northern North America. The peat surface is an undulating complex of sphagnum moss hummocks and deep mossy hollows, supporting an often dense cover of such heath shrubs as leather-leaf, Labrador-tea, and bog-laurel. The only tree of consequence is black spruce. The black spruce is typically only 15 to 25 feet tall and 2 to 5 inches in diameter at maturity. Mature trees are sometimes more than 150 years old. Occasional tamaracks, equally stunted, are sometimes scattered among the spruce. Peat depth is often 5 to 20 feet or more, the water table often stands near the bottoms of the bog hollows, and the bog waters are acid, typically pH 3.5 to 4.0. Many examples of this community are found far out toward the interior of large spruce bogs, some are adjacent to bog lakes, and others occur along boggy streams.

Many of these stunted black spruce bog stands have a multiaged structure, and many of the "young" spruce are "layers" that originated from the lower branches of old trees that took root after becoming overgrown by sphagnum mosses. This form of vegetative reproduction produces the clumpy distribution of spruce one often sees in this community. Other stands are of postfire origin and have an even-aged structure. Some stands occur in areas that were generally logged over, but this type was usually not affected because the trees were too small to be merchantable. The type often integrates with the black spruce bog forest community and with open muskeg. It occurs throughout the region and is not confined to specific bedrock provinces, although it may be more common on granitic terrain and on the Duluth Gabbro because the landscapes there are more favorable to bog formation.

Leather-leaf is by far the most abundant low shrub, followed by Labrador-tea, bog-laurel, bog-rosemary, creeping snowberry, small cranberry, and sometimes a few blueberries. Cotton-grasses are abundant; bog false Solomon's-seal and pitcher-plant are the only other herbs of note. The peat surface is almost entirely blanketed with mosses; *Sphagnum* mosses predominate (*S. fuscum* is often abundant), followed by Schreber's feathermoss, hair-cap moss, and *Dicranum* mosses. Reindeer mosses occur on many of the higher hummocks.

Ash-Elm Swamp Forest

This largely deciduous forest community is dominated by black ash, and until recently American elm shared dominance with ash. The community occurs on wet, intermittently flooded clayey, silty, or sandy soils or on black, mucky, decomposed organic soils. The soils and waters are rich in nutrients washed in from the adjacent uplands and are near neutral in reaction (pH 6.0 to 7.5). Boulders often project above the organic or silty soils. The type is of limited extent, occurring chiefly along streams or in surface drainageways along valley bottoms, frequently near lakeshores. A common location seen by canoeists is on delta soils of larger streams where they enter lakes, often near a portage.

Many forests have multiaged stand structures, probably because most stands have not burned for a long time or were only partially burned by the last fire. Where logging occurred, it usually only removed a few large white pines. The type is not restricted to particular geographic regions but is less common on infertile granitic terrain.

Black ash is the principal overstory dominant in most stands but often has many associates. American elm has recently been nearly eliminated from many stands by Dutch elm disease. Other common overstory associates include white spruce, white pine, paper birch, and sometimes the relatively rare yellow birch, silver maple, basswood, green ash, balsam poplar, and bur oak. The latter rarer species are more frequent in Voyageurs than in the BWCAW or Quetico. Red maple, white cedar, and balsam fir are often abundant in the understory as saplings or in intermediate canopy positions. Tall shrubs are often not dense, but mountain-maple, red osier and pagoda dogwood, willows, speckled alder, high-bush cranberry, beaked hazelnut, downy arrow-wood, red-berried elder, red raspberry, and honeysuckles are often present. Low shrubs are scarce, but poison ivy occasionally occurs in openings, and alder-leaved buckthorn, the vine Virginia creeper, wild black currant, swamp red currant, northern gooseberry, and other species of currants and gooseberries are found in many stands. The herb layer is rich in species, but many are not abundant. Some of the frequent or more interesting species include jewelweed, goldthread, bishop's-cap, twinflower, bunchberry, dewberry, marsh marigold, red baneberry, nodding trillium, tall lungwort, violets, bedstraws, common skullcap, field-mint, purple-stemmed aster, Joe-Pye weed, thoroughwort, sweet coltsfoot, shinleaf, blue flag, purple fringed orchid, lady fern, sensitive fern, rattlesnake fern, other ferns, grasses, field horsetail, forest horsetail, and clubmosses. Many moss species occur in the ground layer but do not cover much area.

Alder-Willow Shrub

This is a nonforest tall-shrub wetland community occurring chiefly along the floodplains of streams and in continuously wet, gently sloping flats. The dominant shrub is speckled alder, but on some sites willows and occasionally other shrubs also occur. Soils are usually sand, silt, or clay, or a black decomposed organic muck. Sites are generally fertile, not acid, but intermittently flooded. The type occurs throughout the region, and although individual stands are often narrow bands, in the aggregate the type covers considerable area. Scattered black spruce, tamarack, white cedar, balsam, or black ash often occur among the alders. Grasses, sedges, iris, several other herbs, ferns, and sometimes cattails and reeds cover the ground.

Marsh and Open Muskeg

This type is really a combination of two rather dissimilar communities, but they are described under this single heading to match the available area statistics (table 4.1). Most of the area is open muskeg. The muskeg community is essentially a sphagnum moss-cotton grass-sedge heath. It usually occurs either as a nearly treeless bog within a larger black spruce bog, or as a nearly treeless semifloating bog that appears to be actively invading a bog lake or stream. In either case the open muskeg community often integrates with a contiguous sphagnum–black spruce community.

The second subgroup is the marsh. Although there are few marshes in the Boundary Waters region, these communities are productive standing-water types supporting grasses, sedges, reeds, cattails, white panicled aster, grass-leaved goldenrod, bog goldenrod, marsh cinquefoil, common skullcap, blue flag, and many other wetland herbs and emergent aquatics. Marshes usually occur on more fertile soils and bedrocks where gently moving groundwaters flow across the land surface, often along active beaver ponds or the meadows of abandoned beaver ponds. Such marshes contrast sharply with the acid, nutrient-poor environments of muskegs.

The open muskeg community is widespread throughout the region. Scattered small, stunted black spruce and tamarack are often present. The pillowlike sphagnum moss hummocks usually support thickets of low heath shrubs, especially leather-leaf, bog-laurel, bog-rosemary, and small cranberry. In a few localities the large cranberry also may be found near lakeshores (Walshe 1980). Bog-birch (or dwarf birch) and sweet gale are often present, especially on the less acid floating bogs adjacent to lakes and streams. The peat surface is spongy, and the water table often stands within the hollows between hummocks. Cotton-grass, sedges, clubmosses, pitcher-plant, and round-leaved and spatula-leaved sundew are common herbs. Rare orchids sometimes found in floating-bog open muskeg include the rose pogonia, grass-pink, dragon's-mouth, and club-spur orchids.

LAKESHORE PLANTS OF MINERAL SOIL AND ROCKY SHORES

Many distinctive plants commonly occur in a narrow fringe between forest and water along the shorelines of lakes and streams, rooted in mineral soil or bedrock crevices. A few of these plants are seldom found elsewhere, whereas many also occur as members of other communities. This chapter would be incomplete without a brief treatment of such plants. I am indebted to the late Shan Walshe (1980) for his notes on the occurrence of Boundary Waters plants. This discussion covers plants that occur on land, not those rooted in shallow water or on floating bog margins, although a few also occur in those environments.

Among the several small trees that often create a shoreline fringe distinct from the adjacent upland forest are white cedar, green ash, and silver maple. The latter two species are common chiefly in the western BWCAW, Voyageurs, and southwestern Quetico. Some of the most common shrubs characteristic of rocky and mineral soil shorelines are sweet gale, speckled alder, leather-leaf, meadow-sweet, red osier dogwood, and winterberry. Common grasses and sedges include big bluestem, beaked sedge, hairy-fruited sedge, broom-like sedge, and Alan Crawford's sedge. Among the many herbs and ferns often found in the shoreline fringe are royal fern, spearwort, bristly crowfoot, blue flag, grass-leaved goldenrod, white panicled aster, flat-topped white aster, Joe-Pye weed, thoroughwort, swamp-loosestrife, field-mint, mad-dog skullcap, common houstonia, New England blue violet, common bugle-weed, northern ragwort, spotted water-hemlock, dodder, and sundrops.

The Dynamic Nature of Plant Communities

Plant communities are not immutable landscape features. In fact, in an ecosystem such as the Boundary Waters region where most natural communities develop following one or more of several natural disturbances, just the time since the last disturbance can have a major influence on the character of communities. The effect of human influence adds even more possibilities for change.

In the Boundary Waters nine major factors may cause important changes in plant communities (excluding for now such longer-term factors as climatic change and plant migrations): windstorms, drought, flooding, fire, insects, mammals, plant diseases, humans (especially logging and postlogging forestry activities), and succession (gradual natural changes in community composition and structure related to the passage of time, in the absence of major disturbances). Later chapters explore in depth the effects of these factors. The purpose here is just to recognize the existence of change to show that the communities described in this chapter are not the only ones.

The first eight of these factors are sources of disturbances that are each capable of triggering changes in the species composition of some plant communities sufficient to change the type to which we would assign the area. When several of these factors interact, as they often do (for example, drought, windstorms, insects, and fire), their combined effects can cause major and very rapid changes in vegetation that may persist for long periods.

For example, a jack pine–fir community that developed gradually after a fire in 1864 may now support a tree layer of old jack pine, aspen, birch, balsam, and spruce with a typical understory vegetation. Assume that the jack pine is under attack by the jack pine budworm, that most of the mature balsam have been recently killed by the spruce budworm, that many aspen and birch are beginning to die from factors associated with old age, and that a major wind-

storm has recently blown down many trees in the area. Assume further that a large forest fire sweeps through the stand in early fall during a major drought. After the fire, there is prolific seedling regeneration of jack pine, aspen, and birch but not of balsam. Also assume that because of the complete burning of the soil organic layer (litter and duff, or humus), the shrubs, herbs, and mosses that colonize the burn are at first a very different assemblage from the prefire understory vegetation. These are all realistic assumptions, as we will see in later chapters. The outcome would then produce a new plant community that for a few decades at least would be quite different from the prefire community.

Succession is more subtle, but over periods of many years, it can also produce changes that would lead us to reassign a community to a new type. For example, the new postfire community just described may eventually see reinvasion by the shade-tolerant balsam fir and by the shrubs and herbs typical of the former jack pine–fir community. The postfire succession will then have gone full circle. The postfire vegetation one usually sees for the first decade or so after an intense fire in a jack pine–black spruce (or in a black spruce–feathermoss community) certainly could not be classified the same as before the fire, and yet very often the original community does redevelop in 30 or 40 years. Long after a new forest is established following fire or windstorms, the aging forest undergoes many complex changes in composition. For example, senescent or dead balsam and spruce become draped with the tree lichen old man's beard, and large stand openings caused by windfalls are often invaded by raspberries and other shrubs. We will revisit the succession process and postdisturbance changes in forest composition later.

To summarize, in a disturbance-driven forest, ecosystem communities do change through perfectly natural processes, and the communities described here do not cover all possibilities. When one adds all the posttreatment vegetation combinations that modern logging and forestry practices create, especially in the first few decades following logging (and large areas of the Boundary Waters, Quetico, and Voyageurs have been recently logged), the total vegetation becomes even more varied.

The plant-community area statistics for the BWCAW in table 4.1 are therefore really snapshots in time, a time band perhaps from about 1952 through the 1990s. The virgin forest areas and the areas logged in the early big-pine logging era could be classified into these communities because the classes fit mature forests best, and most such areas have remained in mature forest because of fire exclusion and a lack of other extensive natural disturbances or logging. There is no way to easily describe the vegetation of recently logged areas. Both succession and natural disturbances are now slowly changing the mix of communities on the landscape even in the virgin forests and early logging areas. The same situation prevails in Quetico and Voyageurs.

Early Forest and Human History

The trees, shrubs, and herbs that now grow in the Boundary Waters region have origins far back in geological history. For example, species that we now associate with the Canadian and Alaskan boreal forest such as white and black spruce, tamarack, jack pine, balsam fir, aspen, and paper birch moved back and forth across Minnesota repeatedly in response to the climatic changes associated with the advances and retreats of the Ice Age continental glaciers. Numerous finds of wood, cones, and other remains of these trees and associated shrubs and herbs beneath thick deposits of glacial till and lake sediments provide the geologic evidence of their occurrence.

Geologic Setting for the Early Postglacial Forests

The paths of advances and retreats of the many ice lobes of the Ice Age glaciers across North America have been the subject of extensive studies ever since Louis Agassiz, the great Swiss geologist, first described the evidence of continental glaciation in Europe a century and a half ago. Minnesota has played a vital role in this research, partly because of the abundance, clarity, and accessibility of glacial features on the landscape: distinctive moraines and eskers, several drumlin fields, thousands of lakes and bogs, three vast lake plains left by former glacial lakes, and the fortunate circumstance that the deposits left by the ice lobes crossing Minnesota from several directions have distinctly different colors, textures, and rock content, making recognition easier.

The sequence of retreats and readvances by the last three ice lobes to override or approach the Boundary Waters influenced the character of the first vegetation to invade the area. The Rainy Lobe from the northeast pushed beyond the present position of the Mississippi River and then retreated far back to the Vermilion Moraine, a distinctive band of hummocky glacial deposits that marks the southwestern edge of the rock-bound landscape of the BWCAW. Later the St. Louis Sublobe of the Des Moines Lobe pushed in from the west, almost reaching the western part of the BWCAW about 12,000 years ago. At the same time the Superior Lobe pushed southwest through the Lake Superior basin (Wright 1972).

By 11,000 years ago the ice margin of the Rainy Lobe stood roughly along the Canadian border. Meanwhile the Des Moines Lobe and St. Louis Sublobe retreated into Canada, and their meltwaters produced Glacial Lake Agassiz in the Red River valley; its waters reached eastward at least to the Voyageurs area and perhaps to Basswood Lake (Wright 1972, 1989). Lake Agassiz drained southward at this time into the Minnesota-Mississippi river system. Most of the BWCAW and Quetico was ice-free, although Lake Agassiz probably still covered much of Quetico's lower terrain, and ice persisted in the Superior basin. The ice then withdrew east of present Lake Nipigon and exposed a lower outlet for Lake Agassiz into the Superior basin and thence to the Atlantic, temporarily lowering Agassiz to the area far north of Quetico. Then about 10,000 years ago the ice readvanced in northwestern Ontario almost to Quetico and in the Superior basin, closing the eastern outlet and expanding Lake Agassiz, which again drained south to the Minnesota River. About 9,500 years ago melting reopened the eastern outlet (Wright 1989). Some low terrain in northwestern Quetico may have remained flooded by Lake Agassiz until nearly 8,000 years ago (Zoltai 1965; Ontario Ministry of Natural Resources 1977). The ice front in the Hudson Bay region was still only about 260 miles northeast of Quetico 8,000 years ago (Bryson et al. 1969).

Sequence of Postglacial Plant Invasions

Quantitative studies of pollen grains and larger plant remains preserved in the bottom muds of glacial lakes have been used by paleoecologists to document the sequence of past plant communities that occupied a region around the lake. Cores of the lake-bottom sediments are taken with a tube outfitted with a piston. The corer can be driven by hand about 3 feet at a time to great depths, using extension rods as needed to penetrate the organic bottom muds, which may be more than 40 feet thick. In the laboratory the cores are sampled at intervals from top to bottom. The samples are treated chemically to concentrate the pollen grains, which are then identified and counted under the microscope. Radiocarbon dating of the organic sediment makes it possible to determine the age of key layers to within a few hundred years, even in sediment as much as 40,000 years old. The result of these studies is a history of the vegetation that occupied the area from the time of origin of the lake to the present.

The best evidence of the first plant invasions along the southern edge of the BWCAW comes from Weber Lake, a small lake located about 25 miles southwest of Isabella in a swale between two drumlins in the Toimi Drumlin Field. The lake probably formed about 17,000 years ago and was later approached to within a few miles on the north by the Rainy Lobe, on the east by the Superior Lobe, and on the

west by the St. Louis Sublobe, all between 16,000 and 12,000 years ago. Organic sedimentation of the lake basin began about 15,000 years ago. For almost 4,000 years until about 11,000 years ago, when the closest glaciers had finally melted back some distance, a treeless herb-dominated tundra vegetation apparently grew in the Weber Lake locality. The pollen record gives no indication of climatic shifts during this long period that saw glaciers advance to within a few miles, retreat for millennia, and return again. The explanation may be that significant warming did not occur locally because of the almost continuous proximity of glacial ice, leaving an unstable rocky landscape that could support only a sparse cover of shrubs, grasses, and sedges (Fries 1962; Wright 1976).

About 10,300 years ago a dwarf birch shrubland developed in the Weber Lake region, before the arrival of trees. This event coincided with the withdrawal of the St. Louis Sublobe to the northwest, the formation of Glacial Lake Agassiz, and the shrinkage of the Rainy Lobe into northeastern Quetico. The end of the Great Ice Age was arriving in the Boundary Waters. Other dated sites farther south indicate that regional warming actually began about 15,000 years ago, but 4,000 years of ice wastage was required to shrink the vast Laurentide ice sheets irrevocably back into Canada, except the Superior Lobe, which still lay in the Superior basin 10,000 years ago (Fries 1962; Wright 1989).

Sometime shortly after 10,000 years ago spruce expanded into the shrubland, and a full spruce forest was soon established in the Weber Lake region. The initial spruce–dwarf birch community probably was an open woodland with only scattered tree cover (Fries 1962; Wright 1976).

Weber Lake remains the only well-dated site in the Boundary Waters area that was open to plant colonization during the full period of ice withdrawal. But beginning about 11,000 years ago, the regional picture was widened at Lake of the Clouds, a small lake in the BWCAW 8 miles southwest of Saganaga Lake (Craig 1972; Swain 1973; Amundson and Wright 1979), and at Myrtle Lake, a tiny bog lake 70 miles west of Ely, just below the upper beach of Glacial Lake Agassiz (Janssen 1968). These three sites give a clear picture of regional forest history from 11,000 years ago until the present, a picture consistent with the continental record of postglacial vegetation changes from scores of other accurately dated sites.

Lake of the Clouds is the first site in North America where annually laminated lake sediments were used to date the sequence of pollen and charcoal and to check the accuracy of radiocarbon dating (Stuiver 1971, 1975). In small deep lakes protected from the wind the oxygenated surface water may not be mixed to the bottom, so that the annual layers of sediment may remain undisturbed by bottom organisms. Lake of the Clouds is a small trout lake 110 feet deep. The lake sediment had 9,349 countable annual layers, plus a fluid section at the top estimated to contain about 200 layers (Craig 1972).

The spruce forest that began to expand sometime after 10,000 years ago probably contained both white and black spruce. Both now occur in Canada to the northern limit of trees. This spruce forest also contained some tamarack, northern white cedar, aspen, and even black ash, elm, and oak. It may be hard to believe that these temperate deciduous trees could be common in a boreal spruce forest, but this association is widely recorded elsewhere in the Midwest, implying that the late-glacial climate was by then already as temperate as today. Clearly the spruce forests of that time have no analogue today (Fries 1962; Janssen 1968; Craig 1972; Amundson and Wright 1979).

Just as the spruce forests were reaching their maximum development about 10,000 to 9,500 years ago, pine (probably jack pine) began invading all three areas. By 9,300 years ago spruce was in steep decline, and jack pine was rapidly taking over the landscape. Red pine may also have been present, but the pollen of jack and red pine cannot be distinguished. Oak, elm, and white cedar decreased markedly after 9,000 years ago. Balsam fir was present, and paper birch arrived at Lake of the Clouds about 9,500 years ago and became almost as abundant as in today's forests by 8,900 years ago. Both green and speckled alder arrived at Lake of the Clouds about 8,300 years ago (Craig 1972; Amundson and Wright 1979). Detailed pollen diagrams also show that a full suite of other shrubs, herbs, grasses, and sedges invaded the region during this period.

Both climatic warming and postglacial plant migrations were clearly operating simultaneously to gradually change the composition of these early pine forests.

THE POSTGLACIAL WARM-DRY PERIOD

From about 8,000 to 4,000 years ago postglacial warming peaked in central North America, with striking effects on the vegetation of most of Minnesota but with less extreme results in the lands north of Lake Superior. In northwestern Minnesota near present Itasca State Park a boreal spruce-poplar forest prevailed soon after deglaciation, from about 12,000 to 11,000 years ago. Then, in a shift similar to that in the Boundary Waters, jack pine forests replaced spruce. On the lowlands only 30 miles west of Itasca the spruce forests were replaced directly by prairie, which persisted until converted to farmland in the twentieth century. About 8,500 years ago, as postglacial warming neared its maximum, the jack pine forests at Itasca and eastward were replaced by oak savanna (McAndrews 1966). The warmer and drier climate persisted until about 4,000 years ago. In Minnesota it is often called the prairie period because the western prairies expanded far eastward in central and southeastern Minnesota as well as in adjacent Iowa and southern Wisconsin.

In northern Minnesota the upland vegetation in the Myrtle Lake locality shifted from jack pine forest to oak savanna about 7,900 years ago. There, only 50 miles southwest of the BWCAW and 45 miles south of Voyageurs, the climate remained sufficiently warm and dry to maintain oak savanna with prairie grasses on the drier uplands until about 7,000 years ago, when closed oak-ironwood-ash-aspen forests developed on the uplands (Janssen 1968).

North of Lake Superior in the Boundary Waters the most significant vegetation changes in the postglacial warm interval began with the arrival of white pine, which reached Weber Lake about 7,200 years ago, and Lake of the Clouds about 6,000 years ago. There it remained throughout the prairie period, during which pollen of grasses, sedges, some prairie herbs, and oak increased, probably mostly representing pollen blown in from prairie and oak savanna to the southwest. Red pine also became a component of many forest stands during this period if it had not arrived earlier. White pine probably reached Myrtle Lake about 6,700 years ago and thereafter became a prominent element on mineral soil sites in that region (Fries 1962; Janssen 1968; Craig 1972; Jacobson 1979).

EXPANSION OF BOREAL FOREST SPECIES

The three pines, white, jack, and red, remained consistently prominent in the Lake of the Clouds region from about 5,500 to 3,000 years ago. Beginning about 3,000 years ago, the pines, especially white pine, began a gradual decline. At about this time spruce, white cedar, and fir increased. Similar changes in forest composition were recorded at Weber Lake. The direction of these changes persisted up to the logging era at the start of the twentieth century. By then there had been a substantial decrease in white pine and significant increases in jack pine and spruce. The relative abundance of the three pines at the time logging began indicates that red pine most likely suffered decreases paralleling those of white pine (Craig 1972; Fries 1962). These changes in forest composition, as well as comparable shifts across North America, are attributed to a cooler and perhaps wetter climate in the past 3,000 years.

CHANGES IN THE POSTGLACIAL
FOREST COMMUNITIES

The pollen records from Lake of the Clouds and Weber Lake show that the forests of the Boundary Waters underwent reasonably continuous changes in species composition and abundance throughout postglacial time. Ecologically significant changes in composition were still under way in the forests at the time of the early big-pine logging in response to the so-called Little Ice Age, a cooler period from A.D. 1600 to 1895, when logging began. If we had not intervened with logging and fire suppression in the twentieth century, more adjustments to climate would likely have occurred. Even with our interventions, subtle changes are still under way. Thus the jack pine–black spruce forests,

the aspen-birch-fir forests, and the stands of old red and white pine in the virgin areas of the Boundary Waters today are part of a dynamic, ever-changing scene.

Records of the migration of white pine from its glacial refuge in the Appalachian Mountains to and across Minnesota and its movements in northern Ontario provide lessons in the factors that influence forest composition. White pine was in the state of Virginia about 13,000 years ago and then spread both north and west, reaching Connecticut by 9,000 years ago, southern Michigan 10,000 years ago, north-central Wisconsin 8,500 years ago, and Cedar Bog Lake just north of Minneapolis 8,000 years ago. By then the postglacial warm interval was approaching its peak, prairie and oak savanna were invading central and northwestern Minnesota, and the dry climate coupled with competition from prairie grasses prevented further northwestward spread of white pine for 5,000 years. White pine probably found its way to the Weber Lake and Lake of the Clouds localities via northwestern Wisconsin and the west end of Lake Superior, reaching the Boundary Waters 6,500 years ago. The westward migration of white pine was not resumed until 3,000 years ago, when climatic cooling again favored it. White pine reached Itasca State Park 2,700 years ago and only became dominant about 2,000 years ago. It was not joined by red pine and jack pine until 1,000 years ago. Southeast of Itasca in Morrison County, white pine reached Billy's Lake only 1,000 to 800 years ago. The loggers that cut the big pine in that region near the turn of the century were probably cutting the first, second, and third generations of white pine to grow there in postglacial time (McAndrews 1966; Jacobson 1979; Davis 1981). In contrast, jack pine reached northwestern Minnesota at least 10,000 years ago from a glacial refuge in the southeastern states, migrating almost twice as fast as white pine (McAndrews 1966; Davis 1981).

The white pine and jack pine records and the records of the early postglacial spruce forests emphasize the individualistic behavior of forest species. Forest communities are not immutable entities that move as units in response to climatic change. Climate was clearly a powerful driving force in shaping the sequence of postglacial vegetation changes, but the rates and paths of migration of individual species can also have major effects on community composition. White pine simply arrived too late in Minnesota to play a role in the early postglacial forests, especially in the west. Many similar examples exist in the records of other species that confirm the individualistic behavior of tree species and reinforce the view that forest communities are in many ways transitory assemblages of plants (Davis 1981; Jacobson, Webb, and Grimm 1987).

Forest and grassland fires must have been important agents in mediating postglacial vegetation changes. We know from the charcoal fragments in Lake of the Clouds sediments that forest fires were a factor in the destruction and regeneration of forests in the Boundary Waters for at least 10,000 years (Swain 1973). Fire clearly can have important differential effects on the survival and regeneration of various trees, shrubs, and ground-layer plants. In some circumstances these effects must have encouraged one species over others, or even a whole class of vegetation over another. I explore these kinds of relationships in depth in later chapters, but here I only make the point that fire must have been one of the key environmental factors that affected postglacial vegetation changes.

In the Boundary Waters region the role of changing fire regimes from 10,000 to 2,000 years ago is difficult to establish in the shifts from spruce to jack pine, or from jack pine to white pine and then back to more jack pine, but there are hints in Swain's (1973) Lake of the Clouds charcoal record that fire was a factor. Cwynar (1978) documented the presence of fire in forests in Algonquin Provincial Park in Ontario from A.D. 770 to 1270, again using charcoal stratigraphy in laminated lake sediments, but because his pollen data do not show a persistent vegetation change over that period, the possibility that fire frequency or severity might be related to such a change cannot be tested. Detailed work on local fire history and climatic changes at Itasca State Park by Clark, using fire-scar dates and close-interval sampling of annually laminated lake sediments for charcoal, shows much promise, but his methods were not integrated with pollen analysis to attack the questions raised here for key periods of postglacial vegetation change (Clark 1989, 1990a).

POSTGLACIAL VEGETATION CHANGES IN WETLANDS

The vegetation of most present Boundary Waters bogs, forested swamps, and treeless marshes has had a very different postglacial history from that of the uplands to which all the foregoing discussions apply. Most such areas started their existence 15,000 to 11,000 years ago as lakes, ponds, or at least intermittently wet bedrock depressions or lowlands. The available evidence indicates that many present thin peatlands then went through stages as grass-sedge meadows and willow-alder wetlands, and in many cases subsequent acidification and colonization by sphagnum mosses and often cedar, tamarack, and finally black spruce trees. Deeper basins mostly went through the classic lake-filling succession: first a bottom sedimentation phase, then a sedge mat stage, invasion of the consolidated sedge-covered peatland by sphagnum mosses and bog shrubs, and finally black spruce or tamarack trees. The history of each peatland depended on the area, depth, water flow, and chemical properties of the basin or wet soils involved. Many peatlands are still passing through some of the stages sketched here in all or portions of their watersheds.

Postglacial climatic changes also apparently affected the course of peatland development. In early postglacial times the climate was probably favorable for peatland expansion, but then it became warm and dry enough to inhibit the development of peat or even to destroy the peat that had already accumulated. Most bog development and peatland expansion occurred primarily after the peak of the postglacial warm interval.

The actual timing of peatland development in Minnesota has been documented best in the Lake Agassiz peatlands west of the Boundary Waters. The site with considerable data closest to the Boundary Waters is the Myrtle Lake Peatland Natural Area, located about 40 miles south of International Falls, where Janssen conducted the studies mentioned earlier and where I did much of my work on peatland development (Janssen 1968; Heinselman 1970). Organic sedimentation of the small Myrtle Lake basin and of the deepest depression elsewhere in the peatland began about 11,000 years ago. There also appears to have been an early period of some peatland development from 10,000 to 8,000 years ago around the edge of the growing peatland by swamp forests of elm, tamarack, black ash, and perhaps some cedar and spruce. Then during the peak of the postglacial warm period the presence of charcoal suggests that much of the accumulated peat was burned, and that sedge and cattail fens and willow shrublands occupied much of the peatland, especially from about 8,000 to 6,000 years ago (Janssens 1992). Beginning perhaps 4,500 years ago, relatively rich tamarack and spruce swamp forests, probably with an alder understory, grew over the peatland. Sphagnum–black spruce bogs expanded about 3,000 years ago.

The Myrtle Lake peatland is 13 miles long and is larger than any peatland in the Boundary Waters. It also differs from the peatlands in the Boundary Waters in three important respects. First, the Lake Agassiz peatlands formed on a vast, nearly level clay plain—the bed of former Lake Agassiz. Second, the lake clays and beach sands on which the peat formed are rich in calcium and other bases derived by glacial action from the limestones of Manitoba. Third, Myrtle Lake is just enough southwest of the Boundary Waters to have been affected more by the dry climate of the postglacial warm period.

In the Boundary Waters the sterile acidic bedrocks and soils that form the substrate for peatland development, the slightly cooler and wetter summers, and the greater local relief did not provide the opportunity for swamping (or paludification) of vast, nearly level areas, yet the abundance of small water-filled basins offered far more opportunities for lake-filling bog development processes, and the sterile acidic environment encouraged the encroachment of sphagnum mosses even on gently sloping bedrock terrain. These factors have led to the postglacial development of countless small peatlands of many sizes and shapes in the Boundary Waters, most of the acidic black spruce–sphagnum bog type. One marker that seems to remain almost the same in both areas, however, is the time of initiation of widespread sphagnum-black spruce bog development. In the Boundary Waters region the late postglacial spruce expansion began about 3,400 years ago (Craig 1972), whereas, as noted earlier, in the Myrtle Lake peatland black

spruce and sphagnum both began to increase about 3,100 years ago. Much of the late postglacial spruce in the pollen record in both areas must have come from peatlands because today in both regions on bog islands the majority of the spruce is black spruce.

The Role of Humans in the Ecosystem before European Settlement

People have been present in at least some portions of North America throughout late-glacial and postglacial time. We know that even the earliest people depended on a variety of animal and plant resources for subsistence and used fire for cooking and other purposes. They lived in an intimate relationship with all components of the ecosystem and in that sense were an integral part of the natural system. Thus a comprehensive understanding of the Boundary Waters ecosystem must include the role of people. Five phases of cultural history are recognized (Johnson 1988):

- The migration of humans from Siberia into North America (15,000 to 12,000 years ago)
- The Paleoindian Tradition (12,000 to 8,000 years ago) and the migration of humans into the Boundary Waters region
- The Eastern Archaic Tradition (8,000 to 2,800 years ago)
- The Woodland Tradition (2,800 to 300 years ago)
- The Voyageurs Era (A.D. 1690 to 1865)

THE MIGRATION OF HUMANS INTO NORTH AMERICA

The timing of the arrival of the first humans in the Americas is still debated. The first Americans came from Siberia via a strip of land connecting Siberia with Alaska (called Beringia) now covered by the Bering Sea due to rising sea levels from melting of the Ice Age glaciers. Geologists place the probable window of opportunity for the invasion in the interval between 20,000 and 12,000 years ago, when ice-free land virtually connected the two continents. Migration southward from Alaska probably came when the Laurentide and Cordilleran ice sheets retreated enough to open the "Alberta corridor." Although little is known about these first migrants into the Americas, they were the ancestors of the first Native Americans to enter the Boundary Waters region.

THE PALEOINDIAN TRADITION
(12,000 TO 8,000 YEARS AGO)

People called the Clovis hunters constituted the earliest known widely distributed cultural group in the Americas. Their lifestyles and artifacts plus those of some related peoples are called the Paleoindian Tradition. The Clovis people were nomadic hunters who pursued the now extinct large Ice Age mammals. A diagnostic artifact of the Clovis is a particular style of fluted chipped-stone projectile point, which has been found at many North American sites as far east as Nova Scotia, in some cases in association with the remains of extinct large mammals, particularly the cold-adapted, grassland-dwelling woolly mammoth and the mastodon, an elephant apparently adapted to more temperate forests or savannas. Other large mammals, now mostly extinct, that roamed the late-glacial open spruce forests included bison, caribou, ground sloth, lion, saber-toothed cat, short-faced bear, tapir, horse, camel, and other large herbivores. Radiocarbon dates from mammoth and mastodon remains and other organic materials associated with the Clovis mostly fall between 12,000 and 9,000 years ago. The Clovis hunters might have been a factor in these extinctions (West 1983).

Solid evidence of Paleoindians in Minnesota is scanty, partly because few studies of its earliest humans were done until the 1980s. Woolly mammoth bones and teeth have been found at several sites in Minnesota, but none has yet been connected with human activity (Johnson 1988). Orrin Shane of the Science Museum of Minnesota located 40 Minnesota fluted points in public and private collections. Most confirmed fluted-point locations were in the southern third of the state. The scarcity of reported Clovis points in the north might be due as much to the difficulty of finding points in heavily forested areas as to a real scarcity or absence of these artifacts. However, the lack of finds in the agricultural areas of northwestern Minnesota, even south-

east of Lake Agassiz, could indicate the virtual absence of Clovis and related early big-game hunters in that region (Orrin Shane, personal communication, 1991). In the Boundary Waters only a narrow tundra-covered area remained continuously ice-free during the early part of the Paleoindian period, when much of Quetico and Voyageurs was mostly still ice-covered.

When the Clovis and related spear-point styles disappeared, they were replaced by a number of new styles. The Plano point, a beautifully chipped stone point without fluting, is widespread in the Boundary Waters and throughout Minnesota. These points date from near the end of the Paleoindian Tradition, between about 10,000 and 7,000 years ago (Steinbring 1974; Johnson 1988). By the sheer abundance of Plano and related points we can guess that the Native American populations of the Boundary Waters increased significantly in that period. The Plano hunters might have been taking white-tailed deer, woodland caribou, moose, elk, or bison, all of which could have occurred either in the jack pine, birch, and spruce forest habitats of the region or in the oak savannas and prairies to the west at the end of the period. Johnson (1988) speculates that populations around the present reservoirs north of Duluth wintered in the forests and hunted the prairies in summer.

On Knife Lake, which forms the border between Minnesota and Ontario in the heart of the BWCAW and Quetico, Paleoindian stone quarries on both the U.S. and Canadian sides are the source of some of the Plano points in the region (Gordon Peters, personal communication, 1991). Just west of Thunder Bay, Ontario, at the Cummins site, a red jasper quarry is a source for many spear points chipped from that rock type. Plano points of jasper are found at the Thunder Bay Brohm site, at South Fowl Lake on the east end of the BWCAW, and at the Houska Point site in Ranier just west of Voyageurs (Steinbring 1974).

The total human population in the Boundary Waters region in Paleoindian times can only be guessed, but the evidence points toward only scattered, small nomadic groups of hunters. Some plant foods such as berries must have been eaten in summer, but these people had no pottery, and they built no shelters that left evidence. What shelter they had must have been only temporary lean-tos or skin tents. There is no evidence of woodworking or the use of watercraft. They must have used fire for cooking and for warmth in winter, but the evidence is scant because in the Boundary Waters surface fire hearths are not well preserved, and good rock shelters do not exist.

THE ARCHAIC TRADITION
(8,000 TO 2,800 YEARS AGO)

With the onset of the postglacial warm-dry interval about 8,000 years ago, human implements and lifestyles began to change. The earliest and best-documented site of the entire Archaic period in Minnesota is the Itasca Park Bison Kill site, with a radiocarbon date of about 8,300 years ago (Shay 1971). The site is 145 miles southwest of the Boundary Waters, but it gives us a glimpse of the people that used the area as the vegetation was shifting from open jack pine forests to oak savanna and prairie. Here, where a stream enters the southern end of Lake Itasca, small groups of hunters killed the now extinct larger species of bison as they forded the stream, perhaps on fall migrations. The hunters butchered the animals on the spot, threw the remains in the lake, and then processed the meat and hides at campsites on a nearby ridge (Shay 1971).

Sedimentation at the end of Lake Itasca at this time, along with peat formation in the 7,000 years since then, preserved many animal remains and artifacts and left sediments that Shay used for pollen studies and radiocarbon dating. Between about 8,300 and 7,000 years ago at least 16 bison were killed and butchered there, indicated by the number of skulls, horns, and bones found. Remains of fish and turtles suggest that these were used as well, perhaps during spring fishing encampments. The skull of a domestic dog was found—the oldest in Minnesota. Other mammals whose remains were recovered include white-tailed deer, moose, wolf, black bear, fisher, otter, beaver, snowshoe hare, and small mammals. Among the artifacts found in the peat or at ridge campsites were a variety of stone projectile points, hide scrapers, knives, choppers, perforators, and other tools. Some toolmaking occurred at the campsites. Shay (1971) postulates that groups of perhaps 25 people

camped intermittently at the site in the fall or spring over several centuries.

Beginning about 7,000 years ago, new types of stone projectile points, polished stone gouges, grooved axes, other new stone tools, and copper points and tools signaled changing lifestyles. This culture and its artifacts are called the Old Copper Complex (Johnson 1988). The new culture spread throughout the Lake Superior region, including the Boundary Waters. The copper came from surface occurrences of native copper and small open pits mostly on Isle Royale and perhaps near Minong, Wisconsin. Stone projectile points were smaller, stemmed, and corner-notched, and not so well finished as earlier. Some may now have had tipped darts thrown with an atlatl. Copper products included various styles of socketed projectile points, knives, gouges, chisels, adzes, harpoons, and awls. They were made simply by hammering raw copper nuggets with hammer stones. Copper technology apparently began in the Boundary Waters about 5,000 years ago. The Old Copper people continued a seminomadic way of life, hunting both large and small game, spearing fish on spawning runs, and probably eating hazelnuts, acorns, berries, and fruits. Given what we know of the vegetation of the Boundary Waters then, white-tailed deer likely replaced caribou as the principal large game. The human population of the region apparently remained small, but the use of typical Old Copper Complex tools persisted until about 3,000 years ago (Johnson 1988).

Several finds of large polished-stone and copper gouges and copper chisels suggest the making of dugout canoes. In Old Copper times white pine and red pine must have provided a ready source of large, easily worked roundwood suitable for that purpose (Steinbring 1974). Thus began the use of the Boundary Waters canoe routes we still know today. We do not know when these waterways first became travel arteries, but it must have been nearly 5,000 years ago, judging from the distribution of Old Copper Complex artifacts along major canoe routes. Significant finds of these artifacts have been documented from South Fowl Lake, the town of Winton, and Crane Lake in the BWCAW area, from Pickerel Lake in Quetico, and from Houska Point on Rainy Lake just west of Voyageurs. A burial near the mouth of the Little Fork River where it joins the Rainy River contained the skeleton of a five-year-old child and two copper projectile points. Copper probably had a supernatural meaning to these early Lake Superior region peoples (Steinbring 1974). The lakes, streams, and connecting portages of the Boundary Waters probably were also major winter travel routes because the energy cost of lengthy overland travel in winter is excessive even with snowshoes.

THE WOODLAND TRADITION
(2,800 TO 300 YEARS AGO)

Beginning about 2,800 years ago, the development of pottery and other changes in technology, subsistence strategies, and social practices produced a new cultural tradition that in the Boundary Waters region persisted in evolving patterns up to the time of European contact about A.D. 1690. There was now a much stronger dependence on fishing and later on wild rice and other plant foods, although hunting both large and small game remained important. The recurrent seasonal use of base camps apparently increased, but the fundamental economic strategy remained the gathering of wild plant and animal foods. In at least the western portions of the region, burying the dead in large mounds became common. This way of life is called the Woodland Tradition. In southern Minnesota, agriculture based on growing corn, squash, and other crops began about 1,100 years ago, and the Mississippian Tradition developed in parallel with the evolving cultures of the north. In the Boundary Waters the growing season was simply too short for corn, and the unfavorable soils and landforms precluded virtually all agriculture up to the time of European contact (Johnson 1988).

Dugout canoes persisted until at least 1,000 years ago, but sometime between then and 500 years ago birch-bark canoes were perfected, surely facilitating mobility in the Boundary Waters (Gordon Peters, personal communication, 1991). The bow and arrow apparently replaced the atlatl and dart in hunting about 1,700 years ago, yielding further gains in efficiency (Shay 1990). Chipped-stone arrowheads were generally stemmed and side-notched. Socketed and perforated harpoons made of deer or moose antlers were used in fishing. Copper tools became much less abundant than in the Archaic, perhaps because the supply was inadequate or because trade was cut off by conflicts. Animal hides were used for clothing up to the time of European contact.

The Woodland Tradition in the Canadian border region is subdivided by Lenius and Olinyk (1990) into Laurel, Blackduck, and Rainy River Composite cultures, distinguished by differences in pottery shapes, decorative markings, and pottery-making methods, as well as by other artifacts, time spans, and inferred subsistence and social practices.

The Laurel culture, named for a former town at the junction of the Big Fork and Rainy rivers, 17 miles west of International Falls, spans the interval from about 2,050 to 1,000 years ago (Lenius and Olinyk 1990). Laurel sites are widespread in the Boundary Waters, especially in the western half. The Grand Mound, preserved as a historic site, is over 100 feet in diameter and 40 feet high, the largest prehistoric burial mound in the upper Midwest. Studies of vertebrate remains in other mounds by Lukens (1973) indicate that moose, bison, white-tailed deer, and black bear were the principal big game taken. Only one possible caribou was reported. Forty percent of all mammal bones were beaver, indicating a strong reliance on this animal for meat and furs, and demonstrating the extent to which the Laurel economy used waterways. Sturgeon, northern pike, and suckers were the most frequently found fish, probably taken by spearing on spring spawning runs in the Rainy and Big Fork rivers, and possibly also through the ice in winter. It is not entirely clear in what seasons the Laurel people used these sites, or how many people camped at them at given times. Spring and early summer use is strongly suggested by the fish taken (Lukens 1973).

Analyses of trace elements in copper tools found at a Laurel site indicate the most probable source of copper tools was the Minong, Wisconsin, region. The Big Rice Lake site north of Virginia was a late summer and early fall wild-rice processing camp used in Laurel, Terminal Woodland, and historic times. A radiocarbon date from a rice-parching pit of A.D. 280 provides an early date for wild-rice harvesting. Again there were copper tools, here possibly of both Minong and Isle Royale origin (Rapp, Allert, and Peters 1990).

Anfinson (1990) believes that the location of many Laurel sites in the Border Lakes Region (as he defined it) implies that wild rice was not a principal resource during much of the period. However, several good wild-rice lakes and streams exist in the BWCAW and Quetico and adjacent areas, and at least some of these have Laurel-period rice camps. Along with sites already mentioned, Laurel sites have been studied at Nett Lake, a famous rice lake west of Orr used by Native Americans to the present day, and at the Pearson site on Lake Vermilion (Stoltman 1973). Other good present-day rice lakes and streams in the BWCAW are Manomin (south of Bayley Bay of Basswood), Big Rice (south of Big Lake), Rice (west of Slim), Rice (west of Isabella), Hula (south of Basswood), and portions of the Moose and Little Indian Sioux rivers, and in Quetico, Kawa Bay of Kawnipi Lake. The eastern BWCAW and portions of the Hunter Island region of Quetico have fewer wild-rice lakes and might have been less inhabited by Woodland people for that reason.

The Blackduck culture apparently overlapped the Laurel broadly both in time and geographically, beginning 500 years later, between about 1,500 and 1,300 years ago, but ending in Minnesota about the same time as the Laurel 1,000 years ago. Blackduck sites and artifacts have been studied at the Smith site on the Rainy River, at several sites in the Leech Lake Indian Reservation region near Deer River, Minnesota, at Pitner's Point and Oak Point Island on Rainy Lake adjacent to Voyageurs, on Isle Royale, at the Cressman site northeast of Quetico, at sites northwest of Thunder Bay, Ontario, on Lake Nipigon, and at numerous sites on Lake of the Woods and northwestward in the Lake Winnipeg region of Manitoba and northern Ontario (Lenius and Olinyk 1990). In addition, numerous apparently small temporary Blackduck campsites have been noted by archaeologists in Voyageurs, the BWCAW, and Quetico.

The Rainy River Composite (Late Woodland) cultures apparently developed through a coalescence of Laurel and Blackduck cultures about 1,000 years ago and persisted in one form or another to about the time of European contact in the late 1600s. The building of large Laurel mounds also seems to have ceased about 1,000 years ago, to be replaced by the building of much smaller mounds seldom

over 4 feet high, attributable to the new composite cultures (Lenius and Olinyk 1990). This coalescence of cultural artifacts and subsequent elaboration of new cultures may reflect the actual sharing of social, political, and religious activities by the peoples involved. Sites where such composite traits have been documented include the McKinstry and Smith mounds on the Rainy River, Oak Point Island mound on Rainy Lake, and the Nett Lake sites, as well as many more to the northwest in the Lake of the Woods and Lake Winnipeg regions of Canada.

The Late Woodland, Terminal Woodland, or Rainy Lake Composite cultures in the Boundary Waters, whatever we choose to call them, were marked by only a few modifications of lifestyle patterns already established in the Laurel and Blackduck periods. Probably most important in terms of subsistence strategies and ecosystem relations were an increased reliance on wild rice as the chief dietary source of carbohydrates, increased emphasis on fish as a protein source, and the use of birch-bark canoes for greater ease of movement in spring, summer, and fall. The Native American people in the Boundary Waters at the time of initial European influence were still living within the natural system. They were not felling the forests, not clearing the land for agriculture, not introducing new plants, not decimating the wildlife, not altering lake and stream levels, and not disrupting the forest ecosystem significantly with unnatural firing of the woods. They were gatherers, fishers, and hunters, dependent on the fruits of the land and waters, shifting their small extended family groups and simple pole and bark-covered dwellings to take advantage of the subsistence opportunities offered by each season. They knew what the land offered and how to procure the necessities of life, but their numbers and demands were small in the total scheme, and the ecosystem continued to function much as it had for millennia.

THE ERA OF THE FUR TRADE AND EUROPEAN INFLUENCE

Following Columbus's discovery of the New World, European products and social pressures gradually diffused into Native American cultures before the first European and African people's contacts with the natives. When the first

Europeans explored the Lake Superior region in the 1600s, such items as steel knives and axes were probably already known to the inhabitants, even if not in general use. Pressures from European settlements in the East also may have been a factor in the strife between the Dakota and the invading Ojibwa (Chippewa), who were already driving out the Dakota when the first whites arrived in search of furs for the insatiable European markets—and in search for that elusive Northwest Passage to the Pacific.

The main target of the fur trade initially was the beaver, whose soft fur was hammered and compressed to make felt hats for the European gentry. The Eurasian beaver had earlier been used but was near extinction. Later, as the North American beaver became scarce, muskrat was also used for felting. Marten, fisher, otter, lynx, fox, wolf, bear, ermine, wolverine, and other species were exploited for fashion furs. The animals were taken primarily by the Indians with snares, nets, traps, spears, bows and arrows, guns, and dogs, over the fall, winter, and early spring, when pelts were prime (Gilman 1982). Late in the era some trapping was done by overwintering or resident whites.

At first Indian canoe groups brought the furs directly to certain posts, where they were traded for goods, some Indians serving as middlemen. Soon an elaborate system of couriers, the French voyageurs, collected the furs from the Indians at remote wintering posts and transported them to major depots, returning with trade goods. The Indians were also the principal canoe builders at first, but later some voyageurs became skilled builders as well. Among the most important trade goods were traps, snare wire, guns, powder and shot, hooks, spearheads, axes, knives, files, kettles, pans, beads, needles, blankets, and brandy.

The story of the fur trade, the voyageurs, and their involvement with the Native Americans is so fascinating and complex that many excellent books and pamphlets on all aspects of the era are available (Nute 1941, 1955; Bolz 1960; Olson 1961; Morse 1962; Wheeler et al. 1975; Treuer 1979; Gilman 1982; Williams 1983; Breining and Bolz 1987; Waters 1987). Appendix B contains a chronological sketch of the fur trade that should help to clarify the impact of the fur trade on the ecosystem and locate sites of activities in the Boundary Waters.

THE IMPACT OF THE FUR TRADE ON WILDLIFE

It is difficult to assess the impact of the fur trade on most mammals because only vague general statements about population levels during the period are available. However, beaver, marten, fisher, and wolverine must have been severely reduced. All four species were taken. Beaver and marten were the prime targets of the trade. The wolverine was extirpated and has not yet returned to the region, although it still exists farther north in Canada and Alaska. Beaver had virtually disappeared from all the upper Midwest and much of southern Ontario before 1900, but the effects of disease epidemics cannot be positively separated from those of trapping. In any case, following years of legal protection, the beaver population of the region began to recover in the 1920s and 1930s and was again strong regionwide by the 1950s. This recovery strongly suggests that overtrapping was a major factor in the decline. Marten and fisher were essentially extirpated from all the Boundary Waters region by 1900, and with total legal protection they returned only after 1950, marten largely since 1970. Again, overtrapping seems to have been a major factor, but vegetation changes due to logging and slash fires also may have adversely influenced marten habitat.

IMPACT OF THE FUR TRADE ON NATIVE AMERICANS

A few immediate and direct effects of European and African cultures and technology on Native Americans can be noted. Contact with European people introduced several new diseases that had disastrous consequences; smallpox probably is the best example. The introduction of alcohol had tragic effects on native societies and was deliberately used by fur traders as a tool in subjugating Native Americans. Brandy for the Native Americans was a major trade item. The introduction of firearms, snare wire, and traps made the Native Americans dependent on trade for guns, powder, shot, wire, and other items, and for the first time perhaps made it possible to overharvest some species of wildlife. The introduction of steel axes, knives, other tools, metal pots, and other household goods of course changed their way of life forever and ultimately led them down the path to modern technology that all of us have followed. It has not been an easy path for them.

About 1890, when mining, logging, and permanent European settlement came to the Boundary Waters region, the Native American population within or near the areas now designated as wilderness or park reserves had mostly settled into a few local enclaves. Some were located on Basswood Lake, Lac La Croix, Lake Vermilion, Grand Portage, Nett Lake, and Kawa Bay of Kawnipi Lake in Quetico.

Without the contributions of these people and their ancestors, the fur trade would have been impossible. The explorers and traders did not really "discover" the canoe routes that were used by the trade. They were shown them by friendly Native Americans whose forebears had used them for untold generations. The canoe routes of the Boundary Waters were home paths to these people long before the gentry of Europe developed a taste for felt hats. Furthermore, the Native Americans themselves harvested the fur-bearing animals they knew so well. Their knowledge of the land and waters and of the habits of all wildlife made the prodigious harvest a reality. Never before had they been driven to take so much of an animal population that the life-giving resource itself was jeopardized. The Native Americans' birch-bark canoes made it all possible. They had developed a watercraft uniquely suited to the lakes and streams of the vast Canadian Shield, a craft so unique that its basic pattern is still used today with little modification over much of northern North America and lately in Europe and Scandinavia as well. Surely the canoe is among their greatest gifts to humankind.

NATIVE AMERICAN PICTOGRAPHS

There are at least 25 pictograph sites in Quetico, 5 or 6 in the BWCAW, and some in Voyageurs. The locations of many of these sites are shown on the canoe route maps available from commercial sources.

The antiquity of the rock paintings is unclear, and no method of determining their age seems available. The pigment used in virtually all paintings is red ochre, derived from red oxide of iron, obtainable in the region from iron-bearing bands in iron-formation bedrock. Colors range from brick red to a rusty orange brown. The pigment seems to have been mixed with water and used as a finger paint. Fish glues or egg fluid might have been used as a binder in mixture with water, but water alone may well have been the only carrier in most cases. Some paintings are badly faded, and others are partially overgrown with lichens, but many are still clear. The best guess is that most are less than 500 years old, because it seems unlikely that the pigments would remain discernible longer than that on exposed rock outcrops. Some in the Lake Superior region are known from historical records to be more than 150 years old. One painting on Darky Lake in Quetico seems to depict a person firing a gun, a clear reference to European contact, but no others contain any hint of European influence (Dewdney and Kidd 1967).

Most paintings occur on vertical rock faces on steep and often large cliffs along lakeshores or streams, just a few feet above the high-water line. The artists must have painted most either while sitting or standing in a canoe or from the ice on a warm day in early spring. The individual paintings are small, generally from a few inches to perhaps 12 inches long, but at many sites they occur in groups, often with 3 or 4 to 10 or more small paintings scattered over perhaps 15 to 50 feet of rock face. The compass direction toward which the paintings face also varies, although many face approximately east. Yet some of the best pictographs (on Lac La Croix and Darky Lake) face west, and a few face in other directions.

The subject matter of most paintings falls into one of five categories described in an illustrated pamphlet distributed by the Ontario Ministry of Natural Resources at Quetico contact stations:
• human handprints
• human figures and human-made objects, including people in canoes, people smoking pipes, and so on
• mammals, birds, fish, turtles, and other objects or impressions of the natural world. (There are many moose, a few caribou, bear, wolf, pelican, and turtles but, perhaps significantly, no white-tailed deer that I know of.)
• supernatural beings, especially Maymayguishi, odd

little men that played tricks on the Native Americans and disappeared into rocks, and Mishipizhiw, the great lynx or water god of the Ojibwa

- abstractions such as thunderbirds and other odd figures or symbols.

Perhaps the finest pictographs are those in the groups on Lac La Croix and Darky Lake in Quetico and on Crooked Lake and North Hegman Lake in the BWCAW. The meanings or purposes for which these paintings were prepared are lost in antiquity. No living Native Americans, even generations ago, seemed able to interpret them. Many occur along major canoe routes that must have been used often by Native Americans centuries ago, just as they are now. But some, such as the North Hegman Lake pictographs, are on small lakes that were difficult to reach from main travel routes in bygone times. Among other things they surely attest to the presence of sensitive Native Americans on both the highways and byways of their world long before our "civilization" changed it forever.

Fire Origin of the Virgin Forests

The virgin forests of the Boundary Waters region were literally "born in fire." Fire largely determined their species composition and structured the forest age classes and spatial patterns of the vegetation mosaic on the landscape. This mosaic is a patchwork of different vegetation types and individual stand-age classes in which the patch sizes and shapes were determined by the interplay of fire with topography and landforms over long periods of time. The landscape-vegetation mosaic is like a giant kaleidoscope, with fire being the principal force that periodically rearranges the patterns of vegetation types. In turn, these vegetation patterns largely determine the habitats available to all land-based wildlife. Fire also influences soil-vegetation nutrient cycles and energy flows and pathways, regulates forest insect populations and many plant-disease organisms, and determines the productivity, diversity, and long-term stability of the ecosystem. In this sense, then, virtually the whole terrestrial ecosystem is fire dependent.

Methods of Determining Fire History

I determined the years of past fires in the virgin forests and the areas they burned by the following five sequential steps (Heinselman 1973):

1 I built a chronology of fire years by sawing small wedges from old fire-scarred trees and by then counting the annual rings on these wedges back to each fire scar

(figures 6.1, 6.2). This technique gives the actual year of the fire that caused each scar.

2 I searched the U.S. General Land Office Survey township reports to find fire evidence noted by the land surveyors between 1873 and 1907 to verify certain fire dates and validate my methods.

3 I determined the ages of major virgin forest stands by counting total tree rings on increment-borer cores (figure 6.3) from trees known to reproduce well after fires: jack pine, red pine, and black spruce. Cores were taken as low as possible on the trunk, extending to the heart, with appropriate additions for height of the boring above the ground. Fire scars on older trees nearby and historical records were used to verify the relation of tree ages to past fires.

4 All major forest stands were mapped by year of origin. Air photos and forest-type maps served as aids in locating stand boundaries in the field. The latter are high-quality maps based on stereoscopic interpretation of 1948 air photos. Many fire boundaries are easily traced on these maps once the contrasting stand ages are established in the field. Interpretation of 1934, 1937, and 1961 air photos was helpful. Where data were unavailable, the stand-origin dates are extrapolations from the nearest similar stands of known origins. My stand-origin maps were combined with the stand-age data from colleagues Lewis Ohmann and Robert Ream and from

Figure 6.1 / The author examining a fire-scarred tree, an important source of information about past fires.

Figure 6.3 / An increment borer being used to obtain a core from a red pine. The ages of major virgin forest stands were determined by counting total tree rings on cores from jack pine, red pine, and black spruce, trees known to reproduce well after fires.

1882
1864
1796
1741
LAC LA CROIX

Figure 6.2 / Wedge sawed from a fire-scarred tree. A chronology of fire years can be built by counting the annual rings in a wedge back to each fire scar. This technique gives the actual year of the fire that caused each scar.

the Superior National Forest, giving us a total data pool covering more than 2,000 locations scattered across all virgin forests in the BWCAW.

5   The final step was the preparation of fire-year maps from these stand-origin maps, field notes, and historical records for all recognizable large fires dating back to 1610. Before 1610, living trees, fire-scar dates, and historical records are virtually nonexistent, but Swain's (1973) lake-sediment charcoal studies indicate that fire has been important throughout postglacial time.

Stand-Origin and Fire-Year Maps

The study area of 1.3 million acres includes the BWCAW plus the Echo Trail and Gunflint Trail road corridors and some adjacent land. In 1948, the base year for the type maps, the area encompassed about 1 million acres of virgin forest. Stand origins were mapped for those virgin areas, even though the original forest has since been cut in many cases. The maps show stand-origin fire years for all the virgin forests in the BWCAW remaining in 1979 after Public Law 95-495 ended logging in the wilderness. They also show prelogging fire-origin years for most areas logged after 1940. Appendix D contains a selected group of stand-origin maps prepared by the author. The entire collection of stand-origin maps has recently been digitized at the University of Minnesota to make the maps accessible to others. Plate 3 presents an example of a digitized map section.

Stand-origin fire years for the 250,000 acres of forests logged in the early big-pine logging era were not obtained, because most field evidence has been destroyed, and reliable prelogging forest-type maps do not exist. But I did map the limits of both this early logging and the more recent pulpwood logging so that the fire history would not be confused with stand origins related to logging. This produced logging-history maps and delimited the uncut virgin areas. I interviewed longtime residents and authorities on the history of the area[1] and studied the Superior National Forest timber-sale records to obtain details of the logging history and to aid field mapping. The logging history is discussed in later chapters.

When the final stand-origin maps were completed, the fire-year maps were prepared (figure 6.4 a–d). These maps include the entire 1-million-acre virgin-forest study area, which gave a wider base for certain fire statistics than just the present virgin forests. The fire-year maps estimate where the larger and more severe fires burned for each fire year. A problem in preparing such maps was to reconstruct the burns that have been overlapped by later fires. Extrapolation was used to determine boundaries for the larger earlier burns since about 1800, and the areas of at least the major burns between 1700 and 1800 are shown approximately. Only three fire years are shown before 1700, and their limits are speculative. Thus, my fire-year maps are a conservative estimate of the actual fire history. As each succeeding fire sweeps the landscape, former stands or scar-bearing trees are obliterated. After about 400 years all tree-ring evidence is gone. Finally, hundreds of creeping surface fires must have scarred few trees, if any. All traces of such fires are already gone, even for fires of the twentieth century.

In addition to the mapped fires there also must have been many fires between 1600 and 1895 in the areas logged for big pine. There is no way of reconstructing most such burn areas, and the fire-year maps do not show such burns. Blank areas on the fire-year maps indicate areas for which firm fire history data are lacking, rather than that no fires occurred there since 1610.

Fire History Record

CULTURAL HISTORY PERIODS

The fire chronology shown in table 6.1 is based on the total body of evidence from stand origins, fire scars, and historical data. The areas of burns and the proportion of virgin forest burned are based on estimates from the fire-year maps for the 1-million-acre virgin-forest study area as it existed in 1948, but they exclude the areas cut in the early big-pine logging era because no data were obtainable from those areas. Note these three points:

- Significant fires occurred somewhere in the area at one- to eight-year intervals from 1926 back to 1739. After 1926 and before 1739, the intervals widen.
- Major fire years, marked by fires burning more than 100 square miles (more than 6 percent of the virgin forest), occurred at much longer intervals.
- Most of the total area burned in the period of record is accounted for by fires in the major fire years.

The data can be grouped by cultural history periods as shown in table 6.2. Effective fire control began soon after the Superior National Forest was created. The last year with major burns in the virgin forests was 1910, so I call the period from 1911 to 1972 the Suppression Period. The period of active settlement, prospecting, and the beginning of logging by people of European origin spanned the years 1868 to 1910, and I call it the Settlement Period. The fire-scar and stand-origin record begins to fade before about 1727; note the widening intervals between fire years before then. Of course such a change might reflect an actual decrease in fire incidence. No records at all were obtained for fires before 1542 because of the absolute limit set by the longevity of trees in the region and the limit of durability of exposed wood in fire-killed snags. The 1542 fire year is based on the estimated year of origin of a fire-scarred pine snag found on Ge-be-on-e-quet Lake that yielded good ring counts on the intervals between several major fire years. As we have seen, Swain's (1973) work shows that there was much fire prior to my record, so I call the period before 1727 the Period of Fading Record, and the period 1727 to 1868 the Presettlement Period with Good Record.

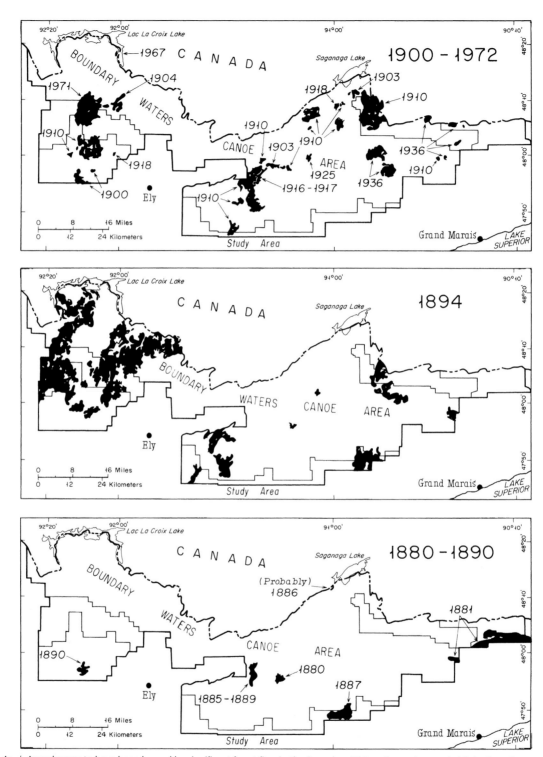

Figure 6.4a / Areas known to have been burned by significant forest fires in the Boundary Waters Canoe Area and vicinity, based on stand-origin maps, field evidence, and historical records. Shaded areas show general areas burned by fires of indicated years. (From M. L. Heinselman 1973, copyright 1973 by University of Washington. Reprinted by permission of the Ecological Society of America.) Fire years, 1880–1972

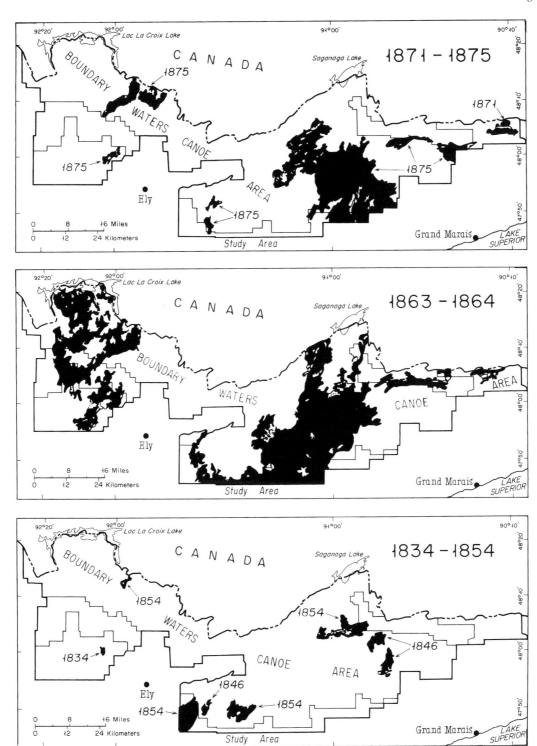

Figure 6.4b / Fire years, 1834–1875

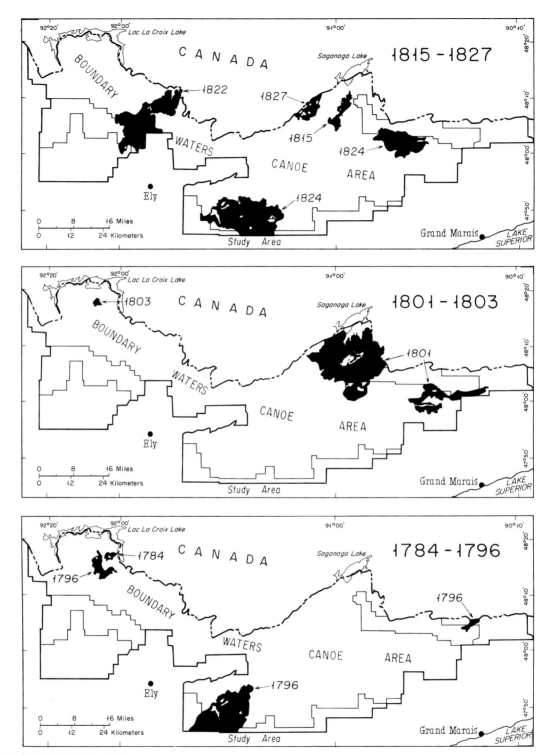

Figure 6.4c / Fire years, 1784–1827

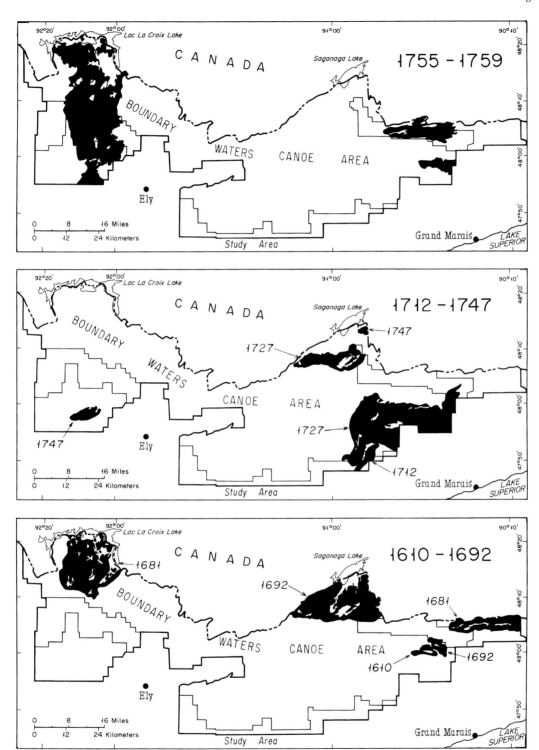

Figure 6.4d / Fire years, 1610–1759.

Table 6.1 / Fire-year data for the virgin forests of the Boundary Waters Canoe Area, A.D. 1542 to 1972

Fire year	Years since previous fire	Fire scars found (no.)	Known area of burns (mi.^{2})	Percentage of virgin forest burned	Fire year	Years since previous fire	Fire scars found (no.)	Known area of burns (mi.^{2})	Percentage of virgin forest burned
1971	4	—	24	1.5	1830	1	1	—	—
1967	31	1	1	.1	1829	2	2	—	—
1936	10	—	16	1.0	1827	3	4	13	.8
1926	1	1	—	—	1824*	2	2	131	8.3
1925	4	—	1	.1	1822	7	2	75	4.7
1921	1	—	1	.1	1815	4	2	12	.8
1920	2	1	—	—	1811	3	1	—	—
1918	1	—	1	.1	1808	1	1	—	—
1917	3	—	4	.3	1807	2	1	—	—
1914	4	1	—	—	1805	2	1	—	—
1910	6	14	80	5.1	1803	2	9	2	.1
1904	1	6	4	.3	1801*	5	5	162	10.3
1903	3	3	4	.3	1796	2	5	92	5.8
1900	6	5	6	.4	1794	4	1	—	—
1894*	2	32	265	16.8	1790	6	7	—	—
1892	2	2	—	—	1784	4	2	3	.2
1890	2	6	4	.3	1780	11	1	—	—
1888	1	5	—	—	1769	3	3	—	—
1887	1	1	10	.6	1766	7	4	—	—
1886	1	2	1	.1	1759^{b}*	4	8	312	19.7
1885	1	1	5	.3	1755	3	6	—	—
1884	1	4	—	—	1752	5	2	—	—
1883	1	3	—	—	1747	5	2	15	.9
1882	1	4	—	—	1742	3	2	—	—
1881	1	3	24	1.5	1739	12	4	—	—
1880	5	7	2	.1	1727*	15	3	207	13.1
1875*	4	23	350	22.2	1712	15	—	9	.6
1871	3	4	10	.6	1697	5	1	—	—
1868	4	3	—	—	1692*	11	2	103	6.5
1864^{a}*	1	50	696	44.1	1681*	33	1	154	9.7
1863	7	8	—	—	1648	11	—	—	—
1856	2	1	—	—	1637	27	1	—	—
1854	8	4	60	3.8	1610	15	—	9	.6
1846	4	5	21	1.3	1595	53	—	—	—
1842	8	1	—	—	1542	?	—	—	—
1834	4	3	2	0.1					

Note Basis for table is the 1-million-acre virgin area defined on 1948 forest-type maps, including some areas outside the BWCA. Some of this forest has since been cut.

^{a} 1863–64 burns cannot be separated on the ground. The total area for both years is given under 1864, which was the major year.

^{b} 1755 and 1759 burns cannot be separated in most cases. Total area for both years is given under 1759.

* = "Major fire year," burning more than 100 square miles.

Source M. L. Heinselman (1973), copyright 1973 by University of Washington. Reprinted by permission of the Ecological Society of America.

Table 6.2 / Fire-year intervals and burn percentages by cultural history periods for the virgin forest of the Boundary Waters Canoe Area, A.D. 1542 to 1972

Cultural period	Interval	Average interval between fires (years)	Average interval between major fires (years)[a]	Burned area accounted for by major fire years[a] (%)	Virgin forest burned per year (%)	Virgin forest burned per century (%)	Length of record (years)
Suppression Period	(1911–1972)	6.1	—	—	.05	5	61
Settlement Period	(1868–1910)	2.1	21	80	1.15	115	42
Presettlement Period with Good Record	(1727–1868)	4.3	28	84	.82	82	141
Presuppression Period with Good Record	(1727–1910)	3.5	26	83	.88	88	183
Period of Fading Record	(1542–1727)	20.6	—	—	.10	10	185
Total period	(1542–1972)	6.1	48	82	0.43	43	430

Note Basis for table is the 1-million-acre virgin area defined on 1948 forest-type maps, including some areas outside the BWCA. Some of this forest has since been cut.

[a] Major fire years are defined as those with burns of over 100 square miles. There were only nine such years: 1894, 1875, 1864, 1824, 1801, 1759, 1727, 1692, 1681.

Source M. L. Heinselman (1973), copyright 1973 by University of Washington. Reprinted by permission of the Ecological Society of America.

When the Presettlement Period with Good Record is compared with the Settlement Period, it is apparent that increased human activity and carelessness with fire during settlement reduced the intervals between fire years from 4.3 to 2.1 years, a change not so great as for Itasca Park, 180 miles to the west (Frissell 1973). The reduction may reflect in part a somewhat faded record for the earlier period. Settlement also resulted in a small increase in the percentage of the virgin forest burned per century.

The average time required for a natural fire regime to burn an area equivalent to the total area of an ecosystem (or of any particular region being considered) is a useful statistic, somewhat analogous to the forester's rotation. I call it Natural Fire Rotation (Heinselman 1973, 1978, 1981a,b). The concept is useful for comparing the role of fire in different ecosystems and for understanding the degree to which the many plant species in an ecosystem might really depend on recurring fire. Van Wagner (1978) used the term Fire Cycle for the same concept. Applying a probability approach, he estimated the Fire Cycle (from my data) at just 50 years, although Baker (1989a) criticized his calculations.

The BWCAW Natural Fire Rotation in presettlement times was about 122 years and in the Settlement Period about 87 years. Fire suppression changed the BWCAW Fire Rotation to about 2,000 years in the 61 years from 1911 to 1972. This is an enormous change in the prevalence of a powerful environmental factor, but fortunately a program to restore fire to its natural role began in 1987 (see chapter 11). Lightning-caused fire may be a semirandom process, and in the BWCAW many areas burned two or more times during a rotation, whereas others escaped for long periods —sometimes as long as 350 years—and some large landscape units may have much longer fire-return intervals than others.

THE LARGEST BWCAW BURNS, 1727 TO 1910

To help in understanding the dynamics of fire-patch generation and turnover, I named all the recognizable separate burns shown on the BWCAW fire-year maps for the period 1727 through 1910 and determined their approximate areas (table 6.3). The 71 burns in this 183-year period covered a gross area of 2,569 square miles (1,644,160 acres), an average

Table 6.3 / Original fire-patch areas in the BWCA virgin forest study area, 1727 to 1910

No.	Fire name	Fire year	Possible area of ignition	Area (mi.^{2})^a
1	Amoeber–Sea Gull lakes	1727	Amoeber Lake?	37
2	Gordon-Brule-Winchell lakes	1727	Sawbill Lake?	170
3	Saganaga Lake	1747	Saganaga Lake?	4
4	Western-Cummings lakes	1747	Western Lake?	11
5	Big Moose-Oyster-La Croix lakes	1755–59	Big Trout–La Croix?	257
6	Gunflint–W. Bearskin lakes	1755–59	Gunflint Lake	41
7	Winchell-Morgan lakes	1755–59	Winchell Lake	14
8	Lady Boot Bay–Kelsey lakes	1784	Lady Boot Bay	3
9	Bald Eagle–Lake 4	1796	Stony River country-south of BWCAW?	77
10	Ge-be-on-e-quet–Oyster-Boulder River	1796	Oyster Lake	12
11	W. Bearskin-Rove lakes	1796	W. Bearskin Lake?	3
12	Gabimichigami-Saganaga lakes	1801	Gabimichigami Lake & Lake of the Clouds?	129
13	Kiskadinna-W. Bearskin-Alder lakes	1801	Kiskadinna Lake?	33
14	Ge-be-on-e-quet–La Croix lakes	1803	Ge-be-on-e-quet Lake	2
15	Gabimichigami-Saganaga lakes	1815	Gabimichigami Lake?	12
16	Hook-Hegman-Crooked lakes	1822	Hook Lake	75
17	Bald Eagle–Isabella lakes	1824	Bald Eagle Lake (west of)?	94
18	Long Island-Rush-Loon lakes	1824	Long Island (or Snipe?) Lake?	37
19	Knife-Cypress lakes	1827	Knife Lake southwest of Amoeber Lake	14
20	Cummings Lake	1834	Cummings Lake	2
21	Bald Eagle–Turtle lakes	1846	Bald Eagle Lake (southwest)	4
22	Auk–Long Island–Cross Bay lakes	1846	Auk (or Mass?) Lake	8
23	S. Temperance–Frule–Long Island lakes	1846	S. Temperance Lake?	9
24	Fox-Crooked lakes	1854	Fox Lake	3
25	Hy 1–Little Gabbro lakes	1854	Stony River country?	22
26	Isabella River–Cargo Lake	1854	Isabella River	14
27	Gabimichigami-Sea Gull-Round lakes	1854	Marble (or Gabimichigami southwest) Lake	21
28	Phantom-Cummings-Big lakes	1863–64	Phantom Lake	51
29	Little Sioux River-La Croix-Crooked complex	1863–64	Little Sioux-Bootleg Lake-Lac La Croix?	176
30	South boundary to N. Kawishiwi River-Alice-Cypress-Saganaga complex	1863–64	Near Town of Isabella?	434
31	Cross Bay-Loon-Duncan-Rose lakes	1863–64	Cross Bay Lake?	27
32	Clearwater-Mountain lakes	1863–64	Clearwater Lake	8
33	Caribou-Mountain-Pine lakes	1871	Caribou Lake	10
34	Mule-Sterling-Sunday-Crooked lakes	1875	Southwest of Mule Lake	33
35	August Creek-Bald Eagle-Clearwater lakes	1875	August Creek area	8
36	South boundary to Alice-Ogishkemuncie-Tuscarora-Cherokee Complex	1875	Insula and Frear-Hog lakes area?	279
37	George-Portage-Poplar lakes	1875	George Lake	12

No.	Fire name	Fire year	Possible area of ignition	Area (mi.^{2})^a
38	Silica-Hook-Rice lakes	1875	Silica Lake	5
39	Horseshoe-Swamp-Crocodile-Pine-Stump lakes	1875	East shore Horseshoe Lake	13
40	Insula to Alice	1880	Insula Lake (northeast side)	2
41	Misquah-Crocodile-Pine-Stump lakes	1881	Misquah-Crocodile lakes?	24
42	Fire to Disappointment lakes	1885–89	South of Fire Lake	5
43	Saganaga Lake	1886	Saganaga Lake (extreme western end)	1
44	Hog Creek to Alton Lake	1887	Hog Creek West	10
45	Western-Glenmore-Schlamm lakes	1890	West of Glenmore Lake	4
46	Oriniack-Sioux River to La Croix Boulder Bay-Crooked complex	1894	Vermilion River (west of Oriniack)	100
47	Chad-Cummings-La Croix Boulder Bay-Crooked complex	1894	Chad-Schlamm-Cummings lakes	103
48	Heart Lake to Omaday Lake	1894	Heart Lake	3
49	Gabbro to Lakes 1, 2, 3 (incl. patch west of Kawishiwi River)	1894	Gabbro Lake	10
50	Bald Eagle-Pietro-Gull-Isabella River	1894	Bald Eagle Lake	10
51	Alice Lake-Kawishiwi River	1894	Alice Lake	1
52	Pace Lake to Sprig Lake	1894	Pace Lake	1
53	Sawbill Trail to Alton, Sawbill, Kelley lakes	1894	Sawbill Trail south of BWCAW	15
54	Snipe-Round lakes to Gunflint-Pine lakes	1894	Round Lake area	9
55	Rib Lake to Gunflint Trail, Ross, Finn, Kiskadinna lakes	1894	West of Rib Lake	10
56	Misquah Lake-Little Trout Lake to Dislocation Lake	1894	Misquah Lake	3
57	Bear-Buck lakes	1900	South of BWCAW (Mud Creek area?)	5
58	Schlamm Lake	1900	East end Schlamm Lake	1
59	Muzzle Lake to Kiana Lake	1903	South of Muzzle Lake	2
60	Saganaga Lake (south shore) to Romance Lake–Sea Gull River	1903	Saganaga Lake (south of Gold Island)	2
61	Mule Lake to Stuart, Bibin lakes, Stuart River	1904	East of Mule Lake, or north of Legend Lake	4
62	Sioux River to Bootleg, Big Moose, Cummings lakes complex	1910	Sioux River or Chad Lake-slash fires?	16
63	Little Isabella River north to Isabella River	1910	Little Isabella River (south of BWCAW)	3
64	Horseshoe-Wilder lakes north to Parent-Disappointment lakes	1910	Southwest of Horseshoe Lake?	21
65	South of Thomas Lake to north end Alice Lake	1910	South end of Thomas Lake	2
66	Knife Lake northeast to Hanson, Ester lakes	1910	Knife Lake south of Amoeber Lake	8
67	Kekekabic Ponds	1910	East end Kekekabic Lake	1
68	Howard Lake north to Rog, Sea Gull lakes	1910	North tip Howard Lake	2
69	Red Rock Lake (east shore)	1910	East shore Red Rock Lake	1
70	Paulson Mine-Sea Gull-Saganaga, Gneiss, Granite lakes	1910	$\frac{1}{2}$ mi. east of Paulson Mine (by old mine)	25
71	Gaskin Lake	1910	Southeast end Gaskin Lake	1
	Total area			2,569

Note Grand total area (1727 to 1910, for 71 burn patches) = 2,569 square miles = 1,644,160 acres; average patch area = 36 square miles = 23,157 acres; maximum patch area = 434 square miles = 277,760 acres; just 8 burns covered 100+ square miles each, and burned 1,648 square miles = 64% of total area.

^{a} Areas are gross areas of the entire fire area, excluding only larger lakes, and not allowing for small skipped areas within burn perimeters not shown on maps.

of 14 square miles per year. The range in original fire-patch areas was from 1 to 434 square miles. I did not attempt to map small fires or age-class patches (under about 20 acres) even on the stand-origin maps, and certainly many small burns were missed, especially for the years before 1875. The average original patch size or actual fire area for the whole period was 36 square miles (23,000 acres). These are gross landscape areas that include small lakes and ponds, streams, and small unburned areas. It is primarily a record of stand-replacing fires and does not include light surface fires that failed to regenerate new stands or leave fire-scar evidence.

Only eight fire patches covered 100 square miles or more during this period, encompassing 1,648 square miles or 64 percent of the total burned area. Thus the fire history is somewhat like that of Yellowstone National Park and the Canadian boreal forests in that much of the age-class patch area was generated by a few very large fires.

The largest single fire patch, number 30, extending from the south boundary of the BWCAW to Alice, Cypress, and Saganaga lakes in 1863–64, had a gross area of about 434 square miles (277,760 acres) within the study area, as nearly as can be determined from stand remnants and fire scars. I was unable to separate possible 1863 fire areas from the 1864 burns. It is also impossible to tell whether most of the burn was produced by one fire or if several fires coalesced to produce this large burned area. The mapped area could certainly have been produced by a single vast fire that started somewhere south of the BWCAW, perhaps near the present village of Isabella. In that case the total fire must have had a gross area of at least 400,000 acres—comparable to the largest of the 1988 Yellowstone fires. The length of this burn from south to north just within the study area is about 30 miles, and it probably extended farther north into Quetico, at least 45 miles from Isabella. The fires may have burned for weeks or even months during the known extreme drought of 1864.

The second largest fire patch, number 36, from the south boundary to Alice, Ogishkemuncie, Little Saganaga, Tuscarora, and the Cherokee lakes in 1875, had a gross area of 279 square miles (178,560 acres) within the study area. It may have started southwest of Sawbill Lake, perhaps near Timber and Frear lakes, and by another start near the east

shore of Lake Insula. The total fire area was certainly more than 300 square miles. It reburned many large areas that had burned only 11 or 12 years earlier in 1863–64. Fire scars for both fires are difficult to find in overlap areas because few older trees survived.

The third largest fire patch, number 5, the Big Moose-Oyster-La Croix fires, was produced by a 1755–59 fire complex that burned from south to north across the whole western BWCAW from the south boundary near Phantom, Clark, and Burntside lakes north across the Echo Trail corridor to Lac La Croix and Iron Lake on the Canadian border, a distance of about 31 miles. The full extent of the fires responsible is probably obscured by extensive logging of big pine in the Burntside Lake area and along most of the western and southern edges of the area. The total area burned is estimated to be at least 257 square miles (164,480 acres). Separate burns in or between 1755 and 1759 could not be mapped, because their tree-ring records were within the range of ring-counting errors or because of possible problems with false or missing rings. These problems are not common in red pine, but ring counts may vary by one to three years on adjacent old fire-scarred trees. Even numerous individual living jack pines date from the 1755 to 1759 fire period.

The Little Sioux River-Lac La Croix-Crooked lakes fire complex of 1863–64 created the fourth largest patch mapped, number 29. It covered about 176 square miles (112,640 acres). It may be the result of two or more ignitions, at least one along the southern Sioux River and perhaps one east of Snow Bay of Lac La Croix. These fires crossed the Echo Trail corridor between Lake Jeanette and the Sioux River and near the Moose River. They also probably crossed into Quetico near Iron Lake and Curtain Falls. The total run from south to north was at least 20 miles. Again I was unable to separate possible 1863 fires from the more probable 1864 burns.

The Sawbill-Gordon-Little Saganaga-Winchell-Brule fire of about 1727 created the fifth largest stand-age-class patch, number 2 at 170 square miles (108,800 acres). Much evidence of this fire's path has certainly been obliterated by later fires. It was necessary to make large jumps between known points, and the limits of this burn are speculative.

The fire may have originated near the south end of Sawbill Lake and spread northeastward about 14 miles before west winds drove it eastward about 20 miles to the edge of the BWCAW and beyond. There the fire left the study area and may have burned considerably more area outside the wilderness.

The Gabimichigami-Saganaga lakes burn of about 1801, number 12, produced the sixth largest stand-age-class patch at 129 square miles or 82,560 acres. It might have resulted from ignitions near Gabimichigami Lake and Lake of the Clouds. Fire scars from both 1801 and 1803 are included. These fires burned eastward to the Granite River, where they probably crossed into Canada. Fire probably crossed northward into Quetico near Swamp Lake just west of Cache Bay of Saganaga as well. Areas near Saganaga and Sea Gull lakes and the Granite River still support a scattered overstory of ancient jack pines and black spruce that came in on this burn. Extensive reburning to the south and east in 1864, 1875, and 1894 masks the limits of these burns.

The seventh largest stand-age-class patch, number 47, was generated by the 1894 Chad-Cummings-La Croix Boulder Bay-Crooked lakes complex of fires that burned about 103 square miles (65,920 acres). These fires ran some 20 miles from south of Cummings Lake northeastward around Big Moose and Big lakes, across the Echo Trail corridor, and on to Boulder Bay of Lac La Croix and Iron and Crooked lakes, where they undoubtedly crossed into Quetico. Vast forests of boreal conifers and aspen-birch of 1894 origin still occupy these areas wherever there has been no subsequent logging or reburning.

Another large 1894 burn generated a 100-square-mile (64,000-acre) stand-age-class patch, number 46, within the study area and must have burned considerable adjacent area as well. This was the eighth largest burn mapped. This Oriniack-Sioux River-La Croix–Ge-be-on-e-quet lakes complex may have started southwest of Oriniack Lake, perhaps along the Vermilion River. The fires entered the study area along a front 10 miles wide on the west and burned northeastward past Lake Jeanette, the Pauness lakes, Shell and Lynx lakes, Loon Lake, and on to Lac La Croix and Ge-be-on-e-quet Lake. Their spot fires may have ignited the Chad-Cummings-Boulder Bay-Crooked lakes

complex as well. These 1894 fires are confirmed in the notes of the U.S. General Land Office surveyor who surveyed Township 65 N, Range 16 W in 1895 (west of the Sioux River, including Maude, Astrid, Picket, and Gustafson lakes)(as quoted in Trygg 1966, 93): "The east two thirds of this township is a barren rock without any Soil to speak of, and all timbers growing thereon [have] been killed by the forest fires of the summer of 1894." In the BWCAW vast forests of jack pine, black spruce, aspen, and birch of 1894 origin now occupy these burns in the region north of Shell, Lynx, and Hustler lakes and south of Lac La Croix.

Two more burns generated extensive virgin-forest age classes that still exist in the BWCAW. The Hook-Hegman-Crooked lakes burn of 1822, number 16, covered a 75-square-mile (48,000-acre) swath from Slim and Hook lakes northeastward past Big Lake, the Hegman lakes, Bear Trap, and Gun lakes to Thursday and Friday bays of Crooked Lake and probably northward into Quetico. The total fire area may have been larger, because it is bordered on the west by extensive 1894 burns that may have obliterated evidence of former 1822 stands. Today many mixed conifer stands of 1822 origin still surround the Hegman lakes, Angleworm and Home lakes, and Thursday Bay of Crooked Lake. Remnant conifer stands of 1822 origin are also common along the Echo Trail from First Lake to Big Lake.

The Bald Eagle–Isabella fire of about 1824, number 17, produced another stand-age-class patch of about 94 square miles (60,160 acres). This fire, which may have started west of Bald Eagle Lake, apparently ran eastward some 18 miles at least to a point about 2 miles east of Lake Isabella. It also moved southeastward beyond the study area south of the Island River and northward to Lake Three and Horseshoe Lake. Forests of this age class still exist around Gull, Pietro, Clearwater, Bald Eagle, and Horseshoe lakes, although they have been much reduced by logging and windstorms.

THE FOREST AGE-CLASS MOSAIC

Perhaps more startling than any of these statistics is the simple fact that in virtually all present virgin forests most overstory trees still consist of the first generation to repopulate the burns, even after more than 80 years of fire control. The intricacies of this age-class mosaic pattern and its fit to the landforms and waterways show in the stand-origin maps.

A clear break in the age-class distribution since 1910 came with fire control. The year classes decreased gradually with time before 1900, punctuated by irregular but declining jumps in year-class areas for the major fire years. This earlier pattern of year classes has been modified by timber cutting, which selectively eliminated certain year classes in areas outside the remaining virgin forests, especially where older pine forests occurred.

Many stands have a simple even-aged overstory structure with one age class of postfire trees still dominant, indicating that the last fire killed virtually all aboveground elements of the former stand. This is the most common situation in jack pine, black spruce, and aspen-birch forests. Fine examples are the 1864 age class of these species on the north, west, and south shores of Lake Insula, the 1894 age classes of jack pine south of Lac La Croix and Crooked Lake, and the 1910 jack pine forests around Amoeber, Topaz, and Cherry lakes and Lake of the Clouds.

Another frequent fire-produced structure consists of two or more overstory age classes, each dating from a separate fire. Such compound stand origins are shown on the stand-origin maps when feasible. Often the older trees tend to be segregated into small groups, or even fair-sized groves. These are common patterns in red and white pine, although large even-aged stands of these trees are also common. Still another common pattern is a rather fine-scale mosaic of two or more age classes. Many good examples of all of these structures can be found in the old red and white pine forests near Boulder Bay and Lady Boot Bay of Lac La Croix and on the islands of Lac La Croix, Saganaga, and Sea Gull lakes. These fire-produced age-class structures also undoubtedly prevailed in the old white and red pine forests cut in the early logging era. The specific year classes that were cut can never be adequately determined, but judging by the age structures of the nearest remaining old stands, many dated from the same fire years as these existing stands: 1610, 1648, 1681, 1692, 1712, 1727, 1739, 1747, 1755–59, 1784, and 1796. Some even older stands probably were cut.

In addition to the fires severe enough to introduce the new stands reflected in figure 6.5, many surface fires in red

and white pine killed a few trees. The average return interval for fires in pine stands where some or all trees survived was 36 years, based on fire-scar evidence. These intervals were extremely variable, however, with some stands showing repeat burns as close as 5 years and others as long as 100 years. Many of these fires burned in the same major fire years that elsewhere killed entire stands, whereas some occurred in years that are seldom reflected in new stands. The old pine stands cut in the early big-pine logging era probably had similar fire histories.

Fire Regimes

SURFACE FIRES AND CROWN FIRES

The kind of fire regime that prevailed in the Boundary Waters wilderness before fire control began (ca. 1910) is revealed by the stand-origin and fire-year maps. Fire regimes are the ecologically significant kinds of fire activity that characterize a specific region over long time periods and leave a stamp on the vegetation. They do not include the many small fires that are soon put out by rains. The elements of a fire regime are

- fire type and intensity, for example, crown fires, severe surface fires, and light surface fires;
- size or area of typical significant fires;
- fire-return intervals, that is, interfire periods in years for typical kinds of landscape units or even for specific geographic areas (Heinselman 1978, 1981b; Kilgore and Heinselman 1990).

Surface fires are fires that burn in the dry needles, leaves, grasses, twigs, and organic matter that cover the soil surface but do not rise into the tops of trees and burn the needles or leaves of living trees. If enough fuel is on the ground, surface fires can kill or severely scar many trees by heating the living (cambium) layer of cells beneath the bark at the base of the tree to lethal temperatures (about 140°F). The rate or intensity at which such fuels are burned can influence the result as well as the total amount of fuel burned (total energy released). When surface fires are in progress, often one can walk along the perimeter of the fire, or even

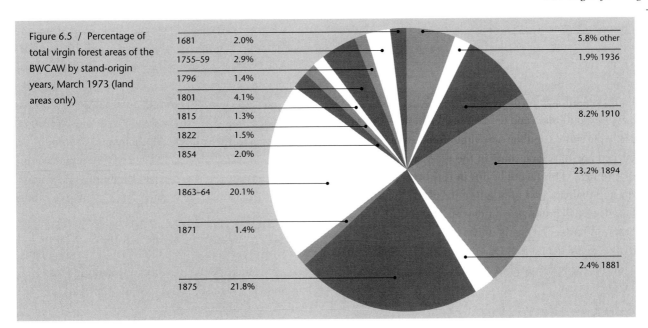

Figure 6.5 / Percentage of total virgin forest areas of the BWCAW by stand-origin years, March 1973 (land areas only)

1681	2.0%
1755–59	2.9%
1796	1.4%
1801	4.1%
1815	1.3%
1822	1.5%
1854	2.0%
1863–64	20.1%
1871	1.4%
1875	21.8%

5.8% other
1.9% 1936
8.2% 1910
23.2% 1894
2.4% 1881

in front of it, without being burned. Such fires are unpredictable, and if a small increase in winds or heavier fuels is encountered, crowning and rapid fire spread can begin with little warning.

Crown fires are fires that rise into the tops of trees and burn the living and dead needles and twigs, often burning the entire tops of trees. A true crown fire leaps from treetop to treetop and consumes most of the finer fuels in nearly all treetops or crowns. It is supported in part by an intense surface fire burning beneath or just behind the advancing flame front in the crowns. A fire in which only an occasional tree is burned to the top is often called torching off, as distinct from a running crown fire. Crown fires in the BWCAW are almost always driven by substantial winds, often more than 15 or 20 miles per hour. Running crown fires may also occur on steep slopes if the fire creates its own winds through uphill convection. Crowning occurs only in forests with abundant conifers, especially long-crowned conifers such as balsam fir, black spruce, white spruce, or cedar with live branches near the ground even in the shade of an overstory of jack pine or red and white pine. These conifers can serve as fire ladders to help loft the flames up into the crowns of the overstory.

Running crown fires can be awesome engines of destruction. With strong winds such fires sometimes consume a narrow cigar-shaped band of forest several miles in length in a single day. If a shift in wind direction then occurs, the fire will begin a new advance on a very wide front. This kind of behavior, occurring over a period of several days or weeks, can expand fires to cover many thousands of acres, as happened in the Yellowstone fires of 1988 (Romme and Despain 1989). Surface fires can also burn very large areas, given long enough periods without suppression measures. Crown fires usually do not consume the trunks of standing live trees but burn off the needles and twigs, producing a scene of dead, blackened snags. Within 2 or 3 years the bark falls off, leaving a forest of mostly uncharred silver grey snags that fall over during the next 10 to 30 years.

The dominant fire regime in the BWCAW was one of large-scale running crown fires or high-intensity surface fires that killed most or all the trees over very large areas at relatively long intervals, resulting in the establishment of new even-aged forests. Some fires, particularly in red and white pine stands, were low-intensity creeping surface fires that killed only portions of stands or individual trees, often leaving fire scars on the survivors. This regime is in contrast to certain forests in the western United States where the natural fire regime was one of frequent, low-intensity surface fires that burned relatively small areas at intervals as close as 5 to 15 years for any given area. Such regimes were typical of the giant sequoia forests of California and of many ponderosa pine forests in the lower elevations of the western mountain states (Heinselman 1981b; Kilgore 1987; Kilgore and Heinselman 1990).

The stand-origin and fire-year maps also show that virtually the entire 1-million-acre virgin-forest study area was burned one to several times in the 377-year period from 1595 to 1972. This record begins in 1595 because that was the approximate year of origin of the oldest living stand found, a small group of red pines on Threemile Island in Sea Gull Lake. The nearly universal occurrence of charcoal on top of the mineral soil but beneath the humus layer confirms the widespread extent of past fires.

FIRE REGIMES OF
MAJOR VEGETATION TYPES

Following is a summary of the fire regimes typical of each major class of forest communities, together with brief sketches of some adaptations of the principal forest trees for survival and regeneration after fire. This summary provides a convenient set of pigeonholes to simplify our view of the fire regimes, but one must not forget that fire is an extremely variable process. Details on the regeneration strategies of Boundary Waters trees, shrubs, herbs, mosses, and lichens are provided in chapter 7.

Jack Pine and Upland Black Spruce Forests

Jack pine and black spruce share a unique adaptation to fire: jack pine have persistent closed cones and black spruce have semiclosed cones. Both also have very light windblown seeds. They are thus the only conifers in the region that can reproduce immediately following crown fires that kill all living individual trees over wide areas. Both have very flammable foliage and thin bark, so they are readily killed by crown fires and severe surface fires. Both can produce viable seed at 10 to 15 years of age. They are not very demanding of either soil moisture or fertility and thus can occupy dry or infertile sites. They may occur either as nearly pure stands or in various mixtures. Associations with aspen, birch, fir, red pine, and other trees are common.

Jack pine and upland black spruce are most abundant on large ridge complexes, where crown fires can run unchecked for considerable distances. Jack pine may occur on any slope exposure, whereas black spruce, demanding more moisture, is more common on flat ridgetops, north-facing slopes, and some lower slopes (especially on shallow soils over granitic bedrock). Both are more common on convex landforms, where water and nutrients tend to run off the site (as opposed to concave landforms, where water and nutrients tend to be concentrated by surface runoff and soil seepage). These are generalizations, and exceptions do occur. Because of its unique adaptability to reproduce after crown fires and its lack of special site requirements, jack pine can be found occasionally on almost any site, but it often loses in competition with other species on the more fertile and moister sites.

The typical fire regime on jack pine–black spruce sites was crown fires or high-intensity surface fires of short return interval that killed most or all trees over large areas. Typical return intervals for specific landforms were in the range of 40 to 100 years, but some stands probably reburned and reproduced only 15 or 20 years after a fire, and some escaped 200 years or more. The average fire-return interval before European settlement for the landforms on which jack pine and upland black spruce are dominant was probably 50 to 75 years.

Aspen-Birch-Conifer Forests

Quaking and bigtooth aspen share two remarkable fire adaptations: both sucker from the roots of fire-killed trees, up to 100 feet from the "dead" parent, and both have tiny, light seeds surrounded by downy hairs that can transport their seeds thousands of feet or even miles, given strong winds and updrafts. Quaking aspen is by far the more abundant of the two, but locally bigtooth may be dominant. Root suckering is the major source of regeneration because suckers outgrow seedlings for the first few years. Seeding is the means by which the aspens may colonize burned sites far from existing potential parents. Seedbeds must be continuously moist during early germination stages, so aspen often fails to colonize dry sites. The aspens, even when large, are readily killed by hot surface fires.

Paper birch has tiny, light winged seeds, easily blown long distances by the wind. It also has highly flammable bark. Surface fires may ignite the loose bark, and fire will then run up the trunks. Birch is thin barked and easily killed by hot surface fires. Fire-killed birches may resprout from the root collar at the base of the trunk but not from the roots away from the tree. Resprouting is the reason birch commonly occurs in clumps of two to five stems.

Balsam fir is a common associate of aspen and birch. It is very easily killed by surface fires and has long, full crowns with very flammable foliage, making it an important fire-ladder species. Balsam seed is winged but fairly heavy, so wind transport is normally not more than a few hundred feet. White spruce is another common associate of aspen and birch. It is sensitive to surface fires and has long flammable crowns and light windblown seeds. Good seed years are very intermittent in white spruce but more dependable in aspen, birch, and fir. White spruce and fir are shade tolerant, whereas aspen and birch are intolerant, especially the aspen. Fir and white spruce must reproduce from surviving seed trees because neither has persistent or closed cones, but their ability to grow in the shade makes them capable of invading aspen-birch (and pine) stands, sometimes many years after fire. Aspen and birch stands may also have mixtures of jack, white, and red pines and northern white cedar. If a stand escapes fire for long periods, the fir, spruce, pine, and cedar may eventually take over the site.

Aspen-birch-conifer mixtures are most common on concave landforms: valleys, fault lines in bedrock ridges, lower slopes, and flats. Yet they may also be associated with the same large ridge complexes that support jack pine–black spruce forests. They simply occupy the more concave drainageways on these landforms because aspen and birch can outcompete jack pine on the moist and fertile sites.

The typical fire regime for these forests was one of high-intensity surface fires that killed most but usually not all stand elements. Where the fir, spruce, or pine component was significant, partial crown fires were common, but aspen and birch alone will not sustain crown fires. Individual conifers often torched off where not enough conifers existed to sustain a running crown fire. Some fir, spruce, and cedar often escaped burning on high-moisture local sites, leaving a nucleus of seed trees to restock the area. Stands that escaped fire for 100 years or more often had enough mature balsam fir to sustain a spruce budworm epidemic, which then increased the probability of ignition. The burns and therefore the age classes in these forests were commonly very large in area. Many stands burned in the same fires that consumed the adjacent jack pine–black spruce stands elsewhere within the same ridge-and-valley complexes. Fire-return intervals probably were a bit longer than in jack pine–black spruce forests; perhaps 50 to 200 years was the full range. Average intervals were about 70 to 110 years.

White and Red Pine Forests

All the forests where one or both of these pines dominated the stands are included here. White and red pine both have nonpersistent cones with light windblown seeds but only intermittent good seed crops. Their principal adaptations to fire are large size, longevity (300 to 400 years), thick, fire-resistant bark, and long branch-free trunks when mature. Survivors must reseed burned areas. Some degree of fire resistance develops by 30 to 50 years of age, and seed is produced by about 50 years.

Stands composed mainly of red pine generally occurred as open groves on convex landforms and on shallow soils over bedrock or on very gravelly or sandy soils, with little shrub cover and few understory trees (figure 6.6). In contrast, many nearly pure white pine stands occurred on flats, in valleys, or on concave lower slopes and on the deeper more fertile soils, with a heavy shrub layer of mountain-maple, alder, or hazelnut and frequently a significant understory of fir, white spruce, or cedar.

The typical fire regime on red pine sites was one of intermittent light surface fires at return intervals of 5 to 50 years, with higher-intensity partial crown fires killing many trees at intervals of perhaps 150 to 250 years. Return intervals of even 300 years for the higher-severity fires needed to open up stands might still allow time for reproduction. The regeneration period for red pine often lasts 10 to 20 years after fire, probably because of the intermittent seed crops and rather exacting seedbed requirements of this species.

The typical fire regime in pure white pine stands involved less frequent underburning than in red pine sites,

Figure 6.6 / Open red pine stand. Stands composed mainly of red pine generally occur as open groves on convex landforms and on shallow soils over bedrock or on very gravelly or sandy soils, with little shrub cover and few understory trees.

and probably longer return intervals for the partial crown fires needed to open up stands for regeneration. Some stands may have escaped underburning for the life of that stand, whereas others experienced light surface fires at 25- to 100-year intervals. High-intensity partial crown fires probably had return intervals of at least 200 to 350 years on many sites. The regeneration period for white pine often lasts 10 to 20 or more years after fire, and because it is more shade tolerant than red pine, white pine may fill in stand openings for a century or more after fire.

For white and red pine forests the fire rotation concept has less meaning than for jack pine–black spruce, or aspen-birch-conifer forests, because white and red pine stands were frequently burned through by light to moderate-intensity surface fires that failed to kill enough overstory trees to induce regeneration. Thus many fires were really not stand-renewal burns, and the forest age structure remained little changed by such fires. If only the stand-renewal burns are counted in fire rotation calculations, then the rotation for red pine sites was probably 150 to 200 years and for white pine sites perhaps 200 to 250 years. If all fires are counted, the rotation was less than 100 years for red pine sites and not much longer for white pine sites. Primarily the physio-graphic location of most red pine–white pine sites accounts for their history of frequent light surface fires and for the longer return intervals for severe fires. These unique fire regimes permitted the survival and regeneration of red and white pine.

Bog and Rich Swamp Forests

Black spruce is the major dominant species on the infertile, acid bog peatlands, and most true bogs have a nearly pure cover of this tree. Tamarack may occur as scattered individuals. The water table in most black spruce bogs is below the peat surface much of the time, and the feathermoss ground layer covering the peat surface beneath many stands becomes tinder-dry in droughts. In bogs where sphagnum mosses are the principal ground cover, the bog surface dries out enough to sustain surface fires only after prolonged and intense drought. Rich swamp forests are usually located in water movement areas where mineral- and oxygen-bearing groundwaters flow from or past mineral soil areas. They have high water tables and often not very deep peat. Northern white cedar, tamarack, and black ash are common trees on such sites, and balsam fir and black spruce are less frequent. Many black spruce bogs directly adjoin upland black spruce, jack pine, or aspen-birch-conifer forest sites, whereas many rich swamp forest sites adjoin white pine or spruce-fir and upland cedar sites.

Given the physiographic characteristics and species composition of these wetland sites, their fire regimes are predictable. Black spruce bog forest sites were often involved in the same major fires that swept the adjacent uplands. Crown fires were usual, and most bog spruce stands are even-aged. Regeneration from seeds in the persistent, semi-closed black spruce cones is usually prompt. Fire-return intervals perhaps averaged a bit longer than for the adjacent uplands, but 100 to 150 years is a good guess. Swamp forests, on the other hand, adjoined upland forests that often had long fire-return intervals and often only surface fires. These swamp sites are usually the last to dry out, even in severe drought. Thus fire was an infrequent visitor to most rich swamp forests. Many escaped fire for centuries. Without a good basis for estimating average fire-return intervals, 200 years or more is my best guess.

Factors Affecting Fire Occurrence and Distribution

FIRE WEATHER, FIRE BEHAVIOR, AND SEASON OF BURNING

The behavior, size, and ecological effects of past fires in the virgin forests depended on many interacting factors. Among the most important were season, preceding weather patterns, weather during the fire, vegetation types, fuel types, and the physical landscape.

We need to understand the weather and climatic factors associated with past fires in the Boundary Waters virgin forests because these fires burned intact natural stands. In contrast, the historic fires of the logging era in the Lake States, about which so many frightening accounts have been written, burned largely on cutover land carrying logging slash and even on some open hay land. Fires in such open areas move very quickly, kill most of any standing seed trees, and burn up most of the tree seeds in the slash. This was the case, for example, with the great Peshtigo, Hinckley, Baudette, and Cloquet–Moose Lake fires (Haines and Sando 1969). Both the behavior and the ecological

effects of such slash fires differ from those in virgin forests because of differences in fuels, in tree seed supplies following the burn, and in remaining overstory cover from snags and living trees.

The climate for a year or more preceding fires influences the nature of the fire. Large high-intensity burns often occur in severe drought. As described earlier, most of the area burned in the BWCAW from before European settlement through 1910 was generated by a few large fires that tended to come along at 10- to 20-year intervals during major droughts, circumstances that set the stage for fires that can burn away most of the soil humus layer. Prolonged drought can convert into ready fuels many plant materials that normally would not burn, or might even be heat sinks, and these add tremendously to total available fuels. For example, in normal or wet summers the green needles of most living pines, spruces, and balsam do not readily ignite without prolonged heating, but in extreme drought they become desiccated to the point where they will torch off dramatically with far less heating than would be required if their internal moisture levels were normal. Also, in extreme drought the green leaves and stems of many understory shrubs and herbs, and even the leaves of broadleaf trees such as aspen, birch, and red maple, become wilted and may dry up, much as they do in the fall, again adding greatly to the total fuel load.

Snowmelt recharges soil moisture reserves in April. But spring fires still occur because the spring green-up is just beginning, the needles of living conifers are very dry until growth begins, and the dead needles, leaves, and grasses from the previous summer dry quickly on the long, warm, sunny days that often come with spring dry spells, especially with humidities lower than 30 percent and winds exceeding 15 to 20 miles per hour (Sando and Haines 1972). Spring fires seldom burn away much of the organic layer, because it is usually still wet and cold or even frozen just below the surface. Given spring drought and the right burning day, however, even crown fires are possible, and some of the largest fires of the late twentieth century in Minnesota have occurred in May and June.

Light surface fires, causing little injury to fire-resistant red pines, are also possible under spring conditions if it is not too dry and the wind is not excessive (Buckman 1964a). This is often called underburning.

Summer fires in most vegetation types require a longer drought buildup and more severe fire weather than spring or fall fires. Late summer and early fall fires come when soil moisture reserves are often much lower. The surface litter and humus layers may be almost totally dried in major droughts and are much more likely to be consumed then. Summer and early fall are normally the heaviest rainfall periods of the year, so it is only in years of exceptional drought such as 1910, 1936, 1961, 1974, and 1976 that major summer or early fall fires can occur. From mid-June through August the herbs, grasses, and shrubs that comprise the undervegetation in many forests are succulent and actively growing, and except in extreme drought they serve as heat sinks, robbing an advancing fire of its energy. The same is true of the foliage of deciduous trees: aspen, birch, red maple, black ash, and oak. Forests of these species are fuel breaks in most summers, but in extreme drought they may carry fire fairly well, especially if they have understories of balsam, spruce, or cedar or have a significant stocking of pine. By mid-August most trees, shrubs, and herbs have completed growth for the season and are beginning to go into dormancy in preparation for winter. Grasses and sedges are curing. With these seasonal changes under way, the desiccation of a major drought can make forests we normally think of as fireproof explosive by late summer.

In prolonged summer drought, evapotranspiration dries out the litter and humus layers, and these become part of the fuel. Snags, fallen trees, and other heavy fuels also may burn. In the past, many summer fires must have been smoldering and slow-moving, as these heavy fuels and organic layers burned with the retardant effect of a green undervegetation. Today most summer fires are easily extinguished before they reach significant size; without control they could burn large areas during prolonged droughts. Some may have even held over into the fall, when more rapid spread is likely. In a very dry year, late summer and fall fires have the potential both to move rapidly and to consume heavy fuels and organic layers. Fall fires after about October 1 are less likely to burn vigorously except in extreme drought, because the daily burning period is shorter due to decreasing day length and nightly frost or dew.

Some nearly pure conifer forests are much less affected by seasonal changes in fuels. Jack pine–black spruce, black spruce–feathermoss, and red pine communities are the best examples. These types have sparse to negligible shrub and herb layers and few broadleaf trees in the tree layer. Coniferous fuels are inherently more flammable because they have significant resins, tars, and other easily ignited compounds in their wood, bark, and needles. Although the moisture content of their needles does increase during the growing season, summer drought can easily dry them and increase their flammability. Furthermore, the feathermoss ground layer in most jack pine–black spruce, black spruce–feathermoss, and some red pine stands dries out in rather short dry spells, as do the pine needles always present on the ground. Fuels experts call these "short time-lag fuels" because they respond so quickly to low humidity and short periods without rain. These communities will burn after short droughts in spring, summer, and fall, although they of course burn more fiercely after prolonged drought. The jack pine–black spruce and black spruce–feathermoss communities are often the most prone to running crown fires.

Lightning ignitions vary seasonally. Usually lightning storms are most frequent in June, July, and August. Thunderstorms are usually associated with invasions of warm, humid Gulf of Mexico air into the upper Midwest, and these are mostly summer events. Most thunderstorms are accompanied by enough rain to extinguish any ignitions, but it is the dry lightning storms during droughts that cause fires.

Weather during fires is a major factor influencing fire behavior. Key factors are humidity, wind speed and direction, temperature, sky conditions, day length, and time of day. Fires tend to be relatively inactive at night and for the first few hours after dawn because of the higher humidity, lower temperature, and light winds that usually prevail then. Crown fires are uncommon at night. Sometimes these nighttime conditions fail to develop, however, and fires may remain active all night. The most extreme fire activity comes with humidity below 15 or 20 percent, winds in excess of 20 miles per hour blowing toward large areas of heavy fuels and highly flammable stands, high temperatures (generally over 80°F), and clear skies, and at midday when days are long (generally before late September). Given such an extreme situation, fires can run several miles in a single day, aided by long-distance spotting and complicated by fire-induced winds, whirls, and strong convection columns. The stand-origin maps indicate that many past fires jumped sizable lakes and streams and other possible natural fire barriers, probably during episodes of the most severe fire weather. Rapid increases in fire size can come with wind shifts after a long fire run because such shifts may turn the long flank into a new and greatly widened flaming front. This kind of fire activity can potentially produce vast blowup fires like the Yellowstone fires of 1988.

FIRE WEATHER AND THE MAJOR FIRE YEARS

Much of the burned area for both the Settlement and Presettlement periods can be accounted for by just a few major fire years. In the Settlement Period, the fires of 1875 and 1894 created 80 percent of the total burn. In the whole Presettlement Period with Good Record, just five fire periods

account for 84 percent of the total: 1863–64, 1824, 1801, 1755–59, and 1727 (figure 6.7). Thus without control measures large areas burned at rather long intervals when weather and fuels combined to yield optimum burning conditions.

The average interval between such major fire years varied only from 21 to 28 years between cultural periods, a difference probably related to climatic circumstances rather than to people. The average interval between major fire years from 1727 to 1910, before suppression, was 26 years, but the interval between fires ranged from 11 to 42 years, and if both 1863 and 1864 are counted, major fires occurred in two successive years.

Important BWCAW fire years in common with Itasca Park, Minnesota, included 1712, 1727, 1759, 1803, 1864, and 1875 (Frissell 1973; Clark 1988, 1989, 1990a), and those in common with Algonquin Park, Ontario, included 1854, 1864, and 1875 (Cwynar 1977).

What were the climatic circumstances associated with past fires, and what can we infer about their ecological effects? First, it is clear from the fire maps, fire-scar dates, and climatic data that the total number of fires was large,

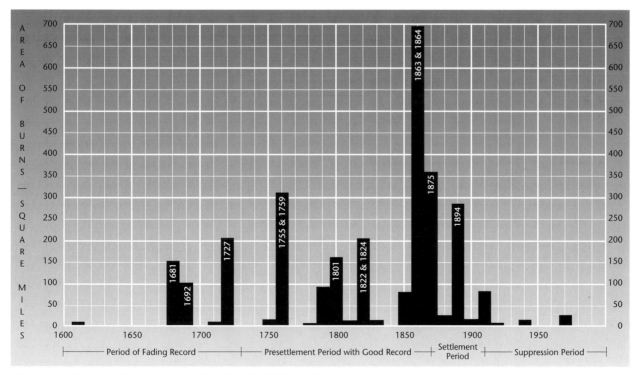

Figure 6.7 / Fire years in the virgin forests of the BWCAW, 1610 to 1972

and that many fires did burn even in years not marked by prolonged regional drought. For example, in the 32 years from 1863 to 1894, fire scars were found for 17 years. For the whole Settlement Period, 1868 to 1910, fire scars were recorded at intervals averaging just 2.1 years (table 6.2). The climatic summaries for Minnesota (Martin 1934a,b) document numerous short-term spring, summer, or fall droughts during these periods. Some of these brief droughts set the stage for fairly large burns in local areas.

Just 5 fire years account for 90 percent of the stand origins still present in the BWCAW that date from the 70 years from 1840 to 1910 for which some weather records are available and suppression was minimal. In fact, 73 percent of all remaining virgin stands still date from these 5 years: 1863, 1864, 1875, 1894, and 1910 (figure 6.5).

Weather records suggest that the fires of 1863 came in the spring or early summer, whereas the 1864 fires may have burned almost the whole season, except perhaps for a few weeks in July. In 1863, Beaver Bay, Fort Ripley, and St. Paul all recorded very light precipitation from April until August. At Fort Ripley, the weather chart for June 1863 notes: "The drought is very severe, the grass upon the prairie is nearly or quite dried. The Mississippi River at the point is lower than it were ever known before" (unpublished records, courtesy of E. L. Kuehnast, Minnesota State Climatologist). Again in the spring of 1864 little rain fell, and the drought persisted until July and returned again in August and September. The fires of these 2 years cannot be separated on the ground, but they consumed the forests thoroughly in most areas where they burned. Remnants of former stands are not common, and large areas are now clothed with even-aged jack pine, spruce, aspen-birch, and sometimes red and white pine stands that reproduced in their wake.

An idea of the regional extent of the 1863–64 droughts can be gleaned from scattered historical records and other fire studies. For example, notes from Samuel Taylor's journal at Fort Garry (now Winnipeg), Manitoba, confirm the severity of the 1863–64 droughts in that region, 300 miles northwest of the Boundary Waters. On July 1, 1863, Taylor wrote: "only 9 bushels (potatoes) from 9 bushels of cut seed owing to dry weather all summer . . ." On August 9,

1864, he wrote: "the fire is burning the hay on all directions the very earth is burning the like is never been known . . ." (from the original journal, courtesy of the Laboratory of Anthropology, University of Manitoba, Winnipeg). On the Cut Foot Sioux Experimental Forest, about 100 miles southwest of the BWCAW, extensive even-aged red pine stands (and jack pine before logging) date from 1863–64 fires. The local lore there refers to "the fire of two summers." At Itasca Park, 180 miles southwest, Frissell (1973) identified large areas burned by 1864 fires. Cwynar (1977) identified 1864 burns in Algonquin Park, Ontario, far to the east. Grange (1965) reports 1,000,000 acres burned by 1864 fires in Wisconsin. The most remote record of 1864 fires comes from the pioneering study of Frederick E. Clements at Estes Park, Colorado (Clements 1910). He concluded that the burns of 1864 were the most extensive of any in his study area.

The droughts of 1863 and 1864 were major climatic anomalies of subcontinental extent. Such major fire periods may have occurred only once in a century or two. In the BWCAW, at least 44 percent of the 1-million-acre virgin-forest study area became involved in the burns of these 2 years, and surely large areas in Quetico and Voyageurs also burned. Thus the fires of 1863–64 in the Boundary Waters region were comparable to or greater in scale than the great Yellowstone fires of 1988 but occurred in the Little Ice Age of the nineteenth century, clearly independent of any global warming caused by fossil-fuel burning.

The next earlier period when a similar climatic and fire sequence may have occurred was 1755–59—more than a century before. There are no climatic data and no eyewitness reports. But the silent testimony of many stands of even-aged forest dating from these years and an abundance of fire scars still identify some of those burns. The forest regeneration that followed these fires must have been similar to that which occupied the 1863–64 burns, because in several areas where ancient jack pines of 1755–59 origin dotted the landscape a few trees remained in the early 1990s, and extensive areas of red and white pine of that age class still exist (figure 6.8).

The 1875 fires must have burned in July, the only month that shows up consistently in the precipitation records as a drought period. The 1894 fires could have burned any time between late June and September, as the climatic data indicate drought persisting most of the summer that year. All stations show severe rainfall deficits for July and August. The great Hinckley fire occurred on September 1, 1894, about 150 miles south of the Boundary Waters. U.S. General Land Office Survey notes locate some of the fires of the summer of 1894 in the Echo Trail region. Most of these fires probably burned in July, August, or early September, because general rains came later that month.

The 1910 fires could have burned anytime between May and early October. The precipitation at St. Paul for 1910 was the least ever recorded. Some northern Minnesota stations recorded fair rains in July, but the drought returned, and the historic Baudette fire occurred on October 10. This was also the year of the great Idaho and Montana fires, again implying a subcontinental drought. The actual dates of the 1910 fires in the Boundary Waters have not been discovered, but several separate fires were clearly involved (figure 6.9). Some probably began as slash fires on logging operations and spread into adjacent virgin stands.

After 1910, fire suppression by Superior National Forest crews greatly reduced the extent of burning, but some fires nevertheless achieved considerable size. The droughts of 1936 and 1976 were similar in severity and regional extent to those of 1863–64 and 1910. The fires of these years have already been described.

The fire history of Quetico and Voyageurs was clearly similar to that of the BWCAW, although we do not yet have as much detail or published stand-origin maps for their remaining virgin forests. More information on the fire history of Quetico is available in Day (1990), Woods and Day (1977), and the seven other unpublished reports by these authors from their 1975–77 fire ecology study of Quetico (in files of Ontario Ministry of Natural Resources, Atikokan). Although I do not have a full list of known fire years for either Quetico or Voyageurs, fires surely burned large areas of each of these parks in some of the same major fire years recorded for the BWCAW and for Itasca and Algonquin parks. That has certainly been true in such recent major drought years as 1936 and 1974. We can safely conclude that in principle the ecological role of fire in Quetico and

Figure 6.8 / Remnant of an old jack pine forest on a 1755 burn near the Echo Trail, 20 miles northwest of Ely, Minnesota. The jack pine in the foreground was 215 years old. Note the advanced succession to balsam fir, white spruce, and paper birch. This photo was taken in 1970. The area burned in a crown fire during the Little Sioux fire in 1971. (From M. L. Heinselman 1973, copyright 1973 by University of Washington. Reprinted by permission of the Ecological Society of America.)

Voyageurs has been the same as that in the BWCAW, even though there were certainly differences in historical details.

FUEL BUILDUP

To understand the possible role of people in increasing fire before European settlement we must consider the interactions among vegetation types, stand ages, vegetation stages, fuels, weather patterns, and the location and frequency of ignitions. Mutch (1970) argues that fire-dependent vegetation types burn with a nonrandom periodicity regulated by their flammability, which in turn is linked to inbred

Figure 6.9 / Jack pine at Wilder Lake dating from 1910. In the year 1910, several separate fires, like the one from which this stand originated, occurred in the Boundary Waters. Some probably began as slash fires on logging operations and spread into adjacent virgin stands.

plant regeneration adaptations requiring fire. My concept of Mutch's ideas is simply that certain factors linked to stand maturation and senescence increase the probability that older stands will burn. Let me outline how these factors may operate:

- Total aboveground biomass in living plants increases with stand age, up to some maximum for each first-generation postfire forest type. Some living stand components are potential fuel, especially in crown fires (foliage, branches, and portions of the bark of trees, as well as shrubs, some herbs, most mosses, and lichens). The time after fire at which biomass peaks varies with forest type, but for most types in the BWCAW it is at least 100 years. For red and white pine stands it may be 150 to 250 years (Loucks 1970; Ohmann and Grigal 1985).

- A general relation exists between time since fire and dry weight of dead wood. Such fuel is initially high following crown fires (snags from the fire-killed stand), but this first peak comes when other fuels are low and fuel arrangement does not favor fire spread (the snags are standing and widely spaced). Then, about 15 years after fire, many snags are down, jackstrawed, and still

dry, sometimes amidst dense thickets of flammable young conifers. Such young forests are not necessarily immune to fire under drought conditions. During a forest's midlife such dead-wood fuels decrease through decomposition of the snags, probably reaching a minimum in the pole stage of stand development 30 to 70 years after fire. At this stage biomass may be relatively high, but fuel arrangement may not be conducive to fire spread, particularly in jack pine, red pine, and aspen stands lacking a balsam or spruce understory. A resurgence of dead wood then occurs as the first-generation trees begin to deteriorate and die at 100 to 300 years after fire. Here fuel arrangement is better, and other fuels also are abundant. Readiness to burn is not a simple function of time since fire but varies widely with stand conditions, weather, and fire behavior. Yet, as we shall see later, in many forests there is a general trend toward increasing flammability with time since the last fire.

- Within 50 to 100 years after fire, an understory of balsam fir, spruce, or cedar may develop beneath the new forest, introducing flammable ladder fuels capable of carrying fire into the crowns of the overstory. They often torch off even when scattered among other trees that lack this feature, such as red pine, aspen, or tall jack pine. Paper birch may have loose scrolls of highly flammable bark that may be lofted far ahead of the main flame front by updrafts, igniting spot fires a quarter mile or more in advance of the fire. Tree lichens that grow on the dead or dying branches of conifers (old man's beard) also aid crown firing and long-distance spread.

- Within 100 to 150 years after fire, balsam may increase enough to sustain a spruce-budworm outbreak, especially if burns are large, because single-age classes of mature balsam would then cover large areas. In the Boundary Waters region the native spruce budworm kills vast areas of old balsam fir and weakens or kills many white spruce, especially in stands largely composed of balsam, which is really the prime host despite the budworm's name. The budworm has been almost continuously epidemic in various areas of the BWCAW and Quetico since 1956. Black spruce is rarely damaged. A close relative, the jack pine budworm, plays a similar role in old jack pine stands, although up to 1992 it had not been as lethal in most Boundary Waters stands. The budworms are defoliators: they eat the new needles that grow from buds each spring. Balsam and jack pine can withstand about three successive years of heavy defoliation, but if heavy feeding continues in subsequent years, tree death begins on a major scale. Stands ravaged by spruce budworm contain much flammable fuel and often support high-intensity fires (Stocks 1987b). The black spruce dwarf mistletoe is a parasitic plant that causes "witches' brooms" on old black spruce, kills many trees, and adds to crown fuels. White pine blister rust, introduced from Europe, kills many individual white pines, especially seedlings, saplings, and smaller trees, but it has not generally been lethal to whole stands. Stand openings created by such outbreaks permit increased sunlight, increased air movement, and rapid drying of fuels (Sando and Haines 1972; Stocks 1987b).
- As the forest ages, the first-generation overstory trees become more susceptible to wind breakage and uprooting. Individuals fall, or (rarely) most of the stand is blown down. The great regional downburst storm of July 15, 1988, caused vast blowdowns in the Boundary Waters.

The down timber from such storms is often suspended above the ground for several years, where it adds much to local fuels. Windstorms of this type do not generally flatten whole forests. Instead they tend to blow down erratic swaths a few hundred feet wide of the oldest, tallest, or most exposed trees. The region over which such blowdowns may extend can be many miles long and almost as wide. Tornadoes are very rare but have occurred. Down trees are an additional source of dead needles, twigs, and wood and offer favorably arranged fuels for ignition and spread. Before European settlement most blowdowns probably burned before decomposition recycled the nutrients in the down timber, but for many decades now most blowdowns have not burned, because of fire control.

- Postfire stands may contain paper birch, which develops loose scrolls and strips of highly flammable bark 50 to 150 years after establishment. Windblown flaming birch bark carries spot fires far out ahead of the main fire.
- Tree diseases such as the heart-rotting fungi, and plant parasites such as black spruce dwarf mistletoe increase with stand age, eventually causing the death of many trees and increased susceptibility of living trees to fire.
- Litter, duff, and humus gradually accumulate on the forest floor as postfire forests mature. Accumulations of 1 to 3 inches are usual within the first 100 years after fire. On upland sites accumulations of 3 to 5 inches or more are possible beneath mixed-conifer stands 250 to 350 years after fires. On cool north-facing lower slopes, seepages, and bog margins, indefinite accumulation and peat formation may occur. During severe drought these organic layers become fuel.

All of these factors tend to increase fuels and the flammability of stands with advancing age. A gradual increase in total dry matter per unit area on the landscape thus occurs up to at least 100 to 300 years after fire. These correlations of fuels with stand age are not simple, however, because some dense conifer stands become highly flammable at 15 to 50 years of age (Sando and Wick 1972; Van Wagner 1977, 1983; Stocks 1987a). In many vegetation types the probability of ignition and of a high-intensity fire does increase as first-generation stands reach maturity and senescence. Once a significant fire occurs, the fuels are reduced, plant growth begins anew, and fuel patterns on the landscape are reordered. The burns themselves thus help control the mosaic (Heinselman 1981a).

These fuel factors, related to vegetation types and stand age and interacting with climatic oscillations, partially regulated the pattern of burns in primeval times. Lightning and people were both sources of ignition, but it mattered little to the ecosystem which was the actual cause. Fuels and weather determined whether a significant fire would occur, and lightning alone was an adequate source of ignition to guarantee that all flammable stands would eventually burn.

LIGHTNING AND PEOPLE AS FIRE SOURCES

In the Boundary Waters lightning is the only significant ignition source not related to human activity. It was likely sufficient to have produced the amount of fire recorded from 1595 until 1910 (when control began), even though many fires were people-caused. Thunderstorms occur about 25 days per year over northeastern Minnesota, chiefly between April and October, especially in midsummer. Duff layers, pine needles, lichens, mosses, and dry snags may be ignited by lightning strikes, but most such fires are extinguished by rains that accompany the storm. Occasional storms with little or no rain occur, however, and if they coincide with drought, forest fires may result.

Until the new prescribed natural-fire-management program began in the BWCAW in 1987, nearly all lightning fires were quickly extinguished by control crews, but the fire records of the Superior National Forest show the potential for major lightning fires. Most lightning fires occur in July and August, although some have been recorded for all months from May through October. For July, 31 percent of all fires in the BWCAW from 1956 to 1970 were lightning-caused. For August the average was 38 percent (Sando 1969). Although this proportion of fires caused by lightning may seem low, it must be remembered that the Boundary Waters hosts 180,000 recreational visits annually, and many campers cook with open fires. Thus the potential for people-caused ignitions is probably greater today than in the voyageurs

era, and perhaps greater than in the settlement era. It must be far greater than in prehistoric times, when the human population was much lower. Viewed in this context, lightning is still a surprisingly important cause of fire. Lightning caused some of the largest fires in the BWCAW in recent decades, such as the Cherokee-Frost Lake fires of 1936 and the Roy Lake and Rice Lake fires of 1976.

By comparison, in the Canadian and Alaskan boreal forests there are only 3 to 10 days with thunderstorms annually, but lightning is an even more important cause of fires there because the human population is lower, and many fires are not suppressed. Johnson and Rowe (1975) report that 85 percent of all fires were lightning-caused in a large region of the Northwest Territories, and lightning fires accounted for 99.9 percent of the total area burned. In the Alaskan interior, lightning accounted for 30 percent of the ignitions and 78 percent of the area burned from 1951 to 1969 (Barney 1971). Unlike the situation in western North America, where many fires may have been set deliberately by Native Americans near camps or villages in precolonial times, in the northeastern United States some investigators believe that native people were not a major cause of forest fires (Russell 1983).

In the Boundary Waters people were primarily an added source of ignitions until about 1910. Thereafter, they also became a major factor in limiting burn size through suppression measures. A relevant question, then, is how much burning would have taken place prior to 1910 if only lightning ignitions had occurred? A direct answer is unobtainable. But given only lightning ignitions, the burn patterns would result from interactions between the number, timing, and locations of ignitions, climatic variations, weather during fires, landform and topographic factors, and the mosaic of fuels on the landscape. The natural fuels mosaic is controlled by vegetation types, stand-age classes, and vegetational stages, but these factors are themselves influenced by past burn patterns. People changed these burn patterns only insofar as their ignitions caused burns that would not otherwise have occurred.

Lightning by itself may be only a semirandom source of ignitions. Ground strikes tend to be more frequent on high ridges. Successful ignition, of course, requires adequate fuels and dry conditions along with strikes. Tall dry snags, good dry tinder such as pine needles, dry lichens, and mosses, or dried soil organic layers may be the actual points of ignition.

The main difference between most white and red pine sites and the jack pine, aspen-birch, and black spruce sites was that fire intensity (not frequency) may have been less in the former. Fewer lightning ignitions may have occurred within the big-pine areas because of their physical location on the landscape, but we must not forget the great size of many fires before European settlement. Those fires roamed far and wide across the landscape. The more protected lower-elevation sites where white and red pine were most abundant must have often been ignited by spot fires from the ridges, even if no direct lightning ignitions occurred within them. Once an ignition did occur within these big-pine forests, either from spot fires or from lightning- or human-caused ignitions, the intensity of the resulting fire was often less on these sites than on the adjacent upland ridge complexes because of their location, topography, soil moisture, or other physical site factors. Stand-killing crown fires or high-intensity surface fires capable of killing most trees were simply less common on white and red pine sites. Of course, we must also remember that mature white and red pine can withstand higher-intensity surface fires because of their thick bark and long, branch-free trunks, adaptations to underburning not possessed by any other trees in the region.

Numerous areas of high soil moisture and better fertility probably also existed where the best nearly pure white-pine stands occurred, and these sites probably did have a history of longer fire-free intervals. Again, was there less fire because of a lack of lightning strikes, or were ignitions simply less probable because of the better moisture and fertility conditions on such sites? A fine example of the latter class of virgin white-pine forests can be seen on the Old Pines Loop trail, east of Disappointment Lake and west of Kiana Lake.

Humans may have been a source of some ignitions through most of postglacial time in the Boundary Waters, but does this really alter the view of fire as a key natural environmental factor? It is widely reported that the Ojibwa (Chippewa) regularly burned the ridges on United States Point in Basswood Lake to encourage blueberry production during the late nineteenth and early twentieth centuries. Other deliberate burning areas may have existed but are not well known. Probably the Ojibwa and earlier the Dakota also made at least some use of fire in hunting and warfare, and certainly these tribes and their ancestors used fire in cooking, for warmth, and for driving off insects. Over the centuries many forest fires may have been ignited by such activities. Yet we should also realize that these people certainly were aware of the effects of fire on their environment and probably avoided burning the forests when it was not to their advantage to do so.

People were present in Minnesota throughout most of postglacial time, perhaps 11,000 years. In the Boundary Waters there is reason to believe that human populations were very small in the distant past, and certainly an increase in human activity occurred in the voyageurs fur-trading era, 1670 to 1800. Yet Swain's (1973) charcoal data from Lake of the Clouds show that forest fire activity fluctuated up and down throughout the past 9,000 years, with no indication of a major upswing in fire after Europeans arrived on the continent. The greatest period of fire activity occurred just before 1400, a century before Columbus reached the Western Hemisphere. Swain's charcoal data and Craig's (1972) pollen data document a forest ecosystem in 1400 similar to that at the time of European settlement, with fire as an active environmental factor from 9,000 years ago up to 1895. Thus if humans added significantly to fire's role in the ecosystem, they did so rather consistently throughout the past 7,000 years, when white and red pine, jack pine, and the other present forest dominants flourished.

If we look still further back into the geological record, we see that many of the Boundary Waters trees and shrubs evolved their adaptations to fire in lightning-fire environments long before humans migrated from Asia to North America via the Bering Land Bridge. This evidence confirms that fire has been a vital factor in the environment of the Boundary Waters vegetation throughout its history. Humans no doubt became an increasing source of ignitions over the last several thousand years, but lightning alone is probably a sufficient source of ignition to produce the fire-dependent forest ecosystem that existed when full-scale settlement of northeastern Minnesota by Europeans began about 1880.

FIRE BARRIERS AND FOREST COMPOSITION

Clear relationships exist between historic fire patterns, forest communities, and several landscape factors. These factors are

- location, size, shape, and compass alignment of lakes, and the abundance of islands in them;
- location, size, shape, and alignment of streams;
- location, size, shape, and alignment of wetlands (forested swamps and peatlands, marshes, muskegs, etc.);
- location, size, height, and alignment of bedrock ridges, glacial moraines, and eskers;
- location, size, relative depth, and alignment of fault lines, valleys, troughs, and other lowlands;
- soil textures (relative content of sand, silt, or clay) and rockiness.

These factors influence fire movements because they relate to either natural firebreaks or fire paths. Some, such as ridges, valleys, wetlands, and soil texture, may also relate to fuels through their influence on slope, aspect, soil moisture, soil depth, fertility, and other factors that affect forest productivity and plant community composition. Alignment of landforms and water bodies is important because fire weather usually comes with west, southwest, or northwest winds that push fires eastward. Even weak fire barriers often stop north-south or westerly spread of fires. But only very large and effective barriers can block spread to the east, southeast, or northeast. These generalizations are based on the stand-origin maps, but each fire was a special case, and many exceptions existed. The following relationships often seem to hold:

- The firebreaks most often effective were large lakes, especially those with few or widely spaced islands. Small or long, narrow lakes aligned east-west often checked north-south spread, but it was chiefly the large, wide lakes that checked west-to-east spread.
- Streams, wetlands, valleys, and troughs frequently checked fire spread, especially to the north or south if aligned on a general west-to-east axis. They were less often effective in preventing west-to-east movements, even when aligned on a north-south axis across a fire's path.
- The areas burned most frequently or intensely were large upland ridge complexes, especially those distant from or west of effective natural firebreaks. Jack pine, black spruce, aspen, birch, and sometimes oak dominate many such areas today. Long west-east ridges can burn full length, serving as fire paths for eastward spread.
- The areas burned least frequently or intensely were swamps, valleys, ravines, the lower slopes of high ridges (especially those facing east or northeast), islands, peninsulas, and the east, north, northeast, or southeast sides of large lakes or streams, especially those with much open water in relation to island area. White pine, red pine, white spruce, northern white cedar, black ash, and fir are more abundant on many such sites. Any site on the favorable side of a possible firebreak is more likely to support these species.
- Under extreme burning conditions with high winds, most fire barriers can be jumped by spot fires. This clearly happened in many cases.

The relation of white and red pine to fire barriers is especially interesting. Both reproduce well after fire and are fire dependent. Both are resistant to moderate surface fires when mature but can be killed by crown fires. Both have only intermittent seed crops and nonpersistent, open cones. Thus after fires, many survivors are necessary to reseed the burned area. White pine is the more prolific seeder. Neither grows well in heavy shade, although white pine is the more shade tolerant. Both seed in well on bare soil or thin organic layers, but white pine can survive on thicker organic layers than can red. These characteristics of red and white pine imply need for a disturbance regime provided by combinations of occasional light surface fires and more severe fires only at long intervals. An occasional surface fire would keep down organic layers and shade-tolerant understory trees such as fir, thus preventing fires severe enough to kill the overstory. If a more severe fire then came along once every 100 to 300 years, killing many but not all overstory pines, it would create the necessary stand openings for regeneration and would assure seed sources. This kind of fire regime prevailed in the BWCAW where many stands of these pines occur today. Similar regimes were documented for these species by Frissell (1973) and Clark (1988, 1989, 1990a) in Itasca Park, by Cwynar (1977, 1978) in Algonquin Park, Ontario, and by Bergeron and Brisson (1990) in Quebec at the northern limit of red pine.

The most common location for red and white pine stands today in the virgin forests of the BWCAW and Quetico is on islands and peninsulas, or on the east, north, northeast, or southeast sides of lakes, streams, swamps, or valleys. Similarly, at the northern limit of its range in Quebec and Ontario red pine is restricted to islands and peninsulas (Bergeron 1991). Fires in such locations may be ignited as spot fires and burn as backfires moving against westerly winds, creeping downslope toward the lakeshore or swamp edge. The known locations of many BWCAW stands of old pine that were cut in the early logging era agree with these patterns. Many existing old red and white pine stands bear scars from the surface fires that burned through them, and many of these fires occurred in the same major fire years that elsewhere killed whole forests over extensive areas. This evidence suggests that the location of such stands ameliorated fire intensity and made the regeneration of red and white pine possible. The average interval between fire scars in such stands is 36 years. Clearly they did see much fire.

Northern white cedar is very fire sensitive and has almost literally been driven to the lakeshores by fire. It is so uncommon on uplands that it has been considered a species requiring high soil moisture and mobile groundwater. But the proof that it can cope with dry sites is that it may be abundant on ridges on certain islands and on other upland sites where fires have been infrequent. Many lakeshores are lined with cedars, but the cedar fringe is usually narrow. A little detective work will quickly reveal the reason: many old cedars are fire-scarred on the side away from the lake, and the younger trees spreading inland usually date from after the fire that scarred such a fringe.

Implications of the Fire History for Understanding the Terrestrial Ecosystem

This chapter has set the stage and established the bounds for understanding the discussion in subsequent chapters of many aspects of the terrestrial ecosystem. To understand the functioning of the ecosystem, the vegetation patterns on the landscape, the dynamics of vegetation changes, the changing habitats and populations of terrestrial mammals, birds, amphibians, reptiles, and insects, and the impact of past logging, fire control, and fire-management programs, one must first understand the natural role of fire and the kinds of fire regimes that prevailed before the natural system was altered during the past 100 years.

The forest age-class patterns and logging history depicted on the stand-origin, logging-history, and fire-year maps are needed to relate them to subsequent discussions of all aspects of the ecosystem. These maps are not without their flaws, especially for remote areas far back in the hills. There stand ages and fire years are based on the forest-type maps, air photo interpretation, or Forest Service inventory-plot ages extrapolated from the nearest fire boundaries we did reach. Undoubtedly many small burns and skipped stands were missed. The age structures of some of the old red and white pine stands were too complex to document fully or to depict on maps at the scales used, and many of the smaller old stands simply had to be assigned to the most probable fire years documented nearby. The real story of this fire history lies in the gross landscape patterns of forest age classes and the patterns and scales of past fire events they reveal. It is these gross patterns that one must comprehend to grasp the impact of fire on the ecosystem. Not long ago forest fires were as vital as rain, snow, wind, and temperature in shaping the ecosystem. How we respond to this new understanding will determine in the most fundamental ways the kind of Boundary Waters ecosystem that future generations will experience.

Forest Ecosystem Processes in Relation to Fire

If the forest ecosystems of the BWCAW, Quetico, and Voyageurs are to be restored as functioning natural systems, then we must understand and provide for the pervasive role of fire in the workings of the natural ecosystem. This chapter examines the processes and function of the ecosystem and explores the role of fire as an integral part of that system (Heinselman 1973, 1981a,b).

Some Basic Principles

"An ecosystem includes all the organisms in an area, their environment, and a series of linkages or interactions between them" (Franklin 1990, 243). The physical environment includes climatic factors as well as water supply, atmospheric chemistry, and the essential inorganic materials obtained from mineral soils. The community of organisms encompasses all living things in the system, including (1) green plants (autotrophs), which furnish the system's energy by fixing the sun's energy in complex organic materials manufactured from carbon dioxide, water, nitrogen, and soil minerals (nutrients) through photosynthesis, and (2) animals, microbes, and fungi (heterotrophs), which depend on green plants for their energy, either directly or indirectly. This second group includes consumers such as wolves, bears, moose, chipmunks, gray jays, and spruce budworms, which feed directly on living things, and decomposers such as bacteria, fungi, and insects, which feed

on dead organic material such as fallen logs, leaves, and needles in the litter and humus layers of the forest floor, as well as feces.

The basic processes of ecosystems—photosynthesis, transpiration (evaporation from living plant leaves and needles), consumption, and decomposition—are generally conducted by living organisms and are driven by environmental factors such as sunlight, moisture, and temperature. In addition are the physical processes of rock weathering, erosion, and evaporation. Fire, flood, and windstorms are also important periodic driving forces in the Boundary Waters ecosystem. Fire, for example, causes instantaneous physical decomposition.

The fluxes among parts of ecosystems are vital to their functioning and are often influenced by human actions, which must be understood to comprehend the impact on the system as a whole. Energy, nutrients, and moisture flow through the system via traceable paths. Living organisms die, decompose to simpler materials, and are recycled in the system or lost through leaching, volatilization, or direct removal by humans. Environmental factors control flow rates. Over the life of a forest stand, gradual changes occur in ecosystem states, processes, flow rates, and pathways. Suppression of lightning fires is a major intervention in the flow rates and pathways of energy and materials in the ecosystem because it alters the natural processes of decomposition and recycling of plant and animal nutrients.

The size and boundaries of ecosystems are arbitrary, and they depend on the purposes of the studies or discussions involved. This chapter focuses on the forest ecosystem of the uplands and lowlands of the Boundary Waters. The lake and stream ecosystems are considered in chapter 14.

The Role of Fire in Biomass Accumulation and Nutrient Cycling

The forest soils of the Laurentian Shield are inherently infertile. Their meager store of available plant nutrients (nitrogen, phosphorus, potassium, calcium, magnesium, iron, sulfur, and many micronutrients) is easily tied up in living plants and undecomposed plant remains. Decomposition processes and animals recycle plant materials slowly, producing carbon dioxide and water and leaving the mineral nutrients in the humus and upper soil layers. In cool northern forests decomposition fails to keep pace with plant growth and death on many sites because of unfavorable temperatures, moisture conditions, and acidity for bacterial and fungal decay and for soil microorganisms. Over the life of a forest stand, the gradual net accumulation of undecomposed plant remains contains much of the nutrient capital in the system (Viereck 1983).

Forests accumulate cellulose and other carbon compounds, nitrogen, and mineral nutrients in the growing trunks, branches, roots, and foliage of living trees. Without fire or other major disturbances, these materials continue to accumulate until the death and decay of individual trees compensate for additional growth. Shrub, herb, and ground-layer plants also have growth and decay cycles, which result in additional net biomass accumulation over time. For example, the feathermosses are great humus builders, particularly in jack pine–black spruce and black spruce–feathermoss communities. Sphagnum mosses and the feathermosses are great peat builders in some peatland communities.

These net biomass accumulations appear as gradually thickening litter and raw humus layers on the forest floor and as the living and standing dead or down portions of trees, shrubs, herbs, mosses, and so on. On many upland sites litter and humus may accumulate to depths of 3 to 6 inches or more in old stands. In some old red and white pine stands and upland white cedar communities the litter plus humus may accumulate to depths of 6 to 8 inches. On peatlands the accumulation process may go on indefinitely. The tendency in the Boundary Waters ecosystem is therefore toward net accumulation of living and dead biomass on the forested landscape, some of which is potential fuel for forest fires. This biomass ties up vital plant nutrients that might otherwise be available for plant growth.

Fire was the great recycling agent before logging and fire control changed the natural system. Fires consumed much of the living and dead plant material at intervals varying from a few to hundreds of years on any given site. The combustion process removes chiefly some of the carbon compounds, converting them back to carbon dioxide and water, which exit the system as gases. Much of the carbon remains on site for a time in standing snags and charcoal. Mineral plant nutrients that were tied up in living and dead needles, leaves, twigs, bark, and the surface soil litter and humus layers are redeposited on the land as ash (phosphorus, potassium, magnesium, calcium, iron, etc.). This nutrient release, coupled with profuse regeneration of the forest through adaptations of all plants to fire, leads to renewed production of plant materials via photosynthesis, completing the cycle. Forest fires also formerly burned many bog forests, reducing the thickness of surface moss layers in peatlands and releasing scarce nutrients for renewed forest growth. Charcoal layers in many peat bogs attest to the periodic occurrence of such fires over the centuries. In broad outlines releasing nutrients is the role of fire in nutrient cycling in northern forests across North America and in many areas of Eurasia (Chapin and Van Cleve 1981; MacLean et al. 1983).

Fires oxidize some organic materials to gases, releasing oxides of carbon, nitrogen, and sulfur. They emit particulate matter in smoke and transfer many mineral elements to the surface soil layer as ash. Some of the particulate matter and minerals may be removed from the burned area by convection. Nitrogen is the most important nutrient often removed from the system through volatilization, but this effect may be offset by postfire changes in nitrogen cycles. Nitrogen is derived from the atmosphere by plant fixation and fallout, and losses can be replaced by natural processes.

Volatilization of phosphorus, potassium, calcium, and magnesium is much less. These inputs to the soil surface and losses to the atmosphere depend on fire intensity and the amount of biomass consumed by the fire (MacLean et al. 1983).

Mineral nutrients deposited in the ash layer usually produce a postfire nutrient pulse or fertilization effect that greatly enhances plant growth, especially in the first 5 to 10 years after fire. The extent of this pulse tends to increase with fire intensity and the amount of fuel (biomass) burned. After fire, a decrease in soil acidity usually improves the availability of phosphorus and many micronutrients. Increases in water-soluble phosphorus, potassium, calcium, and sodium may occur, especially in the upper soil layers. Higher surface-soil temperatures due to direct exposure of the ground to sunlight and to increased absorption of radiation by the blackened soil surface contribute to nutrient mobilization (Ohmann and Grigal 1979; MacLean et al. 1983). On recent burns nutrient concentrations are generally much higher in the stems, leaves, and needles of tree reproduction and in shrubs and herbs than they are in mature forests, partly in response to the postfire nutrient pulse. For most elements tissue concentrations tend to be highest in the first year or two after fire and then gradually decline to levels comparable to those in mature forests (Ohmann and Grigal 1979). This response is important to wildlife nutrition and related to the rapid postfire invasion of new burns by moose and other mammals (Peek 1974).

Some nutrients removed from the land surface by runoff and erosion eventually find their way into streams and lakes, but rapid regrowth of vegetation on burns recaptures most nutrients on the land. In the Boundary Waters ecosystem, nutrient inputs to lakes and streams are often so small that no algal blooms or significant changes in lake water chemistry occur (R. F. Wright 1976). Again, such effects depend on many factors, of which fire intensity, total biomass consumed, the consumption of soil-surface humus (organic matter), soil characteristics, topography (especially slope steepness), depth to impermeable bedrock, surface bedrock, and season of burn are especially important. Spring fires, even high-intensity crown fires, on moderate topography are not likely to result in significant nutrient movements to lakes and streams, whereas high-intensity late summer or fall fires in major droughts on steep bedrock terrain may result in considerable nutrient input to waters (H. E. Wright 1974, 1981; McColl and Grigal 1975, 1977; R. F. Wright 1976; Ohmann and Grigal 1979; Schindler et al. 1990).

Effects of Fire Size and Intensity

Fires may vary in many ways that influence their effects on tree mortality, nutrient release, and regeneration of the plant community. The size of the fire is important, as is the intensity, which depends on the type of fire. Three fire types occur: crown fires, surface fires, and ground fires (fires in deeper surface organic matter and in peat).

Each fire type may vary in intensity (rate of burn and energy released) and area burned. Fire type and intensity control

- mortality of trees, shrubs, herbs, mosses, and lichens;
- opening of closed cones and seed dispersal in jack pine;
- survival of canopy-stored seeds in the cones of jack pine and black spruce and of seeds of other trees;
- kill of stored seeds and vegetative reproductive structures in organic and mineral soils;
- release of carbon and nutrients from the vegetation and organic layers.

The vegetation itself affects the fire, especially by determining the amount and kinds of fuel. The species, age, and density of trees, shrubs, herbs, mosses, and lichens are important variables. For example, the sphagnum mosses are usually moist and rarely burn in the ground layer in lowland plant communities, but the feathermosses dry readily and burn well in jack pine and black spruce forests in the Boundary Waters. Some feathermoss humus layers are as much as 6 inches thick, although 2 to 3 inches is more typical. The long-crowned conifers (balsam, white and black spruce, and white cedar) may have flammable branches near ground level that become fire ladders carrying fire into the canopy. Old forests contain dead timber and are often subject to insect, disease, or parasite attacks and windfall. Dead, dying, and down timber are significant fuel sources.

The season of burning determines the stage of annual growth of the plants and thus affects their ability to survive or to reproduce if killed. It determines when the first reseeding will occur and the timing of vegetative regrowth. It influences the dryness and flammability of soil-surface organic layers, dead twigs, and larger woody fuels, and even living plant foliage. In the Boundary Waters the ground is usually snow-covered from November through April, and fires are only possible when the snow is gone.

The size of a burn affects forest regeneration from seed sources outside the burn. This effect is influenced by the shape and orientation of the burn with respect to landscape features such as ridges, valleys, wetlands, lakes, and streams and by unburned areas inside the burn. On many burns, however, the regrowth comes chiefly from sources inside the burn, hence the size of the total burned area may not be as critical for many plant species as one might think. Nevertheless, the size, shape, and homogeneity of the burn do have major implications for landscape-scale effects.

Finally, the extent to which the litter and humus organic layers are burned is a vital factor influencing regrowth. Exposure of mineral-soil seedbeds favors successful reseeding by jack, red, and white pines, black and white spruce, balsam fir, and most other conifers (LeBarron 1939, 1944; Place 1955; Ahlgren 1959, 1970; Ahlgren and Ahlgren 1960; Horton and Bedell 1960; Fowells 1965). Burning recycles nutrients locked up in organic layers, in some areas the largest source of unavailable nutrients. Nutrient release is more or less proportional to the consumption of these layers by the fire (Ahlgren 1970; Ohmann and Grigal 1979; Van Cleve and Viereck 1981; Viereck 1983; MacLean et al. 1983). Burning the organic layer also increases postfire soil temperatures for several years because the blackened soil surfaces absorb more of the sun's radiation. Soil temperatures are an important factor in nutrient mobilization (MacLean et al. 1983). When mineral soils are exposed by complete burning of the humus, the maximum postfire surface-soil temperatures are lower than in blackened organic soils. Partially burned organic soil layers may become so hot and/or dry on clear summer days that seedlings die (LeBarron 1944; Place 1955; Zasada 1971). Burning of all

of the organic layer kills most of the seeds of plants that rely on seed banks in these layers, whereas partial burning may improve or at least not injure their germination (Moore and Wein 1977; Ohmann and Grigal 1979). Burn depth affects vegetative reproduction from plant structures in the organic layer (Ahlgren and Ahlgren 1960; Buckman 1964b; Ohmann and Grigal 1979).

Plant Strategies for Coping with Fire

Plants native to the Boundary Waters fire-dependent ecosystem have evolved many strategies to survive fires or to reproduce even if killed, and they adapt to cope with the many environmental changes that come with the often large, high-intensity but infrequent fires characteristic of the region. If they had not adapted, they would be rare or extinct. Noble and Slatyer (1977) and Rowe (1983) have developed classifications of plant species' adaptations to fire environments that I modified into lists showing some important adaptations of northern forest species (Heinselman 1981a). The substance of these lists is summarized here for many Boundary Waters species.

CANOPY STORAGE OF SEED
IN PERSISTENT CLOSED CONES

The storage of seeds in persistent closed cones in the crowns of jack pine and black spruce is one of the best known adaptations of trees to lethal crown fires. The cones of most jack pines are sealed shut with resins that melt at the temperatures reached in the trees during crown fires or intense surface fires. The cones remain on the tree indefinitely, and seeds remain viable in the cones for at least 25 years (Beaufait 1960; Fowells 1965). When cones are briefly heated by the intense heat of crown fires, the cone scales flex open and millions of seeds are scattered over the burn within a few weeks after the fire has passed (figure 7.1 a, b). Some cones do partially open without fire, so limited seed is available between fires. Black spruce has slowly opening persistent but only semiclosed cones, borne chiefly at the top of the crown. Some seed is shed every year. After fire, dispersal occurs gradually over the first few years (LeBarron 1939; Wilton 1963; Fowells 1965). These adaptations allow

Figure 7.1a / Closed jack pine cones. The cones of most jack pines are sealed shut with resins that melt at the temperatures reached in the trees during crown fires or intense surface fires.

Figure 7.1b / Open jack pine cones. When jack pine cones are briefly heated by the intense heat of crown fires, the cone scales flex open, and millions of seeds are scattered over the burn.

jack pine and black spruce to reproduce abundantly even when virtually every tree of their species is killed over large areas. Vast quantities of seed are shed on bare mineral soil or thin organic-layer seedbeds that have just been fertilized with ash. Furthermore, the new seedlings are temporarily freed of competition from trees, shrubs, and herbs. The result is often a dramatic restocking of the burn with dense young stands of pine and spruce, although stocking often varies from "dog-hair thickets" of jack pine to widely and unevenly spaced mixtures of both species.

WIND-TRANSPORTED SEEDS AND SPORES

Many Boundary Waters plants recolonize new burns with light windblown seeds or spores. The best examples are the trees and shrubs of the poplar/willow family: quaking aspen, bigtooth aspen, balsam poplar, and the willows, all having tiny seeds transported on silken hair parachutes. With strong enough winds their seeds can travel a mile or more. The seeds of many other trees and some shrubs are winged and often blown 300 feet or more—even farther when wind-driven across hard-packed snow. Species that meet these criteria include both spruces, all three pines, all birch, tamarack, cedar, and the alders. Balsam, maple, and ash seeds are winged, and although heavier than the seeds of the other species listed, still can travel some distance. Many grasses, sedges, and herbs also fit here.

The airborne spores of mosses travel great distances, and the mosses are important in postfire vegetation sequences. *Ceratodon purpureus*, *Funaria hygrometrica*, and *Pohlia nutans* invade immediately after fire on moist sites where the organic layer burned away. Hair-cap moss and the liverwort *Marchantia polymorpha* are also abundant on such sites. The three feathermosses, some species of *Dicranum*, and several other mosses do not appear until a conifer forest overstory is established. The sphagnum mosses also invade through spores, and the clubmosses and horsetails reproduce by spores after fire in some cases.

SEED BANKS IN ORGANIC LAYERS

Both long-lived and shorter-lived seeds in the humus layers of Boundary Waters forests are important in the prompt revegetation of many burns. Several early postfire species germinate and flower profusely in the first one to three years after fire and then bank their seeds in the accumulating organic layer. They are not seen again except in special habitats until the next fire burns the humus sufficiently to permit germination. The clearest examples are pale corydalis, Bicknell's geranium, bristly sarsaparilla, and fringed bindweed (Ahlgren 1960; Ohmann and Grigal 1979; Rowe 1983). These plants are most abundant where only the surface of the humus is burned, but some usually appear even on deeply burned sites.

Birds and mammals transport and deposit much of the seed in organic layers. This is particularly true of pin-cherry, other cherries, red osier dogwood, bunchberry, bearberry, high-bush cranberry, downy arrow-wood, currants, gooseberries, buffalo-berry, and snowberry. The germination of some of these berries is assured only by the passage of their seeds through the gut of a bird or mammal. Their regeneration from seed on burns is favored by fires that do not burn much of the organic layer.

VEGETATIVE REPRODUCTION AFTER FIRE

Vegetative reproduction may occur from root suckers, root crown sprouts, basal stem sprouts, rhizomes, tubers, bulbs, and related structures, and in some lower plants from plant fragments. Root suckers are important in the postfire regeneration of aspens and balsam poplar. Suckers may appear up to at least 100 feet from parent trees. Deep burning of the organic layer may kill much of the aspen root network and thus favor conifer seedlings, but even on such sites some suckering is usual. On many aspen sites tens of thousands of suckers per acre may completely dominate postfire regrowth. Root crown or stem sprouts are impor-

tant in the postfire regeneration of birch, maple, oak, ash, willow, alder, hazelnut, blueberries, Labrador-tea, bearberry, and other woody species. The depth of burn of organic layers is particularly important in alder, hazelnut, willow, and the heath shrubs because deep burning can nearly eliminate their vegetative reproduction (Buckman 1964b; Rowe 1983).

Rhizomes, rootstocks, and other miscellaneous underground plant structures are important in the postfire vegetative regeneration of dogbane, wild lily-of-the-valley, pyrolas, wild sarsaparilla, bunchberry, bluebead-lily, fireweed, blue-joint grass, bracken, clubmosses, horsetails, and other species. The depth of burn of the organic layer is critical for several of these species (Rowe 1983; Viereck 1983).

The regeneration of lichens is not well understood, but reproduction from fragments occurs. Moose, deer, bear, and other mammals may be important in reestablishing reindeer moss and other ground lichens on burns. Tree lichens such as old man's beard might be dispersed by birds, mammals, or wind.

FIRE RESISTANCE STRATEGIES

Most Boundary Waters trees are not fire resistant. All the spruces, aspens, birches, and maples, as well as ash, balsam, white cedar, red oak, and pin oak are relatively thin barked and easily killed through cambial girdling in medium- to high-intensity surface fires, even as large trees. Even moderate surface fires kill many individuals. The only important exceptions are red and white pine and to a lesser extent jack pine and tamarack, and all of these are sensitive to moderate surface fires until they attain basal stem diameters of at least 4 to 6 inches. Large red and white pines usually survive moderate surface fires with little injury because their thick bark insulates the cambium (growing cell layer) from lethal heat, and their long clear trunks help avoid crowning. High-intensity surface fires kill some trees through girdling and cause basal fire scars on many surviving trees. Red pine is somewhat more fire resistant than white pine, and it retains sound basal fire scars much longer than white pine because its resinous wood is more resistant to decay. Large jack pine and tamarack often survive

Table 7.1 / Life history data for principal northern conifer forest trees

Species	Juvenile growth rate	Adult growth rate	Age effective seed production starts (year)	Ordinary lifespan without fire[a] (years)	Maximum longevity[b] (years)	Propagules lost without fire[c] (years)	Shade tolerance	Vegetative propagation after fire
Jack pine	fast	medium	15–20	150–200	250	270	low	no
Red pine	medium	fast	30–60	300	400	400	low	no
White pine	medium	fast	30–50	300–350	500	500	medium	no
Black spruce	medium	slow	15–30	180–220	250	na	medium	no
White spruce	slow	fast	30–50	200–250	300	na	high	no
Balsam fir	slow	fast	25–35	150	200	na	high	no
Northern white cedar	slow	slow	30–40	300	500+	na	high	no
Tamarack	fast	fast	30–40	150–200	250–330	300	low	no
Quaking aspen	fast	fast	25	120–160	200	na	low	yes
Bigtooth aspen	fast	fast	25	100–140?	150?	na	low	yes
Balsam poplar	fast	fast	25?	130–150	200	na	low	yes
Paper birch	fast	fast	25	130–200	230	na	low	yes
Black ash	medium	medium	30–40?	150?	250?	na	low	yes
Red maple	medium	slow		100–150	180?	na	medium	yes

[a] Lifespans and maximum longevities given are for the principal range of the species in the boreal forest and for northern species nearer the limits of their ranges.

[b] Age at which all individuals originating after a given fire would be dead.

[c] na = not applicable. These species are either tolerant enough to reproduce from seed without fire, capable of vegetative reproduction by layering, or have such widely dispersed seeds that they could recolonize areas temporarily lost.

Sources Data from Fowells (1965) and the author's files. This table is modified from Table 23.3, p. 388, in Heinselman (1981a) by permission of Springer-Verlag New York, Inc.

light surface fires, but if the humus layer is dry enough to burn deeply, most trees are killed by girdling even if there is no crown fire.

LIFE HISTORY FACTORS

Juvenile and adult growth rates, age of reproductive maturity, longevity, and shade tolerance influence the relative success of northern trees in fire environments (table 7.1). Early growth rates and age of reproductive maturity set the shortest interfire intervals that still permit seed reproduction after stand-killing fires. For example, jack pine and black spruce bear enough cones to regenerate stands at the

very early ages of 15 to 30 years, about the age at which crown fires become a threat.

Longevity is important for the opposite reason: it sets a maximum interfire interval for reproduction of fire-requiring species. That interval is longer than the average natural fire-return interval over the continental range of each species, thus ensuring that there will almost always be living trees to perpetuate the species no matter how long fire is delayed. Nevertheless, individuals of most species do occasionally attain their maximum age because they happen to become established in nearly fire-free habitats or simply are never struck by a lethal fire, and now because of

The Boundary Waters Canoe Area Wilderness contains more than 1,000 lakes over 10 acres in area, hundreds of small ponds, many miles of streams, about 1,300 miles of canoe routes—lakes, streams, and portages—and thousands of miles of shoreline.

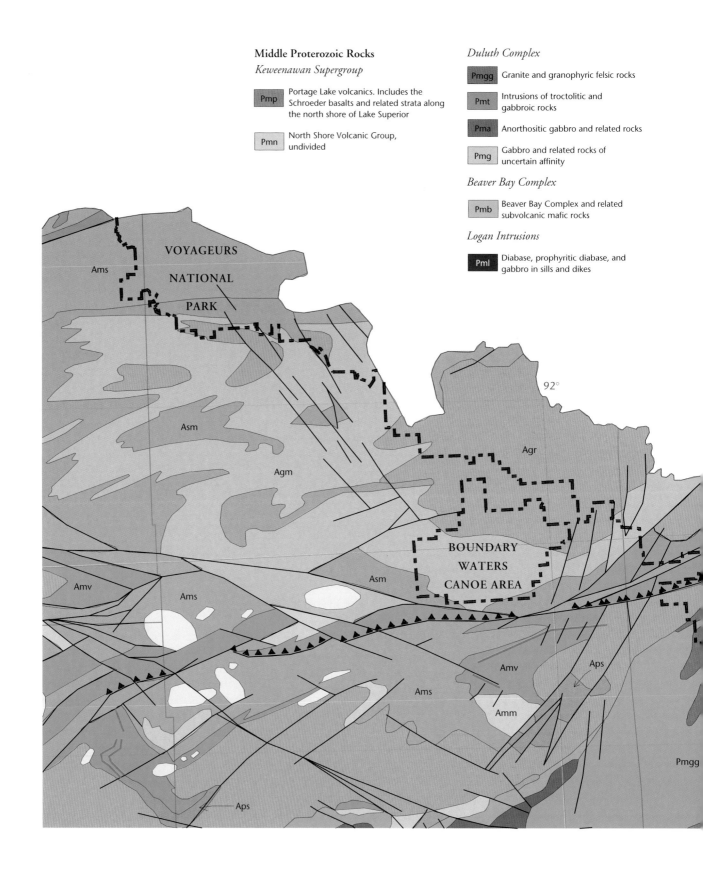

Middle Proterozoic Rocks

Keweenawan Supergroup

| Pmp | Portage Lake volcanics. Includes the Schroeder basalts and related strata along the north shore of Lake Superior |

| Pmn | North Shore Volcanic Group, undivided |

Duluth Complex

| Pmgg | Granite and granophyric felsic rocks |

| Pmt | Intrusions of troctolitic and gabbroic rocks |

| Pma | Anorthositic gabbro and related rocks |

| Pmg | Gabbro and related rocks of uncertain affinity |

Beaver Bay Complex

| Pmb | Beaver Bay Complex and related subvolcanic mafic rocks |

Logan Intrusions

| Pml | Diabase, prophyritic diabase, and gabbro in sills and dikes |

VOYAGEURS

NATIONAL

PARK

Ams

Asm

Agm

92°

Agr

Asm

BOUNDARY
WATERS
CANOE AREA

Amv

Ams

Aps

Amv

Ams

Amm

Aps

Pmgg

Early Proterozoic Rocks

Animikie Group

Peg	Shale, siltstone, feldspathic graywacke, and associated volcaniclastic rocks of the Virginia, Thomson, and Rove formations
Peif	Iron formation. Biwabik and Gunflint iron formations and subjacent units

Late Archean Rocks

Ami	Post-tectonic mafic intrusions
Agd	Late-tectonic to post-tectonic granitoid intrusions of the Algoman orogen
Agr	Pre-tectonic to syntectonic granitoid rocks. Includes portions of the Vermilion Granitic Complex, and the Giants Range and Bemidji batholiths
Agm	Granite-rich migmatite. Includes portions of the Vermilion Granitic Complex
Asm	Paragneiss and schist-rich migmatite
Ast	Saganaga Tonalite

Ams	Metasedimentary rocks, undivided. Includes the Knife Lake Group and Lake Vermilion Formation
Amm	Mixed metavolcanic rocks. Includes the Ely Greenstone and Soudan Iron Formation
Amv	Mafic metavolcanic rocks. Includes the Newton Lake Formation
Aps	Paragneiss, schist, and amphibolite. Metamorphic equivalent of units Amv and Ams; may include components of unit Agr

——————— Inferred geologic contact

——————— Inferred trace of steeply dipping fault

▲▲▲▲ Inferred trace of thrust fault; teeth on upper plate

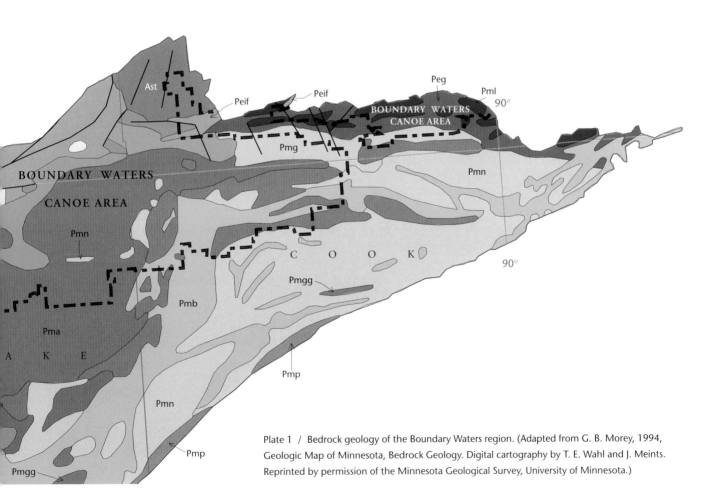

Plate 1 / Bedrock geology of the Boundary Waters region. (Adapted from G. B. Morey, 1994, Geologic Map of Minnesota, Bedrock Geology. Digital cartography by T. E. Wahl and J. Meints. Reprinted by permission of the Minnesota Geological Survey, University of Minnesota.)

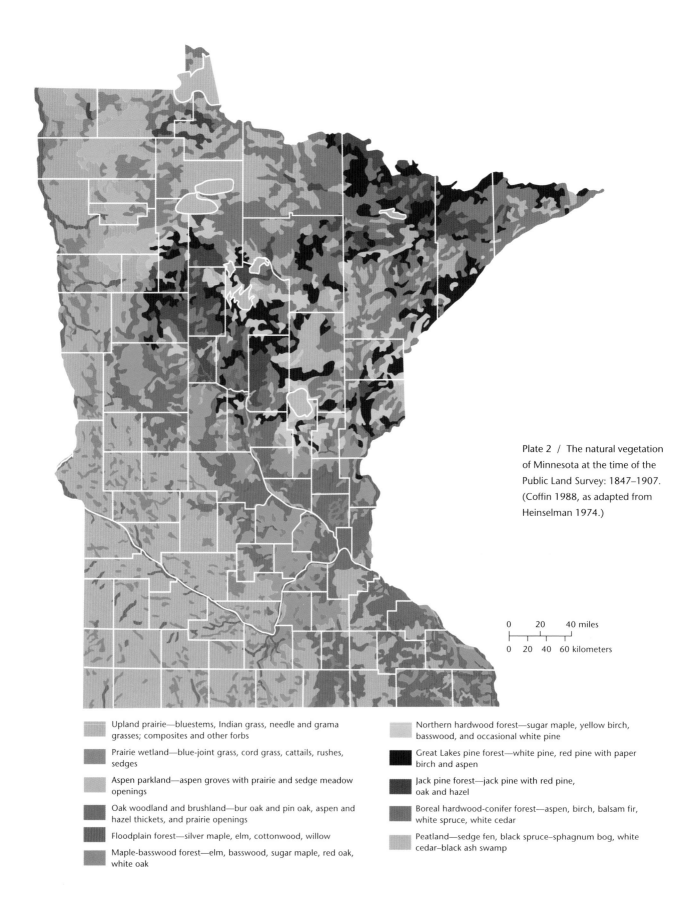

Plate 2 / The natural vegetation of Minnesota at the time of the Public Land Survey: 1847–1907. (Coffin 1988, as adapted from Heinselman 1974.)

0   20   40 miles

0   20   40   60 kilometers

Upland prairie—bluestems, Indian grass, needle and grama grasses; composites and other forbs

Prairie wetland—blue-joint grass, cord grass, cattails, rushes, sedges

Aspen parkland—aspen groves with prairie and sedge meadow openings

Oak woodland and brushland—bur oak and pin oak, aspen and hazel thickets, and prairie openings

Floodplain forest—silver maple, elm, cottonwood, willow

Maple-basswood forest—elm, basswood, sugar maple, red oak, white oak

Northern hardwood forest—sugar maple, yellow birch, basswood, and occasional white pine

Great Lakes pine forest—white pine, red pine with paper birch and aspen

Jack pine forest—jack pine with red pine, oak and hazel

Boreal hardwood-conifer forest—aspen, birch, balsam fir, white spruce, white cedar

Peatland—sedge fen, black spruce–sphagnum bog, white cedar–black ash swamp

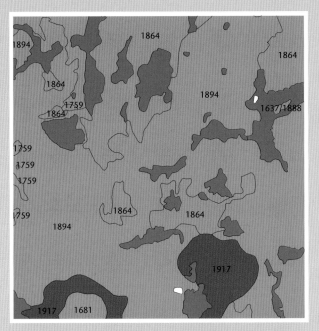

Plate 3 / An example of a digital stand-origin data set. Area shown is a portion of the Takucmich Lake Quadrangle digitized by the University of Minnesota, Remote Sensing Lab, in 1994. Forested areas are colored as to their most recent disturbance: orange for fire and green for logging. Areas are labeled with dates of disturbance, with one area (an island in the northeast portion of the map) being disturbed multiple times. White indicates areas with missing data. (Appendix D contains a selection of the original stand-origin maps prepared by the author.)

Plate 4 / Satellite image data from Landsat Thematic Mapper. Image covers Fourtown Lake Quadrangle and was acquired in June of 1986. Hardwood vegetation appears orange, conifers are dark blue/orange, wetlands are cyan/purple, cutover areas (in southwest corner) are bright cyan/white, and water is black. (Land image reproduced courtesy of Earth Observation Satellite Company, Lanham, Maryland. Image processing by the University of Minnesota, Remote Sensing Lab.)

Plate 5 / Winter on Iron Lake. In the BWCAW and Quetico Provincial Park, real solitude is still achievable for those who penetrate far into the interior, especially in winter. (Photographs courtesy of Dr. J. Arnold Bolz, except where noted.)

Plate 6 / Most winter visitors to the BWCAW and Quetico travel on skis or snowshoes.

Plate 7 / Vermilion River. In most years in the Boundary Waters region the first measurable snowfall occurs by late October. Permanent snow cover is usually established by mid-November, and nearly continuous snow cover remains until mid-April.

Plate 8 / Kahshahpiwi Lake. The Boundary Waters region is a low plateau of modest relief, broken by a labyrinth of lakes and streams and locally by steep cliffs and endless rocky ridges.

Plate 9 / Cliffs on Sea Gull Lake. In most of the region the ridges rise only 50 to 100 feet above the lakes and streams, but in the most rugged areas nearly vertical cliffs rise 200 to 400 feet above the lakes.

Plate 10 / A ground layer of lichens, especially the reindeer mosses *(Cladonia)*, often covers more than half of the otherwise barren bedrock in the nearly treeless lichen-dominated community found in the Boundary Waters region.

Plate 11 / *(opposite)* Wild roses on lichen-covered rocks. Clumps of low shrubs often occur along fractures in the exposed bedrock that makes up about 30 percent of the landscape in the lichen-dominated community.

Plate 12 / Ancient red and white pines keep their lonely vigil over the waterways of the Boundary Waters region.

Plate 13 / Red pine forests were heavily logged from 1895 to about 1940 in many areas of the Boundary Waters region. Thus, good examples of this community are confined largely to the remaining virgin forests of the BWCAW and Quetico.

Plates 14–16 / Winter-green (*below, left*) and blueberries (*below, center*) are two of the low shrubs commonly found in many of the upland forest communities. The stemless lady-slipper (*below, right*), an orchid, is also found in these communities.

Plate 17 / The most common location for white pine stands today in the virgin forests of the BWCAW and Quetico is on islands and peninsulas, or on the east, north, northeast, or southeast sides of lakes, streams, swamps, or valleys.

Plate 18–19 / Quaking aspen (*right photo, green leaves in lower right photo*) and large-toothed aspen (*silver leaves in lower right photo*) are important elements of several upland forest communities. These communities are found in both virgin forests and in areas cut in the early logging era.

Plates 20–21 / Red maple is an important element in two of the upland forest communities: maple-aspen-birch and maple-aspen-birch-fir. These communities occur in both virgin and logged areas throughout the region.

Plate 22 / Golden birch leaves in fall. Paper birch is present in many of the upland forest communities in the Boundary Waters region. In the fir-birch community, paper birch shares dominance with balsam fir. Other common trees in this community include black spruce, white cedar, white spruce, and quaking aspen.

Plates 23–24 / Bunchberry, the most frequent herb in the fir-birch community, has white flowers in spring and red berries in summer.

Plate 25 / Marsh marigolds are most commonly found in mixed conifer swamp forests and ash-elm swamp forests.

Plate 26 / Wild sar-saparilla (*foreground*) is found in the herb layer of the white cedar community.

Plate 27 / Cotton-grass is a common species in black spruce bog forests and tamarack bog forests.

Plate 28 / Labrador-tea (*foreground*), found in several of the lowland plant communities, is the most abundant low shrub in black spruce bog forests.

Plate 29 / The black spruce bog forest occurs throughout the Boundary Waters region and is the most extensive of the lowland plant communities.

Plate 30 / Black spruce–feathermoss forests have a striking, nearly continuous carpet of feathermosses.

Plate 31 / Indian pipe, which obtains nutrients from mycorrhizal fungi that grow on the roots of conifers, is found in black spruce bog forests and black spruce-feathermoss forests.

Plates 32–33 / In the tamarack bog forest, an uncommon community in the Boundary Waters region, the tree layer is often virtually pure tamarack. Black spruce is the most frequent associate. Tamarack needles are bright green in the spring (*left*) and turn yellow in the fall (*left, center*).

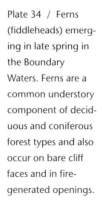

Plate 34 / Ferns (fiddleheads) emerging in late spring in the Boundary Waters. Ferns are a common understory component of deciduous and coniferous forest types and also occur on bare cliff faces and in fire-generated openings.

Plate 35 / Black spruce, sphagnum mosses, and lichens can be found on seepage slopes in the Boundary Waters region.

Plate 36 / Little Sioux Fire, Legend Lake sector, May 1971. The virgin forests of the Boundary Waters region were literally "born in fire." Fire largely determined their species composition and structured the forest age classes and spatial patterns of the vegetation mosaic on the landscape. This landscape-vegetation mosaic is like a giant kaleidoscope, with fire being the principal force that periodically rearranges the patterns of vegetation types.

(*inset*) Large red pines often survive moderate surface fires with little injury because their thick bark insulates the growing cell layer from lethal heat, and their long clear trunks help avoid crowning. Surface fires are unpredictable, however, and if a small increase in winds or heavier fuels is encountered, crowning and rapid fire spread can begin without warning. (Photos by M. L. Heinselman.)

Plate 37 / Coleman Island burn with young jack pine. The cones of most jack pines are sealed shut with resins that melt at the temperatures reached in the trees during crown fires or intense surface fires. When the cones are heated by the fire, the cone scales flex open, and millions of seeds are scattered over the burn. The result is often a dramatic re-stocking of the burn with dense young stands.

Plate 38 / Before logging and fire control, fire was the great recycling agent, consuming much of the living and dead plant material at intervals varying from a few to hundreds of years on any given site. The combustion process removes some of the carbon compounds, converting them back to carbon dioxide and water, but much of the carbon remains on site for a time in standing snags and charcoal.

Plate 39 / (*right*) Fire-denuded soil. The extent to which litter and humus organic layers are burned by fire is a vital factor influencing re-growth. For example, exposure of the mineral-soil seedbeds favors successful reseeding by jack, red, and white pines, black and white spruce, balsam fir, and most other conifers.

Plate 40 / (*far right*) The Little Sioux Fire of May 14–16, 1971, was a crown fire that spread from a slash fire and burned 14,000 acres. Crown fires usually do not consume the trunks of standing live trees but burn off the needles and twigs, producing a scene of dead, black-ened snags.

Plate 41 / Coleman Island burn with abun-dant maple seedlings. Many Boundary Waters plants recolonize new burns with light wind-blown seeds or spores. Maple seeds, although heavier than the seeds of many other species, can still travel some distance.

Plates 42–45 / Native American pictographs are present at about 25 sites in Quetico Provincial Park, 5 or 6 in the BWCAW, and a few in Voyageurs National Park. Most paintings occur on vertical rock faces on steep and often large cliffs along lakeshores or streams, just a few feet above the high-water line, and often must be viewed from the water. Some paintings are badly faded, and others are partially overgrown with lichens, but many are still clear. Among the finest pictographs are those on Crooked Lake in the BWCAW (*left*), and on Darky Lake (*right, top and center*) and Lac La Croix (*bottom right*) in Quetico.

Plate 46 / Waterfall in spring. The network of lakes and streams in the Boundary Waters region reflects an intricate pattern of watersheds, including a major continental divide, which cuts across the eastern end of the region, separating the Hudson Bay watershed from the Lake Superior watershed.

Plates 47–48 / In late summer and fall, beaver in the Boundary Waters cut the trees and shrubs they use to build or repair lodges and dams (*right*) and to supply food caches to carry them through winter. Quaking aspen (*far right*) is by far the favored food.

Plates 49–50 / Common aquatic plants in Boundary Waters lakes and streams include yellow water-lilies (*right*) and white water-lilies (*far right*).

Plate 51 / Wild rice is one of the tall emergent aquatic plants often seen along lakeshores. Wild rice was harvested by Native Americans, and evidence of rice camps has been found at several of the good wild-rice lakes and streams in the region.

Plates 52–54 / A portage in the Boundary Waters requires only a path through the forest with a cleared width of 4 or 5 feet. The most pleasing routes wind around large trees and boulders, where present, and climb or descend ridges with winding switchbacks.

Plate 55 / America's only large lake-land canoeing wilderness, the BWCAW has for decades hosted more visitor-days of use than any other wilderness.

Voices in this land—the music of the wilderness—call us back until our last breath is drawn.

fire control. Long-lived trees such as white and red pine and white spruce have heavy cone crops only once every 3 to 7 years and do not have persistent or closed cones, but their ability to survive 300 to 400 years increases the probability that they will reproduce before they die from age-related factors.

Theoretically, shade-tolerant species might be expected to have greater longevity, slower growth, and later reproductive maturity. Yet balsam, the most abundant species of this type, is notoriously short-lived and invests heavily in early reproduction. Shade tolerance is an advantage in local environments where fire-return intervals are long, and that is where cedar, white spruce, and balsam are most abundant.

BROAD VERSUS NARROW SPECIES NICHES

Some Boundary Waters trees are generalists with multiple survival strategies and broad environmental niches, whereas others are specialists with narrow niches. For example, the continental ranges of trembling aspen, paper birch, jack pine, and black and white spruce (all boreal species) are very large, and they occupy a wide range of soils, geological substrates, and landform situations and mingle with many other trees in various local and regional contexts. All but perhaps white spruce occur in areas with either long or short fire-return intervals, as well as in areas with predominantly crown fires or surface fires. Such species can cope with a broad range of conditions and are much less likely to be eliminated.

Aspen and birch can reproduce both vegetatively and from seed after fire. Black spruce reproduces well from seed, but it can also reproduce vegetatively by layering if fire fails to return for long periods. These multiple strategies ensure success under a wide range of circumstances. Many shrubs, herbs, mosses, and lichens also occupy broad niches and exhibit multiple strategies for coping with fire.

Some species seem to have small niches and are relegated to habitats where generalists are less successful. For example, white cedar is very shade tolerant and long-lived, but it is easily eliminated by fire and thus occupies only sites where interfire intervals are long. If fire (and deer) were eliminated, it might increase (Grigal and Ohmann 1975).

White spruce and balsam are also shade tolerant, and white spruce is long-lived. Both are very fire sensitive but are well adapted to moist fertile sites that often do not burn completely even in large, high-intensity fires. Survivors usually escape in such less fire-prone sites. Their shade tolerance permits them to reinvade the pine and aspen-birch forests of the drier uplands between fires. Fire exclusion also favors these trees.

Red and white pine are also specialists in this ecosystem, which is near the limit of their ranges. They primarily occupy sites subject to combinations of moderately frequent light surface fires and infrequent partial crown fires. This type of site is essential to their survival. If they mingled too freely with the crown fire–prone boreal conifers, they could not persist, because they have no means of reproduction if all adults are killed.

Fire as a Regulator of Insects, Disease, and Windfall

Insect outbreaks, plant disease, and windstorms can increase fuels, but fire itself can change the potential for these factors. For example, a hot fire in a fir-birch or jack pine–fir community that has recently seen much balsam fir mortality from the spruce budworm will usually kill virtually all trees of all species. Balsam is usually absent from the new postfire stand, except where unburned seed trees are nearby. Balsam will slowly creep back into the community over the next 50 years because it is shade tolerant, and for a long time the budworm disappears because its host is gone. Jack pine will reseed from cones on the trees, and birch will both resprout from the root collar and reseed from distant trees because of its light windblown seeds. If the jack pine was under attack by the jack pine budworm, it will be freed from its enemy because jack pine stands rarely sustain heavy populations of this insect until they are at least 50 to 75 years old. Thus fire can have a sanitizing effect, freeing the forest from its insect enemies for a time. This sequence was apparently the usual chain of events before European settlement. But with fire exclusion and other factors increasing the abundance of mature balsam throughout eastern North America, the frequency, severity, and scale of spruce budworm outbreaks has increased dramatically in the latter half of the twentieth century (Blais 1983). On the other hand, bark beetles, wood-boring beetles, and carpenter ants invade fire-injured and fire-killed stands, creating a major food source for woodpeckers and bark-gleaning birds.

Similar principles apply to some plant diseases and parasites. Black spruce dwarf mistletoe, for example, can readily spread from tree to tree via its seeds, which are shot out from tiny flowers with enough force to get to a neighboring tree. But if a crown fire kills the spruce stand, mistletoe dies with it, and when the new spruce forest begins life, it is freed from this parasite for nearly a century because mistletoe must rely on birds and other agents to carry its seeds, a process slow enough to permit the new forest to mature before it is again seriously damaged (Anderson and Kaufert 1959; Irving and French 1971). Fire exclusion is now favoring the spread of mistletoe. Similar stories could be told about other plant parasites and diseases.

Wind-caused tree mortality is often confined primarily to older stands and to individual trees that have root rot, basal rot, stem rot, carpenter ant damage, and so on, or to tall, isolated, and exposed old trees. Rare tornadoes or unusual regional downburst windstorms are less selective in the age classes and condition of areas affected, yet young and middle-aged stands and individuals are usually far less vulnerable to windfall. Again fire has a rejuvenating effect: it eliminates stands prone to wind-caused mortality and replaces them with young and much less susceptible forests. As noted earlier, before European settlement, most major blowdowns and wind-damaged forests probably burned within a few decades.

IS LIGHTNING-CAUSED FIRE RANDOM OR TIME DEPENDENT

It is not entirely clear how the probability of significant lightning-caused fire in the Boundary Waters ecosystem changes for a given locality with time since fire. Are the probability and severity of lightning-caused fire closely linked to fuel accumulation, vegetation changes since fire, and increasing insect, disease, and windstorm mortality with stand age? Or is fire a largely random process, depen-

dent on random lightning ignitions and the vagaries of winds and weather during the burn? Two related questions are involved. Does the probability of a successful lightning ignition increase with time since fire? Do the probabilities for fire intensity and size change with time since fire? There is little doubt that for at least a short period after a major fire, the probabilities of a reburn and of a large high-intensity fire are reduced. But is that period only a decade or two, or is there a continuing rise in probability for ignition, intensity, and fire size? These are important questions both for the understanding of fire as a natural process in the ecosystem and for implementing ecosystem-management programs for the BWCAW, Quetico, and Voyageurs.

The factual background behind these questions was presented in chapter 6. Here is a summary of the arguments pro and con. The arguments for rising probability with time are as follows:

- Total fuel increases with vegetation regrowth after fire, and total living and dead biomass does not peak for at least 100 years in most forest communities.
- The fuel content of the organic layer on the forest floor increases with time, often for more than 100 years.
- The change from bare mineral soil or charred organic matter on the forest floor to continuous carpets of flammable feathermosses or lichens is time dependent. Feathermoss requires the shade of a closed conifer forest overstory and is an important surface fuel in some communities. Continuous feathermoss carpets are usually not well established until 40 or 50 years after fire.
- Tree lichens are time-related fuels, most abundant in old forests.
- Ladder fuels increase with stand age (understories of balsam, spruce, and cedar).
- In aspen-birch and related broadleaf forests flammability increases with stand age if there are parallel increases in conifers in the stands (especially of balsam and spruce).
- Tree death increases with stand age due to insects, disease, mistletoe, and windfall. Dead timber may be more prone to ignition.
- Spruce budworm outbreaks are much more prevalent in old balsam-spruce stands, and the extreme flamma-

bility of budworm-ravaged stands has been documented (Stocks 1987b).

• Changes in the chemistry of fuels with tree age in some species may increase flammability with time since fire (Mutch 1970).

The arguments for randomness are as follows:

• Lightning-strike patterns may be random, or at least not related to stand age.

• Fire paths and spread rates may be largely controlled by wind direction and speed and by temperature and humidity, factors unrelated to stand age.

• Fuel studies, prescribed burning experiments, and field observations by fire-behavior experts indicate that many dense young conifer stands burn well in crown fires, notably jack and red pine stands (Van Wagner 1977, 1983; Stocks 1987a, 1989).

• Given suitable drought conditions, low humidities, and strong winds, spotting by flying brands makes it possible for fires to leap usual fire barriers and non-flammable vegetation.

• Fires create fuel (by killing timber), and such fuels peak early in the new postfire stand's life.

• Fire-cycle (fire-rotation) models that assume randomness fit actual stand-origin data from the BWCAW fairly well (Van Wagner 1978).

• My stand-origin maps for the BWCAW and observations of fires elsewhere in similar ecosystems, including the 1988 Yellowstone fires, suggest that in major droughts most vegetation types may be burned with little regard for age classes.

• The early reproductive maturity of jack pine and black spruce and the suckering ability of the aspens suggest evolution in environments with either very short fire-return intervals or much randomness.

The evidence is obviously mixed. It seems to me that the probability of a successful ignition is higher in most older stands and in wind- or insect-damaged stands than in thrifty young stands. Thus blow-up fires are more likely to begin in senescent stands. Once under way in severe drought and burning conditions, a major fire may burn

many age classes. Ignition in older stands, leading under drought conditions to major fires, seems to be the story in forests of the Boundary Waters region before European settlement and in related Canadian boreal forests. It certainly was also the case in the 1988 Yellowstone fires. Van Wagner (1983) believes that in many boreal forest vegetation types potential fire intensity increases to a maximum 20 or 30 years after stand establishment, then decreases to a lower level through healthy stand maturity, and then rises again as the old stand deteriorates or is invaded by younger conifers (presumably spruce, balsam, or cedar). Many writers have observed that fires often do not burn very intensely in clean, thrifty, middle-aged jack pine or red pine stands, and I agree. In the 1976 drought, however, jack pine stands fitting that description burned fiercely in crown fires with winds of only 15 or 20 miles per hour. On the other hand, given less than maximum burning conditions and drought buildup, fires in the Boundary Waters ecosystem are more likely to start and burn vigorously in old wind- or insect-damaged forests.

Vegetation Change Following Fire

Change is a hallmark of forest communities. Trees, shrubs, herbs, mosses, and lichens grow and die, and each species modifies both its own environment and that of all other plants and animals as it becomes established, grows, and dies. Light, temperature, soil acidity, nutrient cycling rates and pathways, and the structure and composition of the forest community itself all change as forest stands pass through their life stages. Trees are long-lived, and many changes are not obvious even to scientists unless stands are compared that differ in age by many years, even centuries.

SUCCESSION AND THE CLIMAX CONCEPT IN FIRE-DEPENDENT FOREST ECOSYSTEMS

Succession was one of the first theoretical concepts articulated by the emerging science of plant ecology early in the twentieth century (Clements 1916). Lindeman's (1942) seminal paper, "The Trophic-Dynamic Aspect of Ecology," gave new impetus to efforts to quantify the dynamics of succession, efforts that still continue. Odum (1971, 251) defined succession as "an orderly process of community development that involves changes in species structure and community processes with time . . . it is . . . directional, . . . predictable, . . . [and] results from modification of the physical environment by the community. . . . It culminates in a stabilized ecosystem in which maximum biomass . . . and [linkages] between organisms are maintained per unit of available energy flow." That final end point, the stabilized ecosystem, has been called the climax. Over the years a discussion in ecology has continued about the applicability of many aspects of succession theory to various ecosystems, notably the climax concept. Fire-dependent forest ecosystems such as those of the Boundary Waters region present some of the most perplexing cases (McIntosh 1981; Heinselman 1981a).

In the Boundary Waters ecosystem before European settlement, most forests were either maturing following the last fire or being recycled by the next. Although the logging of about half of the virgin forests and 80 years of fire suppression have since changed the natural scene, virgin forests remain in all stages of postfire vegetation change. These postfire changes are often called succession, but there are many problems in applying traditional views of succession to the actual postfire sequences of vegetation in the Boundary Waters. Whether we call it succession or not, however, vegetation change following fire is an important ecosystem process. Here I put aside the formal terminology of succession theory and simply examine the structural and compositional changes that occur after fire as recorded in virgin forest communities of many age classes. The life cycles of several broad classes of plant communities are outlined from their regeneration immediately after fire through maturity to old age, using study-plot data and observations from several areas in the BWCAW and Quetico.

NEAR-BOREAL UPLAND CONIFER FORESTS

The communities here include the jack pine–oak, jack pine–black spruce, jack pine–fir, and black spruce–feathermoss upland types. Before European settlement most fires

of ecological significance in these communities were stand-killing crown fires or high-intensity surface fires that killed most of the aboveground vegetation, and this is still true. A 3- or 4-year postfire establishment period sets the stage for most subsequent vegetation changes. By 10 years the die is cast.

Postfire Establishment Period

Two recent fires in the BWCAW demonstrate the importance of the species composition of the burned stand, the season of burn, and the depth of humus burn in determining the future stand. The Little Sioux fire of May 14–16, 1971, spread from a slash fire and burned 14,000 acres. Two study plots were located about 2 miles west of Ramshead Lake. The Roy Lake fire of August 21–27, 1976, was a lightning-caused late-summer fire after prolonged drought that burned 3,200 acres. Study plots were located on the south shore of Saganaga Lake, the north shore of Sea Gull Lake, and the northeast shore of Grandpa Lake. Although 60 miles apart, both study regions were in granite ridge terrain with thin sandy to bouldery soils, supporting chiefly jack pine, black spruce, trembling aspen, and paper birch stands of postfire origin.

Both Little Sioux study areas (table 7.2) were previously burned in a very large 1864 fire and supported 107-year-old jack pine stands at the time of the 1971 fire. Both burned in an intense crown fire on the evening of May 14. Because it was spring, the humus layer was still wet below the surface, and 1 to 2 inches of organic matter remained unburned over most of the area. Stand 1 was a jack pine–fir community on a gravel-cored sandy ridge, and Stand 2 was a jack pine–black spruce community on a granite bedrock ridge (Ohmann and Grigal 1979).

At Roy Lake I sampled three burned areas, each with different prefire composition and stand ages. Stand 1 on a granite ridge on the north shore of Sea Gull Lake was a jack pine–black spruce community 175 years old dating from an 1801 burn; it burned in a crown fire on August 21, 1976. Stand 2 on a granite ridge on the northeast shore of Grandpa Lake was in a black spruce stand 101 years old, probably of the feathermoss type, dating from an 1875

Table 7.2 / Comparison of prefire composition of two jack pine stands burned in crown fires, May 1971, with regeneration 3 seasons later, Little Sioux fire, Boundary Waters Canoe Area Wilderness

Species	STAND 1 107-year-old jack pine–fir			STAND 2 107-year-old jack pine–black spruce		
	Stand killed by 1971 fire		Regeneration 1973	Stand killed by 1971 fire		Regeneration 1973
	Stocking (trees/acre)	Basal area (ft²/acre)	Stocking (trees/acre)	Stocking (trees/acre)	Basal area (ft²/acre)	Stocking (trees/acre)
Jack pine	288	116	14,488	200	72	32,902
Black spruce	32	2	—	200	30	—
White spruce	32	2	—	—	—	—
Balsam fir	120	7	—	48	1	—
Paper birch	40	4	40	16	1	445
Quaking aspen	—	—	405	—	—	2,104
Bigtooth aspen	—	—	81	—	—	162
Red maple	—	—	—	—	—	567
Other	—	—	41	—	—	485
Total all species	512	131	15,055	464	104	36,665

Note This early-spring fire did not consume much of the organic layer. See text in this chapter for descriptions of fires and burned sites.
Source Data from Ohmann and Grigal (1979).

Table 7.3 / Comparison of prefire composition of three conifer stands burned in crown fires, August 1976, with regeneration 3 seasons later, Roy Lake fire, Boundary Waters Canoe Area Wilderness

Species	STAND 1 175-year-old mixed conifers			STAND 2 101-year-old black spruce			STAND 3 73-year-old jack pine		
	Stand killed by 1976 fire		Regeneration 1979	Stand killed by 1976 fire		Regeneration 1979	Stand killed by 1976 fire		Regeneration 1979
	Stocking (trees/acre)	Basal area (ft²/acre)	Stocking (trees/acre)	Stocking (trees/acre)	Basal area (ft²/acre)	Stocking (trees/acre)	Stocking (trees/acre)	Basal area (ft²/acre)	Stocking (trees/acre)
Jack pine	40	23	11,108	5	2	1,623	1,255	142	97,630
Black spruce	329	35	1,471	562	92	18,295	209	14	2,691
Balsam fir	23	6	—	163	2	—	35	1	—
Red pine	—	—	—	5	20	—	—	—	—
Quaking aspen	20	3	32,025	—	—	10,728	—	—	28,976
Bigtooth aspen	—	—	36	—	—	—	—	—	—
Paper birch	57	5	—	21	2	84	—	—	—
Total all species	469	72	44,640	756	118	30,730	1,499	157	129,297

Note This late-summer fire burned off all of the organic layer. See text for descriptions of fire and burned sites.
Sources Data taken by graduate class (under supervision of M. L. Heinselman) July 1979. J. C. Almendinger compiled these data. This table is based on Table 23.4 in Heinselman (1981a), by permission of Springer-Verlag New York, Inc.

burn; it burned in a crown fire about 5:30 P.M. on August 21. Stand 3 on a granite ridge on the south shore of Saganaga Lake was a jack pine–black spruce community 73 years old dating from a 1903 burn. The fire was a typical crown fire, and burned in a west wind blowing 15 or 20 miles per hour, lofting flames perhaps 25 to 50 feet above the treetops. A half mile of ridge burned in less than two hours. In all three stands the fires killed all trees, shrubs, herbs, and mosses and almost entirely consumed the organic layer (table 7.3).

On the Little Sioux and Roy Lake burns most of the trees that will participate in stand development for at least a half century were established by the end of the 2nd year, and most came in the 1st year. Comparison of prefire stand data with 3rd-year postfire regeneration (tables 7.2, 7.3) tells the story. At Roy Lake, jack pine and black spruce reproduced abundantly on essentially bare mineral soil seedbeds in all three stands. On the Little Sioux, jack pine also reproduced well, although not as abundantly as at Roy Lake, but black spruce failed almost completely. Close inspection showed that most jack pine seedlings on the Little Sioux became established in spots where the organic layer was thin or absent. Some of the failure of black spruce there may be due to seed kill in seared cones in the intense crown fire, but similar intensities at Roy Lake resulted in heavy spruce reproduction. Black spruce reproduction on the Little Sioux is sparse outside the study plots. The near failure on these plots may be partially due to unfavorable seedbeds on hot, dry postfire organic soil, which are especially lethal to tiny black spruce seedlings.

Major seeding-in of aspen on mineral soil occurred at Roy Lake but not on the Little Sioux, again probably due to unfavorable blackened organic seedbeds. Sharp declines in aspen in the 4th and 5th years further reduced the aspen component on the Little Sioux. By 1990 aspen was declining rapidly relative to jack pine and spruce in the Roy Lake stands as well. These stands are near the lakeshore. In 1989, 13 years after the fire, beaver were cutting the aspen heavily for their winter food, and moose were browsing aspen in many areas. A dramatic postfire increase in moose on the Little Sioux also put heavy pressure on aspen and birch there (Peek 1974).

Balsam, the major shade-tolerant potential invader, was eliminated by fire in the study plots of both areas. However, seed sources still exist within about a quarter mile of the burned stands. Thus, after a half century of reinvasion, the tree layer in all of these stands will probably have returned to something approaching prefire composition, except for Little Sioux Stand 2, which will not recover its black spruce component for a long time.

The shrub and herb layers on the Little Sioux virtually recovered to prefire conditions within 5 years (Ohmann and Grigal 1979). Vegetative reproduction of many shrubs and herbs and the germination of seeds stored in the humus occurred because the organic layer was so lightly burned. Fire ephemerals like pale corydalis, Bicknell's geranium, fringed bindweed, and bristly sarsaparilla flowered profusely, but by 1975 they were much reduced. Pin-cherry became a major tall shrub, evidently coming mostly from seed in the humus. Other shrubs and herbs that developed measurable biomass in the first postfire year in these two jack pine communities included wild sarsaparilla, large-leaved aster, bluebead-lily, bunchberry, wintergreen, twinflower, wild lily-of-the-valley, starflower, bracken, beaked hazelnut, and both lowbush and velvet-leaf blueberry. By the 2nd postfire summer the blueberries flowered profusely and bore a heavy crop of delicious fruit. Outstanding blueberry crops continued for about the first 5 postfire years. The fire moss *Funaria* and the liverwort *Marchantia* were not common because little mineral soil was exposed. The principal plants temporarily eliminated were the mature forest mosses and lichens, notably all feathermosses, *Dicranum* mosses, and the reindeer mosses. As Ohmann and Grigal (1979, 19) summarized it, "The major change in stand structure was lowering of the tree canopy from a former height of 10 to 20 m (35 to 70 feet) to 0.1 to 0.2 m (4 to 8 inches) after the first growing season following the fire."

At Roy Lake the nearly complete exposure of mineral-soil seedbeds produced a quite different shrub, herb, and ground-layer vegetation 3 years after the fire. The fire invaders *Marchantia*, *Funaria*, hair-cap moss, and fireweed were abundant, but the fire ephemerals that depend on stored seed in the humus were much less common, except for fringed bindweed. Most shrubs and herbs that reproduce vegetatively were also uncommon, rare, or absent. Shrubs that were present in all three stands included beaked hazelnut, pin-cherry, raspberry, bush-honeysuckle, rose, black currant, and lowbush blueberry. Herbs in all three were fireweed, bristly sarsaparilla, pale corydalis, large-leaved aster, twinflower, fringed bindweed, and grasses and sedges. Many other herbs were present in one or two stands, but not in all three, their occurrence often being related either to small areas of unburned humus or to long-distance transport of seeds by birds or mammals. Among the plants that turned up in this category were three-toothed cinque-foil, wild sarsaparilla, dogbane, pearly everlasting, golden-rods, bunchberry, wild lily-of-the-valley, touch-me-not, bedstraws, pyrolas, wintergreen, pipsissewa, clubmosses, and horsetails. Thus, by the 3rd postfire year a nucleus of most native species existed somewhere in the area, even though many were still uncommon.

To summarize, the Roy Lake late-summer crown fires in a major drought had these effects:

- In Stand 1, the 175-year-old black spruce–jack pine community, heavy restocking of jack pine occurred, with light restocking of black spruce and heavy seedling invasion of quaking aspen.
- In Stand 2, the 101-year-old black spruce–feathermoss community, there was heavy reestablishment of black spruce, light restocking of jack pine, and significant seedling invasion of quaking aspen.
- In Stand 3, the 73-year-old jack pine–black spruce community, very dense restocking of jack pine created a dog-hair sapling stand by the 10th year, with a light understory of suppressed black spruce and moderate stocking of quaking aspen that was being overtaken by jack pine and removed by beaver.

In all three stands the burning-off of the organic layer greatly reduced competition for tree seedlings from shrubs and herbs that reproduce vegetatively or from seed in the humus, yet a small population of most of the expected native species was reestablished by the 3rd postfire year. By the 10th year, all stands were developing closed canopies and understory vegetation that will characterize them for the next few decades.

Canopy-Development Period

This period lasts from about year 10 to year 40. By then the dominant trees have reached more than half of their potential height, and their crowns have grown close together in all but the most open stands. If present, jack pine, aspen, and birch assume dominance, and black spruce, balsam, and white spruce often are overtopped. Nearly pure stands of jack pine or black spruce are common. Snags from the previous fire-killed stand have mostly fallen by the 15th to 20th year, and by the 35th year are mostly in contact with the ground and rotted sufficiently to provide little fuel. Reindeer moss develops on bedrock surfaces in small stand openings by about 30 years. Feathermoss ground layers usually begin to appear beneath closed stands of jack pine and black spruce as scattered patches of Schreber's feathermoss between the 20th and 30th years and often develop into continuous carpets of the three feathermosses plus *Dicranum* mosses between the 30th and 40th years. Natural thinning of very dense young stands of jack pine and/or black spruce occurs continuously from the 1st year, but it may come in waves between the 10th and 40th years due to snag fall, snow breakage, and drought. In the first 10 or 15 years bark girdling by snowshoe hares may also take its toll. By age 30 to 40, tens of thousands of small jack pine and/or black spruce per acre will have died if the initial stand was of the dog-hair type, leaving only 4,000 to 5,000 trees per acre. The Little Sioux and Roy Lake stands will be undergoing all of these changes through the years up to 2011 to 2016. Some observers may see dense young stands as undesirable, and the natural thinning process as wasteful, but we must learn not to impose value judgments on natural processes that have evolved over the millennia.

Shrubs such as green alder, beaked hazelnut, willow, and pin-cherry decrease in vigor as they are overtopped and crowded out by the growing young forest. Some shrubs, such as pin-cherry, may disappear. The fire-ephemeral herbs, liverworts, and mosses also disappear. Most other herbs persist, but if the stands are dense, the herbs are unable to increase because of heavy competition from trees and the expanding feathermoss carpets.

Mature-Stand Period

This period lasts from year 40 to about year 100 to 150, depending on species, local sites, and the vagaries of wind, insects, and other natural factors. Before fire suppression became effective, most stands were recycled by fire sometime in this period if not earlier. Jack pine and black spruce stands in the BWCAW may persist essentially intact for 90 to 130 years, but when fire fails to return, the gradual senescence of dominant individuals usually begins at about 100 years. The mature-stand period may last nearly a century, however, and really cannot be said to have ended until senescence begins to cause stand breakup. A continuing gradual decline in total numbers of trees occurs in the stands as the stronger individuals grow in diameter and height. Maximum basal area is usually achieved somewhere between the 35th and 75th year. In many stands total aboveground biomass continues to increase until at least 100 years because trees add more mass in their upper trunks and crowns than is lost through death of weaker trees, and understory trees and shrubs continue to grow.

The most widespread age classes of boreal conifers now present in the BWCAW will be in the mature-stand period between 1990 and 2030 on burns dating from fires in 1864, 1875, 1894, 1910, and 1936. The same situation prevails in Quetico. Even the vast Kawnipi Lake burn of 1936 now has very extensive jack pine and black spruce forests in the mature-stand phase. After passing through the stand-establishment and canopy-development periods as thus described, the life cycle of the boreal conifers becomes a very real process.

There is little change in species composition of the tree layer that can be called succession in this period. In jack pine–black spruce communities most of the spruce will remain in suppressed, intermediate, or codominant crown positions, but age studies in the stands show that most spruce are of the same age class as the jack pine. They seeded in with the pine after the last fire, just as did the black spruce at Roy Lake in 1976. The same is true of most paper birch and white spruce. In other words, much of what looks like succession is just suppression. Balsam fir may begin a true invasion into jack pine–fir stands and some jack pine–black spruce stands early in the period, but this process usually does not progress far until the senescence period.

Feathermoss carpets, where important, become consolidated and thicken up in this period. This is the time when raw humus layers may reach their maxima. Small rocky openings that supported patches of reindeer moss may be overgrown by feathermosses late in the period. The shrub and herb layers may add a few species, but the principal change is an increase in cover. Abundance is due to rising tree crown heights and small decreases in overhead shade late in the period. Rare plants such as the stemless lady-slipper may be seen in mature stands. Herbs that often peak in abundance here include several ferns, wild sarsaparilla, large-leaved aster, bluebead-lily, bunchberry, starflower, and violets.

Senescence Period

This period begins between the 100th and 150th year and lasts until fire returns, or until the character of the community is greatly changed by stand breakup, generally by the 250th year. Death of overstory trees is at first gradual, but eventually they are subject to insect attacks or death by unknown causes, or are windthrown or wind-broken due to heart rot, root rot, or unusually violent storms. Early in the period black spruce and occasionally white spruce finally overtake jack pine and may become codominant. In the BWCAW three late-stage stands dating from a large 1727 fire in the Gordon-Davis-Winchell lakes region still contained one or two living jack pines more than 245 years old when last visited. Scattered large black and white spruce of the same age class also existed. These stands are now more than 260 years old, and in one of the Gordon Lake stands the last known jack pine had died probably about 1980. In such old communities little by little the original postfire overstory trees die, and after 200 years only a few old jack pine, spruce, aspen, or birch still tower above the balsam saplings, shrubs, sprout aspen and birch, and the jumbled fallen trunks that characterize such old stands. Before fire exclusion, such stands were a rarity. Now several areas exist in the BWCAW on 1727, 1755, 1759, and 1801–3 burns.

As stand breakup progresses, tall shrubs such as mountain-maple, beaked hazelnut, pin-cherry, and mountain-ash may increase in openings created by tree falls. Feathermoss carpets shrink as they become fragmented by down trees, smothered by leaf fall from shrubs and paper birch, or damaged by excessive light in tree-fall openings. The rare American yew may appear. Herb diversity and abundance may decrease somewhat. The only change that perhaps might be called succession is a sharp increase in balsam fir in most late-stage areas. The very existence of many old stands of this type is an event that probably has not occurred in thousands of years. Spruce budworm outbreaks have now been killing the balsam in most such areas for decades, increasing the probability that fire will eventually return to recycle the system, playing out the ancient drama of the north again. A faintly similar sequence of events led to the great Yellowstone fires of 1988.

RED AND WHITE PINE FORESTS

Historical Overview

Before the early big-pine logging era began, forests dominated by varying percentages of red and white pine occupied about 25 to 30 percent of the BWCAW, and a similar situation existed in Quetico and Voyageurs. Logging has now reduced them to about 5 percent of the area. But these communities have high aesthetic value, are still common along lakeshores, on islands, and at campsites, and add a vital element to the diversity of the total ecosystem.

Before European settlement many older red pine and mixed white and red pine stands on the drier sites were subject to repeated surface fires of light to moderate intensity at intervals ranging from 10 to 50 years on specific sites. Such fires consumed the accumulated pine needles, litter, and upper humus layers and killed shrubs and invading shade-tolerant conifers and hardwoods such as balsam, spruce, cedar, birch, and red maple, but they usually only scarred or left uninjured pines more than 30 or 40 years old. Younger pine seedlings and saplings were often killed. From an ecosystem perspective these underburnings released nutrients and reduced fuel accumulations and ladder fuels that might threaten crown fires that could kill all overstory pines. Perhaps once every 100 to 200 years, higher-intensity fires struck these stands and killed large patches of mature pines, setting the stage for regeneration.

On moister sites, where nearly pure white pine stands are more likely, there was less underburning, perhaps none. When fire finally came, perhaps at intervals as long as 150 to 250 years, it was of higher intensity, often killing large patches of old pine and again setting the stage for regeneration. This historical context provides a basis for understanding the life cycles of these forests.

Postfire Establishment Period

Red and white pine do not seem as peculiarly adapted to freshly burned seedbeds as jack pine, but white pine seedlings are more tolerant of light shade. Both red and white pine establish well on the bare mineral-soil seedbeds created by summer fires, and their somewhat greater shade tolerance in the sapling stage means that they can take advantage of smaller fire-created stand openings for several years. These traits are vital because red and white pine have good seed crops only at variable intervals of 3 to 7 years, and their cones shed most of their seed the first fall and winter and then are dropped (Fowells 1965). These seeding habits mean that enough parent trees must survive within seed-fall range (about 500 feet). The optimum situation probably has irregular stand openings no more than a few hundred feet across, or partial stand kills that leave good seed trees scattered in patches over the burn. Because of these factors, effective reseeding of burns by red and white pine usually requires 5 to 10 years, and sometimes as long as 15 to 25 years. If there are enough small stand openings, as there often are along lakeshores, the more shade-tolerant white pine may continue to seed in for many decades.

Here are some examples. On the Little Sioux burn north of Lamb Lake, the south and east edges of a large stand of old red and white pine were heavily burned in a crown fire, killing a wide band of big pines. Aspen and paper birch initially invaded in the open burn adjacent to the unburned stand, with little seeding-in of pine for the first 4 or 5 years. In the next 14 years, many seedlings of both white and red pine came in, and by 1992 a patchy ring of young pines was appearing around much of the old stand. The aspen and birch are serious competition for some of the pines, but a beaver colony on Lamb Lake may eventually cut most of the aspen and birch.

On the Roy Lake fire a small grove of mostly red pines on a peninsula on the south shore of Saganaga Lake was burned through in a partial crown fire, killing most trees but leaving several vigorous seed trees along the lakeshore. Several red pine seedlings were found in 1979, and by 1992 a group of young red pines and some white pine and white cedar seedlings were developing to replace the former grove. Here the main competition was a dense growth of jack pine seedlings that came in beginning about 50 feet from the lakeshore. The white pine and cedar seed apparently blew across the ice from an island just to the west. Other examples exist to the south along the west side of this peninsula.

On numerous sites in Quetico and the BWCAW on large 1936 burns, such as along the shoreline of Kawnipi Lake, and on recently burned islands and lakeshores (camper fires), red and white pine have reproduced effectively since the logging era. I do not share the concern that aspen and birch have increased in the Boundary Waters because of logging so much that the natural regeneration of red and white pine through fire will be precluded by competition from them, at least not in the many virgin forest groves of these pines that still exist (Ahlgren 1976; Ahlgren and Ahlgren 1984). It is a different story in logged areas where the big pines were virtually eliminated by cutting and where aspen and birch have occupied sites for many decades. On such sites regeneration of red and white pine would usually require seeding or planting if these species are to be restored in less than centuries.

Canopy-Development Period

This period usually lasts from about the 25th to the 60th postfire year. In nature red and white pine usually do not form dense even-aged sapling thickets as does jack pine, probably because they are less prolific and slower seeders. Crown closure may occur anytime in the period, depending on stand density. The most common tree associates are jack pine, aspen, paper birch, and occasionally white and black spruce. Both red and white pine usually attain seed-bearing age late in the period. Before European settle-

ment it seems likely from fire-scar evidence that on the drier red pine sites many stands of young pines were thinned by light surface fires from the 30th to 50th year after a fire. Such fires would have eliminated many smaller, weaker pines and the thinner-barked jack pine, aspen, and birch. If the surface fires were very intense, even the young red and white pines would have been killed, however, because at this age they still do not have very thick bark. If the seed source for the stand was in part the surviving old red or white pines within the heavily burned area, some of these parent trees can still be seen towering above the new stand. They may bear fire scars that date the fire responsible for the new stand.

Mature-Stand Period

This period runs from about the 60th to the 250th post-establishment year, although it varies considerably with the actual age of onset of senescence. Many stands begin life with some aspen, birch, jack pine, spruce, or balsam as competitors. But the big pines finally gain dominance over virtually all other species. If surface fires fail to eliminate most other trees in the first 60 years, the probability of such a fire is greater in the nearly two centuries available before senescence begins. Many old stands today still bear fire scars that testify to one or more fires that probably did eliminate other species in this period. Otherwise time will tell, for only white spruce and white cedar are long-lived enough to persist beyond 250 years. This is also the period in which unusually severe surface fires or partial crown fires could strike all of or portions of many stands, creating new semi-open areas that bring in yet another age class of the big pines. Such is the sequence of events that produced the adjoining groves of red and/or white pine of different age classes that we see today in the Lac La Croix region of the BWCAW and elsewhere in the BWCAW and Quetico.

Today we find thick layers of pine needles and raw humus beneath most old pine stands, often with dense thickets of young balsam in the understory. These conditions probably did not exist in many mature stands before European settlement because light surface fires kept the fuels and undergrowth in check in many areas, especially in red pine stands. Chance events may have allowed particular stands to escape underburning for the 50 to 100 years that set them up for fires with enough intensity to kill part of the stand and bring in a new generation.

Senescence Period

White and red pine are the longest-lived trees in the Boundary Waters region, excepting white cedar. Few of these big pines probably die of old age alone. Most die of secondary causes such as wind uprooting, wind breakage (often related to heart rot or old fire scars), disease, and insects. Formerly the cause was fire directly.

The oldest pine for which I obtained a reliable age was in a group of three red pines on Threemile Island in Sea Gull Lake. The only tree that was sound to the heart was a gnarled red pine 24 inches in diameter that yielded an age of 371 years in 1968, putting its year of origin at 1597. The two other old red pines in the group were rotten and could not be dated, but the largest was 31.7 inches in diameter. When I visited this stand in 1992, only one of the old pines was still standing, the one I had obtained the age from, then approximately 395 years old. The other two that were clearly of the same age were already wind-broken when I visited the site in 1979. Many white pines found elsewhere in the BWCAW and Quetico were much larger than these red pines, some over 41 inches in diameter. Some may be older, but all had heart rot and could not be accurately aged. This information is the basis for my placing the maximum life span of red and white pine in the BWCAW close to 400 years.

Even without fire these old red pines on Threemile Island will not be the last of their kind on the island, because the area in which they grew supported other groups of younger pines of several age classes nearby, each dating from later fires that had left fire scars on old pines in the vicinity. These scars placed the fires that produced the younger age classes at 1692, 1727, and 1801. Fire brought in each age class, and without fire the system will someday literally run out of age classes. The senescence period, which usually lasts about a century, barring fire, is the last opportunity for fire to regenerate a specific stand.

Another senescent red pine stand was studied on the southwest shore of Boulder Bay of Lac La Croix. Most trees in this stand became established shortly after a fire in about 1681. The stand showed no evidence of surface fires for the last 202 years when studied in 1969. Several trees uphill from the lakeshore bore scars from fires in 1755 and 1767, evidently the last significant fires in the stand. No pine regeneration from those fires was present, probably because the stand was not opened up enough and was too dense (it was only about 70 years old when the 1755 underburn occurred). In 1969 a few old pines were wind-broken, uprooted, or dead standing, but most trees appeared vigorous, and stocking and basal area (which relate to standing volume and biomass) were high (table 7.4). Scattered white pine and white and black spruce 30 to 150 years old were present in the understory. There were some paper birch and balsam saplings, all 60 years or less in age, with only a sparse shrub layer of green alder and hazelnut, a scanty herb layer, and a ground layer mostly of Schreber's feathermoss and *Dicranum* mosses. Thus, at 288 years since establishment, this stand still showed only minimal evidence of succession to fir-spruce-birch, despite 202 years without significant fire.

Several groves of 1681 and 1755 origin containing mixed red and white pine on Voyageur's Island in Saganaga Lake were breaking up from windfall when photographed in 1992. Others were still relatively intact. In some of these stands a fairly dense understory of balsam and paper birch was established. Many such balsam understories have been killed by the spruce budworm in recent decades, generating horrendous fuel accumulations.

The oldest white pine community studied was on a narrow strip of land between Gaskin and Winchell lakes on the shore of Gaskin, just northwest of the Winchell-Gaskin portage. Its location had evidently protected the stand from fire for some 360 years—longer than any other site I studied in detail. A scattered overstory of huge old white pines made the stand still appear to be a pine forest, but the vegetation shed much light on the ultimate fate of senescent white pine in the absence of fire, because the process of stand breakup was far advanced. The largest white pine was 41 inches in diameter and more than 100 feet tall. All five trees bored for ages had heart rot, but all

Table 7.4 / Stand structure by species and age ranges for a 283-year-old red pine stand originating after a fire in 1681

Species	Diameter range (in.)	Trees per acre (no.)	Basal area per acre (ft²)	Sample tree ages by crown position class (years)			
				Dominant	Codominant	Intermediate	Suppressed
Red pine	2–22	155	180	283	278	280	106–266
White pine	1–14	285	20	—	—	153	32–142
Black spruce	1–6	90	6	—	—	103	56–96
White spruce	1–10	10	3	—	—	156	—
Balsam fir	1–4	90	3	—	—	—	30–44
Paper birch	1–4	175	3	—	—	—	21–60
Total	1–22	805	215	283	278	103–280	21–266

Note Ground fires burned through the stand in 1755 and 1767; no evidence of fire since. Stand A-8, Boulder Bay, Lac La Croix, Boundary Waters Canoe Area. Data taken 1969; includes all trees over 1 in. DBH.
Source Table 9 from M. L. Heinselman (1973), copyright 1973 by University of Washington. Reprinted by permission of the Ecological Society of America.

Table 7.5 / Stand structure by species and age ranges for a 360-year-old white pine stand showing advanced succession to fir-spruce-cedar-birch

Species	Diameter range (in.)	Trees per acre (no.)	Basal area per acre (ft²)	Sample tree ages by crown position class (years)			
				Dominant	Codominant	Intermediate	Suppressed
White pine	33–41	5	33	323–368	—	—	—
White spruce	18–25	10	26	178–185	—	—	—
White cedar	1–22	30	28	—	250–296	—	37–96
Balsam fir	1–13	675	69	—	99	95–121	38–85
Paper birch	10–16	20	22	—	160–162	96	—
Total	1–41	740	178	178–368	99–296	95–121	37–96

Note Stand A-5, Gaskin Lake, Boundary Waters Canoe Area. This stand escaped fire longer than any other studied; last significant fire A.D. 1595 to 1610. Data taken 1969; includes all trees over 1 in. DBH.
Source Table 10 from M. L. Heinselman (1973), copyright 1973 by University of Washington. Reprinted by permission of the Ecological Society of America.

borings gave estimated ages between 323 and 368 years (table 7.5). No fire scars were detectable. Charcoal was found below the humus, and given the nearly even-aged overstory, I am convinced the stand was of postfire origin, probably following a fire between about 1595 and 1610. Beneath the old pines the main overstory trees were white cedars up to 296 years old and 22 inches in diameter, white spruce up to 185 years old and 25 inches in diameter, and paper birch up to 162 years old and 16 inches in diameter. The understory was mostly balsam 121 years old and up to 13

inches in diameter. Spruce budworm injury was only moderate on the balsam. Tall shrubs were mostly mountain-maple and beaked hazelnut of medium density. The herbs were typical of white pine forests, and the ground was partially blanketed by all three feathermosses, *Dicranum* moss, haircap moss, and *Mnium*. The litter plus humus layer ranged from 1 to 4 inches in depth.

This site definitely supported a well-stocked white pine community within the past century because the area was still crisscrossed with the rotting trunks of many large trees in various stages of decay. Virtually all the white pines were reported to be down in 1988. Thus, without fire this site only lost its pine community some 380 years after stand establishment, and succession to a balsam fir, white cedar, white spruce, and paper birch community is now complete.

BROADLEAF-CONIFER FORESTS

Considered here are all the virgin-forest upland plant communities with a strong overstory component of broadleaf trees, most also having a major conifer element at some time in their life cycles. Included are the aspen-birch, maple-aspen-birch, maple-aspen-birch-fir, and fir-birch communities. These communities need some conifers in the stands to carry significant fire, except in extreme drought.

Postfire Establishment Period

This period usually lasts only 3 or 4 years because tree regeneration is either vegetative and occurs mostly in the first postfire season or is from widely distributed wind-blown seed within the first few years while seedbeds are still favorable. Fires that regenerate these communities may be high-intensity surface fires, usually in spring or fall, that burn the leaf litter and woody surface fuels, or more often they are partial crown fires fed by budworm-killed understory balsam and the torching-off of living conifers (figure 7.2).

If the organic layer is not too deeply burned, both aspen species sucker vigorously from the root network that laces the subsurface at the interface between the humus and mineral soil. Suckering is most vigorous if virtually all living aspen of all sizes are killed above ground by the fire. For example, in their aspen-birch Stand 6, Ohmann and Grigal (1979) found 48,361 quaking aspen stems per acre, mostly suckers, in the first postfire season. There were another 13,962 stems per acre of bigtooth aspen. Natural attrition reduces these extremely dense sucker stands rapidly in the first few years: by the 5th year the total aspen stem count in Ohmann and Grigal's Stand 6 was down to 14,690 stems per acre. The stronger aspen suckers commonly grow 2 to 4 feet in height the 1st year. Seedlings grow much more slowly the 1st year but soon catch up.

Paper birch sprouts from the root collar, just above the ground line at the base of the fire-killed tree. Commonly there are several sprouts, the origin of the birch clumps we so often see in northern forests. Red maple and oak sprout

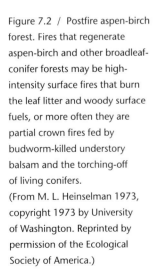

Figure 7.2 / Postfire aspen-birch forest. Fires that regenerate aspen-birch and other broadleaf-conifer forests may be high-intensity surface fires that burn the leaf litter and woody surface fuels, or more often they are partial crown fires fed by budworm-killed understory balsam and the torching-off of living conifers. (From M. L. Heinselman 1973, copyright 1973 by University of Washington. Reprinted by permission of the Ecological Society of America.)

in a similar fashion. If jack pine or black spruce are to be in the stand, most seed in during the first year or two. Balsam and white spruce must normally seed in from un-burned areas and are usually scarce in the first few post-fire years.

If aspen or birch are to invade areas not occupied before the fire, they come via their light wind blown seeds. Some invasion of conifer sites by this means occurs on most burns, but in virgin areas where conifer seed sources have not been lost through logging, the conifers usually regain their dominance in a few decades.

Shrub, herb, and ground-layer vegetation changes follow patterns similar in principle to those in conifer forests (Ohmann and Grigal 1979).

Canopy-Development Period

This phase usually lasts only from about the 5th through 25th postfire years, because aspen and birch have such rapid juvenile growth. It is an important period for game habitat. If conifers intolerant of shade, such as jack pine, red pine, and even black spruce, are to remain in the stand, they must attain codominance with the aspen and birch in this period unless they happen to occupy a stand opening such as a small area of rock outcrop.

Mature-Stand Period

This period lasts from about the 25th year until significant stand deterioration begins, usually about 100 to 125 years after fire. The length of this period may surprise some readers who have repeatedly heard how short-lived the aspens and paper birch are. I was surprised to discover in my stand-origin mapping of the virgin forests of the BWCAW that quaking aspen is nearly as long-lived as jack pine. And jack pine itself is much longer-lived in the Boundary Waters region than the forestry literature suggests. For example, we repeatedly encountered perfectly intact stands of aspen, birch, and jack pine of 1864 origin between 1966 and 1972, when the aspen were well beyond 100 years in age. Many of the larger aspen do develop significant heart rot (from the fungus *Fomes igniarius*) after about age 70, but in many stands this has little effect on the community until it begins to cause stem breakage from wind, often well after age 100.

By about the 40th or 50th year, many stands in this community group do begin to develop a significant balsam understory. And by the 90th to 100th postfire year, the balsam may have sustained a spruce budworm infestation severe enough to kill many of the larger trees, perhaps nature's way of setting the stage for recycling the system, for this is the time when during a drought such stands will reburn with enough intensity to regenerate the community. This sequence is precisely what happened in the Little Sioux fire. Before European settlement this was probably the usual course of events.

Senescence Period

Without fire these broadleaf-conifer communities pass slowly into a stand breakup phase that has usually run its course by the 200th postfire year. Quaking aspen and paper birch rarely live more than 200 years in this region, which means that virtually all the first-generation dominants will have died. Stand breakup was certainly a rare event before European settlement, but now, because of some 80 years of fire exclusion, it is occurring in many areas on 1755, 1759, 1796, and 1801 burns. Succession to fir-spruce-birch-cedar communities is the likely outcome on many sites. In some stands, however, the breakup of the aspen-birch overstory may come so suddenly, due to a major windstorm, for example, that open areas large enough to promote aspen suckering result. In such cases a heterogeneous mixture of age classes of aspen, birch, balsam, spruce, and red maple may occupy the site for a long time. This is largely speculation because stand breakup of this kind is just now beginning to occur on a significant scale. Where balsam is a major component of such stands, as it usually is, their future is very uncertain because repeated waves of balsam mortality from the spruce budworm are so probable.

BOG AND SWAMP CONIFER FORESTS

Black spruce bog forests formerly often burned in the same fires that swept adjacent upland conifer stands. Burning of bog forests has also occurred on a limited scale in some recent fires in the wilderness, but I am not aware of detailed studies of such cases. However, the postfire history of bog fires can be reconstructed from the research that William Johnston and I did on the use of prescribed fire in regenerating bog spruce on the Big Falls Experimental Forest (Johnston 1971), by working backwards from the age structure of present bog spruce stands in the BWCAW, and from informal observations on a few recent burns.

The first question about fires in bog stands always concerns the peat: Will it catch fire and all burn away? The answer for natural undrained bogs is no. In all but the most extreme drought the water table is close enough to the surface (usually less than 2 feet, even in a dry year) that capillary rise in the peat and sphagnum moss will keep the peat moist (Heinselman 1963). Typically only an occasional hummock and 2 or 3 inches of dry feathermoss and surface peat may be burned away.

On peatlands black spruce has the same persistent, semiclosed cone habit as upland spruce, making the seed supply dependable, and moist burned moss and peat seedbeds are optimum surfaces for the germination and establishment of spruce. Little serious competition from shrubs, herbs, or other tree species develops on most burned acid-bog sites, but if there was a speckled alder shrub layer in the burned stand, alder will usually resprout and be accompanied by some grass and sedge regrowth.

In years with only slightly below normal rainfall most bog forests will not carry fire well in the spring and summer. But in many bog spruce forests charcoal in the peat, usually only 4 to 6 inches below the green moss surface, attests to the forest fire that established the present spruce stand. On the better sites most bog spruce stands in the postfire age range of 40 to 90 years have scant surface fuels other than feathermosses, which cover perhaps 40 to 60 percent of the forest floor, and the trees are well pruned. What is needed then are ladder fuels and highly flammable crowns. Young stands have the ladder fuels until a few years after crown closure, at perhaps 20 to 30 years of age. Early senescent stands, often between the 130th and 180th postfire year, may develop ladder fuels in a partial understory of second-generation spruce in stand openings, and they may also have some dead and down trees, standing dead trees, and mistletoe-infested partially dead crowns.

At this stage the stands become much more susceptible to crown fires.

Crown fires in drought years, then, appear to be the kind of fire responsible for most of the pure, even-aged bog spruce forests so prevalent in the Boundary Waters today. The 1864 year class is prominent in the BWCAW, for example. In the past some young stands and many senescent stands were probably common types burned. If fire fails to come, bog spruce forests gradually break down from basal stem rots, wind breakage, uprooting, and mistletoe-caused mortality. Black spruce is longer-lived on peatlands than on mineral soils, however, and many stands remain relatively intact until 180 to 200 years. As stand breakup progresses, spruce regeneration gradually fills the gaps with young trees of both seedling and layer origin. Spruce really has no competitors on the more acid bog sites, and gradually these old stands develop into clumpy, mistletoe-infested, all-aged forests. Such old forests often seem to develop more sphagnum moss ground cover at the expense of the feathermosses, and they have a denser low shrub cover of Labrador-tea and leather-leaf. Only fire will re-establish the thrifty even-aged spruce community we still see so often in Boundary Waters bogs.

I have no good information on the postfire vegetation changes in mixed conifer swamp forests, tamarack bog forests, ash-elm swamp forests, alder-willow wetlands, or marsh and open muskeg. All do burn under some circumstances, but they are much less fire-prone than black spruce bog forests. A general observation is that the early postfire vegetation often involves grass-sedge and/or alder-willow shrub growth and a gradual return of tree cover.

What Does Postfire Vegetation Change Tell Us about Succession in the Boundary Waters Ecosystem?

The traditional meaning of succession is a consistent, directional sequence of changes over time in the species composition of a community, accompanied by parallel structural and functional changes. Such changes occur over the post-fire lifetimes of certain Boundary Waters communities. For example, in many cases the fire ephemerals, such as pale corydalis, liverworts, and the fire mosses, proliferate briefly in the first 3 or 4 postfire years, but often many of the herbs and shrubs that will persist through the life of the stand also appear in this same period. Usually most of the trees that will dominate the forest until fire returns become established in this brief period. For red and white pine and white spruce this establishment period can last 10 to 20 years, but often these trees also come in promptly. In some communities the feathermosses invade and form dense carpets beginning 30 or 40 years postfire, a clear successional change. There also are nutrient-cycling changes as mosses invade, organic matter accumulates on the forest floor, and the maturing forest ties up nutrients. If fire's return is long delayed (as through suppression of natural lightning fires), the shade-tolerant balsam, white cedar, and red maple may invade on uplands, and even black spruce on some sites. Many differences in the crown positions of trees in the canopy that may look like succession are just the result of differences in species growth rates, potential size, and longevity.

Cooper (1913) long ago identified a white spruce-balsam fir-paper birch community as the potential climax forest on Isle Royale in Lake Superior. Much discussion of possible climax communities for northeastern Minnesota followed. Except for the addition of white cedar to the list of probable climax dominants by Ohmann and Ream (1971) and Grigal and Ohmann (1975), Cooper's list remains intact. What does it really mean to identify a list of shade-tolerant trees that might in theory replace all others in the absence of major disturbances if we recognize that the forests have been recycled by fire at short intervals for at least 9,000 years (Swain 1973)? As Ohmann and Ream (1971, 27) said, "the differences in the structure and composition of the plant communities of the virgin vegetation of the BWCA are primarily due to differences in the elapsed time since the last major wildfire disturbance, and [to] the composition of the vegetation [burned]." Ohmann and Ream and I were struck by the prophetic words of Loucks (1970, 25), who pointed out that the interruption by modern peoples of the natural processes of forest community renewal through periodic disturbances such as fire "will in all likelihood be the greatest upset of the ecosystem of all time. . . . It is an upset which is moving us unalterably toward decreased diversity and decreased productivity at a time when we can least afford it."

What we need most to see in the Boundary Waters forest ecosystem is a landscape view of the patchlike mosaic of forest communities and age classes resulting from hundreds of years of fire-mediated stand renewal. When we understand how the patch-turnover process and the scale of patch sizes are important to the regional diversity of the whole ecosystem, only then will we recognize the true meaning of the phrase "a fire-dependent ecosystem." The climax-forest hypothesis has little relevance to the nature of the natural ecosystem before European settlement because fire usually renewed the forest before the postfire pioneer tree species disappeared through successional replacement.

The Big-Pine Logging Era: 1895 to 1930

The present ecosystem of the Boundary Waters region was affected by the work of the early loggers who sought the big white and red pines, as well as by the more recent mechanized logging for pulpwood and sawtimber that ended with the passage of the legistative act Public Law 95-495 in 1978. The logging era is part of the dramatic social history of the region. The ingenious methods of the early loggers have a certain fascination in themselves that is heightened when evidence of their work is seen in the woods.

Following the decline of the fur trade about 1830, a half century of rising exploration, prospecting for minerals, timber looking, and claim staking ensued. Travel was still entirely by canoe and on foot until a wagon road, the Vermilion Trail, was built from Duluth to Lake Vermilion in 1869, prompted by the short-lived and ill-fated Vermilion Gold Rush. Although little gold was found, this activity led to the discovery of rich iron ore at what are now the towns of Tower, Soudan, and Ely. In 1884 Charlemagne Tower and George Stone built the Duluth, Mesabi, and Iron Range Railroad (DM and IR) from Two Harbors to the first mine at Soudan. By 1888 the rails had reached Ely, heralding a new era of mining, settlement, and logging (USFS 1974; Brownelle 1982; *Ely Echo* 1988).

On the Vermilion Range the underground mines required large amounts of timbering and lagging to shore up the shafts, tunnels, and other workings. Lumber was an essential ingredient for the homes and shops of the burgeoning new towns. The first sawmill in the region was built near Tower on Lake Vermilion by the Howe Lumber Company about 1890, and the first significant logging in what is now the BWCAW occurred in the Trout Lake area north of Lake Vermilion about 1895 (Interview with Leslie Beatty, 1967, by author), principally white pine for lumber and red pine for mining timbers.

In those days the ecological role of fire was little appreciated. Most government reports considered the forests to have been "destroyed" by the fires of the nineteenth century because of human carelessness. Yet the regenerated stands already established on those burns were to become a hotly contested timber resource in less than a century. For example, consider this excerpt from a public domain withdrawal report of E. A. Braniff (1903, 2):

> The lands were once covered with a forest of conifers, but almost all of it has been burned over and replaced by a dense growth of aspen and paper birch. The original stand of conifers was neither heavy nor composed of valuable species. Judged from what remains of it, the chief species were jack pine, white spruce, and balsam fir, with the jack pine pre-dominant. White pine and red pine never formed any considerable part of the stand in the great bulk of the lands. . . . At present there are two

great types of forest, the aspen and birch, and the jack pine. The aspen and birch is the type that has succeeded the fires, the jack pine is mostly part of the original forest.

The area to which this statement applies includes the region from lakes Malberg and Alice west to Insula and Hudson, a region supporting much virgin forest more than 100 years old today. It also pertains to the vast region south of these lakes from which hundreds of thousands of cords of jack pine and spruce pulpwood have been harvested in the past 40 years.

A slightly more sophisticated attitude toward fire is evidenced in the following description of the public domain from the withdrawal report of S. M. Higgins (1908, 2–5):

> The commercial forest in this area is much broken up by burns. . . . For some twenty years cruisers have gone over this land selecting all the best descriptions. Perhaps 150,000 acres of the alienated lands are covered with a growth of white, Norway, and jack pine, spruce, tamarack and balsam, which will average a cut of 5,000 feet per acre. The bulk of the public lands are found on burnings from one to sixty years old. . . .
>
> Jack pine, balsam and spruce in mixed stand comprise most of the merchantable forest. White and Norway pine excepting in a few locations occur scattered throughout the stand. Tamarack and spruce occupy the wooded swamp lands. Cedar is found only in small quantities.
>
> There is a plentiful regeneration of balsam and spruce in the mature stand. A dense reproduction of jack pine, white birch and poplar follows the fire. . . . Perhaps one-half the burns within the forest are covered with stands of this description from forty to sixty years old, with a diameter of four to six inches. As this stand begins to thin out with age balsam and spruce regeneration comes in. No better guide could be had for the division of the mature forest from the forest following the burn than the alienated and public lands. . . . Fire has destroyed the mature timber on more than half the proposed area.

The areas described by Higgins include the land south of Lac La Croix and Crooked Lake, and the area south-

west, south, and southeast of Saganaga Lake. His descriptions can easily be visualized by one familiar with these areas today. Areas dating from the burns of 1875 or earlier were Higgins's forests "forty to sixty years old." The burns of 1894 and 1903–4 would have still looked barren in 1908, and the 1910 fires had not yet occurred. The "alienated lands" covered with pine that he referred to were the tracts later cut for sawtimber, or in some cases patches of big pine that were later acquired by the government and remain intact today.

H. B. Ayres of the U.S. Geological Survey prepared one of the more ecologically perceptive early descriptions. His small-scale map showing the locations of merchantable timber and burned-over regions in 1899 is the only such map based on fieldwork covering the entire Boundary Waters before logging (Ayres 1899, 684–85):

> much of the so-called virgin forest has been burned and is now in the various stages of restocking. . . . Where undisturbed by cutting, the forest of to-day differs from that of a hundred years ago only as affected directly or indirectly by fire. The oldest woods are fire scattered, especially where composed of young or middle-aged pine, having large trees scattered among it. These large trees have almost invariably been marked by fire at a date older than the younger portion of the forest. . . .
>
> Thus it is seen that fires are not a novelty in these old woods, but have for hundreds of years been a prominent factor in their history. The coming of the whites and the general distribution of trappers and "couriers du bois" through the woods by the Hudson Bay Company and the American Fur Company 100 to 140 years ago seem to have been prolific of fires, for a very large proportion of the trees of the older uniform forests are 100 to 140 years of age, and must have started during that period.

The General Land Office Survey

The U.S. General Land Office was surveying the public domain land of northeastern Minnesota just before and during the early pine-logging era. This work involved "running" the main township and range lines with a staff compass and "chain" (distance measure) to block the region into square townships six miles on a side. Later each township was subdivided into 36 sections, or square miles. Surveying had to be completed prior to legal settlement, although some "pre-emption settlement" occurred before some townships were surveyed. In the Boundary Waters region such surveying lasted from 1873 to about 1907. The surveyors marked and described "witness trees" (usually pine) at all section corners, half-mile "quarter corners," and all "meander corners" where lines crossed lakes or streams. They also wrote general descriptions of each township and of features along section lines and developed a map showing lakes, streams, and other major land features.

The witness-tree notes and descriptions became a rich source of information for prospectors, timber cruisers, and settlers—and for later historians and scientists interested in the character of the forests and land before logging and land settlement. In the Boundary Waters region the surveyors traveled by canoe and on foot in summer and on snowshoes in winter. The project was incredibly arduous, but it opened the wilderness for logging, mining, and settlement and left a legacy of information about ecological conditions in the era from 1873 to 1895, when most of northeastern Minnesota was virtually untouched.

Francis J. Marschner (1930), an early U.S. Department of Agriculture economist, mapped the "Original Forests" of Minnesota from the General Land Office survey notes in the late 1920s. His map is the only published map showing in some detail the vegetation of the state before settlement or logging (plate 2). It has been resurrected and republished with an extensive text (Heinselman 1974). The map shows white and Norway (red) pine as a forest type, and most of the early logging for sawtimber occurred in areas of this type. Aspen-birch-conifer mixtures and jack pine forests occupied far more of the total landscape than did old white and red pine. They were not logged, either because they were not marketable or because the areas had been recently burned and the timber was too small.

Only about a quarter of the area on the early maps contained large contiguous stands of mature white and/or red pine when logging began. The balance of the forest area was either in young timber, recent burns, stands too small

or too far from water to permit profitable logging, or in species not of interest to the loggers. Extensive old pine stands like those in the southeastern Lac La Croix area were saved from the loggers only by the last-minute withdrawals of public domain land by President Roosevelt in 1902, 1905, and 1908.

Marschner's map shows the species composition of the forests for each township at the time of the original Land Office Survey. Because the townships were surveyed over a period of years, the map is not a snapshot of the vegetation at a specific moment, but a collage of "pictures" taken between 1873 and 1907. Many of the forests that Marschner mapped are the very same stands that are still there today in the remaining virgin areas. They originated after the fires of 1801, 1822, 1854, 1863–64, 1875, and 1894 but were still too young or of the wrong species to interest the early loggers. Some of these forests were later replaced by new stands that followed fires in 1894, 1910, 1936, 1971, 1974, or 1976.

Logging in the Vermilion-Trout-Pine Lakes Region

The first significant logging in what is now the BWCAW took place near Big Trout Lake north of Lake Vermilion about 1895. The white and red pine logs were cut during the winter and skidded or sleigh-hauled with horses directly to Lake Vermilion, or they were banked on the ice of Trout Lake for spring rafting and driving into Lake Vermilion. A logging dam and sluiceway were built by James Beatty at the outlet of Trout Lake in Portage Bay to sluice the logs when the spring snowmelt raised the water level enough. In the early 1980s remains of this dam and sluiceway were still evident at the canoe portage from Trout Lake to Vermilion. The logs were then rafted with steam-powered tugs across Lake Vermilion to the mines and sawmills near the present town of Tower.

Leslie Beatty worked as a boy in his father's logging camp on Trout Lake, probably the first such camp in the BWCAW, built about 1895 (interview with L. Beatty, 1967, by author). This camp was on a small knoll in the bay just south of the outlet of Pine Creek into Trout Lake. In the early 1980s this site was still an open grassy area, and a few metal objects and other remains from the camp were easily seen. James Beatty later became a state forest ranger and then land commissioner of St. Louis County. He was one of the principal authorities on the logging history of the Lake Vermilion-Trout Lake and Crane Lake-Lac La Croix regions.

Logging in the Lake Vermilion-Trout Lake area continued into the early 1920s. The Howe Lumber Company was succeeded by the Tower Lumber Company, which operated a mill in Tower from about 1900 until 1920 and was the last to cut timber in the Trout Lake area. Martin Gunderson, the Alger-Smith Company, and other firms had operations in the region as well. Later most of the lumber and mine timbers produced by these firms was exported via the DM and IR railroad to Two Harbors, where it was shipped to eastern and midwestern markets.

Fires in the new slashings of the cutover lands north of Lake Vermilion were common, and U.S. Forest Service records for 1920 and 1923 show large burns southeast of Trout Lake and between Lake Vermilion and the southwest side of Pine Lake. In addition, J. W. Trygg, former U.S. Forest Service ranger in Ely, reported fires in this area in 1925 and 1926. Certainly slash fires occurred as well, but rough maps of only these burns have survived. For example, the forest age classes still present northeast of Triumph Lake attest to large 1910 fires that may have started in slashings to the southwest.

The Tower Lumber Company found it was not economical to sleigh-haul their logs from Pine Lake to Lake Vermilion. Instead, they built a short temporary railroad from Pine Lake to Lake Vermilion and hoisted their logs out of Pine Lake onto railcars. These in turn dumped the logs into Lake Vermilion for rafting to Tower (interview with L. Beatty, 1967, by author). Large pine far to the northeast of Big Trout and Pine lakes around Triumph Lake and north of Chad Lake was brought out to Lake Vermilion via a long sleigh-haul road through the swamps to Chad Lake, across the ice on Chad Lake, and then south through the swamps to Pine Lake. From there the logs were driven into Trout Lake via Pine Creek, then rafted across Trout Lake to the flume at the dam in Portage Bay (interview with J. W. Trygg, 1967, by author). It is not clear why the Tower Lumber Company could not drive logs out Pine Creek instead of building the railroad to Lake Vermilion. Perhaps in some years the water flow in Pine Creek was too low.

Logging in the Burntside-Fall-Basswood-Knife-Kawishiwi Region

THE ST. CROIX LUMBER COMPANY

A large segment of the early logging industry that operated in the present BWCAW was centered in the Ely area, especially at Winton. In 1893 Sam Knox, Robert V. Whiteside, and W. C. Winton built the first sawmill in Winton, which became a major lumber-producing center for the next 30 years. This mill was operated as the Knox Lumber Company until 1899, when it was purchased by the Terrinus Brothers of Stillwater, Minnesota, and thereafter called the St. Croix Lumber Company. In 1911 the mill was sold to Edward Hines of Chicago, who had major interests in Wisconsin and elsewhere. It was closed in 1923.

The Knox Lumber Company and its successor the St. Croix operated in a large region chiefly east and south of Winton and in the Burntside-Shagawa area. Within the present BWCAW the St. Croix logged the big pine along the east shores of Fall Lake eastward to the Wood Lake area, in the North and South Kawishiwi River and Clearwater Lake areas, and in the lakes One, Two, Three, Four region. Most of their logs were sleigh-hauled to the nearest lake or stream with drainages to Fall Lake and were driven to the mill with the aid of an ingenious and extensive series of cheaply constructed log and lumber dams and sluiceways, as on the North Kawishiwi River between Lake One and Farm Lake, at the northwest outlet of Lake One, and at the outlet of Lake Two into Lake One. Remnants of these structures still exist at most of these sites. The company also built a logging dam at the outlet of Garden Lake in 1902–3.

The skidding of logs from stump to sleigh-haul roads was done with horses. Carefully graded and iced sleigh-haul roads then led from the cutting areas to the nearest waterway suitable for driving logs to the mill. Most sleighs were drawn by one to several teams of horses. Haul roads were usually only a mile or two long and often across frozen swamps that required no grading or rock removal. All log hauling and most cutting was done during the winter.

Toward the end of the early logging era, some firms, including the St. Croix Lumber Company, used steam haulers instead of horses. They resembled our present Caterpillar tractors, having steel crawler treads of similar design. The steersman, who sat over the front runners, had to keep them centered between the iced ruts that were essential for control of the sled train. One of the longest steam-hauler routes used by the St. Croix within the Boundary Waters ran from Wood Lake westward 4 or 5 miles through the swamps all the way to Fall Lake. Such sleigh-haul roads terminated either on the ice of a lake or stream or at nearby "banking grounds."

When water levels and flows were suitable during the spring flood, or driving, season, the logs were dumped into the water at the banking grounds, generally in early May. If a sizable lake had to be crossed, the logs were made into booms and towed to the natural stream outlet or to the next flume or sluiceway.

The St. Croix mill in Winton was the largest sawmill ever built near the Boundary Waters. Each year it sawed close to 50 million board feet of lumber, lath, and crating during the sawing season, which ran from spring through summer into the fall. A planing mill kept some of the mill crew busy year-round. When the sawmill finally closed in 1923, it had produced nearly a billion board feet of lumber, which was shipped by rail via Duluth or Two Harbors to midwestern and eastern markets.

In 1923 major fires burned over many of the St. Croix Company's slashings in the Fernberg Road area east of Winton, including a long strip within the present BWCAW from the east side of Fall Lake eastward to Wood Lake. An earlier slash fire in 1910 burned eastward along the North Kawishiwi River from Pickerel Lake almost to Lake One. These and many unrecorded slash fires converted many of the former white and red pine forests logged by the St. Croix into paper birch and aspen stands containing few conifers, a condition that still persists today.

The St. Croix Lumber Company also cut certain areas deep within the Boundary Waters near Thomas, Fraser,

and Kekekabic lakes, but those areas were related to the Swallow and Hopkins operations discussed in the next section. Some of the largest and most interesting St. Croix operations were in the Stony River area south of the Boundary Waters, but they are beyond the scope of this book. Most of the areas cut within the present BWCAW by the St. Croix or its predecessor the Knox Lumber Company were cut between about 1896 and 1912. A few patches may have been cut as late as 1922.[2]

THE SWALLOW AND HOPKINS COMPANY

In 1898 George Swallow of Minneapolis and Louis Hopkins of Duluth engaged Sam Simpson to build a sawmill on Fall Lake at the east edge of Winton and begin logging operations on their timber holdings in the Fall-Basswood lakes area. Simpson was succeeded by G. H. Good until the mill shut down in 1922. This company gradually extended its operations eastward and westward from Basswood Lake and eventually logged more of the original white and red pine land within the present BWCAW than any other firm. The area cut encompassed most of the lands on the U.S. side of the international boundary from the east end of Crooked Lake eastward almost to the east end of Knife Lake and extended southward to Thomas, Ima, Disappointment, Snowbank, Moose, Wind, Fall, Horse, and Fourtown lakes. Considerable timber was also cut in the western Burntside Lake area, including small areas within the BWCAW east of Crab and Slim lakes. The mill produced about 30 million board feet of lumber yearly in its better years, about 600 million feet over its 24-year lifetime.

Swallow and Hopkins had to develop some unique transportation methods to move its logs into its Fall Lake millpond because most of its timber holdings were downstream from Fall Lake (which drains into Basswood Lake). They also had to raft log booms across several large lakes. The solution to the first problem was to link Fall Lake to Basswood with a railroad portage capable of transporting millions of board feet of logs yearly. A temporary logging railroad from Fall Lake to Pipestone Bay of Basswood Lake was used from 1899 to 1900. Another short rail portage was built from the northeast end of Fall Lake to Ella Hall Lake about the same time. Then, to reach their timber holdings in the upper Basswood Lake area and farther upstream in the Moose-Ensign-Snowbank-Ima and Knife Lake regions, they built the Four Mile Portage in 1901 from Fall Lake to Hoist Bay of Basswood Lake. Hoist Bay gets its name from the Swallow and Hopkins hoist that loaded logs onto railroad cars at the Basswood Lake terminus of this line. A 40-ton Brooks locomotive and a smaller switch engine were used on the portage. The Brooks engine, which burned wood for fuel, moved several carloads of logs each trip. This railroad was also used for moving camp supplies, which were transferred over the Prairie Portage on rails by winching.[3]

The movement of large log rafts across such major lakes as Basswood, Fall, Moose, Birch, Ensign, Snowbank, Ima, and Knife was accomplished by several means. Swallow and Hopkins had large steam-powered tugs on Fall and Basswood lakes to tow log rafts encircled by booms, as well as to haul supplies for the camps and to tow supply barges to Prairie Portage. Horse-powered winches mounted on huge rafts were also used. J. W. Trygg of Ely recalled that these rafts were up to 40 feet square, so that horses could walk a circle around the capstan that wound up the winch rope onto a drum. The raft was attached to the boom with a rope, and men in a rowboat took an anchor forward in the desired direction with up to a quarter mile of rope attached to it. When this rope was fully extended, the anchor was dropped, the boat returned to the raft, and the horses were started on their trips around the capstan. When the raft and log boom reached the anchor, the process was repeated until the lake was crossed.

Low-head log dams and sluiceways were constructed up the international boundary chain from Basswood Lake to Knife Lake and up the Newfound-Ensign-Gibson-Cattyman-Jordan-Ima lakes chain. The Prairie Portage dam, which backs up Moose, Newfound, Sucker, and Birch lakes, was built in 1902. This old wooden dam washed out in 1968 and was rebuilt by the U.S. Forest Service in 1975 in concrete. The Fall Lake dam was built jointly by Swallow and Hopkins and the St. Croix Company in 1902–3 to raise the water level in their millponds and to facilitate log rafting on the lake. The timber from the Wood-Hula-Indiana lakes area cut by Swallow and Hopkins was sluiced

out to Wind Bay of Basswood Lake via Hula Creek. Other Swallow and Hopkins dams and sluiceways east of Basswood Lake, now essentially disintegrated but still evident, were located between Newfound Lake and Splash-Ensign lakes, between Gibson and Cattyman lakes, at the outlet of Ima Lake, at the outlet of Big Knife Lake, and on the Knife River canoe route between Knife and Carp lakes. This long series of waterways was skillfully used by Swallow and Hopkins crews each spring and summer to float, drive, or raft logs out to the Hoist Bay railroad hoist and rail portage. When the logs were dumped into Fall Lake, they were rafted by steam tug for the final 7 miles to the Winton millpond.

Logs in the woods were skidded in winter with single horses or teams to sleigh-haul roads and thence to the nearest waterway for banking in preparation for the spring drive. Some of the later and longer hauls employed steam haulers. J. W. Trygg said that one Swallow and Hopkins steam hauler sank into a bog about a mile south of Jordan Lake. When Trygg last saw this machine in the 1940s, only its smokestack was still protruding. A flume was built at the outlet of Wind Lake, but it failed to move the logs for lack of water (interview with J. W. Trygg, 1967, by author).

In 1910 Swallow and Hopkins sold all of its dams, sluices, camps, and other facilities east of Basswood Lake to the St. Croix Lumber Company. The sale also included the Four Mile Portage and Prairie Portage facilities. By this time Swallow and Hopkins had cut all the pine in that region except for scattered pockets and some larger stands in the Kekekabic-Fraser-Thomas lakes area. St. Croix crews cut the remaining accessible timber in these areas by about 1916 (interview with William H. Magie, 1967, by author). To get the logs out of the Fraser Lake area, sleigh-haul roads were built from Trinity and Mosquito lakes to Hatchet Lake. From Hatchet Lake to Basswood Lake, the St. Croix used the dams and sluiceways already constructed by Swallow and Hopkins to float their logs out to the Four Mile Portage at Hoist Bay. The Four Mile Railroad was operated by the St. Croix Company until 1920.

At the eastern end of these Swallow and Hopkins–St. Croix operations, the cutting crews generally logged to the crests of ridges above the lakes on which they were booming logs. Horses could not skid or sleigh-haul logs uphill. If waterways were not available for moving logs, some timber was passed up. Similar circumstances account for occasional patches of uncut old-growth pine throughout the logged-over regions of the Boundary Waters. Other reasons for skipping occasional stands probably included land-ownership problems and the end of a cutting season followed by camp abandonment before the next winter. Some patches of large old pine in the Fraser-Thomas lakes area probably owe their survival to such circumstances.

One of the last Swallow and Hopkins–St. Croix camps stood on the shore of Fraser Lake in a small northwest bay by the portage to Trinity Lake. Large old white pines were still growing not far northeast of the camp in 1982. All that remained of the camp were the outlines of several buildings marked by straight narrow ridges of rotted logs and earth, densely overgrown with small trees, brush, and grass. Swallow and Hopkins Camp 25 is said to have stood in the northeast bay of Newfound Lake, about a half mile southwest of the portage to Splash Lake. Many other camps must have been built east of Basswood Lake, but these are the only ones I have clearly identified. Trygg said that Swallow and Hopkins operated more than 50 logging camps in its total operation, each having about 100 men.

After the sale of its eastern operations to the St. Croix Company in 1910, the Swallow and Hopkins Company concentrated its logging largely in the region northwest of Winton, around Jackfish Bay of Basswood Lake and Horse and Fourtown lakes. Good-quality white and red pine stands existed north of Jackfish Bay and elsewhere in the area, and the logs were skidded or sleigh-hauled to the nearest large lakes for booming. To get the logs to the mill, however, would have required long sleigh-hauls on adverse grades and/or long and difficult rafting operations on Basswood Lake if alternate means were not found. To solve these problems, Swallow and Hopkins built a railroad from its Winton mill to Jackfish Bay in 1912. Spurs were extended northward to Horse and Fourtown lakes and westward to Grassy and Picket lakes. Camps were built on Horse, Fourtown, and Picket lakes and elsewhere in the region. Most of these camps were operated until 1921 by Swallow and Hopkins (interviews with Magie and Trygg, 1967, by author).

The Winton mill did not operate at full capacity after World War I.

In 1922 Swallow and Hopkins sold its mill, railroad, camps, and all other properties to the Cloquet Lumber Company, which dismantled the mill. With the closure of that mill and the St. Croix mill (1923), the once-booming lumber center of Winton ended its reign. My father, who had business in Winton in those days, described the size of the industry in Winton in the 1916 to 1920 era. The mental pictures of such accounts are difficult to contrast with the quiet little village we know today.

With the completion of logging in the various areas cut by Swallow and Hopkins came the inevitable slash fires. In 1910 large fires swept the area west of Moose Lake from Wood Lake north past Wind Lake to Merriam Bay of Basswood Lake and northeastward to Sucker Lake. The area east of Moose Lake and north of Snowbank Lake also burned in 1910. On the South Arm of Knife Lake large fires in 1910 swept eastward into the uncut public domain lands beyond the Swallow and Hopkins cuttings. These fires probably originated in slashings. Large areas burned in 1919 around Disappointment, Parent, and Snowbank lakes and northeastward from Ensign Lake to Kekekabic Lake. To the west, big fires occurred on both sides of Jackfish Bay in 1923, as well as west of Pipestone Bay and Newton Lake and south of Back Bay. The area east and south of Fourtown Lake burned in 1920. A large fire burned north of Sandpit Lake in 1917. Many of these fires may have been set deliberately to burn off the logging slash in compliance with state slash-burning laws, but their effect on subsequent forest composition was major and unfortunate, as I describe later.

THE CLOQUET LUMBER COMPANY

The Cloquet Lumber Company took over the logging operations, camps, and railroads of the Swallow and Hopkins Company in 1922. The Cloquet Lumber Company and the Northern Lumber Company were apparently both controlled by Weyerhaeuser interests and had sawmills in Cloquet. The General Logging Company was the actual legal entity that carried on the logging for these Weyerhaeuser firms. To this day the road that now traverses their old railroad grade is known locally as the "Cloquet Line."

At this time significant patches of uncut big white and red pine still existed north of Horse and Fourtown lakes, west of Fourtown, northwestward around Angleworm, Home, Gull, and Gun lakes, and in the Picket-Grassy lakes area.

The Cloquet Lumber Company had no sawmill in the Ely-Winton area but instead used a linkage of the Swallow and Hopkins Horse Lake railroad with the main line of the DM and IR railroad to ship its logs to Cloquet. The Horse Lake-Fourtown-Jackfish Bay railroad system was eventually extended northwestward to a landing on the west side of Gun Lake within the present BWCAW. A short spur was also built to the east side of Angleworm Lake and another to within about a quarter mile of the east side of Home Lake. Some of this final railroad work was already done by Swallow and Hopkins crews and completed by the General Logging Company. These rail landings marked the end of rail penetration into the wilderness in the Ely area. At one point there were plans to extend the railroad all the way to Curtain Falls, or even Lac La Croix. The surveying for such a route was never done, according to William H. Magie (interview, 1967, by author). These plans were never carried out, probably because timber volumes were low in the region, the government owned most of the land, and a major controversy over road building in the Boundary Waters was raging by 1926.

Some of the General Logging Company operations centered out of the Horse Lake camp run by Jack Halliday and the Fourtown Lake camp run by Frank Carter. The northern limit of cutting reached by General Logging Company crews, or in some cases perhaps by the earlier Swallow and Hopkins crews, is a ragged line running northeastward from just south of Beartrap Lake to Wagosh, Chippewa, Gypo, and Jackfish lakes, and then east from the northern end of Jackfish Lake to the extreme southeastern end of Crooked Lake. Removal of logs from the most northerly points must have posed difficult logistical problems for the loggers. According to Magie, the logs in the northeast sector were hauled out in winter either with a steam hauler or perhaps on a temporary winter rail spur, with the ties simply laid in the snow on the frozen ground. Temporary rail spurs of this type were often used toward the end of the logging era. The rails were picked up for use elsewhere before the ground thawed in the spring.

Some logs were hoisted out of the Basswood River near the pictured rocks below Lower Basswood Falls, according to Magie. It is not clear just when this northern limit was reached, but it was probably about 1925 or 1926 (interview with Magie, 1967, by author). Logs from the Moosecamp Lake area were driven into Fourtown Lake. Remnants of a dam and flume at the outlet of Moosecamp Lake still existed in the 1970s.

In the west around Angleworm and Home lakes much of the land and timber was owned by the federal government and administered by the new Superior National Forest, a circumstance that probably prevented Swallow and Hopkins, General Logging, and subsequent operators in the area from cutting all of the mature pine in one large operation, as had been the practice elsewhere. Logging of pine timber in this western area continued sporadically into the 1970s. The General Logging Company and Swallow and Hopkins crews did cut some big pine on the east side of Angleworm and Home lakes and around Gull Lake, but much of the pine in this area had originated after a fire in 1822 and was probably too small to interest these firms. A body of timber lying west of Gun and Boot lakes and east of the railroad was not cut, because it was largely jack pine, spruce, and balsam fir of 1822 origin and was evidently unmerchantable.

About 1926 most of the merchantable pine tributary to the Cloquet Line railroad spurs had been cut. The camps were closed, and logging declined to a very low level. The rail line was still used in the late 1930s by the U.S. Forest Service for access to their Angleworm Lookout Tower and Crooked Lake Cabin, using a small gasoline-powered speeder. About 1940 the rails were removed, and the last direct evidence of railroad logging in the Ely-Winton area was gone.

OLIVER IRON MINING COMPANY OPERATIONS IN THE BURNTSIDE AREA

The Oliver Iron Mining Company, a division of U.S. Steel Corporation, conducted fairly extensive logging operations in the Crab Lake region of the present BWCAW between about 1912 and 1916. The general areas cut included the shores and adjacent backcountry around Crab, Little Crab, Clark, Meat, Korb, Jig, and Maxine lakes. Some of the areas near Burntside Lake were cut by Swallow and Hopkins crews, who were working in the area at the same time. Oliver cut primarily red pine mining timbers for use in its underground mines at Ely and for trestle construction in its open-pit mines. Oliver also cut both white and red pine sawlogs and boom poles for log rafting on Burntside Lake. The timber was sleigh-hauled to Burntside Lake and then rafted across the lake to the railroad on Hoist Bay at the southwest end of Burntside Lake.

In the winter of 1913–14, Samuel A. Graham, later a distinguished forest entomologist and professor of forestry at the University of Michigan, worked in Oliver's Camp 24 in the Crab Lake area. His logging camp cut more than 1 million board feet of timber from Sections 11 and 12 on the north side of Crab Lake and the east side of Little Crab Lake. On this operation Oliver's crews practiced a method of slash disposal uncommon at the time. They lopped the slash into short lengths with axes and then burned it progressively as the logging proceeded. This practice left the area nearly free of logging slash and resulted in the burning of only a small fraction of the ground surface.

Today much of the area cut by his camp is stocked with second-growth red and white pine that dates from the years of these operations. Evidently the new forest arose either from seed on the ground at the time of cutting or from small seedlings already established on the ground and not killed by the logging. All merchantable pines were cut, and Graham believed that not enough seed-bearing trees were left to account for the resulting regeneration by seeding-in after the logging.[4] If similar slash-disposal practices had been used on all logging operations in the early logging era, the second-growth forests of Minnesota might have looked very different today. Instead of vast areas of nearly pure aspen and birch where white and red pine once grew, we might have had far more pine.[5]

Logging in the Little Vermilion-Loon-Lac La Croix Region

THE RAT PORTAGE LUMBER COMPANY

A firm based at Rat Portage (now Kenora), Ontario, known as the Rat Portage Lumber Company, conducted extensive logging operations along the international boundary from Lake of the Woods east to about the Loon River between 1885 and 1915. They cut very little timber on the American side within the present BWCAW but possibly did cut a few stands of white and red pine on Little Vermilion Lake and the Loon River around the turn of the century. They skidded their logs directly onto the ice of the boundary waters and then drove and rafted the logs all the way to Rat Portage via Sand Point, Namakan, and Rainy lakes, the Rainy River, and Lake of the Woods. Tugs powered with steam engines were used to pull the log booms across the big lakes. This firm operated a major sawmill at Rat Portage, which cut lumber used in the building of Winnipeg and many other Canadian prairie communities and farms. Their operations had little effect on the present Boundary Waters region because of its great distance from their base, but their operations were far-flung and impressive and probably had a greater impact in Voyageurs.

THE VIRGINIA AND RAINY LAKE COMPANY

Shortly before 1910 the Virginia and Rainy Lake Lumber Company was formed by Edward Hines through a consolidation with Cook and O'Brien and other interests. Hines hired Sam Cusson to run the sawmill and logging operations. A large sawmill was built in Virginia, Minnesota, and the logs were transported to the mill by railroad. The headquarters for logging operations and rail transportation were in Cusson (now a tiny rail siding north of Orr, named for Sam Cusson). In 1922 or 1923, Cusson died and was replaced by Thomas Whitten, who had just completed his career as manager of the St. Croix Lumber Company of Winton (interview with E. M. Heinselman, 1967, by author).

The Virginia and Rainy Lake Company logged a vast region largely west, southwest, and northwest of the present BWCAW. Their operations extended into the BWCAW in a narrow band running from west of Little Vermilion Lake eastward to the Loon River, Loon Lake, Range Line Lake, and Hustler Lake and thence back westward through Shell Lake, the south end of Loon Lake, and Wolfpack Lake. Their total operating area extended northward at least to Namakan and Kabetogama lakes, southwest to several miles west of Ash Lake, southward to Pelican Lake, the town of Gheen, and eastward to Myrtle Lake, the town of Buyck, Picket Lake, and the Hunting Shack River. The period of operation was from about 1910 to 1929.[6]

Echo Lake was a major rail terminus from which rail spurs reached up into the present BWCAW in the Loon River area. A main rail line linked Echo Lake with Cusson and with the sawmill in Virginia. Logs from within the present BWCAW were landed for rail shipment at two or three points on the Loon River and at several camps along the Echo River just west of the present BWCAW. An elaborate system of temporary rail spurs—some probably laid on frozen ground in the winter and removed before the spring thaw—was used to log the area just west of the BWCAW, where lakes and rivers suitable for rafting and driving were scarce. Within the BWCAW most of the logs were sleigh-hauled to water and driven to hoists where they were put on railcars.

The Virginia and Rainy Lake Company operated a total of some 143 logging camps over its lifetime from 1910 through 1929. Of these, only 5 or 6 were located within the present BWCAW, according to a complete listing of these camps by Leslie Beatty (list compiled in 1967; copy in author's files). They were Camps 39, 42, 43, 56, and 70, and a possible unnumbered 6th camp on Lady Boot Bay of Lac La Croix. A rail spur from the Echo Lake branch line was built to "56 Rapids" on the Loon River about 1915, and Camps 42 and 43 on Loon Lake were opened that year. In 1916 Camp 56 opened at 56 Rapids. About this time a dam and sluiceway were built at the outlet of Loon Lake at Loon Falls to sluice logs down the river to a hoist at Camp 56, where logs from the Loon Lake area were loaded on railcars. Remnants of the dam still existed in the 1960s. Meanwhile, the lower Loon River area was also being logged out of Camp 39, which was built in 1914 or 1915 about a half mile south of the south end of Little Vermilion Lake. A rail spur apparently was built to this camp too, and logs were hoisted there as well. In 1918 or 1919, Camp 70 was built on the middle Loon River to receive logs cut south of that area that could not be efficiently brought to these earlier camps. A short rail spur from the line that served Camp 56 was built to Camp 70, and logs may have been

hoisted there from the Loon River also. According to Leslie Beatty, the actual years that operations were conducted out of these camps were as follows: Camp 39, 1915 to 1917; Camp 42, 1915 to 1918; Camp 43, 1915 to 1917; Camp 56, 1916 to 1920; and Camp 70, 1919 to 1920.

The operations out of Camp 43 were the most complex and far-flung. In the Shell-Lynx-Hustler-Range Line lakes region, the Virginia and Rainy Lake Company owned scattered tracts of big white and red pine. The intervening land was mostly part of the new Superior National Forest and contained a few sections of state land as well. These publicly owned lands had mostly burned in the great fires of 1863–64 or 1894 that swept the Lac La Croix region well before logging began. Thus they supported mostly very young pine stands of no interest to loggers. A few stands of merchantable pine on national forest or state land may have been sold to the company, but most of the small patches of big pine that did exist on public land were never cut and still exist today. No company other than Virginia and Rainy Lake logged in the area then. According to Beatty, whose father was fishing commercially in Lac La Croix at the time, all the logs from these scattered stands of big pine were sleigh-hauled with horses into Camp 43 on Loon Lake. From there they were rafted across Loon Lake to the sluice, driven to the 56 Rapids hoist, and put on railcars. Beatty Portage between Loon Lake and Lac La Croix is named for James Beatty, whose fishing camp was located on the portage at the time. This portage was not connected with logging. According to Beatty, the fishing for lake trout and walleyes was excellent in those days. The Little Indian Sioux River was not used for log driving in these operations and remains free of the damage often caused by dams, sluices, high spring floods, and lost logs.

The timber tributary to the other camps within the Boundary Waters was also sleigh-hauled with horses or steam-haulers to the nearest drivable waterway or directly to the camp hoists, and from there it was shipped out by rail to Virginia. In the west, some of the timber was undoubtedly loaded onto rails near camps 42, 55, or 67 outside the BWCAW. These camps were also operating in the 1915 to 1919 era. At least some of the Virginia and Rainy Lake camps were ultimately dismantled by the U.S. Forest

Service. Diary notes of forest guard Uno Tikkala describe his work in tearing down the Camp 43 buildings in 1921 to obtain lumber for building several Forest Service structures (White 1974).

The last significant operation in the Lac La Croix area occurred between 1924 and 1929 in the southern tip of Lady Boot Bay. Apparently a small Superior National Forest timber sale of white and red pine involving three tracts aggregating 160 acres was made here in 1924. The company that cut the timber may have also owned small adjacent tracts. The actual area cut seems to involve a little more land than the three tracts I located in an old Superior National Forest cutting-areas atlas, but the total logged area is not more than 400 acres. According to both J. W. Trygg and Leslie Beatty, the area was logged by Virginia and Rainy Lake, and the logs were rafted northwestward across Lac La Croix into Canada and then driven down the Namakan River into Namakan Lake and hoisted onto railcars, probably at Virginia and Rainy Lake's main hoist in Hoist Bay of Namakan Lake in what is now Voyageurs National Park. This last log drive in the Boundary Waters took place in 1929, according to Trygg and Beatty. About 1 million board feet of logs were involved.

When the Virginia and Rainy Lake operations were completed, or in some cases even before logging was over, the inevitable slash fires again swept many of the cutovers. Thousands of acres burned in 1917 southwest of Little Vermilion Lake, southwest of Loon Lake, and south of Camp 56. Some of these areas burned again in 1923, along with areas from Echo Lake northeastward to Camp 56. Most of the 1923 burns were west of the present BWCAW. In addition to these fires on the American side, the 1923 fires jumped the Loon River near Camp 70 and ran northeastward through Ontario to Beatty Portage. These slash fires killed most of the surviving pines and other conifers, and burned tree seeds in the slash and on the ground. The slash fire converted what might have been a fairly satisfactory second-growth pine forest into a poor aspen-birch forest containing few conifers. The contrast in present vegetation between the areas west of the Sioux River that burned in these slash fires and the areas cut on Hustler Lake that did not burn is truly dramatic.

Logging in the Brule-Gunflint-Pigeon River Region

GENERAL LOGGING COMPANY OPERATIONS

In the northeast the General Logging Company was the logging arm of the Northern Lumber Company of Cloquet, a Weyerhaeuser firm. About the turn of the century the Alger-Smith Company had built a logging railroad from Duluth to Two Island Lake in Cook County, via Finland, Cramer, Wanless, and Cascade Lake. In 1918 the Northern Lumber Company acquired the upper end of this Alger Smith line to gain access to its extensive white pine holdings located from Brule Lake northeastward to the Canadian border around Rose and Clearwater lakes.

The General Logging Company then extended the old Alger-Smith railroad through its holdings all the way to Poplar, Hungry Jack, Clearwater, and Daniels lakes to its final terminus at Rose Lake on the international boundary. Short lines and spurs were built to Brule and Juno lakes, to Lower Trout, Marshall, and Swan lakes, to Flour, East Bearskin, and Alder lakes, and to Caribou and Deer lakes. Cascade Lake became the company's headquarters for railroad and logging operations, with a railroad roundhouse, warehouses, offices, and residences.

By the summer of 1929, logging was well along in the Cascade-Homer-Juno-Brule lakes area. Camp 3 was a major work camp, located at the site of the former resort on the south side of Brule Lake, just southwest of the public access and canoe landing. A log hoist was located on the site of the public access to load logs cut within the Brule Lake watershed and boomed on the lake. At least five camps had been set up on the north shore of Brule Lake and on the Cone lakes. These were Camps 4, 5, 6, 7, and 8. At about the same time, logging had progressed to Swan Lake. Logging had also occurred farther north around East and West Bearskin and Hungry Jack lakes, around the west end of Clearwater Lake, near Flour, Caribou, Deer, and Moon lakes, and up the east shore of Daniels Lake to Rose Lake.

At this point three unanticipated circumstances combined to bring an early end to these far-flung operations. First, the Brule Lake fires of 1929 killed much of the remaining timber in that area and forced changes in operating plans. Second, the Great Depression began, and lumber demand and prices collapsed. Third, the amount of heart rot in the big white pine in the Gunflint Trail region was much greater than had been estimated, so much of the remaining timber was not profitable to log.

On July 22, 1929, smoke was spotted near Star Lake along the General Logging Company's railroad from Cascade Lake to Camp 3. The fire probably was started by sparks from one of two engines that were hauling cars out to the junction with the main line at Cascade Lake. Logging had been going on in the area for a decade, and there was much slash in the logged areas. This fire is the only major slash fire in the big-pine logging era for which detailed records are available. The Superior National Forest by 1929 had a strong fire-protection and control organization, the fire was within the national forest boundaries, and much national forest land ultimately burned. Forest Service crews were heavily involved in fighting the fire, and full reports were filed.[7]

A substantial drought prevailed during the summer of 1929, and thus the logging slash and remaining pine forests were tinder-dry. A west wind was blowing at 20 miles per hour during the early afternoon. In spite of prompt action by company crews and Forest Service personnel, the fire escaped and quickly jumped Star Lake. Then about 4:00 P.M. the wind shifted to the north-northwest, driving the fire southeast down the railroad grade toward Tomash Lake and Camp 1. By 6:00 P.M. Camp 1 had burned.

Logging crews were in the woods because railroad logging using short spurs made summer operations possible. The company and the Forest Service put in quick telephone calls for help to man the fire lines, and by 6:30 P.M. a train from Swan Lake Camp arrived at Cascade Lake with 35 men. By 8:00 P.M. 150 more men were brought down from the Flour Lake Camp 30 miles to the northeast. By the next afternoon when Assistant Forest Supervisor Raymond Harmon from Ely took charge of the fire, more than 200 men were on the lines, including 66 men brought up from Duluth to the Sawbill Trail by bus and then ferried to Cascade Lake by railroad.

For the next several days the winds shifted back and forth and no rains came. Despite valiant efforts by the company and Forest Service crews, the fire enlarged considerably in several sectors. On July 29 the Cascade Lake railroad base and warehouses were saved only by strenuous efforts by a large force of firefighters. On July 30 the fire jumped Juno Lake and nearly trapped a fire crew camped on the south shore of Brule Lake near the Juno Lake railroad spur. The men narrowly escaped with their lives when a company "Alligator" (a long, narrow boat) reached them just in time.

On July 31 a new fire north of Brule Lake was spotted from the air just east of the Cone lakes near Camp 8. The Brule Lake fires were among the first major fires during which an airplane was used for observation, greatly enhancing the Forest Service's ability to keep track of the fire's progress and move crews effectively. Men were dispatched to the new fire at once, but it escaped initial attack and eventually burned more than a square mile. The official report notes that log booms on Brule Lake hampered boat travel by the fire crews that were ferried across the lake to the Camp 8 fire and eastward or westward to work on the flanks of the main Camp 3 fire. Obviously much timber had already been cut north of Brule Lake and along its eastern shorelines to generate those large concentrations of logs.

On August 7 the first good rains fell—0.48 inch. Favorable weather continued, and the fire was soon under control. In the end some 25,000 acres were burned, of which 4,448 acres were national forest lands. Similar dramatic stories could no doubt be told of many earlier slash fires in the Boundary Waters, but documentation is lacking.

A considerable amount of white and red pine timber was killed by the fire. This forced the General Logging Company to modify its cutting plans and concentrate on salvage of the fire-killed timber, much of which was still usable if it could be cut before insects and rot damaged it too much. That change in operating plans must have been difficult for the company.

At the same time, the Great Depression began with the stock market crash of October 29, 1929; lumber markets collapsed, prices fell, and it became much more important that logging and mill costs be kept down. About this time it also became apparent that the quality of the old white pine on the General Logging Company's operations was not good. A combination of over-mature stands, unfavorable climatic conditions for white pine in this northern region, and many stands with a history of fire injuries that introduced heart rot had apparently caused excessive defects that seriously affected the yield of lumber obtainable from a given gross volume of timber.[8] This problem was common in the Northern Lumber Company's holdings in the Gunflint region. Logging continued on a declining scale for a few more years, but by 1931 the General Logging Company's railroad logging efforts in the region were essentially over. The rails were removed from their lines about the beginning of World War II.

The cessation of operations by the General Logging Company's Brule-Gunflint camps marked the end of the railroad logging era in the present BWCAW.

PIGEON RIVER

LUMBER COMPANY OPERATIONS

The Pigeon River Lumber Company was a Canadian firm operating out of the Port Arthur-Fort William area (now Thunder Bay). Their crews constructed a series of dams and flumes on the Pigeon River that enabled them to drive logs cut on either side of the border all the way down to Lake Superior. From there the logs were rafted to their sawmill. They operated along the border from about 1905 until recent times, but most of their logging in the present BWCAW occurred between about 1914 and 1920. Some of their dams and sluiceways still existed on the Pigeon River in the early 1980s. This company cut big pine on the Fowl lakes, Moose, John, East Pike, and McFarland lakes, and the east end of Pine Lake. I do not have specific records of slash fires in their operating areas, but it is evident on the ground that some of their slashings did burn.

The Hughes Brothers Company also cut some stands in the same general area operated by Pigeon River, but the center of their operations was farther east, largely outside the present wilderness. Their operations near the Boundary Waters occurred between about 1917 and 1920.

Ecological Effects of the Early Logging

Several effects of the early logging operations were different from those of more recent operations. First, no year-round roads were built, no tractors were used for log skidding, no mechanical ground preparation was used to prepare logged areas for planting or seeding, and no herbicides were ever used to control postlogging vegetation. Thus there was virtually no disturbance of the natural soil profile and little direct effect of logging on the ground vegetation. A few year-round railroad grades involved cuts, fill, blasting, and ballasting with gravel that left permanent scars on the landscape.

Second, dams and sluiceways were built on numerous streams and lake outlets within the present BWCAW, and log driving and rafting were widely practiced, but most were small low-head structures built largely of wood and sometimes brush, earth, and a minimal amount of local rock. Typically the lakes or streams were raised only a few feet. With a few notable exceptions, such as the Prairie Portage Dam, Fall Lake Dam, and Garden Lake Dam, most of these structures were partially washed out after the log drives were completed, failed to hold back much water, and today are gone entirely or hardly recognizable. The streambeds in their vicinity have in most cases resumed their original courses. Some of the larger lakes and streams experienced significant changes in water levels, changes that drowned out the forests near shore, leaving much dead timber, and changed shoreline and lake-bottom conditions. Major lakes where changes occurred include Moose, Newfound, Sucker, Birch, Knife, Fall, and Big Trout. Knife and Big Trout lakes have now virtually returned to former levels with little shoreline damage, partly because their shores are solid bedrock in many places. The Moose-Sucker-Birch chain has been altered by the Prairie Portage concrete dam, an unfortunate but reversible change. One other effect of log driving and rafting that has not entirely disappeared is the accumulations of bark on the bottoms of some streams and lakes and the large numbers of lost logs that remain in many lakes. Some pine logs were "sinkers" and others were lost for various reasons. Once waterlogged, such logs will last for centuries, and many still exist on the bottoms of lakes and streams in which logs were driven.

The use of horses in skidding did result in significant plant introductions in certain areas. The horses were fed oats and other farm-grown feeds that inevitably contained minor mixtures of weed seed, such as several species of clover, thistle, plantain, dandelion, and several grasses. These non-native species have persisted at almost all old logging camp sites, and many have become established generally on open sites within the logged regions. Some of these species have now become ubiquitous throughout the region, even in areas never logged, although fortunately in such areas none has yet become dominant.

The most important general effect of the early pine logging has been a major reduction from 15 percent to 5 percent of the landscape occupied by mature white and red pine forests. This situation is dynamic, however, and the coverage of mature red pine stands is now on the increase, as I will discuss later.

Conversion of pine stands to aspen and birch forests most often occurred where large areas were virtually clearcut of all mature pines and then burned in a high-intensity slash fire during the growing season. Such fires killed most remaining mature pines that might have served as seed trees, killed pine and other seeds on the ground and in cones in the slash, and killed any seedlings already established beneath the old trees. Fire per se did not prevent regeneration of white and red pine and other conifers, because as we have seen fire itself often creates favorable seedbeds for these trees. But the destruction of all living pine and of existing pine seed supplies did prevent their regeneration.

In areas where no high-intensity running fires occurred and if other circumstances were favorable, good pine regeneration often resulted. Such forests are now 60 to 95 years old, their age depending on the time of logging of each area. Favorable circumstances included at least one or more of the following:

- Pine and other conifer seedlings were present on the site at the time of logging and were not killed by the felling or skidding operations. These circumstances could easily occur, especially with winter logging and

horse-skidding, because the snow protected the soil and seedlings, and the horses and logs passed over only a fraction of the ground surface.

- Mature white and red pines were left on or near the site in sufficient numbers to restock the area wherever seedbeds were suitable. This situation occasionally occurred, especially where seed trees were left and subsequent light surface fires produced favorable seedbeds without killing the seed trees.
- Seed was on the ground at the time of logging in sufficient quantity to restock the area. This circumstance probably occurred only occasionally because white and red pine have only intermittent good seed years, and their seeds are mostly shed during the first winter after the cones mature.

Thus logging would have to occur during the first winter after a good seed year, and the postlogging seedbed would have to be favorable and not burned while the seedlings were young and unable to survive surface fires. Despite these rather rigorous requirements for successful regeneration, one or more of these circumstances did exist in many areas. Accurate surveys are not available, but I would estimate that fully a third of the areas logged in the early big-pine horse-logging era within the present BWCAW are now fairly well stocked with white and red pine.

One other general factor influencing the effect of the early logging is that in most regions of any size that were logged for big pine, no more than half of the land supported stands of mature pine and was therefore logged. The intervening areas supported stands of other species such as jack pine, black spruce, aspen, paper birch, white spruce, balsam fir, and black ash or elm and here and there the lichen-dominated communities of nearly treeless rock outcrops or the sphagnum-dominated communities of open bogs. Such areas were not often directly affected by logging operations. Sometimes a railroad grade or sleigh-haul road passed through them, but they were not the targets of the loggers. Many such areas were burned in the slash fires that swept the logged regions, but fire was no stranger to most of the vegetation involved. The postfire vegetation in these plant communities often is the same as it might have been if there had been no logging of adjacent pine stands. For example, there are many jack pine, black spruce, or aspen-birch stands within regions generally logged for white and red pine that are virtually indistinguishable from larger tracts of virgin forest of the same age class in regions that were not logged.

Within the logged regions in these early pine operations, fully half the total land surface may be occupied by vegetation that was not changed substantially by the logging. In some cases, where no slash fires occurred, the same trees are still there—they are simply 60 to 95 years older now. Where general fires but no logging occurred in the substantial areas between the old pine stands, the present forest is still the result of a natural environmental factor: fire. Only the age class of the vegetation was changed. We may be offended by the knowledge that such fires were often set by the loggers, either accidentally or deliberately. Did the plant communities that resulted really know the difference between a logger's escaped slash fire and fire resulting from a lightning strike? I think not. As we shall see shortly, the more recent pulpwood logging operations employing trucks, tractors, and gravel roads often caused greater changes in the ecosystem than did the early logging operations described in this chapter.

The Pulpwood Logging Era: 1935 to 1978

As the early big-pine logging era drew to a close, five factors evolving simultaneously produced a new type of logging in the present BWCAW:

- the creation of the Superior National Forest and the gradual development of a timber-management program by the U.S. Forest Service, a program soon constrained by public concerns about the impact of logging on the wilderness
- the gradual maturing of the extensive young forests of jack pine and black spruce on the old public domain lands
- the gradual development of a wood pulp and paper industry in Minnesota and adjacent states that generated markets for smaller timber and for species not cut in the big-pine logging era
- the gradual improvement of gasoline- and diesel-powered crawler tractors and of large gasoline- and diesel-powered trucks and associated mechanical logging equipment capable of economically harvesting smaller timber and transporting it out of the woods on roads instead of by stream driving or by railroad
- the gradual development of an all-weather road system linking the Superior National Forest timber with pulpwood markets, at first through rail and Lake Superior shipping, but ultimately with direct woods-to-mill truck hauls

When President Theodore Roosevelt created the Superior National Forest in 1909, a major motivation was to protect the remaining public domain land from the timber industry. Yet most of the mature white and red pine timber was already in the hands of the timber companies. A few timber sales were made to companies that happened to be cutting close to mature government timber, but initially these sales were on a small scale. The major activities of the Superior National Forest from its inception until at least 1938 were fire control, the gradual acquisition of tax-forfeited timber lands within the forest, and the development of a forest road network. Tree planting, plantation care, and timber-stand improvement also became major activities after the Civilian Conservation Corps and other Great Depression emergency jobs programs began about 1933. A network of fire-lookout towers was constructed, including four towers within the present BWCAW: Sioux River Lookout (at Devils Cascade), Angleworm Lookout, Kekekabic Lookout, and Brule Lake Lookout. Cabins were built at several towers to house the lookouts. Foot trails and telephone lines were also built between cabins and towers for fire control and other purposes.

The new Forest Service cadre of trained foresters became remarkably proficient at detecting and extinguishing forest fires. To be sure, there were a few large fires, but the average area burned per year was dramatically reduced. This program had its desired effect. By 1940 many stands of spruce, jack pine, aspen, birch, and balsam that had originated after the fires of 1822, 1824, 1854, 1863, 1864, and 1875 were maturing. A significant timber resource now existed on the old public domain, if only markets could be found, and if less costly ways could be found to get the timber to market.

While the timber resource was growing and fire-control programs were being perfected, a new public concern for the unique wilderness qualities of the Boundary Waters was also developing, leading to laws and administrative regulations. Public concern over road building produced the first tentative Forest Service identification of a "wilderness area" in 1926 and led Secretary of Agriculture W. M. Jardine to promise that the Forest Service "will leave not less than 1,000 square miles of the best canoe country . . . without roads of any character" (Jardine 1926). In 1930 Congress passed the Shipstead-Newton-Nolan Act, which forbade logging within 400 feet of lakes and streams in a vast area including even more area than the present BWCAW.

By 1938 the Forest Service, under the guidance of Robert Marshall as its Chief of Recreation, had set up three units of the forest as official "Roadless Primitive Areas" under new secretary of agriculture regulations. These roadless areas were designed to protect the wilderness character of the Boundary Waters and included the lands initially identified as "wilderness areas" in accord with the Jardine policy, plus additional tax-forfeited land along the Canadian border that had by now been included within the Superior's boundaries. Timber cutting was not initially excluded from any of the roadless areas, except for the Shipstead-Newton-Nolan Act reserves. In 1941 protection from logging was extended administratively to a 362,000-acre irregular no-cutting area along the international boundary from Little Vermilion Lake in the west to Mountain Lake in the east.

While these programs and policies were evolving, the forest products industries in Minnesota were undergoing major changes. By 1932 most of the big sawmills had ceased operations, but a gradual shift to pulp and paper manufacturing and to the production of crating lumber, poles, posts, and pilings was under way. These new industries developed slowly during the 1930s because of depressed economic conditions, but with the outbreak of World War II, timber markets picked up dramatically. Pulp and/or paper mills had been built at Cloquet and Brainerd by the Weyerhaeuser interests (Northwest Paper Company), at International Falls by the Backus interests (Minnesota and Ontario Paper Company, 1885), at Grand Rapids (Blandin Paper Company), and at Sartell (Watab Paper Company). In addition, a large pulp and paper industry had developed in Wisconsin and Michigan, with some mills located near Great Lakes ports. At first spruce pulpwood (chiefly black spruce) was used almost exclusively in the groundwood process. At about the time of World War II, however, the kraft process and other technological changes created a demand for pine pulpwood (chiefly jack pine) and ultimately also for aspen and other woods. Crating lumber from jack pine was also in demand during the war. Thus species that were not cut in the original big-pine sawlog operations were salable by 1940, and these species existed in abundance on the original public domain lands within the new roadless areas.

Early Pulpwood and Associated Big-Pine Logging

The mid-1930s saw little logging of any kind in the present BWCAW. In 1939 a small logging operation by Carlson and Oppel just west of Angleworm Lake north of the Echo Trail may have marked the beginning of truck wood logging in the Boundary Waters. No year-round roads were built. The timber was hauled out on a winter road from the Echo Trail northeastward down the Spring Creek Draw 3 miles to the cutting area. Much of the land and timber cut in this operation was privately owned. The Spring Creek Draw winter logging road ultimately led to many conflicts with wilderness values, for it served as access for logging as far north as Beartrap Lake, 6 miles northeast of the Echo Trail.

The development of diesel- and gasoline-powered crawler tractors with a bulldozer blade made the clearing of winter truck haul roads feasible in the late 1930s. Trees were still felled, limbed, and bucked up with handsaws and axes, and horses were often still used for skidding the logs to a landing. The haul to markets or railroad sidings was accomplished with trucks that could be driven over frozen roads directly from the log landing to year-round public gravel roads and hard-surfaced highways. These "winter roads" were built by first clearing the route with a bulldozer, usually in December after some snow had accumulated and the ground was frozen. The dozer cleared away stumps, fallen logs, and protruding rocks and leveled and compacted the snow and organic matter on the forest floor, facilitating deep-freezing of the roadbed. After a week or two of subzero weather, the road was again leveled and plowed and was then ready for truck hauling. Even deep peatlands, open bogs, lakes, and sluggish streams could be traversed by such roads in January, February, and March after prolonged cold had sufficiently thickened the soil frost or lake and stream ice. Winter roads were normally laid out to follow lowlands because this minimized grades and the need to bulldoze much soil or rock to obtain a level surface.

Early in the 1940s, Jacob Pete, an Ely logger, began a series of relatively small logging operations on the east side of Angleworm Lake. In this case the old Cloquet Line railroad grade was available as a roadbed. The right-of-way was still owned by the Cloquet-based General Logging Company. The old bridges were planked and repaired, and much gravel was hauled in to surface the grade. The road could then be used for both summer and winter truck hauling, a practice continued intermittently into the 1970s by various firms. Pete evidently cut a combination of sawlogs, pine mining timbers, pulpwood, and other products. He set up a temporary sawmill on the east shore of Angleworm Lake. Remnants of the sawdust pile still remained in the 1980s. Pete's crews cut several tracts in the present BWCAW, from near the south end of Angleworm Lake north to an area northeast of Home Lake.

In 1941 and 1942, and probably in subsequent years, Harry Homer Sr., another Ely logger, cut timber in the Cummings Lake region south of Big Moose Lake and the Echo Trail and west of the North Arm of Burntside Lake. Four tracts were located just north of the northeast bay of Cummings Lake near the portage to Big Moose Lake, and at least four more were located east of Cummings Lake along the Korb River and along the northeast shore of Jig

Lake. Some or most of these tracts were owned by the Oliver Iron Mining Company. Much of the timber cut was probably red pine for mine timbers in the underground iron mines in Ely and the Tower-Soudan area, which were being operated at full capacity to supply steel for the war effort. Significant stands of red pine of 1755 and 1747 origin still exist in this general region, and it was probably those age classes that were cut, along with other trees for pulpwood, sawlogs, and perhaps other products. Some timber was hauled out via the Coxey Pond winter road to the North Arm of Burntside Lake, and some from the tracts north of Cummings Lake may have been hauled northward to the Echo Trail via a long winter road through the bogs east of Big Moose Lake. About the same time, state land was logged south of Coxey Pond and near Silica Lake. This timber was also brought out via the Coxey Pond road to the North Arm of Burntside Lake. A logging camp was built near the portage between Silica Lake and Coxey Pond, and a temporary sawmill was set up near Silica Lake. In about 1943 and 1944, the Oliver Iron Mining Company also logged its land in Section 30 west of Angleworm Lake on the west side of the Spring Creek Draw. This timber again came out via the Spring Creek winter road.

In 1944 the North Star Timber Company began a long series of winter logging operations in the Davis Lake region west of Winchell Lake and north of Brule Lake. North Star, the Minnesota logging subsidiary of Kimberly-Clark Corporation, was primarily interested in pulpwood, especially spruce. The wood was hauled out by truck across the ice of Davis, Pup, Trump, and Winchell lakes, the Cone lakes, and perhaps Wahnigan, Mulligan, and Lily lakes to Brule Lake, where the winter route joined the old Brule Lake General Logging Company railroad grade. This operation, which lasted until 1950, began in the era when pulpwood was cut mainly by "piece-cutters," who used Swedish bow saws to cut the pulpwood into 8-foot "sticks." The men were paid according to the number of sticks cut each day. Toward the end of these operations, gasoline-powered chain saws were coming into general use in the woods, and some were no doubt used here. North Star's pulpwood was trucked to either the Grand Marais harbor or the Sugar Loaf Landing, located between Taconite Harbor and Little

Marais, where it was made into large booms and rafted across Lake Superior to ports on the Michigan side. During their period of operation in the Davis Lake area, North Star cut several thousand acres. Most of the timber came from federal timber sales.

In August and September 1946, the Superior National Forest began the construction of one of the first year-round timber access roads into the Superior roadless areas. The bridge across the Brule River on the old General Logging Company railroad grade about 3 miles east of Horseshoe Lake was not usable, and the grade was overgrown with brush from that point northwestward to Poplar Lake. The bridge was repaired, the railroad grade was cleared of brush for about a half mile to the northwest, and clearing the right-of-way was started for a road to be built to the west. The Horseshoe-Vista lakes big white pine stands were cut between about 1947 and 1953, and most of the region north of that area up to Swamp, Lizz, and Poplar lakes was also cut over between 1946 and 1963. This logging was conducted through a series of small sales to several loggers. The road eventually penetrated some 3.5 miles west to the Horseshoe-Vista lakes portage, which was crossed to provide access to big white pine southwest of Vista Lake.

The old white pine stands that were cut mostly dated from forest fires in 1692 and 1755–59, with a few stands dating from 1801 burns, and perhaps a few groves from fires as long ago as 1610. These Shipstead-Newton-Nolan reserves left remnants of the virgin forests in all areas cut in the pulpwood logging era, and they also screened the logged areas and roads from canoe travelers. From 1940 to 1960, few winter visitors came to the Boundary Waters other than local fishermen. The full impact of modern logging was therefore not recognized by most canoeists until 1960 to 1970, when logging roads and portage crossings became widespread and when winter recreational use of the area became more common.

The Tomahawk Sale

Beginning late in World War II, the U.S. Forest Service was also developing plans to log a large region of virgin timber centering on Lake Isabella, both inside and out-

side the roadless areas. The main interest was in jack pine and black spruce pulpwood and in pine crating, pallet lumber, and related rough-sawn products. Large areas to the southwest outside the roadless area had been sold to the Tomahawk Timber Company (which represented several Wisconsin firms) between 1941 and 1945. By 1945 cutting on these sales had progressed eastward to about the Little Isabella River, along what is now Forest Road 173 (the Tomahawk Road). In the roadless area large areas of mature jack pine and spruce originated after fires in 1824, 1854, 1864, and 1875 north, east, and west of Lake Isabella. These age classes also occupied large areas south of the roadless area. By the summer of 1945 logging of these age classes on the old public domain lands of the Superior had progressed northeastward from the village of Isabella along the Dumbell River almost to Sylvania, Bunny, and Plum lakes, using the then new Forest Road 174 (the Dumbell River Road) for access. I was working as a timber scaler for the Superior in logging camps on this road in June and July of 1945, and it was obvious at that point that more timber sales would soon be needed to the north to keep the Dumbell River and Tomahawk Road camps in operation.

Planning proceeded for extending a railroad and the supporting road systems into the Sylvania–Lake Isabella area to provide access to more timber. By the time these plans developed into actual programs, the war was over, but the logging went forward. On December 19, 1945, a vast area of federal timber within the roadless area, north, east, and west of Lake Isabella, was sold to the Tomahawk Timber Company. The sale encompassed about 130 square miles of land and water, with a net land area of some 73,000 acres in federal ownership. Logging of this area continued for two decades.

By 1948 the Duluth, Mesabi and Iron Range Railroad had been extended to within a few hundred feet of Lake Isabella, the Tomahawk Road had been extended to the same area, and the construction of a temporary logging town called Forest Center at the rail terminus had begun. The Tomahawk Road was closed to the general public for more than a decade thereafter and was not shown on Superior National Forest maps available to the public until the 1960s. Thus public awareness of the scale of logging oper-

116 ations in the Forest Center area was slow to develop. The Silver Island Lake unit of the roadless area was deleted in 1948 to accommodate the Forest Center developments and additional logging and road building southeast of Forest Center (figure 9.1).

A new 1948 Plan of Management for the roadless areas called for preventing further intrusion of motorboats, aircraft, and roads into the Boundary Waters but allowed timber harvest to be continued "without unnecessary restrictions" (U.S. Forest Service 1948). The gravel road network being built north of Forest Center in the roadless area was considered "temporary" and not a contradiction of this policy, of the Jardine policy of 1926, or of the 1939 roadless area regulations. Yet within a few years, a system of main gravel haul roads extended as far as 15 or 20 miles to the northeast of Lake Isabella, and other roads penetrated some 7 or 8 miles to the northwest. Logging was eventually conducted almost year-round on these operations, and a spider web of spur roads was bulldozed from the main roads back into almost every 40-acre tract of federal land within the sale area. The road network is shown in figure 9.1. These roads were never shown on the Superior National Forest's recreational maps available to the general public.

The Forest Service claimed that logging in the road-less area northeast of Forest Center was necessary to salvage a large 1949 blowdown of timber near Polly Lake, but the great extent of the Tomahawk Sale of 1945 suggests that the actual motivation was a desire to organize a systematic harvest of mature timber throughout the region. Blowdowns were simply used to justify the "need" for the program to anyone who questioned the wisdom of such extensive logging in the Boundary Waters. Ultimately this logging involved clear-cutting and road building as far north as the southern shores of Hudson, Insula, Fishdance, Malberg, and Koma lakes. Chain saws were used to cut the timber on most of the Forest Center operations, creating much noise that could not be easily avoided. Again, the 400-foot lakeshore reserves required by the Shipstead-Newton-Nolan Act screened the logging from the direct view of most canoeists. To its credit, the Forest Service often kept logging even farther back from certain high-use wilderness lakes such as Hudson and Insula, a fact that certainly postponed the inevitable negative reaction when canoeists finally realized the extent to which the wilderness was being exploited for timber and filled with roads. The existence of a town, roads, and a railhead at Forest Center, and of roads and portage crossings by roads in the Perent Lake-Kawishiwi Lake-Isabella River area, effectively

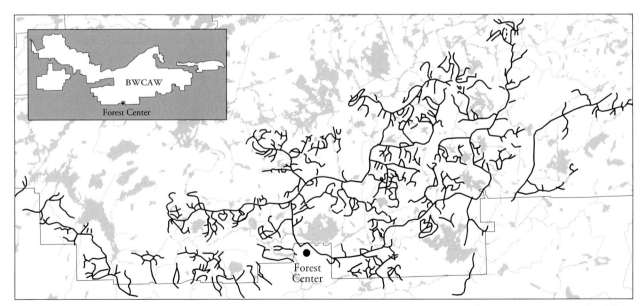

Figure 9.1 / Logging roads near Forest Center. (Original map by M. L. Heinselman. Digitized by University of Minnesota, Remote Sensing Lab in 1994.)

destroyed the wilderness character of the south half of the former circle canoe route originating at Lake One. The southern part of that route was little used by wilderness-seeking canoeists in the 1950s and 1960s because of this destruction.

Pulpwood logging on the Tomahawk Sale involved almost total clear-cutting of blocks of jack pine and spruce covering hundreds of contiguous acres. Many upland pine areas were replanted to red pine, even though the natural vegetation had been jack pine. However, many tracts were not replanted at all. Where much aspen and birch were mixed with pine and spruce, the aspen and birch were often left standing because of the poor market for those species. Balsam fir was also usually left. Thus many cutover areas were converted from even-aged mixed stands containing much pine and spruce to ragged, uneven-aged stands with an overstory of scattered aspen and birch and an under-story of balsam fir, small aspen and birch thickets, and such shrubs as hazelnut and alder.

Where pine was replanted, in some cases the soil was first cleared of stumps, shrubs, and unmerchantable trees with giant bulldozer-like "rock-rakes." This practice often removed the topsoil and left huge "windrows" of stumps, boulders, and organic matter on the landscape at intervals of a few hundred feet. In some areas within the wilderness mixtures of the herbicides 2,4-D and 2,4,5-T were applied to kill the aspen, birch, and shrubs competing with planted red pine and spruce. Of course many nontarget shrubs and herbs, including many native wildflowers, were also killed on the sprayed areas. Herbicides were commonly used from the mid–1950s until the late 1960s, but the total area treated with herbicides and/or rock-raking within the Boundary Waters was only a few thousand acres. The total area planted to red pine and other conifers on these sale areas was also only a fraction of the total area logged.

Other Significant Timber Sales

While the Forest Center operations were developing, large-scale logging was also beginning in the roadless areas west of Ely, both north and south of the Echo Trail. In the 1940s the Nekoosa-Edwards Paper Company of Wisconsin began

a large operation west of Wolfpack Lake and north of Lake Jeanette. This logging encompassed about 7 square miles, some of which had been partially logged earlier for big pine by the Virginia and Rainy Lake Company. It was not near canoe routes, and its location in a far corner of the Boundary Waters attracted little notice.

A more obtrusive group of logging operations began on state land west of Burntside Lake in the Phantom-Battle lakes area about 1950. Here a series of timber sales to the Northwest Paper Company and others eventually resulted in the clear-cutting of some 15 square miles within the Burntside State Forest. These lands were within the road-less area and largely surrounded by federal land, some of which was also logged. The timber cut was mostly jack pine and spruce of 1863–64 or 1894 origin, plus scattered patches of red and white pine, mostly of 1755 origin. Toward the western edge of the logged area, some of the timber had originated after fires in about 1900, probably escaped slash fires from the early big-pine cutovers to the south and west. A logging camp (Palmquist's Camp) was built at the portage between Phantom and Battle lakes. The gravel road that served this camp and the timber operations to the north skirted the shores of Phantom and Sprite lakes, and some fill was even used to cross the northeast tip of Phantom Lake. Several canoe portages were crossed by logging roads. A sawmill also operated for several years on the road northwest of Battle Lake. It may have sawn some of the scattered red and white pine that was cut along with the pulpwood. Extensive pine plantations were put in by the state north and west of Battle Lake. Some operations were still in progress at this locality in 1964 when the first major controversy over recent logging in the Boundary Waters erupted, and small operations were still under way west of Cummings Lake when Public Law 95-495 was passed in 1978.

In 1947 the Oliver Iron Mining Company began cutting its timber along the northeast end of Slim Lake. This was a small operation within the roadless area, and less than a square mile was cut over by 1951. In 1952 and 1953 about 200 acres were cut northwest of Slim Lake and north of Rice Lake. These operations were mostly in red, white, and jack pine of 1822 origin, and the logs were probably used primarily for mining timber. The remains of a logging camp and an old rusting vehicle can still be found not far inland from the northeast shore of Slim Lake. No gravel roads were built to the site; it was a winter operation.

The Minnesota Division of Forestry also sold the timber on most of its scattered blocks of ownership within or adjacent to the federal Tomahawk Sale operations out of Forest Center. State sales in these areas occurred in 1950 and 1954, including several tracts aggregating about 2 square miles south of Perent Lake.

In 1950 the Northwest Paper Company purchased the timber on a large federal sale block south of the Isabella River and west of Forest Center. This block was partially within the roadless area and partially outside along the Tomahawk Road. Within the roadless area, it extended from just east of Bog Lake south of Bald Eagle Lake. It encompassed about 15 square miles of timberlands within the area, supporting mostly jack pine, spruce, aspen, birch, and fir dating from fires in 1796, 1824, 1854, 1864, 1875, 1894, and 1910. All but the 1910 age class were eventually cut over, but much of the aspen, birch, and fir was left standing. Most of the logging within the roadless area did not occur until after 1955. A permanent gravel access road was constructed along the south boundary of the roadless area during the early 1950s. Two segments of this road "accidentally" penetrated the roadless area to a depth of about ⅛ mile, the easterly penetration being about 1 mile in length. These segments of Forest Road 381 were deleted from the wilderness by Public Law 95-495.

The Finn Lake Sales

In 1954 the focus of new timber sale activity shifted back to the Gunflint Trail region with the awarding of the vast Finn Lake Sale block to Consolidated Papers of Wisconsin. This sale encompassed some 38 square miles of federal timberlands, plus about a square mile of state land. The tract ran from Caribou Lake—just south of Poplar Lake—westward to Long Island Lake and southward to Cash, Winchell, and Gaskin lakes. It also included land around such well-known canoeing lakes as Lizz, Meeds, Rush, Banadad, Finn, Henson, Kiskadinna, Omega, Moon, Mus-

keg, Otto, Horseshoe, Pillsbery, and Allen. The timber was a complex mixture of jack pine, black and white spruce, white and red pine, northern white cedar, balsam fir, aspen, and birch. These forests dated from fires in 1801, 1824, 1875, and 1894, and had scattered patches of still older white and red pine.

Access to the Finn Lake block was via a new year-round gravel road that entered the roadless area from the old General Logging Company railroad grade about a mile southeast of the east end of Poplar Lake. This road headed westward, weaving in and out of the roadless area to near the southwest side of Poplar Lake, at which point it divided into three branches. The north branch followed the edge of the roadless area—again weaving in and out of the area—for some 11 miles westward, where it joined the so-called Rib Lake Trail, another logging road entering the roadless area from the Gunflint Trail just southwest of the west end of Loon Lake. The central stem of the road system headed west from a point just north of Meeds Lake for about 7 miles, passing just south of Rush and Banadad lakes, at which point it swung southwestward, crossing the west end of Finn Lake over a large fill and culverts, thence winding southwestward across the Muskeg-Kiskadinna lakes portage to a point about 1 mile east of Cash Lake. The total length of this main stem from the entrance gate on the General Logging Company railroad grade was about 14 miles. The south branch headed south from the east end of Meeds Lake for about a mile and then swung southwestward between Pillsbery and Allen lakes along the west end of Gaskin Lake and down almost to Winchell Lake to a terminus just south of the Otto Lakes. The full road system just described, with its branches, crossed canoe portages between Poplar and Skipper, Poplar and Lizz, Meeds and Caribou, Horseshoe and Allen, Pillsbery and Allen, Gaskin and Henson, Rush and Banadad, and Kiskadinna and Muskeg lakes.

Cutting on the Finn Lake block began in 1954 during the era when trees were felled, limbed, and cut into logs by piece-cutters using chain saws, and ended about 1972 in a new and more mechanized logging era when trees were felled with large four-wheel-drive feller-bunchers that cut the trees and hauled them out of the woods full-length to landings, where they sometimes were loaded onto trucks almost full-length, only the tops and limbs being removed. Consolidated Papers trucked its logs to the Grand Marais harbor or to Sugar Loaf Landing. From these points the logs were made up into rafts and towed across Lake Superior to Ashland, Wisconsin, where they were loaded onto railroad cars for shipment to Consolidated's paper mills at Wisconsin Rapids or Biron, Wisconsin. This practice continued until the end of the 1972 rafting season (Timber Producers Association Bulletin 1971).

Other Sales

Logging began about 1954 and 1955 in two cutting units in the roadless area just west and south of Little Gabbro Lake. By 1960 virtually all the federal and state timber in the roadless area west of both Gabbro and Bald Eagle lakes had been sold. The Spruce Road (Forest Road 181) was extended several miles from its original terminus east of State Highway 1. It eventually ended at a gate about 1.5 miles south of Gabbro Lake, from which point a network of "temporary" logging roads led several miles southeastward into the roadless area. Cutting in this area persisted into the 1970s. As part of the operation, a short spur was constructed that led about a mile northeastward off the Spruce Road to the shore of Little Gabbro Lake. When first bulldozed in the late 1950s, this road had no gate at the roadless area boundary and was soon used by local people as an unofficial new entry point into the Boundary Waters. There were no regulations excluding motorboats in those days, and the site soon became a motorboat launching area. Within a few years several motorboats were being cached on the lakeshore both at this point and off a second road to Little Gabbro. The forests that were logged in the Gabbro–Bald Eagle sales mostly originated following fires in 1824, 1846, 1864, and 1875. Most of the timber cut was jack pine and spruce. Much aspen, birch, and fir were left standing in portions of the sale areas.

At essentially the same time that the Finn Lake, Gabbro–Bald Eagle, and Forest Center blocks were being logged, another sale began north of the Echo Trail and some 25 miles northwest of Ely. This was the so-called Blandin Sale,

covering about 5 square miles within the roadless area, primarily around Ramshead, Lamb, and Nina Moose lakes and west of the Moose River. The federal timber in the area was purchased by the Blandin Paper Company of Grand Rapids, Minnesota. Cutting on the northern end of this operation east of Ramshead Lake began about 1956 and ended about 1965; the southern area south of Lamb Lake along Meander Creek was cut between 1960 and 1966. A bulldozed winter road was built from the Meander Lake Picnic Ground road (Forest Road 467) northeastward into the roadless area to a point about a quarter mile west of the north end of Nina Moose Lake. At this point the main road branched into a complex network of spur roads that reached northward almost to the point where Ramshead Creek joins the Moose River. The main road crossed the Nina Moose–Lamb Lake portage about a quarter mile west of Nina Moose Lake. The timber cut on this operation was generally much older than that typical of pulpwood-era operations. The most abundant age class was jack pine, spruce, and red and white pine that had originated after fires in 1755. There was also some still older red and white pine between Ramshead and Nina Moose lakes that dated from fires in 1681. Much of this oldest pine was left standing in a wide lakeshore reserve east of Ramshead Lake and north of Lamb Lake, where it still existed in 1993, except for a portion of the stand killed by the 1971 Little Sioux fire.

In 1958 the Superior National Forest changed the name of the Superior roadless areas to the Boundary Waters Canoe Area (BWCA) because that name "better described the actual qualities of the area." About the same time the Superior National Forest also launched the most ambitious program of new timber sales within the BWCA since the Tomahawk Sale of 1948. The first of these new sales was the vast West Tofte block, sold to the St. Regis Paper Company in 1959. The original sale boundaries encompassed about 80 square miles, extending from the south boundary of the BWCA south of the Lady Chain of Lakes northward to Frost Lake and to within 1 mile of Little Saganaga Lake. From east to west the sale extended from Alton, Sawbill, and Cherokee lakes west to Hazel and Knight lakes. Cutting on this sale began about 1960, at first confined to the southwestern end, near the Lady Chain. Most

120

of the timber in the sale area dated from fires in 1863–64 and 1875. The main year-round graveled access road crossed the Hazel-Knight lakes portage and bridged Phoebe Creek. Much of the area was not heavily stocked with conifers, and there were large areas of aspen and birch.

The West Tofte Sale was followed in 1961 by the East Tofte Sale, which originally encompassed some 22 square miles within the BWCA east of Sawbill, Ada, and Cherokee lakes and south of Cherokee, South Temperance, and Brule lakes. In 1960 and 1962 there were sizable state timber sales adjacent to the East Tofte block, east of Kelly Lake. Also in 1962 there was a sizable federal timber sale south of Shell Lake and east of the Little Indian Sioux River (the Shell Lake Sale), and another east of the Sioux River but south of the Echo Trail along Bellow Creek. In 1963 more federal tracts were sold in the Bellow Creek area, and a strip of federal timber was sold just south of Cummings Lake, adjoining the extensive Burntside State Forest sales. In early 1964 still another federal sale was made along Jerry Creek, north of the Echo Trail, just west of the Stuart River canoe route. Another large federal sale along the Lac La Croix hiking trail (later called the Stuart Lake Trail) was proposed in the early 1960s, and construction of a timber access road into the area was begun, but this sale was withdrawn after public protests.

The Selke Committee

By 1964 the BWCA was alive with logging operations from east to west; several new sales had just been made but were not yet active, and there were rumors of still more in the planning stage. The many portage crossings by logging roads and the recent appearance of several culverts and bridges across canoe routes had made canoeists painfully aware of the direct impacts of logging on their wilderness experiences. The logging roads were said by the Forest Service to be temporary and were closed to the public, but there were numerous reports of unauthorized vehicular use of certain roads for hunting, fishing, or other recreation by local residents. Most roads did have gates or chains across them at the former roadless area boundary, but these

were often torn down or left open. Several new boat access points to the BWCA had also been created by roads built primarily for logging. Some of these, such as the Gabbro Lake, Forest Center, and Kawishiwi Lake roads, had bisected formerly remote, continuous canoe routes. Some people were also concerned about the loss of natural ecosystem values inherent in logging and road building on lands that had never been directly altered by human action before. These people pointed to the damage to the wilderness character of the region being logged and questioned whether the value of the timber could justify such losses in our nation's only dedicated canoe area. By early 1964 the Wilderness Act was being hotly debated in the U.S. Congress, and the BWCA was one of the areas to be included in the National Wilderness System under bills before the Congress. In addition, motorboat and snowmobile use was growing rapidly on many lakes that had never seen motorized recreational use before.

By the spring of 1964, a group of people, largely from the Twin Cities, were calling upon Secretary of Agriculture Orville L. Freeman, a former Minnesota governor, to stop the logging and the spread of motorboats and snowmobiles in the Boundary Waters. This group, led by Clayton G. Rudd, president of the Natural History Society of Minnesota, called themselves the Conservation Affiliates. The ad hoc committee was drawn largely from the Natural History Society, the Izaak Walton League, the Minnesota Conservation Federation, and other organizations. Glen Ross of the Izaak Walton League and Homer Luick of the Conservation Federation were among the other most active Twin Cities leaders.

On May 21, 1964, Secretary Freeman announced the appointment of a special Boundary Waters Canoe Area review committee, chaired by George A. Selke, who had served as Minnesota's commissioner of conservation while Freeman was governor. In addition to the chair, the committee consisted of Wayne Olson, then Minnesota's conservation commissioner; Raymond Haik, vice president of the Minnesota Division of the Izaak Walton League, Minneapolis; Rollie Johnson, news director, WCCO-TV, Minneapolis; John Vukelich, county supervisor, St. Louis

County, Minnesota; and David J. Winton, chairman of the board of Winton Lumber Company, Minneapolis.

On September 3, 1964, while the Selke committee was deliberating, the U.S. Congress passed and President Johnson signed the Wilderness Act. This law included the Boundary Waters Canoe Area in the new National Wilderness Preservation System as one of the "instant wildernesses" set up by the act, but paragraph 4(d)(5) of the act left much discretion to the secretary of agriculture regarding logging and motorboat use in the BWCA:

> Other provisions of this Act to the contrary notwithstanding, the management of the Boundary Waters Canoe Area . . . shall be in accordance with regulations established by the Secretary of Agriculture in accordance with the general principle of maintaining, without unnecessary restrictions on other uses, including that of timber, the primitive character of the area, particularly in the vicinity of lakes, streams and portages: Provided, that nothing in this Act shall preclude the continuance within the area of any already established use of motorboats.

The BWCA now had a new status as one of our nation's first congressionally mandated wilderness areas, but paragraph 4(d)(5) left it an orphan in the wilderness system, the only area singled out for such major exceptions in management policy.

The Selke committee released its report on December 15, 1964, recommending significant increases in the area closed to logging. Secretary Freeman accepted the report and most of its recommendations. Before announcing his decisions on future BWCA regulations, Freeman allowed a one-year period for public comment. The proposed motorboat and snowmobile regulations were particularly controversial.

The Freeman Directive

On December 15, 1965, Secretary Freeman issued his directive implementing the Selke committee's recommendations. This order, since known as the Freeman Directive, was a detailed and comprehensive set of regulations implementing

both the Wilderness Act and the Selke committee's recommendations. Concerning logging, the order increased the no-cutting zones by 150,000 acres immediately and designated 100,000 acres for addition in 1975 after logging contracts in those areas were completed. This increase brought the total area closed to logging up to 512,000 acres in 1965, and to 612,000 acres by 1975. Motorboats and snowmobiles were for the first time limited to designated routes, but more than half of the water area was left open to motors.

A few key paragraphs from this order that concerned the forest ecosystem read as follows (U.S Forest Service 1974, 68–69):

Code of Federal Regulations, Section 293.16 Special Provisions Governing the Boundary Waters Canoe Area, Superior National Forest:

> Subject to existing private rights, the lands now owned or hereafter acquired by the United States within the Boundary Waters Canoe Area of the Superior National Forest, Minnesota, as formerly designated under Reg. U–3 (36 CFR 294.1) and incorporated into the National Wilderness Preservation System under the Wilderness Act of September 3, 1964, shall be administered in accordance with this Regulation for the general purpose of maintaining, without unnecessary restrictions on other uses, including that of timber, the primitive character of the area, particularly in the vicinity of lakes, streams and portages.

A In the management of the timber resources of the Boundary Waters Canoe Area, two zones are established:

> 1 An Interior Zone, in which there will be no commercial harvesting of timber. The boundaries of this Zone are defined on an official map dated the same date as that on which this Regulation is promulgated, which map shows the specific boundaries established January 12, 1965, and the boundaries of the additional area which is to be progressively added by the Chief of the Forest Service between January 12, 1965, and December 31, 1975.

> 2 A Portal Zone which will include all of the Boundary Waters Canoe Area not designated as Interior

Zone. Timber harvesting is permitted in the Portal Zone under conditions designed to protect and maintain primitive recreational values. Timber within 400 feet of the shorelines of lakes and streams suitable for boat or canoe travel, or any portage connecting such waters will be specifically excluded from harvesting, and timber harvesting operations will be designed to avoid unnecessary crossings of portages. Timber sales plans will incorporate suitable provisions for prompt and appropriate cover restoration . . .

B   Except as provided in the Wilderness Act, in this Regulation, and in Section 294.2 of Title 36, Code of Federal Regulations, and subject to existing private rights, there shall be no commercial enterprises and no permanent roads within the Boundary Waters Canoe Area, and there shall be no temporary roads, no use of motor vehicles, motorized equipment, or motorboats, no landing of aircraft, and no other form of mechanical transport . . .

2   In the Portal Zone temporary roads and the use of motorized equipment and mechanical transport for the authorized travel and removal of forest products will be permitted in accordance with special conditions established by the Chief, Forest Service, but such use of the roads for other purposes is prohibited . . .

The Freeman Directive served to govern the management of the BWCA for the next 13 years, until the passage of Public Law 95-495 in 1978. Several important tracts of virgin forest were added to the no-cutting area (the new interior zone) in 1965. Most significant was an area in the west from Loon Lake eastward to Oyster Lake and Lake Agnes, and the area just north of Stuart Lake. Most of that area had not been logged. Another significant area was north and west of Cherokee Lake. Most of the other additions to the no-cut zone had already been logged either in the big-pine logging era or in the post–World War II period. The areas to be added to the no-cut zones in 1975 were mostly either already cutover or currently under contract. Some 200,000 acres of virgin forest were left in the portal zone subject to continued logging. These areas included not only considerable acres already under contract but also at least 180,000 acres not yet subject to contracts.

New Timber Sales after Freeman's Directive

Even with all these areas under contract, the Superior soon let additional large contracts in the portal zone. The first was the Old Road Sale to Consolidated Papers in 1966. This sale encompassed some 2,380 acres east of the old Cloquet Line railroad grade northwest of Ely, west of Gun, Fairy, Boot, and Fourtown lakes. About 300 acres of adjacent state timber northeast of Holy Lake were also sold. The net area to be logged on the federal sale was about 1,200 acres (U.S. Forest Service 1974). Much of the timber dated from a fire in 1822 and consisted of large jack pine, spruce, aspen, birch, and fir.

The next sale was the so-called Sunnydale Sale located south of Oyster Lake and west of Ramshead Lake and Lake Agnes in the Lac La Croix region. This sale, made on March 28, 1968, to the Northwest Paper Company, originally encompassed an area 5 miles long, running diagonally southwest from just south of Oyster Lake to the BWCA boundary east of Woksapiwi Lake. The sale was later modified, but it originally encompassed about 4,000 acres. Most of the timber was jack pine, black and white spruce, aspen, birch, and balsam dating from a fire in 1864. There were also scattered patches of red and white pine and other species dating from a 1755 burn. The sale straddled the Sioux-Hustler hiking trail. The logging plan called for a road that would have penetrated almost to Oyster Lake, into a region totally free of roads up to that time.

The last large federal timber sale to make a deep incursion into virgin area was the Beartrap Sale of December 30, 1968, to the Kainz Logging Company of Ely. This tract was located about 5 miles up the now infamous Spring Creek Draw winter road, just southwest of Beartrap Lake. It encompassed some 1,150 acres of federal timber, of which about 900 acres were to be logged (U.S. Forest Service 1974). Adjoining tracts owned by St. Louis County, the state of Minnesota, and the U.S. Steel Corporation were also involved, making the total area to be logged nearer 1,500 acres. The timber was mostly red, white, and jack pine that originated after a fire in 1822. There was also some aspen, birch, jack pine, and spruce that originated after fires in 1894 that had burned through some stands. The

Kainz brothers operated a sawmill in Ely, and their primary interest was probably in the pine sawtimber.

In addition to these new sales, there were smaller federal sales to Consolidated Papers in 1967 and 1968 to the north and south of Perent Lake in an area already heavily logged in connection with the Forest Center operations, and in 1969 a new sale to the Northwest Paper Company, called Trail Block, south of the Isabella River and west of Forest Center, and contiguous with the larger Northwest Sale of 1950. About the same time, U.S. Steel Corporation was logging a group of inholdings within the BWCA to the north and south of the Echo Trail. Some of these U.S. Steel operations probably began as early as 1960, but many of them were still active in the late 1960s. They were located north of the Echo Trail between Mule Lake and Nina Moose Lake, south of the Echo Trail near Serenade Lake, and west of Big Moose Lake. The Serenade Lake operation involved a gravel road that penetrated about 2 miles into the present BWCAW, but the other operations used winter roads through the swamps. Much of the timber cut by U.S. Steel was large red pine.

Most of the timber operations in the BWCA in the late 1960s and 1970s employed highly mechanized logging techniques. Large rubber-tired four-wheel-drive skidders, feller-bunchers, and various other kinds of tree harvesters were used to cut the trees and remove them from the woods, often in full-tree lengths. On some operations the entire tree—trunk, limbs, tops, and needles or leaves—was transported from the stump to a central landing, where long semitrailers or full trailer trucks could be loaded. There the tops and limbs were cut off with chain saws or special machines, and the full tree trunk was then loaded onto a waiting truck. This method removed all the accumulated nutrients and organic matter in the tops from the forest and concentrated them in high debris piles at the landings. These debris piles were usually burned later, but some were simply left to rot. Such techniques removed a significant percentage of the nutrient capital from the forest, a practice that could impoverish poor soils if repeated a few times. Rock-raking also became a more common practice for preparing cutover lands for tree planting during this period.

The Logging Trials under Judge Miles Lord

On November 24, 1972, the Minnesota Public Interest Research Group (MPIRG), a statewide student-supported organization centered at the University of Minnesota, filed a lawsuit in federal district court in Minneapolis (*MPIRG* v. *Butz*). Quoting the National Environmental Policy Act (NEPA), the suit sought a court order to require an environmental impact statement (EIS) before renewal of logging contracts and requested an injunction to halt all logging of virgin forest in the BWCA pending completion of the EIS.

On April 16, 1973, Judge Miles Lord found that portions of seven timber sales were indeed major incursions into the remaining large blocks of virgin forests and that logging of such tracts in the BWCA constituted major federal actions requiring an EIS under NEPA. Accordingly, he issued injunctions against further logging on all or portions of each of those seven sales, pending completion of an EIS by the U.S. Forest Service. The sales enjoined were

- Beartrap Sale, the entire sale
- East Tofte Sale, the north end only, generally the area from Clam Lake north to Cherokee Lake
- Jerry Creek Sale, all of the sale except the southwest end where logging was nearly completed
- Old Road Sale, the entire sale
- Shell Lake Sale, the northeast portion where logging had not begun
- Sunnydale Sale, all of the sale within the BWCA
- West Tofte Sale, all the sale east of the portage from Kelso to Lujenida lakes, and the northeast end of the main sale area.

In his lengthy legal opinion, which included a detailed discussion of wilderness vegetation policies and the natural role of fire, Judge Lord made it evident that he did not believe the Wilderness Act permitted logging of the remaining large blocks of virgin forest in the BWCA.

After the EIS was released, on August 19, 1974, MPIRG filed a second lawsuit, and the Sierra Club soon joined as a coplaintiff. This time the suit charged that logging within large contiguous tracts of BWCA virgin forest was

124 a violation of the Wilderness Act and sought a permanent injunction against such operations, including the seven timber sales previously enjoined. The adequacy of the Forest Service's management plan and EIS were also challenged. Judge Lord issued a temporary injunction against logging on the seven active sales on September 18, 1974, and the trial commenced on November 4, 1974.

On August 13, 1975, Judge Lord rendered his decision in *MPIRG and Sierra Club* v. *Butz et al.*, the suit for a permanent injunction against logging. He ruled in favor of the plaintiffs on virtually all counts. The six remaining timber sales were all enjoined from further incursions into the remaining virgin forests (the Old Road Sale had been released during the trial as not a significant incursion). More important, he found that any further timber cutting within the remaining large contiguous blocks of virgin forest violated the intent of the Wilderness Act of 1964 and was therefore illegal. The Forest Service was permanently enjoined from conducting further sales within these large virgin areas. If this decision could withstand the appeals process, logging in the BWCA had been dealt a major blow, because most of the merchantable timber was within the virgin areas.

The Boundary Waters Wilderness Act

On October 24, 1975, Representative James Oberstar announced that he was introducing a bill in Congress to resolve the long-standing BWCA lawsuits and disputes (H.R. 10247). His bill would have given full wilderness status to some 600,000 acres of the BWCA, but it would also have removed the other 400,000 acres from the wilderness system and made it a National Recreation Area, open to logging and motorized uses and lacking the many other protections and objectives of the wilderness system.

Representative Donald Fraser introduced H.R. 14576 in the U.S. House of Representatives on June 28, 1976. The Fraser bill was simple in concept: it would have made a full wilderness area of the entire existing BWCA, ending all logging, administrative cutting, motorized recreation, and mining.

On August 30, 1976, the Eighth Circuit Court of Appeals overturned Judge Lord's logging decision. By December 1976, the injunctions had been lifted, the winter roads were frozen solid, and logging was imminent on several of the previously enjoined sales. On December 29, 1976, Representative Oberstar announced that, with the U.S. Forest Service acting as mediator, he had persuaded Boise Cascade, Abitibi Corporation (the new owners of the East and West Tofte sale contracts), Potlatch Forests (Northwest Paper), and Kainz Lumber Company to suspend cutting on their timber contracts for six months so that Congress could consider the issue without confrontations or ongoing damage to the ecosystem. As a practical matter the moratorium would last until September 15, 1977, because meanwhile the Forest Service had imposed a ban on logging during the summer canoeing season.

In November 1976, the Carter-Mondale administration was elected. When the Washington, D.C. hearings finally occurred on the Fraser and Oberstar bills in September 1977, the administration unveiled a proposed bill that would have terminated all logging. After the hearings, the logging moratorium was extended.

The administration proposal became the model for a new draft bill unveiled in March 1978 under the sponsorship of Phillip Burton of California, chair of Interior's National Parks and Insular Affairs subcommittee, and Minnesota's Representative Bruce Vento of St. Paul. The Burton-Vento bill called for termination of logging. On April 10, 1978, the full Interior Committee voted to send the Burton-Vento bill to the House floor with its logging ban intact. On June 5, 1978, the House of Representatives passed H.R. 12250, an amended version of the Burton-Vento bill that still incorporated the key logging language.

On October 15, 1978, in the last hours of the Ninety-fifth Congress, both the House and Senate passed a further amended version of H.R. 12250 that still contained provisions for the termination of logging. Six days later on October 21, 1978, President Jimmy Carter signed the bill, and Public Law 95-495 became a law of the land.

With respect to logging, Public Law 95-495 accomplished the following:

• Paragraph 4(d)(5) of the Wilderness Act was repealed and superseded by provisions of Public Law 95-495.

- The secretary of agriculture was directed to terminate all timber sale contracts in the BWCAW within one year, and there was to be no further logging of the virgin forest areas formerly enjoined by the federal district court.
- Ameliorative measures were to be taken, including land and cover restoration on logged areas, to "make the imprint of man's work substantially unnoticeable."
- The logging companies were given either substitute timber or compensation for losses.
- An annual appropriation of $11,000,000 was authorized for the intensification of forestry on national forest, state, and county lands outside the BWCAW in Minnesota through the year 1990.

Thus ended some 93 years of logging in portions of the Boundary Waters. The last logging that I am aware of, other than the authorized 1-year cleanup of the six enjoined sales, was on a St. Louis County timber sale during the winter of 1978–79 within an addition to the BWCAW just northwest of Big Moose Lake. About 160 acres of virgin pine and spruce were clear-cut on this operation. It was within the 1-year termination period authorized by the act, but it illustrates the problem created by county inholdings, of which the U.S. Forest Service has little effective control.

Ecological Effects of the Pulpwood Logging Era

The legacy of the pulpwood logging era in the BWCAW is damage to the natural landscape and ecosystem substantially exceeding that of the early big-pine logging. Many of the extensive jack pine forest areas that were logged on the Tomahawk Sale and several other large sales did not regenerate to jack pine. Some limited areas were reseeded to this species or came back naturally, but many were either planted to red pine and white spruce or left to the scattered aspen, birch, fir, and shrubs that were not removed by the loggers. Thus there was a semipermanent shift in species composition of the forest on large areas, especially where herbicides or rock-raking were used.

Perhaps as serious is the temporary road system within the former portal zone. Literally hundreds of miles of gravel roads existed, and far more bulldozed and slightly graded dirt spur roads. Some of the main gravel roads had significant cuts and fills not removed in the ameliorative measures that were taken. These road grades will surely exist for hundreds of years. Fortunately, however, nature will partially heal these scars rather quickly, because bare gravel and earth are excellent seedbeds for most native trees and shrubs, and many are already coming back to tree cover. After a few decades, the most noticeable evidence of these roads will be their leveled surfaces and cuts and fills. The Forest Service did remove many culverts and most bridges, restoring natural drainage patterns. In some areas the Forest Service also planted trees on the abandoned roadbed, especially near portage crossings. Some old roads have been designated as "hiking trails" and will evidently be kept open.

From the standpoint of terrestrial wildlife habitat and populations, the effects were complex and will be discussed in chapters 12 and 13. Many of these effects relate to changes in the gross landscape patterns of forest age classes, and in the percentage of the landscape converted from conifer forest to aspen-birch-fir and other communities with a lesser percentage of conifers than the virgin forests contained. In general, all logged areas were converted to young age classes over a span of about 30 to 40 years, and many areas were converted to forest communities with a greatly changed species composition, often involving reduced representation of native conifers in the overstory canopy. Such changes benefited some species of mammals and birds and had negative effects on others.

The positive side of the story is the extent of the still remaining virgin forest areas. Public Law 95-495 came soon enough to save slightly more than half of the BWCAW from logging. The remaining virgin areas are identified, and their stand-origin years are shown on maps. (A selection of these maps is in appendix D.) My estimate is that some 545,000 acres of landscape in large contiguous areas have never been logged or otherwise significantly altered by people. The actual area of virgin forest, excluding lakes, marshes, treeless bogs, and barren rock fields, is about 400,000 acres. These figures include the areas within the enjoined timber sales that were not logged, plus several virgin areas within the 50,000 acres of additions to the

BWCAW affected by Public Law 95-495. These are minimum figures for truly virgin forest because numerous virgin stands of a few acres to several hundred acres occur within the logged regions. Such areas were not cut, because the species present were not wanted, because the timber was too small, or because of several other reasons, some of which are unique to particular tracts. It has not been feasible to map or locate such stands on the ground. As a rule, for perhaps another decade or two, one can assume that an area was not logged if no stumps are present within the stand in question. Some stumps will usually persist for roughly a century in this part of Minnesota, especially if the cut trees were pine or cedar. Aspen, spruce, fir, and birch stumps rot away quickly. Logged areas can also readily be seen on aerial photographs taken within 20 or 30 years after the cutting. Of course, in the BWCAW the presence of abandoned roads is an indication that logging did occur, especially if there is a pattern of spur roads fanning out from a main haul road. Some roads, however, passed through stands that were not cut.

The Dynamic Forest Mosaic Yesterday and Today

As we have seen, the virgin forests of the Boundary Waters are a patchwork of various stand-age classes and forest communities resulting from a long history of fires of various sizes, shapes, and intensities. Sometimes the community boundaries coincide with age-class boundaries, and sometimes they do not. The reason is that fire does its work on a landscape base that includes topography, soils, and landforms, factors that influence nutrient and moisture availability and local climates, determine fire barriers, and interact with fire behavior, intensity, and long-distance spread. These factors influence fire effects and postfire forest-community composition as well.

Many of the virgin forest patches and stand boundaries can be seen from a canoe or along a portage. They are even more visible from an airplane or on air photos, and they can be seen to some extent on satellite multispectral images (plate 4). The total picture is a mosaic of patches, much like the patches on a quilt or the patterns in a child's kaleidoscope. Fire is the force that rearranges the patches, now much less frequently than in the past. Patterns also exist in the forest vegetation of logged areas in the Boundary Waters, Quetico, and Voyageurs, but the nature of these patterns and their causes are quite different.

The nature, scale, and dynamics of the forest vegetation mosaic have much to do with the productivity, diversity, and stability of the Boundary Waters ecosystem. The goal of this chapter is to describe the complex interactions that produced the mosaic, the changes it is undergoing, and the implications of the new mosaic pattern for the future of the ecosystem. These aspects are first examined in the virgin forests that originated before European settlement, to show how the natural system works. The examination is done from the viewpoint of the new discipline of landscape ecology, standing back and looking at the shifting mosaic of forest communities and age classes from a total ecosystem perspective.

The Forest Mosaic before European Settlement

The stand-origin maps (see appendix D for a selection) and fire-year maps (figure 6.4a–d) give us valuable tools to look back in time. From them we have at least a partial record of how fire regulated the distribution of forest age classes on specific BWCAW landscape units and on the total landscape from about 1610 to 1910, a 300-year period when there was no significant human fire control. The very processes that created the age-class mosaic produced a record clouded by the overlapping of earlier fires by later fires. I probably missed many fires of the period 1610 to 1727, and the boundaries of most fires in that era are uncertain at best. For this discussion I use the maps and data for the period 1727 through 1910 for most purposes. The period 1868 through 1910 includes most of what I call the Settlement Period, but my analysis of fire occurrence suggests that European settlement activities did not markedly increase the percentage of the virgin areas burned per century. Several large areas of the present virgin forest did originate from fires in that period. For these reasons I use the entire period from 1727 through 1910 for this discussion and note any effects that might be due to settlement activities.

EFFECTS OF PATCH SIZE AND SHAPE

The size of a stand-age-class patch is initially defined by the burned area of the stand-killing crown fire or high-intensity surface fire that caused the replacement of a previous forest community. A patch may be anywhere from an acre or less to hundreds of square miles in area. Its external boundaries are typically irregular in shape, reflecting the varied fuel, weather, and landscape factors that caused the fire to move in various directions and then finally go out in particular places. Often, for example, a patch edge will coincide for some distance with a lakeshore, stream, valley bottom, or wetland margin. Within a burn the numerous unburned or partially burned areas may make the new stand-age class look something like Swiss cheese when viewed from aircraft or on air photos. The skipped areas are seen as patches themselves, but they no longer outline the fire that created their age class.

The landscapes of the Boundary Waters were crisscrossed repeatedly by stand-replacing fires that generated new age-class patches and reduced earlier patches to remnants that no longer fully outlined the fires that created them. This process of stand-age-class generation and modification by fire produced the forest-age-class mosaic of today in the remaining virgin forests of the Boundary Waters.

The stand-origin and fire-year maps show the effects of this process and help to visualize it. Even a research fire ecologist needs to see real crown fires in action and explore many recent burns to decipher successfully the forest-age-class mosaic and visualize past fire movements. It helps to think like a forest fire. Where did that fire start? Where did it go? Where did it finally go out? Unless there are living witnesses or historical records, we must determine the answers from the patterns of remnant patches and fire-scarred trees still present on the landscape. Only the last

fire on a given landscape still shows its full boundaries as a stand-age class. To reconstruct earlier burns requires detective work—the older the burn, the fewer the clues. For example, on the stand-origin map for the Takucmich Lake quadrangle (figure D.1), all the final fire perimeters are shown only for the fires of 1894. What areas did the fires of 1864 or 1755 burn? The edge of a burn is usually shown only where stands of that age class adjoin older forests or the edge of a nonforest area such as a lake. Where an age class adjoins younger stands, the possibility of an overlapping burn must be considered. The fire-year maps give the best visual feel for the initial range in sizes and shapes of burns before European settlement, but the stand-origin maps provide a better look at fine-scale variations in burn intensities and skipped areas and the long-term effects of reburning on the total vegetation mosaic.

Patch size and shape and uniformity of the burn depend on fuel continuity, drought severity, landform factors, and weather at the time of the burn. Severe drought, high temperatures, high winds, low humidity, and unbroken expanses of fuel on uniform terrain make for large, uniform, high-severity burns. Areas burned at night with low winds or during and just after light rains or heavy dew may show less overstory kill and in some cases less consumption of the organic layer. Even though the Boundary Waters is not mountainous, terrain factors often induce variable fire effects. The bases of slopes, valley bottoms, lakeshore areas, north slopes, and lowlands or wetlands are more often skipped by fires or burned at lower intensity and with less organic-matter consumption than are ridges, south slopes, and large gently rolling uplands. Areas so situated that they happen to be burned by a fire backing against the wind as opposed to a head fire also often show less severe fire effects. All of these factors, plus the important differential effects of fuels and seed sources of the forest community and age class burned, produce the variations in patch size, shape, and uniformity in postfire plant communities.

Turner and Romme (1994) point out that variations in burn patch size and fire severity may have important differential effects on the death and reestablishment of plant species and communities. Depending on burn severity and organic-matter consumption, the effects of fire are often quite different for species with light, highly dispersed seeds or spores in contrast to those that reproduce from seeds or other structures in organic layers or from canopy-stored seeds (Rowe 1983). Shade-tolerant species such as balsam or cedar must reinvade heavily burned areas from the edge of the burn and are thus sensitive to patch size and fire severity, as are fire-resistant species such as red and white pine. Large high-severity burns with few unburned areas are initially repopulated by trees with canopy-stored seeds such as jack pine and black spruce if present in the burned stand, or else by invaders with light seeds such as aspen and birch. As described in chapters 4 and 7, there also is a whole suite of shrubs, herbs, and mosses with varying degrees of adaptation to patch size, burn severities, and distance to unburned seed-source areas.

THE CHANGING COMPOSITION OF THE AGE-CLASS MOSAIC

When surface fires burn through stands of thick-barked red and white pine more than about 60 years old, many trees may survive even intense surface fires with local crowning out. As shown in chapters 6 and 7, fires of the latter type often opened up stands sufficiently to permit survival of enough seed trees to restock the burned-out openings. The size of the open areas regenerated by this process varied from small irregular patches of only an acre or so to much larger areas hundreds of acres in extent. In the latter cases, scattered groups of old seed trees must have survived the fire throughout the area. This mechanism created the groves of multi-age-class red and white pines so often seen in the virgin forests today.

This process of stand renewal created a mosaic of forest age classes quite different from that resulting from the large stand-replacing crown fires typical of the extensive boreal conifer-broadleaf areas, which typically regenerated to vast even-aged stands of jack pine, black spruce, aspen, and birch, with only islands of unburned older forest here and there, or an occasional surviving older tree. At the time logging began in 1895, about a quarter of the present BWCAW was occupied by red and white pine stands, most of which must have exhibited multi-age-class structures.

The old red and white pine groves in the Boulder Bay-Lady Boot Bay-Coleman Island region of Lac La Croix and near Oyster Lake, Lake Agnes, and the Boulder River offer excellent opportunities to see a full range of fire-created stand-age-class structures, which can be appreciated by study of the stand-origin maps and then by canoe and on foot. For example, in the Coleman Island and Lake Agnes regions (figures D.2 and D.4) many patches date from fires in 1681, 1755–59, 1784, and 1796. Such groves or extensive forests of red and white pine adjoin younger forest patches dating from fires in 1864 or 1894. Many of the older patches are designated by double or triple age-class notations, with the top date indicating the year of the fire from which the oldest overstory trees date. Some stands were not visited but were mapped from forest-type maps and air photos. For these stands the dates shown are extrapolations from the pattern of fires and stand origins elsewhere in the locality.

Where two or more age classes were identified, at least three possible stand-age-class structures may exist. Perhaps the most common is for the oldest pines to occur in small groups and as scattered individuals within a stand that consists mainly of their progeny, a frequent combination in the Lac La Croix region being a few 1681 veterans within a stand largely of 1755–59 origin. In this case some of the old veterans have fire scars that date the younger stand. Sometimes few living seed trees remain, and the stand consists almost entirely of ancient veterans. Another common structure consists of small groves of one age class, often covering only an acre or less, merging imperceptibly into adjoining stands of a different age. Still another possibility is a patchwork of adjoining stands of different ages, each covering several acres, and sometimes of different species composition, but still covering an area small enough that it is not feasible to map the separate age classes at the scale of a USGS quadrangle. Mapping is even more difficult when all three possible age structures exist in an area of old pines covering less than a square mile.

It is not feasible to map all the age-structure variability in most multiaged areas of old pines, because of the limitations of map scales as well as the enormity of the fieldwork required to work out the details in each stand. The stand-origin maps do give a picture of age-structure variations within the larger patches of virgin red and white pine, and they clarify the overall pattern of the fire-created age-class mosaic in the extensive areas of old pine. If anything, the actual stand-origin picture in many stands is even more complex than that shown on the maps. Frissell (1973) documented similar stand-age structures in virgin red and white pine at Itasca State Park, Minnesota, as did Cwynar (1977) in Algonquin Provincial Park, Ontario.

FORMER AGE-CLASS MOSAICS OF AREAS CUT IN THE BIG-PINE LOGGING ERA

We have no effective means of reconstructing the age-class mosaic of the approximately 184,000 acres of upland forest in the BWCAW logged in the big-pine logging era between 1895 and 1940. We know that much but not all of that area was occupied by groves and in some areas by continuous stands of mature white and red pine that probably had a fire history similar to that just outlined. At least some of the oldest pine stands cut in the early years probably dated from fires in about 1610, 1595, or even earlier. However, many stands probably dated from later fires. Most stands that originated after fires in the 1800s would not have contained many trees large enough to interest the loggers and were probably not cut. Many of the logged areas presumably supported a complex mosaic of multiaged groves of pines similar to the remaining stands of virgin white and red pine in the BWCAW. Some areas, especially of old white pine, may not have had significant fire activity since the fire that initiated the stand, but probably most stands had seen one or more surface fires of varying intensity. Many old pines probably bore fire scars that could have been used to reconstruct the fire history of these areas by the methods used in the present virgin areas. That option was foreclosed by the early logging, and the age structure of the forest mosaic in those areas will remain unknown. However, the scenario outlined here checks well with the description of the pine lands of the region by Ayres in 1899.

The stands of big pine that were cut must have been interspersed with areas of younger age classes of white and red pine, jack pine, black spruce, aspen, birch, balsam, and red maple, just like the virgin pine areas of the BWCAW and Quetico today. Those intervening areas probably supported stands that dated from fires in 1801–3, 1815, 1822, 1824, 1827, 1834, 1846, 1854, 1863–64, and 1875. In addition, there must have been at least some areas within the mosaics of the logged area that were in recent burns dating from the fires of 1894, 1900, 1903, 1904, and 1910. Much of the land that supported these younger age classes apparently reburned in the same fires that burned the big-pine slashings nearby, making it difficult to map out local areas that were not logged. The presence of old stumps is proof of logging, but failure to find stumps leaves uncertainty unless the stand-age class predates logging in the vicinity.

PATCH TURNOVER BEFORE EUROPEAN SETTLEMENT

The turnover of stand-age-class patches in the forest mosaic with the passage of time was obviously a more complex process in white and red pine areas than in the single-age-class areas of boreal conifer-broadleaf forests. Many burns in the big-pine areas were probably light to moderate surface fires that burned out seedlings and saplings of balsam, spruce, cedar, and red maple and shrub understories but only scarred a few old pines and perhaps killed small understory pines and occasional mature trees. Then at much longer intervals more severe fires killed large patches of old pine, leaving veterans here and there as well as nearly intact groves nearby. Thus in red and white pine stands some fires probably left the age-class mosaic intact over considerable areas, and others generated small new age-class patches here and there, or at least added a new age-class component to some stands. Then after long intervals, perhaps often as long as from 1755 to 1864 (109 years), a major drought was accompanied by numerous ignitions and episodes of weather favorable for high-intensity large-scale fires that produced major reshuffling of the age-class mosaic, as did the fires of 1681, 1755, and 1864 in the Lac La Croix region.

The possible effects on the age-class mosaic of the 1863–64 fires are interesting. These fires did generate vast new age classes of jack pine, black spruce, and aspen-birch forests but only occasional new stands of red and white pine. Did this reflect the severity of the burns? Were more old pine stands eliminated than were regenerated by these fires? Were significant areas that had been in white and red pine for centuries converted to jack pine–black spruce and aspen–birch? It is difficult to answer these questions from field evidence, but some of the General Land Office Survey notes taken between 1875 and 1895 suggest these possibilities. There is no guarantee that fire will always simply rearrange the age-class mosaic without significantly changing the distribution of forest communities on the landscape. We do know from paleobotanical evidence that no truly major shift in forest composition occurred, but it is likely that certain fire years produced some net change in forest-community areas.

The fire-year maps provide a basis for educated guesses at the age-class mosaic just before the 1863–64 fires in many virgin areas now occupied by boreal conifer-broadleaf forests if we assume that the previous forests were as now largely composed of single-age-class stands of these species. With my calculated fire rotation of about 100 years, perhaps three-quarters of the landscape of the BWCAW saw a nearly complete reshuffling of the age-class mosaic in a century or less. No such simple reconstruction is possible for the multi-age-class red and white pine portions of the total vegetation mosaic that exist today. We do not know what areas of these species may have been lost, nor what age classes may have disappeared from the existing multiaged mosaic either as a result of the 1863–64 fires or through mortality in the ensuing century. We do know that many of the existing areas of old pine have been there for centuries, but describing their age-class turnover history quantitatively is not a simple matter.

FADING OF PATCH DISTINCTNESS WITH TIME

When an intense crown fire burns a swath through a mature stand of trees, say a 70-year-old jack pine–black spruce forest, the contrast between the remaining unburned stand and the new burn is dramatic. The comparison is between a field of fire-blackened snags and a 65-foot-tall stand of green pines and spruce. Forty years after the fire, the snags

are down, many are decayed, and the new stand is about 40 feet tall, still dense but beginning to thin. The adjacent stand that did not burn is now 110 years old, has grown only a few feet more in height, and is showing the first signs of senescence. A few dominant jack pines have died standing, and a few have been uprooted. Some codominant black spruce may be filling the gaps, and balsam seedlings and saplings are appearing in the new stand openings. The contrast between the young forest and the old is still evident to a perceptive observer, but many canoeists would paddle by without recognizing the fire boundary. A century after the fire, the "new" forest is 75 feet tall and has opened up through gradual death of suppressed trees, balsam saplings are coming in, and here and there a big jack pine or spruce has died. In the 170-year-old adjoining forest jack pine and black spruce are still dominant but have grown little in height, and many have died. Much balsam has matured, but the spruce budworm has killed many, and new balsam saplings are filling the gaps. A forester or ecologist should be able to recognize the fire boundary if actively looking for it, but most casual visitors would never notice.

This fading of the difference between stand-age classes with the passing of time after fire is of more than historic or aesthetic interest. It homogenizes the mosaic of vegetation and fuels and has biological significance for many plants and animals. Fading of the stand-age-class boundaries over vast areas could potentially lead to even larger fires than occurred before European settlement. Some fire boundaries were certainly difficult to see even in presettlement times, and some stands escaped fire for long periods. Fire frequency then was high enough that many stands must have contrasted sharply with adjoining age classes. New burns were common at intervals of only a decade or two and certainly broke up the fuels mosaic to a considerable extent at times.

Today after 80 years of fire suppression, many stand-age-class boundaries are like those in the last stage of the preceding hypothetical example. A case in point is the boundary between the 1863–64 year classes and the 1894 year classes in the Lac La Croix region. In the 1920s and 1930s the perimeter of the 1894 burns must have been very clear. Even in the late 1960s, when I traced those boundaries, I could usually see a distinct contrast at the fire perimeter. Today both age classes are old enough that dominant trees have nearly reached their maximum heights, and senescence is under way. The structure of their plant communities, their forest fuels, and their potential as habitat for many plants, birds, and mammals have been homogenized by the changes that accompany forest maturation and the onset of senescence. Turner and Romme (1994) have shown through landscape modeling that a qualitative shift from a fragmented vegetation and fuels mosaic to a connected mosaic occurs when about 60 percent of the landscape contains susceptible fuels. As time passes, and few significant burns occur in the Boundary Waters because of fire suppression, the vegetation and fuels gradually lose their diversity as the age-class mosaic slowly fades away.

Stability of the Patch Mosaic before European Settlement

The literature concerning forest ecosystems subject to disturbance regimes is replete with discussions of the effect of various kinds of disturbance on the stability of the system. Several writers suggest that even though such events as fires or windstorms repeatedly set back succession in portions of an ecosystem, over some larger area the system as a whole may be in a dynamic steady state (Cooper 1913; Heinselman 1973; Wright 1974; Foster 1983).

Such a landscape-scale equilibrium, which Bormann and Likens (1979) called a "shifting-mosaic steady state," might be looked for in the fire-dependent ecosystems of large wilderness areas and parks such as the BWCAW, Quetico, and Yellowstone. Pickett and White (1985) hypothesized that equilibrium is most likely in systems that experience frequent small-scale disturbances over relatively large areas as opposed to those with infrequent but large-scale disturbances. Through simulation modeling, Shugart and West (1981) found that a landscape should be at least 50 times the size of individual disturbance patches to accommodate the disturbances while still keeping the total land-

scape in quasi-equilibrium (Urban, O'Neill, and Shugart 1987). According to Urban, O'Neill, and Shugart (1987, 125), "In a national park that is large enough to incorporate wildfire, a constant and predictable proportion of fire-successional vegetation (perhaps critical habitat for some species) is maintained. Conversely, a park that is too small to incorporate a natural wildfire regime does not lend itself to straightforward predictions of the relative abundance of patch types." To meet Shugart and West's criterion for a landscape in equilibrium with fire, a protected Boundary Waters reserve subject to the fire regime that existed before European settlement would have to encompass about 20 million acres to accommodate occasional fire patches as large as 400,000 acres. That is an area as large as the entire forested region of Minnesota. In a smaller area there apparently would be large fluctuations over time in the proportion of the area occupied by various age classes and forest communities.

Turner and Romme (1994) note that the criteria for equilibrium or steady-state conditions have not been consistent among researchers. Various authors have defined these ideas to involve one or more of the following conditions: persistence of all species, no net change in biomass, and distributions of stand-age classes or successional stages that show little or no change over time.

A test of the stability of presettlement stand-age-class distributions in the BWCAW has actually been made by Baker (1989a,b), and similar tests have been made for portions of Yellowstone Park by Romme (1982), Romme and Despain (1989), and Turner and Romme (1994). Baker used data for the period 1727 to 1868 derived from my small-scale published fire-year maps (Heinselman 1973) to make his determinations for the BWCAW. Both reserves failed to meet the test for stable or equilibrium systems by the age-class distribution criterion.

This criterion requires a nearly constant proportion of the area in new burns, young stands, middle-aged stands, and old stands over a time span long enough to test the concept of equilibrium. The size of the park or wilderness is itself a factor influencing determinations of whether a stable patch distribution exists. For example, what conclusion would Baker have reached if he had considered the contiguous BWCAW, Quetico, and Voyageurs reserves to be a single ecological unit in his test? (He could not do this, because fire-year maps are not available for Quetico and Voyageurs for the period 1727–1868.) If all three areas had been included, the area to be evaluated for patch mosaic stability would have more than doubled. Baker dealt with this question by subdividing the BWCAW into several units and looking at the effect of increasing area on the stability of the patch mosaic. He concluded that there is no minimum area on which the mosaic pattern would have been stable.

Baker found that stability in the BWCAW was precluded not so much by the size of the fires or by too frequent burning of some areas, but by the failure of certain areas to burn at all in the entire period. He believes that it is primarily spatial heterogeneity in the environment or in the vegetation that precluded a stable patch mosaic. This conclusion may be correct, given the data he used, but the much greater detail on age-class-patch mosaics and logging history on my stand-origin maps might have led to a different analysis of the fire history and possibly to different conclusions if the maps had been available to Baker.

In reality the BWCAW before European settlement had three kinds of fire regimes that produced distinctly different forest communities and age-class mosaics within geographically identifiable subunits of the wilderness. This situation could not have been clear to Baker. At the time logging began in 1895, about a quarter of the total land area or 30 percent of the upland area was occupied by a complex of forest stands composed largely of multiaged groves of white and red pine (table 10.1). All but 17.5 percent of that virgin big-pine area was logged, mostly before 1940. The remaining virgin white and red pine areas clearly indicate that the logged big-pine stands must have had multiage structures. Furthermore, we know the old pine stands were concentrated near the larger lakes and streams, or downwind from them, on sites where fire intensity and behavior probably were ameliorated by their location on the landscape.

- Fire regime 1 consisted of light- to moderate-intensity surface fires at intervals of 10 to 50 years, and more severe fires that brought in new stand-age-class ele-

ments only at longer intervals, perhaps 150 to 200 years. Even these more severe fires rarely generated whole new age classes over thousands of contiguous acres. Virgin stands of old-growth red and white pine that were subject to this kind of fire regime still cover some 5 percent of the upland forest of the BWCAW, and a similar percentage of Quetico's forests. They constitute a rare and endangered old-growth forest unique in the eastern United States and western Ontario, deserving special attention in wilderness fire-management programs.

- Fire regime 2 was one of predominantly stand-replacing crown fires in boreal conifer-broadleaf forest complexes. These were the areas subject to the classic large-scale crown fires that came chiefly in major drought years, establishing new forest age classes over large areas. It apparently was the dominant fire regime over perhaps two-thirds of the BWCAW from 1727 to 1910, the period with the most reliable stand-origin data.

- Fire regime 3 is much less distinct, poorly known, and more ubiquitous in occurrence. It prevailed on the lowland and wetland forest sites occupied by mixed conifer swamp, ash-elm, tamarack bog, and some of the larger and wetter black spruce peatland communities. These sites apparently had regimes of long return-interval but fairly high-intensity surface fires or partial crown fires. Some black spruce bog forest communities had fire regimes similar to and linked to adjacent upland boreal conifer-broadleaf forests.

Fires in a single major fire year, or even a single large fire, might have burned all three kinds of areas, but the outcome in terms of stand replacement was often quite different.

PAST CLIMATIC CHANGE AND PATCH MOSAIC STABILITY

Climatic shifts sufficient to influence fire regimes must also be considered in any discussion of the long-term stability of forest age-class and community mosaics (Clark 1988, 1989, 1990a; Turner and Romme 1994). If we use a time period long enough to encompass periods with sig-

Table 10.1 / Areas of the Boundary Waters Canoe Area Wilderness occupied by virgin white and red pine forests in 1895 and 1979

Total upland forest, 1979	735,900 acres
Total upland forest logged, 1895–1940	184,000 acres
Percentage of total upland forest logged, 1895–1940	25.0%
Area of virgin red pine communities, 1979	17,700 acres
Area of virgin aspen-birch-white pine communities, 1979	21,400 acres
Total virgin white and red pine communities, 1979	39,100 acres
Total land area of virgin upland forest, all types, 1979	370,400 acres
Percentage of virgin upland in white and red pine, 1979	10.6%
Percentage of total upland in virgin white and red pine, 1979	5.3%
Total land area of BWCAW (excluding lakes, streams), 1979	904,000 acres
Percentage of total land in virgin white and red pine, 1979	4.3%
Total upland in white and red pine communities, 1895	223,100 acres
Percentage of total upland forest in white and red pine, 1895	30.3%
Percentage of total land area in white and red pine, 1895	24.7%
Area of virgin white and red pine 1979 as percentage of that in 1895	17.5%
Area in stands of all species dating from 1796 or earlier[a]	33,952 acres
Area in stands of all species dating from 1822 or earlier	62,528 acres
Percentage of total land in stands dating from 1796 or earlier	3.8%
Percentage of total land in stands dating from 1822 or earlier	6.9%

Note Virgin forests are those never logged, cleared, or otherwise directly altered by people. Nearly all areas have burned within the past 400 years, and most stands date from or formerly dated from one or more of these past fires. Areas are gross land areas that include some intermingled areas of young stands, but most of the area is or was in stands of 1822 or earlier origin, and much of it is or was in stands of 1796 or earlier origin. The virgin areas also exclude scattered areas of virgin white and red pine within the 400-ft. Shipstead-Newton-Nolan Act lakeshore reserves in areas of federal and state land logged after 1930.

[a] Figures for 1796 and 1822 or earlier origins given here do not include small areas in these age classes added to the BWCAW in 1978 under Public Law 95-49. Much of the area in these age classes is in red and white pine communities, especially that in stands of 1796 or earlier origin.

nificantly different climates in testing the stability of patch mosaics, we run the risk that some of the variability in age-class distributions will be due to climatic change instead of to shorter-term variations in droughts, fuels, vegetation, weather during fires, and the vagaries of ignition patterns.

Through precise charcoal analyses of annually laminated lake sediments and matching fire-scar dates, Clark (1988, 1989) has shown that fire frequency and severity have varied substantially in northwestern Minnesota in response

to climate between A.D. 1240 and 1980. These studies at Deming Lake and other lakes in Itasca State Park document climatic shifts from cool-moist until about 1420 to warm-dry from 1420 to 1600 and then back to cool-moist during the "Little Ice Age" from 1600 to 1900, when the present warmer and drier climate started. These differing climates were reflected in fire regimes that produced maxima in fire frequency and severity between about 1440 and 1600, followed by both decreased fire frequency and longer spacing between periodic episodes of major fires during the Little Ice Age. There still were several strong charcoal peaks during the Little Ice Age. These came around 1620, 1705, 1790, and 1880, close to periods of maximum fire activity documented by tree-ring data for Itasca obtained by Frissell (1973) and Clark and from the BWCAW by myself.

That Clark's results probably apply in principle to the Boundary Waters some 180 miles to the east of Itasca is indicated by similar results from the earlier and less detailed pollen and charcoal studies of Craig (1972) and Swain (1973) at Lake of the Clouds. Swain's pollen data suggest that spruce was increasing slightly while white pine was slowly decreasing during the Little Ice Age. Craig's pollen data show a gradual decrease in white pine up to the present from its postglacial peak about 4,300 years ago. This decrease is consistent with Clark's findings, with pollen and macrofossil studies in Ontario east of Lake Superior (Liu 1990) that show a decrease in white pine and an increase in spruce and jack pine beginning about 3,000 years ago near the edge of the boreal forest, and with a general southward increase in spruce in eastern North America over the past 3,000 years documented by many other paleoecological studies (Jacobson, Webb, and Grimm 1987). Thus it is likely that at the time logging began in the Boundary Waters, white pine and probably red pine were decreasing in response to climatic cooling and perhaps changed fire regimes, while the boreal spruces and perhaps jack pine were increasing.

WAS THE FOREST COMMUNITY AND AGE-CLASS MOSAIC EVER STABLE?

After the foregoing discussions of the many factors that influence the vegetation and age-class mosaic one might wonder whether the mosaic was ever stable, and whether it matters anyway. To deal with those questions, we first must recognize that change is a hallmark of natural systems.

We do know from pollen and macrofossil studies of lake sediments that over some undefined larger region centered in northeastern Minnesota, the forest vegetation retained essentially its present species composition for about 3,000 years, even though the relative abundance of some important trees shifted back and forth (Fries 1962; Craig 1972; Swain 1973). For many species there have not been drastic changes for even longer periods. White pine, for example, first attained population levels close to those at the time of European settlement about 6,000 years ago and did not experience a catastrophic decline until the logging era. By the time logging started, white pine had decreased to possibly half its peak abundance, which came some 4,500 years ago. Increases in spruce, northern white cedar, and perhaps jack pine in the past 3,000 years were significant and probably came in part at the expense of white and red pine, but these were gradual and natural adjustments to relatively small climatic shifts.

Such changes are not to be compared to the changes in the total vegetation of northeastern Minnesota wrought by the logging industry in the past 100 years, which are orders of magnitude greater than the changes that had occurred in the preceding 3,000 years. The recorded gradual and natural shifts in relative abundance of trees, shrubs, and herbs over the past 6,000 years came in an environment including periodic fires that burned over most of the landscape at least once a century. In this sense there was a quasi-stable fire-dependent ecosystem over the entire life of the present forest complex, with only gradual shifts in the relative abundance of species as the climatic environment itself slowly changed (Wright 1974). Thus, given a large enough region, the fluctuations in stand-age classes and forest-community composition induced by climate and weather-related variations in fire size and intensity did not result in catastrophic changes in the total forest mosaic over millennia, even though at some smaller scale there undoubtedly were large changes at times.

Our interest in the long-term stability of the forest community and age-class mosaic is twofold. First, we want to understand how the natural system works; and second, we need to know how we can best provide for the continued functioning of the natural system in the BWCAW, Quetico, and Voyageurs, given their area constraints, the condition of their biotas, and their present social and economic settings. I return to these interests when I consider the present forest mosaic and the fire-management options available.

Is the Climate Still Favorable for the Renewal of the Virgin Forests through Natural Fire?

The present virgin forests mostly originated before European settlement in response to the climate and fire regimes of the Little Ice Age. The climate of the twentieth century might have produced fire regimes significantly different from those that regenerated the existing virgin forests if the regimes had not been altered by fire suppression. The warm-dry climate of the early twentieth century appears unprecedented in the last 2,000 years, and in the past lesser changes altered fire regimes significantly at Itasca State Park (Clark 1988, 1989, 1990a,b).

Even small changes in temperature and precipitation can directly affect such basic ecosystem processes as biomass production and organic-matter accumulation, but the indirect effect of such climatic changes on fire frequency and severity could have crucial implications for the reproductive success of trees with narrow fire-regime requirements. Red and white pine, for example, need occasional fire-free intervals of 20 to 40 (or even 60) years for new trees to reach fire-resistant sizes, and the twentieth-century climate might not have allowed enough such opportunities, Clark believes. The Boundary Waters is much farther from the prairie/forest transition zone than Itasca, and perhaps the changes in fire regimes would not have been as great as at Itasca.

Perhaps the best indication that the climate itself is still favorable for the fire-mediated regeneration of most Boundary Waters trees is the success of these species on the burns of 1903, 1904, 1910, 1917, 1918, 1929, 1936, 1961, 1974, and 1976, the major twentieth-century fire years. Numerous examples of the successful regeneration of virtually all tree species on many burns of these years can be found in the BWCAW and Quetico, even though fire suppression has dramatically limited the total area of such burns. This observation, of course, does not answer Clark's concern that shortened interfire intervals might have reduced the number of mature white and red pines enough to cause significant declines if suppression had not reduced fire frequency. Thus the question remains, would a natural fire regime in the twentieth century have caused significant

shifts in the forest community and age-class mosaic? A clear answer may be unobtainable, but in any case, as we shall discover in the next chapter, this may not be a concern that should affect fire-management policies and programs.

Would a Climax Forest Be More Diverse and Stable than a Fire-Renewed Forest Mosaic?

According to the early ecologists (Clements 1916), the "climax" is the final outcome of plant successions that result in a community so well adjusted to the prevailing climate and other environmental factors that it is self-reproducing and self-maintaining in the absence of major disturbances. It is fair to say that to this day the climax concept, which is still taught in many schools, has so pervaded the popular view of forest ecology that the very idea of a climax forest is surrounded with a certain aura of reverence that closes many minds to the known facts of forest history. Even some ecologists still suffer from a fixation on succession and climax. Is it surprising then that the interested layperson is confused? With that introduction, let us look at the climax concept as it has been applied to the forests of the northern Lake Superior region.

Cooper (1913) made the first extensive studies of forest succession in the region in his landmark work on Isle Royale. He defined a white spruce-balsam fir-paper birch climax forest community for the island, although he also made many other perceptive observations of vegetation change, including postfire changes. Numerous later studies have refined the views of succession in the region (e.g., Buell and Niering 1957; Ohmann and Ream 1971), but except for the addition of northern white cedar to the list of important late successional trees, Cooper's list of climax species remains essentially intact. In the last few decades, however, most forest ecologists and others in related disciplines have focused more on ecosystem processes and functions, vegetation classification, and the actual record of vegetation development as recorded by tree-ring, pollen, macrofossil, and charcoal analyses.

Early disagreements can be found in the literature with respect to the end point of succession, such as Bergman and Stallard's (1916) espousal of a white pine climax, but for northeastern Minnesota and adjacent Ontario a consensus has long existed that in the absence of fire, blowdowns, or other major disturbances, some combination of balsam fir, white spruce, black spruce, white cedar, and paper birch would eventually occupy most sites. The pines and aspen are unable to reproduce successfully beneath the deep shade of these species, and when the pines and aspen eventually die, the shade-tolerant balsam, spruce, and cedar tend to replace them.

In the real world many problems exist with this simple scenario. The most serious is that it fails to recognize the prevalence of fire as an integral part of the natural environment. Studies in the BWCAW failed to turn up any significant upland forest areas lacking evidence of past fire, or even lacking at least some overstory trees that dated from the last fire. Even white spruce, balsam, and cedar often seed in directly on new burns, so their presence does not necessarily indicate an old self-replacing forest.

Furthermore, balsam and white spruce are extremely vulnerable to the spruce budworm, which periodically decimates their populations, especially where old stands develop over large areas (Hardy, Mainville, and Schmitt 1986). Spruce and balsam are also very shallow-rooted and thus prone to windthrow. When old fir-spruce stands are ravaged by the budworm and/or are wind-damaged, their fire potential increases significantly (Stocks 1987b).

White pine and red pine can persist without fire for up to 350 or possibly even 400 years for occasional individuals, but without a fire that creates favorable conditions for stand renewal, most stands will eventually be replaced by balsam and spruce as the old pines die. Jack pine can persist as scattered individuals for up to about 250 years on some sites, but most stands have virtually lost their jack pine component by 200 years after fire. Postfire upland black spruce stands also generally break up by 200 years, but because black spruce is much more shade tolerant than jack pine, there often is considerable spruce regeneration even without fire, although balsam often virtually takes over the site. Aspen-birch stands normally break up by 130 to 180 years after fire, and again balsam is the most common replacement.

If fire were excluded from the Boundary Waters ecosystem for additional centuries, we can foresee a timetable for the homogenization of most virgin upland forests to a balsam-spruce-birch complex. The vast jack pine, upland black spruce, and aspen forests of 1863–64 origin would be largely replaced by the year 2065. The 1894 stands of these trees would be gone by 2100. The 1910 stands would be gone by 2115. And most of the present virgin red and white pine stands, which date largely from fires of 1796 or earlier, would be replaced between 2000 and 2200. Even the 1822, 1864, and 1894 stands of the big pines would be gone by 2300.

Consider what this hypothetical climax forest would be like. All three pines and aspen would be virtually lost from the system. Vast upland areas now occupied by these species would be dominated by a complex of balsam fir, scattered white and black spruce, paper birch, white cedar, and probably a few red maples. Peatland forests would probably be dominated by all-aged stands of mistletoe-ravaged black spruce, and on the richer swamp sites by cedar. As the dying pines, upland black spruce, and aspen succumbed, a jumble of down timbers would occupy large areas as each age class in turn met its fate. The balsam and spruce that largely replaced them would soon be engulfed in a nearly perpetual spruce budworm outbreak as more and more of the landscape became occupied by the budworm's host species.

This scenario could be a recipe for fire disasters unlike any the ecosystem has experienced. Clark's (1989) data certainly suggest that such a long fire-free interval would lead to fires of greater than normal intensity. Stock's (1987b) data on fire behavior in budworm-killed balsam indicate that at times of extensive budworm-caused mortality the fire potential would be great. Turner and Romme (1994) argue convincingly that as the vegetation becomes homogenized by the fading of the presettlement fire-generated age-class mosaic, the fuels would become connected across much of the landscape, leading to the potential for fires to roam at will over most upland and many peatland areas. There have been very large fires before, as we have seen, but now seed sources for the pines would be gone and the fire-sensitive balsam, white spruce, and cedar could be easily eliminated by fire over vast areas. The landscape would then lie open to colonization by the light-seeded aspens and to sprouters like birch, alder, willow, and hazel. The final result might be a vegetation unlike any that has existed in postglacial time, except perhaps for that of the most heavily burned-over former pine lands in the cutover counties of Minnesota in the 1920s.

It should be clear from this discussion that the climax balsam-spruce-birch-cedar forest, if it did develop through fire exclusion, would possess much less diversity in species, age classes, and structure than did the presettlement fire-generated forest mosaic. It would also be less stable through greater vulnerability to fire, insect destruction, and windthrow. If widespread fires did finally occur, as surely they would, the vegetation could then be even further destabilized and reduced in species diversity.

This scenario helps to show the direction in which fire exclusion is taking the virgin forests of the Boundary Waters. In reality there is no possibility of excluding fire so completely for so long that all the consequences discussed here would occur. The diversity and stability in the natural system owed its existence to the fire-generated mosaic of age classes and forest communities on the landscape. The within-stand diversity in any one vegetation type is often quite low in these near-boreal northern forests. It is the heterogeneity of the total mix of forest communities and stand-age classes on the landscape that produces the natural diversity necessary to sustain all native plants and animals in the ecosystem.

Biodiversity Values of the Virgin Red and White Pine and Boreal Forests of the Boundary Waters Reserves

Before leaving the subject of the changing patterns and stability of the forest mosaic of the Boundary Waters reserves, I should emphasize certain truly unique values of the remaining virgin forests. The BWCAW, Quetico, and Voyageurs together encompass the last large remnants of virgin red and white pine old-growth forests on the continent within fully protected wilderness reserves large enough to perpetuate this vanishing ecosystem through natural processes, including fire. Rough estimates of the area of

these old forests only for the BWCAW are shown in table 10.1, but within all three reserves there is probably a total of at least 50,000 acres. These forests together constitute a rare, endangered, and vanishing ecosystem resource unique on the continent. They once covered many millions of acres from Maine and New Brunswick westward to the prairies of Minnesota and Manitoba, and they contribute immeasurably to the biodiversity of the entire Boundary Waters regional ecosystem.

In 1990 I tried to assess the total old-growth forest resources of the BWCAW as a contribution to the discussion of the need for preservation of old growth in Minnesota. Table 10.1 summarizes some of the data. If we accept that all stands originating from fires in 1822 or earlier qualify as old growth, then in 1979 there were about 62,000 acres of virgin old-growth forests of all tree species combined in the BWCAW. Of these areas, some 33,000 acres dated from fires in 1796 or earlier. An estimated 39,100 acres of virgin forest in the white and red pine communities existed in 1979. An uncertain fraction of those communities occurred in forests originating from fires of 1822 or earlier. Estimates of the area of these old-growth red and white pine stands cannot be made with any precision from the data available. It is known that much of the forest of 1796 or earlier origin is comprised of old red and white pine groves, and some of the forest of 1801–3, 1815, and 1822 origin is also red and white pine. A rough approximation is that between 20,000 and 30,000 acres of virgin old-growth red and white pine are still present in the BWCAW.

I know where most of these stands are. A count of virgin red and white pine stands of 1822 origin or older on the 1948–54 Superior National Forest type maps, using the stand-origin maps as a guide, identified 329 individual stands over about 10 acres in area, some in large patches. Many of these stands were still there in 1992.

The largest concentrations of old red and white pine stands occur in the Lac La Croix region of the BWCAW. Here, near Boulder Bay, Lady Boot Bay, Fish Stake Narrows, Coleman Island, and the other eastern islands of Lac La Croix, the Boulder River, Lake Agnes, Ge-be-on-e-quet Lake, and Oyster Lake, about 6,400 acres of more or less contiguous red and white pine groves date from fires in

1801–3 or earlier, primarily 1784, 1755–59, and 1681, although the age structures of some groves are complex, and there is evidence of several other fires. Other BWCAW areas with extensive stands of old virgin pine that exhibit the range of age structures discussed in this chapter include the islands of Saganaga and Sea Gull lakes, and Duncan, Daniels, Rose, and Clearwater lakes. Still more locations where fine stands can be seen include Ramshead and Lamb lakes, the north end of Big Moose Lake, the east end of Cummings Lake, the north shore of Alder Lake, portions of Gaskin, Winchell, Horseshoe, and Cliff lakes, and the Old Pines Trail southeast of Disappointment Lake. Many other examples occur elsewhere. The stand-origin maps are the best guides. These areas escaped logging for a variety of reasons. Some were withdrawn from entry under the land laws in the early land withdrawals by President Theodore Roosevelt before the logging companies obtained cutting rights, and were then included in the first no-cutting areas designated by the Superior National Forest. Others were just too small in area or too remote to interest the timber companies. In other cases the Forest Service simply never put them up for sale before they were included in no-cutting areas or before Public Law 95-495 ended logging. Many fine stands were cut even after World War II.

Although I have no figures, Quetico must contain about as much old red and white pine as the BWCAW. For ex-ample, consider the north shores of Basswood and Knife lakes, and Kahshahpiwi, Yum Yum, Sarah, Brent, McIn-tyre, Darky, Camel, Argo, (Canadian) Agnes, and Emer-ald lakes, and portions of the Man Lakes chain.

Although it may be harder to see, the remaining virgin boreal conifer-broadleaf forests of the BWCAW and Quetico are also a vanishing ecosystem resource in the entire Great Lakes–St. Lawrence forest region. Where else are there extensive contiguous virgin forests of jack pine, black and white spruce, balsam fir, northern white cedar, aspen and paper birch within large nature reserves closed to logging? These forests, in their way, display just as remarkable adjust-ments to the climate, soils, geology, topography of the landscape, and fire as do the virgin red and white pine groves. The record of how that adjustment occurred over the centuries can still be read at the landscape scale in the patch mosaic of the virgin boreal forests. The total area of these virgin forests within the BWCAW and Quetico is of course much larger than that in virgin red and white pine. The boreal forests require a much larger land base to dis-play their adaptations to climate, landscape, and fire. Like the wolf, bald eagle, peregrine falcon, pine marten, and woodland caribou, the old-growth virgin red and white pine forests and the virgin boreal conifer-broadleaf forests of the Boundary Waters are truly rare and endangered eco-system elements from almost any perspective.

CHAPTER II

Fire-Management Programs to Maintain and Restore the Natural Forest Mosaic

Today the mosaic of forest communities and stand-age-class patches in the Boundary Waters is a product of three quite different histories affecting the mosaic itself and influencing the kinds of efforts needed to maintain or restore natural conditions:

- About half of the BWCAW and Quetico area is in virgin forests, where the distribution of communities reflects natural adjustments to soils, topography, local climate, and past fire regimes, even though the area occupied by particular communities and age classes has been modified by fire suppression.
- About a quarter of the forests of the BWCAW, Quetico, and Voyageurs are composed of communities modified by the early big-pine logging and subsequent slash fires.
- About a quarter of the forests of the BWCAW and Quetico and a considerable fraction of Voyageurs were logged for pulpwood and sawtimber after about 1945, and in these areas many communities were further modified by heavy equipment, tree planting, and sometimes herbicides and mechanical soil preparation.

These three histories have produced vegetation conditions that are significant in understanding the present forest mosaic and in constraining vegetation policy options for the reserves.

Status of the Forest Mosaic

THE VIRGIN FOREST AREAS

For the virgin forests of the BWCAW, we have a breakdown of the estimated areas occupied by each of the plant communities described in chapter 4 (table 4.1). The data on which the area estimates for the upland communities are based were collected between 1966 and 1974. Area data will probably change little in the next decade or so because most of these communities change quite slowly without logging or other large-scale direct artificial disturbances and with few fires. The lowland-type estimates are based on still older data, but most lowland communities change even more gradually. The percentage of the present virgin areas occupied by red and white pine communities (4.3 percent) is much lower now than it was for the total BWCAW before logging (24.7 percent) because the areas originally occupied by these big pines were sought out by the timber companies. But the proportion of red and white pine in the present virgin areas is the result of natural factors and has not been altered by logging within those specific areas.

The fire-driven renewal of stand-age classes in the virgin forest areas before European settlement has been virtually blocked by fire suppression since 1910 except for the relatively small fires of 1914, 1917, 1918, 1925, 1929, 1936, 1967,

1971, 1974, 1976, 1987, 1988, and 1991, as shown in the stand-origin maps. The virgin-forest landscape is therefore occupied especially by the age-class patches generated by the few major stand-replacing fires of the nineteenth century: 1894, 1875, 1863–64, and 1801–3.

The Cherokee Lake and Frost Lake fires of 1936 in the BWCAW give a good idea of the forest communities that could have been expected if larger burns in that major drought year had occurred. On the vast Kawnipi Lake burn of 1936 in Quetico, the scene has changed from one of fire-blackened snags as far as the eye could see to the present dense forest. The 1976 Roy Lake burn on Saganaga and Sea Gull lakes, the 1976 Fraser Lake burn on Fraser, Sagus, and Raven lakes in the BWCAW, and the 1961 Saganagons Lake burn in Quetico involved stand-replacing crown fires that consumed mature jack pine–black spruce and aspen-birch-fir forests. The Fraser Lake fire also burned a considerable area of white pine of 1875.

The multiaged groves of red and white pine that were maintained and renewed over the centuries by periodic light underburns and occasional more intense surface fires or partial crown fires are still there, but few have had significant fire since 1910. Many of these stands have developed dense understories of balsam, spruce, and sometimes cedar over the past half century, although that condition is more prevalent on fertile white pine sites than in red pine stands. On many sites the accumulation of humus, pine needles, twigs, and dead and down trees now constitutes a surface fuel potential considerably greater than would be present if one or more surface burns had occurred since 1910. Many stands, especially of red pine, have not had much successful recruitment of new age classes since then. Some, however, do have thickets of suppressed red or white pine saplings and poles here and there that might have developed into successful trees if they had been thinned by the kinds of surface fires that formerly burned through such stands every 20 to 50 years. Many trees of the oldest age classes (1648, 1681, 1692, 1727) are now becoming senescent. Numerous old pines have recently died standing, and more are clearly near death or have been windthrown, either by uprooting or breakage of the trunk. The overstory pines

of 1595 and 1610 are already virtually gone, replaced either by balsam, spruce, birch, and cedar or by younger red or white pines. On drier south, southeast, or southwest slopes and lakeshores where open red and/or white pine stands occur, some successful recruitment of saplings and poles of both big pines may be found. White pine blister rust, an imported European fungus present in the region since early in the twentieth century, has killed many white pines both large and small, but fortunately the fungus does not seem to be threatening the species with extinction here.

Quetico has had several large burns in its virgin areas in the twentieth century, for example, the Kawnipi, Saganagons, Camel, and Man lakes fires. Together these and other burns generated enough new age-class patches so that the virgin forest mosaic may not be so far different from a natural age structure. However, fire suppression has certainly produced a dearth of younger stands in Quetico also.

On the smaller islands, points, and peninsulas of lakes within the virgin forest, small camper-caused fires seem to have burned a higher percentage of the area than of comparable mainland areas. Fire-scars and age-class evidence suggest that such sites burned infrequently in the past, and the recent frequency of fires in these locations is clearly unnatural.

The fire rotation for the total virgin forest area of the present BWCAW after fire control became effective in 1911 was about 2,000 years up to 1987, when natural fire management began. This compares with a rotation of 100 years or less before European settlement. If continued, such a drastic reduction in fire would make it impossible to perpetuate even a semblance of the natural vegetation-age-class mosaic in the remaining virgin forests. The vast areas of boreal jack pine, black spruce, and aspen-birch forest originating in 1801–3, 1822, 1854, 1863–64, 1875, 1881, and 1894 are already senescent on a scale no doubt far beyond anything the ecosystem has experienced in the last 6,000 years. The oldest age classes are already in the last stages of conversion to unstable balsam-spruce-birch communities, and many of the younger stands are well on their way. Most of the older white and red pine groves lack the younger age-class components they must soon have if they are to persist long into the future. None of these conditions is unnatural in itself, of course. Large areas of old forests have always existed. It is the scale of the changes and the 80-year gap in the recruitment of new age classes that is unnatural. A natural, fire-generated mosaic of forest communities and age-class patches still exists on the landscape, but it has been virtually "frozen in time" for 80 years.

AREAS CUT IN THE BIG-PINE LOGGING ERA

In the areas logged between 1895 and 1940, the proportion of the upland area occupied by the various forest communities is substantially different today from that in the virgin forests of the BWCAW and from what it must have been before logging. The various jack pine- and red pine-dominated communities are less extensive than in the virgin areas, and the aspen and paper birch communities are larger. The stocking of white pine in the aspen-birch-white pine communities is much lower in the cutover areas, with vastly fewer large old pines. The lowland plant communities may not have been directly altered by cutting, but sleigh-haul roads often crossed them, and many lowlands burned in slash fires on adjacent uplands.

We do not have detailed data on the present age-class mosaic of the early logging areas because the age structure of their forests relates primarily to the time of logging or to the time of the last significant slash fire. We have generalized maps of many of the cutting areas and of the larger slash fires. Thus most upland stands date from between 1910 and 1930. In some cutover tracts enclaves exist where only an occasional big pine was cut or where no cutting occurred at all. If no slash fire spread into the stands, the present overstory trees may date from a prelogging fire. The lowland forests that were not cut within otherwise logged regions are also enclaves of virgin forest, some of considerable extent.

Some stands cut for big white and/or red pine have regenerated to a community similar to many virgin stands, especially if they were cut in the winter, so that the tree felling and skidding did little direct damage to the ground-layer vegetation except along narrow skid trails. If pine seedlings and saplings were present on the site and if no slash fire occurred after cutting, an adequate stocking of

the native pines may have occurred immediately after logging. Seed on the ground or from a good cone crop in the slash could regenerate if no subsequent slash fire occurred and if rainfall was adequate the next spring. Several good white and/or red pine seed trees left uncut could also provide seed. In a stand with only a few large merchantable pines, the smaller trees may not have been seriously injured by felling or skidding or killed by slash fires.

Otherwise, the cutover areas today support a variety of aspen-birch-fir, maple-birch, or jack pine and black spruce communities. So few white and/or red pines have survived that the big pines have little prospect of recovering to their former abundance for many decades if not centuries without deliberate seeding or planting. Restoration of the natural fire regime in such areas is probably not feasible, because of their altered vegetation and fuels mosaic. Even if fire could be reintroduced at natural frequencies and intensities, an adequate seed source for white and red pine would be missing.

AREAS LOGGED BETWEEN 1940 AND 1979

The areas logged in the BWCAW between 1940 and the termination of logging in 1979 were mostly jack pine and black spruce cut for pulpwood with mechanized logging practices quite different from those of the early big-pine operations. Aspen pulpwood was usually not taken, because of low demand before 1965.

The uplands are a heterogeneous mix of small patches of uncut virgin forest and larger cutover areas that were subjected to various postlogging regeneration practices (including no treatment at all). Most of the better-site black spruce bog forests that were cut are regenerating to a vegetation similar at least in species composition to the original type.

By 1940 the majority of the land in the present BWCAW was owned by the federal government, although the state and counties owned considerable land. Some private inholdings were logged, particularly by the U.S. Steel Corporation, which did little or no regeneration work following cutting.

On federal and state pine and spruce timber sales, large patches of aspen, birch, and balsam were usually left uncut, and red pine and/or spruce might have been planted in the skid roads and secondary haul roads. Aspen suckers, birch sprouts, and balsam seedlings generally took over much of the cutover area.

In pure jack pine and spruce stands all merchantable trees were clear-cut, and the slash was burned, followed by seeding of jack pine or sometimes planting of red pine and/or white spruce. In some areas the soil was prepared for planting with large disks or rock rakes mounted on crawler tractors. Some areas were sprayed with herbicides to kill the competing aspen, birch, or shrubs, although hand-cutting was used locally. The Minnesota Forest Service (now Minnesota Department of Natural Resources) established large areas of successful red pine plantations northwest of Phantom Lake on the Burntside State Forest by these means. Northeast of Lake Isabella the U.S. Forest Service aerial-sprayed a few areas with herbicides before planting to kill overstory aspen, birch, balsam, and shrubs.

Similar practices were often followed after groves of old white and red pine were cut. Where younger age classes of red or white pine were intermingled with the old pines, however, the younger pines were often left standing. White pine was not planted, because of concerns that blister rust would kill most trees.

Often no seeding or planting was done, leaving the area to reproduce to whatever species volunteered, in many cases primarily aspen, birch, and balsam, and in other cases variable restocking of the species that were removed.

In many of the peatlands cut for black spruce pulpwood, the best sites and therefore the largest trees were in a band around the bog, whereas the poorer sites tended to occur toward the center. The band of larger trees was clear-cut, leaving the stunted bog spruce in the center untouched. Those central bog areas are today small islands of virgin bog vegetation. The perimeter of the bog that was cut is often quite well restocked through natural seeding by black spruce, although some of the most fertile sites came back to heavy stands of speckled alder with low stocking of spruce.

One other effect of these operations should again be noted: the legacy of abandoned roads. Where gravel roads crossed drainages in lowlands or peatlands, the natural drainage of considerable areas was often impeded, fre-quently to the point where trees died and the whole plant community was altered upslope from the fill. Removal of culverts has helped restore drainage in some cases, but in other cases the effects remain. These old roadbeds have also become heavily used unnatural travel lanes for large mammals such as moose and wolves, patterns that may persist for a long time.

Thus the most recent logging episode resulted in a very heterogeneous forest mosaic and in varying degrees of alteration of the natural ecosystem in the logged areas. Possibly one of the most unnatural effects is the near elimination of jack pine from large areas where it was formerly the dominant tree. Another important change is the planting of numerous pure, dense, even-aged red pine stands on sites previously occupied by the boreal conifers. These plantations may remain unnaturally vulnerable to fire for some time. The area occupied by multiaged stands of aspen, paper birch, and balsam has increased at the expense of the boreal conifers and large old white and red pine. In a way, logging has broken up the age-class mosaic much as fires might have done it.

The Shipstead-Newton-Nolan Reserves

The federal Shipstead-Newton-Nolan Act of 1930 prohibited the logging of lakeshores, islands, and streamsides to a breadth of 400 feet from the waterway. A similar state law applies to state areas. The resulting strips were administratively widened to the top of "the military crest" in the late 1950s even where the ridgetop was more than 400 feet back.

The Shipstead-Newton-Nolan reserves at the very least preserve a seed source of virgin forest species along waterways, and they may give some visitors a feeling of being in an undisturbed wilderness environment while on the water or at campsites within logged regions. Locally they have also saved small groves or groups of mature white and red pine, which occur more frequently near waterways. However, some of these uncut strips of older forest are breaking up through senescence or windfall induced by their exposure from the clear-cuts behind them, especially old stands of jack pine and black spruce.

Present Fire-Management Policies in the Boundary Waters Wilderness and Park Reserves

The need to restore fire to its natural role in the forest eco-systems of the three major nature reserves of the Boundary Waters region has been discussed since 1970. The three responsible agencies recognize the vital role of fire in the region's natural ecosystem. In 1987 the Superior National Forest and Voyageurs National Park instituted a major first step toward allowing lightning-ignited fires to play a more natural role. By 1992 Quetico was developing fire-management plans that might allow some fires to burn (Friends of Quetico Park 1989; field discussions with Terry Curran, Quetico Ecologist, 1992).

THE BWCAW FIRE-MANAGEMENT PLAN

According to the Superior National Forest's fire-management plan for the BWCAW (U.S. Forest Service 1991a), lightning-ignited fires that meet preplanned prescriptions are declared Prescribed Natural Fires (PNFs) and are monitored daily to insure that they remain under prescription. If they do not, partial or complete suppression is initiated. Lightning fires that fail to meet the initial criteria are declared wildfires and are suppressed if possible, as are all fires caused by people. A beginning goal of 1,500 acres per year or 15,000 acres per decade was set. Safety of wilderness visitors and protection of lives, developed property, and forest resource values on the periphery of the wilderness have top priority. The plan was reviewed and updated in 1989 and will be reviewed annually thereafter, following directives resulting from the 1988 Yellowstone fires and other large western wilderness fires. Planned ignitions to augment lightning fires were being studied, for the plan's prescriptions could not restore the fire rotation or natural fuel conditions that existed before European settlement even if the burn-area target was achieved.

The Superior's plan is a cautious first step, as it should be, toward restoring fire's natural role (Lasko 1991). The stated primary objectives of the plan (U.S. Forest Service 1991a, 8) are to

(1) permit lightning caused fires to play, as nearly as possible, their natural ecological role within wilderness

and (2) reduce to an acceptable level the risks and conse-quences of wildfire within wilderness or escaping from wilderness.

Secondary benefits are:

A   The restoration and maintenance of the natural vegetative mosaics that have evolved through fire for enhancement of primitive recreation, viewing, and wildlife habitat.

B   Habitat improvement of the threatened Gray Wolf by improving habitat of preferred prey species.

C   Reduction of suppression costs.

D   Establishing and maintaining a public awareness that fire is a natural and essential component of the BWCAW ecosystem.

The prescription criteria are as follows:

• The fire must be caused by lightning.

• Human life and/or private property and developed sites will be protected. If there are significant threats the fire will be suppressed.

• The extent of drought buildup is assessed. If unaccept-able, the fire is suppressed. Sophisticated parameters such as the Energy Release Component, 10:00 A.M. fuel-moisture content, and Palmer Drought Index are employed. The known thresholds for probable large fires by these criteria are used in decision making.

• Current and forecasted fire weather and behavior are evaluated initially and daily thereafter. If either weather or behavior would cause the fire to exceed prescriptions, the fire is suppressed.

• The impacts of smoke on resorts, towns, wilderness users, and Canada are evaluated daily. If unacceptable, it may be necessary to partially or totally suppress the fire.

• If fires pose unacceptable inconvenience, annoyance, or economic hardship to visitors or local communities, these socioeconomic and political impacts are considered.

• If fires threaten to cross the wilderness boundary or the international boundary, they are suppressed.

• The availability of personnel and equipment to take action on each fire is assessed for the ranger district, forest, eastern region, and nation. If forces are stretched too thin, the fire is suppressed.

- A cumulative risk assessment that considers the total interrelated effects of all the prescription criteria is made both initially and in daily monitoring. If the cumulative risk is excessive, the fire is suppressed.
- If the total amount of fire activity in the wilderness and elsewhere on the Superior National Forest is too great, new fires are suppressed even if they otherwise meet the criteria.

A fire plan is prepared for each PNF, identifying specific limits to the fire's growth, considering natural fire barriers and problem areas. If a fire exceeds or threatens to exceed these "trigger points," that sector is suppressed. The plan contains much information about the prescription criteria and other factors, as well as quantitative data to be used in applying some of the criteria. As time passes, the plan will certainly undergo many changes.

The initial plan was implemented in 1987. By fall 1992 more than 25 lightning fires had been declared PNFs. In 1987, 11 fires burned a total of 135 acres; in 1988, 9 burned 694 acres; in 1990, 1 burned about 100 acres; and in 1991, about 5 burned a total of about 800 acres. Some of these first 26 fires smoldered for weeks or even months, but only 5 burned enough area or achieved enough intensity to create significant ecological effects. Descriptions of those five follow:

1 The Section 21 Fire of June 2–23, 1987: This 90-acre fire burned most of a high rocky granite island in Lac La Croix located about a mile north of Boulder Bay and a mile east of Toe Lake. Several virgin-forest plant communities were burned, including a patchy red pine community with some old overstory pines dating from previous fires in about 1681 and 1755 and patches of younger red and white pine possibly either dating from a light burn in 1864 or 1894 or entering stand openings in the last 50 years. Patches of younger paper birch, aspen, and jack pine also occurred in some of the more level areas. The fire burned lazily for the first 10 days, but as the drought intensified, most of the burn occurred between June 16 and 21. Some torching off of individual pines produced smoke columns reaching altitudes up to 5,000 feet. The fire killed most of the

birch, aspen, jack pine, and younger red and white pine saplings, and perhaps 30 to 40 percent of the larger overstory red and white pine. Surviving old pines are well distributed over the island, and much regeneration of all species was evident in 1989.

2 The Boulder Fire of May 30 to June 18, 1988: This 175-acre fire burned the bedrock peninsula that creates a reverse bend in the Boulder River at the north end of Lake Agnes, south of Boulder Bay of Lac La Croix. It was a classic underburn beneath old red and white pine that dated from fires in 1681 and 1755. Local surface fires may have occurred in 1766, 1796, 1864, and 1894, when areas nearby burned, but no significant fires had occurred since 1894 and perhaps earlier. Most of the old pine stands were well stocked, and the accumulated organic layer and dead and down woody material was heavy in many places. The organic layer still held some moisture at depth, and the fire weather was not severe. Consequently, flame lengths were short, and crown scorch and torching-off of overstory pines were limited. Some big pines with exposed butt rot were burned through and felled by the fire, and some were killed by excessive heat at the ground line (cambial girdling), but 80 to 90 survived. Killing of understory balsam, spruce, cedar, shrubs, and occasional pine saplings was nearly total in most places. Thus, this fire reduced the organic layer, eliminated understory competition and most understory ladder fuels, and created a few openings large enough to permit regeneration, but it did not open up the area enough to introduce a new age class of red and white pine. The fire was extinguished by rains in mid-June. It never jumped the narrow Boulder River.

3 The Wabang Fire of May 30 to June 16, 1988: This 485-acre fire burned a high granite ridge complex south of Lady Boot Bay of Lac La Croix, between Arch, Wabang, and Yabut lakes. It was ignited by the same lightning storm that started the Boulder Fire. The ridgetop was occupied by jack pine and black spruce communities of 1894 or later origin, and in places by open lichen-covered bedrock. Depressions on the ridgetop were occupied by large sphagnum–black spruce bogs. The lower slopes were partially occupied by patches of old

146

white and red pine dating from fires in 1681 and 1755, with understories of aspen, birch, balsam, spruce, and red maple. On the south slopes were extensive aspen stands. In the jack pine communities the fire varied from a light underburn to occasional small crowned-out patches. Stand kill varied from little to total, with about half of the area largely killed. Jack pine regeneration was coming into the killed-out patches in 1989, but many areas have too many surviving trees to induce new growth. Most of the black spruce bogs were not burned. Most of the old white and red pine groups on the slopes had moderate- to high-intensity surface burns, with some crown scorch and mortality. The aspen stands saw mostly sporadic light surface fires with only occasional trees killed. Some of the lichen communities were burned, others were skipped. Thus, this fire left a very heterogeneous mix of new plant communities, fire-modified old stands, and unburned patches. It was extinguished by the same rains as the Boulder Fire.

4   The Baldpate Fire of June 19 to July 29, 1991: This 496-acre lightning fire burned in jack pine of 1894 origin on a rolling granite ridge and bog complex about a mile northeast of Baldpate Lake, 2 miles northeast of Big Lake and the Echo Trail. The ignition and the entire fire were in a large area of patchy 1988 blowdown extending more or less continuously to the east, northeast, and west for several miles. Furthermore, the 1894 jack pine extended essentially continuously northeastward to Crooked Lake on the Canadian border, indicating that the 1894 fire had burned that entire region, now encompassing more than 20,000 acres of jack pine–black spruce and aspen-birch forest. Fuels were not extremely dry, and the fire danger was only moderate, so the fire was declared a PNF. The fire burned slowly and sporadically for two weeks, occasionally torching off patches of blowdown pine and spruce, slowly expanding the burned area to the northeast and somewhat to the south and west. At the end of June, with only occasional light rains since the fire began, a decision was made to begin containment on some of the fire perimeter. Before such action was taken, however, rains began, and by July 3, Ely recorded 1.39 inches. Thereafter aerial

monitoring detected no activity, and the fire was declared out at the end of July. This fire clearly had the potential to burn very large areas if a major drought had developed. In 1992 I found the burn to be somewhat patchy, with incomplete consumption of many blowdown patches, and many surviving pines and spruce in some areas.

5   The Gun Lake Fire of July 30 to August 12, 1991: This 125-acre surface fire and underburn occurred in mixed red, white, and jack pines of 1755 and 1864 origin east of the portage from Gun Lake to Lac La Croix, and between Tesaker and Trygg lakes. Ignition was from a lightning-struck tree. The fire moved slowly at first, attaining 18 acres by August 3. By August 6 about 65 acres had burned. Residents of the Lac La Croix Village and Handberg's resort on the Canadian side of Lac La Croix were concerned about the smoke. On August 6 and 7 a burnout was conducted along the Gun Lake–Lac La Croix portage, a monitoring crew was kept on the fire, and the fire reached the shore of Lac La Croix along the portage. The fire consumed some of the larger fuels and much of the organic layer. Flame lengths averaged about 2 feet on August 7. Torching-off of larger trees was minimal. By August 8 about 125 acres had burned, and the fire crew thereafter contained the fire within that perimeter. By August 12 the fire was essentially out.

THE VOYAGEURS NATIONAL PARK FIRE-MANAGEMENT PLAN

The Voyageurs National Park fire plan was revised and updated in 1989 (Voyageurs National Park 1989). Voyageurs is subdivided into three kinds of fire-management units:

1   A Prescribed Natural Fire Management Unit covers most of the park. Here lightning-ignited fires are allowed to burn under prescribed weather conditions, subject to monitoring, unless they threaten life, property, developed sites, or endangered or threatened species or might escape from the unit. The unit is designed

to maximize the area in which natural fire can play its role, for much of the unit is on the Kabetogama Peninsula almost entirely surrounded by very wide lakes. Management-ignited fires are to be used here only if research shows that the natural fire program does not encourage regeneration of white and red pine, or if enough critical habitat is not being created to permit the continued survival of threatened or endangered animals.

2   More than 30 Conditional Fire Management Units, each averaging 1 or 2 square miles in area, are located along the park's south boundary or close to certain developments. Many lightning-ignited fires originating within or outside these units will be allowed to burn if they remain within prescription, unless they threaten life, private property, developed park sites, cultural or archaeological resources, or threatened or endangered species or might escape from the unit. The prescriptions are similar in principle to those of the Superior National Forest. Management-ignited fires will be used to supplement lightning-caused fires, recognizing that the plan's restrictions will prevent attainment of a natural fire rotation.

3   Several Fire Suppression Units, each about a square mile in area, surround major enclaves of development. Here all wildfires, regardless of origin, will be suppressed. Mechanical fuel manipulation and management-ignited prescribed fires will be used to reduce fuels and maintain the mosaic of vegetation and wildlife habitat in approximately natural condition. As of 1992 two sizable wildfires burning outside prescriptions had burned about 800 acres. Also several management-ignited burns in mature red and white pine were successfully conducted to reduce fuel accumulations and establish more natural understory conditions conducive to pine regeneration.

Prospects for Fire Management

Fire-management objectives, policies, and programs for the Boundary Waters wilderness and park reserves, and for wilderness and national parks nationwide, progressed

remarkably in the 1980s. They even survived the test of the dramatic western fires of 1988. The BWCAW and Voyageurs plans are conservative and realistic first steps toward restoring fire to its natural role. Reintroducing fire in a large wilderness where it has been excluded for 80 years is an awesome assignment.

If there were no need to protect human lives, property, and commercial resources, and no legacy of vegetation and fuel changes due to decades of fire exclusion, then wilderness fire management would be a simple matter. But forest fires in a fire-dependent ecosystem can be an awesome, destructive, and potentially deadly force. The basic objective, then, must be *to restore fire to its natural role in the ecosystem to the maximum extent feasible, consistent with protection of human life, property, and commercial resources outside the wilderness.*

Note that the objective is not to produce a particular set or mosaic of plant communities or to create specific kinds of wildlife habitat. Rather it is to let nature take its course, consistent with safety constraints. The Wilderness Act clearly states that a wilderness is to be an area where "the earth and its community of life are untrammeled by man . . . an area of undeveloped Federal land retaining its primeval character and influence . . . which is protected and managed so as to preserve its natural conditions . . ." (U.S. Public Law 88-577). In the words of Howard Zahniser, one of the principal framers of the 1964 Wilderness Act, we are to be "guardians, not gardeners." The BWCA was included in the original 1964 act, but with exceptions that permitted commercial logging under certain vague restrictions. Logging was finally banned by Public Law 95-495 in 1978. That law incorporates the protections of the original 1964 act and provides "for the protection, enhancement, and preservation of the natural values of the lakes, waterways and associated forested areas," and calls for "protecting the special qualities of the area as a natural forest lakeland wilderness ecosystem of major esthetic, cultural, scientific, recreational and educational value to the Nation" (U.S. Public Law 95-495). Thus, there is a clear mandate to maintain or where necessary to restore the natural ecosystem of the BWCAW, with all that implies for a fire-dependent ecosystem.

The Superior National Forest's 1989–91 fire plan acknowledges that its 1,500-acre annual burn area target falls short of achieving a natural fire rotation even if fully attained. In fact it would produce roughly a 590-year rotation if calculated for the total forest area of the BWCAW. If the plan's fires are confined to the virgin forests, as perhaps they should be at first because these are the forests most affected by fire exclusion, then the rotation would still be about 300 years for the virgin forests alone. These figures contrast with my estimated rotation of 100 years before European settlement or Van Wagner's 50 years, and with the actual fire rotation for the virgin forests of the BWCAW from 1911 until 1987 of about 2,000 years. The plan's prescriptions virtually preclude running crown fires, yet the historic evidence indicates that much of the burned area in the past was achieved by just such fires. Intense surface fires or crown fires are essential to clean out senescent old stands and make way for new generations of trees. Even if the plan allowed for substantial burning by escaped wildfires during severe droughts and fire weather, say 10,000 acres per decade, about the average for the 1970–90 period, the new fire rotation would still be about 360 years for the full BWCAW, or 180 years for the virgin areas alone if most of the fires occurred there. These rotations are still too long to perpetuate the boreal conifer-broadleaf forests and too long for white and red pine. These facts are mentioned not to criticize the plan, because it is only prudent to start a burning program cautiously, but to assess realistically what the present plan can accomplish in restoring fire to its natural role.

The plan may result in significant underburning in red and white pine (of the kind that occurred in the Boulder and Wabang fires) if lightning ignites enough stands and restores natural fuel conditions. In contrast, the unnaturally large fuel accumulations and understories of balsam, spruce, and cedar ladder fuels due to fire exclusion in some stands may cause unnaturally high mortality in the red and white pine overstories. Also, the fire dispatcher and district ranger must make difficult choices when a lightning fire is detected. Many fires that have the potential to burn significant areas occur in weather that exceeds prescriptions. If stands are chosen on a truly random basis, it is unlikely that a natural number of red and white pine underburns will occur, because these forests occupy only about 8 percent of the forest area. Thus, only 20 percent or less of the naturally expected area of underburns in red and white pine would be allowed to burn. If more are allowed because they are deemed easier to control, then "nature's allocation" of fires by vegetation types will be frustrated. In the long run, a more ominous problem for these big pines is the likelihood that some fires will crown out and kill entire groves, and yet not enough high-intensity fires in total will occur to bring in a natural proportion of new age classes.

Most of these problems are inherent in any plan that allows less than all natural ignitions to burn. On the other hand, if all lightning ignitions were allowed to burn (certainly not a prudent option), the resulting vegetation and forest-age-class mosaic would probably not be fully "natural," because of changed fuels and vegetation due to 80 years of fire exclusion. This is especially true for the groves of old red and white pine—a rare element in the biodiversity of the region. We have produced a dilemma that is not easily avoided.

In Quetico a two-year research study in the virgin forests of the Hunter Island region in 1975–76 found that from 1860 to 1920, fire burned given areas at an average frequency of 78 years. At recent rates of burning, the fire rotation has averaged 870 years (Day 1990). Thus, Quetico faces the same questions as the BWCAW regarding fire policy, although the age-class mosaic in the remaining virgin forests is not so far out of balance, because there have been more large fires in the past 60 years than in the BWCAW.

Voyageurs may suffer somewhat less. Its large Prescribed Natural Fire Management Unit is well surrounded by large lakes, especially on its north and east sides. As a practical matter, however, the end result might be similar because of the recognized need to protect private inholdings and developed areas. The plan also allows for some management-ignited fires, a provision that will help alleviate some problems with red and white pine stands. Unfortunately, however, Voyageurs has less virgin-forest area, and this situation further complicates fire's ecological effects, as we shall see later.

ARE THE BWCAW, QUETICO, AND VOYAGEURS LARGE ENOUGH TO ACCOMMODATE A NATURAL FIRE REGIME?

The BWCAW alone is clearly not large enough to accommodate burns as large as some that occurred in the period from 1727 to 1910. If we assume that lightning ignitions produced these burns, then a natural fire regime could not be attained if fires are suppressed outside the wilderness. As discussed in chapter 10, 64 percent of the area burned between 1727 and 1910 in the BWCAW was generated by just 8 large burns, each exceeding 100 square miles (64,000 acres). The largest of these burn patches covered 434 square miles, and for the 71 mapped burns 1 square mile or larger in area, the average patch size was 36 square miles, or 23,000 acres. Several of the largest burns appear to have originated outside the wilderness, and several crossed the Echo Trail or Gunflint Trail corridors. Several large fires also probably crossed the international boundary into Quetico, and some no doubt entered from Canada. Thus, suppression of all fires outside the BWCAW, including those that threaten to cross the road corridors or the international boundary, will produce a fire rotation significantly longer than did the natural regime. Of course a policy that allows fires to move freely into and out of the wilderness is intolerable. So we must settle for something less than a natural fire regime and longer than natural fire rotations if we rely only on lightning ignitions.

If Quetico adopts a natural-fire-management program, what would be the effect on fire regimes of managing fire in the BWCAW and Quetico under a cooperative international agreement that provided for accepting fires crossing the border under specified conditions? Clearly such a policy would help increase the area in both nations where suppression actions would not automatically be taken. But it might not make as much difference as one might think, because much of the international boundary falls along large, wide lakes that would often be fire barriers. Quetico has a significantly better opportunity to safely approach a natural fire regime with lightning ignitions than does the BWCAW because Quetico is more compact and not cut up by developed road corridors.

Voyageurs is not contiguous with either the BWCAW or Quetico, although the southeast tip of Voyageurs virtually touches the BWCAW. Cooperative fire programs among the three organizations obviously are advantageous (and already exist), but the opportunity to accept Voyageurs' natural fire program fires in the BWCAW or vice versa would rarely arise. Fortunately, although Voyageurs is much smaller than the other two units, it has an excellent opportunity to allow large fires on the Kabetogama Peninsula. Furthermore, many fires on the peninsula before European settlement likely started there rather than moved in from surrounding areas.

The converse to the questions addressed here must also be asked. Would lightning-ignited, stand-replacing fires as large as those in 1863–64 and in a few other major fire years be ecologically acceptable today, even if they could be accommodated safely? This is a sticky policy problem involving the whole question of how we should attempt to maintain the natural forest community and age-class-patch mosaic at the landscape level. The problem is that what we have to work with is a somewhat damaged fragment of the original natural ecosystem of a vastly larger region. Would fires burning a third of the entire area in one or two fire years threaten the natural biodiversity of the ecosystem? The answer is unclear, but a risk exists. The proportion of the BWCAW, Quetico, and Voyageurs occupied by the red pine and white pine communities and even the jack pine and black spruce communities is now much reduced through logging. The possibility exists that vast fires in a single major drought year might eliminate many of the red and white pine communities because of excessive fuel loads due to fire exclusion. Even if that kind of loss of diversity did not result, would it be good ecosystem-preservation policy to convert a third of the remaining forest ecosystem reserves to a single age class? I will revisit this question again from other angles, because it is fundamental to a sound landscape-ecology policy for these few remnants of the region's natural ecosystem. If we are to restore fire to something approaching the natural regime and natural rotation without such vast burns, then we must burn approximately the same average area per century with more but smaller stand-replacing fires. Perhaps a maximum patch size limit of 25,000 to 50,000 acres should be incorporated into future plans as fire-management capabilities improve. It will be better to maintain a full range of patch diversity in forest communities and age classes on a smaller scale than existed before European settlement than to risk irretrievable loss of some diversity in two or three vast burns.

CAN FIRE PROGRAMS BE DEVISED FOR THE VIRGIN FORESTS TO SAFELY ACCOMMODATE MORE LARGE-CROWN FIRES, REDUCE UNNATURAL FUELS, AND APPROACH A NATURAL FIRE ROTATION?

I believe that unnaturally heavy fuel loads due to fire exclusion in many old-growth red and white pine stands could be reduced safely with a program of management-ignited prescribed underburns. If such stands have not had an underburn for more than 40 or 50 years, and especially if they also have thick organic layers, sapling or pole understories of balsam, spruce, or cedar ladder fuels, extensive budworm-killed understories, or thickets of small pines, then they probably qualify as having unnatural fuel loads. Of course, we will never know which stands might have had underburns in the past 80 years if a natural fire regime had prevailed. The ecological justification for intervening with prescribed ignitions is that we have created unnatural fuel loads and locked up nutrients in these stands by excluding fire and thereby jeopardized their health and their survival when lightning fires do burn in them. These unnatural fuel accumulations are not only a threat to fire-control efforts and the safety of resources and developments outside the wilderness, but they also pose a major threat to the survival of rare and endangered ecosystem resources. Once a successful underburn has occurred, we should rely on lightning ignitions for future burns unless the loss of

potential ignitions from outside the wilderness is important in given areas. I am convinced that management-ignited underburns are feasible, based on the experience of Buckman (1964a) on the Cutfoot Sioux Experimental Forest in the 1950s and 1960s, on my observations of wildfire effects in the BWCAW and Quetico, and on recent experience in Voyageurs. The expertise to write the prescriptions and to conduct such burns exists among the natural-resource professionals. We must just make the decision that these kinds of burns will be used to restore fire to its natural role in red and white pine communities. The old-growth red and white pine groves of the Boundary Waters reserves are among the most endangered forest communities of the entire Great Lakes region of the United States and Canada. They are an irreplaceable element in the biodiversity of the region.

The truly difficult fire-management problem will be to provide safely for enough crown fires in virgin upland boreal conifer-broadleaf forests and peatland conifer stands to approach the natural fire rotation. In the BWCAW and Quetico these forests are already reaching senescence over vast regions, and such changes become more evident with each passing year.

Running crown fires were undoubtedly the natural agents that produced the vast stands of jack pine, black spruce, aspen, and paper birch that now cover much of the BWCAW's virgin forests north and south of the Echo Trail, and from Hudson, Insula, Alice, Malberg, Wine, and Cherokee lakes north to Knife, Cypress, and Saganaga lakes and the Gunflint Trail. We can surmise this from the present age and stand structure of the forests, from historical reports, and from the weather records of some of the fire years. What makes a natural-fire program in these forests even more difficult is the realization that nearly all of these stands were reproduced by vast fires that burned in just a few of the most severe drought years in the past two centuries, years like 1863, 1864, 1875, 1894, and 1910. How can we safely duplicate the ecological effects of such fires on the scale needed to restore conditions even close to the natural fire rotation?

The honest answer is that no simple solution exists. Several positive steps might be taken to provide more stand-replacing crown fires, or we can suppress all fires that have the potential to become large crown fires. Either course carries risks of even larger fires. The suppression option also carries serious ecological consequences for the wilderness ecosystem if we even partially succeed. This dilemma is not peculiar to the Boundary Waters wilderness and park reserves. As we learned in 1988, it applies equally to Yellowstone, the Bob Marshall Wilderness complex in Montana, and to dozens more of America's and Canada's favorite wilderness areas and national parks (Heinselman 1985; Kilgore 1987; Kilgore and Heinselman 1990). Steps that might be taken to accommodate more high-intensity fires in virgin jack pine, black spruce, balsam-spruce, and aspen-birch-conifer forests are suggested.

First, we need a policy and program to address the fire-control situation near the wilderness boundary, especially where it adjoins or approaches developed areas or private property. In such areas a program of management-ignited prescribed fires is needed to reduce high-risk fuels such as those in budworm-killed stands, recent blowdowns, and senescent jack pine–black spruce stands. If successful burns can be carried out in the most critical high-risk areas, then the chance that a wilderness fire will endanger lives or destroy developed property along the wilderness perimeter will be reduced (Arno and Brown 1989). Defense strategies for critical areas should also be preplanned. In some cases timber sales or noncommercial fuel-modification projects in areas just outside the wilderness adjacent to or within developed areas might also make sense. Such work is particularly needed in those relatively few areas where developments are located just east, southeast, south, northeast, or north of high-risk fuels that extend far back into the wilderness. The U.S. Forest Service, National Park Service, Ontario Ministry of Natural Resources, and Minnesota Department of Natural Resources have the expertise to prepare the plans for the management-ignited fires and to conduct the burns.

A second possible approach to allow more crown fires and high-intensity surface fires is a combination program of management-ignited crown fires and preplanned prescribed natural fires in virgin boreal conifer-broadleaf forests. Such fires would be located deep in the wilderness,

but only where fire managers believed the fire could be herded into defensible natural firebreaks that would limit the fire area to something that could be handled. Initially the burning units might be limited to a few hundred to a thousand acres. Maybe either deliberate ignitions or fortunate lightning ignitions would occur at points west or south of large lakes where reasonably good natural fire barriers also exist to the northeast and southeast. Fire planners might make a systematic study of all virgin forest areas in the BWCAW for feasible burning areas and map out all candidate areas. A program of management-ignited prescribed fires would then be set up, with the sequence of burns beginning with the smallest and most easily defended units first. If a lightning ignition occurred in one of the units, it would be allowed to burn unless it exceeded prescriptions. The prescription criteria for these units would be less stringent than those for the present wildernesswide prescribed natural fire program. This difference is essential to achieve intensities needed to induce stand-killing crown fires or intense surface fires. The purpose would be to safely restore stand-replacing crown fires to the ecosystem under burning conditions of less than maximum drought and fire weather. If this can be done, the goal of more but smaller crown fires can be achieved and the possibility of vast wildfires perhaps reduced.

To test this idea, I studied the BWCAW topographic and vegetation maps to identify 10 virgin boreal forest areas that present a reasonably secure situation where crown fires of a few hundred to a thousand acres might be feasible. The criteria used in selecting areas were as follows:

- The site must permit burning at least a few hundred acres.
- It must be feasible to burn the area with a west, southwest, or northwest wind (that is, the site must be on the west or southwest side of a good-sized lake).
- There must be an expanse of open water downwind at least a quarter mile wide.
- The forest must be primarily mature or senescent stands of upland boreal conifer-broadleaf species (jack pine, black spruce, aspen, birch, or balsam of an 1894 or earlier origin).
- The site must not be near enough to any wilderness

boundary or structures to pose a threat to areas outside the BWCAW or to Forest Service or private structures within the wilderness. Areas with some intermingled land owned by the state or the counties were not ruled out, because cooperative agreements are possible and land exchanges are likely in the future.

These criteria may sound easy to meet, but ideal sites are difficult to find. The greatest problem is locating sites that clearly have no flammable vegetation downwind within range of spot fires. Most possible sites have some mainland or islands too close offshore in at least one potentially hazardous direction (east, northeast, or southeast). This situation, of course, explains precisely why so many past fires jumped such water barriers. Despite these problems, here are 10 areas that might work as starters for such a program:

1 The ridge complex northeast of Takucmich Lake fronting on Lac La Croix in Secs. 29, 30, 31, 32, T.68 N., R.14 W., in mostly jack pine, aspen, and birch of 1894 origin.

2 The land between Pocket Lake and Lac La Croix northeast of Pocket and fronting on Lac La Croix in Secs. 34, 35, T.68 N., R.14 W., and Secs. 2, 3, T.67 N., R.14 W., in mostly jack pine, aspen, and birch of 1864 and 1894 origin.

3 The peninsula on the west side of Ge-be-on-e-quet Lake in Secs. 15, 16, 21, 22, T.67 N., R.14 W., in mostly jack pine and black spruce, with some white pine and balsam. The stands date from 1894 fires except for a few old white pines.

4 The peninsula on the southwest side of Lake Agnes (south of the portage to Oyster Creek) in Sec. 12, T.66 N., R.14 W., in mostly jack pine, aspen, birch, and black spruce of 1864 origin.

5 Part of the southwest side of Thursday Bay of Crooked Lake in Secs. 20, 29, T.66 N., R.11 W., in mostly jack pine of 1894 origin.

6 Part of the southwest side of Friday Bay of Crooked Lake in Secs. 24, 25, T.66 N., R.12 W., in mostly 1894 jack pine.

7 The peninsula on the south side of Saturday Bay of Crooked Lake in Secs. 22, 23, T.66 N., R.12 W., in mostly 1894 jack pine, aspen, and birch.

8 Some of the land on the west side of Sunday Bay of Crooked Lake in Sec. 17, T.66 N., R.12 W., in mostly 1894 jack pine and aspen.

9 The peninsula on the west side of Lake Insula in Secs. 23, 26, T.63 N., R.8 W., in 1864 jack pine, aspen, and birch.

10 The northeast end of American Point on Saganaga Lake in Secs. 9, 10, 15, 16, T.66 N., R.5 W., in mostly senescent jack pine, black spruce, aspen, birch, and balsam originating after a fire in 1801–3.

Crown-fire research, including many experimental crown fires in various forest communities similar to those in the BWCAW, has been under way in Ontario and elsewhere in Canada for many years. The weather, fuel moisture, forest vegetation, age relations, stand structure, and other conditions necessary for the initiation of crown fires and high-intensity surface fires are quite well known for the fuel types in the Boundary Waters. Prescriptions that might be used for burns or for subsequent fires in a continuing program should be based on the work of Van Wagner (1977, 1983, 1987), Stocks (1987a,b, 1989), Roussopoulos (1978), and other relevant new work in the United States and Canada. The problem with such fires is not so much knowing the threshold conditions for crown fires and high-intensity surface fires as the sobering fact that the latitude between conditions suitable for manageable crown fires as opposed to unmanageable wildfires is not large. The margin for error is small, and the consequences of error might be considerable under some circumstances. Because the window of opportunity for suitable weather can be narrow, it will often be essential to get the fire over with quickly, both to capitalize on the weather before it rains and to avoid the possibility that continuing drought or worsening fire weather will cause an escape and a large wildfire.

Another problem is that such fires often must be conducted at times when at least some other prescribed natural fires or wildfires outside wilderness will be burning. This means that local or regional fire-management forces may already be busy. Forces are not unlimited, and this situation could mean the priority will go to wildfires. This situation must be faced in advance. The only answer is a special cadre of wilderness or park fire specialists who are not subject to call for wildland fires outside wilderness.

If all the steps discussed are taken, a new BWCAW program of management-ignited and lightning-caused crown fires and high-intensity surface fires that might produce some 30,000 acres of burned area per decade can be envisioned in the near future. This program would be in addition to the prescribed underburning needed to reduce fuels to natural levels in red and white pine. Assume that most of this burning would be confined to the virgin forest areas because these are the areas most heavily affected by fire suppression in the past 80 years.

Even with these programs, the inevitable major drought years will come, and some wildfires will escape. However, these programs should help reduce the frequency and size of wildfires because at least the most recent burns will act as fire barriers. If prescribed burning or mechanical fuel modification around developments on the wilderness edge are also done, then the likelihood of injuries or property losses there should be small. But even young conifers on new burns will carry crown fires under worst-case scenarios when more than about ten years old (Stocks 1987a). There is no guarantee against an eventual year when wildfires burning under conditions far exceeding prescriptions will burn truly large areas, conceivably 100,000 acres or more. It is to be hoped that such fires will not leave the wilderness. We must also realize that the potential for very large fires still exists outside wilderness in the region, entirely apart from wilderness fire programs. Proof of this potential is examples like the 1976 Huntersville fire in Minnesota and the 1974 wildfires in northwestern Ontario (Stocks 1975).

To predict fire rotations for the BWCAW under an enlarged fire-management program, it would be prudent to make a liberal allowance for wildfires burning outside prescriptions. If an allowance of 10,000 acres per decade is used, the total fire program suggested here might produce a decade-average burned area of some 40,000 acres. This translates to a fire rotation of about 112 years for the virgin areas, not far from my figure of 100 years for before European settlement but still very far from Van Wagner's 50-year rotation. This prediction assumes that most of the burning will be confined to the virgin forests. If some occurs in logged areas, the rotation for the virgin areas will be correspondingly longer. If such a program is instituted, but no effort is made to confine the fires to the virgin areas, then for a decade-average burn of 40,000 acres, the rotation for the whole BWCAW, including the virgin areas, would be about 225 years. Eventually such a program would have to be expanded to include the logged areas. When it is, the decade-average burn target would have to be increased to about 80,000 acres, plus a wildfire allowance of 10,000 acres, to achieve a 100-year rotation for the whole BWCAW. Restoring fire to the logged areas, however, is not a high-priority need.

WHAT SHOULD BE THE FIRE-MANAGEMENT POLICIES FOR LOGGED AREAS?

For at least two reasons, the fire programs for areas logged either in the early logging era or since 1940 should be different from those for the virgin areas. First, the forests in these areas are mostly much younger than those in the virgin areas because they originated after the logging or after subsequent slash fires. Most date from 1917 or later, and perhaps 100,000 acres or more date from 1945 to 1978. Such forests have not yet been pushed unnaturally into senescence by fire exclusion as have many areas of virgin forest. In fact, the recently logged areas contain most of the young forests in the BWCAW, Quetico, and Voyageurs. Second, the forest communities in many of these areas have been unnaturally altered by logging, slash fires, and in some cases by tree planting, herbicides, and other practices. If any management funds are available to restore natural conditions to these areas, it would make much more sense to reverse some of these changes than to engage in fire restoration work that might simply exacerbate past unnatural effects.

Perhaps the greatest ecological need in the logged areas is to replace the red and white pine seed sources that were lost in areas cut in the big-pine logging era and in some recently cut areas. A major problem here is simply that there are few or no seed trees of these pines in many areas.

154 If fire is used, it could only be used effectively to burn out the present competing forest vegetation in small patches prior to seeding or planting of red and white pine. If such work is done, it is vital that the pine seed sources be from local collections because one of the most important long-term values of wilderness and park reserves is their gene pools of naturally adapted species and ecotypes.

Another uncommon but important exception is the case of those relatively few red and white pine stands that did reproduce well immediately after logging around the turn of the century. Some of these stands are now 80 or 90 years old and have never had an underburn because of fire suppression. If a lightning ignition occurs in such stands, it should qualify as a prescribed natural fire if it otherwise meets prescription criteria. If a program of management-ignited underburns is undertaken to reduce unnatural fuels, some of these stands might be considered.

Other than work such as that just outlined, any fire funds available for the logged areas would probably be best spent in suppressing fires that threaten to burn large areas, at least for the next few decades. Eventually the vegetation of most of these areas will return to something more closely resembling what it might have been without the impact of logging. When that occurs, it will be time to reevaluate the role of fire and include logged areas in a prescribed natural-fire program.

CAN WE CONTROL

POTENTIALLY LARGE FIRES?

The Superior National Forest has a remarkable record of keeping wilderness fires small in the context of a fire-dependent ecosystem where fires burned an average of at least 90,000 acres per decade before 1900. Many large fires occurred in logging slash and semiopen second-growth lands in the early years of the forest. Much of the burned area in those fires was then owned by the timber companies, and the Forest Service had little control over their activities. The last of the big slash fires in what is now the BWCAW was the Brule Lake fire of 1929, which burned some 25,000 acres, of which only 4,448 acres were national forest lands. Much of the burn was outside the present wilderness. Shortly after this fire, the Great Depression began, virtually all the big timber on private land had been cut, and the era of the big sawmills in Minnesota ended. With the depression also came the expansion of the national forests, acquisition of abandoned and tax-delinquent private timberlands, and the Civilian Conservation Corps (CCC) program with its camps and large pools of manpower.

Then came the extreme drought years of the 1930s. Many fires in the Superior National Forest were caused by both lightning and people, but only the adjacent Cherokee and Frost Lake fires of 1936 south of the Gunflint Trail reached significant size on the U.S. side of the border. Both were lightning-caused, late-summer fires in old budworm-killed balsam and other senescent and mature forest fuels. At least some of the burned forest appears to have been of 1727 postfire origin. Both fires were fought valiantly by crews of up to 800 CCC men, supervised by Forest Service professionals. Despite extreme drought and adverse fire weather, the Cherokee fire was held to 3,200 acres and the Frost Lake fire to 3,500 acres. These fires were fought with hand tools and gasoline-powered pumps. Pontoon-equipped aircraft were used for aerial observation and transport of key supervisory personnel, but crews and most supplies were moved to the fires on foot and by canoe. Regional and Superior National Forest crews were heavily overcommitted on other fires in addition to these. Given the extreme drought conditions, it is a real tribute to the crews and their supervisors that these fires did not become much larger. A large fire in Ontario north of Rose Lake, called the "Canadian Outbreak," burned during the same period in 1936. It ultimately jumped the international boundary on Rose Lake, was fought vigorously from the start, and burned only 900 acres on the U.S. side (Heinselman 1973).

The next large fire in the present BWCAW occurred 35 years later, when on May 14, 1971, the Little Sioux fire broke out on a Forest Service timber sale east of the Little Indian Sioux River, 2 miles south of the Echo Trail. The origin was a holdover fire from an April slash burn. This spring fire occurred after a short drought, on a day of extreme fire danger with a relative humidity of 15 percent and southwest winds gusting to 30 miles per hour. The fire burned 14,628 acres in three days, but nearly 60 percent of its final size was attained that first unusually hazardous day. About 65 percent of the burned area was recently logged land. Rates of spread exceeding a mile per hour the first day were due in part to large open areas of untreated logging slash, treeless grass-sedge marshland, and spot fires that started as much as a half mile ahead of the main fire (Sando and Haines 1972). More than half of the fire was outside the BWCAW in the Echo Trail corridor, which was crossed the first day. Only about 3,000 acres of virgin forest in the wilderness ultimately burned. Bulldozers, aerial water bombing, and handmade fire line construction by more than 200 men were employed, but the fire was really extinguished by a heavy rain the morning of May 17, followed by a 4-inch snowfall later that week. Much of the dramatic behavior of this fire was due to effects of recent logging, which will not be repeated in the Boundary Waters wilderness and park reserves. But in the northern end of the fire in the BWCAW, some 3,000 acres of virgin jack pine, aspen, birch, budworm-infested balsam, and black spruce of 1864 origin were killed by running crown fires. These areas have since reproduced well, in many cases to the original plant communities. On the north shore of Lamb Lake the edge of a large stand of red and white pine of 1681 and 1755 origin was also killed by crown fire. The big pines are still slowly returning to that burn. Other areas in the same stand were underburned with little injury to overstory trees.

The next large fires came in 1974, a drought year in which 516 wildfires burned 1,079,000 acres of forest in northwestern Ontario; one of the largest fires was only 100 miles northwest of Quetico (Stocks 1975). In the BWCAW the largest was the 1,006-acre camper-caused Prayer Lake fire of July 27. It started about 2:30 P.M. on the east side of the channel leading from Saganaga Lake into the Sea Gull River and the Trail's End developments at the end of the Gunflint Trail. Driven by strong west-northwest winds, the fire crowned out in mixed conifer-broadleaf stands of 1801–3 origin and then ran rapidly 2 miles eastward through a complex of mostly jack pine and other boreal conifers of 1910, 1903, 1864, and 1801–3 origin, jumping Maraboeuf Lake and crossing into Ontario by 8:30 P.M. Most of the area burned in that first day's run, although the fire widened about another quarter mile along its north

edge before final control on July 30. Spot fires burned significant areas in Canada as well. The fire was fought by 270 people, using 20 boats, 12 pumps, and 2 Beaver pontoon aircraft, the latter used for water bombing, transport, and aerial observation. The area has since reproduced well to jack pine, aspen, birch, black spruce, and other species.

The Plume Lake fire burned only about 40 acres in the BWCAW, but it is noteworthy because it was a spot fire from a much larger lightning fire that started near Other Man Lake in Quetico. Driven by strong northwest winds, this fire jumped the international boundary in four or five places between Cypress and Swamp lakes about 4:00 P.M. on July 27, 1974, the same day the Prayer Lake fire started. It was fought vigorously beginning the next morning with ground forces and pumpers and never made any significant runs.

In 1975 there was little fire activity in the BWCAW, but the next year, 1976, the drought returned with a vengeance. Minnesota saw one of the driest summers ever recorded. On August 21 a dry lightning storm passed over the Saganaga Lake area in the eastern BWCAW about 7:30 A.M. At 10:42 A.M. the Forest Service's morning aerial patrol spotted a fire burning vigorously in mixed boreal conifers of 1815 origin about a mile west-southwest of Roy Lake, in the wilderness. A strong wind was blowing from the west, and the Trail's End complex of canoe outfitters, resorts, summer homes, and a large Forest Service campground lay only 2 miles to the east on the edge of the wilderness. Hundreds of people lived or worked there, and the developments were worth millions of dollars. The only continuous fire barrier between the point of ignition and these developments was the narrow Sea Gull River, which forms the BWCAW boundary and the edge of the developed area. The Trail's End complex is the northern end of the Gunflint Trail corridor, surrounded on three sides by wilderness. A crisis was in the making.

In the first 24 hours, the Roy Lake fire roared 2 miles through jack pine, spruce, balsam, and cedar of 1815 and 1801–3 origin, reached the Sea Gull River, and threatened to engulf the entire Trail's End complex. Firebrands rained down on the roofs of buildings and into the old boreal conifer stands that hugged all developments. Residents and fire-suppression teams poured water on buildings and jumped on every little blaze that popped up in the surrounding woods. Despite these efforts, a sizable spot fire developed in Trail's End Campground. A massive attack finally extinguished the blaze before it became a threat to the whole area. By August 23 the wind had shifted to the south, and the fire moved northward toward Saganaga Lake on a 2-mile front, soon entering a much younger complex of jack pine, black spruce, aspen, and birch of 1903 origin. On August 25 the wind shifted to the southwest and picked up to 15 or 20 miles per hour in midafternoon. Between 3:00 and 6:00 P.M., a slow-moving crown fire roared eastward through about 100 acres of 1903 jack pine–black spruce stands along the south shore of Saganaga Lake. Fortunately these winds did not persist, and fire lines constructed between Romance Lake and Saganaga Lake held, else Trail's End might have been threatened again. The fire made a few more short advances to the west, southwest, and northeast on August 26 and 27 but was finally controlled on August 28. The final burned area encompassed 3,380 acres of virgin jack pine, black spruce, balsam, cedar, aspen, and birch forest of 1801–3, 1815, and 1903 origin. Most stands were killed by crown fires or high-intensity surface fires, but there were the usual small skipped or partially burned areas here and there. As described in chapter 7, natural regeneration of the entire fire area is proceeding well. The fire was fought by 350 firefighters, 28 Forest Service supervisory professionals, and 65 camp facilities workers, with 23 pumps, 2 engines, 5 air tankers, and 2 helicopters. The total cost of suppression exceeded a million dollars. Fortunately there were no deaths, serious injuries, or significant structural or other property losses.

Two other 1976 BWCAW fires burned just after the Roy Lake fire. The first was the 1,190-acre Rice Lake fire, ignited by a lightning storm the afternoon of August 30. It was detected promptly by air reconnaissance and attacked at once by a B-17 water bomber and ground forces. The fire was within the area of the former vast Tomahawk Timber Sale and later logging operations northwest of Isabella Lake. A road system was still usable for truck and tractor access. Despite these advantages, the extremely dry fuels, including explosive budworm-killed and injured spruce

and balsam and windblown birch bark, proved too much for the initial forces of suppression. Riding on westerly winds, the fire ran more than a mile to the east-northeast that first day, advancing at about a half mile per hour until dark. Most of the burn area was generated the first two days. Eventually 19 crews of firefighters, 8 crawler tractors, helicopters, and air tankers using fire-retarding slurry were used. Much bulldozed fire line was built around key fire-perimeter areas, and the entire fire was encircled with hose lines, requiring a total of 30 miles of hose. These massive efforts were deemed necessary because of the extreme dryness of the fuels. The fire was controlled on September 7, but mop-up continued until about September 20.

The other 1976 fire of note was the 1,025-acre Fraser Lake fire, of incendiary origin. This fire started on September 7 along the northeast shore of Fraser Lake. It was discovered by air patrol at 3:41 P.M., attacked at 4:50 P.M. with a 1,000-gallon water drop from an air tanker, but still escaped the initial attack. Driven by west winds, the fire eventually burned a swath some 2 miles long to the north side of Raven Lake. It was fought with large crews of firefighters aided by air tankers, with some 410 people ultimately involved. Suppression costs exceeded half a million dollars. Much of the burn was in virgin white pine of 1875 origin. The fire crowned out or burned too deeply in the organic matter around the bases of most of the white pine, killing most trees over extensive areas. There are numerous living seed trees in some areas, but it is too early to predict the ultimate composition of the new stands. It seems likely in this case that there will be a long period of increased aspen and birch before many conifers return on some portions of the burn. There had been no underburns in the white pine stands since their establishment, and the resulting heavy organic layer could have contributed to their demise.

This detailed summary of the largest fires in the BWCAW since the 1920s brings out several key points about our ability to control wilderness fires in the Boundary Waters ecosystem:

- The U.S. Forest Service has a remarkable record of extinguishing most fires before they attain significant size.
- The Forest Service controlled those few BWCAW fires that did escape initial attack in severe fire weather before they became truly "large," especially in the context of

a natural ecosystem with a clear potential for fires exceeding 100,000 acres.

- The Forest Service has so far never had a BWCAW lightning-caused fire that burned private structures or injured people outside the wilderness. Structures have been lost, but only in fires originating outside the wilderness. Two cabins were burned on Meander Lake by the Little Sioux fire, but it was an escaped Forest Service slash-burning fire.

- The downside of this record is that control of the few larger BWCAW fires that did escape initial attack was made at great cost, not only in dollars but in human effort and massive use of modern technological equipment.

The lesson in this record is that the technical and physical capability exists to suppress most wilderness fires, even in severe drought, but if a massive control effort becomes necessary to suppress a large escaped prescribed natural fire or a management-ignited fire, the cost and disruption to normal national forest activities could be great.

WILL NATURE DO IT FOR US IF WE FAIL TO ADOPT EFFECTIVE FIRE PROGRAMS?

Until fire control became effective in the Boundary Waters in the late 1930s, vast forest fires swept portions of the area during major droughts that occurred at 10- to 30-year intervals. The whole forest ecosystem was adapted to these recurring fires, and many key forest species require fire for their regeneration. For more than half a century, in record droughts, we have succeeded in holding even fires with great potential to a few thousand acres. Also, we found controlling large fires difficult and very costly. Our response to this dilemma so far is to develop fire programs that will hold average annual burn areas far below natural levels and will keep fires small and, if possible, limited to moderate burning conditions.

We now ask the ultimate question: If we continue to limit burning to a fraction of the fire rotation before European settlement, will nature sooner or later catch up by burning truly vast areas in one or two major fire years? Are we going to see a year like 1988 in Yellowstone? If there is a serious risk of such an outcome, would the risks to human lives and costs in property and resource values outside the wilderness be greater than the risks and costs of a more aggressive and effective natural-fire management program?

These questions cannot be answered with certainty. Yet the possibility of vast fires is real and is increased yearly by fire suppression. We have not yet pushed most of the older virgin forests over the brink into terminal senescence and stand breakup. Very large areas will reach those conditions in the next 30 to 70 years. Much of the fuel in those old stands will be lost through decomposition, but on some sites fuels will probably continue to increase. Individual tree windfalls and even extensive areas of blowdown will occur on a scale not seen before. Spruce budworm and jack pine budworm populations may reach epidemic levels more frequently and in a higher percentage of the total landscape. An order-of-magnitude increase in these conditions may occur as the forest mosaic on the landscape loses its diversity and as the differences among stand-age-class patches fade with time. Such a multiplication of the effects of widespread forest senescence can be expected if Turner (1989) and Turner and Romme (1994) are correct in suggesting that susceptibility to these kinds of disturbances may increase as the vegetation becomes homogenized.

A more ominous implication is the possibility that a single forest fire can become "critical" and propagate across the entire landscape if the area is characterized by relatively flat terrain with contiguous forest "connected" by susceptible fuels occupying more than 60 percent of the landscape (Turner and Romme 1994). This is certainly the kind of forest we are generating by continuing to withhold fire from most of the BWCAW landscape.

One can argue that the forests of the region have always been "contiguous and connected" in this sense. But the level of "susceptibility" of fuels to fire and their "connectedness" is headed for a much higher degree than existed before European settlement. Then, at any one time large areas were occupied by recent burns and by large patches of forest in various stages of maturation and senescence. Quite possibly, the loss of this patch diversity will produce a fire potential significantly greater than existed before European settlement.

Once fires in the region reach a certain critical size in extreme fire weather, perhaps 5,000 acres, they are very difficult to control. Firefighters can often only defend critical sectors where homes or other structures are located. This situation developed in Yellowstone in 1988. Very large fires are constrained mainly by the fuels mosaic on the landscape and by changes in burning weather. Many are controlled only by heavy rains, a spell of cold, wet weather, or by the arrival of fall rains or snow. The latter is what terminated the 1988 Yellowstone outbreak. The advance of large fires may be blocked in certain directions by wide natural barriers such as the widest sections of Lac La Croix, Saganaga, and Basswood lakes in the BWCAW, Pickerel in Quetico, and Rainy, Namakan, and Kabetogama lakes in Voyageurs. But in extreme drought, most truly large fires continue to move on more than one front unless they run out of explosive fuels or are extinguished by weather changes. Skillful burning-out operations can sometimes stop the advance of a sector by depriving the fire of fuels during a lull in burning conditions, but such work is risky and often results in increasing the area burned.

Fires of the kind just described do occur now in the western mountain states, Alaska, and interior Canada. The Dryden Ontario No. 18 fire complex resulted from three lightning fires ignited on June 29, 1974. They all started in a vast 100,000-acre blowdown in senescent jack pine and black spruce located about 100 miles northwest of the BWCAW between Lake of the Woods and Eagle Lake. Driven by southwest winds gusting over 34 miles per hour, two of these fires coalesced during the first afternoon. The final burned area was 79,864 acres, much of it in the blowdown (Stocks 1975).

What are the lessons from this Canadian fire record? There is little cause to doubt that similar blowdowns in old jack pine, black spruce, and balsam in the BWCAW or Quetico could result in comparable or even larger fires in the next 10 to 40 years. The terrain is similar, the forests are nearly identical over very large areas, and the Boundary Waters is equally subject to large blowdowns and lightning ignitions. With water bombing as a first attack weapon, we just might be lucky enough to check all the potentially large fires before they become too large to suppress. Chances are our luck will sooner or later run out. We will be living dangerously if we fail to move aggressively into more proactive fire-management programs that could restore a more natural patch mosaic of forest communities and age classes to the landscapes of the BWCAW and Quetico, and in the process break up the vast areas of unnaturally homogeneous connected forest fuels. If we do not, nature may very well do it for us. If we wait too long, the result could be an unnaturally large holocaust that would reduce the biodiversity of the wilderness.

What if we succeed in holding back large fires and preventing most stand-replacing crown fires, thereby putting these wilderness ecosystems on a much longer fire rotation than many of the trees and other plant species are adapted to? As shown earlier in this chapter and in chapters 4, 7, and 10, we would be forcing totally unnatural and unprecedented successional changes onto the whole plant ecosystem. The outcome, bought through heavy fire-suppression costs, would be a highly unstable forest devoid of its natural diversity and ultimately lacking in many of the most characteristic, rare, and scenic forest communities we associate with the Boundary Waters landscape. The consequences for land-based wildlife would be equally disastrous.

HOW DOES THE THREAT OF GLOBAL WARMING RELATE TO FIRE MANAGEMENT?

Everyone is familiar with the concern that global increases in atmospheric carbon dioxide, chlorofluorocarbons, methane, and other greenhouse gases may cause significant increases in the earth's temperature unless immediate steps are taken to reduce the accumulation of these gases. Many atmospheric scientists believe that current and near-term projected increases in greenhouse gases may have already committed the earth to some degree of warming. Efforts have been made to estimate future increases in carbon dioxide, and computer models predict what future climates and vegetation might look like, assuming various levels of greenhouse gases. I examine these vital questions in detail in chapter 16, but here I consider briefly what climatic change might mean for Boundary Waters fire-management programs.

Even the near-term possible effects of climatic change on Boundary Waters forests and fire-management programs are challenging. Many climate modelers predict a temperature rise of about 2°C (3.6°F) within 50 or 60 years. Even if precipitation remains unchanged or increases slightly, higher temperatures would reduce effective soil moisture. The BWCAW climate might be much like that of central Minnesota, say the Brainerd area, by 2050. Jack pine, aspen, paper birch, red maple, the oaks, and red and white pine might still grow reasonably well, but spruce, balsam, and cedar might be severely stressed and begin to die during droughts. Soil organic layers and dead and down woody fuels might dry out more often and reach lower moisture levels than they now do. The probability of large fires would rise, and fire intensities would be greater, at least in the first fires to burn each site after such a change.

Davis warns that simple extrapolation of present vegetation zones to expected new climatic situations is invalid. She points out that the record of postglacial plant migrations shows that plant species, including the trees of the Boundary Waters, react individually to changing climates. They do not move as intact plant communities. Thus we should expect that a new climatic regime may produce assemblages of plants that do not now exist together anywhere (Davis 1981, 1989a, 1990; Davis and Zabinski 1992). Given the climate that may develop, fire could turn out to be one of the principal environmental factors that determines just how such a reshuffling of plant species occurs.

The prospect of climatic change does not lessen the need for aggressive fire-management programs. On the contrary, we need to help fire play its role in response to whatever changes develop in the coming decades. If we try to withhold fire as one of the agents of change, then the prospect of a holocaust that we cannot control and that might eliminate otherwise adapted species will increase.

Much progress has been made in understanding the natural role of fire in forest ecosystems in the past few decades. Fire-control technology and its application to wilderness and park-management programs have seen a parallel increase. We now have a much better base on which to build as we face the complex issues of changing societal goals for wildlands and a changing global environment. Progress has also been made in the critical area of informing the general public about the natural role of fire in forest and prairie ecosystems and the importance of fire management. Much more needs to be done in that area. The old Smokey Bear images are still alive in the minds of too many people. Without public understanding and support, fire-management programs are doomed to failure. Strong public support exists for wilderness, and the public will support natural-fire management programs if they understand how vital those programs are. The ecosystems of the Boundary Waters Canoe Area Wilderness, Quetico Provincial Park, and Voyageurs National Park are too valuable to entrust to anything less than the most enlightened and sophisticated fire programs we can devise.

The Role of Mammals in the Ecosystem

The terrestrial and aquatic mammals of the Boundary Waters are a fascinating integral part of the ecosystem. As either primary consumers (herbivores) or secondary consumers (carnivores) or both (omnivores), they ultimately depend on plants, and some have important reciprocal effects on plant communities. The species composition and productivity of the vegetation in the virgin forests depend in turn on past fire frequency, the fertility of the soils, the geological substrates and waters, and the rates of nutrient cycling on the landscape. In this chapter, critical links to the vegetation side of the ecosystem and to the fire and logging history are noted as well as relationships between species, such as predator-prey, and diseases.

The Moose-Deer-Caribou-Beaver-Wolf System

Before about 1880, the principal large herbivores of the Boundary Waters were the moose, woodland caribou, and beaver. White-tailed deer were present but apparently rare. With the beginning of European settlement and large-scale logging about 1890, the mix of large herbivores in northeastern Minnesota began a series of shifts that continues to this day. During all this time the wolf has remained the principal predator of these herbivores, but populations have fluctuated in response to regional vegetation changes and to complex interactions between predator-prey, climatic, and disease factors, human activities, and other vari-

ables. This story is best understood through profiles of each species.

MOOSE

The moose, like all deer, is a ruminant. It has a series of complex stomachs, the first being the rumen, where microbes partially digest and detoxify leaves, twigs, conifer needles, and aquatic plants, which are then regurgitated, chewed as a cud, and mixed with saliva for further digestion. Moose are expert swimmers and waders and do much feeding on aquatic plants, their principal source of salt (sodium), particularly in this region, where the content of sodium in the soils and vegetation is low (Jordan 1987). In spring, moose in the Boundary Waters feed on the forbs that are the first to show new growth. In early summer, they switch to leaves and twig tips of quaking aspen, mountain-maple, choke- and pin-cherry, paper birch, juneberry, and beaked hazelnut. Submerged aquatics become important in June and early July. In early fall, red osier dogwood is favored. As leaves dry and fall, ferns and other forbs are taken. Winter browse is primarily twigs of the same species as in summer, as well as balsam fir, white pine, and northern white cedar (Peek 1971).

Moose prefer regions with many lakes, ponds, and streams and a high proportion of aspen stands and lowland forests. Large burns or clear-cuts covering at least several hundred acres containing areas of young aspen and birch provide optimum forage for 15 to 20 years after disturbance. In severe winters, access to dense conifer stands for bedding becomes important, and upland stands with balsam are preferred for browsing (Peek 1971). The highest moose populations in the BWCAW in recent decades have been in areas cut for pulpwood between 1948 and 1978, such as the vast Tomahawk Sale, and on recent burns, such as the Little Sioux. At high populations, as on Isle Royale in Lake Superior, moose browsing of balsam saplings and other preferred winter foods can severely reduce the successful regeneration of such trees and shrubs (Brandner, Peterson, and Risenhoover 1990).

Moose have surprisingly small home ranges for such large animals. Many spend most of their lives in a few square miles. Some yearlings, however, disperse considerable distances, a factor in rapid population increases often seen on new burns (Peek 1971, 1974). Their long legs and thick winter coats make moose much better adapted than deer to deep snows and severe winter temperatures. These traits make it possible for moose to feed in large open burns or logged areas and still escape wolves even when snow depths exceed 18 inches (Peek 1971, 1974; Telfer and Kelsall 1984).

On the Little Sioux burn of 1971 in the Echo Trail area within and adjacent to the BWCAW, moose increased rapidly through 1973, at first through immigration of both sexes, especially yearlings dispersing from nearby range. By 1973 the good nutrition provided by new growth on the burn evidently increased fecundity because the percentage of cows with twins rose from none in 1971 and 1972 to 42 percent by 1973. The moose population of the study area of 27,000 acres increased from an estimated 17 animals before the fire to 112 in 1973 (Irwin 1974; Peek 1974). Data collected by Irwin (1974) indicate that many moose ranged on open areas of the Little Sioux burn from May through September. In October they began shifting to the edges of the burn or to unburned forests off the burn, probably to be near winter browse and to shelter from cold in stands of balsam and spruce.

A tiny parasitic brain worm (*Parelaphostrongylus tenuis*), carried without ill effects by white-tailed deer, is fatal to moose and caribou. First-stage larval brain worms in deer

pellets enter snails and slugs as their intermediate hosts, and there they develop to the infective stage. When snails and slugs become active in the spring, infective larvae may be ingested by feeding deer, moose, or caribou. The worms migrate via the spinal cord to the meninges (outer covering) of the brain, where they burrow into brain tissues. Prior to death, such animals wander aimlessly, showing little fear of humans. Moose and caribou populations may suffer serious mortality in areas with high numbers of infected deer. This parasite may be an important cause of the moose decline that began early in the 1900s (Karns 1967a,b).

The moose population did not recover significantly until the deer population in the wilderness reserves collapsed as early as 1950 as a result of habitat deterioration caused by maturing forests and succession on the early logging areas and on the extensive burns of 1863–64, 1875, 1894, and 1910. Wolf predation compounded the effects of habitat deterioration during a series of severe winters between 1965 and 1976. These habitat and weather changes were unfavorable to moose as well, but moose were not so seriously affected by snow depths and low temperatures as were deer, and they were thus better able to cope with wolves (Mech et al. 1987).

In the mid-1980s the winter tick (*Dermacenter albipictus*) caused some moose mortality in northwestern Minnesota. By late winter 1991 it was apparent that the northeastern herd had suffered about a 45 percent population decrease, evidently due primarily to the winter tick (Fredric Thunhorst, Minn. Department of Natural Resources, personal communication, 1991).

The wolf is the major predator of moose in the Boundary Waters, but wolves take primarily the weakest calves, plus old, diseased, or injured adults. In the southern and western BWCAW, most packs depended primarily on deer and took few moose until after the virtual elimination of wintering deer by 1977 (Nelson and Mech 1986b). At that point, some BWCAW wolf packs developed larger territories and switched to moose (Mech 1986). Certain areas deep in the virgin forests of the BWCAW, such as the Little Saganaga Lake area, and probably some areas of Quetico never had significant wintering deer. Wolf packs using those areas may always have taken some moose (Mech and Karns 1977).

Black bear also may take some newborn and weak calves, although this is not well documented.

Statistically controlled aerial censusing of moose since 1962 showed that the estimated moose population in the northeastern Minnesota census area fluctuated at just under 3,000 until 1966–67 (Karns 1967a) and had more than doubled by 1988, when about 2,000 lived in the BWCAW alone, mostly in low density because of poor habitat. The Little Sioux burn became a high-density area soon after the 1971 fire and remained so until about 1989.

Limited permit hunting of moose began in Minnesota in 1971 and continued in alternate years until 1991, when the season was temporarily closed in the northeast because of the tick-related population decline that cut the herd to about 3,700 moose. From the late 1970s through 1989, around 100 to 150 moose per season were taken in the BWCAW, mostly from the high-density areas from Gabbro and Bald Eagle lakes eastward through the Tomahawk and Tofte Block timber sale areas to the Gunflint Trail. The BWCAW take in 1989 was about 126 moose. Quetico and Voyageurs are closed to hunting, and there was little hunting in the more remote northern sections of the BWCAW, if only because of the difficulty in portaging out such a large weight of meat.

WHITE-TAILED DEER

White-tailed deer were a staple in the diet of Native Americans 1,900 to 2,500 years ago in the Rainy River area and near Nett Lake, close to Voyageurs (Lukens 1963). In 1880, when European settlement began, deer were apparently rare in most sections of the BWCAW (Peek 1971), and since 1900, regional populations have fluctuated wildly (Stenlund 1955; Erickson et al. 1961; Mech and Karns 1977; Nelson and Mech 1986b).

Deer are much smaller and shorter-legged than moose or caribou and are thus not so well adapted to deep snow (Telfer and Kelsall 1984). Their continental distribution is largely south of the boreal forest, so their productivity in the BWCAW region is less than it is in the heart of their range farther south. The brain worm (*P. tenuis*) is normal in deer, which are the primary carriers of this serious parasite of moose and caribou (Karns 1967b).

During much of the year, deer feed, move about, and rest both day and night, although there are often activity peaks near dawn and dusk. In severe winter periods, however, they feed chiefly during warmer daylight hours and bed beneath balsam, spruce, or cedar at night. In areas of heavy snow, as in the eastern BWCAW near Saganaga Lake, deer leave in the winter (unless they are fed at the lodges nearby).

In the Boundary Waters, the best spring, summer, and fall deer range is in aspen-birch and mixed conifer-broadleaf forests, with 20 to 50 percent of the area in small recently clear-cut areas or new burns, each perhaps 15 to 30 acres in area. By 20 years after logging or fire, the forest has regrown to the point that range quality is reduced. On the Little Sioux burn 2 and 3 years after the fire, major summer foods for deer included asters, fireweed, pale pea, clover, goldenrod, and jewelweed. In June deer also spent much time in streams and ponds feeding on water-milfoil and pond lilies as a source of sodium. In late summer and fall they used more browse, especially red maple, paper birch, pin-cherry, and bush-honeysuckle. Jack pine seedlings and sweet fern were much used in early winter. From May through October, deer preferred the burn, but from November through April, much of their activity was confined to unburned forests along the edge of the burn or beyond (Irwin 1974). Before European settlement, the forests did include large areas of favored forest communities, but the burns were mostly much too large for deer; the forest mosaic favored moose and caribou, not deer.

Before the virtual collapse of the deer population between 1968 and 1977, deer occupied summer ranges in moderate numbers throughout the Boundary Waters. Populations were high in some of the early logging areas and on some of the later burns in the virgin areas of the BWCAW. By the 1950s deer were declining in the Gunflint region, but at the same time, populations were increasing on the new cutovers of the Tomahawk Sale and other large pulpwood operations along the south side of the BWCAW. This trend continued until the severe winter of 1968–69, when the population went into a steep decline statewide. But pockets of good populations in the BWCAW, such as on the Little Sioux burn, persisted until about 1974.

The subsequent collapse of the deer population in the Boundary Waters has several linked primary causes. First, the maturing of forests in the early logging areas and on recent burns in the virgin areas, plus succession to balsam, reduced the quantity and quality of both summer and winter foods. This led to poor nutrition, lowered fawn production, and an excess of male fawns. Second, a series of severe winters with deep snow between 1968 and 1977 placed cumulative stresses on an already vulnerable deer herd (Mech et al. 1987; DelGiudice, Nelson, and Mech 1991). And finally, with increased hunting pressure on does (until bucks-only hunting began in 1974) as well as wolf predation, the BWCAW deer population dwindled to a tiny remnant within a decade (Mech and Karns 1977; Nelson and Mech 1986a,b). Telemetry studies of radio-collared wolves and deer, begun in 1968 and 1974, documented the collapse and initial stages of recovery of part of the BWCAW deer population and gave fascinating insights into the movement patterns and behavior of deer and wolves (Hoskinson and Mech 1976; Mech and Karns 1977; Nelson and Mech 1981, 1986a,b, 1987; Nelson 1990).

Many deer in the region migrate 5 to 20 miles into winter yards, where they congregate in loose groups of 50 or more and tramp out trails that help them escape wolves and move about while feeding. Yarding is now understood to be an antipredator strategy (Nelson and Mech 1981, 1991). Wintering areas are often in cedar swamps, dense mixed lowland conifer stands, or aspen-birch-balsam areas. High deer concentrations can change the vegetation composition in such traditional wintering areas. Cedar commonly shows a distinct browse line in deer yards as well as in swamps and along lakeshores in some BWCAW areas, a clear indication of present or past heavy deer use.

In spring, about 80 percent of deer in the yards studied migrated directly to their traditional summer ranges, taking a few days at most. Fawns are born and reared on these ranges. Yearlings disperse and colonize new or vacant habitats, for example, in buffer zones between wolf pack territories (Mech 1977a; Rogers et al. 1980).

The return to winter yards comes in November with the arrival of cold, snowy weather. Migration patterns and home ranges are traditional, passed on from parents to off-spring, and most deer do not move onto the ranges of deer from adjacent yards. The populations of each yard are more or less discrete, and considerable inbreeding seems to occur (Nelson and Mech 1987).

A deer population decline similar to that in the BWCAW also occurred in Quetico, where hunting is not allowed, and to a lesser extent in Voyageurs. The deer population remained significantly higher in the northwestern Superior National Forest than in areas to the east adjacent to the lightly hunted BWCAW. Greater average snow depths in the east may be a partial explanation for this difference, as well as greater wolf densities.

With a return to milder winters after 1978, a gradual increase in deer populations occurred throughout northeastern Minnesota. The shift to bucks-only hunting and later to limited permit hunting of antlerless deer was no doubt also a factor in the regional deer recovery. By 1986 to 1988, an estimated 0.65 to 1.30 deer per square mile were summering in the north-central BWCAW area studied by Nelson, but deer were still rare farther north (Nelson 1990). There still were few or no wintering deer in most of the interior in 1990. I saw no deer and very few tracks or droppings on long canoe trips into the Hunter Island region of Quetico every fall from 1982 to 1992. By 1986 the Minnesota deer census showed higher deer populations in some areas of the Superior National Forest near the Boundary Waters, especially west of Ely.

WOODLAND CARIBOU

Caribou occupied a vital niche in the ecosystem until the early years of the twentieth century. They are no longer present in Minnesota, but it may be possible to restore them to the BWCAW. Understanding their problems deepens our knowledge of the system. The woodland subspecies is a magnificent boreal deer, intermediate in size between moose and white-tails. Caribou are well adapted to deep snow and cold. Their dense underfur, covered by hair filled with air bubbles, provides excellent insulation and makes them buoyant, strong swimmers. Large, rounded, sharp hooves with large dewclaws give good support on snow and aid digging in snow for food (Fashingbauer 1965; Hazard 1982; Telfer and Kelsall 1984). Woodland caribou generally have larger home ranges than moose or deer and tend to wander in small bands, particularly in winter. Some populations migrate 5 to 50 miles or more between summer and winter ranges; others do not move appreciably. In summer caribou are often solitary (Darby et al. 1989).

Until about 1800, caribou occurred as far south in Minnesota as Mille Lacs and Kanabec counties, but by 1880, they were confined to the northeast and the big-bog region north of the Red Lakes. They were still common in Lake and Cook counties in 1885. Land Office Survey notes by George Stuntz, dated July 30, 1892, for Township 59, Range 11, describing the Snowshoe Lake Bog (6 to 9 miles southeast of Babbitt), state that "great numbers of caribou (American Reindeer) live in these swamps on the mosses [lichens] that grow in great abundance. If these animals are to be preserved a park by 10 square miles should be fenced and guarded as they are fast disappearing before the Winchester rifles of hunters" (as quoted in Trygg 1966, 53). Thereafter the population collapse was rapid. Caribou hunting in Minnesota was prohibited in 1905. Individuals have occasionally been sighted since then near Lake Superior and the Canadian border, most recently in 1981. They probably wandered from the herd in the Lake Nipigon area, 150 miles to the northeast (Mech, Nelson, and Drabik 1982).

Why did the caribou disappear from the Boundary Waters and fail to return after hunting was stopped in Minnesota and Ontario? The excessive hunting by settlers, prospectors, and loggers was probably a major factor in the initial decline. Another important cause was probably the brain worm, to which caribou are extremely vulnerable (Anderson 1972). Today there is little overlap in the ranges of white-tailed deer and caribou anywhere in North America, suggesting that the brain worm may be more lethal to caribou than moose (Bergerud and Mercer 1989). The Slate Islands in Lake Superior have no deer, and the caribou are free of the brain worm. The Nipigon-Armstrong population also is in a region essentially devoid of deer. There is evidence that a low deer population existed in northeastern Minnesota before the caribou decline, but their final demise coincided with a manyfold increase in deer, even if the decline began before the deer upsurge.

Predation is another important factor regulating caribou populations. Wolf, lynx, and bear are present in the BWCAW and can be effective caribou predators, primarily on calves during their first year. Woodland caribou prefer to use islands, lakeshores, and open bogs as calving areas, apparently to avoid predators. The caribou's opportunity to detect predators early is probably better in such open sites, and wolves have difficulty killing caribou in water. The Nipigon population, which is subject to wolf predation, uses islands. Also, wolves have difficulty taking adult caribou in winter (Bergerud 1971, 1985; Bergerud and Mercer 1989; Darby et al. 1989).

Interest in reintroducing caribou has been developing in Minnesota. Studies were made to locate a possible region for release that would meet these criteria: suitable habitat, including food resources and secure calving areas; very low deer density, and very low brain worm larval infection in deer pellets; and wolf density as low as possible. By a process of elimination, the Little Saganaga Lake region of the BWCAW was tentatively selected as the only acceptable site (Gogan, Jordan, and Nelson 1990).

By 1988 private funding through the North Central Caribou Corporation stimulated a new cooperative effort involving the Minnesota Department of Natural Resources, U.S. Forest Service, U.S. Fish and Wildlife Service, and University of Minnesota and Ontario biologists. New assessments of brain worm problems, wolf predation potential, and caribou habitat were under way in an enlarged possible release area in the Little Saganaga Lake region. Collections of deer fecal pellet groups in that region and in distant deer wintering areas in 1989 and 1990 indicated infection rates by first-stage brain worm larvae of 25 to 60 percent in various areas (Jordan and Pitt 1989; Pitt and Jordan 1991). However, deer were extremely scarce in the possible release region, and it is likely that the brain worm infections in deer occurred in and near the wintering yards, not in the Little Saganaga Lake region. Very large areas to the north and northwest in Quetico also harbored virtually no deer and offered promising habitat. Thus, the brain worm and habitat situations seemed favorable. Wolf predation remained a concern. The Little Saganaga Lake site was selected because the deer population was very low and brain worm larval infection in fecal pellets was only 5 percent. The large number of islands might afford calving sites safe from wolves. Wolf density was near 1 per 10 square miles and declining rapidly. Very large areas to the north and northwest in Quetico also harbored virtually no deer and offered promising habitat.

After 80 years of effort in Ontario and the United States to restore the BWCAW-Quetico-Voyageurs ecosystem, the balance between human pressures, vegetation, caribou, competing herbivores, and predators is still so tenuous that the caribou's future remains in doubt. But the chances for a successful release look favorable, and if the effort goes forward, perhaps it will succeed.

BEAVER

The beaver is a fascinating member of the Boundary Waters ecosystem, with surprisingly important effects on other elements of the system for such a small animal. In the Boundary Waters most colonies live in lodges built of sticks and mud piled several feet high against a lakeshore, but some lodges are freestanding domes in shallow-water ponds or streams. On a few streams, such as Quetico's Wawiag River, colonies may live in burrows in the streambank, but such sites are uncommon. Lodge and burrow entrances are underwater and lead to low, fairly long rooms where winter temperatures rarely fall below freezing.

In summer, beavers eat water-lilies, sedges, reeds, cattail, arrowhead, pondweed, grasses, and leaves and new-growth twigs of some deciduous species. Roots, rhizomes, and tubers are much used. In late summer and fall, beaver cut the trees and shrubs they use to build or repair lodges and dams and to supply food caches to carry them through winter. Quaking aspen is by far the favored food, followed by willow and mountain-ash. Paper birch and balsam poplar are less favored, and speckled alder is cut largely for construction (Longley and Moyle 1963). Sometimes aspens 15 inches in diameter and 75 feet tall are felled and debarked, and the treetops are consumed, or made accessible to other browsers, such as moose and hare. Saplings are less desirable because they contain toxic compounds. The food cache is generally sunk in front of the lodge in late September and October. Beaver remain active all winter, feeding on their cache and on aquatic plants beneath the ice. Waterways bordered with aspen-birch forests provide optimum habitat for beaver. In the ecosystem before European settlement, such forests were the result of forest fires. Beaver return to burned-over watersheds within 5 or 10 years after fire to exploit the small trees of early postfire forests.

The wolf is the most effective predator of beaver, which often are a small but important part of the wolf's diet. Most beaver are probably taken when they are inland, cutting trees and shrubs (Mech 1970). Beaver are wary of this risk, however, and in the Boundary Waters they seldom cut trees more than 200 to 300 feet from water. On the Slate Islands, where no wolves occur, beaver make trails to alternative cutting areas up to a half mile from water.

Dams are built to raise water levels to increase security and provide more space under the ice. Wood, rocks, and mud are used to build the dams higher and higher as the water level rises. In the process, streams and lowlands that otherwise would be impassable are made deep enough for canoes. Large areas may be flooded, killing the trees and expanding habitats for waterfowl and moose (Heinselman 1961; Naiman, Melillo, and Hobbie 1986). When beavers exhaust their food resources, the colony may abandon the site. The dam will break for lack of maintenance, but the legacy is a wet meadow on the sediment accumulated behind the dam.

The beaver population of much of North America including Minnesota was decimated by the fur trade. The BWCAW region was gradually repopulated from 1880 to 1920. Beaver die-offs caused by tularemia occur occasionally, as in 1951–52 (Longley and Moyle 1963). Trapping in the BWCAW in the interior has never been extensive. The population increased again between about 1955 and 1970, but in recent years more and more lakes and ponds are losing beaver colonies through loss of available winter foods. As forests mature, aspen and birch stands near lakeshores and streams are felled by beaver and replaced by conifers that beaver do not use. This is a perfectly natural sequence, but before European settlement, such aspen-birch stands were periodically renewed by fires that often burned right down to the lake or stream. With fire suppression, this renewal process has been virtually halted, and little by little the beaver habitat is disappearing from the waterways.

WOLF

The gray wolf is now one of the rarest mammals in the United States, save in Alaska. In 1991 Minnesota still had the only truly viable population in the lower 48 states, although there were some animals in Wisconsin, Michigan, Montana, and Idaho, and some of these populations are growing. The wolves in the Boundary Waters area have been more intensively studied than those anywhere else in the world. Because of protection, the wolf population in Minnesota has grown to an estimated 1,550 to 1,750 (Cohn 1990). Of these, perhaps 200 live in the BWCAW, Voyageurs, and the road corridors immediately adjacent to those reserves. Quetico has perhaps another 100 wolves. A continuous population exists northward in Ontario and elsewhere in Canada and Alaska. Full protection under the federal Endangered Species Act came in August 1974.

In Minnesota 62 percent of wolves possess some coyote-type mitochondrial DNA (genetic material), indicating that hybridization with coyotes has occurred in the past, perhaps recently when coyotes invaded the cutover region. The matings that introduced coyote DNA were between male wolves and female coyotes (Lehman et al. 1991). Three diseases, canine parvovirus, Lyme disease, and heartworm, may pose serious problems for wolves (Mech 1991).

Wolves are strongly territorial. Packs defend their territories by scent-marking the boundaries with urine and feces, by howling, and by driving off and sometimes killing trespassing wolves. Mech and co-workers mapped and followed changes in the territories of some 14 wolf packs that hunted the east-central BWCAW and immediate environs between 1967 and 1991. Pack territories varied from 48 to 120 square miles. Most packs had fairly stable territory boundaries over periods of several years, but there were substantial changes in boundaries, loss of some packs, and expansion of certain territories with the collapse of the BWCAW deer population between 1969 and 1977 (Mech 1970, 1973, 1977b, 1986, 1991; Harrington and Mech 1979).

The general location of some of the packs studied is evident from their names: Glenmore Lake, Newton Lake,

Pagami Lake, Greenstone Lake, Ensign Lake, Thomas Lake, Quadga Lake, Maniwaki Lake, Knife Lake, Canadian Point, Sawbill Lake, Wood Lake, Little Gabbro Lake, and Malberg Lake. The largest packs were the Ensign Lake at 15 during the winter of 1971–72, which declined and had a complex history thereafter; the Maniwaki Lake at 14 in the winter of 1969–70, which dropped to 9 by the winter of 1971–72; and the Knife Lake at 13 in the winter of 1968–69. Spring pack sizes are usually smaller because of the loss of dispersers and the death of some members (Mech 1973, 1977b, 1986). In addition, a pack that traditionally hunts the Nina Moose Lake region of the BWCAW had 15 members in 1951, according to Stenlund (1955), and a pack of at least 6 was near Cruiser Lake in Voyageurs in the summer of 1987. I have also seen and heard wolves elsewhere in the BWCAW and encountered tracks and scats throughout the BWCAW and Quetico in many years of work and recreational canoe trips, fall hikes, and snowshoe treks. Thus, although wolf studies have not covered the entire Boundary Waters, certainly packs were present throughout the area as of 1991.

The principal prey in the Boundary Waters are deer, moose, and formerly caribou. Beaver are a small but at times significant food source. Wolves occasionally take snowshoe hares, porcupine, grouse, mice, and other small mammals and birds, but these are not an important portion of the diet. Wolves are capable of fasting for several weeks when they have difficulty taking prey, and of gorging heavily when kills are made. No attacks on humans by healthy wild wolves are documented in North America.

From 1920 until about 1970, deer were by far the most important prey in the region, but with the deer decline from 1969 to 1977, many BWCAW packs either disappeared or restructured their territories and shifted primarily to moose. Moose are not only a more challenging prey but exist at much lower densities than deer. Wolves occasionally are killed by moose, and rarely even by deer. Packs that depend on a moose economy must have larger territories, and a larger pack size is advantageous. A year after the heavy snow and cold winter of 1968–69, in which many deer were taken by wolves and considerable surplus killing occurred, the wolf population in the central BWCAW increased. The deer population was so decimated, the range so poor, and the succeeding winters so severe, that wintering deer in much of the BWCAW were eliminated by 1972–73. In those few areas where remnants existed, they continued to decline until at least 1975. Packs living primarily on deer consequently also declined. A pack must take about 15 deer per wolf annually, and that kill rate was simply no longer possible after 1969. The inevitable result was starvation and stress in most wolf packs (Olson 1938b; Stenlund 1955; Mech 1966, 1986, 1991; Mech and Karns 1977; Nelson and Mech 1985; Mech and Nelson 1990b). The winter wolf population in Mech's central Superior National Forest study area east of Ely fell from a peak of 87 in 1969–70 to only 35 by 1983–84. For packs feeding primarily on deer, the decline was even greater, from 87 to 23. After 1984, the population remained essentially stable through 1988 (Mech 1977b, 1986; DelGiudice, Mech, and Seal 1991).

The history of the Malberg Lake Pack is an instructive example of the kinds of population adjustments that occurred during this period. Before 1977, the northeastern part of Mech's study area had lost its wintering deer and its deer-killing wolves. The area supported a good moose herd, however, and by the winter of 1977–78, wolves had begun recolonizing the area. That winter 2 wolves were identified as the Malberg Lake Pack. By the winter of 1982–83, the pack had 12 members, preying exclusively on moose and occupying 20 percent of the study area. Then in spring 1984, 4 Malberg Lake Pack wolves split off and colonized the southeastern half of the territory, expanded farther to the southeast, and grew to 7 by spring 1985. This pack was renamed the Maniwaki Lake Pack because it had reoccupied most of the former range of a pack by that name that had 14 members in winter 1969–70 but had died out by 1984. Also, by winter 1984–85, a new pack of 5, the Quadga Lake Pack, was colonizing the southwestern 20 percent of the Malberg Lake Pack's territory and expanding southwestward. It is unclear whether the wolves preying on moose came from a moose-killing population farther north or dispersed from deer-killing packs and learned to use moose. These kinds of adjustments allowed the wolf population to stabilize at about 1 wolf per 17 square miles by 1986, down from about 1 per 10 square miles before the

decline (Mech 1986). Trends were probably similar in Quetico and Voyageurs.

The importance of interactions among vegetation, prey-population changes, winter severity, and wolf populations in the Boundary Waters should be clear from the preceding sections on deer, moose, caribou, and beaver. The wolf's future is inextricably tied to the fate of its prey, whose welfare depends heavily on the status of the vegetation mosaic on the landscape. Thus, in the final analysis the wolf is as dependent on the forest community and stand-age-class structure of the vegetation mosaic as is its prey. Fire exclusion has generated a wave of forest maturation, senescence, and succession to balsam that is reducing food resources for prey and predator alike.

Black Bear

Black bears are the only bears in the Boundary Waters; grizzlies may have occurred in extreme western Minnesota before European settlement, but not in the northeast. Bears have acute hearing, an exceptional sense of smell, color vision, and soft foot pads that permit them to move quietly —traits that help them avoid people. They can run as fast as 25 miles per hour (Rogers 1977a; Fair and Rogers 1990).

Bears, like humans, are omnivorous: they eat both plant and animal matter. They concentrate on carbohydrate-rich berries, fruits, and nuts in the fall to build up the body fat they must accumulate to survive the winter denning period. In the Boundary Waters, blueberry, pin-cherry, choke-cherry, juneberry, raspberry, wild sarsaparilla, hazelnuts, and in a few areas, acorns of red and northern pin oak are especially favored. Mountain-ash berries and bunchberries are eaten where available. Ant eggs, ants, grubs, tent caterpillars, other insects, fish, occasional small mammals, and carrion are their principal sources of protein and fat. They rarely prey on larger mammals but do take deer fawns and even moose and caribou calves. The weight gains that bears must make before denning are largely attained during the summer berry crop season, and their success at producing cubs depends on their weight as they begin hibernation (Rogers 1977a, 1978, 1981; Arimond 1979, 1980; Fair and Rogers 1990).

Most of the important berries bears rely on are found in greatest abundance in open areas or low-density forests, and in virgin forests primarily on recent burns. For example, blueberries are generally most abundant and of best quality two to six years after fire in jack pine and black spruce forests. The scarcity of recent burns in the present virgin areas of the BWCAW and Quetico due to fire control undoubtedly poses food-resource problems for bears in many years. Sarsaparilla is found in mature forests, however, so a mosaic of young and mature stands provides optimum habitat. Access to large, rough-barked, limby trees is important to cub survival. Cubs climb such trees to escape danger on signal from their mothers, and large white pines are preferred. Refuge trees are remembered sites in a bear's territory (Fair and Rogers 1990; Rogers 1991).

Because hazelnuts and acorns are the only fall nut crops in the Boundary Waters and are only occasionally or locally abundant, bears must usually turn to greens and whatever animal matter they can find to fill out their fall diets. It is in years of poor summer berry crops and fall nut crops that canoeists have the most problems with bears raiding campsites for food and that homeowners on the edge of the wilderness are troubled with nuisance bears. Scarcity of fall foods means that Boundary Waters bears must slow their activity and begin to prepare their dens in September and go into hibernation by late October (Rogers 1976, 1977a, 1981; Fair and Rogers 1990).

Dens are usually made in burrows, caves, rock crevices, or hollow logs or dug under fallen trees or brush. Openings are just large enough to permit the bear to enter, and the chamber is usually 3 to 5 feet wide and 2 to 3 feet high. The main insulation is the bear's own thick fur, but nests of leaves, grass, cedar bark, and so on also protect bears from the cold ground. Snow cover helps limit the low temperature in the den to only a few degrees below freezing except in winters with scant snow. Bears den alone except for females with cubs (Rogers 1981, 1987; Fair and Rogers 1990).

Boundary Waters bears commonly go 5 to 7 months without eating, depending on summer and fall food availability. They cut their metabolic rate nearly in half while still maintaining body temperatures at 88° to 98°F, just a little below their summer temperatures of 100° to 101°F. Their body fat is consumed over winter with little loss of flesh. During denning, they do not eat or drink, they defecate and urinate very occasionally, and their heart rates sometimes fall to as low as 8 beats per minute. Respiration may fall to only 1 breath every 45 seconds. The little urea produced is broken down and its nitrogen reutilized to synthesize amino acids needed to maintain body proteins. In spite of these changes, bears are easily awakened if disturbed during hibernation. By spring, most bears have lost 15 to 25 percent of their body weight. Females suckling cubs sometimes lose as much as 40 percent. Despite this incredible drain, denning deaths are rare (Rogers 1977a, 1981, 1987; Wolfe et al. 1982; Fair and Rogers 1990).

Female bears reach reproductive age at 3 to 8 years and continue to have cubs at 2- to 4-year intervals until age 20 years or more. Age of maturity and intervals between litters vary with food supply. The breeding season is in June and July, but embryo development is delayed until the last 3 months of pregnancy. Two to four cubs are born in the mother's den in January. They weigh less than a pound, are almost naked, and are suckled in the den. By April, when the family leaves the den, cubs weigh 4 to 8 pounds and can climb trees to escape predators such as wolves. Cubs are suckled through July and remain with their mother over the next winter (Rogers 1977a, 1987; Fair and Rogers 1990). Watching a mother bear feeding on blueberries with her two cubs is a rare treat. They seem almost human as they walk about in a recently logged area looking for choice clusters of berries, which they deftly strip from the bushes with their mouths, climb trees when strange sounds are heard, or watch and listen for oncoming cars before crossing a nearby highway.

Cubs usually leave their mothers in June of their 2nd year. Females tend to settle near their mother's territory, but males disperse, often more than 100 miles, before settling. Males are aggressive toward other males during the mating season and range over large areas that include the territories of several females. Males leave scent on "bear trees" by scratching, biting, or rubbing selected trees. Both sexes are promiscuous. Female territories average 3.7 square miles and are defended against other females. Adults of both sexes tend to be solitary except in the breeding season or when feeding in areas of unusual food abundance. In late summer, both males and females often leave their usual ranges and move many miles to feed in areas of unusual food availability such as blueberry patches, oak stands with acorns, or, outside the wilderness, garbage dumps. Males often travel farther than females on these fall foragings. They later return to their home ranges for denning (Rogers 1977b, 1987; Fair and Rogers 1990).

During periods of extreme food shortages, cub and yearling mortality increases greatly. For example, Rogers (1977b) found that after the 1974–76 drought in the Boundary Waters, 88 percent of cubs born during the 3rd consecutive year of food scarcity died before reaching 1.5 years of age. During such periods, lean females either had no cubs or their cubs died at unusually high rates. In Roger's study area near Ely, the population fell 35 percent from 1 bear per 1.7 square miles to 1 per 2.4 square miles by June 1977. More than 90 percent of cub and yearling mortality was from natural causes. In 1990 the black bear population of the BWCAW was about 700 animals (Rogers 1976, 1977a,b; Fair and Rogers 1990).

Most adult bear deaths in northeastern Minnesota are caused by people, primarily by hunters and by the shooting of nuisance bears (Rogers 1977a,b). In the more remote regions of the BWCAW and Quetico, human-caused mortality may be less important, and many adults may live 10 to 20 years. Rogers had one radio-collared bear 26 years old. Even many wilderness bears are shot because they raid campsites, or because they leave the wilderness in search of food during years of scarcity.

Bears are good swimmers and often patronize island campsites. Keeping a clean camp, burning all food scraps, and hanging food packs on high ropes between trees will prevent most losses. But at campsites where particular bears have been successful, visits are likely even if no food is available. Attacks on people are very rare but have occurred. During an 18-year study of bear-human interactions, Rogers did not receive a single attack report in 18 million visitor days of BWCAW use. The very next year a single emaciated female attacked two visitors on successive days. Both recovered. Most visiting bears can be driven from campsites by

yelling, waving arms, and banging pans. If this fails, the campsite should be abandoned. Bears may threaten campers by blowing, clacking their teeth, slapping the ground or trees, or making short rushes toward them. These are almost always bluffs, according to Rogers, and black bears virtually never attack persons during or after such threats (Rogers 1987; Fair and Rogers 1990). Bears are fascinating members of the natural wilderness ecosystem and if respected and treated as wild animals, add much interest to visitors' trips.

Insectivores

Five shrews occur in the Boundary Waters: the masked shrew, arctic shrew, northern water shrew, pygmy shrew, and short-tailed shrew. All are very small, and the pygmy shrew is the world's smallest mammal at a total length of only 3 to 4 inches, including the tail. These shrews might be mistaken for mice because of their small size and generally brown, gray, or blackish coats, but they have long slim snouts, tiny eyes, and very different habits. All have voracious appetites, feeding every few hours day and night, winter and summer. In winter, they forage primarily in the litter layer beneath the snow. All apparently eat some combination of adult and larval insects, spiders, centipedes, sow bugs, snails, slugs, mice, other shrews, and a certain amount of vegetation, particularly seeds in winter.

The arctic shrew and other shrews may help limit outbreaks of the larch sawfly, a serious defoliator of tamarack, by eating overwintering sawfly larvae found in the surface organic layers of bogs. The water shrew lives near water and swims readily, but it depends at least in part on slugs, earthworms, and spiders found on land. The shrews are preyed on by hawks and owls (Hazard 1982).

The star-nosed mole is a bizarre-looking blackish mole, with a nose ending in a disk fringed with 22 pink fleshy papillae. It lives in wet meadows, swamps, and bogs. It is a good swimmer and feeds mainly on aquatic invertebrates. Rarely seen, it is active year-round both day and night, often above ground. However, its burrows in organic soils frequently end under water. In winter it may swim under the ice (Hazard 1982; Siderits 1981).

Bats

Six species of bat inhabit the Boundary Waters: the little brown bat, eastern long-eared bat, silver-haired bat, big brown bat, red bat, and hoary bat. They eat primarily such flying insects as moths, mayflies, and beetles, hunting in late evening and after dark. In the wilderness they roost in trees, rock crevices, and caves. Many probably migrate to caves, mines, and buildings located far south of the Boundary Waters to hibernate for the winter. The hibernation sites for many Minnesota bat colonies are not known. Bats are long-lived, some living 20 years or more. Females generally raise only one or two offspring each year (Hazard 1982).

Snowshoe Hare

The snowshoe hare inhabits all of boreal North America and is named for its large furry hind feet that offer support on soft snow. It is the only member of the rabbit and hare family in the Boundary Waters. In summer, its coat is grayish brown, but a white winter coat develops in November, usually coinciding with the arrival of permanent snow cover. It tends to be solitary, and its home range covers only a few acres (Gunderson and Beer 1953). Snowshoes are prolific. Breeding begins in March and continues into August, with females raising litters of three or four young, three or four times each season. This high reproductive potential is balanced in the long run by mortality, but the snowshoe population fluctuations offer classic examples of the complex interrelations among herbivore prey species reproductive capacity, food sources, predation, and other mortality factors.

The snowshoe hare population cycle has been widely studied (Grange 1949; Keith and Windberg 1978; Akcakaya 1992). Variations in the abundance of snowshoes of up to sevenfold between highs and lows tend to come at intervals of 7 to 11 years and may have dramatic effects on the abundance of the hare's principal predators: the Canada lynx, bobcat, fisher, and the barred, great gray, and great horned owls (Hazard 1982; Powell 1982). The regularity and amplitude of population cycles are stronger in the far

north than in the Boundary Waters. These fluctuations are still not well understood.

During summer, hares feed on a wide variety of herbaceous plants, especially large-leaved aster and twisted-stalk. They also take deciduous leaves. In winter, snowshoes feed on the bark, small stems, and twigs of aspen, paper birch, jack pine, alder, and northern white cedar. In the dormant season, when deciduous leaves are lacking, hares require cover from predators; hence, they are most often found near thickets of white or black spruce or northern white cedar with foliated limbs extending to the ground or snow surface. Thus, damage to hardwood seedlings will be greatest in forests of mixed hardwood-conifers and in lowlands where low conifers are common. During population highs, hares can remove nearly all small seedlings of paper birch, jack pine, and white cedar. Although new seedlings arise and survive during population lows, this impact at the very least can slow down some aspects of forest development (Grange 1949; Akcakaya 1992).

In the forests before European settlement and in the virgin forests of the BWCAW and Quetico, forest fires were the principal agent that generated the dense young stands of aspen, birch, willow, and jack pine so favorable to hares. Fires often result in short-term reductions in hare populations because of reduced food supplies and cover, but new highs soon occur (Keith and Surrendi 1971). Predators increase during population highs, and when declines are under way, predation exacerbates downward trends. The high levels of predators that build up tend to keep hares low for several years beyond their own ability to rebound. When hare populations fall to very low levels, the lynx, bobcat, and owl populations are ultimately affected, and reduced predation then aids the recovery of the snowshoes (Grange 1949; Hazard 1982; Akcakaya 1992).

I have watched the snowshoe populations fluctuate in northeastern Minnesota for more than half a century, and it seemed that the highs of the 1920s, 1930s, 1940s, and 1950s were much higher than those of later decades. Great increases in the young aspen stands and palatable shrubs came in the wake of the early logging and slash fires, habitat changes very favorable to the snowshoe. In the forests of the Boundary Waters before European settlement, snowshoes undoubtedly reached their highest populations on recent burns. Bark girdling of young aspen, jack pine, and other trees and shrubs by hares is often an important factor in the thinning of over-dense thickets of young trees on recent burns (Grange 1949) and must have been important in regulating forest stand density in primeval times. Now, with fire exclusion and the end of logging in the BWCAW, Quetico, and Voyageurs, the stand renewal process has virtually stopped, and the area of optimum habitat for hares is rapidly declining. As the snowshoe population peaks fall to lower and lower levels, the impact on their predators must also be substantial.

Small Rodents

The red squirrel is the most conspicuous small mammal in the Boundary Waters, seen summer and winter, for it does not hibernate. It occurs primarily in mature conifers, especially in jack pine and black and white spruce. Red squirrels subsist chiefly on conifer seeds and are particularly fond of pines, both spruces, and cedar (Hazard 1982). They are active in the daytime year-round and in fall spend much time caching hoards of pine and spruce cones for winter use. They are solitary and defend feeding areas against other red squirrels; their chattering and scolding is one of the most characteristic sounds of the Boundary Waters. Enormous amounts of conifer seeds are consumed, and their activities probably affect seed availability for the regeneration of some trees, at least locally. The peculiar bunchy appearance of black spruce crowns is due to clipping of cone-laden branches by squirrels. Red squirrels are important agents in the long-distance transport of black spruce dwarf mistletoe, an often fatal parasite of spruce in older bog spruce forests. The sticky mistletoe seeds attach readily to the squirrel fur. The red squirrel's most successful predators are the pine marten and fisher, and there may have been declines in its population after these predators returned to the Boundary Waters in the 1960s and 1970s (Siderits 1981; Hazard 1982; Ostry, Nicholls, and French 1983).

The northern flying squirrel is nocturnal and seldom seen in the Boundary Waters, even though it is quite common and remains active in the winter. It prefers pine, spruce,

and balsam forests or mixed aspen-birch-conifer stands and feeds primarily on the seeds of conifers just as the red squirrel does. These squirrels do not really fly. They simply glide from tree to tree on the folds of skin that connect their front and rear legs (Siderits 1981; Hazard 1982).

Two chipmunks occur in the Boundary Waters. The least chipmunk is more likely to be found on steep semi-open rocky sites with a partial cover of pines or spruce, whereas the eastern chipmunk is more common in mature mixed hardwood and conifer stands and dense brushy areas. Both eat seeds, nuts, fruits, mushrooms, insects, bird eggs, nestling birds, and even small mice and frogs. Both hibernate from October to April, and their body temperatures may fall to near freezing at times. They awaken frequently, however, and eat from food caches in their burrows. The eastern chipmunk's repeated low barklike call and the least chipmunk's repeated "chip-chip-chip" notes are familiar sounds in the Boundary Waters (Siderits 1981; Hazard 1982).

The woodchuck is the largest of the squirrel family in the Boundary Waters. The only larger rodents are the beaver and porcupine. Woodchucks are not abundant but occur in forests and along streams and valleys throughout the area. We may think of the woodchuck as characteristic of the eastern deciduous forests, but their range also extends northward to Labrador, Hudson Bay, and the Yukon. They live primarily on green vegetation, dig extensive burrows, and are deep hibernators (Hazard 1982).

The woodland deer mouse is familiar to many canoeists because of its fondness for late-evening campfire dinners and the contents of food packs. It has large ears, white underparts and feet, and a long tail. A nocturnal species, it shows up at dusk at many heavily used campsites. Like most small rodents, it has several litters per year. Its natural foods are conifer and other seeds, nuts, berries, buds, insects, and other invertebrates. It generally prefers conifer forests but is also common in lichen-covered or grassy habitats and is abundant on recent burns and logged areas. It can climb trees and shrubs, and it nests in trees and stumps. On many sites the deer mouse is often the most abundant small mammal, but it is subject to frequent population fluctuations. It can be a significant factor influencing jack pine, black spruce, and other conifer regeneration, especially on new burns and in open areas if seed fall is not abundant. Deer mice are a significant food resource for many of the smaller mammalian predators and for several species of hawks and owls (Beer, Lukens, and Olson 1954; Beer, Brander, and Cushwa 1973; Ahlgren 1966; Krefting and Ahlgren 1974; Buech et al. 1977; Siderits 1981; Hazard 1982).

The southern bog lemming is a small mouselike mammal with ears nearly concealed by fur and a short tail. It inhabits tamarack and spruce bogs and wet grassy meadows and feeds primarily on grasses, sedges, and the leaves, twigs, and berries of the bog heath shrubs, including blueberries (Siderits 1981; Hazard 1982).

The red-backed vole is a small, chunky boreal rodent with short ears and tail, gray undersides, brown sides, and a reddish brown back. It prefers mixed conifer swamp forests, spruce and tamarack bogs, and moist upland conifer forests with feathermoss ground layers, but it will also occupy blowdowns and recent burns in jack pine and black spruce. The red-back is one of the most abundant small mammals in the virgin forests of the region. It is active both day and night and feeds on greens, seeds, nuts, bark, and some insects. Like the deer mouse, it can influence tree seed supplies when it is abundant (Beer, Lukens, and Olson 1954; Beer, Brander, and Cushwa 1973; Ahlgren 1966; Books 1972; Powell 1972; Krefting and Ahlgren 1974; Buech et al. 1977; Siderits 1981; Hazard 1982).

The meadow vole is the common meadow "mouse," most abundant in open grassy areas, which are not a major habitat in the Boundary Waters. It is present throughout the region but not abundant in closed-canopy conifer forests. Females can breed when only 25 days old. The meadow vole feeds on green plants and some insects (Siderits 1981; Hazard 1982).

The rock or yellownosed vole is a rare resident of the Boundary Waters, known only from a few isolated locations. It occurs primarily in fields of glacial boulders and on steep rocky slopes, but it is also known to use a shrubby upland area without rocks in Cook County. It is thought to be primarily vegetarian (Siderits 1981; Hazard 1982).

The meadow jumping mouse and the woodland jumping mouse have powerful hind legs and long tails and can

jump several feet if alarmed. The meadow jumper prefers open, semiforested, and early post-disturbance areas with rank grassy or herbaceous vegetation, whereas the woodland species prefers closed spruce-fir, jack pine, or mixed conifer-broadleaf forests and shrubby areas near water. Both eat fruits, seeds, and insects. Unlike most mice, voles, and lemmings, the jumping mice are hibernators and survive the long winter on their body fat (Siderits 1981; Hazard 1982).

The Effect of Recent Burns on Small Mammals

One might expect that small mammals would be eliminated by large high-intensity forest fires, and that recolonization of burns would be a slow process, but neither seems to be the case. Two separate surveys of ground-dwelling small mammals on the 1971 Little Sioux burn, begun about three weeks after the fire, found little difference in densities on and just outside the burn. Red-backed voles, woodland deer mice, and least chipmunks were active even on the most severely burned sites. Because this was a spring fire, with incomplete burning of the damp organic layer, survival was possible in burrows. Regrowth of vegetation was prompt because the propagules of many plants survived in the partially burned organic layer. Surveys repeated in September 1971 and 1972 had results similar to those of the initial trapping study, showing populations of red-backed vole, woodland deer mouse, meadow vole, masked shrew, least chipmunk, and meadow jumping mouse (Books 1972).

Buech and co-workers (1977) found a different situation on the 1976 Roy Lake burn in the Saganaga Lake area of the BWCAW. During this late-August fire in a severe drought, high-intensity fires consumed the entire organic layer on slopes and ridges and left few unburned areas except in some draws and wetlands. A postfire trapping survey of small mammals found that the total small-mammal population was reduced to an average of 16 percent of the prefire population in all forest communities. No chipmunks or rock voles were found on the burn. In the aspen-fir-spruce community, red-backed voles, which depend heavily on green vegetation, were reduced to 16 percent of their unburned-area populations, deer mice to only 8 percent, and masked shrews to 40 percent. In the jack pine community, red-backs were reduced to only 8 percent, but the primarily seed-eating deer mice increased to 175 percent, presumably as a response to the abundant new-fallen jack pine and black spruce seeds, which otherwise were the source of the dense regeneration of these trees (see chapter 7).

Krefting and Ahlgren (1974) documented populations of small mammals each fall for 13 years on two wildfire areas in jack pine and black spruce south of Ely. The woodland deer mouse was the most abundant small mammal for the first 7 years on both burns, but thereafter vegetation changes apparently favored red-backed voles. Eastern chipmunks were abundant on one burn for most of the period but not so abundant on the other. The meadow vole, masked shrew, and meadow jumping mouse had erratic populations on both burns. Ahlgren (1966) also reported similar responses of deer mice and red-backs to fire in jack pine forests in an earlier study. Each species seems to have its optimum forest community and postfire stand-development stage. The adjustment of populations after fire is complex, yet seems to follow a general pattern.

An interesting sidelight on the whole question of the effect of forest disturbance and stand maturity on small mammals comes from Powell's (1972) comparison of red-backed vole populations in a standing mature conifer-broadleaf forest on Basswood Lake with those in an adjacent tornado blowdown. One year after the blowdown, he found that red-back voles were three times as abundant in the blowdown as in the standing forest. Comparison of the sexual maturity of the two populations indicated that many of the red-backs in the blowdown were juveniles, perhaps driven out of the standing forest by social pressures. The mature forest might still be the preferred habitat of the resident population.

None of the studies just reviewed dealt with the larger small mammals such as the snowshoe hare, red squirrel, flying squirrel, woodchuck, or their smaller predators, because the censusing methods used for small mammals are not appropriate for them. Both squirrels vacate severely burned crown fire areas for some 15 to 30 years until the

various trees in the new forest begin to bear seed. Their optimum habitat seems to develop at least 50 to 100 years after fire in most forest communities. On the other hand, snowshoe hare populations often peak within the first 10 or 15 years after fire. The proportion of the populations of these somewhat larger small mammals killed by high-intensity crown fires is unknown. Many individuals escape by moving into areas skipped by the fire or to the edge of the burn. Some may find refuge in burrows and similar underground shelters. Many snowshoe hares were observed hopping calmly ahead of the Little Sioux fire in 1971. In any event, fires do not eliminate any of these species for long, and in the long run, fires are essential to maintaining their habitats (Keith and Surrendi 1971).

Muskrat

The muskrat forages and builds its houses in marshes and along the edges of ponds, streams, and lakes. Much smaller than the beaver, the muskrat subsists primarily on vegetation, especially cattails, bulrushes, and sedges. In winter, muskrats work out of their houses or burrows and eat stored foods and roots beneath the ice and occasionally small fish and clams. Muskrat houses are made of vegetation but not of sticks and stones and should not be confused with beaver lodges. The houses usually rest on the bottom in shallow water. Muskrats are not as abundant in the Boundary Waters as beaver, probably because the marshy habitat they prefer is not common in most of the region. Mink are probably their most successful predators (Siderits 1981; Hazard 1982).

Porcupine

The porcupine's quills are really modified hairs and cannot be thrown at attackers, as some people believe. Quills are most strongly developed on the back and tail, are finely barbed, and readily penetrate an assailant's skin. Once barbs have entered skin, the animal's activity tends to work them more deeply into flesh. The nose and underbelly lack well-developed quills, and it is the nose that capable predators usually attack (Powell 1982). Porcupines are very slow and clumsy on the ground but are excellent tree climbers and will usually climb a tree if pursued. In the Boundary Waters porcupines feed on the new leaves of aspen in the spring, on a variety of green and woody vegetation in summer, and on the bark of all three pines in winter. The porcupine can deform pines through its winter bark girdling of the upper main stem. They tend to spend weeks feeding in a grove of pines. They do not hibernate, but they tend to den up in cold weather.

By the 1930s, trapping had virtually eliminated the porcupine's principal predator, the fisher, and the porcupine became unusually abundant in the Boundary Waters. With protection, the fisher regained its former levels in the 1960s, leading to a dramatic decline in the porcupine. On the other hand, studies in Minnesota suggest that wolves, coyotes, and bobcats feed on porcupines more than does the fisher (Berg 1987). Unlike most rodents, porcupines breed only once a year and usually have only one pup, so their reproductive potential is low. To compensate, they are quite long-lived if they escape predators. Porcupines love salty wood and formerly often gnawed canoe paddles while the unwary campers were sleeping. Now porcupines are scarce in the Boundary Waters, and seeing one is a rare treat (Siderits 1981; Hazard 1982).

Smaller Carnivores

The coyote is rare in the Boundary Waters because its larger relative, the wolf, often kills coyotes within its territory. Thus in northeastern Minnesota, coyotes tend to occur mainly near settlements and farms where wolves are less common. This member of the dog family is a species distinct from the gray wolf. Interbreeding with wolves is rare, although female coyotes apparently do occasionally mate with wolves. In the Boundary Waters, the coyote is a recent invader from the prairies of western Minnesota. Adults weigh 25 to 40 pounds. They prey primarily on mice, voles, chipmunks, snowshoe hares, porcupines, and ground-nesting birds and eat much carrion. Coyotes do not form packs in Minnesota as do wolves (Siderits 1981; Hazard 1982; Lehman et al. 1991).

The red fox is a common native of the Boundary Waters. It is much smaller and shorter legged than either the wolf

or coyote. It feeds on chipmunks, squirrels, hares, mice, voles, woodchucks, songbirds, grouse, snakes, turtles, frogs, and fish, as well as much carrion. From spring through fall it also feeds on insects, fruits, and berries. Females have litters of four to six pups in March or April, and the pair cares for its family until fall, when the young disperse (Siderits 1981; Hazard 1982).

The Canada lynx is rare in the Boundary Waters except during "invasions," which tend to occur at about 10-year intervals, perhaps because of population pressures and shortages of its principal prey, the snowshoe hare. It is the boreal and arctic equivalent of the bobcat, and in the Boundary Waters, the lynx is near the southern limit of its usual range. In addition to hares, its food includes carrion, grouse, squirrels, and occasionally deer fawns, foxes, and porcupines. Home ranges, based on radio-tracking data from the Boundary Waters region, ranged from 20 to 47 square miles for females and 56 to 94 square miles for males (Mech 1980). The longest movement ever documented for the species was by a radio-collared female who traveled from near Isabella to northwest of Red Lake, Ontario, some 300 miles. Hunting and trapping of lynx in northeastern Minnesota was permitted until 1983 (Mech 1977c, 1980; Siderits 1981; Hazard 1982).

Lynx populations tend to peak at the end of or just after the high point in the snowshoe hare cycle. Where lynx are the major predator, they apparently push the hare population lower and hold it down longer, although the decline itself may be initiated by food shortage or other factors. Hare and lynx fluctuations are more pronounced in the far north than in the Boundary Waters region near their southern limit (Akcakaya 1992).

The bobcat is similar to the lynx in size and general appearance. Near the northern limit of its range in the Boundary Waters, the bobcat is nevertheless more abundant than the lynx, except perhaps in years of lynx "invasions." Its main prey is the snowshoe hare, and its other foods and hunting habits are much the same as those of the lynx. Hunting and trapping of bobcats has been permitted in Minnesota for many years. Their populations do not fluctuate as wildly as those of the lynx (Siderits 1981; Hazard 1982).

The pine marten is about the size of a mink and has large ears and a reddish to yellowish brown coat. It is primarily a denizen of boreal conifer forests, its range in the Midwest extending just to the Lake Superior region. Marten are mostly nocturnal and hunt both in trees and on the ground. Easily trapped, this valuable furbearer was virtually eliminated from Minnesota shortly after 1900. Taking of marten was prohibited in 1927, and by the 1950s, reports of marten were again coming from Lake and Cook counties. A strong population recovery occurred in northeastern Minnesota in the 1970s. As of 1989, limited marten trapping was permitted northeast of a line from Duluth to Baudette, including the BWCAW.

The marten decline coincided with the destruction of the white and red pine forests of northern Minnesota and with widespread fires that greatly reduced the area of mature conifer forests. Even in the uncut virgin forests of the BWCAW, and probably of Quetico, the fires of 1863–64, 1875, 1894, and 1910 reduced the extent of mature conifers. However, the return of marten to all of northeastern Minnesota, despite the logging of much of the remaining virgin black spruce and jack pine forests between 1945 and 1975, strongly suggests that trapping or some factor other than forest composition was the major cause of the near extirpation of marten earlier in the century (Mech and Rogers 1977; Siderits 1981; Hazard 1982; Berg 1987). The marten's major prey are squirrels, chipmunks, mice, voles, shrews, and snowshoe hares. Birds, insects, fruits, and berries are also eaten. Of these, only tree squirrels are strongly tied to mature conifer forests. Radio-telemetry studies of marten near the BWCAW southeast of Ely indicate that although jack pine, black spruce, red pine, and balsam stands are the primary habitat, aspen-birch and mixed conifer-broadleaf stands are also used (Mech and Rogers 1977).

The fisher is a larger dark brown to nearly black relative of the marten, almost as big as a fox. Its range is chiefly the boreal forest, but it is now reestablished in Wisconsin and Michigan and ranges south at least as far as Cloquet in Minnesota. Its prey includes snowshoe hare, mice, squirrels, other small mammals, birds, and porcupines, although recent Minnesota studies found porcupine remains in only about 3 percent of stomachs examined (Siderits 1981; Haz-

ard 1982; Powell 1982; Berg 1987). Fisher also eat carrion and some vegetation. They do not eat fish. The reported low percentage of porcupine in the diet of Minnesota fisher may reflect the recent scarcity of porcupines relative to other prey, because many other studies have found porcupine to be an important food (Powell 1982). Fisher are solitary except during the breeding season and when rearing young.

Like the marten, the fisher was virtually eliminated from Minnesota in the early twentieth century and extirpated from Wisconsin and Michigan by about 1934. Trapping and habitat changes associated with logging are the probable causes (Powell 1982). With protection from trapping and a large reintroduction effort in Michigan and Wisconsin to control the porcupine, the fisher experienced a dramatic recovery, beginning in Minnesota in the 1960s. A limited trapping season has been held in Minnesota in most years since 1977. Fishers occupy a wide range of forest communities and age classes, including conifers, mixed conifer-broadleaf stands, and even chiefly hardwood forests (Powell 1982; Berg 1987).

The short-tailed weasel, long-tailed weasel, and least weasel may all occur in the Boundary Waters, although the least weasel has a sparse and sporadic distribution. All have brown backs and sides with white underparts in summer, and they turn white in winter. The least weasel is the world's smallest mammalian carnivore, and females of the larger short-tailed weasel (also called ermine) weigh no more than a chipmunk. The short-tailed and least species are primarily boreal and arctic in distribution, whereas the long-tailed extends southward. All three prey heavily on voles and mice. The short-tailed weasel also takes chipmunks, shrews, hares, birds, snakes, frogs, insects, and earthworms, and the long-tailed weasel preys on the short-tailed and least weasels. The weasels are secretive and are seldom seen (Siderits 1981; Hazard 1982; Berg 1987).

The mink is a blackish brown, bushy-tailed, semiaquatic member of the weasel family, about the size of a gray squirrel. Solitary and largely nocturnal hunters, they stalk the shores of lakes and streams, preying on muskrats, frogs, fish, crayfish, and waterfowl and other birds. They also hunt inland for hares and squirrels. Very adaptable and widespread in distribution, the mink is the most familiar member of the weasel family to most of us (Siderits 1981; Hazard 1982).

The striped skunk is not very abundant in the Boundary Waters. It is sometimes found along lakes and streams, where it feeds on insects, earthworms, mollusks, bird eggs, carrion, fruits, and nuts. The skunk is solitary and largely nocturnal and dens underground during the cold months, but it is not a hibernator. It is preyed on by great horned owls (Siderits 1981; Hazard 1982).

The river otter is a large aquatic member of the weasel family with a brown coat, short legs, webbed feet, small hidden ears, and a long, thick tail. It lives along lakes and streams and is often seen with its slim head raised well above the water, peering curiously at passing canoeists. While people watching, it may utter a series of soft barks. Families of two to five may be encountered. Otters love to slide down banks into the water in summer and down snowbanks in winter. Many live in burrows, chiefly along lakeshores and streambanks. Their principal foods are fish, crayfish, frogs, tadpoles, salamanders, and occasionally a muskrat or beaver (Gunderson and Beer 1953; Siderits 1981; Hazard 1982).

In addition to the mammals discussed in this chapter, there are occasional reports of cougar, wolverine, badger, and raccoon in the Boundary Waters. Those of cougar and wolverine since 1900 are unverified and of questionable authenticity (Hazard 1982; Birney 1974). These animals are too rare to warrant detailed treatment. Except for the wolverine, most were probably not regular breeding residents within the past few centuries. The raccoon has been extending its range northeastward in Minnesota in recent decades and may occur in small numbers along the south-central and southwestern edges of the BWCAW.

The Role of Birds in the Ecosystem

Because of its location in the center of North America, the Boundary Waters region is host to a large assemblage of bird species. Most are not permanent residents. The 188 bird species that occur regularly in the area can be grouped into four general categories:

- permanent year-round residents (18 species)
- warm-season-only resident breeding birds (110 species)
- regular migrants that pass through but do not stay to breed (about 50 species)
- winter visitors and winter invaders that breed elsewhere (10 species)

Many more species occur in the Boundary Waters from late May through early August than in other seasons.

So many species occur within the region that this chapter provides details only for the most abundant or interesting species, and for some whose roles in the ecosystem are known. Much of the information in this chapter is based on the booklet *Birds of the Superior National Forest* (Green, Niemi, and Siderits 1978), Terres's (1980) *The Audubon Society Encyclopedia of North American Birds*, Janssen's (1987) *Birds in Minnesota*, and Benyus's (1989) *Northwoods Wildlife*.

Following the species reviews are accounts of the effects of forest fires and postfire vegetation changes on bird populations and species diversity, the effects of blowdowns and insect outbreaks on bird populations, and the special problems faced by Boundary Waters breeding birds wintering in the Caribbean islands, Mexico, and Central and South America.

Permanent Residents

To survive year-round in the Boundary Waters, birds must withstand the severe cold of winter and be able to find dependable food resources in a frozen, snow-covered landscape for five or six months every year. Only 18 species meet that test on a regular basis, although 6 species of breeding finches are erratic invaders in this season.

The two resident grouse, the spruce grouse and ruffed grouse, have different habitat requirements. Both range far north into the Canadian boreal forest, but the spruce grouse barely ranges into the northern United States, whereas the ruffed grouse occurs much farther south.

Ruffed grouse, the more abundant species, is most often found in aspen-birch or aspen-birch-conifer forests or in alder and willow lowland shrub areas close to aspen-birch stands. In April and early May, males defend breeding territories by "drumming"—beating the air with their wings while standing on a large log or rock. Males prefer drumming territories in dense small aspen stands 10 to 25 years old, and hens come to the male's drumming log. The hens prefer older aspen stands with little ground cover for nesting, often building their nests at the base of a tree. Broods of seven to nine chicks hatch in early June, and the hen then moves them to nearby speckled-alder lowlands or dense 5- to 15-year-old aspen, where the chicks feed on insects and earthworms through the summer. Chicks can fly at a very early age. By September, they are mature, and broods begin to break up. Few grouse live beyond their 2nd year, and maximum longevity is about 8 years (Gullion 1989; Harrison 1978).

Aspen flower buds and the buds of birch and hazelnut are the most important ruffed grouse winter foods. Flower buds of male quaking aspen are the most nutritious foods available. Male trees often occur in groups that may cover an acre or more, because all trees in such clones originated through root-suckering from genetically identical parent trees killed by the last fire in the area. Grouse can often be seen high in the crowns of male aspens in such cloned groves, even on the coldest winter evenings (Gullion 1989).

The optimum stand-age class of aspen differs for each phase of the bird's annual life cycle. Before European settlement, frequent forest fires often produced several age classes of aspen relatively close together, and the essential young stands were seldom far away. Today most remaining virgin forests lack the needed diversity of aspen age classes because of fire exclusion, and few young stands exist. The result is very low ruffed grouse populations in most of the virgin forest of the BWCAW and Quetico (Gullion 1989).

The most effective strategy for the ruffed grouse to escape both cold and predators is to dive into 10 inches or more of soft snow to spend the night well insulated, warmed by the earth's heat, and out of sight. If deep, soft snow is lacking or if hard crusts persist too long, overwinter survival may be very low, principally because of predation. The most effective winter predators are great horned owls, barred owls, goshawks, and in some years great gray and snowy owls. Foxes, bobcats, and lynx also take some grouse, especially when snowshoe hares are infrequent. Although we know much about the habitat factors that favor grouse abundance, the underlying causes of their pronounced roughly 10-year cycles of abundance remain elusive (Gullion 1989).

The spruce grouse prefers black spruce bog forests and upland black spruce–jack pine stands. In the Boundary Waters it is near the southern limit of its range and is much less common than the ruffed grouse. It is remarkably unwary of humans. Both species of grouse pick fine gravel to aid their gizzards in grinding buds and other hard foods. They may be encountered on gravelly portages during the late afternoon (Peterson 1980).

The goshawk is a rare year-round breeding resident. It is an important predator of grouse and many small mammals, but it also feeds on the red squirrels and crows that eat grouse eggs. The goshawk is noted for its ability to dodge around trees and other obstacles in dense forest as it pursues its prey. The main breeding range lies north of the Boundary Waters region in the Canadian boreal forest (Green, Niemi, and Siderits 1978; Peterson 1980; Terres 1980; Gullion 1989).

Four owls, the great horned owl, barred owl, great gray owl, and boreal owl, nest in the region at least occasionally, spend the winter there, and are significant predators. The barred owl's characteristic hooting is a common sound echoing across the lakes on still evenings. All Boundary Waters owls feed on small mammals and birds. The great gray, with a wingspread of 5 feet, is the largest North American owl, but it has a relatively small body weight. The owls are primarily nighttime hunters, but the great gray is also active in the day (Green, Niemi, and Siderits 1978; Peterson 1980; Benyus 1989).

Radio-telemetry studies indicate that barred owls, perhaps the most common species, maintain nearly exclusive home ranges, expelling intruders and advertising occupancy of their territories by hooting. Home-range boundaries in a given area may persist with little change for at least two decades. Mated pairs occupy closely overlapping ranges. Young and dispersing barred owls are apparently nonterritorial—they are essentially homeless, looking for ranges they can occupy (Nicholls and Fuller 1987).

The very tame and tiny boreal owl, about the size of a robin, has its primary range in the Canadian boreal forests, but it breeds regularly in the Boundary Waters. Its nesting requirements seem closely tied to older diverse forests; it nests in old woodpecker holes high up in large old aspens. Large white and red pines nearby may be important for perching. Periodic winter irruptions or invasions of boreal owls occur and may be followed by large die-offs caused by starvation.

Five woodpeckers comprise another group of year-round residents: the pileated, hairy, downy, black-backed, and three-toed woodpeckers. All five woodpeckers feed on insect larvae and adults hidden in tree bark crevices, under the bark, or in galleries in the wood itself. Common targets include bark beetles, wood-boring beetles, and carpenter ants. Berries and nuts are also eaten. All species drum on dead trees to advertise territories and attract mates. All also nest and roost in cavities excavated in dead snags or living trees with heart rot.

Large areas of recently killed or severely injured trees on new burns and blowdowns harbor vast hordes of wood borers and bark beetles that attract these woodpeckers. For example, on the Little Sioux burn of 1971, all five species became abundant within a year or two. Even the rare black-backed and very rare three-toed species became relatively common, yet both are boreal conifer forest species near their southern limit in the Boundary Waters. Such abundant food resources seem to lead to increased woodpecker populations if the affected areas are large enough. However, a burned forest only retains high beetle populations for a few years. When the prime feeding years have passed, the woodpeckers must move on to new burns or blowdowns or face reduced food resources. Before European settlement, there always were new burns within a decade or less, but with fire exclusion, this source of foods virtually disappeared, and the regional populations of these woodpeckers have probably declined. Today they are still abundant on new burns but most occur in mature and senescent stands where dead and dying trees may harbor enough insects.

The gray jay (Canada jay or whiskey jack) is familiar to most canoeists in the Boundary Waters. This friendly "camp robber" manages to eke out a living during the winter months and even nests in late March while snow still covers the landscape. Individual jay home ranges cover about 20 to 50 acres. Populations vary strongly from year to year. The gray jay is widely distributed across the boreal forests of North America and barely reaches south of Canada. It is most abundant in upland jack pine and black spruce forests and in spruce bogs, where its natural foods include seeds, berries, insects, mushrooms, lichens, bird eggs, and carrion. Gray jays are important agents in spreading the seeds of the parasitic black spruce dwarf mistletoe from infected trees. The sticky coating on the seeds readily adheres to the jay's feathers as it searches spruce tops for insects or as it nests in the "witches' brooms" caused by mistletoe (Green, Niemi, and Siderits 1978; Peterson 1980; Ostry, Nicholls, and French 1983; Janssen 1987; Benyus 1989).

The common raven is another prominent boreal species in the Boundary Waters that does not occur much south of Canada except in the high mountains. Ravens are larger than crows and have rounded tails as opposed to the crow's square-ended tail. They have a very different repertoire of calls, ranging from a hoarse croak to a clear bell-like tinkle. Pairs mate for life. Nests are built on high cliffs or high in a tall pine or spruce and may be 4 feet across. Nest building begins in late February and early March, and eggs are laid by late March. Young leave the nest in late May or early June. The raven is primarily a scavenger. It is remarkably intelligent and sometimes seems to follow wolf packs. Adults seem to establish 15- to 25-square-mile "dominions" within which they establish and defend nest sites, use traditional roosts, and cache food for future use.

The black-capped chickadee and boreal chickadee are active, little, year-round residents. Their cheerful calls, "chick-a-dee-dee-dee" (black-capped) or "chick-che-day-day" (boreal), are welcome sounds to snowshoers and cross-country skiers. The black-capped occurs in the boreal region but also ranges much farther south. Both species nest in May in cavities in rotting small trees, usually not far above ground. They feed on seeds and insects and in winter can be seen methodically searching branchlets and bark crevices. The heartbeat rates of boreal chickadees rise markedly during winter cold spells, an adaptation that enables these tiny birds to feed actively even when temperatures are far below zero (Green, Niemi, and Siderits 1978; Harrison 1978; Benyus 1989; Green 1991).

Some white-breasted and red-breasted nuthatches are also year-round residents; the red-breasted species is fairly common, the white-breasted very rare. Both are cavity-nesting bark gleaners that obtain much of their food by creeping head-down on tree trunks looking for insects.

They also eat seeds. Many red-breasted nuthatches migrate southward in about November, but some remain in the Boundary Waters, and irregular winter invasions occur (Green, Niemi, and Siderits 1978; Peterson 1980).

Warm-Season Resident Breeding Birds

RESIDENT BREEDING WATERFOWL

The common loon is perhaps the most characteristic bird of the Boundary Waters. Most of the North American breeding range of the common loon lies in the lake regions of northern states and the Canadian and Alaskan boreal forest and arctic tundra (Peterson 1980).

In the Boundary Waters nearly every sizable lake has its family of loons, and many of the larger lakes have several pairs. Loons arrive on their nesting lakes within a few days of ice-out, generally in early May. Males usually arrive first and set up and defend territories at once. Loons are monogamous, and the pair remains together until fall, both participating in nest building, incubation of eggs, and care of young. Territories range from about 10 to 300 acres and average some 50 acres. Loons feed primarily on fish and must see their prey. Thus they select areas with relatively clear water. They can dive well over 100 feet, but most of their fishing is done in water 6 to 20 feet deep. The territory defended seems to include only as much area as the pair needs at given stages of parenting. After chicks are hatched, territories may be expanded to include new areas needed for "nurseries" (McIntyre 1988).

Islands or backwater bays are preferred for nesting. Nests are built almost at the water's edge, usually with a short steep slope to the water so the incubating parent can slide silently into the lake if an intruder approaches. Some overhanging foliage or other cover is helpful to screen the nest from gulls, ravens, and other birds that might molest the nest. Eggs are laid in May or early June, and chicks hatch about June 20 and mid-July (Olson and Marshall 1952; Titus and Van Druff 1981; McIntyre 1988).

A few days after the eggs have hatched, the chicks are moved to a nursery area where they usually stay for 2 weeks or more. They depend on the parents for food for many weeks but gradually learn to fish for themselves. They can fly at about 3 months and leave the BWCAW by late September. Chicks are vulnerable to gulls, large northern pike, big snapping turtles, starvation, and other problems. In Minnesota loon pairs average only about 0.30 to 0.90 chicks per year raised to the flight stage. If they make it through the first year, many loons apparently live 7 to 10 years and even as long as 20 to 30 years (McIntyre 1988).

Adult loons have a complex repertoire of vocalizations that can be reduced to four basic types: hoots, wails, tremolos, and yodels (McIntyre 1988). Hoots are short soft notes among loons close to each other, apparently used to keep in touch. Wails are the long, mournful calls that sometimes sound almost like wolf howls. Pairs also use wails to get together when separated, and males use them to lure the female to shore for mating. Most wailing and other calling occurs at night, tending to peak just before midnight. Tremolos are "laughing" calls, given in three variations involving frequency changes. On the water tremolos are alarm calls; the higher the frequency the more likely the bird will leave (often underwater) (McIntyre 1988). Perhaps the most spectacular display by loons is the running on water, diving, and penguin-dancing by extremely agitated individuals in defense of their young, accompanied by constant frantic tremolos (Crowley and Link 1987). Canoeists who encounter such activity at close range should leave the area at once.

As fall approaches, adults may gather in social groups of 3 or 4 to 15 or 20, often in the morning. Adult tremolos and wails decrease as the chicks mature, and by mid-September little such calling occurs. In late September and early October, groups of 20 to as many as several hundred adult loons gather at traditional "staging areas" and engage in group feeding, often for many days. These gatherings are clearly in preparation for migration (McIntyre 1988). In the BWCAW-Quetico area, Merriam Bay and Bayley Bay of Basswood Lake are often used as staging areas. I saw groups of at least 100 to 250 birds in these bays between October 8 and 10 in several years in the 1980s and in 1990. Most adult loons in the Boundary Waters depart for their wintering areas sometime in October.

Banding data indicate that many of the Boundary Waters loons winter along Florida's Gulf coast, but some probably winter inland on the Great Lakes and on some of the larger southern reservoir lakes. Juveniles do not participate in the fall staging but apparently depart singly or in small groups later than the adults. It is not clear whether juveniles use the same wintering areas as their parents. Loons face many hazards from pesticides, industrial chemicals, oil spills, and commercial fishing nets on their migrations and in their wintering areas (McIntyre 1988).

McIntyre (1988) cites studies that suggest that loons can adapt to a considerable degree to human disturbance from water-based recreation activities, both motorized and nonmotorized. More ominous, however, is the threat from acid rain and mercury pollution over much of the loon's breeding range in eastern North America. Acid rain could ultimately eliminate fish from many lakes, and this would be fatal to loons. Mercury bioaccumulates in the tissues and organs of fish and is further concentrated in fish-eating birds like the loon. Mercury tends to concentrate particularly in nerve tissues, where it may seriously interfere with motor functions and normal behavior, rendering the birds helpless. This is a growing problem in many northern lakes and in the loon's wintering areas (McIntyre 1988).

The pied-billed grebe is a very rare summer breeder on some lakes, especially those with marshy bays. Much smaller than a loon or most ducks, it is an incredibly adept diver that subsists on small aquatic life.

The common merganser is perhaps the most abundant breeding duck in the Boundary Waters and may sometimes be confused with the rarer hooded merganser, which also breeds in the area. Both nest in tree cavities, but the common merganser also nests on cliffs or in rock piles along lakeshores and streams. Common mergansers breed in the extreme northern regions of the lower 48 states and across much of the Canadian boreal forest region. They are among the very first ducks to arrive in the spring, just as the ice goes out. Mature mergansers are usually reluctant to fly when approached and will swim rapidly away, croaking repeatedly. Mergansers are skillful diving ducks and live chiefly on small fish, insects, fish eggs, and crustaceans. Some remain in the Boundary Waters until late October or November before migrating to open water on the Atlantic coast and the southern states (Kortright 1943; Harrison 1975; Harrison 1978; Green, Niemi, and Siderits 1978; Peterson 1980).

The black duck is still probably the second most abundant breeding duck in the Boundary Waters despite drastic population declines in the latter half of the twentieth century. Black ducks are "dabbling" ducks, tipping "bottoms up" in shallow water to feed on aquatic plants such as pondweeds, grasses, sedges, water-shield, water-lilies, wild celery, wild rice, and to a much lesser extent insects, mollusks, and crustaceans. Blacks nest primarily on land, both in grassy swamps near the water's edge and in dense shrubs or forest some distance from shore. Ducklings can fly by August. In the Boundary Waters blacks are most often found in shallow beaver ponds and marshy streams. The black duck is a close relative of the mallard. Both species rise almost vertically, usually with loud quacking, when surprised along a shoreline. Resident blacks often arrive on their Boundary Waters breeding waters in late April or early May soon after ice-out and depart in October or early November. They winter along the Atlantic coast, the Great Lakes, and in the southeastern states. Overhunting, pollution, and wetland destruction on their winter ranges, as well as acid rain, pose serious threats to this once most characteristic duck of the Canadian Shield's lakes and streams (Kortright 1943; Green, Niemi, and Siderits 1978; Harrison 1978).

Several other ducks breed in varying numbers in the rather uncommon marshy lakes and streams of the Boundary Waters and in beaver ponds. The mallard is the most common. The mallard and black duck are so close genetically that they hybridize readily. Blue-winged teal, common goldeneyes, hooded mergansers, ring-necked ducks, wood ducks, and American wigeon are the other species occasionally seen during the summer breeding season. Wood ducks and goldeneyes are tree-nesters. Ring-necks and goldeneyes, being divers, breed occasionally in the larger open-water lakes in addition to small lakes and beaver ponds.

The great blue heron, American bittern, killdeer, spotted sandpiper, common snipe, woodcock, and herring gull are the most common breeding birds in this group. The black tern is a very rare summer breeder, apparently breeding only in the western edge of the Boundary Waters.

The great blue heron breeds in rookeries in the tops of tall trees. The adults are solitary hunters and fishers, often seen wading along lakeshores and streams looking for small fish, frogs, and other aquatic life. The great blue heron winters in the southern states, along the Gulf of Mexico, and even in northern South America (Green, Niemi, and Siderits 1978; Harrison 1978; Peterson 1980).

The American bittern inhabits marshes, where frogs are its principal food. The Boundary Waters may be one region where the bittern's habitat is still largely unaltered, although it is scarce because of unfavorable geological factors (Coffin and Pfannmuller 1988).

The little spotted sandpiper, while uncommon, is often seen flitting ahead of a canoe close to the water. It nests in open sites or low growth near lakeshores and feeds on small fish, crustaceans, insects, and worms. Its breeding range covers most of Canada and the United States except the far south. It winters in the Gulf states, Mexico, and South America (Green, Niemi, and Siderits 1978; Harrison 1978; Peterson 1980; Terres 1980).

The common snipe inhabits wet, grassy forest openings, where it is an insect-eating ground-feeder from late April to late September or mid-October (Green, Niemi, and Siderits 1978; Janssen 1987).

The American woodcock arrives in April or May and departs for its wintering areas in the southeastern states in September and October. It is primarily a bird of the eastern deciduous forest and is uncommon in the boreal conifer forest communities of the Boundary Waters. It can be found in brushy areas near aspen-birch and mixed conifer-broadleaf stands. It is an insectivorous ground-feeder (Green, Niemi, and Siderits 1978; Peterson 1980; Janssen 1987).

The herring gull is the principal gull seen on Boundary Waters lakes, where it nests commonly on barren rock islets, often in colonies. A scavenger, this gull has become accustomed to the ways of canoeists and usually can be depended on to clean up fish entrails left on an exposed rock a few hundred feet from camp, unless ravens, vultures, eagles, otters, mink, or bears beat them to it. They arrive in the Boundary Waters soon after ice-out, and some remain until at least late October, when they depart for wintering areas chiefly along the Mississippi valley and in the Gulf states (Green, Niemi, and Siderits 1978; Harrison 1978; Peterson 1980).

FOREST-DWELLING BREEDING SUMMER RESIDENTS

In addition to the year-round residents and water-related breeding birds described above, 92 species of chiefly forest-dwelling birds breed in the Boundary Waters but leave in winter.

The turkey vulture is a carrion-eating scavenger that breeds regularly in portions of the Boundary Waters. With a wingspread of as much as 6 feet, it can be mistaken for an eagle, but its small red turkeylike head and its habit of soaring with wings in a broad upswept V clearly distinguish it from even immature eagles. Vultures are sometimes seen along lakeshores, feeding on dead fish or soaring above the rocky ridges. They generally arrive in late April and depart in September or early October, wintering from Illinois southward (Peterson 1980; Janssen 1987).

Nine species of hawks, eagles, and falcons breed in the area but migrate southward out of the region during at least the coldest winter months. All are predators (or raptors), feeding primarily on birds, mammals, or fish. The osprey usually nests along lakeshores in tall snags, subsisting chiefly on fish. It is our only raptor that plunges into the water from considerable heights to take fish. It is rare in the Boundary Waters, yet in 1989, 71 nest sites were identified to the south in the Superior National Forest, producing 46 young—a good recovery from its population low in the 1960s and early 1970s due to pesticides. Most spring arrivals are in April and fall departures in September (Peterson 1980; Terres 1980; Janssen 1987; Coffin and Pfannmuller 1988; U.S. Forest Service 1991b).

The bald eagle is still classified as threatened in Minnesota, but it has made a remarkable recovery in the Boundary Waters since the bottom of its DDT-induced decline in 1970, when only about 10 active eagle nests remained on the Superior National Forest. In 1989 the forest's annual eagle survey located 74 active nests, producing 86 young bald eagles. Most of these nests were in the BWCAW. Similar increases have occurred in Quetico and Voyageurs. Most nests are in tall old white or red pines near lakeshores or streams because fish are the eagle's primary food source. It also takes some small mammals and birds and utilizes carrion, especially dead fish and wolf-killed deer and moose. Nests are used year after year and may be several feet high and up to 8 feet across. Most of the Boundary Waters eagles migrate in October and November to wintering areas in the Mississippi valley, along the Great Lakes, and southward to the Gulf coast. Occasional individuals may be seen in the BWCAW even in December and January. They return to their nest sites in late February or March, and one or two chicks may be hatched about May. Eagles do not breed until three years old and can live many decades if not shot or poisoned by environmental pollutants. With a wingspread of 7 to 8 feet, the bald eagle is the region's largest bird (Green, Niemi, and Siderits 1978; Harrison 1978; Peterson 1980; Janssen 1987; Coffin and Pfannmuller 1988; U.S. Forest Service 1991b).

The sharp-shinned hawk and northern harrier (marsh hawk) are slim-bodied, long-tailed hawks that prey on small birds and mammals. The sharp-shinned is about the size of a gray jay and particularly characteristic of mixed-conifer forests, whereas the northern harrier is crow-sized and preys in open and semi-open habitats such as cattail and sedge marshes and bogs. Spring arrivals tend to peak in April, and fall departures in September (Green, Niemi, and Siderits 1978; Peterson 1980; Terres 1980; Janssen 1987).

The broad-winged hawk is the most common hawk in the Boundary Waters region, and, like the much rarer red-tailed hawk, belongs to the genus *Buteo*, a group of fairly large, chunky-bodied, broad-winged, and broad-tailed hawks that do much soaring. Broad-wings are crow-sized and hunt from perches, often in broadleaf forests, taking small mammals, snakes, frogs, and insects. Most nesting pairs tend to arrive in the Boundary Waters in April or early May and may be seen migrating south in large soaring flocks in September and early October. Broad-wings nest throughout the eastern mixed and deciduous forests and winter in the Tropics. Red-tails are larger, with a wingspread of about 4 feet, and often hunt in open disturbed areas. They nest throughout most of North America and winter mostly in the United States (Robbins, Bruun, and Zim 1966; Green, Niemi, and Siderits 1978; Peterson 1980; Terres 1980; Janssen 1987; Green 1991).

Three species of falcons nest in the Boundary Waters, or at least did so until recently: the American kestrel, the merlin, and the peregrine falcon. The robin-sized kestrel hunts primarily in forest openings such as burns, blowdowns, open wetlands, and lakeshores and is rare in the Boundary Waters. The slightly larger merlin is more numerous. It takes small birds and insects in forests, on islands, and near lakeshores. The kestrel and merlin generally arrive in the Boundary Waters about mid-April and depart southward in October. Merlins are occasionally seen in winter as well. The peregrine falcon was formerly a breeding summer resident (a few pairs) but was extirpated from all of Minnesota and adjacent regions by DDT in the 1960s. The last nesting in the BWCAW was reported in 1964. Larger than either the merlin or American kestrel, peregrines prey on small to duck-sized birds. One of the fastest birds on earth, peregrines have been clocked at 62 miles per hour in level flight and more than 175 miles per hour in dives (Terres 1980). It was reintroduced into the wild in Minnesota, including in Cook County beginning in 1984, and breeding pairs should be watched for in the Boundary Waters. It was still listed both nationally and in Minnesota as endangered in 1992 (Robbins, Bruun, and Zim 1966; Green, Niemi, and Siderits. 1978; Peterson 1980; Janssen 1987; Coffin and Pfannmuller 1988).

The black-billed cuckoo is an uncommon insect-eating resident of largely broadleaf forests and forest edges that obtains its food by foliage gleaning. During and just after outbreaks of forest tent caterpillar in aspen stands, cuckoo populations may increase markedly. It winters in South America. Spring arrivals peak in late May, and the fall migration is from August through September (Green, Niemi, and Siderits 1978; Janssen 1987)

Two owls, the long-eared owl and northern saw-whet owl, are breeding summer residents of the Boundary Waters, but unlike the other owls, they migrate southward beyond the area in winter and are then essentially absent. The saw-whet is uncommon as a breeder and is a very rare winter visitor. It is a small owl that hunts by night in conifer and mixed forests, taking small rodents, birds, and other vertebrates. The long-eared owl, considerably larger and a very rare breeder in the Boundary Waters, hunts in mixed conifer-broadleaf forests. Spring arrivals tend to peak in April for both species, and the fall exodus peaks in October (Robbins, Bruun, and Zim 1966; Green, Niemi, and Siderits 1978; Peterson 1980; Janssen 1987).

The common nighthawk is occasionally seen chasing insects over lakes and cliffs near dusk on summer evenings. As it dives, its wings produce a whirring hum. It is a ground nester that selects open rock outcrops for nesting and may become locally quite common on barren rocky ridges following high-intensity crown fires that temporarily denude rocky ridges. It winters in South America. The related insectivorous whip-poor-will is a very rare breeding resident, but it may occasionally be heard on summer evenings along heavily forested lakeshores, singing the song that imitates its name. It is near the northern limit of its breeding range in the Boundary Waters and winters from the Gulf states to Honduras (Robbins, Bruun, and Zim 1966; Green, Niemi, and Siderits 1978; Janssen 1987).

The ruby-throated hummingbird is an uncommon resident of forest openings in the Boundary Waters, where it seeks nectar-yielding flowering plants. This smallest of all native birds is near the northern limit of its range in the Boundary Waters and winters in Mexico and Central America (Green, Niemi, and Siderits 1978; Peterson 1980; Janssen 1987).

The belted kingfisher is an uncommon but very visible fish-eating summer resident that seeks its prey by perching and flying along lakeshores and streams, calling as it flies in its hoarse rattling voice. It nests in burrows that it excavates in gravel and sand banks (Green, Niemi, and Siderits 1978; Janssen 1987).

Two members of the woodpecker family, the yellow-bellied sapsucker and the northern flicker, are common breeding summer residents that, unlike the other woodpeckers, migrate southward beyond the Boundary Waters in winter. Sapsuckers are bark probers that feed on tree sap and on insects such as spruce budworm and moths of the forest tent caterpillar. Sapsuckers often cause significant injury to trees by girdling them with holes, particularly paper birch and young pines. Sapsuckers winter mostly in Central America and the West Indies. The flickers are ground feeders that subsist on insects (especially ants) and berries. In the Boundary Waters a sure sign of approaching fall and winter is the gathering of flickers into small groups in August and early September, accompanied by much calling. The peak of the fall migration comes in late September. They winter from southern Minnesota south to the Gulf states (Green, Niemi, and Siderits 1978; Peterson 1980; Terres 1980; Janssen 1987).

The tyrant flycatcher family includes seven species that breed regularly in the Boundary Waters: the olive-sided flycatcher, eastern wood-pewee, yellow-bellied flycatcher, alder flycatcher, least flycatcher, eastern phoebe, and eastern kingbird. All take insects on the wing; thus they usually do not arrive on their Boundary Waters breeding grounds until mid-May or early June and must depart for their wintering areas in Central and South America in August or early September, when flying insect populations plummet. Their habitat preferences differ somewhat, so that direct competition for the same insects is lessened.

Of the two swallows, the more common tree swallow nests in tree cavities and old woodpecker holes, usually near ponds, lakeshores, or streams. The barn swallow may nest in rock overhangs near water. Both are aerial insect feeders, usually arriving in the region in late April or May and departing southward in August or September (Green, Niemi, and Siderits 1978; Harrison 1978; Peterson 1980; Janssen 1987).

The blue jay is a common summer breeding resident of the Boundary Waters. Unlike the gray jay, the blue jay is near the northern edge of its range here, and most individuals move either southward out of the area or to feeders in nearby towns for at least the coldest winter months. Many leave the Boundary Waters in October and return in late April. They prefer aspen-birch, pine, and pine-oak forests. Foods include pine seeds, other seeds, acorns (scarce in the region), fruits and berries, insects, bird eggs, snails, frogs, and minnows (Green, Niemi, and Siderits 1978; Peterson 1980; Janssen 1987; *Audubon* 1990).

The American crow is a fairly common nester in the Boundary Waters and far northward in the Canadian boreal forest. Unlike the larger but outwardly similar raven, virtually all crows migrate southward and winter from southern Minnesota to the Gulf of Mexico (Green, Niemi, and Siderits 1978; Janssen 1987).

The secretive little brown creeper breeds in the old-growth mountain forests in the eastern and western United States, as well as in the mixed conifer forests adjacent to the eastern U.S.–Canadian border. It also appears on new burns. It is an uncommon but regular nester in the Boundary Waters. A bark gleaner, it finds insects on the trunks of old trees by creeping upward, spiraling around the tree as it goes. It places its nest in crevices behind flaking bark of old trees (Green, Niemi, and Siderits 1978; Peterson 1980; Janssen 1987).

Three wrens breed in the Boundary Waters: the house wren, winter wren, and sedge wren (short-billed marsh wren). The fairly common winter wren is an insectivorous ground and foliage gleaner of brushy forests and swamps from April or late May to September or October. The house wren is a rare resident of forest openings, and the sedge wren is a very rare resident of marshes and grassy openings, both from May to September (Green, Niemi, and Siderits 1978; Peterson 1980; Janssen 1987).

The golden-crowned kinglet and ruby-crowned kinglet feed on insects gleaned chiefly from the needles of conifers. The breeding ranges of both stretch far northward into the Canadian and Alaskan boreal forests, the ruby-crowned being the more widespread in the far north. Both species arrive mostly between late March and mid-May and depart between mid-September and the end of October (Green, Niemi, and Siderits 1978; Peterson 1980; Janssen 1987).

The thrush family is represented in the Boundary Waters by summer-breeding populations of the veery, Swainson's thrush, hermit thrush, and robin. The veery is an abundant ground nester in aspen-birch-red maple and mixed broadleaf-conifer forests and along streams and lakeshores in black ash-willow-alder swamps, where it feeds on insects and berries on the ground. Much of its breeding range is in Great Lakes-New England mixed deciduous-conifer forests. Most spring arrivals are in May, and most birds leave between early August and mid-September. Veerys winter in Central America and northern South America.

Swainson's thrush feeds on insects and berries in conifer forests and bogs. It is the most common thrush in the conifer-dominated parts of the Boundary Waters. Its breeding range is largely in the Canadian and Alaskan boreal forest. Most spring migrants arrive between late April and early June, and the fall migration occurs chiefly in August and September. This thrush winters from southern Mexico to Argentina.

The hermit thrush is a fairly common ground nester and ground feeder in pine, black spruce–tamarack, and mixed forest communities, where it feeds on insects and berries. Its breeding range includes much of the Canadian boreal forest, the Great Lakes-New England area, and the western mountains. Spring migrants arrive chiefly in late April and early May, and the fall migration peaks in the first half of October. It winters chiefly in the southern states.

The robin feeds on insects, earthworms, and berries. Its breeding range includes most of North America north of Mexico, including even some areas of arctic tundra. Most robins arrive in the Boundary Waters in April or early May and depart from late September to late October for wintering grounds in the southern states. The robin and veery are among the eight most abundant breeding birds in the Boundary Waters (Robbins, Bruun, and Zim 1966; Green, Niemi, and Siderits 1978; Peterson 1980; Terres 1980; Farrand 1983; Janssen 1987; Benyus 1989; Green 1991).

The mockingbird-thrasher family is represented by the gray catbird and the brown thrasher. Both are summer breeders and are most often found in brushy forest openings, the catbird especially near lakes and streams and in alder-willow lowland communities. Both are near the northern limit of their range in the Boundary Waters (Green, Niemi, and Siderits 1978; Peterson 1980; Janssen 1987).

The cedar waxwing feeds on insects it fly-catches or gleans from foliage at forest edges, and on the berries of such shrubs as high-bush cranberry and mountain-ash. It usually arrives about middle to late May and departs from mid-October to mid-November. It winters in flocks from central Minnesota southward to the Gulf states, Mexico, and beyond. The similar Bohemian waxwing breeds in western Canada and Alaska but winters in the Boundary Waters and may be locally abundant during irregular winter invasion years (Green, Niemi, and Siderits 1978; Farrand 1983; Janssen 1987).

The starling, introduced to North America from Europe in 1890, became a common resident in the cities and towns of northern Minnesota in the 1940s and 1950s. It is probably the only introduced bird having breeding populations in the wild in the Boundary Waters. It is still rare beyond villages and is found only occasionally in forest openings and along lakeshores (Green, Niemi, and Siderits 1978; Janssen 1987).

Three vireos are breeding summer residents of the Boundary Waters, the red-eyed vireo, solitary vireo, and Philadelphia vireo. The very common red-eyed vireo is a foliage gleaner, feeding on insects high in the canopy of aspen-birch and red maple communities. It is abundant throughout the eastern deciduous forest and much of the Canadian boreal forest. Males sing constantly all day, uttering a series of short robinlike phrases. Most vireos arrive in middle to late May and depart for their South American wintering areas between August and early October.

The solitary vireo is an uncommon bird that feeds on foliage insects in conifer forests. The northern Great Lakes forests are near the southern edge of its breeding range, which is largely in the Canadian boreal forest and the eastern and western mountains. Most birds arrive in the Boundary Waters in May and leave for their winter ranges in the Gulf states, Mexico, and Central America in late August and early September.

The Philadelphia vireo is a very rare resident of brushy broadleaf forest edges and alder-willow swamps. Its breeding range is largely in the southern Canadian boreal forest. Spring arrivals are mostly in middle to late May, and the fall migration peaks in early and mid-September. The winter range is in Mexico and Central America (Robbins, Bruun, and Zim 1966; Green, Niemi, and Siderits 1978; Peterson

1980; Terres 1980; Farrand 1983; Janssen 1987; Benyus 1989; Green 1991.)

Twenty-four species of wood warblers are breeding summer residents in the Boundary Waters, at least in some areas in many years (table 13.1). Four species, the Nashville warbler, chestnut-sided warbler, mourning warbler, and ovenbird are (or recently were) among the eight most abundant breeding birds in the region, and many more warblers are common or fairly common in much of the area. Furthermore, all species are insect-eating predators, and despite their small size, as a group they play an important role in the dynamics of nutrient cycling, energy flow, and insect populations of the forest ecosystem. Many species also eat some berries and seeds. The territorial singing of a myriad of male warblers enlivens early summer mornings for Boundary Waters visitors. These tiny birds spend only a few short months each year raising their offspring in the Boundary Waters and then make perilous journeys of many thousands of miles to their winter homes, which are for most species in the tropical forests of Mexico, the Caribbean islands, or Central and South America. The orange-crowned and blackpoll warblers regularly migrate through the Boundary Waters to their far northern breeding grounds but do not nest here.

In the Boundary Waters the peak of spring arrivals for most species comes about mid-May. Exceptions are the Connecticut, Wilson's, mourning, and Canada warblers, which usually arrive later in May, and the yellow-rumped, black-and-white, palm, and pine warblers, which often arrive in early May or even late April. The breeding and nesting season when the males do their singing runs from mid-May through June for most species. In July the singing stops, broods of young are fed, adults moult, and preparation for migration begins. For several species the first migrants leave in mid-July, and for many species the departures peak in August and early September. Only two warblers tend to leave later, from late September through early or mid-October, the yellow-rumped and palm warblers (Green, Niemi, and Siderits 1978; Janssen 1987).

Most warblers search for larval or adult insects on the needles or leaves of the trees and shrubs of their preferred habitats (foliage gleaners). A few are flycatchers, bark glean-

Table 13.1 / Abundance, habitat preferences, and feeding strategies of warblers in the Boundary Waters region

Species	Abundance	Habitat	Feeding strategy	Canopy level
BOREAL WARBLERS				
Tennessee	U	Brushy openings in conifer forests	Foliage gleaner	Upper
Cape May	U	Fir-spruce forests, bogs	Foliage gleaner	Upper
Yellow-rumped	C	Conifer forests, bogs	Foliage gleaner, berry feeder	Ground to tops
Bay-breasted	R	Conifer forests, bogs	Foliage gleaner	Middle
Palm	VR	Open bogs	Foliage gleaner	On ground
Connecticut	R	Bogs	Foliage gleaner	Some ground feeding
Wilson's	VR	Brushy swamps	Flycatcher	Near ground
NORTHERN FOREST WARBLERS				
Nashville	A	Brushy edges, openings, conifer forests	Foliage gleaner	Upper
Magnolia	FC	Young conifer forests	Foliage gleaner	Inner growth
Black-throated blue	R	Broadleaf forests	Flycatcher?	?
Black-throated green	FC	Mature conifer, aspen-birch forests	Foliage gleaner	?
Blackburnian	FC	Conifer forests	Foliage gleaner	Upper
Chestnut-sided	A	Brushy openings, edges, burns, aspen-birch	Foliage gleaner	Ground to tops
Northern waterthrush	U	River, lake edges, swamps	Foliage gleaner, ground feeder	On ground
Mourning	A	Brushy openings, edges, burns	Ground feeder, foliage feeder	On ground
Canada	FC	Brushy forests, swamps	Flycatcher, foliage gleaner	Near ground
WIDESPREAD AND/OR EASTERN DECIDUOUS FOREST WARBLERS				
Black-and-white	C	Forests	Bark gleaner	Tree trunks
Golden-winged	VR	Brushy openings, broadleaf forests	Foliage gleaner	Shrubs to tops
Northern parula	FC	Conifer forests	Foliage gleaner	Upper
Yellow	R	Brushy edges near water	Foliage gleaner	In shrubs
Pine	VR	Mature red, white, jack pine	Foliage gleaner	Ground to tops
Ovenbird	A	Broadleaf and mixed forests	Ground feeder, foliage gleaner	Mostly on ground
Common yellowthroat	C	Marshes, bogs, brushy shores	Foliage gleaner	In shrubs
American redstart	FC	Open broadleaf forests	Foliage gleaner, flycatcher	?

Note Abundance codes: A = abundant, C = common, FC = fairly common, U = uncommon, R = rare, VR = very rare.

Sources Adapted from Table 2, Green, Niemi, and Siderits (1978), with additional information from Rusterholz (1973); Wiens (1975); Terres (1980); Farrand (1983); Janssen (1987); and Green (1991).

ers, or ground feeders in addition to or instead of being foliage gleaners. For this remarkable assemblage of forest-dwelling, insect-eating warblers, two additional factors reduce interspecies competition for food. First, there is a considerable spread in the kinds of forest, bog, shrubland, or lakeshore habitats preferred by the various species. Second, important differences exist between some species in feeding patterns within forest stands. Some tend to concentrate their searching for insects high in the treetops, while others work the middle of the crowns or near the ground (table 13.1).

Data from breeding-bird censuses in northeastern North America and in the northwestern Canadian boreal forest regions summarized by Wiens (1975) suggest that warblers comprise at least half of the individuals of all birds in the Boundary Waters. The Minnesota Copper-Nickel Study just south and west of Ely estimated the average number of pairs of warblers of all species in recent clear-cuts and open bogs at 1,295 per square mile, in closed broadleaf and conifer stands at 1,729 to 2,223 pairs per square mile, and in shrub and young broadleaf communities at 2,470 to 3,705 pairs per square mile (Green, Niemi, and Siderits 1978). Using these estimates as approximations for the Boundary Waters, we can put the number of warblers at somewhere between 1,300 and 2,200 adults per square mile during the breeding season. After the young are fledged but before migration begins, the total number could easily be more than double that. Extrapolating from the land area of the BWCAW and using 1,700 adults per square mile as a general average, we can estimate the total BWCAW warbler population as easily 2,300,000 breeding adults and 5,000,000 adults and young combined just before migration begins.

Warblers are major predators of the spruce budworm, an important defoliating insect causing much mortality in balsam fir and white spruce stands. Four Boundary Waters warblers, the Tennessee, Cape May, bay-breasted, and blackburnian, feed so avidly on budworms that the increased food resources during outbreaks often cause sharp population increases of these warblers during and following outbreaks. Some of the increases may be due to warbler population movements, but much of the increase is prob-

ably due to greater reproductive success. Predation by warblers and other birds apparently cannot control budworm epidemics once an outbreak is under way. Between outbreaks of endemic budworm populations, however, warbler predation may help hold these insects in check. The situation may be similar for the jack pine budworm (Wiens 1975; Green, Niemi, and Siderits 1978; Farrand 1983).

The scarlet tanager, an uncommon breeding summer resident, is the region's only tanager. It is a foliage-gleaning insect feeder occasionally found in aspen-birch-red maple forests. The spring migration peaks in late May. Most departures for winter ranges in Central and South America come in August and September (Green, Niemi, and Siderits 1978; Janssen 1987).

The cardinal subfamily has only two summer breeding residents in the Boundary Waters. The rose-breasted grosbeak is a common foliage-gleaning insect feeder that also regularly eats fruits and seeds. Most often found in aspen-birch-red maple forests in the Boundary Waters, it works the full canopy from forest floor to treetops and may be found in young stands and the edges of openings as well as in mature forests. Spring arrivals peak in mid-May, and fall departures peak in early September. They winter from Mexico to South America. The indigo bunting is a rare insect-eating breeder in brushy forest openings. Spring arrivals peak in middle to late May, and most fall migrants leave in early September. It also winters from Mexico to northern South America (Green, Niemi, and Siderits 1978; Terres 1980; Farrand 1983; Janssen 1987; Benyus 1989; Green 1991).

The large sparrow subfamily is represented in the Boundary Waters by eight breeding summer residents, most of which subsist primarily on seeds and on foliage insects (Green, Niemi, and Siderits 1978; Terres 1980; Farrand 1983; Janssen 1987; Benyus 1989; Green 1991). The chipping sparrow is a common inhabitant of conifer forest edges and bogs from late April to late August and September. It breeds over most of North America from the open subarctic spruce forests of far northern Canada to Central America, and it winters from the southern states to Nicaragua.

The clay-colored sparrow is a rare denizen of brushy forest openings, lakeshores, and recent burns from early

May to middle or late September. It breeds from Michigan and southwestern Ontario to British Columbia and Colorado, putting the Boundary Waters on the fringe of its range. It winters from south Texas through Mexico.

Le Conte's sparrow is a very rare breeding resident of sedge meadows in the Boundary Waters from May through September. It also breeds far northward into the arctic tundra and westward on the northern Great Plains. It winters across the southeastern states.

The song sparrow is a common ground-nesting breeder in brushy openings, often along lake, pond, and stream shores. Its summer diet consists of such insects as beetles, grasshoppers, ants, wasps, caterpillars, and flies, as well as seeds. Territories are usually less than an acre in area. It arrives in early to mid-April, and the fall migration is in late September and early October. The breeding range covers much of the Canadian boreal forest and the northern United States. Wintering occurs from Iowa and southern Wisconsin across the United States to both coasts and southward into Mexico.

Lincoln's sparrow, a rare breeder in open bogs and recent burns in the Boundary Waters, breeds primarily in the Canadian and Alaskan boreal forest region and high western mountains. It winters from the western Gulf states to California, south to Guatemala. It arrives in late April and early May and leaves from mid-September to early October.

Swamp sparrows are fairly common breeding residents of brushy swamps, marshes, shrubby sedge fens, and bogs in the Boundary Waters, which is well within their main breeding range that also includes most of the Canadian boreal forest region. They winter from Nebraska through southern Wisconsin to Massachusetts and south to the Gulf states. Spring migration is in late April, and departures are mostly in late September and early October.

The white-throated sparrow, one of the most abundant breeding birds in the Boundary Waters, utters a haunting whistlelike series of notes that symbolize the vastness of the northern forests it claims as its summer home. It is found most frequently in conifer and mixed conifer-aspen-birch forests and associated forest openings and recent burns. A ground nester, it rarely raises more than

one brood a year. It feeds mainly on seeds and fruits. It arrives in late April and early May, and the peak of fall migration comes in late September and early October. The breeding range is primarily in the Canadian boreal forest, and the winter range is mostly from Missouri to Massachusetts and southward to the Gulf states.

The dark-eyed junco is an uncommon breeding resident of conifer forest edges, burns, and bogs in the Boundary Waters. It breeds primarily in the Canadian and Alaskan boreal forests and southward in the eastern and western mountains. It searches for seeds and insects in the forest litter. The spring migration peaks around mid-April, and fall departures peak in October. It winters from the Dakotas and southern Minnesota east to New England and south to the Gulf states and northern Mexico.

As a group, the sparrows are among the most voracious consumers of forest tree seeds. Juncos and some other sparrows have been implicated in consuming significant portions of the seed fall of conifers on logged areas (Wiens 1975). They may well have a similar impact in burned standing forests under some circumstances. Seed-consuming birds, along with mice and voles, may be important factors influencing the stand density of newly established tree seedlings on fresh burns and blowdown areas. The timing of seed fall on burns and blowdowns with respect to fall or spring flocks of migrating sparrows is probably crucial in determining their impact on seed supplies. If most of the seed fall occurs over winter after sparrows have left, then only the spring germination period will be available for seed eating. However, some birds are also known to feed on germinating young conifers (Wiens 1975). On many burns, jack pine and black spruce seed supplies are so abundant that birds and mice apparently cannot reduce an initial seedling density below that necessary to produce a fully stocked forest. In the postfire establishment of red and white pine and white spruce, restocking may be limited by seed supplies.

Four members of the blackbird-oriole subfamily are breeding summer residents of the Boundary Waters (Green, Niemi, and Siderits 1978; Farrand 1983; Janssen 1987). The familiar red-winged blackbird is a fairly common resident of cattail and grass-sedge marshes, marshy lakeshores, and pond and stream edges, where they feed on insects and seeds. Most spring migrants arrive in April, and the fall exodus comes between late September and early November. They winter from southern Minnesota to Central America. The rusty blackbird is a very rare resident of conifer forests along alder-edged streams. It also winters in the states south of Minnesota.

The common grackle is an uncommon breeding resident of brushy shorelines, and it too feeds on insects and seeds. Its range and migration times are very similar to those of the red-wing.

The brown-headed cowbird is an uncommon breeding resident with a peculiar means of providing for its young. The females lay their eggs in the active nests of other species, often warblers, thrushes, vireos, and sparrows. Thereafter they abandon the eggs, relying on the pair tending the parasitized nest to rear their young along with their own. A single female may lay eggs in the nests of several other birds each year. The cowbird is increasing in many regions because it is well adapted to human-modified environments. They probably do not breed in the contiguous forests of the Boundary Waters. Its nest parasitizing is causing population declines in some host species in fragmented forests. Most cowbirds arrive in the Boundary Waters region in April and leave in late June and July soon after they have dropped their eggs in hosts' nests. They breed throughout the United States and winter from the Southwest to Iowa and New England, south into Mexico.

The finch family is represented in the Boundary Waters by six breeding summer residents (Green, Niemi, and Siderits 1978; Terres 1980; Farrand 1983; Janssen 1987). The purple finch is a fairly common nesting species in conifer and mixed conifer-broadleaf forests. Its breeding range includes the conifer forests of the Pacific Northwest, much of the Canadian boreal forest, and most of the Great Lakes–St. Lawrence River region. The eastern winter range includes all the eastern United States except northern Minnesota, south to the Gulf coast.

The red crossbill and white-winged crossbill are both extremely rare and erratic breeders in the Boundary Waters; they are seldom seen in summer, but breeding has been confirmed. Both breed in the Canadian boreal forests, and the white-winged also breeds in the western mountains. The Boundary Waters is on the southern fringe of their ranges. Both species are nomadic wanderers in all seasons, tending to winter primarily within their breeding ranges but appearing occasionally as far south as the southern states. In occasional invasion years they may be fairly numerous in the Boundary Waters in winter. Both literally have crossed bills, adapted to opening the cones of spruce and pine to get the seeds, which are their principal food. The red crossbill prefers pine seeds and is found chiefly in jack, red, and white pine stands, whereas the white-winged feeds on both pine and spruce. Crossbills are very tame and fond of Boundary Waters fireplace ashes, which they seem to eat for the calcium and salt content (Robbins, Bruun, and Zim 1966; Terres 1980).

The pine siskin is an uncommon breeder in the Boundary Waters in conifer forests, where it eats tree seeds. Like the crossbills, it is an erratic wanderer within and beyond its main breeding range, which is in the Canadian and Alaskan boreal forests, the northern Great Lakes–St. Lawrence River region, and the western mountains. It winters sporadically within the breeding range, including the Boundary Waters, and southward to the Gulf states. It often moves in flocks of 50 or more.

The American goldfinch is a fairly common breeder in the Boundary Waters, particularly in forest openings and edges, where it feeds on the seeds of many ground-cover herbs, shrubs, and broadleaf trees. It breeds across the northern two-thirds of the United States and into southern Canada. The goldfinch winters from the southwestern states to southern Minnesota, New England, and southward to the Gulf of Mexico and northern Mexico.

In the Boundary Waters the evening grosbeak is a fairly common breeder in conifer forests, where it feeds heavily on seeds and fruits. Some insects, including the spruce budworm, are eaten in summer. Its breeding range covers a narrow band across the northern United States and southern Canada, plus the western mountains. Like the other finches, it is an erratic migrant and wanderer. It winters sporadically within its breeding range southward to the Gulf of Mexico and is an occasional winter visitor in the Boundary Waters. Evening grosbeaks tend to move in small flocks and are often seen on gravel roads eating deicing salt.

Migrants and Invaders Not Breeding in the Area

There are about 50 bird species that migrate through the Boundary Waters each year, most in both spring and fall, but do not remain to nest. Many are enroute from wintering areas south of the Boundary Waters to breeding grounds in the Canadian-Alaskan boreal forests, subarctic, or high-arctic, or returning from those areas in the fall. Some are moving to or from the Canadian prairies. Individuals, pairs, or flocks of many species linger briefly for resting or feeding and so enhance the numbers and variety of bird life in the Boundary Waters during the spring and fall migrations. Some of the larger waterfowl, waders, and raptors also provide spectacular views of migrating flocks or individuals in autumn or spring, and some ducks are the quarry of local hunters. Individuals of several species are summer visitors.

The annual fall migration of Canada geese and snow geese is one of the events that heralds the onset of freezing temperatures and approaching winter. The first flocks of Canadas are usually seen about mid-September. They are seldom seen on the water, because few flocks stop to rest here, and even when they do, they usually remain only overnight. In late September or October the approach of a strong cold front with north winds and snow squalls seems to trigger massed flights. These can be spectacular events, with dozens of large vees or long strings of Canadas and snows passing southward within view in a single day.

In addition to the regular nonbreeding migrants, there are about 10 species that are winter visitors, usually showing up as individuals or small flocks, or as sporadic winter invaders that often appear in larger numbers at intervals of several years or even decades (table 13.2). The reasons for such invasions are not always clear but may relate to population pressures, food scarcity, or weather factors in a species' breeding range, or to changes in food resources, weather, or other factors in the Boundary Waters.

The migrant nonresident winter visitors and invaders, in particular the large raptors, add a fascinating touch of variety and surprise to a season otherwise hardly remarkable for its bird life. The rough-legged hawk and golden eagle are not seen often. During invasion years, snowy owls tend to arrive earlier in the fall and linger later in spring. They are daytime hunters, typically seen as lone individuals waiting on a low perch for mice, voles, lemmings, or hares to show themselves (Robbins, Bruun, and Zim 1966). The Boundary Waters is just south of the normal breeding range of the boreal northern hawk owl, and it may be seen during invasions, which tend to come once or twice a decade.

The pine grosbeak breeds in the closed Canadian boreal forests, open subarctic spruce-lichen woodlands, and high western mountains. It is a common to uncommon fall migrant and winter visitor in the Boundary Waters, especially in periodic invasion years. In the Boundary Waters it eats the fruits of mountain-ash and sumac and the buds of red maple and birch.

The common redpoll breeds in arctic and subarctic tundra, but it winters in the northern states and in invasion years can be a common winter visitor in the Boundary Waters. It is a seedeater and often moves in large flocks, feeding on the seeds of birch, alder, and other trees and herbs (Farrand 1983; Janssen 1987).

The Effects of Forest Fires on Bird Habitat, Abundance, and Species Diversity

In the ecosystem before European settlement, Boundary Waters birds obviously coexisted with recurrent large-scale forest fires and fire regimes that produced a natural fire rotation near 100 years. In fact, many of the species nest today in great numbers in far northern Canadian and Alaskan boreal forests, where lightning fire regimes similar to the Boundary Waters' presettlement regime still prevail. What effect do large fires have on the habitats and populations of the many bird species? Hints are in some of the preceding species accounts. Studies in and adjacent to the BWCAW provide much of the information available for forests similar to these in the Boundary Waters.

Bergstedt and Niemi (1974) documented postfire breeding-bird populations in burned aspen and jack pine forests three years after the large high-intensity Little Sioux fire

Table 13.2 / Birds seen regularly in the Boundary Waters region as migrants, visitors, or sporadic invaders, but not breeding there

Species	Status	Season of occurrence			
		Spring	Summer	Fall	Winter
WATERFOWL					
Horned grebe	Migrant, visitor	Apr–May	Visitor	Aug–Nov	—
Red-necked grebe	Migrant	Apr–May	—	Aug–Nov	—
Double-crested cormorant	Migrant, visitor	Apr–June	Visitor	Sept–Nov	—
Tundra swan	Migrant, visitor	Apr–May	Visitor	Oct–Nov	—
Snow goose	Migrant	Mar–May	—	Sept–Nov	—
Canada goose	Migrant, visitor	Mar–May	Visitor	Sept–Nov	—
Green-winged teal	Migrant, visitor	Apr–May	Visitor	Aug–Nov	—
Northern pintail	Migrant	Mar–May	—	Sept–Nov	—
Northern shoveler	Migrant	Apr–May	—	Sept–Nov	—
Canvasback	Migrant, visitor	Apr–May	Visitor	Sept–Nov	—
Redhead	Migrant	Apr–May	—	Sept–Nov	—
Greater scaup	Migrant	Mar–June	—	Sept–Nov	—
Lesser scaup	Migrant, visitor	Mar–June	Visitor	Sept–Nov	—
Oldsquaw	Migrant	May	—	Oct	—
Surf scoter	Migrant	Apr–June	—	Oct–Nov	—
White-winged scoter	Migrant	Apr–June	—	Oct–Nov	—
Bufflehead	Migrant	Mar–May	—	Sept–Nov	—
Red-breasted merganser	Migrant	Mar–May	—	Oct–Dec	—
Ruddy duck	Migrant, visitor	Apr–May	Visitor	Sept–Nov	—
HAWKS AND EAGLES					
Cooper's hawk	Migrant (threatened)	Mar–May	—	Sept–Oct	—
Rough-legged hawk	Migrant, winter visitor	Mar–Apr	—	Sept–Oct	Uncommon visitor
Golden eagle	Migrant, winter visitor	Feb–Apr	—	Oct–Nov	Casual visitor
American coot	Migrant, visitor	Apr–May	Visitor	Sept–Nov	—
Sandhill crane	Migrant (very rare)	Apr–May	—	Sept–Nov	—
PLOVERS					
Black-bellied plover	Migrant	May–June	—	Aug–Nov	—
Lesser golden plover	Migrant	May–June	—	Aug–Nov	—
Semipalmated plover	Migrant	May–June	—	July–Sept	—
SANDPIPERS AND TURNSTONES					
Greater yellowlegs	Migrant	Apr–May	—	July–Nov	—
Lesser yellowlegs	Migrant	Apr–May	—	July–Oct	—
Solitary sandpiper	Migrant	Apr–June	—	July–Oct	—
Whimbrel	Migrant	May–June	—	Aug-Sept	—
Ruddy turnstone	Migrant	May–June	—	July–Sept	—
Red knot	Migrant	May–June	—	July–Sept	—
Sanderling	Migrant	May–June	—	July–Oct	—
Semipalmated sandpiper	Migrant	May–June	—	July–Oct	—
Least sandpiper	Migrant	May–June	—	July–Oct	—
White-rumped sandpiper	Migrant	May–June	—	July–Sept	—
Baird's sandpiper	Migrant	Apr–June	—	July–Sept	—
Pectoral sandpiper	Migrant	Apr–June	—	July–Oct	—

Species	Status	Season of occurrence			
		Spring	Summer	Fall	Winter
SANDPIPERS AND TURNSTONES (CONT.)					
Dunlin	Migrant	May–June	—	July–Oct	—
Stilt sandpiper	Migrant	May	—	July–Sept	—
Buff-breasted sandpiper	Migrant	May	—	July–Sept	—
DOWITCHERS					
Short-billed dowitcher	Migrant	May–June	—	July–Sept	—
Long-billed dowitcher	Migrant	May–June	—	July–Sept	—
GULLS					
Bonaparte's gull	Migrant, visitor	Apr–June	Visitor	July–Nov	—
Ring-billed gull	Migrant	Mar–May	—	Aug–Dec	—
Glaucous gull	Migrant	May	—	Nov	—
OWLS					
Snowy owl	Uncommon winter visitor, irregular invasions	Until early May	—	After mid-Oct	Invasions Oct–May
Northern hawk owl	Winter visitor, rare invasions	Until early May	—	After early Oct	Visitor Oct–May
THRUSHES					
Gray-cheeked thrush	Migrant	May–June	—	Aug–Oct	—
PIPITS					
Water pipit	Migrant	May	—	Sept–Nov	—
WAXWINGS					
Bohemian Waxwing	Erratic winter visitor	Until mid-Apr	—	After early Oct	Irregular invasions
SHRIKES					
Northern Shrike	Winter visitor	Until Apr	—	After early Oct	Uncommon visitor
WARBLERS					
Orange-crowned warbler	Migrant	Apr–May	—	Aug–Oct	—
Blackpoll warbler	Migrant	May–June	—	Aug–Oct	—
SPARROWS, LONGSPURS, BUNTINGS					
American tree sparrow	Migrant	Apr–May	—	Sept–Nov	—
Fox sparrow	Migrant	Apr–May	—	Sept–Nov	—
White-crowned sparrow	Migrant	Apr–June	—	Sept–Oct	—
Harris' sparrow	Migrant	Apr–May	—	Sept–Oct	—
Lapland longspur	Migrant	Mar–May	—	Sept–Nov	—
Snow bunting	Migrant, rare winter visitor	Mar–Apr	—	Oct–Nov	Rare visitor
FINCHES					
Pine grosbeak	Common migrant, winter visitor	Until early April	—	After mid-Oct	Invasions Oct–Apr
Common redpoll	Common migrant, winter visitor	Until late April	—	After mid-Oct	Invasions Oct–Apr
Hoary redpoll	Rare migrant, winter visitor	Until mid April	—	After late-Oct	Invasions Oct–Apr

Sources Based on information from Green, Niemi, and Siderits (1978) and Janssen (1987).

of May 1971. A breeding-bird census in burned aspen forest (with dense regrowth of aspen, red maple, paper birch, shrubs, and herbs) revealed 16 nesting species with a combined total of 228 territorial males per 100 acres—a good population. Most abundant were chestnut-sided warbler, mourning warbler, least flycatcher, white-throated sparrow, house wren, and red-eyed vireo. Other nesters present in low numbers were yellow-bellied sapsucker, blue jay, rose-breasted grosbeak, ruffed grouse, hairy woodpecker, veery, blackburnian warbler, ovenbird, common yellow-throat, and chipping sparrow. Nine more species visited the study plot but were not nesters.

A similar census of a three-year-old burned jack pine community on the Little Sioux burn found a population of 187 territorial males per 100 acres, comprised of 9 nesting species. The chestnut-sided warbler again was most abundant, followed by white-throated sparrow, house wren, song sparrow, red-eyed vireo, and common grackle, plus a few mourning warblers, common flickers, and brown thrashers. Nine additional species were visitors. The most abundant species in both the aspen and jack pine plots are known to be adapted to edge habitats and forest openings—no surprises there. Both insectivores and seedeaters were represented. The very low numbers of ovenbird and veery, species usually abundant in older closed forests, were expected. Many warblers characteristic of older forests were missing. Total numbers of breeding birds in both communities were within the lower ranges of populations reported by others for closed forests of aspen and jack pine elsewhere in Minnesota and Ontario (Bergstedt and Niemi 1974).

In further studies on the Little Sioux burn, Niemi (1978) assessed bird populations on both burned and adjacent unburned areas in a wider range of forest communities in 1973, 1974, and 1975. About 107 species were found in unburned areas, compared to 91 on the burn. Fifty-four species decreased on the burn, 17 increased, and 42 showed no change. Most woodpeckers increased or at least were more conspicuous on the burn, including the rare black-backed three-toed and red-headed species. Woodpeckers were undoubtedly attracted by the myriad of wood-boring beetles that proliferated in fire-killed trees throughout the

burn and by bark beetles that invaded dead and fire-injured trees. Cedar waxwings were common in both areas but increased on the burn in 1975 in response to bumper crops of blueberries, juneberries, and pin-cherries. The vireos and warblers were the groups reduced most by fire, notably the usually abundant red-eyed vireo, Nashville and blackburnian warblers, and ovenbird. The chestnut-sided and mourning warbler, both adapted to shrub and edge habitats, became superabundant on the burn. Cowbirds were common in both burned and unburned habitats. Some sparrows increased after fire, others declined.

Through a coincidence, Apfelbaum and Haney (1981) were able to assess bird populations before and after an intense crown fire on a plot within the Roy Lake burn of August 1976 in the BWCAW. This plot, in a 73-year-old jack pine stand, was intensively studied in June 1976 and surveyed again the next spring. Eight species with territories on the burn were not present before the fire: most prominent were the white-throated sparrow, dark-eyed junco, and black-backed three-toed woodpecker; others included the olive-sided flycatcher, robin, and Swainson's thrush. Five species disappeared: red-eyed vireo, solitary vireo, red-breasted nuthatch, ovenbird, and winter wren. Bay-breasted, blackburnian, and yellow-rumped warblers, boreal chickadees, and ruby-crowned kinglets decreased in importance while brown creepers increased.

In a wider study, Apfelbaum and Haney (1986) surveyed breeding-bird territories across a full spectrum of postfire upland-forest age classes in the eastern BWCAW and Quetico. Study areas included sites burned 1, 2, 3, 7, 15, 23, 67, 73, 112, 175, 176, 366, 367, and 370 years before the survey. The authors viewed this as a forest successional sequence, but even the oldest forests still had some first-generation postfire trees in the overstory, so it can be considered simply an array of postfire forest age classes. This study is the only one for the Boundary Waters that directly assesses changes in bird populations and species diversity in relation to time since fire.

The bird communities of this forest-age-class array fell into four more or less distinct postfire groups in terms of species richness (number of territorial species) and density (number of individuals per 15.4-acre study grid plot). The

1- to 23-year-old stands (yearly successional jack pine–aspen) had as high bird diversity as the 112- to 176-year-old forests (mature and senescent jack pine-spruce-fir-aspen-birch), but half the bird density. The 67- to 73-year-old stands (intermediate aged jack pine–aspen pole timber) had a third fewer species than the 1- to 23-year-old stands, but similar bird density. Stands 200 or more years after fire (mostly old-growth red and white pine) had lower diversity and density than 112- to 176-year-old stands.

Successional trends were apparent in the importance values calculated for each bird species by Apfelbaum and Haney. One- to 23-year-old burns were dominated by white-throated sparrows, chestnut-sided warblers, mourning warblers, and black-backed three-toed woodpeckers. Olive-sided flycatchers and other flycatchers were most abundant in the first three postfire years. In 67- and 73-year-old stands, blackburnian and bay-breasted warblers had the highest importance values. The red-eyed vireo was also an important canopy species, and ovenbirds were important among ground-shrub foragers. In the 112-year-old stand, the bird species were similar to those in 67- and 73-year-old stands, but importance ranks differed, and species richness and density were similar to that in the 175- and 176-year-old stands. In the heavier spruce and fir of the 112-year-old stand, bay-breasted warblers were more important than blackburnians, and red-eyed vireos were about equal in importance to black-throated green and black-throated blue warblers. Golden-crowned kinglets, brown creepers, and ovenbirds were also important. In the 175- and 176-year-old stands, more species of tree-foliage gleaners were found than in the other age classes, most important being blackburnian and bay-breasted warblers. Ground-brush foragers such as the ovenbird, white-throated sparrow, Swainson's thrush, and chestnut-sided warbler were also more important as a group. In old-growth forests ground-brush foragers were more important than in the 67- to 73-year-old or 112- to 176-year-old age classes, and tree-foliage searchers were also important. Canada and parula warblers seemed especially characteristic.

For the total upland forest landscape, it appears from the studies of Apfelbaum and Haney and of Bergstedt and Niemi that the maximum number of species (species rich-

ness) would be achieved on a landscape with a good mix of postfire forest age classes scattered over the whole area. There would need to be many new burns, young stands, and mature forests and many areas of old growth. That conclusion probably applies to total populations of all species at the landscape scale. Some species are characteristic primarily of recent burns, others of mature forests, and some of very old stands. Many species are adapted to a fairly wide spectrum of forest communities and age classes, but many also seem to have optimum breeding habitats found only in a portion of the total range on the landscape. These findings should not surprise us, for to succeed on the landscape before European settlement, a bird species had to find suitable breeding habitat somewhere in a complex of forest communities and postfire age classes covering the full range of possibilities, and the greatest number of species and individuals could be accommodated if there was a diversity of habitat requirements among the available bird species. Over the ages, those species succeeded that were adapted to available habitats. Now, by changing the relative proportions of the forest age classes and communities on the landscape through logging and fire exclusion, we are altering the mix of habitats available to breeding birds and thus probably also altering the relative abundance of many bird species.

The Effects of Blowdowns and Forest Insect Outbreaks on Bird Habitat, Abundance, and Species Diversity

Large-scale forest blowdowns, such as those of 1988 in the BWCAW and Quetico, obviously alter bird habitat over substantial areas. Before European settlement such blowdowns probably were "cleaned up" by forest fires within a decade or two, because blowdowns in conifer forests are extremely flammable. Fire suppression has greatly increased the area of blowdown that regrows to new forest stands without the intervention of fire. No known studies directly address the effects of blowdowns on birds. However, with a general knowledge of the changes in vegetation produced by blowdowns, and with bird data from burns that produced somewhat similar effects on forest stand structures, composition, and density, one can speculate on the probable effects.

The many dead, dying, and injured trees resulting from blowdowns generate hordes of bark beetles and wood-boring beetles that must create a significant food resource for the several species of woodpeckers native to the Boundary Waters. Such increases in foods often persist for a decade or so, but eventually new forest growth takes over, and the forest insect populations return to more normal suites of species and population levels. I would expect local areas of abundance of woodpeckers to develop and persist at least several years near large pockets of blowdown. Many blowdowns soon develop into semi-open shrubby habitat similar to forest edges. This kind of habitat persists for at least a decade after major blowdowns, sometimes much longer. Some of the many bird species adapted to open areas and forest edge habitats probably attain locally higher populations in affected areas.

Large-scale outbreaks of the spruce budworm, jack pine budworm, forest tent caterpillar, and larch sawfly in the Boundary Waters sometimes have widespread effects on the populations of certain birds. These effects may be both short-term and long-term if an outbreak results in the death of whole forest stands over wide areas. In the Boundary Waters the spruce budworm has been epidemic over large areas in such years as 1943–44, 1954–64, and 1968–71 and in more localized areas in most years since 1972 (Hardy, Mainville, and Schmitt 1986). Fire suppression may be increasing the frequency and intensity of these outbreaks by encouraging succession to balsam fir on a scale that would not have occurred under the fire regimes and fire rotations that existed before European settlement. As we have noted, populations of certain birds often increase markedly during and toward the end of such outbreaks, in the Boundary Waters notably the Tennessee, Cape May, bay-breasted, and blackburnian warblers. This response probably results in part from better nesting success due to increased food resources, although some population increases could be caused by population shifts into outbreak areas (Wiens 1975).

The jack pine budworm, forest tent caterpillar, and larch sawfly also become incredibly abundant during periodic outbreaks, probably causing significant bird population responses at times. The best known seems to be increases in the black-billed cuckoo during and after forest tent caterpillar outbreaks (Janssen 1987). The populations of other birds may be affected in very different ways by the changed environments of aspen-birch forests during these dramatic episodes of complete defoliation. Tree mortality is usually not great, however, and most forest tent caterpillar outbreaks last only about two years in given regions. During larch sawfly outbreaks in tamarack bogs, the grosbeaks, finches, and sparrows may be more important as sawfly predators than are the warblers (Dawson 1979).

Population Declines of Neotropical Forest Migrants

There is a growing body of evidence that the populations of many bird species breeding in the eastern United States and Canada and wintering in Mexico, Central America, the West Indies, or South America are declining. Many Boundary Waters breeding birds spend their winters in these regions. Species dependent on tropical or subtropical forests for winter habitat in areas of deforestation are declining, while those dependent on open "scrub" vegetation seem to be maintaining their populations. The causes of the declines are complex and probably due to multiple factors on the wintering ranges, along migration routes, and on at least some of the breeding ranges in the United States and Canada. Among the factors that seem to be important are

- clearance of tropical forests for cattle grazing and cultivation of corn, sugarcane, and soybeans
- destruction of tropical forests through slash-and-burn farming
- destruction of tropical forests through logging for timber, mining, petroleum operations, urbanization, dam construction, and related development work
- forest clearance for agriculture, urbanization, reservoirs, highways, and so on in the southern and midwestern United States and southeastern Canada
- fragmentation of the remaining forests in the eastern United States and southeastern Canada due to the same factors

- wetlands drainage and the conversion of wetlands to agricultural, urban, or transportation corridors along migration routes in the United States and Canada
- forest fragmentation due to clear-cut logging on the breeding ranges and along migration routes in the United States, Canada, and Mexico (Robbins et al. 1989; Terborgh 1989)

Destruction of tropical forests on wintering ranges can have a disproportionate effect on particular species because many wintering areas are relatively small compared to a species' vast northern forest breeding grounds in the northern United States and Canadian boreal forests. More than half of all Neotropical migrants winter in Mexico and the Bahamas, Cuba, and other islands of the West Indies. Other species winter in the relatively small areas of Central America. For example, the ovenbird, Cape May warbler, and northern parula winter primarily in the West Indies; the bay-breasted, black-throated green, golden-winged, Tennessee, and chestnut-sided warblers and least flycatcher winter primarily in Central America; Wilson's warbler winters primarily in Mexico, Guatemala, and Belize; and the olive-sided flycatcher, veery, rose-breasted grosbeak, black-billed cuckoo, scarlet tanager, and the Canada and blackburnian warblers winter chiefly in northern South America (Terborgh 1989). All of these species have shown recent declines (table 13.3) (Robbins et al. 1989).

Forest fragmentation on breeding ranges in the eastern deciduous forest of the United States and southern Canada is causing decreases and even local disappearance of some species over wide areas. These declines are related in part to increases in edge habitat caused by reducing forests to isolated blocks and narrow corridors. Predation on nests and nestlings along forest edges by raccoons, skunks, cats, jays, ravens, crows, and other species is much greater than in the interior of large forest areas. Many Neotropical migrants are especially vulnerable to such predation because they nest on or near the ground instead of in tree cavities or in protected nests high in trees. Many do not renest if the first nesting fails. Parasitism of nests by brown cowbirds is also much higher along forest edges and in small isolated tracts as opposed to the interior of large

Table 13.3 / Trends in North American populations of some Neotropical migrant songbirds nesting in the BWCAW, 1966–87

Species	Population trends 1966–78	Percent per year 1978–87
Black-billed cuckoo	13.4	-5.9
Olive-sided flycatcher	3.6	-5.7
Eastern wood-pewee	-2.1	-0.7
Least flycatcher	-1.6	-0.2
Veery	1.6	-2.4
Gray catbird	0.6	-1.4
Golden-winged warbler	-2.2	-1.9
Tennessee warbler	18.6	-11.6
Northern parula warbler	1.2	-2.1
Chestnut-sided warbler	2.2	-3.8
Cape May warbler	19.3	-2.3
Black-throated green warbler	0.3	-3.1
Blackburnian warbler	1.3	-1.1
Bay-breasted warbler	10.2	-15.8
American redstart	1.3	-1.2
Ovenbird	1.0	-1.0
Mourning warbler	1.1	-1.6
Common yellowthroat	0.2	-1.9
Wilson's warbler	9.8	-6.5
Canada warbler	-2.7	-2.7
Scarlet tanager	2.6	-1.2
Rose-breasted grosbeak	6.1	-4.1
Indigo bunting	0.4	-0.7

Source Data from Robbins et al. (1989).

forests (Terborgh 1989; Robbins et al. 1989; Wilcove 1990).

The habitat needs of Neotropical migrants while enroute from their breeding grounds to wintering ranges are not well known but are thought to be another piece of the story behind declining populations. Forest fragmentation and loss of coastal upland habitats along major migration routes may be factors in the declines. Many species must rest and refuel along the long and perilous routes between their northern forest summer homes and tropical wintering areas. Efforts are under way to fill this knowledge gap (Nicholls 1990).

The BWCAW, Quetico, and Voyageurs together constitute one of the largest enclaves of protected forest in eastern North America, and the nesting areas of Neotropical migrants within their borders are not subject to most of the problems just outlined. Unfortunately, their bird populations are not immune to habitat destruction on the wintering grounds, along migration routes, or in breeding areas in unprotected forests elsewhere. Forest senescence and succession within the Boundary Waters reserves due to fire exclusion may in the short run be improving the habitat for some species, such as many warblers. But in the long run, the vegetation changes induced by changed fire regimes will surely have new and unforeseen effects on many species.

How these habitat changes, both within and beyond the Boundary Waters ecosystem, are affecting bird populations is still unknown. Fortunately, new cooperative population monitoring programs and habitat studies were begun in Minnesota and nationwide in 1989 and 1990, involving states, universities, federal agencies, and private foundations. It is to be hoped that we will soon have better information on the status of each species, and better knowledge of what actions must be taken to stem these alarming declines (National Fish and Wildlife Foundation 1991; Niemi et al. 1991). It is depressing to realize that the fate of many of the Boundary Waters most abundant and characteristic breeding birds may hinge on events in faraway regions, but that is a reality of the interconnectedness of the global ecosystems.

The Lake and Stream Ecosystems

The network of lakes and streams in the Boundary Waters region reflects an intricate pattern of small and medium-sized watersheds that ultimately lead either to Hudson Bay or to the Great Lakes–St. Lawrence River drainage. All the waters of Quetico and Voyageurs converge into the Rainy River system, which leads eventually to Hudson Bay. The eastern third of the BWCAW lies across a continental divide that separates the Hudson Bay watershed from the Great Lakes–St. Lawrence River watershed, giving the BWCAW a more complex array of watersheds (figure 14.1).

The smaller watersheds occur within or straddle several geological landform regions and give rise to a variety of different lake and stream types. Differences among lakes in the Boundary Waters region influence the kinds of fish and other aquatic life they support. In this chapter, these variables are grouped for discussion into five categories, with the recognition that all factors interact: landscape setting, physical form of the basin, temperature and oxygen, productivity, and fish populations. I then classify lakes into seven types based on the variables in these categories. (Specific information on BWCAW lakes in this chapter is based on Minnesota Department of Natural Resources [MDNR] lake survey reports, courtesy of MDNR.)

The Landscape Setting of the Lake

Significant differences in the bedrock types and in the resulting topography in each bedrock region affect lake types. The chemical composition of the rocks influences the chemical content of the runoff waters that enter lakes and streams, in turn affecting their acidity and available nutrients for aquatic plants. Likewise the composition and depth of surface soils and underlying glacial drifts influence runoff and groundwater chemistry. In general, the least fertile lakes occur on granitic bedrock, such as the Vermilion Granite in the western BWCAW and similar rocks in much of Quetico and Voyageurs. Some of the more fertile soils in the BWCAW are associated with the Knife Lake Group of rocks from Fall Lake, the Moose Lake chain, and Snowbank Lake northeast to Knife and Cypress lakes, and with the Rove Formation and Logan intrusions east of the Gunflint Trail. The Duluth Complex generally produces lakes of low to intermediate fertility. In Quetico the Poobah Lake Complex consists of unusual alkaline potassium syenites that undoubtedly influence the chemical properties of lake water.

Most soils in the Boundary Waters are formed on glacial deposits derived largely from the local bedrock and thus have chemical properties reflecting these source rocks. Locally some soils formed on Glacial Lake Agassiz clays are more fertile than the predominant local bedrock and soil types. Examples are the pockets of glacial lake clays in low-lying terrain in the western BWCAW and in Quetico and Voyageurs in otherwise very infertile granitic terrain (R.F. Wright 1976). Another case is the Wawiag River in Quetico, also in Glacial Lake Agassiz clays and silts.

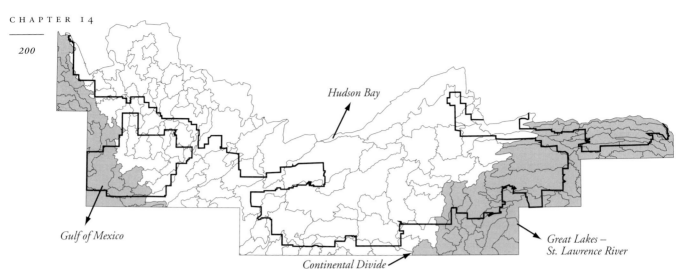

Hudson Bay

Gulf of Mexico

Great Lakes –
St. Lawrence River

Continental Divide

Figure 14.1 / The complex array of watersheds in the BWCAW, which eventually flow to Hudson Bay, to the Great Lakes—St.Lawrence River, or to the Gulf of Mexico. (Data courtesy of the Minnesota Department of Natural Resources, Division of Waters. Map by Stephen Lime, Department of Forest Resources, University of Minnesota.)

Each bedrock type also tends to produce characteristic landforms with typical ridge and hollow patterns and relief and typical lake-basin shapes, sizes, and depths, distribution of islands and reefs, and so on. Lakes on the Rove Formation tend to be long, narrow, and deep, with few islands and with plunging shorelines rimmed by high cliffs, especially along their south shores. Pine, Clearwater, and Mountain lakes are good examples.

Lakes on granitic bedrock often have irregular shapes with roundish bays and many islands and peninsulas. Many are shallow, but some of the larger lakes have deep basins. They may be surrounded by low, rounded bedrock hills and frequent bogs. Basswood, Crooked, Big Trout, Lac La Croix, Ge-be-on-e-quet, and Agnes lakes are BWCAW examples. Argo, McIntyre, Sturgeon, Brent, and Russell lakes are Quetico examples.

Lakes on the Knife Lake Group of rocks tend to have linear branch bays and small linear islands. They vary in depth but usually have some deep troughs. Many are surrounded by steep, high bedrock ridges. Examples are Ensign, Knife, Kekekabic, and Cherry lakes.

On the Duluth Complex (mostly gabbro) the lakes vary greatly in shape, but many are roundish or spiderlike with many bays, points, and rounded islands. Most are surrounded by low, rounded hills and often by large bogs. Most are relatively shallow compared to lakes on other bed-

rock types. Typical examples are Gabbro, Bald Eagle, and Isabella lakes, the One-Two-Three-Four chain of lakes, Insula, Alice, Malberg, Polly, and Phoebe lakes. However, Ima, Thomas, Fraser, Little Saganaga, Gillis, Tuscarora, and Cherokee lakes are deep trout lakes.

Where major faults occur (displacement of bedrock by shifting of the earth's crust), steep slopes and plunging shorelines are typical of the local bedrock. The line of contact between two different bedrock types is also often associated with steep topography and abrupt changes in lake shorelines and depths. The Kahshahpiwi-Keefer chain of lakes in Quetico is an example of both effects.

Generally lakes located at or near the headwaters of a watershed receive less inflow from the land and therefore depend more for nutrients on the chemical content of rainwater, snowfall, and dry atmospheric fallout and are less fertile. Other factors being equal, a lake at the headwaters of a watershed with a small catchment in relation to its size will be less fertile. Meander and Dogfish lakes north of the Echo Trail are examples (R.F. Wright 1976).

Sphagnum–black spruce bogs generally have very acid surface waters (pH 3.5 to 4.5) and are high in humic acids and dissolved humic substances and low in plant nutrients. Bog waters are usually light yellow brown or tea-colored, and lakes with a significant percentage of their watershed occupied by bogs or receiving significant flows from bog areas tend to have tea-colored, slightly acid waters and low alkalinity. The runoff waters from cedar swamps and aspen-birch forests tend to be clear, neutral in acidity, and rich in nutrients, whereas the runoff from jack pine–black spruce forests is acidic and lower in nutrients.

The Physical Form of the Lake Basin

Lake depth determines summer water temperatures and influences the percentage of the lake available for the growth of many plants and animals. Some lakes are only 5 to 20 feet deep over their entire area, Big Moose Lake, for example. Others have large areas deeper than 100 feet. Saganaga Lake has the greatest maximum depth of all mapped lakes in the BWCAW. The deepest point, 284 feet, is on the Ontario side of the main basin. Generally a lake must have large areas at least 70 to 80 feet deep to support lake trout, burbot, and other cold-water fish.

In the Boundary Waters, that portion of a lake's area less than 15 feet deep, called the littoral area, supports shallow-water plants and animals. Such areas generally occur in a band around the shore and around islands, but in some lakes extensive reefs and large areas of the bottom are within this high-productivity zone. Lake Three has 44 percent littoral area; Perent Lake, 76 percent; Big Moose Lake, nearly 100 percent; and Gabimichigami Lake, only 12 percent. The bottom in shallow areas is the habitat for many plants and animals, and its character affects the spawning success for many species of fish. Bottoms vary from smooth rock shelves to boulder, gravel, sand, or muck and may be vegetated or barren.

Total lake area may also be a factor for species of fish such as walleyes that require room to move about and for large predatory fish that may need a large prey base to support significant numbers. A chain of small lakes interconnected by streams passable to most fish, like portions of the Kawishiwi River system, may mitigate the effect of small lake size (Johnson et al. 1977).

Water clarity influences the depth to which light penetrates at intensities sufficient to support various aquatic plants, and it varies greatly in the Boundary Waters region. Clarity is measured with a white metal disk (Secchi disk) lowered to the depth at which it can no longer be seen. In the Boundary Waters this depth is only 3 to 6 feet in brown-water lakes such as Gabbro, Isabella, and Perent but reaches 30 feet in very clear lakes like Mountain Lake (MDNR lake survey reports). Brown-water lakes and streams generally receive significant flows from acid bogs and are colored by humic substances. Lakes situated at or near the headwaters of a watershed are often clear unless the headwaters area happens to be dominated by bogs. Algae may impart a bluish or greenish tinge to very clear lake waters.

Water Temperature and Oxygen Factors

Deeper lakes in the Boundary Waters develop strong thermal stratification during the warm season because warm water is less dense then cold, but only down to 39°F (4°C), below which it becomes lighter again. When the ice melts in late April or early May, the coldest water, at 32°F, is at first on the surface. As the spring sun warms the surface, the wind mixes the entire water mass to a uniform density and a temperature of 39°F. This is the spring turnover, which replenishes the bottom water with oxygen (Goldman and Horne 1983).

Then, as the sun continues to warm the surface water, thermal stratification begins, in most lakes usually in late May or early June. Wind-mixing of this warmer water usually extends only to a depth of 15 to 30 feet. Below this warm upper water (the epilimnion) is a relatively rapid drop in temperature through the thermocline to a bottom layer of uniformly cold water (the hypolimnion). The epilimnion may have a temperature 65° to 75°F, depending on the date, recent sky conditions, and air temperatures, and the hypolimnion temperature may be 40° to 50°F even on the hottest July or August days. Temperatures lower than about 55°F are vital to the survival of lake trout and other cold-water fish.

Oxygen is gradually depleted within and below the thermocline in many lakes as the summer progresses, because these waters have no direct access to the atmosphere, and microbial decay of organic matter consumes oxygen. Many native fish and other aquatic organisms cannot tolerate dissolved oxygen levels below about 2 parts per million and trout cannot tolerate conditions below 5 parts per million. In many lakes less than about 60 feet deep, oxygen within and below the thermocline often falls below 5 parts per million by midsummer and may be virtually gone by late summer. However, shallow lakes do not always develop thermoclines, and oxygen may be adequate to the bottom.

As fall approaches, the sun's elevation declines, days shorten, and heat input to the lakes decreases. Between early September and early October—earlier for shallow lakes than large deep lakes—most lakes lose their thermoclines and attain essentially uniform temperatures from top to bottom. The cooled surface waters sink and become mixed with deeper waters by winds. The oxygen supply is fully replenished, and the excess carbon dioxide that accumulated below the thermocline is released.

After lake water temperatures fall to 39°F from top to bottom in late October, colder but lighter water accumulates at the surface, usually reaching about 34°F by early November. Then, on a cold night in November a skim of ice forms over lakes, and the long period of winter stagnation begins. By middle to late winter, the ice layer is usually 20 to 36 inches thick on most lakes, depending both on winter temperatures and snow cover on the ice (deep snow insulates the ice from the cold). Oxygen replenishment and carbon dioxide release are prevented by the ice cover. With some oxygen generated through photosynthesis by algae, most of the larger lakes have adequate oxygen through the winter, but some ponds and very shallow lakes become oxygen deficient, especially in winters with prolonged deep snow on the ice.

Strong water flows through a lake, as occur along major river systems such as the Maligne River and Basswood-Rainy river systems, may alter thermal and oxygen regimes, especially in shallow areas at times of unusually strong flow. In winter, ice thickness and oxygen levels may be atypical near major waterfalls or rapids that rarely freeze over.

Lake Productivity

The basic energy source for all lake organisms is the sun, which drives photosynthesis by algae and other green aquatic plants, the source of all primary production. All animal organisms are consumers. Water clarity in lakes determines the depth to which light intensity will support photosynthesis, and in the Boundary Waters region there are significant differences in clarity in this respect.

Photosynthesis requires a balanced suite of plant nutrients, including phosphorus, which is very scarce in Boundary Waters lakes and limits the growth of algae and other aquatic plants. The lands within a lake's watershed receive a significant percentage of their annual supply of cations and phosphorus from atmospheric fallout. Weathering of minerals and storage contribute the remainder. Most of these nutrients are recycled by the forest vegetation annually, and only a small fraction is lost in runoff to lakes. Nevertheless, the input of cations from runoff contributes much of the cation supply to lakes, although most of the phosphorus comes from atmospheric fallout (R.F. Wright 1976). Thus the production of plant biomass in Boundary Waters lakes is inherently low, and small differences in phosphorus inputs from their watersheds are important.

The acidity or alkalinity of lake water, measured as the negative log of the hydrogen ion concentration (pH), is a major factor influencing nutrient availability. The pH scale ranges from 0 to 14, with values below 7 denoting increasing acidity, and above 7 increasing alkalinity, 7 being neutral. Boundary Waters lakes generally have a pH between 6.5 and 7.5. Acidity below pH 4 or 5 severely limits plant and animal diversity and growth. Carbon dioxide and water are the basic ingredients of organic compounds, and carbon dioxide availability can also limit productivity in some situations (Goldman and Horne 1983).

Total alkalinity (expressed in parts per million as calcium carbonate) is widely used as a proxy for nutrient availability. The range of total alkalinity in Minnesota lakes is from 5 parts per million or less in the least fertile soft water lakes of the Boundary Waters to more than 200 parts per million in some fertile hard water lakes of western counties. Most BWCAW lakes have alkalinities between about 6 and 25 parts per million, but some are below 5 parts per million. Thus most are very infertile soft-water (oligotrophic) lakes. Total alkalinity is also an indicator of the buffering capacity of a lake against acidification by acid deposition (acid rain). Alkalinities below about 5 parts per million combined with pH values below 6.0 suggest vulnerability to acidification (Thornton, Payer, and Matta 1982).

Given the history of frequent high-intensity, stand-replacing forest fires in the Boundary Waters, we also need to understand the role of fires in the nutrient regimes of lakes. The high-intensity Little Sioux fire in spring of 1971 burned two-thirds of the virgin forest surrounding Meander Lake, changing nutrient cycling on the lake's watershed and increasing the export of potassium by 265 percent and phosphorus by 93 percent (R. F. Wright 1976). The increased export represented only a small fraction of the nutrient capital on the landscape. Increased potassium had little impact on the lake because it does not limit algal growth. Phosphorus loading increased by only 38 percent, because most still came from atmospheric fallout. No significant increase in phosphorus concentrations in lake water was found, apparently because the phosphorus was quickly taken up by organic matter. The lake remained a clear, nutrient-poor water body. A companion study by McColl and Grigal (1975), involving different research methods, also found no increase in the phosphorus concentration in Meander Lake.

A high-intensity fire in late summer or fall of a very dry year might result in larger inputs of nutrients. Fall fires may consume nearly all of the organic layer, exposing mineral soils to erosion, especially on steep terrain or watersheds that are large relative to the size of the lake. Postfire rainfall intensity, especially in the first year after the fire, is also important. Obviously, however, the history of fires over the past 9,300 years shows that even high-intensity fall fires have not permanently degraded water quality.

Tiny floating algae of many forms, called phytoplankton, are the foundation of the food web in lakes. Wide seasonal and irregular increases in the abundance are called blooms. Some species are also active beneath the ice in winter. Oxygen is a by-product of photosynthesis and is vital for aquatic animals. Winter algal activity can furnish some oxygen at a time when absorption from the atmosphere is precluded by the ice cover (Goldman and Horne 1983). In the Boundary Waters many species of small forage fish and the fry of predaceous larger sport fish feed in whole or in part on algae and other phytoplankton (Phil-

lips, Schmid, and Underhill 1982). Like all plants, the phytoplankton depend on adequate light, carbon dioxide, and nutrients for maximum growth. But productivity is limited in most lakes by nutrient shortages, unfavorable ratios of littoral area to total lake area, cold deep waters, and five months of ice cover. Phosphorus and nitrogen are most often the limiting nutrients.

Very small free-floating and swimming animals, collectively called zooplankton, such as protozoans, rotifers, and crustaceans, are the primary consumers (herbivores) that feed on algae and other phytoplankton. Some feed in part on the eggs and young of their own or other species of zooplankters, but as a group they serve a vital function in the food web by converting carbohydrates generated by the phytoplankton into a source of protein and other foods needed by larger aquatic animals. The tiny water flea (*Daphnia*), often seen in water taken near shore in the Boundary Waters, is one of the most common zooplankters. The opossum shrimp is a boreal cold-water species that survives warm summers below the thermocline of deep trout lakes. Many zooplankters are inactive in winter. In forms such as the water flea, adults die off in the fall, and the species overwinters in a resting-egg stage (Goldman and Horne 1983). Many minnows and the young of larger fish feed in whole or in part on the zooplankton (Phillips, Schmid, and Underhill 1982). Again, productivity in most Boundary Waters lakes is low, limited by the scarcity of phytoplankton.

Along Boundary Waters lakeshores and in streams, such larger bottom organisms as the larvae (nymphs) of dragonflies, dobsonflies, stone flies, mayflies, blackflies, and other insects plus nematode worms, leeches, crayfish, snails, and clams are also part of the food web. So are the brown, yellow, gray, and green sponges (the green ones harbor algae in their bodies and extract food from them [Nelson 1989]). The tadpoles and adults of frogs, toads, and salamanders also live along shorelines, and the painted turtle and snapping turtle frequent the shallows and shores of most lakes and streams. The adults of some aquatic insects such as mayflies become food for fish and other vertebrates as they emerge from the water. Again, productivity is low in most waters. Blackflies breed primarily in fast-flowing streams, not in calm lake water, but you will surely be attacked by them at your lakeshore campsite in late May and June.

Rooted higher aquatic plants are not abundant in most Boundary Waters lakes and streams because of unsuitable or infertile rocky bottoms, narrow littoral zones due to steep shorelines, and a general lack of sufficiently shallow areas. A full suite of aquatics does occur, however, and some shallow lakes and bays of deeper lakes are well vegetated. Among the tall emergent aquatics often seen along lakeshores are the common reed grass, bulrushes, spike-rush, sedges, and, in some shallow muck-bottom lakes and streams, wild rice. Common low emergents and floating-leaf plants include the arrowheads, pipewort, bur-reeds, bladderworts, water-smartweed, pondweeds, water-shield, and six species of water-lilies. Submerged aquatics include water-milfoil, water nymph, common waterweed, and tapegrass. The free-floating duckweeds occur chiefly in beaver ponds (Walshe 1980). Most of these aquatics are not heavily used directly for food by fish and other aquatic animals. However, the seeds of several species, notably wild rice, are widely used as foods by waterfowl and other birds; the tubers and other parts of several species are important foods for beaver, muskrat, moose, and deer; and many invertebrates and fish use their foliage for protection from predators and as sites for egg laying. The decaying leaves and stems of many species also become part of the detritus used as food by bottom organisms (the benthos) important in the food web (Goldman and Horne 1983).

Native crayfish feed on some of the higher aquatic plants but do not limit the plant growth. The rusty crayfish, a southern species accidentally introduced by fishermen using it as bait, had by 1991 appeared in Fall Lake and the Moose-Newfound-Sucker lakes chain in the BWCAW and in Lake Vermilion. Larger, more aggressive, and possessing a harder exoskeleton than the native crayfish, the rusty crayfish has wreaked havoc with vegetation and fish populations in many northern Wisconsin lakes, where it is an effective predator near the top of the food chain (Lodge, Beckel, and Mugnuson 1985). Whether the rusty poses similar threats to Boundary Waters lakes and streams remained unclear as of 1991.

Fish Populations of the Lakes and Streams

About 50 fish species with breeding populations occur in the Boundary Waters region, and at least 4 or 5 exotic trout are maintained in a few lakes by stocking. Among the established breeders, the smallmouth bass and rainbow smelt and perhaps the largemouth bass and crappie did not occur before about 1930, when they were introduced either deliberately (bass) or accidentally (smelt) at various times and places. In addition, walleye and lake trout have been stocked in many lakes in the BWCAW and Voyageurs, in some cases in waters where they did not exist previously.

The principal sport fish are the lake trout, walleye, northern pike, and smallmouth bass, all of which as adults are predators on smaller species and even on their own young. Largemouth bass and black crappie are not present in many waters and are often scarce where they do occur. Many of the other species are small forage fish that serve as prey for the larger predators. The following discussions are not a guide to fishing but an effort to place the key fish species in the ecosystem and to describe their relationship to lake types.

The lake trout, a boreal North American char, is the most demanding cold-water species. Many trout lakes are located high in their watersheds, have clear waters, are surrounded by high rocky ridges, and have plunging shorelines. In the early spring and late fall, trout inhabit the shallows, but when surface waters are warmer than about 55°F, they usually remain in or below the thermocline. Oxygen levels must be above 5 parts per million.

The lake trout is potentially one of the largest fish; Minnesota's angling record is 43 pounds. In recent years most have weighed 2 to 5 pounds. Lake trout grow slowly, requiring 15 years to reach 9 or 10 pounds. They reach reproductive age at 6 or 7 years. Trout spawn in October after waters in the shallows drop to the 50°F range. They deposit their eggs at night in crevices between boulders, in gravel on reefs, or in shallows usually 5 to 20 feet deep. The young hatch in late February or later and seek deeper water in about a month when the yolk sac is absorbed. Adults disperse after spawning and may move long distances. Lake trout feed on crustaceans, sponges, insects, and many fish species, including young smallmouth bass and small lake trout, but in the Boundary Waters, the cisco, a cold-water fish inhabiting most trout lakes, may be the most important food of adults. Young trout feed heavily on such zooplankton as opossum shrimp and water fleas. Burbot, small lake trout, and other fish sometimes eat trout eggs. Hatchery-reared trout have been introduced into many BWCAW lakes or added to maintain populations in the face of heavy fishing pressure. However, some natural trout lakes have never been stocked (Phillips, Schmid, and Underhill 1982; Trippel and Beamish 1989).

The northern pike, a most voracious predator, is the most widely distributed fish in Quetico and probably in the BWCAW as well. Northern pike clearly tolerate warmer water than lake trout. They are present in lakes of all sizes and depths on all geological landforms and in both brownwater and clear lakes. They often frequent weedy shallow waters into early summer and return to the shallows early in the fall, but usually they move into deeper, cooler water in midsummer, sometimes as deep as 100 feet. Northern pike vie with lake trout for size records. They spawn in early spring as soon as the ice goes out in grassy or marshy shallows. The sticky eggs adhere to vegetation and hatch in 12 to 14 days. After their yolk sac is absorbed, the young feed on zooplankton and insect larvae for 7 to 10 days and then switch to fish. Adults will eat any fish, frog, bird, or mammal a third to a half their own size. Females reach sexual maturity at about 4 years and tend to be larger than males (Scott and Crossman 1973; Crossman 1976; Phillips, Schmid, and Underhill 1982).

The walleye is the second most widespread fish in Quetico and probably also in the BWCAW. Walleyes tolerate warm waters and are found in many shallow lakes and streams with either clear or brown waters, as well as in deep, clear lakes, especially with areas of gravel, sand, or rocky bottoms. In the 1930s and 1940s, walleyes were widely stocked and have since become established in many BWCAW and Quetico lakes where they did not naturally occur. In the Boundary Waters most adults weigh 1 to 4 pounds. Females are larger than males. The walleye is Minnesota's official state fish.

Female walleyes reach sexual maturity at 3 to 6 years.

Maximum age is about 15 to 20 years. Spawning occurs in late April or early May soon after the ice goes out, especially in gravelly or rocky riffles, and may extend up rivers. Such sites provide water movement needed to clean and aerate the eggs, which hatch in 12 to 18 days.

The tiny fry grow to 4 or 5 inches by the end of the first season. They first eat mostly zooplankton but soon switch to small perch and minnows or cannibalize their siblings. By late summer, they move to the bottom in 20 to 30 feet of water. Adults feed on yellow perch, ciscoes, several minnows, rock bass, and smaller walleyes, plus insects, frogs, snails, crayfish, and small mammals. The eyes of walleyes are sensitive to strong light, and in clear water most feeding occurs early and late in the day and at night. During midday, walleyes tend to move into deeper water or seek the shade of cliffs or overhanging vegetation. Northern pike are the most important predator on adults. Perch, sauger, smallmouth bass, northern pike, and lake whitefish compete with walleyes for food (Scott and Crossman 1973; Crossman 1976; Phillips, Schmid, and Underhill 1982; MDNR lake surveys 1976–90).

The smallmouth bass did not occur in most of the Boundary Waters region before about 1940. Its northward spread after introduction has had profound implications for the fish populations of the region, which I discuss later in this chapter. Its range prior to stocking was restricted to the upper Mississippi River drainage and the Great Lakes–St. Lawrence system (Scott and Crossman 1973). The waterfalls along Minnesota's Lake Superior north shore were barriers to migration into the lakes of the eastern BWCAW from Lake Superior, and the Mississippi drainage is separated from the BWCAW-Quetico area by the Laurentian Divide.

Smallmouth bass is a warm-water fish, but it inhabits somewhat cooler waters than the largemouth bass. It prefers lakes and streams with rocky bottoms and rocky or gravelly shoals and shorelines. In deep lakes it remains largely in the warmer waters above the thermocline at depths of 15 to 20 feet during midsummer. It becomes inactive in the fall when water temperatures drop to about 55°F and remains inactive all winter. Growth is slow in the Boundary Waters; about 7 years is required to reach lengths of 15 inches and weights near 2 pounds (Crossman 1976). Individuals larger than 5 pounds are rarely taken in the Boundary Waters. The Minnesota record is 8 pounds, from a northwestern county.

Female smallmouth bass attain sexual maturity at about 4 to 6 years. Spawning occurs in late May or early June when waters in the shallows reach 60° to 65°F. Males build nests in gravelly or sandy bottoms by fanning out a depression with their tails. Eggs and sperm are deposited in the nest, whereupon the male guards the eggs and later the tiny fry. Males often return to the same nest or nearby in subsequent years. Smallmouth bass feed on crayfish, small fish, minnows, leeches, and insects such as immature dragonflies, mayflies, midges, caddis flies, and stone flies. They take some immature walleyes, but fish are a smaller fraction of their diet than crayfish and insects. Their most effective predators are probably northern pike (Scott and Crossman 1973; Crossman 1976; Johnson and Hale 1977; Phillips, Schmid, and Underhill 1982).

The white sucker ranges from subarctic and boreal North America to the northern Gulf states and New Mexico. It inhabits shallow lakes and streams as well as the shallower areas of many deep trout lakes and is sometimes collected in deep-water test nets. Most adults are 8 to 20 inches long and weigh about 0.5 to 3 pounds. Small suckers are among the most important food fish taken by northern pike, walleye, smallmouth bass, lake trout, and burbot. The white sucker spawns on gravel bottoms in May in small tributary streams and shallows of lakes. The tiny fry begin feeding on near-surface plankton and small invertebrates, but they gradually shift to various small larvae, snails, and clams (Scott and Crossman 1973; Crossman 1976; Phillips, Schmid, and Underhill 1982). The related longnose sucker is present in some lakes, including Saganaga and Sea Gull.

The yellow perch is found in varied habitats in lakes and streams of all sizes. Perch tolerate warm water well. Most adults are only 5 to 9 inches long, making them ideal food for walleye, northern pike, bass, and trout. They spawn in mid-May and early June in weedy shallow water. Tens of thousands of eggs are laid in long gelatinous folded tubes. They are predators, often moving in large schools and feeding in the daytime on minnows, insects, snails,

fish eggs and fry, leeches, and crayfish (Crossman 1976; Phillips, Schmid, and Underhill 1982).

The cisco is a small cold-water species confined in the BWCAW and Quetico to deep cold lakes inhabited by lake trout, for which it is a prime food. The typical cisco is a slim, roundish fish seldom exceeding 14 inches and 0.75 pound. A larger form, called tullibee, is heavier-bodied and may reach lengths of 20 inches and weights up to 5 pounds. In summer ciscoes inhabit the same cold oxygenated waters below the thermocline that lake trout do, and like trout they use the shallows in spring and fall. They spawn at night in late fall just before freeze-up, gathering in schools in 6 to 9 feet of water. The zooplankton, especially crustaceans, are their chief food. They also use larval insects and emerging aquatic insects during spring hatches, and larger ciscoes may eat newly hatched lake trout or trout eggs. Where lake whitefish occur in the same waters, ciscoes are often very stunted, not exceeding 6 inches in length (Crossman 1976; Phillips, Schmid, and Underhill 1982; Trippel and Beamish 1989).

The lake whitefish inhabits some deep trout lakes of the BWCAW and Quetico. Like the cisco, it belongs to the salmon family but is normally larger. Adults are usually 12 to 20 inches long, weighing 1 to 3 pounds. Some lakes have dwarf populations that mature at 6 to 8 inches. Whitefish are a valuable food for northern pike and lake trout. Spawning occurs in late fall shortly before freeze-up in gravelly or rocky shallows, but the eggs do not hatch until spring. Larvae feed on plankton but switch to snails, clams, and insect larvae when 3 to 4 inches long. Adults are also bottom feeders, but they often leave the depths briefly in June and July to feed on emerging mayflies and midges (Crossman 1976; Phillips, Schmid, and Underhill 1982).

The lake sturgeon is the region's largest fish—a 162-pounder was taken in the Rainy River in 1968. But commercial fishing, last conducted in Lac La Croix from 1959 to 1968, depleted this sparsely distributed fish. Sturgeon feed on snails, clams, crayfish, and insects in productive shallows. They are very slow growing and long-lived. At 20 to 30 years, the age of sexual maturity, they are 3 to 4 feet long but weigh only 10 to 18 pounds. At 50 years they are a little over 5 feet long and weigh around 50 to 60 pounds.

Spawning occurs in late May and June in shallow rapids where these huge fish sometimes leap out of the water (Crossman 1976; Phillips, Schmid, and Underhill 1982).

The burbot, eelpout, or lawyer is a cold-water inland codfish ranging from the arctic coast of North America to the northern United States. It is present in many deep trout lakes and some shallower lakes. It reaches lengths up to 23 inches and weights up to 10 pounds. It spawns beneath the ice in midwinter in the shallows of lakes and streams. A bottom-feeding predator, it feeds mostly at night on insects, crayfish, small fish, and the eggs of other fish, and it may compete with trout in some lakes (Crossman 1976; Phillips, Schmid, and Underhill 1982).

There are about 35 more fish species in the Boundary Waters. Most are very small types one might call minnows, although only 15 species actually belong to the minnow family. Many occupy important places in lake and stream ecosystems as herbivores, feeding on algae, other small plants, and zooplankton, and they serve as protein sources for larger fish.

Several sunfish family members smaller than bass are not very abundant. Introductions may be the source of the crappies now found in some lakes, but the species could be native to some lakes. Four sunfish occur mostly in ponds, small weedy shallow lakes, and weedy shallow bays of a few larger lakes. The rock bass, really another sunfish, is much more widely distributed and abundant, frequenting rocky shallows. These members of the sunfish family feed on insects, crustaceans, snails, and small fish. They in turn become food sources for the larger predators, especially bass and northern pike. All spawn in nests from June to August (Crossman 1976; Phillips, Schmid, and Underhill 1982).

The rainbow smelt is now established in several Boundary Waters lakes, apparently the result of releases by fishermen for bait, now illegal. A cold-water species that feeds on zooplankton and small fish, the smelt may be a serious food competitor of lake trout, walleye, and other predatory fish and may eat the fry of trout and other cold-water species. At the same time, it has become a prime forage species for lake trout in Burntside and Saganaga lakes.

The tadpole madtom is the region's only common member of the catfish family. It is no larger than a small tad-pole. It has poison pectoral spines. It inhabits slow-moving streams such as sections of the BWCAW's Moose River and small weedy lakes and ponds.

The uncommon native silver lamprey is the region's only member of this parasitic fish family and should not be confused with the exotic sea lamprey that wrecked Lake Superior's fishery. The silver lamprey lives only 12 to 20 months and reaches lengths of no more than 13 inches. Occasionally its scars are seen on northern pike (Crossman 1976).

Fish Population Structures before 1938 and Today

Population structure is the combination of fish species in a lake or stream and the relative abundance of the various species. The relative abundance of the four large predators in the Boundary Waters (lake trout, walleye, northern pike, and smallmouth bass) along with the burbot in a given water is of great biological significance because the top predators in an ecosystem influence the structure of their prey populations, and these in turn influence populations of the smallest animals and plants at the base of the food chain.

Major changes have occurred in both the species composition and size-class structure of the fish populations in many BWCAW and Quetico lakes and rivers since about 1938, when substantial documentation was initiated. Before 1938, smallmouth bass were absent or uncommon in most of the region. Walleyes were absent from many lakes where they have since been planted, or to which they migrated as a result of plantings elsewhere. The invasion of both species into additional lakes may still be going on, and the invasion of smelt as well. Natural fish migrations occurred during and after the retreat of the continental ice sheet and the formation and drainage of such large late-glacial lakes as Lake Agassiz and high-water stages of Lake Superior (Crossman 1976). These fish migrations were complex and followed several pathways at various times. The situation in 1938 was still the result of two natural limiting factors. First, only those fish species were present that could swim there via available waterways; and second, only those succeeded that were adapted to the climate and the lake and stream habitats and to competition with other species. This process had been under way for the 12,000 years since the glacial period, and movements and population adjustments were probably still going on when we began to produce rapid change by releasing new species and selectively reducing some populations by commercial and sportfishing. Before 1938, the fish population structure of many lakes was simpler than today. The final outcome of recent introductions is unknown.

Attempts have been made to relate the fish populations of the Laurentian Shield region of Canada and the northeastern United States to the characteristics of the varied lake and stream environments of that vast region. Such efforts are complicated by the recent introduction of smallmouth bass and walleyes into many waters (Johnson et al. 1977). Before 1938, the top predators in many lakes were only the lake trout or the northern pike or both; in other lakes, they were walleyes plus northerns; and in some large lakes, all of these. Lakes containing only walleye as a top predator apparently were rare. Now the situation is more complicated and less stable.

There are now 15 possible combinations of the four most abundant large predatory fish in the Boundary Waters according to a survey of Quetico lakes (Crossman 1976) and 180 BWCAW lakes in Lake County (Minn. Dept. of Natural Resources 1990) (table 14.1). Both sets of data have limitations. The Quetico data are from lake surveys before 1976, and the invasion of additional lakes by smallmouth bass has continued into the 1990s. The Lake County data are based in part on more recent surveys, but the fishing guide from which they came may not report a species with numbers too low to offer fishers fair catches, and smallmouth bass expansion is probably still occurring in the BWCAW. Both data sets may also underrepresent smallmouth bass because this fish is undersampled by the netting techniques used in surveys. The BWCAW data are not a cross section of the whole BWCAW because they do not include the lakes in Cook and St. Louis counties.

The most frequent combination of top predators in both data sets is walleye-northern pike together (30 percent of BWCAW lakes, 23 percent of Quetico lakes), a combination that may have been increased by walleye stocking.

The second most frequent situation in the BWCAW data is northern pike alone (29 percent of lakes, but in Quetico only 10 percent). In Quetico the second most frequent combination is all four predators together (17 percent). The trout-bass combination did not occur in either data set, but three Quetico lakes may now qualify. The trout-pike-bass, walleye-bass, trout-walleye, and trout-walleye-bass combinations are also very uncommon, representing no more than 1 to 2 percent of lakes in either data set. In the BWCAW set, trout occurred most frequently alone (7 percent of lakes), but in the Quetico set, trout occurred most often with all four predators together. Walleye alone is also an uncommon situation, occurring in only about 2 percent of lakes.

Two studies provide information on actual structural changes in BWCAW fish populations. The changes resulted from two new factors that began to affect fish populations shortly after 1938. First, between about 1930 and 1952 smallmouth bass and walleye were introduced or had migrated into many waters where they had not existed previously. And second, selective fishing pressure on lake trout, walleye, and northern pike increased dramatically after 1938.

Increased fishing pressure was due to five factors:

- Roads and automobiles improved dramatically shortly before and after World War II, and several new roads giving direct access to BWCAW lakes, such as the Gunflint Trail, were completed by 1938.
- Outboard motors, including small, easily portaged models usable on canoes, were improved and less costly by 1940. By 1950, aluminum canoes and boats became widely available. BWCAW motorboat use was not significantly curtailed until 1978 to 1984.
- Beginning about 1940, fly-in fishing and fly-in resorts and cabins proliferated in the roadless areas. Between 1945 and 1950, they became the source of dramatic increases in "take out a limit" fishing.
- Snowmobiles became widely used in the BWCAW about 1960. Between 1960 and 1975, snowmobilers became a major source of winter fishing pressure on lake trout.
- By 1950, use of remote lakes by canoeists, many of whom were fishers, was increasing dramatically, not leveling out until the 1980s.

Table 14.1 / Number and percentage of BWCAW lakes in Lake County, Minnesota, and Quetico Provincial Park with reported populations of lake trout, walleye, northern pike, and smallmouth bass

Combination of top predator gamefish	Lake County BWCAW lakes		Quetico Provincial Park lakes	
	Number	Percentage	Number	Percentage
Trout-bass	0	0.0	0	0.0
Trout only	12	6.7	5	2.6
Trout-walleye-pike	5	2.8	18	9.2
Trout-walleye-pike-bass	4	2.2	33	16.9
Trout-pike	4	2.2	15	7.7
Trout-pike-bass	0	0.0	2	1.0
Bass only	2	1.1	7	3.6
Pike only	52	28.9	20	10.3
Pike-bass	2	1.1	5	2.6
Walleye only	3	1.7	5	2.6
Walleye-pike	54	30.0	45	23.1
Walleye-pike-bass	16	8.9	15	7.7
Walleye-bass	0	0.0	4	2.1
Trout-walleye	1	0.6	3	1.5
Trout-walleye-bass	2	1.1	1	0.5
Subtotal	157	87.3	178	91.4
Perch, sunfish, crappie, largemouth	13	7.2	17	8.7
Reclaimed for stream trout	4	2.2	—	—
Muskie only (planted)	1	0.6	—	—
No fish present	5	2.8	—	—
TOTAL LAKES	180	100.0	195	100.0
Total lakes with lake trout	28	15.6	77	39.5
Total lakes with smallmouth bass	26	14.4	67	34.4
Total lakes with walleye	85	47.2	124	63.6
Total lakes with northern pike	137	76.1	153	78.5

Sources Data for Quetico Provincial Park from Crossman (1976); data for Lake County, Minnesota, BWCAW lakes from Minn. Dept. of Natural Resources (1990).

Before 1938, fishing pressure was so light in most of the BWCAW and Quetico that fish populations in most lakes and streams were little altered by the selective removal of larger lake trout, walleye, and northern pike by fishers. A few large lakes such as Lac La Croix saw sporadic commercial fishing, but even these efforts did not last long enough to seriously alter most fish populations except for sturgeon. Before 1940, large catches of walleye, lake trout, and big northern pike were easily taken. Truly large lake trout were frequently taken from such lakes as Lac La Croix, Basswood, McIntyre, Snowbank, Knife, Saganaga, and Gunflint.

When lake trout–northern pike lakes were invaded by or stocked with both walleyes and smallmouth bass after 1938, these introductions plus rising fishing pressure caused major shifts in the populations of large predatory fish, with walleye and smallmouth bass partially replacing lake trout and northerns, without much change in total biomass. These structural changes may well have also involved forage fish used by the large predators. When new fish species are introduced to an ecosystem, the available resources are inevitably partitioned in new ways, and the final outcome is difficult to predict.

Another wave of structural change in fish populations has resulted from the stocking of smallmouth bass in former walleye and walleye–northern pike lakes, or from the migration of the exotic smallmouth bass into such lakes from introductions elsewhere. Long-term studies of four walleye lakes stocked with smallmouth bass have documented some of the changes that may result from such introductions (Johnson and Hale 1977). Hungry Jack Lake on the Gunflint Trail, Big Lake on the Echo Trail, and Pike and Two Island lakes north of Grand Marais were all originally walleye lakes, first stocked with smallmouth bass between 1945 and 1948. All lakes had good white sucker and perch populations—important as food for walleye—and some had small numbers of rock bass, sunfish, whitefish, and northern pike, as well as darters, dace, mudminnows, bluntnose minnow, stickleback, and sculpin. The study ran for about 20 years, beginning and ending in different years in each lake.

In all four lakes, smallmouth bass gradually increased to peaks in 9 to 15 years and then decreased to low populations in the subsequent 2 to 4 years. In Big, Hungry Jack, and Two Island lakes, walleyes decreased as the bass increased and remained low after bass declined. But in Pike Lake, walleye and bass increased together, and walleye continued to increase even after the bass declined. Perch increased dramatically in Hungry Jack Lake after the bass declined. Spawning times and sites of smallmouths and walleye did not overlap. Diets of bass and walleyes were similar in Pike Lake, where this was studied, but walleye fed more heavily on fish, and bass more heavily on crayfish, while both fed heavily on insects. Smallmouth bass

did consume some young walleyes, but in this lake walleyes nevertheless continued to increase. The decrease in walleyes as bass increased in three of the four lakes, followed by the decline of bass in all lakes, was probably not the result of competition between bass and walleyes for the same food resources, the authors believed. Instead, competition among bass seems to account for changed growth rates and for some of the decline of bass, and competition among walleyes may account for decreases in walleye growth rates. Predation by smallmouth bass on young walleye may have been a factor in the failure of walleye year classes and their decline in three of the four lakes. The authors could not account for the sharp drop in bass populations, but they note that decreases are expected when a species increases above the carrying capacity of the environment, and when various causes of death then check populations. In any case, here is documentation that in three of four lakes where smallmouth bass were introduced into walleye lakes, the outcome after 15 or 20 years was not only much lower walleye populations but low bass populations as well (Johnson and Hale 1977). Some variation of the outcomes in these four lakes may well have occurred in many other lakes in the BWCAW and Quetico as the smallmouth bass has proliferated and migrated to new waters.

Lake Types in the Boundary Waters Region

The foregoing discussions point to a need for a more organized understanding of the wide differences in lake characteristics within the Boundary Waters. Two approaches have often been taken toward recognizing what are usually called lake types. The simpler and more common approach is just to characterize lakes by the dominant fish species of interest, usually the top predator game fish. Up to this point that custom has been followed—calling lakes trout lakes, walleye lakes, northern pike lakes, bass lakes, and so on. The problem with this approach is that there are many important differences among lakes within these simple groupings, and the spread of smallmouth bass and walleyes to lakes they did not formerly occupy has blurred the meaning of these terms. The other approach is to group lakes by certain limnological characteristics, such as soft-water lakes and hard-water lakes. Or better yet, combine the two approaches and talk about soft-water walleye lakes (the Boundary Waters) and hard-water walleye lakes (western Minnesota). Fisheries managers and researchers know these simple approaches do not account for much variation among lakes. There have been efforts to develop better lake classifications and to study the factors that account for differences among lakes in productivity and in the fish they support.

For 2,496 Ontario lakes, including 221 from the Atikokan–Thunder Bay regions, Johnson and co-workers (1977) examined the relationship of 12 physical and chemical characteristics to the 15 possible combinations of the presence of walleye, northern pike, lake trout, and smallmouth bass in order to determine which characteristics best distinguish lakes supporting the various combinations. After eliminating some correlated variables and those lakes with many missing measurements, they developed a statistical scheme to relate the 15 combinations of four dominant predatory game fish to area, elevation, mean depth, shoreline development, water clarity, pH, and alkalinity. The analysis identified some of the factors related to fish occurrence when the data were stratified on the basis of climate as it affects the distribution of smallmouth bass (some lakes were beyond the northern limit of bass).

Lakes with lake trout differed from nontrout lakes in having greater depth, clearer water, and lower total dissolved solids. Trout-only and trout-bass lakes had oxygen concentrations below the thermocline averaging 6.0 and 6.5 parts per million, but bass-only, pike-only, walleye-pike, and walleye-pike-bass lakes averaged 2.9, 3.8, 4.2, and 3.9 parts per million. Larger trout lakes usually contained walleye and northern pike, or both plus smallmouth bass. The characteristics of such lakes with and without bass were similar, and the authors note that in northwestern Ontario, which includes Quetico, lakes such as Lac La Croix and Basswood were originally trout-walleye-pike lakes. Smaller trout lakes are most likely to be trout only or trout-bass lakes. The authors (Johnson et al. 1977, 1,599) state: "Apparently no hard evidence exists that demonstrates that smallmouth bass are detrimental to lake trout populations." Trout-pike and trout-pike-bass lakes were

similar to those that also had walleye, except that their areas were considerably smaller. The trout-pike-bass combination was rare in northwestern Ontario, just as it is in the BWCAW and Quetico (table 14.1), suggesting that bass have trouble invading such lakes (Johnson et al. 1977).

Walleye-pike lakes averaged smaller than trout-pike lakes, but size may not be a key difference because the smaller walleye-pike lakes also had higher dissolved solids and were shallower. A factor that may mitigate the adverse effect of small lake size for walleyes, the authors note, is the occurrence of small interconnected shallow lakes in flatter terrain, which may give walleyes needed living space, as opposed to the less satisfactory environment of poorly connected small lakes in rugged terrain (Johnson et al. 1977). In the BWCAW, the Kawishiwi River chain from Lake One all the way to its headwaters at Kawishiwi Lake is an example of interconnected shallow walleye-pike lakes in low-relief terrain, whereas the less well connected deeper small lakes in steep terrain east of Knife Lake, including Amoeber, Topaz, Cherry, Lunar, Lake of the Clouds, Hanson, Ester, Rabbit, and Gijikiki are mostly trout-only, trout-pike, or trout-walleye lakes, although smallmouth bass are now in several of these.

Only 169 of 839 lakes with trout also had walleye in the study by Johnson and co-workers, but these often were the larger lakes. They believe a deep, cold, infertile (oligotrophic) trout lake is more likely to contain enough shallow bays and shoals suitable for walleye if it is large than if it is small. Large complex lakes simply have more diverse habitats and are likely to support more fish species, a principle that certainly fits such large lakes as Basswood, Lac La Croix, and Pickerel. Lakes supporting trout, walleye, and northern pike had the largest average area (2,768 acres), followed closely by lakes supporting all four species (2,352 acres). Those areas are a little greater than the area of the South Arm of Knife Lake (2,224 acres), which supports all four species.

Shallower lakes, richer in total dissolved solids, with favorable shoreline and other habitat factors, had a much higher frequency of walleye than did trout lakes in the study, but smallmouths were found about equally in these two types. The lakes with the smallest average area were

212

the pike-only and bass-only lakes, which averaged only 90 acres in area. Pike-bass lakes at 237 acres averaged larger than pike-only lakes. Small lake area seems to be the only clue to why pike-only lakes lack walleyes. Johnson and co-workers speculate that larger lakes may have sufficient wave action to expose gravel and boulder bottom for walleye spawning, that "living room" itself may be a need, or that perhaps the chances of walleye surviving with northern pike are simply better in larger lakes. The 553 walleye-pike lakes and 178 walleye-pike-bass lakes in the study averaged about 608 acres in area, had littoral areas averaging 77 percent and 65 percent respectively, and Secchi-disk water-clarity depths averaging 7.9 feet and 10.2 feet respectively. There was no difference in walleye-pike lakes with and without bass other than location, because, as in the Boundary Waters, smallmouth bass were recent introductions in many lakes. The 476 pike-only lakes were the shallowest, with average depths of only 10.2 feet and maximum depths averaging 40 feet, compared to all lakes with trout, which had average maximum depths around 100 feet.

The 799 walleye-pike, walleye-pike-bass, and walleye-bass lakes as a group included most of the lakes with walleyes and had the following average characteristics: area, 605 acres; average depth, 13 feet; Secchi-disk water clarity, 8.5 feet; alkalinity, 29 parts per million; total dissolved solids, 58 parts per million; plus shoreline and other physical lake factors favorable for walleye. Alkalinities averaged higher than in most walleye lakes in the Boundary Waters, probably because the sampled lakes included some with substantially higher fertility than is typical for BWCAW walleye lakes.

To summarize this discussion of lake types and relate it directly to the Boundary Waters, the lakes and streams are organized into eight groups, using as guides a sampling of Minnesota Department of Natural Resources BWCAW lake survey reports, lake-depth maps, topographic maps, geologic maps, the Quetico fish occurrence lists of Crossman (1976), the Lake County fish occurrence list, general knowledge of the Boundary Waters, and the Johnson et al. (1977) study. Typical lakes usually have most but not necessarily all of the listed characteristics. Intermediate cases fall between groups (tables 14.2–14.9).

The Threat of Airborne Toxic Chemicals

At least up to 1991, the lakes and rivers of the Boundary Waters were relatively free from water pollution entering these waters directly from land-based industrial, urban, domestic, or agricultural sources. There are or have been problems with pollution originating outside the wilderness reserves from mine waste drainage, urban sewage, and summer-home septic systems, but these have either been corrected (by the Ely sewage treatment plant) or do not yet significantly affect water quality within the wilderness areas. Acid rain and airborne mercury, on the other hand, pose threats to aquatic life in Boundary Waters lakes and streams. Fortunately, neither had yet become an overwhelming problem as of the early 1990s, but no treatment of the aquatic ecosystems of the region would be complete without discussion of these threats.

ACID DEPOSITION

Unpolluted rain or snow has a slightly acid pH of about 5.6 through the effect of carbon dioxide in the air. Rain or snow with a pH lower than 5.6 has been acidified by pollutants, usually sulfur dioxide and nitrogen oxides emitted to the atmosphere by the burning of coal, fuel oil, and gasoline in power plants, automobiles, trucks, aircraft, and so on, or by oil refineries, copper-nickel smelters, and other industries. In the Boundary Waters nitrogen oxides are smaller sources of acidity than sulfur dioxide. Furthermore, nitrates and ammonia derived from nitrogen oxides are scarce plant nutrients used by both land and aquatic plants. Thus sulfur dioxide, which forms sulfuric acid in the atmosphere, is the major pollutant of concern. Acids are deposited by rain and snow in wet forms but also as dry fallout. Thus it is more accurate to call the process acid deposition than acid rain, although wet deposition predominates (Thornton, Payer, and Matta 1982).

Several large coal-fired power plants exist in northeastern Minnesota and one at Atikokan, Ontario, just north of Quetico, as well as several large plants near the Twin Cities. It was the proposal by Ontario Hydro in 1976 to build an 800-megawatt plant without scrubbers at Atikokan, so close to Quetico and the BWCAW, that initially

Table 14.2 / Characteristics of small, deep, cold lakes suitable for lake trout, cisco, white sucker; high in watershed; and often not favorable for walleye or northern pike

1	Depth	One or more large deep basins with maximum depth at least 70–80 feet; typical lakes usually with extensive areas 60–100 feet or deeper.
2	Temperature profile	Summer water temperatures below thermocline consistently below 53°F in one or more deeper basins even in hottest summers; mid- to late-summer temperatures generally 41°–48°F below thermocline. Summer temperatures from surface to thermocline often 65°–78°F.
3	Oxygen profile	Summer oxygen levels generally 6–10 ppm below thermocline except very near bottom in some lakes.
4	Water clarity and color	Secchi-disk clarity usually 15–30 feet; color usually clear to light brown or light green.
5	Fertility	Total alkalinity usually 5–20 ppm; pH 6.0–7.5; total phosphorus usually near 0.010 ppm.
6	Basin characteristics	Lake area 50–1,500 acres, occasionally up to 2,500 acres; shorelines mostly steep; often a few islands; littoral area small, generally 10–40% but variable.
7	Bottom characteristics	Near-shore bottom mostly bare bedrock, rubble, or boulders, a few shallow muck-bottom bays may be present; deep basin bottom mostly organic ooze.
8	Spawning areas	Some near-shore shallows or submerged reefs usually present with rubble, boulder, cobble, or gravel bottom in 5–15 feet of water for lake trout spawning; bottom types and depths suitable for cisco, whitefish, white sucker usually present, the latter often in small tributary streams. If northern pike occur, some emergent vegetation present near shore, in marshy bays, tributary streams, or connected lakes.
9	Aquatic vegetation	Sparse, confined to occasional mucky bays, near-shore shallows, and vicinity of inlet streams, where bottom will support rooted plants.
10	Inlets, outlets, flow volumes	Inlet and outlet streams usually small, low volume, often with steep gradients; often choked with boulders. If lake is at head of watershed, inlet flows may only represent seasonal runoff from adjacent slopes and springs.
11	Location in watershed	Often located high in local group of watersheds; if the lake is one of a series of connected lakes, it is usually high enough in chain that inlet and outlet flows are low. Often surrounded by high ridges, steep cliffs on one or more sides of basin; ridges may attain some of highest elevations in local area.
12	Geology, landforms	In bwcaw most frequent on Knife Lake Group of bedrock northeast and south of Knife Lake, along and near northern edge of Duluth Gabbro, and on Rove Formation north and east of Gunflint Trail; occasional in deep basins on Vermilion Granites south of Lac La Croix. Often associated with bedrock faults and along juncture of adjoining bedrock types. In Quetico most common on granites, syenites, and related rocks correlated with Vermilion Granite, especially along faults in Hunter Island and west to southwest of Pickerel Lake; and on metavolcanic bedrock and local iron formation northwest of Knife Lake.
13	Fish species present	Most common large predators: lake trout, burbot, in some lakes also northern pike (usually not abundant); smallmouth bass and walleye sometimes present, probably introduced into or migrated to lake after 1945. Most common larger forage species are white sucker and cisco (tullibee); less common are whitefish and perch. Few to several species of small forage fish may be present, such as shiners, darters, dace, and sculpin.
14	Typical lakes	In bwcaw: Kekekebic, Clearwater, Mountain, Hanson, Ester, Gabimichigami, Peter, Gillis, Winchell, Takucmich; in Quetico: Emerald, Plough, Louisa, Hurlburt, Argo, Cone, Elk. Such lakes have native lake trout, most lack walleyes, several have northern pike and/or smallmouths. In 1982 Mountain Lake had one of the best self-sustaining lake trout populations in the bwcaw, perhaps because it still had not been invaded by either walleyes or smallmouth bass, but walleyes were present just downstream in Moose Lake (Crossman 1976; mdnr lake survey reports).

Table 14.3 / Characteristics of large, deep, cold lakes suitable for lake trout, better connected to stream systems, and supporting more diverse fish populations

1	Depth	One or more large deep basins with maximum depth at least 70–80 feet; typical lakes usually with extensive areas 60–100 feet or deeper, but also with large areas of shallower water 20–40 feet deep.
2	Temperature profile	Summer water temperatures below thermocline consistently below 53°F in one or more deeper basins even in hottest summers; mid- to late-summer temperatures generally 41°–48°F below thermocline in deep basins; in extensive shallower areas summer temperatures may range 45°–60°F at depths of 20–40 feet, and the thermocline may not persist in some areas. Summer temperatures above thermocline often 65°–78°F
3	Oxygen profile	Summer oxygen levels below thermocline consistently above 5 ppm virtually to bottom in one or more large deep basins. In extensive shallow areas, late summer oxygen may fall below 2 ppm below thermocline at depths of 20–25 feet.
4	Water clarity and color	Secchi-disk clarity usually 15–30 feet except in larger shallow bays or inlets, where it may be 7–10 feet, especially if there is bog drainage into shallows. Color generally clear to light green or light brown.
5	Fertility	Total alkalinity usually 5–20 ppm; pH 6.0–7.5; total phosphorus near 0.010 ppm.
6	Basin characteristics	Lake area usually 1,000–10,000 acres, occasionally 20,000 acres; shorelines mostly steep but gently sloping in shallow bays or along part of perimeter; often many islands present. Littoral area limited except in shallow bays and around some islands, generally 15–45% of an entire lake but varies greatly.
7	Bottom characteristics	Near-shore bottom mostly bare bedrock and boulders, except in larger shallow bays, which may have gravel, sand, or muck bottom; deep basin bottom mostly organic ooze.
8	Spawning areas	Some near-shore shallows or submerged reefs adjacent to deep basins present with boulders, cobble, or gravel bottom in 5–15 feet of water suitable for trout; gravel-bottom shallows along shorelines or in inlet streams for walleyes, rocky shallows for smallmouths, and often emergent grass-sedge marshes in a few shallow bays for northern pike; bottom types and depths suitable for cisco, whitefish, white sucker, and perch also may be present.
9	Aquatic vegetation	Generally sparse, except where rooted on the mucky bottoms of fairly extensive shallower bays in some lakes and near inlet streams.
10	Inlets, outlets, flow volumes	Inlet and outlet streams variable in volume, depending on position of lake in watershed
11	Location in watershed	Generally in midwatershed positions; usually not in main stem of large flow system. Often with high ridges on one or more sides but seldom located at or near the highest position in watershed.
12	Geology, landforms	In BWCAW occurs on Saganaga, Snowbank, and Vermilion granitic rocks, on Knife Lake Group of rocks, and along northern edge of Duluth Complex. In Quetico on granites, syenites, and related rocks coextensive with Vermilion Granites of BWCAW, along junctures of these rocks with belts of gneiss, schist, graywacke, and related rocks that cut across Quetico, and on Poobah Lake Complex. On many lakes the landscape is one of rolling bedrock hills, but in some cases, as on Kahshahpiwi Lake, where there are significant faults, some shoreline may be marked by nearly vertical cliffs more than 100 feet above lake.
13	Fish species present	All four large predatory game fish—lake trout, walleye, northern pike, and smallmouth bass—often present, plus burbot. Trout and pike probably native to all of these waters, walleye native to many but introduced to Saganaga and Sea Gull lakes; smallmouth introduced or migrated to lakes where present. Other species often present include white sucker, cisco, whitefish, perch, rock bass, bluegill, and few to several species of small forage fish such as shiners, darters, dace, bluntnose minnow, and sculpin. Largemouth bass uncommon.
14	Typical lakes	In BWCAW: Sea Gull, Saganaga, Knife, Snowbank, Thomas, Ima, Big Trout; in Quetico: Agnes, Kahshahpiwi, Burt, Brent, McIntyre, Sarah, Robinson, Darky, Poobah, Jean, Orianna, and That Man.

Table 14.4 / Characteristics of very large lakes with strong flow volumes and diverse habitats

1 Depth	One or more large deep basins with maximum depth at least 100 feet; usually with extensive areas 60–100 feet or deeper and also with large areas 20–40 feet deep or less. Major depth factor is great variability and the presence of large shallows as well as some deeps.
2 Temperature profile	Summer water temperatures below thermocline consistently below 53°F in one or more deeper basins even in hottest summers; mid- to late-summer temperatures generally 41°–48°F below thermocline in deep basins; in extensive shallower areas summer temperatures may range 45°–60°F at depths of 20–40 feet, and the thermocline may not persist in some areas. Summer temperatures from surface to thermocline often 65°–78°F.
3 Oxygen profile	Summer oxygen levels below thermocline consistently above 5 ppm virtually to bottom in one or more large deep basins. In extensive shallow areas, late summer oxygen may fall below 2 ppm below thermocline at depths of 20–25 feet.
4 Water clarity and color	Secchi-disk clarity varies from 6–20 feet or more in the various bays and main water bodies. Generally 10–20 feet or more in main basin carrying flows through lake; often 6–10 feet in shallow bays or inlets isolated from main basin, especially where there is bog drainage into shallows. Color generally clear to light green or light brown, but water more strongly colored in some bays isolated from main basins.
5 Fertility	Total alkalinity ranges at least 6–30 ppm; pH 6.5–7.8.
6 Basin characteristics	Lake area varies from near 10,000 acres to 220,000 acres; shorelines vary from steep to very gently sloping in shallow bays or along part of perimeter; islands abundant in most lakes. Littoral area extensive in portions of most lakes; probably ranges 20–50% of an entire lake, but from as low as 14% to as high as 70% in various bays. Some bays of lakes such as Basswood and Lac La Croix are really distinct but connected waters.
7 Bottom characteristics	Near-shore bottom extremely varied, from bare bedrock or boulders around the perimeter of many bays and islands to gravel, sand, or muck bottom in larger shallow bays; deep basin bottom mostly organic ooze.
8 Spawning areas	In most lakes, near-shore shallows or submerged reefs adjacent to deep basins occur with rubble, boulder, cobble, or gravel bottom at depths suitable for trout; gravel-bottom shallows occur along shorelines or in inlet streams for walleyes, rocky shallows for smallmouth bass, and emergent grass-sedge marshes in shallow bays for northern pike; bottom types and depths suitable for spawning of cisco, whitefish, white sucker, perch, and other species generally present.
9 Aquatic vegetation	Generally sparse, except where rooted on the mucky bottoms of the often extensive shallower bays in these large lakes.
10 Inlets, outlets, flow volumes	Inlet and outlet stream volumes vary, but usually fed by one or more high-volume inlets. Several lakes have falls, rapids, or dams at inlets, outlets, or both.
11 Location in watershed	On main stem of flow path of a large watershed, usually far downstream from headwaters lakes.
12 Geology, landforms	In BWCAW occurs on Vermilion Granite, in Quetico primarily on related granites, in Voyageurs on several bedrock types. In all three areas these lakes occupy very large complex bedrock basins and receive inflowing waters from diverse bedrock regions.
13 Fish species present	All four large predatory game fish—lake trout, walleye, northern pike, and smallmouth bass—usually present, plus burbot and sauger in some lakes. Trout, pike, and walleye probably native to all of these waters; smallmouth bass introduced or migrated to lakes where present. Other species often present: sturgeon, silver lamprey, white sucker, cisco, whitefish, perch, rock bass, black crappie, bluegill, other sunfish, tadpole madtom, and many small forage fish such as shiners, darters, dace, bluntnose minnow, and sculpin. Largemouth bass introduced if present, uncommon or absent in most waters.
14 Typical lakes	In BWCAW: Basswood, Crooked, Lac La Croix; in Quetico: Pickerel, Saganagons, Kawnipi, Sturgeon, Quetico, Beaverhouse, McAree; in Voyageurs: Namakan, Rainy, Kabetogama, Sand Point. (Kabetogama has no deep basins, but the Kettle Falls dam made it a very large bay of Namakan, which has extensive deeps.)

Table 14.5 / Characteristics of medium to small, shallow walleye-northern pike lakes in well-connected stream systems

1	Depth	Typically large areas of main lake range between 10 and 50 feet; often there are extensive waters 5–10 feet deep or less; maximum depths often 60 feet or more, but some productive lakes have maximum depths of only 15 or 20 feet.
2	Temperature profile	Some shallower lakes and smaller lakes with strong flows do not develop thermoclines that persist through summer. In deeper lakes mid- to late-summer temperatures below thermocline range between about 42° and 55°F in basins 40–60 feet or more in depth. In extensive shallower areas, summer temperatures may range between 60° and 75°F at depths of 5–25 feet, and thermoclines may not persist. Surface summer temperatures often 65°–78°F.
3	Oxygen profile	Where thermoclines develop, late-summer oxygen levels below thermocline often fall below 2 ppm at depths below about 25 feet, but some lakes retain oxygen above 5 ppm to depths of 50 feet or more in most summers. Above thermoclines and in extensive shallow areas, late-summer oxygen usually remains in the 6–9 ppm range from surface to depths of 20–25 feet.
4	Water clarity and color	Secchi-disk clarity ranges from 4 to at least 15 feet, but most lakes are 6–12 feet. Color usually light brown to strongly tea-colored, but some lakes are light green or nearly clear. Waters often more strongly colored in boggy bays.
5	Fertility	Total alkalinity ranges at least 6–30 ppm; pH ranges 6.5–7.5, but most lakes are near 7.0.
6	Basin characteristics	Lake area varies from 100 acres or less to more than 3,000 acres; most are 200–1,000 acres. Shorelines vary from gently sloping in shallow bays or along part of perimeter to steep, rocky slopes or even low but vertical cliffs. Islands abundant in some lakes, nearly absent in others. Littoral area extensive in most lakes; probably ranges 25–80% of an entire lake, but most are 35–65%.
7	Bottom characteristics	Near-shore bottom varies, from bare bedrock, boulders, or gravel around perimeter of some bays and islands, to sand or muck bottom in shallow bays. Connected stream bottom varies from gravel and rock to sand or muck.
8	Spawning areas	Gravel-bottom shallows suitable for walleye occur along shorelines or in inlet or outlet streams, and emergent grass-sedge marshes suitable for northern pike occur in shallow bays or in connected lakes or streams nearby. Bottom and depths suitable for spawning of white sucker, perch, and other species usually present or available in connected waters.
9	Aquatic vegetation	Often abundant on the mucky bottoms of shallower bays and sometimes near inlet streams.
10	Inlets, outlets, flow volumes	Inlet and outlet stream volumes vary, but many lakes have low-volume inlets and outlets, often marked by small rapids or riffles near lake and placid canoeable sections between lakes.
11	Location in watershed	On main stem or tributary flow paths of streams issuing from large watersheds; may occur at any point from headwaters lakes to far downstream in system, but usually in a series of limnologically similar interconnected lakes.
12	Geology, landforms	In BWCAW occurs chiefly on Duluth Gabbro Complex and on the Vermilion Granite; in Quetico on related granites, along contacts of the granites with the Quetico Gneissic Belt rocks, or on the latter. Typical settings are along lowlands among low, rolling bedrock hills, with small lake basins interconnected by short, often winding streams.
13	Fish species present	Walleye and northern pike are chief predators; smallmouth bass introduced or migrated into some waters. Other species often present include yellow perch, white sucker, rock bass, tadpole madtom, and small forage fish such as shiners, darters, dace, bluntnose minnow, fathead minnow, trout perch, and log perch.
14	Typical lakes	In BWCAW: Kawishiwi River system and tributaries, including Gabbro, Bald Eagle, Isabella, Perent, One, Two, Three, Four, Hudson, Insula, Alice, Malberg, Polly, Kawishiwi, Phoebe, Grace; Moose-Portage-Stuart rivers system, including Big, Nina Moose, Agnes, Stuart; plus Pocket, Finger, Horse, Fourtown, Boot, Gun, Angleworm, Home, Beartrap, Thunder. In Quetico: Russell, Chatterton, Keats, Shelley, Kenney, Wet (shallow members of Falls Chain), Fred, Nan, Camel, Veron, Delahey, Eag, Cub, Baird, Metacryst, Cutty (Cutty Creek system), Fern, Bud, Beg, Bisk (Pickerel River system), Anubis, Bird (east channel, Agnes River), Conmee, and Suzanette.

Table 14.6 / Characteristics of small, often more isolated northern pike lakes

1	Depth	Much of main basin between 5 and 20 feet, but may be extensive shallower waters less than 5 feet deep. Maximum depths frequently 30–50 feet or more, but some lakes do not exceed 10 feet.
2	Temperature profile	In deeper lakes mid- to late-summer temperatures below thermocline probably range 45°–60°F in basins 30–50 feet or more deep. In shallower areas summer temperatures may range 60°–75°F at depths of 5–25 feet, and thermocline may not persist. Surface summer temperatures often 65°–78°F.
3	Oxygen profile	Where thermoclines develop, late-summer oxygen levels below thermocline often fall below 2 ppm at depths below about 25 feet, but some lakes probably retain oxygen above 5 ppm to depths of 40 feet or more in most summers. Above thermoclines and in shallow areas, late-summer oxygen usually remains in the 6–9 ppm range from surface to depths of 20 feet.
4	Water clarity and color	Secchi-disk clarity probably ranges 5–15 feet. Color often light brown to tea-colored, but some lakes are light green or nearly clear. Waters often more strongly colored in boggy bays.
5	Fertility	Total alkalinity probably 6–30 ppm; pH probably 6.5–7.5.
6	Basin characteristics	Lake area varies from 50 acres or less to more than 1,000 acres in a few larger pike lakes in Quetico; most are probably 60–300 acres. Shorelines vary from gently sloping in shallow bays or along part of perimeter to steep, rocky slopes or even low vertical cliffs. Islands present in some lakes, absent in others. Littoral area extensive in most lakes, probably 30–80% or more.
7	Bottom characteristics	Near-shore bottom varies, from bare bedrock, boulders, or gravel around perimeter of some bays and islands, to sand or muck bottom in shallow bays. Connected stream bottom varies from gravel and rock to sand or muck.
8	Spawning areas	Grass-sedge marshes suitable for northern pike spawning occur in shallow bays or in connected lakes or streams nearby. Bottom types and depths suitable for white sucker, perch, and smaller forage fish usually present or available in connected waters.
9	Aquatic vegetation	Often abundant on the mucky bottoms of shallower bays and sometimes near inlet streams.
10	Inlets, outlets, flow volumes	Inlet and outlet streams often very small, carrying low volumes over rocky or marshy streambed.
11	Location in watershed	Often high in a local watershed near or among headwaters lakes not well connected to nearby lakes.
12	Geology, landforms	In BWCAW occurs chiefly on Duluth Gabbro Complex and on the Vermilion Granite; in Quetico on related granites, along contacts of the granites with the Quetico Gneissic Belt rocks, or on the latter. Typical setting are among rolling bedrock hills, in small lake basins often poorly connected with the regional watershed.
13	Fish species present	Northern pike is chief predator; smallmouth bass introduced or migrated to some waters. Others often present: yellow perch, white sucker, rock bass, sunfish, tadpole madtom, small forage fish such as shiners, darters, dace, bluntnose minnow, fathead minnow, log perch. Truly large northern pike (over 20 pounds) occur primarily in the bigger lakes, but a few very large individuals are present in some of these small pike-only lakes.
14	Typical lakes	In BWCAW: Arrow, Baskatong, Bonnie, Boulder, Clearwater (near Bald Eagle), Elton, Fire, Fish, Gift, Gerund, Keneu, Kiana, Nawakwa, Pietro, Rocky, Spoon, Turtle. In Quetico: Baptism, Edge, Howard, Lakin, Lynx, Trousers, Wicksteed.

sparked the acid-rain discussion in Minnesota and Ontario (Glass and Loucks 1980). As a result, in 1979 the first international conference on acid precipitation in North America was held at Toronto. The Atikokan plant was not initially built to its planned 800-megawatt size, and as of 1991 had not been expanded. However, computer models of atmospheric transport of sulfates have since demonstrated the extent of long-distance transport of acid precipitation to the Boundary Waters region. Source regions contributing more than 5 percent of the sulfate deposition at Ely in 1980

Table 14.7 / Characteristics of small, shallow ponds (panfish-bass ponds)

1	Depth	5–15 feet deep.
2	Temperature profile	No temperature data available. Warm-water lakes lacking thermoclines.
3	Oxygen profile	No oxygen data available. Many do not freeze out, perhaps because they have good flows of oxygenated water.
4	Water clarity and color	Not available.
5	Fertility	Not available.
6	Basin characteristics	Most are less than 100 acres in area. These are mostly very small lakes and beaver ponds.
7	Bottom characteristics	Not available.
8	Spawning areas	Not available.
9	Aquatic vegetation	Not available.
10	Inlets, outlets, flow volumes	Not available.
11	Location in watershed	Not available.
12	Geology, landforms	Not available.
13	Fish species present	Typically sunfish, yellow perch, occasionally largemouth and/or smallmouth bass, sometimes white sucker, and usually several species of shiners, dace, darters, etc.
14	Typical lakes	Not available.

were Minnesota, 16 percent; Wisconsin, 9 percent; Texas, 9 percent; Alberta, 7 percent; Missouri, 7 percent; and Manitoba, 7 percent; leaving 45 percent for all other sources (Roberts 1988).

Normal lakewater in the Boundary Waters is nearly neutral in reaction, with a pH usually between about 6.5 and 7.5. As we have seen, however, the lakes have very soft water, with total alkalinity usually between about 5 and 20 parts per million, and thus many have little buffering capacity to resist acidification. Acid deposition can gradually neutralize the alkalinity in a lake until virtually none remains. Once this natural alkalinity is nearly used up, a lake's acidity can rapidly increase with continued acid inputs. Thus alkalinity is a measure of a lake's sensitivity to acid deposition.

The Minnesota Pollution Control Agency (MPCA) developed the following classification of lake sensitivity, based on alkalinity (Thornton, Payer, and Matta 1982):

1   Acidified lakes: alkalinity zero, pH usually below 5.0, water often very clear, fish severely stressed or absent;

snails, clams, frogs, insects, and many other organisms may be gone.

2   Naturally acidic lakes: highly colored lakes, strongly tea-colored due to organic acids from bogs, with no alkalinity. Many strongly colored lakes do have some remaining alkalinity, but such lakes are vulnerable to acidification.

3   Extremely sensitive lakes: alkalinity more than zero but less than 5 parts per million; may eventually be acidified with continued acid inputs at current levels.

4   Moderately sensitive lakes: alkalinity 5 to 10 parts per million. Long-term continued acid deposition may damage some of these lakes.

5   Potentially sensitive lakes: alkalinity 10 to 20 parts per million. A few of these lakes may be damaged by long-term deposition at current levels, but most may not show effects unless acid loadings increase.

6   Nonsensitive lakes: alkalinity greater than 20 parts per million; probably enough buffering to neutralize acid deposition indefinitely.

Table 14.8 / Characteristics of wild-rice lakes and streams

1	Depth	Good rice waters fluctuate within depths of 1–4 feet. Big Rice Lake, for example, has maximum depths of only about 6 feet, and most of the lake is only 2–4 feet deep in normal years.
2	Temperature profile	Not available.
3	Oxygen profile	Not available.
4	Water clarity and color	Not available.
5	Fertility	Not available.
6	Basin characteristics	Lake areas 100–400 acres.
7	Bottom characteristics	Mucky organic bottom sediments.
8	Spawning areas	Not available.
9	Aquatic vegetation	Not available.
10	Inlets, outlets, flow volumes	Not available.
11	Location in watershed	Not available.
12	Geology, landforms	Not available.
13	Fish species present	Not available.
14	Typical lakes	In the BWCAW: Rice Lake (10 miles northwest of Ely), Big Rice (12 miles northwest of Ely), Manomin (20 miles northeast of Ely), Hula (2 miles south of Basswood), Lapond and Duck (just west of Big Lake, south of the Echo Trail), and Rice (2 miles west of Lake Isabella). There are also extensive stands of rice in Back Bay and Rice Bay of Basswood Lake. Other lakes and several streams in the BWCAW and Quetico also have good rice stands in many years. Examples are the stretch of the Moose River from Nina Moose Lake north to Lake Agnes, and the Little Indian Sioux River south of the Echo Trail.

As of 1982, no lakes in Minnesota were reported by the MPCA to be already acidified or naturally acidic according to these criteria. Data from 1,338 BWCAW lakes indicate that 23 percent were extremely sensitive, 43 percent moderately sensitive, and 25 percent potentially sensitive. This leaves just 9 percent in the nonsensitive class (Thornton, Payer, and Matta 1982; Glass and Loucks 1980). Lakes in the BWCAW and Quetico are the most sensitive to acidification in all of Minnesota and adjacent Ontario because of their low alkalinities and the generally low buffering capacity of the bedrock and thin glacial soils of the region.

The annual average acidity of precipitation falling on the Boundary Waters ranged between about pH 4.8 and 4.9 in 1985, according to data presented at the 1986 hearings on rules for control of acid deposition. Summer rainfall tends to be slightly less acid than winter snowfall. The annual fallout of wet sulfate deposition in the region was about 9 pounds per acre (10 kg/hectare) (MPCA 1985; Rob-

erts 1988). Fortunately, the acidity of precipitation in the Boundary Waters is not yet as great as that responsible for fish kills in the northeastern United States, eastern Canada, and Norway, where the pH of precipitation ranged between about 4.2 and 4.5. The annual deposition of wet sulfate averaged about three times as much as the Boundary Waters was receiving in the early 1980s (MPCA 1985; Roberts 1988).

Despite lower annual sulfate loadings than in regions where fish die-outs have occurred, the spring snowmelt in the Boundary Waters produces short-term pulses of acidity in streams and near lakeshores approaching levels known to harm fish and other aquatic organisms. Sulfates and nitrates accumulated in the snowpack are released in meltwater as a strong pulse generally between about March 25 and late April. The watershed snowpacks of two lakes studied in March 1982 had a weighted average pH of 3.95. Stream alkalinities may decrease as much as 70 percent to 85 percent, and pH may fall considerably during the peak of

Table 14.9 / Characteristics of rivers and streams

1	Depth	Rivers and small streams vary widely.
2	Temperature profile	Not available.
3	Oxygen profile	Not available.
4	Water clarity and color	Most rivers and smaller streams have light brown tea-colored waters from bog seepage, but some are quite clear.
5	Fertility	Not available; however, the Wawiag River in Quetico is cut through Lake Agassiz silts and clays and is therefore rich in plant nutrients.
6	Basin characteristics	Not available.
7	Bottom characteristics	Bottom types vary widely from bedrock to boulders, cobble, gravel, sand, silt, and muck.
8	Spawning areas	Not available.
9	Aquatic vegetation	The smallest streams are often interrupted here and there by beaver dams, and many are fringed with tall grasses, sedges, bulrush, wild rice beds, or lily pads.
10	Inlets, outlets, flow volumes	Rivers and small streams vary widely in flow volume and speed. The Maligne, Namakan, and Basswood rivers carry the largest volumes of water and have numerous falls and rapids.
11	Location in watershed	Not available.
12	Geology, landforms	Some waters pass through narrow, high-walled bedrock gorges; some wind slowly through miles of black spruce and tamarack bogs and alder-willow floodplain communities.
13	Fish species present	The larger rivers and streams support many fish species, including walleye, northern pike, smallmouth bass, yellow perch, white sucker, rock bass, sunfish, shiners, bluntnose minnow, tadpole madtom, darters, dace, and log perch. Clams, turtles, frogs, toads, and salamanders abound.
14	Typical lakes	In the BWCAW: several small streams navigable in part by canoe are genuine flowing waters for at least several miles; the Moose-Boulder, Little Indian Sioux, Isabella, Horse, Beartrap, Dahlgren, Perent, Frost, and Louse rivers, and short sections of the Kawishiwi system. In Quetico: the Maligne River between Sturgeon Lake and Lac La Croix, the Quetico and Namakan rivers along the west edge of Quetico, and the Darky and Wawiag rivers. Along the international boundary, short sections of the Basswood, Loon, Pine, and Granite rivers also qualify. Also, many small but very short streams occur in both areas but are too numerous to catalog, e.g., Oyster Creek in the BWCAW.

snowmelt runoff (Heiskary and Payer 1983). These short-term increases in acidity and losses of buffering come when many fish species are spawning and other vulnerable aquatic organisms such as snails, clams, sponges, frogs, toads, and salamanders in lakes, streams, and temporary ponds are at crucial stages in their life cycles.

The effects of lake acidification on aquatic life are well known from experience in the northeastern United States, eastern Canada, and Norway, from laboratory studies, and from the long-term experimental field studies of Schindler and associates in the Experimental Lakes Area near Kenora, Ontario (Beamish and Harvey 1972; Braekke 1976; Thorn-ton, Payer, and Matta 1982; Schindler et al. 1985). Beginning in 1976, Schindler's group slowly lowered the pH of an Ontario trout lake from 6.8 to 5.0 by gradually adding sulfuric acid, while carefully documenting changes in all ecosystem components and comparing them to untreated control lakes. This research showed that some impacts occur earlier in the acidification process (at higher pH levels) than previously believed.

- In 1978 at pH 5.9, opossum shrimp, a vital food of young trout, virtually disappeared, and fathead minnow failed to reproduce.
- In 1979 at pH 5.6, the biomass of phytoplankton in-

creased, a filamentous alga not seen before appeared, fathead minnow became nearly extinct due to reproductive failure, the exoskeletons of crayfish became softer, slimy sculpin declined, and young-of-the-year white sucker and trout actually increased.

- In 1980 at pH 5.6, phytoplankton increased again and further species shifts occurred, zooplankton species changed, biomass increased, trout failed to reproduce and their condition declined, pearl dace and white sucker increased, and crayfish became infested with fungi and failed to reproduce.

- In 1981 at pH 5.0, some waterfleas disappeared but zooplankton and phytoplankton biomass remained high, white sucker reproduction failed, dace reproduction nearly failed, sculpins were very rare, lake trout reproduction failed again and their condition declined further, and crayfish exoskeletons became very soft and the population dwindled.

- In 1982 pH was kept at 5.1, trout condition became very poor, crayfish were almost gone, no fish species reproduced, leeches were rare, but zooplankton and phytoplankton biomass remained essentially stable.

- In 1983 with pH still at 5.1, phytoplankton remained stable, but crayfish, leeches, and mayflies were absent, no fish reproduction succeeded, and although lake trout adults were still common, their condition was now poorer than any seen in the region, and cannibalism increased, probably because of the scarcity of minnows and bottom crustaceans.

Over the eight years, concentrations of calcium, manganese, and aluminum increased in lake water, but contrary to usual predictions, phosphorus did not decrease. The results also show that the early stages of acidification do not cause significant kills of adult fish, even when the food web is so severely disrupted that extinction of most fish will occur within a decade. The most reliable early indication that potentially lethal acidification is under way may be changes in the populations of bottom animals (crustaceans), sensitive minnows such as fathead, and certain species of algae (Schindler et al. 1985).

The effects of lake acidification on many of the Bound-

Table 14.10 / Effects of acidity on Boundary Waters fish species

Water pH	Effects
6.5	Walleye spawning inhibited
5.8	Lake trout spawning inhibited
5.5	Smallmouth bass disappear
5.2	Walleye, burbot, lake trout disappear
5.0	Spawning inhibited in many fish
4.7	Northern pike, white sucker, brown bullhead, pumpkinseed, sunfish, and rock bass disappear
4.5	Perch and cisco spawning inhibited
3.5	Perch disappear
3.0	Toxic to all fish

Sources Thornton et al. (1982); after Beamish (1976); Beamish et al. (1975); EIFAC (1969).

ary Waters fish species are shown in table 14.10. Some of the information in this table comes from the La Cloche Mountains area in Ontario, where Beamish and Harvey (1972) carefully documented the demise of entire fish populations in several lakes largely as the result of acid deposition from the infamous Sudbury copper-nickel smelters. The more subtle loss of fish populations from long-term acidification of more than 100 brook trout and lake trout lakes in the Adirondack Mountains of New York (Schofield 1976) shows that acid deposition from sources hundreds of miles away can have the same effect. The loss of trout and salmon from hundreds of lakes and streams in southern Norway from acid deposition derived primarily from industrial sources in Europe and the British Isles is another example (Braekke 1976). All of these data and histories taken together suggest that if the input of sulfates to Boundary Waters lakes increases significantly, we can expect to see many of the more sensitive lakes begin to lose their fish populations. The first species to go would likely be the smallmouth bass, followed in order by walleye, lake trout, burbot, northern pike, white sucker, sunfish, rock bass, cisco, and finally even yellow perch. Other vital members of the food web such as certain zooplankters, snails, clams, leeches, aquatic insects, crayfish and other crustaceans, frogs, toads, and salamanders are very vulnerable to acidification, and many species disappear at pH levels higher than those for many fish (MPCA 1985).

Nationally, progress toward reducing acid deposition was dismal until the Clean Air Act Amendments of 1990 finally offered some hope, but Minnesota's Acid Precipitation Act of 1980 (ch. 490, Minn. Laws 411) was the first such state legislation in the nation. It was followed by the Acid Deposition Control Act of 1982, which directed the MPCA to develop and publish a list of acid-sensitive areas by 1983, and to establish an acid-deposition standard to protect sensitive areas and promulgate regulations to protect those areas (Laws of Minn, ch. 482; 116.42–45). On July 1, 1986, pursuant to that mandate, the MPCA Citizens Board adopted an Acid Deposition Standard of 11 kilograms of wet sulfate deposition per hectare per year and regulations to attain that standard (Roberts 1988).

Minnesota's sulfate deposition standard was set at a level calculated to avoid acidification of the most sensitive BWCAW lakes, but only by a narrow margin. It allowed slight increases in sulfate loadings in some areas. Between 1987 and 1991, there were episodes of acid deposition in northeastern Minnesota with pH values in the 4.7 range and sulfate loadings that exceeded the deposition standard by 2 or 3 kilograms per hectare per year. Research and legislative and regulatory processes in Minnesota repeatedly demonstrated the critical importance of controlling distant sources of acid deposition. Minnesota alone cannot protect Boundary Waters lakes from acid deposition. The problem is national and international in scope and can really be fully addressed only with adequate steps at those levels. In 1991 Ontario was proposing a sulfate deposition standard of 8 or 9 kilograms per hectare per year, even lower than the Minnesota standard. But Minnesota's efforts defined the problem, brought monitoring procedures to track changes in lake alkalinity, pH, and acid deposition, and in the long term may bring some reductions in sulfur dioxide emissions and sulfate deposition. The threats from acid deposition are real, but the Boundary Waters lakes are not yet seriously affected. A reduction in acid deposition is predicted for Minnesota by the MPCA as a result of the federal Clean Air Act amendments of 1990.

MERCURY DEPOSITION

Concentrations of mercury in fish in some Boundary Waters lakes have reached levels that can cause health problems in humans using fish as food. Minute background levels of mercury are present in most lakes, apparently derived from natural watershed sources, but most of it comes from airborne pollutants in rain and snow. Analyses of lake sediments show that mercury deposition rates have increased above threefold since European settlement. Sources of atmospheric mercury include coal burning in power plants, mercury additives in latex paints, and waste incinerators. Incinerator waste sources that could be removed for recycling include button and alkaline batteries, fluorescent bulbs, and mercury switches (Swain 1989).

Rain and snow in the Boundary Waters have mercury concentrations of about 19 nanograms per liter of water, but most mercury falling on land becomes bound in soils, and much of it falling on lakes quickly enters bottom sediments, so that lake-water concentrations are only about 3 nanograms per liter. Lakes with large watersheds receive more mercury per unit area than those with small watersheds. Before mercury enters lake food webs, it must be converted to methylmercury by complex processes that vary with lake-water chemical properties. Zooplankters and other small food organisms then take up minute quantities of methylmercury in their feeding, and the concentration of mercury is biomagnified up the food chain as these animals are eaten by small forage fish, and those in turn by the large predators, notably walleye, northern pike, and lake trout. The older and larger the fish, the higher the fish mercury level may become. Lakes with low alkalinity and lower pH (below 7.0) and waters colored yellow or brown by humic acids derived from bogs or forest soils often have fish with higher mercury levels, perhaps because of increased persistence of mercury in their waters or higher methylation rates (Swain 1989; Swain and Helwig 1989).

The accumulation of mercury in fish tissues has already reached the point where the Minnesota Department of Health's annual fish consumption advisories contain recommended limits on the eating of fish from many Boundary Waters lakes. Three levels of advisories are issued: (1) eat no more than one fish meal per week, (2) eat no more than one fish meal per month, and (3) eat no fish. Mercury levels vary enough by fish species and sizes that the advisories for each lake are by species and length class. The 1989 fish consumption advisory recommended at least some limits on fish consumption from the following BWCAW lakes: Adams, Alpine, Alton, Amber, Basswood, Big Moose, Brule, Caribou, Crane, Davis, Disappointment, East Bearskin, Fat, Frost, Gabimichigami, Ge-be-on-e-quet, Kawishiwi, Lac La Croix, Loon, Moose, Morgan, North Cone, One, Oyster, Parent, Round, Rush, Saganaga, Sand Point, Sandpit, Sea Gull, Slim, Snowbank, South, Stuart, and Trout. Fish had still not been tested from most BWCAW lakes in 1989, and a lake's absence from this list is no guarantee that its fish do not contain elevated mercury levels. In fact, the high percentage of tested lakes with advisories suggests that most BWCAW lakes have mercury problems. For many BWCAW lakes the consumption advisories are only for larger fish of one or two species, usually walleye, northern pike, lake trout, or smallmouth bass. The absence of a species from the list for a given lake may simply mean that no fish or not enough fish were tested.

Mercury can cause serious nervous system damage in humans, especially in children under age six and in the unborn. Pregnant women, breast-feeding women, women who may become pregnant in the next several years, and children under age six are warned to follow the advisories carefully, and to eat no fish from the "one meal a month" and "no fish" categories (Helwig and Heiskary 1985; Minnesota Dept. of Health 1989).

Unlike humans who may read and heed such advisories, many fish-eating birds and mammals that may be at risk are without protection. Species that face potentially lethal effects include the loon, mergansers, bald eagle, osprey, kingfisher, sea gulls, great blue heron, otter, mink, and probably others. Control of mercury emissions is urgent, but long-distance transport may be as much a problem in controlling mercury here as it is with acid rain.

National or international action may be essential, but control of regional U.S. and Canadian mercury sources is obviously urgent.

Summation

In spite of all of the changes, impacts, and problems we have examined, the lake and stream ecosystems of the BWCAW and Quetico are probably as close to their natural state before European settlement as those of any wilderness area or national park south of Alaska and far northern Canada. Water pollution is minimal except for the effects of acid deposition and mercury, most native fish and other aquatic organisms are still present in most waters, and exotic fish still do not dominate many waters. We should cease all stocking of non-native fish and even avoid further stocking of native species in lakes that have never been stocked—and there are still many. For among the most vital resources of wilderness areas are their gene pools of native species. There is growing evidence of genetically distinct locally adapted stocks of many fish species, often with better growth or survival than nonlocal stocks of the same species (Goodman 1991). We may not yet know much about this phenomenon for the Boundary Waters, but it would be tragic if we lost the genetic traits of adapted stocks in Boundary Waters lakes through indiscriminate planting of poorly adapted strains. Of the major game fish and top predators, the lake trout is closest to "living on the edge." The Boundary Waters region is virtually the southwestern limit of the natural range of this widespread boreal species, and, like the caribou, it is therefore very sensitive to habitat changes or potential new competitors and diseases. But, unlike the caribou, the lake trout still thrives in some BWCAW and many Quetico lakes. It is a barometer species, a canary for the lake ecosystems, and so far we have not pushed it over the edge as we did the caribou. The lakes of the Boundary Waters are perhaps its most precious and unique resource. Let us hope we can prevent their further degradation and correct past mistakes as much as possible.

Visitor Impacts on the Ecosystem

As a prelude to discussing visitor impacts, consider what values these impacts might threaten. The Wilderness Act of 1964 defines wilderness as an area "where the earth and its community of life are untrammeled by man . . . an area of undeveloped . . . land retaining its primeval character and influence without permanent improvements, . . . which is protected and managed so as to preserve its natural conditions, . . . which generally appears to have been affected primarily by the forces of nature, with the imprint of man's work substantially unnoticeable; has outstanding opportunities for solitude or a primitive and unconfined type of recreation; . . . and may also contain ecological, geological, or other features of scientific, educational, scenic, or historical value" (U.S. Public Law 88-577).

The Boundary Waters Canoe Area Wilderness Act (U.S. Public Law 95-495) finds it necessary "to provide for the protection, enhancement, and preservation of the natural values of the lakes, waterways, and associated forest areas, and for the orderly management of public use and enjoyment of that area as wilderness, . . . while at the same time protecting the special qualities of the area as a natural forest-lakeland wilderness ecosystem of major esthetic, scientific, recreational, and educational value to the Nation." The section on purposes (sec. 2) calls "for such measures as will . . . (1) provide for the protection and management of the fish and wildlife of the wilderness so as to enhance public enjoyment and appreciation of the unique biotic resources of the region, (2) protect and enhance the natural values

and environmental quality of the lakes, streams, shorelines and associated forest areas of the wilderness, (3) maintain high water quality in such areas . . . "

These statutory findings and purposes indicate what resources and values the American people intended to protect and make available for nondestructive uses in the BWCAW by designating it a wilderness. The following values and their associated resources or activities are either expressly stated or implied in these mandates:

- The natural functioning and biodiversity of the ecosystem, including its forest communities, lakes and streams, fish, wildlife, soils, and geological landforms.
- The genetic resources of its native plants and animals, including all trees, shrubs, herbs, mosses, and lichens, and all fish, mammals, birds, reptiles, amphibians, and insects (the gene pools of all organisms).
- Opportunities for scientific research into the status and functioning of all of the area's natural ecosystem components and the total ecosystem itself (Franklin 1987).
- Opportunities for use of the area's natural ecosystem as an outdoor laboratory for teaching in the natural and social sciences, arts, and literature at all levels from grade school to graduate studies by university students.
- Opportunities for visitors to experience the inspirational and spiritual values of the area's natural ecosystem and for those who will never visit to know that it is there (existence value).
- Opportunities for artists, photographers, and writers

to receive creative inspiration from the natural scenes of the area.

- Opportunities for visitors to experience the beauty, solitude, silence, and natural sounds of the wilderness.
- Opportunities for visitors to experience the physical, social, and psychological challenges of travel, camping, and living in a vast natural lake-land ecosystem.
- Opportunities for visitors to enjoy primitive and unconfined recreation in a lake-land wilderness setting, including such activities as canoeing, hiking, skiing, snowshoeing, dogsledding, rock climbing, wildlife viewing, fishing, berry picking, and hunting.

Some of these categories overlap and may conflict, but their identification will help in assessing the visitor activities that might affect the ecosystem and the vital role the wilderness areas of the Boundary Waters region play. I highlighted the statutory mandates for the BWCAW, but with some changes the discussion also applies to Quetico and Voyageurs (hunting is prohibited, and they have somewhat different statutory and administrative guidelines). These wilderness values range from actual ecosystem components, through values clearly ecosystem-linked, to human social and psychological values and opportunities—a deliberate arrangement because we will make distinctions on those bases. All wilderness-related values and opportunities ultimately depend on the quality of the wilderness ecosystem for their uniqueness, and wilderness management must first of all perpetuate the natural ecosystem (Hendee 1990; Hendee and von Koch 1990). Activities that can be served by nonwilderness areas should probably be concentrated in such areas (Hendee, Stankey, and Lucas 1990).

Kinds of Visitor Impacts

Some visitor activities and visitor use levels may adversely affect the social and psychological experiences of other visitors but not necessarily affect the natural ecosystem. Examples are noisy behavior, litter on portages and campsites, congestion on portages or at lakeshore landings, sights of other parties on remote lakes, presence of large groups, and difficulty in finding unoccupied campsites. Obviously we should be concerned about visitor impacts that detract from other visitors' enjoyment of the wilderness as well as with alterations of the natural ecosystem. In fact, because the BWCAW is America's most heavily visited wilderness, a rich literature dating back to 1960 is concerned with the social and psychological aspects of visitation and to a lesser extent with ecosystem impacts (Lime et al. 1990). Visitor use levels tend to be related to adverse impacts both on visitors' experiences and on the natural ecosystem, and thus both kinds of impacts are strongly intertwined. It is beyond the scope of this book to deal directly with the social and psychological aspects of Boundary Waters visitation. The focus here is on the ecosystem.

The effects of visitors on the ecosystem include impacts attributable to:

- disturbance of vegetation, soils, and geology at campsites and on portages, lakeshore landings, and trails (Cole 1987)
- the taking of fish, wildlife, berries, and wild rice
- visitor disturbance of wildlife
- user-caused forest fires
- reduced water quality

In contrast, the social and psychological impacts of visitation include:

- loss of solitude and other wilderness values due to high use levels and the associated sights and sounds of many people moving about
- the inconvenience and loss of a sense of remoteness caused by crowding on portages and at portage landings
- loss of solitude and feelings of remoteness due to the large number of campsites and their close spacing and intersite visibility on some lakes
- scarcity of unoccupied campsites on some lakes during periods of high visitation
- noisy or otherwise objectionable behavior by some visitors
- the social and psychological impacts of large vs. small groups
- the effect of frequency of encounters with other groups on visitors' satisfactions and perceptions of wilderness
- the relative impact of encountering motorized vs. nonmotorized visitors
- poor fishing or hunting due to excessive fish or game harvests by visitors

226

• difficulty in seeing wildlife due to disturbance of wildlife by other visitors

History of Visitor Use

Most adverse ecosystem impacts caused by visitors also become social and psychological impacts when they reach a certain severity level. For example, the early stages of campsite deterioration may not be objectionable to many users, but when trees begin to die and the ground becomes bare and muddy or dusty, such campsites detract from most visitors' experiences. Many ecosystem impacts are directly related to the intensity and duration of the visitor activities that cause them. We need to understand the kinds of visitor activities and use levels that produce specific effects and what steps might be taken to prevent or mitigate unacceptable impacts.

Fortunately the record of growing recreational use of the Boundary Waters is well documented so it is possible to relate many visitor impacts to specific kinds and levels of use. Before World War II, recreational use of the Boundary Waters was very light by today's standards. But beginning immediately after the war, use increased so rapidly that in the late 1950s the U.S. Forest Service sponsored the pioneering studies of Robert C. Lucas on the recreational use and carrying capacity of the BWCA (Lucas 1962, 1964a,b,c).

His work produced the first reliable estimates of use levels by paddling canoeists and motorboat and motor-canoe visitors, as well as the first detailed analysis of these diverse user groups' activities and perceptions of wilderness attractions and acceptable levels of use from the psychosocial and environmental viewpoints. The benchmark year for Lucas's use data was 1961, and his prophecy that growing use was producing user conflicts and soon might tax the recreational and environmental carrying capacity of the BWCAW was fulfilled in the following decades.

Figures 15.1 and 15.2 give a picture of the trends in recreational use in the BWCAW from 1967 to 1993 by various types of users: paddling canoeists, motorboaters and motor-canoeists, hikers, snowmobilers, and others. To properly interpret these graphs, it is important to understand the definitions of user groups, visits, and visitor-days, the changes in use periods covered by permit data between 1961 and 1993, changes in user regulations and permit rules, and changes in statistical treatment of the permit data on which the graphs are based. A *group* or *party* is a number of people traveling together. In 1993 a group could vary in size from 1 to 10 persons in the BWCAW. Overnight groups are those camping at least 1 night in the wilderness. Day users are persons who do not camp overnight. A *visit* is 1 person traveling in the BWCAW for any length of stay. For example, a group of 4 people staying 1 day would be counted

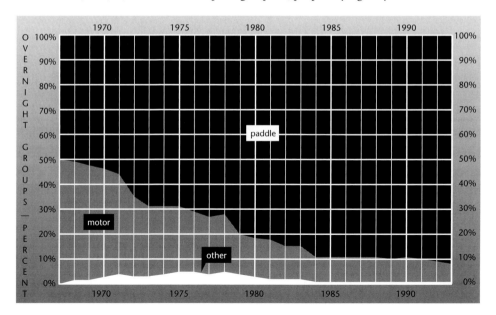

Figure 15.1 / Change in overnight use in the BWCAW, 1967–93, by mode of travel. (Data from Superior National Forest permit and recreational use summaries.)

Figure 15.2 / Change in recreational use in the BWCAW, 1967–91. (Data from Superior National Forest permit and recreational use summaries.)

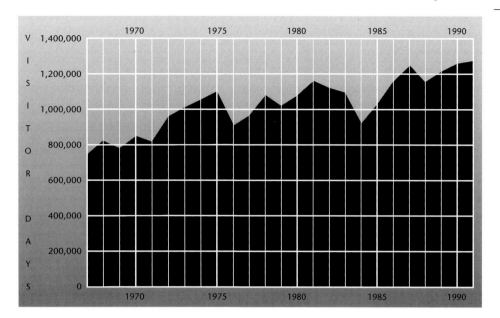

as 4 visits. If they stay 3 days, their use is still counted as 4 visits. A *visitor-day* is a 12-hour use period, that is, 1 person visiting the area for 12 hours or less. Persons remaining overnight accrue multiple visitor-days. For example, a group of 4 staying 1 night and most of the 1st and 2nd days would accrue 12 visitor-days: 4 for the 1st day, 4 for the night, and 4 for the 2nd day.

Despite many regulations designed to control both the amount and type of recreational use, the BWCAW saw a nearly threefold increase in use from 1961 to the early 1990s. Most of this growth occurred between 1961 and 1975, but even after the 1978 motor restrictions, canoe and motorboat camping (overnight groups) and day use still continued to climb into the 1990s. After the 1984 phasedowns, motorboat camping dropped to a third of the 1972–75 peak but then began to increase again. In terms of environmental impact, the data on overnight camper groups are the most meaningful, and that use increased from about 9,000 groups in 1961 to more than 28,000 in 1993. With an average group size of 4 persons, this translates into more than 100,000 people camping in the backcountry for an average length of stay of about 5 days each, or 500,000 camper days per year. Most of that growth was use by paddling canoeists, who by 1993 accounted for 90 percent of overnight use. Winter use is poorly documented because

permits were not required after 1979, but skiing, snowshoeing, dogsledding, and winter camping also have grown.

Perhaps because it is America's only large lake-land canoeing wilderness, and because it is near many large population centers, the BWCAW has for decades hosted more visitor-days of use than any other wilderness, about 10 percent of all national forest wilderness visitor-day use (Soderberg 1987). Quetico receives only about a fifth as much use as the BWCAW. In 1989 only 4,515 overnight groups were recorded, and in 1990 overnight campers spent some 115,649 camper-nights in the interior. Quetico use also has been growing for decades, however, and some areas in the Hunter Island region are very heavily used, mostly by Americans (figure 15.3).

Visitor Activities and Use Patterns

To understand the impact of visitors on the ecosystem, we need to take a closer look at actual visitor activities, their temporal and spatial distribution, and the facilities and resources that accommodate them. The network of lakes and streams in the BWCAW and Quetico gives visitors a virtually unlimited choice of routes and activities.

Although the BWCAW was supposedly managed as a wilderness canoe area beginning with the Jardine policy

Figure 15.3 / Quetico Park
visitation by entry station,
May–August, 1985–93.
(Data from Ontario Ministry
of Natural Resources.)

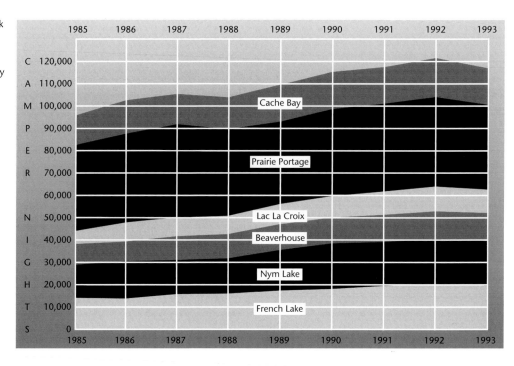

of 1926, there were no restrictions on motorized visitor travel until 1965. In 1965 motorboats and snowmobiles were restricted to designated lakes and streams, but those motor areas still encompassed 62 percent of the water surface. The Boundary Waters Wilderness Act of 1978 phased down motor use to 33 percent of the water surface in 1978 and to 24 percent when the last phaseout (Sea Gull Lake) occurs in 1999. Snowmobiles were phased out in 1984 except for two access routes to Canada. Quetico banned all motorized visitor travel in 1979 except for designated lakes where natives from the Lac La Croix First Nation guide motorized guests. This history still influences the distribution and kinds of visitor uses that occur in both areas. First Lucas (1964b) and then Stankey (1973) and Lime and co-workers (Lime 1975; Lime, Fox, et al. 1990; Lime and Lewis 1992) found that wilderness-seeking canoeists prefer to avoid motorboat parties. Many do not feel they are "in the wilderness" until they have reached areas where motors are absent. Adelman, Heberlein, and Bonnicksen (1982) found that 71 percent of paddlers disliked meeting or seeing motorboat users in the BWCAW, whereas only 8 percent of motorboat users disliked meeting or seeing paddlers. Thus some of the largest and most ecologically

pristine lakes such as Saganaga, Sea Gull, Clearwater, Basswood, and some of Lac La Croix are not seen as wilderness by many canoeists and are shunned as destination lakes for that reason.

Many of the BWCAW motor routes begin at entry-point lakes with parking lots and outfitter facilities, routes that must also be traversed by many canoeists headed for nonmotorized interior lakes (the Fall-Newton-Basswood route, the Moose Lake chain, Snowbank, Saganaga, Sea Gull, Little Vermilion to Lac La Croix, Big Trout, Clearwater, East Bearskin). At several of these motorized access routes, outfitters offer high-speed towboat services to rush wilderness-seeking canoeists through these congested motor lakes, adding further to the perception that such lakes are not really wilderness.

Motorboat groups go mostly to fish, and the lakes where motors are permitted are largely the domain of both day-use and camping motorized fishing parties, especially in the spring and early summer, when fishing is generally best. Lucas (1964b) found that fishing was a major reason given for visiting the area by many motorized parties, whereas paddling canoeists more frequently cited the wilderness qualities of the area as a major reason for their visit. This difference in motivation still holds. Wilderness-seeking canoeists see a much smaller proportion of the total area as meeting their subjective definitions of wilderness than do motorized groups, and they also express more concern about meeting too many parties or large groups in the backcountry (Lucas 1964b; Stankey 1973; Lime 1975; Lime, Fox, et al. 1990; Lime and Lewis 1992; Lewis 1993).

The evolving regulations on motor use have gradually changed the population of open-water-season visitors in the BWCAW and Quetico from a nearly even mix of canoeists and motorized parties to a preponderance of canoeists. For 1961–66 Lucas found about half of all BWCAW camper groups to be motorized. By 1972 about 65 percent of overnight groups were paddling canoeists, and by 1993 about 90 percent were paddlers and 10 percent motorized. Most motorboaters come from local northern Minnesota communities (figure 15.4). The proportion of BWCAW motorized visitors is higher for day users, who account for nearly half of total visitor-days. Day motorboaters and motor-canoeists use the entry points for motor routes, and many reach Basswood Lake, which must be crossed by canoeists headed for nonmotorized lakes beyond (the Quetico side of Basswood Lake is closed to motors, as is the western segment of the border route in the BWCAW). Since 1979, Quetico

visitors have all been paddlers except for the motorized fishing parties guided by the Lac La Croix First Nation on a few western lakes.

Consumptive uses of natural resources by visitors in some areas of the BWCAW have included (besides fishing) the hunting of moose, deer, bear, ruffed and spruce grouse, and ducks; trapping of beaver and other mammals; and the harvesting of wild rice, blueberries, and other berries. Most berry picking is done by visitors for recreation and food supplements, but some day visitors pick berries for home use. Hunting and trapping by visitors are prohibited in Quetico and Voyageurs, but in Quetico registered traplines are operated in some areas by the Lac La Croix First Nation and others. The Lac La Croix First Nation also has hunting rights in some areas and may use snowmobiles in trapping and hunting there. Most hunting and trapping in the BWCAW occur near the exterior boundaries because of the difficulties of penetrating far into the interior, especially after the fall freeze-up. The moose season generally begins in early October in years when hunting is permitted. From about 1977 through at least 1990, deer were so uncommon in the BWCAW that very little deer hunting occurred, and in any case the firearms deer season comes in early November, when freeze-up is often under way.

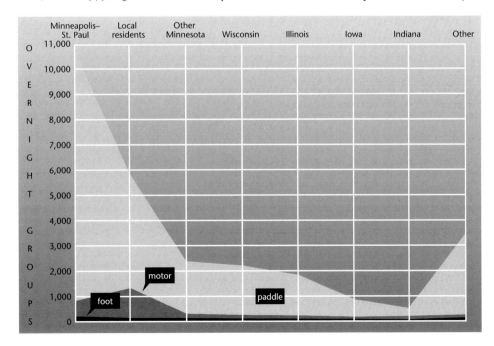

Figure 15.4 / Mode of travel of groups entering the BWCAW by place of origin in 1990 (overnight use only. Data from Superior National Forest permit and recreational use summaries.)

The open-water season generally begins in the first week of May, but the first heavy-use period comes with the opening of the general fishing season, in Minnesota normally the weekend closest to May 15. Other heavy-use periods include Memorial Day, the Fourth of July, Labor Day, and most of July and August. Very few canoe trips occur after about October 1 in either the BWCAW or Quetico (table 15.1).

Of the overnight visitor groups in the 1980s and early 1990s, about a third consisted of 2 persons, about 20 percent of 4 persons, about 16 percent of 5 or 6 persons, and about 17 percent of 7 or more persons. Lone individuals are rare, as is the case in other wilderness areas (Lime et al. 1990). Median group size for all BWCAW overnight groups in 1991 was 4 persons (Lime and Lewis 1992)(figure 15.5).

In 1988 about 44 percent of BWCAW overnight groups consisted of family members, 43 percent friends, 8 percent members of organizations (youth groups, churches, clubs, environmental groups), and 5 percent individuals. Males predominate, but participation by females is increasing, and by 1988 they were about 30 percent of all overnight group members (Lime, Fox, et al. 1990). All ages participate, although youths 13 to 18 and young adults are most strongly represented. Half of all overnight users are between 16 and 35, and 16 percent are 15 or younger. It is not uncommon to see families with children aged 5 to 12 or persons 55 to 75 years old. Physically handicapped groups also participate. Some 88 percent of visitors responding to Lime's 1988 and 1991 surveys were repeat users (Lime, Fox, et al. 1990; Lime and Lewis 1992).

Average length of stay for overnight visitors is about 4 nights, and there is a wide spectrum of behavior. Many visitors penetrate only 1 to 3 portages into the interior, or camp on entry-point lake chains requiring no portages. Many groups take 5 to 15 portages and stay 5 to 10 days. Some visitors travel far into the interior of the BWCAW or Quetico, taking 20 to 40 or more portages and staying 2 to 3 weeks. Most youth-organization groups have a size of 6 to 10 persons and stay 6 to 10 days or more, often penetrating deep into the wilderness. Lime and co-workers (1990) found that 25 percent of BWCAW overnight groups camped 3 nights or less, 27 percent camped 4 nights, 41 per-

Table 15.1 / Percentage of BWCAW groups by month for selected years

	1990	1993
May	15%	13%
June	23%	22%
July	22%	23%
August	27%	28%
September	13%	14%

Source Superior National Forest permit and recreational use summaries.

cent camped 5 to 7 nights, and 6 percent camped 8 to 15 or more nights. Some groups make a base camp on a particular lake their 1st or 2nd night out and take side trips from that campsite for the remainder of their trip. Others move camp almost every day.

About 18 hiking trails exist in the BWCAW, but hiking is largely confined to late summer and fall because of bug problems earlier. Only about 1 percent of overnight campers were hikers in 1993.

Most winter visitors are cross-country skiers, but dog-sledding is growing in popularity, and snowshoeing is still a common activity. Much of this winter activity is day use, perhaps with a noon cookout over a campfire. Some day trips are also for fishing through the ice, usually for lake trout. Winter camping, sometimes for several days, is for truly hardy and experienced winter visitors. Some camping is offered by professional dogsledding guides. The routes followed by winter visitors include some maintained ski trails that wind through forests and cross lakes and bogs, but the routes far into the interior are mostly the same lakes and portages followed by summer visitors except for detours around thin ice near rapids and other known danger spots. Snowmobiling was fairly common on a few routes until phased out in 1984. Some of that activity was focused on lake-trout fishing in remote interior lakes.

The Resource Base, Facilities, and Regulations

The BWCAW has about 1,200 miles of canoe routes, with hundreds of maintained portages linking more than 1,000

Figure 15.5 / Percentage of BWCAW and Quetico overnight groups by party size. (BWCAW data from Lime et al. 1990; Lime and Lewis 1992; and Superior National Forest permit and recreational use summaries. Quetico data from Ontario Ministry of Natural Resources.)

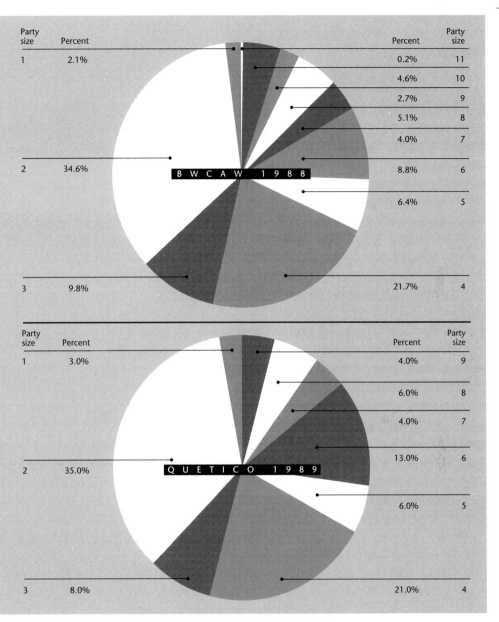

BWCAW 1988

Party size	Percent
1	2.1%
2	34.6%
3	9.8%

Percent	Party size
0.2%	11
4.6%	10
2.7%	9
5.1%	8
4.0%	7
8.8%	6
6.4%	5
21.7%	4

QUETICO 1989

Party size	Percent
1	3.0%
2	35.0%
3	8.0%

Percent	Party size
4.0%	9
6.0%	8
4.0%	7
13.0%	6
6.0%	5
21.0%	4

lakes into an interconnected system. The 18 hiking trails have a combined length of about 200 miles. The two longest are the Kekekabic Trail (35 miles) and the Border Route Trail (33 miles). Some trails are recently abandoned logging roads. Quetico has even more lakes, and the total mileage of canoe routes is probably greater than in the BWCAW. In Quetico portage construction and maintenance are less extensive, and much maintenance is simply done by visitors as they encounter windfalls or new water areas over the portages. Many lakes in Quetico and some in the BWCAW still have no portages to them. Visitors wishing to see these lakes must carry their canoes and gear through "the bush," traveling by compass and map, an art known as bushwhacking by those few who practice it. Otherwise, essentially no cross-country travel exists, because of the difficulty of traversing the brushy, rocky, sometimes rugged, sometimes boggy, and often windfall-strewn backcountry. A few hunters and trappers penetrate the edges of the BWCAW for a mile or two, but even most of them stick to trails, old logging roads, and lakes and streams. Visitor impacts on land are confined almost entirely to the vicinity of campsites, portages, trails, onshore lunch sites, and wood-gathering areas near lakeshores.

The Superior National Forest and Quetico Provincial Park have gradually developed similar and quite sophisticated user regulations in attempts to maintain quality wilderness experiences for visitors while still accommodating their ever-growing clientele (Anderson and Lime 1984). I discuss the BWCAW and Quetico programs separately because of the differences.

Before 1966 the BWCAW had few regulations other than fire safety rules. Visitors selected their own campsites, cleared tent pads, and built fireplaces from rocks. On heavily used routes a few campsites had fire grates, pit toilets, and even picnic tables maintained by the Forest Service. A good system of portages had been built by the Civilian Conservation Corps in many areas, but some areas had only little-used informal trails between lakes. After the Selke committee hearings and Wilderness Act of 1964 and the Freeman Directive of 1965, the Forest Service developed a formal set of regulations governing motorcraft and snowmobile routes and other recreational practices, and in 1966, instituted a mandatory (but free) permit system. Congress also funded a new program of social, geographic, and ecological research in the BWCA in 1966. By 1970 it was becoming painfully obvious that visitors' experiences and campsite resources were being seriously affected by existing use levels and visitor travel patterns. This conclusion was corroborated by the skyrocketing visitor use revealed by visitor registration, by the new visitor-attitude studies of Stankey (1973) and Lime and co-workers (Lime 1972, 1975; Lime et al. 1990; Lime and Lewis 1992), and by the campsite deterioration studies of Merriam's University of Minnesota graduate students (McCool, Merriam, and Cushwa 1969; Merriam et al. 1973; Merriam and Smith 1974; Marion 1984; Marion and Merriam 1985a,b).

The Forest Service responded with a program of new user regulations worked out in consultations among Forest Service and university research people and local outfitting and resort businesses, with the dual goals of reducing visitor congestion and protecting campsites, portages, and lakeshore landings from overuse, litter, and sanitation problems (Lime et al. 1990). Four new measures were implemented between 1968 and 1976:

1 Beginning in 1971, a "designated campsites" rule was instituted on heavy-use routes. By 1975 the rule was extended to the entire BWCAW. The Forest Service installed steel fire grates and simple box latrine pit toilets at suitable old user-built campsites and built new campsites with these facilities as standard practice. Old campsites on small islands and other ecologically sensitive sites were closed. Two University of Minnesota students, Stephen McCool and Timothy Knopp, had mapped all old user-established campsites in 1967–68, so the Forest Service knew the precise location of nearly 2,000 campsites, including the new ones they were installing. The new rule required visitors to camp only at approved campsites, identifiable by a Forest Service fire grate and pit toilet, and to build campfires only in immovable fire grates, which have steel legs driven into holes bored into bedrock or set in concrete. Toilets at first consisted of a simple wooden box seat with cover, set over a pit about 4 feet deep, but these boxes are now replaced by lightweight fiberglass box toilets. One, two, or three leveled tent pads are usually present at each site. Visitors are not required to register for specific sites. They may camp at approved sites of their own choosing. To aid visitors in locating sites, the Forest Service worked with map supply firms to produce high-quality maps for the entire BWCAW to show the location of some 2,000 approved campsites on U.S. Geological Survey topographic maps. Maps are updated regularly as old campsites are closed or new ones developed. This program has done much to limit campsite impacts to suitable sites and to solve sanitation and user-caused fire problems. The only exceptions to this rule are for campers with permits to camp in a few "Primitive Management Areas" and along certain hiking trails where there are no designated campsites, and for winter campers.

2 In 1973 a "can and bottle ban" was instituted. This regulation prohibits the use of nonburnable food and beverage containers, including returnable beverage bottles

even if deposits were charged. Containers of fuel, insect repellents, medicines, and other personal items are allowed. A program of cleaning up campsites and removing accumulated cans and bottles from previous years had been implemented earlier. This new rule combined with "pack it out" education efforts has gone far toward eliminating litter, especially at campsites.

3 In 1969 a maximum group size limit of 15 persons was instituted, and in 1975 the limit was lowered to 10 persons.

4 In 1976 a sophisticated visitor distribution system was instituted, using entry-point quotas on visitor numbers as a mechanism to redistribute visitor use and impacts throughout the wilderness. Visitor permits had been required since 1966, compliance was good, and the new program simply built on the already established visitor contact by limiting the number of permits for each entry point to the specified visitor capacity of the routes served by each entry point. There were about 70 entry points to the BWCAW by 1976, but in 1975 about 55 percent of all groups used just 5, and just 1 (Moose Lake east of Ely) received 20 percent of all entries. Use was also heavily concentrated on holiday weekends and in the first three weeks of August. These patterns caused unacceptable concentrations of use on some routes and lakes, especially during high-use periods, and visitors were heavily affecting campsites in those areas. Some other entry points and routes were little used. Action was needed (Hulbert and Higgins 1977; Lime 1977). The response was the Visitor Distribution System.

DESIGN OF THE BWCAW
VISITOR DISTRIBUTION SYSTEM

The system was the idea of George Peterson, then of Northwestern University, and David Lime, then Recreation Research Project Leader, U.S. Forest Service, St. Paul. Peterson was initially an urban transportation-planning engineer with a background in freeway traffic modeling and control and with long personal experience with BWCAW canoe trips and visitor congestion. He and his students reasoned that the principles of freeway traffic-flow control might fit

the BWCAW visitor congestion situation if the needed data could be assembled. The data included the travel patterns and campsites used by visitors coming from each of the entry points, the locations of all entry points, the prevailing rates of entry for all entry points over a typical season, and some means of simulating possible changes in travel patterns with various changes in entry rates. In 1971 Lime collected data on travel patterns and visitor attitudes and behavior for the BWCAW by asking users to complete trip diaries consisting of maps and a questionnaire (Lime 1975, 1977). Visitor permits provided other needed data.

Given these data, Peterson's student Gorman Gilbert developed a computer model employing Markov renewal theory that permits managers to simulate the travel movements and campsite occupancy of visitors as they circulate from lake to lake, assuming varying entry rates from the many possible entry points (Gilbert, Peterson, and Lime 1972; Gilbert, Peterson, and Schofer 1972; Hulbert and Higgins 1977). By simulating by computer a wide range of visitor entry rates at various entry points for an entire season, one can find the optimum combination of entry-point quotas for all dates that reduces visitor concentrations to a minimum. This solution must then be weighed by BWCAW management against real-world travel and vacation preferences of the region's visitors and the economic and social impacts of revised quotas on local communities and on outfitting and resort businesses. Entry-point quotas can then be set to distribute visitor use to minimize environmental impacts, optimize the social and psychological experiences of visitors, and avoid major economic disruptions (Peterson 1977).

The initial model was further refined through experience with actual visitor responses to entry-point quotas. By the late 1980s, the number of entry points had increased to 87, but with periodic updating, this computer-modeling approach has remained the backbone of the BWCAW visitor distribution system. A computer-based visitor reservation system also is employed, so visitors can reserve dates and entry points. The system has evened out use considerably but so far has failed to eliminate concentrations of visitors on many favorite lakes during heavy-use periods (Lime and Lewis 1992).

Persons not familiar with the BWCAW but knowledgeable about other wilderness areas might believe that these quotas, rules, and regulations would destroy one's appreciation of the area. After all, regulations are the antithesis of wilderness. But the rules have been designed to minimize their impact on visitors' choices and sense of freedom after a group enters the area. After visitors have pushed off from their entry point, they may go anywhere and exit anywhere in the entire BWCAW. Visitors may camp at anytime, provided the site has a fire grate and toilet. The travel model used in setting entry-point quotas is based on average visitor behavior, allowing for many very different visitor movements from each entry point. If the entry point desired is filled for the date visitors planned to start their trip, they have two choices. They can change the date and try again, or they can find an entry point that is open for the chosen date. So far the entire BWCAW has never been declared full, but that day may come. Use levels are reaching the point where visitors' sense of being "in the wilderness" is lost in many areas during high-use periods even if environmental impacts are tolerable.

ENTRY-POINT QUOTAS, CAMPSITE DENSITY, AND CARRYING CAPACITY

The aim of the Visitor Distribution System is to limit entries to levels within the carrying capacity of the lakes, streams, and portages that receive visitors from given entry points, considering the predicted travel behavior of visitors from other entry points who use the same areas. The definition of carrying capacity is the key here, and so far a very simple definition has been used: limiting maximum use to a percentage occupancy of the campsites in the area served by the entry points. Initially capacity was set at 67 percent occupancy to allow campers flexibility in finding unoccupied sites (Higgins 1977). Later, as use exceeded this level, the limit was increased to 85 percent occupancy (Marion and Sober 1987). Assuming that the assigned quotas will actually hold use to such levels, the question that must be faced is whether the number and location of campsites established on a given lake really reflect that lake's carrying capacity. This problem involves complex questions about ecosystem impacts and social and psychological aspects of visitor use for which there are no easy answers.

The numbers and locations of BWCAW campsites with fire grates and toilets on given lakes as of the early 1990s were the result of several factors, some of which have little to do with either social or ecological carrying capacity. Many campsites were old user-established sites that tended to be most abundant on the most heavily used routes and best fishing lakes. Most such sites were aesthetically pleasing and fairly resistant to visitor impact, and the Forest Service simply installed fire grates and toilets to make them official. Old sites on small islands along main travel routes and in other ecologically sensitive locations were closed. Some new sites were established along these same heavily used routes and interior lakes between 1967 and 1980 in attempts to keep up with the rapidly increasing demand.

Both social and environmental resource impacts were considered in locating newly established sites, but the density of sites in itself was apparently seldom the controlling factor. Some of the factors that were considered in locating new campsites and in determining a lake's "capacity" were as follows:

- general terrain of the lake and site
- possible impact of the site on cultural resources such as archaeological sites and pictographs
- proximity of eagle nests or other wildlife impacts
- soil depth adequate for a pit toilet
- a satisfactory canoe landing not subject to severe erosion
- no intersite visibility, to enhance solitude
- water-quality concerns
- size and shape of the lake

These criteria were developed gradually beginning about 1968. By 1980 each ranger district had developed maps of possible sites that could potentially meet such criteria. By 1980, 2,145 campsites had toilets and fire grates, but not all met the criteria.

Lakes still lightly used in the 1967–80 era had few old campsites, and few new ones were built because they were not needed. One or two campsites were established on many small interior lakes that had none previously. Fewer new campsites have been built since about 1980, and those are mostly replacements for closed sites. It is fair to say that as of 1991 the location and density of campsites still primarily reflected the long established preferences of visitors for certain routes and lakes. Perhaps that is as it should be, but an 85 percent occupancy rate of those campsites hardly reflects rationally established ecological or social carrying capacities of the lakes concerned. For the most part campsite numbers on given lakes are little more than an artifact of the history of use of the BWCAW in the 1960–80 era and the budgets and judgment of the Forest Service staff involved.

Additional questions that must be asked to determine a lake's ecological carrying capacity include:

• How many campsites per mile of shoreline are appropriate in terms of ecological impacts to the shoreline ecosystems?

• What percentage of the shoreline ecosystem can be committed to campsites without unacceptable damage to the soils, vegetation, water quality, and wildlife of the area?

• How many visitor-nights of campsite use per square mile of lake surface area can be tolerated in terms of direct campsite impacts and the associated camper impacts on water quality, fish population structures, and wildlife?

To further explore the relationship between campsite density and use levels on various routes, the numbers of campsites were counted on many individual lakes along both heavily used and lightly used routes. It was soon apparent that the lakes with the highest density of campsites were almost all on routes serving canoe or motorboat groups originating at high-use entry points, or at the junction of routes far into the interior where canoeists from two or more heavily used entry points tend to meet. This finding is no surprise, because if the campsites were not that abundant, these routes could not support the high entry rates at the access points that feed them. Campsite numbers generally have been allocated to lakes on the basis of past use levels instead of criteria based primarily on either environmental or social carrying-capacity analyses.

An objective measure of the effect of entry-point quotas on use levels is the change in use levels and rank order of

the most heavily used entry points in 1993 for the period 1972–93, shown in table 15.2. In 1990 the 12 most heavily used entry points accounted for 65 percent of use by overnight groups, whereas in 1972, before quotas and reservations were instituted, these same entry points accounted for 72 percent of all group use (day and overnight users). The Forest Service did not summarize use data by entry point for overnight groups for 1972, 1976, or 1980, nor data for all groups by entry point for 1986, 1988, or 1990. We therefore must compare data for overnight groups in 1986, 1988, and 1990 with those for all groups for 1972, 1976, and 1980. However, when the percentage of groups is used as the basis for comparison, the figures in table 15.2 are close to those that truly comparable data would give, and they reveal shifts in use among entry points even though the percentage of total use accounted for by these entry points as a group decreased only slightly.

Several notable shifts in use seem due largely to the effects of Public Law 95-495 in reducing motor use after 1978. For example, Moose Lake remained the most heavily used entry point throughout the period, but its share of use fell from 22 percent in 1972 to 12 percent in 1990, probably because some motor use was lost after the 1984 motor phaseouts, and also because many canoeists chose new motor-free entry points such as nearby Lake One after 1978. Note that the rank of Lake One shifted from 5th in 1972 to 2nd in 1990 despite the loss of all of its motor use. The data for Brule Lake dramatically demonstrate how canoeists respond to the elimination of motors. In 1985, when motors were still allowed, 705 groups entered there, including 250 motor groups; but motors were phased out in 1986, and in 1990, 1,063 paddler groups entered at Brule, a 134 percent increase in paddlers in just 5 years. Brule Lake rose in rank from 11th in 1986 to 8th in 1990. Many of the shifts in use between entry points over the 18 years from 1972 to 1990 may have been due to new motor regulations and changed user perceptions of where to find quality wilderness experiences, and not directly to entry point quotas under the Visitor Distribution System. In fact, in 1985 only 31 percent of the available quotas were used for the May 1 to September 30 season. The entry points with quotas filled most often in 1993 were generally not the ones

Table 15.2 / Percentage of user groups using the BWCAW entry points that were most heavily used in 1993 and the rank of those entry points for selected years between 1972 and 1993

Entry point	1972		1976		1980		1986		1988		1990		1993	
	%	Rank	%	Rank	%	Rank	%	Rank	%	Rank	%	Rank	%	Rank
Moose Lake	21.5	1	19.2	1	17.5	1	14.2	1	12.8	1	12.4	1	12.9	1
Lake One	5.7	5	5.7	6	7.0	4	9.3	2	9.8	2	9.2	2	9.3	2
Sawbill Lake	4.7	6	6.7	4	6.5	5	7.1	3	6.8	3	6.7	3	6.4	3
Saganaga Lake	9.1	3	7.4	3	7.5	3	6.3	4	6.4	4	6.2	4	6.1	4
Fall Lake	12.9	2	9.8	2	10.9	2	5.2	6	4.9	6	4.7	6	4.9	5
Sea Gull Lake	4.1	8	3.5	7	4.8	6	5.4	5	5.5	5	5.2	5	4.6	6
Moose River North	2.2	9	2.1	12	2.7	8	4.1	7	3.7	7	4.0	7	4.1	7
Mudro / Range Lake	—	—	—	—	—	—	3.9	8	3.6	8	3.7	9	3.8	8
Brule Lake	2.0	10	2.6	9	2.3	9	2.8	11	3.6	9	3.7	8	3.8	9
Kawishiwi Lake	1.2	16	1.7	15	1.8	12	2.5	12	2.7	11	2.8	11	3.0	10
Indian Sioux North	1.3	15	1.8	14	1.9	11	2.4	13	2.3	13	2.3	13	2.7	11
Snowbank Lake	1.8	11	2.2	11	2.2	10	2.8	10	2.6	12	2.7	12	2.1	12
Trout Lake	6.2	4	6.4	5	4.3	7	3.1	9	3.2	10	3.4	10	1.3	—
Little Vermilion Lake	4.1	7	2.6	8	1.4	15	1.1	24	1.1	24	1.0	25	1.1	—

Note For 1972–80, the percentage is of all user groups; for 1986–93, the percentage is of overnight groups.
Source Superior National Forest recreational use summaries.

that feed the most heavily used routes (table 15.3). Only 4 of the entry points on this list were among the 12 most heavily used (figure 15.6): Lake One, Sea Gull, Mudro, and Snowbank. The reservation system as applied through 1991 redistributed use primarily during a few peak use periods. It has not been a ceiling on total use and only rarely on the use of many individual routes.

Quetico Park Visitor Regulations and Use Levels

Some Quetico regulations parallel those of the BWCAW, and others are less or more stringent. Quetico use levels are much lower than those in the BWCAW. Quetico has required Ontario fishing licenses and visitor contacts at its entry stations since at least as long ago as 1939. Formal visitor permits have been required since at least 1956. A visitor distribution program and reservation system similar in principle to the BWCAW system was implemented in 1977 (Wilson 1977). George Peterson was a principal technical consultant as he had been in the BWCAW. A can and bottle ban, essentially the same as that in the BWCAW, was also instituted in 1977. The 1992 group size limit of 9 persons (1 less than the 1992 BWCAW limit) was established in 1977. A partial ban on motorboat use began in 1975, and all visitor motor use was banned in 1979 except for parties guided by Lac La Croix First Nation guides on a few western lakes. Visitor use of snowmobiles has long been prohibited.

Quetico does not have established campsites with fire

Table 15.3 / BWCAW entry points with quotas filled most often in 1993

1	Mudro Lake	11	Cross Bay Lake–Ham Lake
2	Sea Gull Lake	12	South Kawishiwi River
3	South Hegman Lake	13	Larch Creek
4	Snowbank Lake	14	Daniels Lake
5	Bower Trout Lake	15	Duncan Lake
6	Little Gabbro Lake	16	Baker Lake
7	Lizz Lake	17	Homer Lake
8	Pine Lake	18	Moose River/Portage River
9	John Lake	19	South Farm Lake
10	Snake River	20	Lake One

Source Superior National Forest permit and recreational use summaries.

grates or toilets. Visitors are not required to camp at previously used sites, although in practice most camping occurs on existing user-established sites, some of which probably date from the voyageurs era or earlier use by indigenous peoples. Most campsites have cleared spots for one to four

tents, and fireplaces built of rocks found onsite. Close to 2,000 such sites probably exist in Quetico, but in the more remote and lightly used lakes some sites are not used in many years, and some small or very remote lakes have no recognizable campsites. There are regulations concerning proper disposal of human wastes and fish entrails, controlling litter, removing flammable fuels around new fireplace sites, extinguishing campfires, and prohibiting cutting boughs and other live vegetation.

In 1991 Quetico had just 6 entry stations for interior park trips, in sharp contrast to the BWCAW's 87 (figure 15.7). Three are along the U.S. border. From 1985 through 1993, canoe camper groups in Quetico averaged only about a fifth of total overnight groups in the BWCAW, but total camper nights increased from 101,039 in 1985 to 116,673 in 1993. Most Quetico visitors come from the United States, especially those visiting the southern half of Quetico, where use is heaviest (figure 15.8). The visitor distribution program does a fairly good job of limiting entries in the central Hunter Island region north of Ely, but still that area receives twice as much use as other regions of Quetico. As in the BWCAW, most use occurs between mid-May and early September.

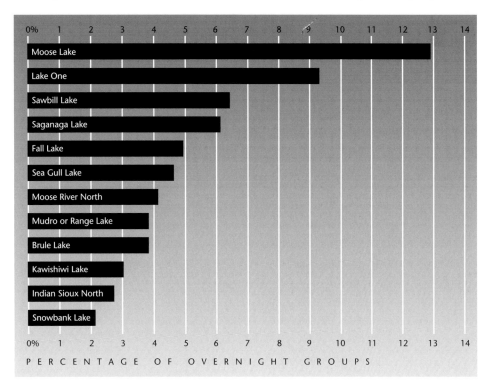

Figure 15.6 / Percentage of overnight groups using the 12 most heavily used BWCAW entry points, 1993. (Data from Superior National Forest permit and recreational use summaries.)

238 **Visitor Impacts at Campsites**

Most of the visitor impact to land-based ecosystems occurs at campsites. In a study of 96 well-established campsites in the BWCAW, a central heavy-use area averaged about 2,368 square feet (220 square meters), or 0.054 acre (Marion and Merriam 1985a). This central area includes the lakeshore landing and paths to the site, the fireplace cooking area, tent pads, and surrounding areas and paths connecting all of these features. The range in campsite sizes that Marion (1984) found in his study was from 452 to 6,199 square feet. The average site area of 0.054 acre implies that the 2,000 BWCAW campsites directly affect just 120 acres, or 0.011 percent of the 922,000-acre total land area of the wilderness.

My own more subjective assessment of impact areas includes the path to the toilet, an area around the toilet used for replacement toilet pits, and a large firewood gathering area surrounding the campsite. That much larger area has not been measured in campsite studies and is much more diffuse and variable, but the total impact area defined rarely exceeds about an acre, and probably averages closer to a half acre. If this larger area is taken as the impact area, the total land area affected by the 2,000 BWCAW campsites is still only about 1,100 acres, or 0.10 percent of the land area of the wilderness. Thus from a strict area perspective, campsites can hardly be seen as a significant threat to the terrestrial ecosystems of the region.

A major problem with that perspective, of course, is that visitors spend much of their time at campsites, and if the natural values of the campsite area are damaged or lost, the visitor's perception of the integrity of the wilderness is correspondingly injured. In addition some visitor effects at campsites such as water pollution and escaped campfires may have wider impacts on aquatic and terrestrial ecosystems. If we consider lakeshore forest ecosystems to be a significant subset of the total forest ecosystem, then the fraction of shoreline forest area affected by campsites is much higher than the percentages given earlier. On lakes like Insula or Ensign, the fraction of shoreline forest affected by campsites is many times these figures. I have no camp-

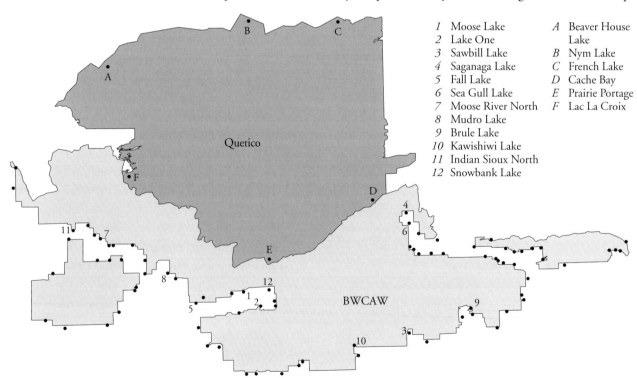

1	Moose Lake	*A*	Beaver House
2	Lake One		Lake
3	Sawbill Lake	*B*	Nym Lake
4	Saganaga Lake	*C*	French Lake
5	Fall Lake	*D*	Cache Bay
6	Sea Gull Lake	*E*	Prairie Portage
7	Moose River North	*F*	Lac La Croix
8	Mudro Lake		
9	Brule Lake		
10	Kawishiwi Lake		
11	Indian Sioux North		
12	Snowbank Lake		

Figure 15.7 / The 12 most heavily used entry points in the BWCAW in 1993 (*1–12*) and Quetico access zones (*A–F*). (Map by Stephen Lime, Department of Forest Resources, University of Minnesota.)

Figure 15.8 / Quetico interior camper groups by access zone and place of origin, 1993. (Data from Ontario Ministry of Natural Resources.)

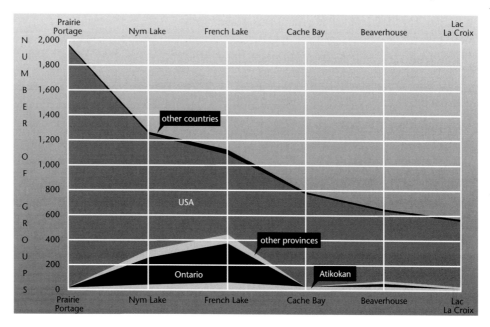

site data for Quetico or Voyageurs, but the situation there is similar in principle to that outlined for the BWCAW. Quetico probably has fewer large campsites and fewer with heavy impacts.

Before looking at how visitors affect campsites, consider what a good Boundary Waters campsite looks like. First, a good warm-season campsite is not necessarily a good site for winter, early spring, or late fall. For the latter seasons a south-facing exposure, heavy forest cover for protection from the wind, and a supply of firewood are vital. Summer is the season most Forest Service sites are intended to serve. An ideal summer site has most or all of the following attributes:

- The location is in an open stand of red pine with little underbrush, well elevated above the lake on a point or island, facing south, east, or west. North-facing points are also excellent if the weather is hot. Such sites tend to be more bug-free and dry and afford a good view of the lake and of sunrises and sunsets.
- The canoe landing is on bare bedrock with a gentle rise to the fireplace area, and there are safe sites to store canoes overnight nearby. There is a deep spot nearby for obtaining clean water for cooking, washing, and putting out campfires. A bedrock landing assures that the landing will not erode from user traffic. Drinking water should be obtained far from shore.

- The fireplace and eating area is on a somewhat elevated bare bedrock knoll close to and with a good view of the lake, with some morning and evening shade from nearby large red or white pines. Bedrock prevents wear and erosion around this heavy traffic area, and rains tend to keep the area clean. Sitting on clean bedrock while eating is more pleasant, cleaner, and more sanitary than sitting on bare earth.
- Tent sites are on well-drained sandy or loamy soils back a bit from the cooking area, preferably in a stand of thrifty younger pines, and the tent pads should be well covered with pine needles.
- The toilet is screened by vegetation and at least 100 to 200 feet back from the lake on a well drained sandy or loamy soil.
- The location has an open bedrock ridge high above the lake yet close to the campsite to serve as a "sitting rock" where one can take in sunsets, sunrises, the northern lights, approaching storms, and wildlife, an added feature that the ideal campsite would surely have. This is also an area where the group can gather without disturbing the campsite.
- A location for swimming is desirable for sites used between about June 15 and September 5. A bedrock shelf for wading out, or a sheer drop-off for diving are possi-

bilities. The ideal is probably a south-facing sand beach near the site, but not immediately in front, because sand soon winds up in tents, food, packsacks, and fishing reels.

Many BWCAW lakes on the Vermilion Granite and the Saganaga Batholith and Quetico lakes on related granitic bedrock, as well as BWCAW lakes on the Duluth Gabbro, have frequent bedrock outcrops along lakeshores that make campsites similar to the ideal one just described. The shorelines of most lakes on the Knife Lake Group of rocks and on the Rove Formation offer few good campsite locations. The bedrock there is often badly fractured, tilted, or jumbled, presenting few flat or rounded rock surfaces for landings, fireplace sites, or sitting rocks. Many shorelines are simply too steep for camping. Aspen-birch stands on the Knife Lake rocks make particularly poor campsites. Sites in brushy, low-lying aspen-birch stands in back bays lack views and are insect-ridden and unpleasant in hot weather. The Forest Service has learned that visitors shun these sites unless all others are occupied.

With this background, let us see how visitors affect campsites, and how important such impacts are. Campsite impacts have probably been studied longer and more intensively in the BWCAW than in any other wilderness, beginning with the pioneering work of Sidney Frissell in the early 1960s (Frissell and Duncan 1965). A study by Merriam and students showed how the condition of 23 newly established campsites changed over five years (Merriam et al. 1973; Merriam and Smith 1974). They found, as have others (Cole 1987, 1990a,b), that new campsites soon experienced loss of ground vegetation, increases in bare mineral soil, soil compaction, trees with exposed roots, dead trees, and expansion of site areas. These factors were measured quantitatively and integrated into a five-step impact-stage rating scheme. Many changes from natural conditions occurred within the first two or three years after site development and then tended to level off. Most of the increase in impact stage occurred during the first 500 to 600 visitor days of camping use. Aspen-birch sites deteriorated to the greatest degree after five years of use, followed in order by jack pine, spruce-fir, red and white pine, white cedar, and open sites.

Site expansion was probably the most striking result of continued camper use. All but one of 22 forested sites showed expansion within the five-year study period. Ten were expanded more than 50 percent and four over 100 percent. Much of the expansion was caused by parties seeking new tent sites because older ones on bare soil were dusty or muddy, or by large groups needing additional tent sites. If suitable new tent sites could not be found around the perimeter of the original site, larger parties often established satellite sites some distance away and developed paths to the original site. Merriam's team noted that one large vigorous party may expand a site so effectively that the site will not return to its earlier configuration regardless of future party size (Merriam et al. 1973).

In another study, the condition of 96 BWCAW campsites at least five years old was compared to that of 96 undisturbed nearby control sites of similar age (Marion and Merriam 1985a,b). On the average campsite, 84 percent of trees within the main campsite use area had exposed roots, and over half of all trees had moderate to severe direct visitor damage such as broken or cut-off branches, trunk scars, stripped bark (especially birches), or axe or knife girdling. The campsites had 95 percent fewer tree seedlings than did their matched control plots. Seedlings tended to occur only near rocks, shrubs, or the edge of the campsite area, places where campers were less likely to trample them. Saplings (small established trees) were virtually absent: only 1 per hectare occurred on campsites, compared to 836 per hectare on control plots. Roughly twice as many standing dead trees and stumps occurred for a given area on campsites as on control plots. Dense vegetative ground cover showed a 76 percent reduction. Sparse cover increased 14 percent, producing an overall loss of 58 percent of the ground cover. In primary-use areas the litter layer (needles, leaves, twigs, etc.) normally covering bare soil was virtually gone as a result of trampling. Much more vegetative ground cover remained on campsites with sparse tree cover than on sites with dense canopies. Heavily used sites tended to have many more non-native grasses and herbs in their ground cover, some of the most abundant being common weeds such as dandelion, white clover, timothy, chickweed, and plantain. Twenty-two non-native species were found, and 62 percent of campsites had at least one. Soil compaction, measured by bulk density and with penetrometers, was higher than on control sites, and the thickness of soil organic layers was 66 percent less than on controls. At least one satellite tent site was found on 42 percent of campsites.

The percentage of a campsite occupied by bare mineral soil was clearly related to visitor use levels, averaging 3 percent on low-use sites, 9 percent on moderate-use sites, and 18 percent on high-use sites. Low-use was defined as 0 to 12 nights per year, moderate as 20 to 40, and high as more than 60 (Marion 1984; Cole 1987; Marion and Merriam 1985a,b). Campsite expansion was also associated with use levels. Low-use sites averaged 1,119 square feet, whereas high-use sites averaged 3,735 square feet. Use levels were also significantly related to tree damage, number of tree stumps, tree seedling abundance, loss of vegetative cover, floristic changes, thickness of soil organic layers, and soil compaction. These findings suggest that campsite impacts could be reduced by reducing BWCAW use levels. But Marion stresses that for all variables except exposed soil, organic layer thickness, soil-penetration resistance, and campsite size, most of the change occurs with low use, and the differences between high and low use are small. Thus only major reductions in total use would have much effect on campsite conditions, and resting old campsites by rotating them with new ones would quickly degrade new sites and simply increase the total area of degraded shoreline ecosystems.

None of the campsite studies dealt with firewood gathering directly. The principal effects of this activity are probably reductions of the input of woody debris to surface litter layers and soil organic layers, and a general expansion of the campsite area. Although these are not major impacts, they add to the unnatural appearance of campsites and concentrate some of the system's nutrients at the fireplace, where most are eventually washed into the lake. However, there is really no shortage of firewood in the BWCAW or Quetico. After all, in the BWCAW alone the forests are capable of growing several hundred thousand cords of wood per year. The impact of wood gathering would be minimal if visitors simply dispersed their gathering to areas away from campsites and back from the lakeshores.

Cole (1990b) has succinctly summarized the nature of visitor impacts on wilderness campsites and the dilemmas of campsite management. His seven "principles to guide wilderness campsite management" fit many BWCAW and Quetico situations, and his relevant points rephrased are as follows:

- Campsite impacts are complex: When new sites are opened, visitors start a complex sequence of changes in soils and vegetation through direct, indirect, and cyclic effects. Vegetation is lost through trampling. A "vicious circle" results from the increased runoff and loss of organic layers. These in turn increase susceptibility to compaction, leading to erosion that may continue even without visitor use.

- Impact at frequently used campsites is inevitable, but some impacts can be limited or mitigated to a degree, for example, by requiring all fires to be confined to Forest Service fireplaces with fire grates.

- Impact occurs rapidly and recovery occurs slowly, as can be seen on old closed BWCAW sites. Any new sites must be selected according to their susceptibility to impacts. Rotation of sites is not a viable option in the face of heavy use.

- Impacts occur rapidly on newly established sites, but the rate of change levels off. This relationship fits the BWCAW, as we saw in the studies reported by Merriam and co-workers (1973), Merriam and Smith (1974), and Marion and Merriam (1985a,b). This finding means that for use levels above some critical point there will be less impact on the total ecosystem if use is concentrated on as few campsites as possible. Making more campsites to "spread the use" will simply degrade more shoreline. In Quetico and the Primitive Management Areas in the BWCAW, where users can make their own campsites, visitors should camp only where others have camped unless use levels are so low that such sites recover completely before they are used again.

- Certain sites are more durable than others: whenever new campsites are established, they must be on sites as resistant to wear as possible.

- Certain users cause less impact than others. Large groups cause campsite expansion and rapid deterioration of new campsites. Groups that use gas stoves for cooking cause less impact than those who use wood for fuel or for warmth or pleasure. The behavior and knowledge of individuals is also important in limiting direct visitor damage of trees with axes, knives, nails, and so on, in minimizing other impacts, and for Quetico in selecting campsites. In Quetico and in BWCAW Primitive Management Areas, visitors using new or lightly used sites should keep length of stays short, return logs or rocks used to their original locations, scatter charcoal at the fire site, and camouflage disturbances or, better, make no fires and move nothing.

- Campsite monitoring data are vital to professional wilderness management. Monitoring the condition of wilderness campsites gives managers a solid factual basis for assessing the effectiveness of their campsite policies and programs (Cole 1990b).

WATER QUALITY AND CAMPSITES

In the late 1960s and early 1970s, concerns were expressed that high visitor use in the BWCAW might cause water pollution and health problems. In connection with the campsite impact studies of Merriam and his students, a study of water quality at campsites was conducted in 1970 by John King on the Moose Lake chain and the Lake Isabella–Isabella River areas of the BWCAW (King 1971; King and Mace 1974; Merriam et al. 1973). Water samples were taken from near shore at campsites and from control sites away from the campsites but also near shore. Four high-use, four medium-use, and two low-use campsites were sampled. Samples were analyzed for fecal coliform bacteria, phosphates, oxygen, pH, nitrates, and total nitrogen. The analyses revealed somewhat higher coliform counts near campsites than on controls for all use levels. The differences between campsite and control counts were greater for high- and medium-use campsites than for low-use campsites, suggesting a relationship between use levels and coliform bacteria abundance near campsites. However, the actual bacterial counts on the low-use campsites averaged higher than those for the high-use sites both near campsites and at control sites. Counts for all campsite use levels were somewhat above the U.S. Department of Health limit of 2.2 organisms per 100 milliliters for safe drinking water. High-use sites averaged 4.61 organisms per 100 milliliters, medium-use sites averaged 6.63 per 100 milliliters, and low-use sites averaged 5.83 per 100 milliliters. Controls averaged within drinking-water limits except for the low-use area.

An informal check of water quality by the Superior National Forest that essentially repeated King's 1970 study on the Moose Lake chain was made in the late 1980s. Water samples were analyzed for fecal coliform bacteria for samples taken near campsites and also from midlake. The results were similar to King's. The near-campsite waters tested somewhat above drinking-water standards, whereas those from midlake met the standard (Robert Berrisford, Superior National Forest hydrologist, personal communication, 1991).

If activities at campsites are in fact the cause of elevated coliform counts, the actual sources remain unknown. Possible human sources include swimming, bathing in the lake, washing clothing in the lake, and seepage from Forest Service pit toilets. The latter source is unlikely at most sites because toilet pits are usually well back from the lake in suitable soils. It is encouraging to know that despite the very heavy recreational use of lakes like those on the Moose Lake chain, water from the middle of the lake still meets drinking-water standards for coliform bacteria.

There was concern in the late 1960s that phosphates in detergents used by campers for washing dishes and clothing might add nutrients to lakes, eventually causing eutrophication and unnaturally high algal blooms. King's study did find somewhat elevated phosphate levels and increased turbidity near campsites. However, the use of phosphates in detergents has since been drastically curtailed by federal and state regulations, and that problem is under control. The other variables studied showed no effects from campsite use (King and Mace 1974; Merriam et al. 1973).

The intestinal flagellate parasite *Giardia lamblia*, which causes abdominal problems in humans, may be present in some Boundary Waters lakes and streams. The disease caused by this organism, called giardiasis, is endemic in most of eastern Europe and Asia, where humans are acclimated to it and rarely show symptoms. Infection can occur from drinking water containing only a few *Giardia* cysts.

It may have been introduced to the Boundary Waters after World War II, for it is also established in many other wilderness areas in the United States and Canada. *Giardia* is difficult to detect in lake water, and as of 1991, its distribution in the Boundary Waters was still poorly understood (Robert Berrisford, Superior National Forest hydrologist, personal communcation, 1991; Joan Rose, University of Arizona, unpublished research). Other mammals, notably beaver, muskrat, coyote, dog (and possibly wolf), cat, deer, and wading aquatic birds are hosts, but their involvement in transmitting the disease to humans is unclear (Spofford 1986). *Giardia* cysts are most likely to be present near lakeshores and in small shallow ponds and streams. The incidence of giardiasis was low among BWCAW visitors in the 1980s. Only 7 to 21 cases per year were reported in the BWCAW counties of St. Louis, Lake, and Cook between 1982 and 1989 (Minn. Dept. of Health, n.d.). Nevertheless, prudence dictates that visitors treat drinking water before use. Water obtained from the middle of large deep lakes is most likely to be free of both *Giardia* and unsafe levels of coliform bacteria. The U.S. Forest Service recommends obtaining water from midlake and treating all drinking and cooking water by boiling or other approved means.

In the long run the greatest threats to water quality in the Boundary Waters may come not from wilderness campers but from airborne toxins such as mercury, pesticides, and some industrial chemicals or their by-products; acid precipitation; and urban and domestic sewage generated by communities, homes, and businesses around the perimeter of the areas. In addition, seepage of heavy metals and other toxic materials from mine dumps, tailings basins, abandoned open pits, and other facilities would be major threats if sulfide-bearing deposits are mined for copper, nickel, or gold within the watersheds of the wilderness areas.

Mitigation of Impacts and Campsite Management

Wilderness researchers and managers have responded to the challenge of deteriorating campsites by developing a sophisticated program of assessing campsite conditions and taking corrective actions. The foundation of these programs is the Limits of Acceptable Change (LAC) concept for wilderness planning developed by a group of researchers working with the U.S. Forest Service's Wilderness Management Research Unit (Stankey et al. 1985) and embraced by both the U.S. Forest Service and National Park Service (Marion, Cole, and Reynolds 1985). The core of this concept is recognition that management programs should be based on clearly stated objectives involving limits to changes in wilderness ecosystem resources and in visitors' social and psychological experiences that can be measured objectively against field conditions (Stankey, McCool, and Stokes 1990).

Briefly, the LAC planning and management process involves nine steps (Stankey, McCool, and Stokes 1990):

1 Identify issues and concerns.
2 Define and describe Opportunity Classes (for the BWCAW these were tentatively identified as primitive, semiprimitive nonmotorized, and semiprimitive motorized).
3 Select measurable indicators of resource and social conditions.
4 Inventory existing resource and social conditions.
5 Specify standards for resource and social indicators.
6 Identify alternative opportunity-class allocations; decide which standards might apply to specific areas.
7 Identify management actions for each alternative.
8 Evaluate and select alternatives.
9 Implement actions and monitor conditions.

The Superior National Forest began applying the LAC process to social, campsite, and other resource conditions in the BWCAW in 1989 and has already taken the process through step four for campsites (Lime 1991). A complete inventory of all 2,000 approved Forest Service campsites in the BWCAW was accomplished in 1989–90 with objectively measured criteria to establish current conditions and to provide a factual basis for setting standards in step five. The nine condition indicators measured in the inventory at each campsite and the average values for all 2,000 approved Forest Service campsites are shown in table 15.4.

A permanent computerized database contains these data for each campsite, identified by site number, lake where located, and the lake's area. This and other databases on campsites, water bodies, and the terrestrial system have recently been incorporated in a geographical information system (GIS). The Forest Service has on file detailed instructions for measuring each variable. In addition a card-file record for each campsite, begun some years earlier, contains maps and other historical data. The LAC process calls for monitoring changes in conditions, and the plan is to remeasure the campsites at some standard interval, perhaps 8 or 10 years.

Monitoring BWCAW campsites and rehabilitating or closing severely degraded sites was recognized as essential long before the LAC planning process was adopted. The Superior National Forest began such a program in 1975. Campsites are often "rehabilitated" by field personnel trained in such work. Helpful actions include the following:

- Place rocks, soil, and organic matter in eroding areas to stop or divert water running across bare soil.
- Place boulders or large down trees so that they close off eroding multiple lakeshore landings and restrict visitor traffic to a single landing and path to the campsite across bedrock or other less erodible ground. Plant native trees or shrubs in closed-off areas.
- Place large boulders or down trees around the campsite perimeter in locations where they will prevent campsite expansion. Plant native trees and shrubs near the campsite perimeter close to logs, dead trees, or boulders where visitors cannot trample them.
- Move the fire grate/fireplace onto bedrock near the front of the campsite to confine heavy traffic to nonerodible ground and to limit the size of high-use areas.
- Establish two good elevated tent pads in favorable spots and eliminate undesirable tent sites with large boulders or down trees.

This campsite program was developed by Paul Smith, retired backcountry manager, Superior National Forest (Marion and Sober 1987; James Hinds, Wilderness Management Specialist, Superior National Forest, personal communication, 1991).

Another means of reducing BWCAW campsite impacts is to reduce quotas on entry points that feed the most heavily used routes. These routes generally have the most heavily used campsites as well as the highest density of campsites. Such a move might retard the long-term trend

Table 15.4 / Average values of condition indicators for 2,000 Forest Service campsites

Condition indicator	Average value
Shoreline disturbance (lineal feet)	18
Campsite area (square feet)	2,712
Nonvegetated area (square feet)	1,777
Exposed mineral soil (square feet)	772
Trees damaged (number)	9
Total trees (number)	28
Trees with roots exposed (number)	9
Trails leading from site (number)	3
Erosion level (3-step rating scale)	2

Sources Marion (1991); James Hinds, Superior National Forest, personal communication, 1991.

toward an end point when many campsites will become essentially barren, nearly treeless open areas. At the same time, the quality of visitors' experiences on these routes would improve. Except for their excessive use, these routes cross some of the finest wilderness in the BWCAW. This approach would be self-defeating, however, if more visitors are shifted to lightly used entry points. Then there would be virtually nowhere in the entire BWCAW where visitors could find campsites in good condition. A significant reduction in total use can be achieved by reducing use on the most heavily affected areas while holding use in the remainder of the wilderness at current levels. Such a move would protect campsites and shoreline ecosystems, to say nothing of visitor experiences.

Visitor Impacts on Portages and Trails

Portages and trails in the BWCAW were generally in good to fairly good condition in 1993. In Quetico the portages on lightly used routes were mostly in good condition, but on heavily used routes in the Hunter Island region some portages are badly eroded.

A portage or trail in the Boundary Waters requires only a path through the forest with a cleared width of 4 or 5 feet and an actual tread way less than 2 feet wide. The most pleasing routes wind around large trees and boulders, where present, and climb or descend ridges with winding switch-backs. The only construction required on most segments is the clearing out of smaller trees, brush, and down timber, removal of small rocks directly in the path, and occasional shovel work in low spots to elevate the path a bit and provide a durable surface with some drainage. For steep slopes, water bars consisting of partially buried rocks or logs are angled across the path to divert water that tends to run down the path. Ideally, portages and trails should go around wetlands. Two half logs laid side by side on top of cross logs, repeated as often as required, were frequently used on the softest and wettest segments in the BWCAW until recently. Now a minimum of such work is done, but where heavy traffic on very wet mucky peat justifies it, two parallel treated planks spiked onto treated cross logs are used. In the backcountry, and especially in Quetico, many bog and swamp crossings have little work of that type. In many areas of the BWCAW the portages were originally built to a higher standard than that described here, by the Civilian Conservation Corps or by subsequent Forest Service crews. In Quetico most portages have never had significant construction work other than tree and brush removal from the tread way and enough clearing to permit passage of canoes between trees.

Once a portage is opened, use will keep it open, and little maintenance is required except for removing occasional large windfalls or repairing serious erosion. Portage and trail maintenance consists simply of cutting out windfalls (with bow saws and axes in the BWCAW), repairing or replacing water bars as needed, shoveling some dirt or gravel onto occasional soft or eroded spots in the tread way, and replacing rotten logs with treated planks on bog crossings. The only areas where somewhat higher standards may be needed are heavily used portages near entry points where foot traffic wears down the tread way. There a graveled tread way with simple drainage and water bars may be needed to maintain a path that will not become an eroding quagmire or boulder field.

In Quetico most of these measures have not been taken, even on heavily used routes. The lack of construction or main-tenance is really no problem as long as truly large wind-falls are periodically cut out. Visitors cut out or go around small down trees, and if traffic is light enough, the lack of drainage, fill, and water bars on the tread way causes few problems. Many backcountry portages still have some vegetation on the tread way that helps prevent erosion. On heavily used portages, erosion of the tread way is gradually turning many Quetico portages into fields of boulders, occasional muddy pools, and steep slopes with loose gravel, rock, and large boulders. The portage from Meadows Lake to Agnes is an example.

The damage to the total wilderness ecosystem from heavily traveled, eroded portages is miniscule, but the impact on visitors' experiences is significant. One result is an in-evitable widening of the tread way and of the total affected area as visitors seek safe paths around boulders and wet places. Repair and reconstruction of such portages, if under-taken, will probably be more costly than maintenance might have been.

Effects of Fish, Game, Berry, and Rice Harvests

The harvests of deer, moose, bear, ducks, grouse, and fur-bearers by visitors in the BWCAW and Quetico may not be much higher now than were those by Native Americans before the arrival of European peoples, both because of game and trapping regulations and because of the diffi-culty of access to most of the wilderness. Moose and deer are no more abundant in Quetico where they are not hunt-ed than in the BWCAW where they are. The taking of deer, moose, and beaver probably does reduce the biomass of prey available to wolves, however. No quantitative analyses of such an effect exist for the whole BWCAW, but some potential wolf food is exported from the ecosystem. Other species dependent on carrion, such as ravens, eagles, vul-tures, and several mammals, must also be affected to a degree. Visitors at times disturb eagles, osprey, loons, and other sensitive birds and mammals, but at this time they are probably not causing major impacts on any species.

Harvests of wild rice are carefully regulated, and there is little indication of a decline in its abundance. Nutrients are exported from the ecosystem, of course. The amount of rice available as food for waterfowl may be reduced significantly in some areas. Berry harvests are small, but blueberry picking around the perimeter of the BWCAW may very well reduce the supply available to bears. The significance of the blueberry reduction to the bear population is unknown.

The taking of fish by visitors clearly has a major impact on the aquatic ecosystems of the BWCAW, Quetico, and Voyageurs. One effect is the export of biomass of fish from the ecosystem. The removal of a large food and energy resource clearly affects the lake and stream ecosystems in significant but complex ways. A second effect is the differential mortality imposed on various fish species and age classes by the selective removal of a few species (primarily walleye, lake trout, northern pike, and smallmouth bass). In the BWCAW the fishery is heavily exploited in lakes such as Basswood, Big Trout, Saganaga, Sea Gull, Lac La Croix, and Snowbank. In such lakes the balance among fish species is certainly under heavy human control. Lake trout populations particularly have been dwindling for decades (see chapter 14). Important questions are, how many person hours of fishing effort per acre per year can each lake tolerate without unacceptable impacts on the structure and species composition of its fish population, and how do such impacts relate to entry-point quotas for specific entry points?

The Impact of Visitor-Caused Forest Fires

Visitor-caused fires are mostly escaped campsite or lunch-stop fires and almost always occur along lakeshores or on islands. These are the very places where the frequency of stand-replacing crown fires was the lowest before European settlement (chapter 6). The frequency of human ignitions on such sites has increased far more than in the backcountry away from lakes. Camper fires seem to be preferentially in older red and white pine stands near campsites. If such fires only caused underburns and rarely killed the old pines, they might replicate many of the fires that brought in new age classes of red and white pine before European settlement. However, many of them crown and kill most or all of the old pines, perhaps because fire control has kept fire

out of most of these old shoreline and island pine forests for nearly a century, and they have now developed thick litter layers as well as understories of balsam fir, spruce, and cedar that act as ladder fuels to induce crowning in the overstory pines. Fires of this kind undoubtedly occurred in the past. But, if fuels have been unnaturally augmented by fire exclusion, and if the incidence of such fires is unnaturally high, a disproportionate share of old red and white pine stands could be lost at the very time when their abundance in the area has been drastically reduced by logging. All camper fires in these old shoreline pine stands should be suppressed, especially those that occur in conditions severe enough to induce crowning. Management-ignited light underburns should be used to reduce heavy fuels to levels more like those thought to have existed before European settlement. Then, when a lightning ignition does occur during a real drought, the probability is higher that sufficient red or white pine seed trees will survive to reproduce the stand, just as they did in presettlement times.

Other rare shoreline and island forest communities possibly threatened by the high incidence of camper fires include very old white cedar and spruce-fir-cedar communities. Such communities are probably there simply because fire rarely visited the sites. Some may not have burned for 200 to 300 years. It would be tragic to allow visitor-caused fires to reduce the shoreline and island diversity that the communities represent.

Visitor Information and Education Programs

Many visitors lack the needed information to choose the routes and areas within a wilderness that best meet their trip objectives (Lime and Lucas 1977; Bright and Manfredo 1989). They may select the same heavily traveled routes that others do simply because such routes are better known or they have used them before or because outfitters have recommended them. Well-planned visitor information campaigns can influence visitor distribution, but the managers' objectives must be clear, and poorly planned efforts can be ineffective or even self-defeating (Lime and Lucas 1977; Lucas 1981).

Managers must first decide whether they simply wish to help visitors make route choices that meet their expectations and capabilities, or if they hope to change visitor distribution patterns in ways that will reduce undesirable visitor concentrations, campsite impacts, and conflicts, perhaps on specific lakes or routes. To be effective, information must reach visitors before they make route decisions, and it must reach a large segment of the potential users of the area (Lime and Lucas 1977). For a heavily visited wilderness like the BWCAW, simply redistributing use from heavily to lightly used routes may not be a sensible objective. If successful, the redistribution might just spread impacts to more campsites and fish populations, bring excessive visitor encounters, and destroy the solitude of the remaining areas where high-quality wilderness experiences are still available. We already know that up to three-fourths of longtime BWCAW visitors and even many beginners change routes because of depreciative behavior of others, wilderness resource degradation, litter, and excessive encounters, especially with large groups and motorboaters (Anderson 1980, 1981; Lime and Lewis 1992).

From the standpoint of campsite impact, the real problem may simply be that already too many feet are pounding the campsites and using the resources of the whole area. Moving those impacts around may only mean that more areas will become severely degraded. If this is the problem, then information programs geared to shifting use must be carefully planned only to steer visitors away from a few "choke points" where visitor concentrations are intolerable. The programs must be coupled with steps to reverse the increase in total visitor use before wilderness resources and visitors' experiences are damaged further.

Visitor education programs hold much promise for helping visitors appreciate the natural ecosystem and minimize their impacts on campsites and other natural resources. The Forest Service and cooperating outfitters have for many years used visitor contacts at BWCAW permit-issuing stations to inform users of the rules and regulations to protect the ecosystem, using verbal explanations, displays, and picture books. A slide tape on minimum-impact camping also has been used to help new users and large groups under-stand the value of thoughtful wilderness behavior. Posters carry similar messages at entry points (Soderberg 1987).

In the mid-1980s the Superior National Forest experimented with a BWCAW User Education Program of direct off-site contacts in advance of trips with users in urban areas, including the Twin Cities, from which 40 percent of all overnight groups came in 1990. Among the approaches tried was an intensive four-hour training course in minimum-impact camping and wilderness ethics designed by volunteers and presented by BWCAW managers with volunteer help (Soderberg 1987). The course, taught at nature centers, schools, camps, outfitters, stores, conferences, and workshops, was intended to reach the leaders of the youth, church, and other organizational groups because these large groups were believed to cause greater impacts on campsites and other resources than small groups. It was also hoped that leaders would pass on their new knowledge of wilderness ethics to group members, multiplying the number of visitors reached. Evaluators of the program found that participants had significantly improved knowledge, attitudes, intended behavior, and beliefs concerning minimum-impact camping, both immediately after the course and three months later (Jones 1987; Jones and McAvoy 1987; Schomaker 1990).

New efforts by nonprofit outdoor and environmental groups, outfitters, and the Forest Service are being developed to inform users through video programs and other modern media (McAvoy, Schatz, and Lime 1991). If they reach enough visitors, such programs should help considerably to reduce campsite expansion, tree damage, litter, escaped campfires, excessive use of firewood, and wood gathering near campsites. They should also help minimize impacts from new campsites in the Primitive Management Areas of the BWCAW and in lightly used areas in Quetico, where users still camp on sites not previously used.

Such programs cannot prevent the inevitable impact of excessive numbers of visitors. If too many people use wilderness areas, minimum-impact camping techniques and good behavior, even if practiced by all visitors, simply cannot eliminate the effects of too many feet on lakeshore, portage, and trailside ecosystems. There must be upper limits on use levels, or all the good intentions and educational programs will come to little.

Early in 1994, the Superior National Forest began implementing a new BWCAW management plan after an environmental impact statement. The plan will reduce the visitor-group size limit from 10 to 9 persons (and limit the number of watercraft per group to 4), operate the visitor distribution program at 67 percent campsite occupancy (instead of 85 percent), reduce entry-point quotas on some routes, and maintain approximately 2,000 campsites. The plan might finally halt the 40-year trend of growing visitor impacts on the ecosystem and on visitors' experiences.

Tomorrow's Wilderness

What does the future hold for the Boundary Waters ecosystem? It is clouded with many new uncertainties traceable to human activities. Nature is never static, and we cannot reasonably expect to restore an ecosystem to an exact replica of its status at some specific point in the past. We have only recently begun to recognize the many complex human impacts on the natural ecosystems of the Boundary Waters on both regional and local scales. A growing number of new global forces may alter all natural systems at rates unprecedented in the history of our planet. The future of natural landscapes is literally in human hands.

Two possible paths are seen. One is straight and familiar, involving few turns not already taken, but it leads inexorably to the disintegration of the natural ecosystems of the Boundary Waters region as we currently know them. The other is a long, difficult, and winding path never followed before.

People had a role in the ecosystem through most of postglacial time; the first Americans lived within the natural system as consumers with only modest impacts on ecosystem processes and functioning until late in the fur trade era. Within the last 150 years, however, humans have begun to influence some of the most basic factors that life depends on—the chemical composition of the atmosphere, temperature, rainfall, storminess, fire, nutrient cycling, and lakewater chemistry—to say nothing of our vastly increased ability to fell the forests and harvest the fish and wildlife.

To understand the possible futures for the Boundary Waters ecosystem, we must look in a more organized fashion at what we are doing to the total system. Perhaps we can then see how tomorrow's wilderness might still be as beautiful, challenging, and rewarding for our children as it has been for us.

The Threat of Global Climate Change

Perhaps the most pervasive changes in the Boundary Waters ecosystem are posed by the so-called "greenhouse effect." A formal foundation for greenhouse theory was set out in 1896 by the Swedish scientist Arrhenius, who calculated that a doubling of atmospheric carbon dioxide should warm the earth 5°C (9°F) (Ramanathan 1988). Several trace gases emitted to the atmosphere at increasing rates by human activities absorb the sun's infrared heat-producing rays and reradiate much of that heat back to earth. This has been dubbed the "greenhouse effect." The most abundant and effective of these gases are carbon dioxide (CO_2), methane, nitrous oxide, and ozone. Chlorofluorocarbons (CFCs) also contribute to surface warming by destroying the stratospheric ozone layer, allowing more radiation to reach the ground, where it is trapped by greenhouse gases in the lower atmosphere. Most of the world's atmospheric scientists believe that the buildup of these gases will produce significant global climatic changes at rates unprecedented

Table 16.1 / Predicted changes in eastern North American temperatures and precipitation, and predicted BWCAW temperatures and precipitation in 2100, based on three global climate models

	Parameter	GISS model	GFDL model	OSU model
Predicted changes in mean temperature and precipitation, eastern North America, by 2100	January temperature (°F)	+11.7	+12.2	+8.1
	July temperature (°F)	+5.4	+11.5	+6.1
	Annual precipitation (in.)	+2.2	+1.9	+2.7
Predicted BWCAW mean temperatures and precipitation in 2100	January temperature (°F)	13.7	14.2	10.1
	July temperature (°F)	71.4	77.5	72.1
	Annual precipitation (in.)	28.2	27.9	28.7

Note Calculated from data in Overpeck, Bartlein, and Webb (1991), assuming doubled greenhouse gases, based on three general circulation model scenarios for eastern North America. The climate models are NASA's GISS; Geophysics Fluid Dynamics Laboratory (GFDL) of NOAA; and Oregon State University (OSU). Expected 2100 BWCAW temperatures and precipitation assume predicted increases for eastern North America are valid for BWCAW. They were calculated by adding the increases to existing means from Baker and Kuehnast (1978) and Baker, Kuehnast, and Zandlo (1985).

Table 16.2 / Predicted changes in central North American temperatures and precipitation, and predicted BWCAW temperatures in 2030, based on three global climate models

	Parameter	CCC model	GFDL model	UKMO model
Predicted changes in mean temperature and precipitation, central North America, by 2030	Winter temperature (°F)	+7.2	+3.6	+7.2
	Summer temperature (°F)	+3.6	+3.6	+5.4
	Winter precipitation (%)	0	+15	+10
	Summer precipitation (%)	−5	−5	−10
Predicted BWCAW mean temperatures in 2030	Winter temperature (°F)	14.2	10.6	14.2
	Summer temperature (°F)	66.6	66.6	68.4

Note Calculated from data in Karl, Heim, and Quayle (1991), based on three global climate models, assuming greenhouse gas emissions are not controlled. The climate models are Canadian Climate Centre (CCC); Geophysics Fluid Dynamics Laboratory of NOAA (GFDL); and United Kingdom Meterological Office (UKMO). The BWCAW is near the northeastern edge of the regions covered by these models. The estimates were scaled to correspond to a mean global warming of 1.8°C (3.2°F) for 2030. Winter and summer predicted mean temperatures for 2030 were obtained by adding present winter and summer means from Baker, Kuehnast, and Zandlo (1985) to the estimated winter and summer increases from Karl, Heim, and Quayle (1991). Winter = Dec., Jan., Feb; Summer = June, July, Aug.

since the Ice Age unless immediate steps are taken to reverse the trend. We are inadvertently conducting a grand global-scale physical and chemical experiment to determine if Arrhenius was right (Ramanathan 1988).

General circulation models (GCMs) are used to simulate the effects of increased greenhouse gases on global and regional climates. With doubled greenhouse gases, Overpeck, Bartlein, and Webb (1991) predict that January temperatures would increase in eastern North America by 8.1°

to 12.2°F (table 16.1), implying winter temperatures in the BWCAW similar to those today along the Minnesota-Iowa border. July increases of 5.4° to 11.5°F imply BWCAW summers as warm as those now experienced somewhere between eastern Nebraska and the Twin Cities. Mean annual precipitation would also increase, but only by 2 or 3 inches. Such changes would produce a BWCAW climate in 2100 like that a bit west of Mason City, Iowa, today. In that area the pre–European settlement vegetation was tallgrass prairie on the uplands and wet prairie and marsh on poorly drained soils, with scattered oak groves on the uplands and with cottonwood, box elder, willow, elm, and ash along streams (Marschner 1930; Heinselman 1974). Some models predict that summer precipitation will decrease over central North America, perhaps making summer droughts even stronger than would the scenarios just outlined (Karl, Heim, and Quayle 1991).

How rapidly might these changes occur? Based on the three models discussed by Karl, Heim, and Quayle (1991) (table 16.2), winter temperatures predicted for the BWCAW for 2030 would be similar to those experienced from 1950 to 1980 at Mille Lacs Lake, the Twin Cities, or Rochester. Summer temperatures would be like those between 1950 and 1980 in Pine City or Brainerd. Winter snowfall might be the same as or 10 to 15 percent heavier than in the recent past, but summers would see 5 to 10 percent less rainfall, and when combined with higher temperatures, the moisture available for plants would be substantially less than in the 1950–80 era. These may not seem like large changes, but such predicted changes within just 40 years are unprecedented in the previous thousands of years.

What evidence is there that such changes are under way? Detailed analyses of central North American climate records for the years 1895 to 1989 indicate that temperatures had increased and precipitation had decreased by small amounts in both winter and summer. Weather is so variable from year to year that the changes were not yet statistically significant. The inherent variability of climate means that we cannot be sure until 2000 or 2010 that the temperature changes predicted in tables 16.1 and 16.2 are occurring. For precipitation we may not be sure until 2030 (Karl, Heim, and Quayle 1991). By then it may be very late to take corrective action.

GROWTH RESPONSES OF PLANTS TO CARBON DIOXIDE LEVELS

What do we know about the probable effects of global climatic change on the biotic components of the Boundary Waters ecosystem?

Photosynthesis is a temperature-dependent process driven by the sun's energy and is the source of all life. Green plants, using the sun's radiant energy mediated by their chlorophyll, synthesize the initial organic constituents of all living matter from the carbon dioxide of the atmosphere, water, nitrogen, and many elements derived from the mineral soil. Plants are the producers of the real world. All animals, from the one-celled paramecium to moose, wolves, and humans, ultimately depend on green plants. The atmosphere, the water derived from the oceans as rain or snow, and the mineral elements thus furnish the basic building materials for all plants and animals.

These climatic changes resulting from increased CO_2 will affect photosynthesis and plant growth in several ways. Increased atmospheric CO_2 directly increases rates of photosynthesis in most plants, including at least some species of spruce and pine and many broadleaf trees such as oaks. The increase in turn depends on temperature, and most plants show increases in photosynthesis only above 64°F. Thus the growth rates of many plants may be enhanced somewhat with doubled CO_2 if temperature or water availability does not limit responses. Water-use efficiency also increases somewhat with increased CO_2. Some plants become acclimated to increased CO_2 and show decreasing response rates with time, whereas others show no acclimation. These effects are known chiefly from laboratory experiments and vary widely with species. Little is known about the effects of long-term exposure of wild vegetation to increased CO_2 levels, or about the additional effects on decomposition, nutrient balance, and competition among plant species (Mooney et al. 1991). Thus we still know relatively little about what ecosystem-level changes might be caused by the effects of increased CO_2 on plant growth.

HOW MIGHT BOUNDARY WATERS FORESTS RESPOND TO RAPID CLIMATIC CHANGE?

What is known about the ability of Boundary Waters trees, shrubs, and herbs or their potential replacement species to respond to the rapid climatic changes predicted with global warming? To grasp the dimensions of this question, we first need to consider the kinds of vegetation changes and range movements by trees and other plants implied by the climate scenarios we have discussed, shown in tables 16.1 and 16.2.

Because the Boundary Waters region lies along the transition (ecotone) between the boreal forest and Great Lakes–Saint Lawrence forest regions, most plants in the Boundary Waters are near the southern or northern limit of their natural ranges. Many boreal trees, shrubs, and herbs are at early risk because plants near their southern limit will probably be the first to feel the effects of rising temperatures and changed precipitation patterns (Davis and Zabinski 1992). New seedlings of some species are generally more vulnerable than adults, but adults might die from increased drought severity or frequency, or perhaps from winter killing of needles due to excessive temperature fluctuations above and below freezing. Changed frequencies of such key disturbance factors as fire, windstorms, or insect defoliation might also be critical. Sooner or later such species would disappear.

Average July isotherms roughly parallel the southern limits of most boreal trees from Minnesota to the Atlantic Ocean and are rough estimators of their present climatic limits. For example, natural stands of black and white spruce, balsam fir, and balsam poplar are rare beyond the 70°F July average isotherm. In Minnesota this isotherm runs from Chisago County west-northwestward to just south of Mille Lacs Lake and thence to just north of Fargo, North Dakota. Natural stands of not only spruce and fir but also tamarack, northern white cedar, and paper birch are rare south of that line. At about Detroit Lakes, however, precipitation becomes limiting, and the western limits of these trees turn northward, passing into Manitoba about 40 miles east of North Dakota. The three GCM scenarios for 2100 shown in table 16.1 predict July means well above 70°F. Under these scenarios, we must expect that black and white spruce, balsam fir, and balsam poplar will not survive indefinitely in the climate predicted for the Boundary Waters region by 2100. The temperature tolerances of jack pine, tamarack, northern white cedar, paper birch, and trembling aspen are slightly higher, but their abundances would apparently decrease dramatically under those climate-warming scenarios. Red pine and black ash are Great Lakes forest species, but they are limited by about

the 71°F and 73°F July isotherms respectively (Fowells 1965) and might also disappear or become rare under all three scenarios.

What trees might replace these? The list of candidates includes sugar maple, red maple, silver maple, box elder, bigtooth aspen, northern red oak, northern pin oak, bur oak, basswood, yellow birch, green ash, and white pine. These species now occur within portions of the Boundary Waters region or within 20 or 30 miles to the south along Lake Superior's north-shore highlands. All now have populations within or very close to the temperature and precipitation ranges forecast by the climate models. Species found farther south and east, such as eastern cottonwood, white ash, ironwood, and several species of oak and hickory, might eventually colonize the area. Of the present abundant boreal trees, only quaking aspen might have a chance if their present temperature and precipitation tolerances are valid predictors.

How do these speculations square with vegetation and climate modeling by ecologists studying the potential effects of greenhouse warming in central North America? Different approaches to modeling the effect of climatic change on forests of the Boundary Waters region or adjacent areas all lead to similar conclusions. A doubling of CO_2 is predicted to cause the upland boreal tree species to die out and be replaced by oak savanna or possibly by stunted oak with scattered white or jack pine on the vast majority of upland sites (Pastor and Post 1988; Botkin, Nisbet, and Reynales 1989; Overpeck, Bartlein, and Webb 1991; Botkin and Nisbet 1992; Davis and Zabinski 1992). The present stately groves of tall red and white pine and vast upland spruce-fir forests would disappear because of drought stress; on moderately moist sites, where water stress is less likely, sugar maple and yellow birch would be likely dominants. The present bog and swamp forests of black spruce, tamarack, and northern white cedar might become treeless sedge and grass meadows. These conclusions also closely match my analysis of the likely outcome based on what we know of the present ranges and climatic tolerances of the existing tree species. The timescale for such changes varies with the models and investigators, but all predict that by at least 2100, the climate would be driving the forests toward such compositional changes, and some predict that noticeable changes will occur by 2030 unless greenhouse gas emissions are sharply reduced very soon.

CAN PLANTS RESPOND FAST ENOUGH TO TRACK CLIMATIC CHANGE?

What we know about the rates and patterns of plant movements in Minnesota in response to the climatic changes of the past 16,000 years must give us pause. The climatic changes projected for doubled CO_2 by 2100 would require plant responses several times more rapid than those that occurred over most of postglacial time. The postglacial pollen record shows that each tree species moved at its own pace, each encountering different factors that changed its rates of movement in various areas over time (Davis 1981, 1989a, 1989b, 1990; Davis and Zabinski 1992). This finding is surely true as well for most shrubs and herbs. The greenhouse climate may present a fast-moving target to migrating plants. Species still adapted 50 years from now might be in trouble in a century if the climate changes as dramatically as models suggest.

Sugar maple would have to move northward 25 to 50 miles to populate the BWCAW in any abundance, as much as 80 miles to populate all of Quetico, and 500 miles to occupy all of its projected new range west of Hudson Bay (Davis and Zabinski 1992). Basswood would have similar problems. Yellow birch, now rare but present in much of the BWCAW, is very rare or absent in most of Quetico. It might find a more favorable climate, at least at first, but it would have to increase very rapidly to become a significant element in the new forests. Northern red oak, northern pin oak, and bur oak now have modest presence in the western BWCAW and Voyageurs but are very rare or absent in much of the eastern BWCAW and in most of Quetico, except in the southwest from Basswood Lake to Lac La Croix. Yet these are the trees that may soon be best adapted to the new climate of the entire area if we do not move quickly to reduce greenhouse gas emissions.

How fast can trees expand their ranges or sparse local populations without human aid? The fastest documented movement is 125 miles per century for spruce, which moved rapidly into northwestern Canada 9,000 years ago (Davis and Zabinski 1992). Both white and black spruce have very light wind-dispersed seeds, and black spruce bears viable seed when 10 to 15 years old. In contrast, the oaks, beech, and hickories bear seeds in heavy nuts dispersed to a distance only by birds such as jays or by mammals such as squirrels. For beech, whose migration rates have been carefully studied, the postglacial dispersal rate is about 12 miles per century (Davis and Zabinski 1992). Similar rates for the oaks can be expected. The minimum age for seed production in bur oak is about 35 years, in red oak 25 years. Good production begins at about 50 years in many oaks, and good acorn years occur every 2 to 5 years. Sugar maple seeds (winged samaras) are fairly heavy and do not disperse readily over long distances. Light seed crops begin when trees reach ages of 40 to 60 years; good production begins at 70 to 100 years. Good seed crops occur at 2- to 5-year intervals (Fowells 1965).

These life history traits suggest that occupation of potential new ranges in the Boundary Waters region by sugar maple and the oaks could require centuries unless aided by people. Red maple, which already has a fairly good presence in much of the region and might remain adapted to the projected climates, would probably be in a better position to expand its populations quickly. Quaking aspen and bigtooth aspen might still be marginally adapted to the new climate, at least early in the warming era, and their very light wind-dispersed seeds make them good candidates to occupy new open areas that may appear with death of the boreal conifers.

Another problem that makes prediction of vegetation changes under greenhouse warming uncertain is the likely existence of climatically specialized "ecotypes" in some tree species, and perhaps in shrubs and herbs as well. Adaptations to specific combinations of day length and temperature regimes have been demonstrated in several tree species, for example. Even though a species grew south of the BWCAW in climates similar to the new BWCAW climate and has populations in the BWCAW, those local BWCAW populations might not be adapted to the new climate. Such variation occurs in jack pine, but little is known about the situation for most species. Present patterns of ecotypic variation have developed over millennia through gradual genetic changes within species, but the projected climatic changes for the next century are far too fast for evolution to keep pace (Davis and Zabinski 1992).

HOW WOULD CHANGED DISTURBANCE REGIMES INFLUENCE THE ECOSYSTEM?

If greenhouse warming occurs as predicted, and if precipitation increases very little or even decreases in summer as many models project, major changes are foreseen in fire regimes. As the climate warms, two factors will interact simultaneously to increase the probability of more frequent, higher-intensity, and perhaps larger forest fires. First, the precipitation-evaporation balance will shift to a climate with lower effective moisture for plant growth. Soil-moisture reserves will be exhausted earlier in the summer, and when droughts come, they will probably be more protracted and more severe. Soil organic layers and surface litter will be dried to critical levels more frequently and for longer periods. All living vegetation will be dried to the wilting point more often. Second, as warming progresses, mortality of the existing boreal conifers, red and white pine, and aspen-birch will accelerate, gradually increasing woody fuel loads on much of the landscape.

A third set of factors may also increase the probability of frequent large fires. If the fire rotation is not quickly shortened to provide for stand renewal in large areas of the present extensive jack pine, black spruce, and aspen-birch-fir forests of 1863–64, 1875, 1894, and 1910 origin, the senescence and breakup of these forests will likely coincide with increasing drought and stand mortality due to climatic change. Furthermore, the vast old forests of these species will become increasingly vulnerable to blowdowns, just at a time when the greenhouse climate may be producing a higher incidence of strong windstorms. The spruce budworm, jack pine budworm, bark beetles, and other insects and tree diseases may also find conditions optimal for major outbreaks in these old forests (Botkin, Nisbet, and Reynales 1989; Graham, Turner, and Dale 1990; Davis and Zabinski 1992).

If this scenario develops, there may come a time when all of these factors in conjunction will result in numerous large high-intensity forest fires that will sweep virtually all the old boreal conifer forests of the BWCAW and Quetico in spite of the best fire-control efforts that can be mustered. Most old stands and many younger ones might well burn in high-intensity crown fires between 2050 and 2080. In other words, vast forest fires on scales not seen even before European settlement may be the primary agents of death for the boreal conifers instead of gradual tree-by-tree or selective stand mortality due to drought or increased insect and disease losses triggered by climatic change. The BWCAW and Quetico may see a succession of years like 1988 in Yellowstone. The difference may be that climatic change, not normal drought recurrence, will be responsible.

HOW WOULD SHRUBS, HERBS, GRASSES, MOSSES, AND LICHENS RESPOND TO CLIMATIC CHANGE AND CHANGED FIRE REGIMES?

The feathermosses and many forest herbs depend on a conifer forest overstory cover. In addition, many shrubs, herbs, mosses, and lichens of the BWCAW region are boreal species adapted to cold climates and do not occur much farther south. Many herbs also have relatively heavy seeds and probably could not move northward rapidly enough to track climatic change. Some are relatively rare and are confined to particular habitats, most particularly the steep cliffs of the Rove Formation in the Gunflint Trail area (Coffin and Pfannmuller 1988). These traits, singly or in combination, mean that many understory plants would be severely affected by greenhouse warming and fires that eliminate the boreal conifers and decimate the northern pines. Davis (1990) and Davis and Zabinski (1992) emphasize that such circumstances mean that many herbs and other understory plants face even greater risks of local or regional or even total extinction from global warming than do the trees. Many others would surely be eliminated or become very rare over vast regions if greenhouse gas emissions are not reduced sharply and if warming occurs as rapidly as projected. Many potential new immigrants from southern populations might eventually colonize the Boundary Waters region but could not track the pace of climatic change and might need centuries to achieve substantial populations.

A few more comments may help to show the magnitude of the vegetational changes in store if we fail to control the greenhouse gases. Less is known about the mechanisms or possible rates of dispersal of most understory plants than of the commercially important trees. For most species little is known of their possible climate or habitat tolerances or of probable reactions to the changed plant competition and nutrient situations they may face. Little is known about how to aerial-seed, cultivate, transplant, or otherwise move species that may be in danger of extinction or extirpation (Davis 1989a, 1990; Davis and Zabinski 1992).

The boreal forest and bog plants that might be eliminated or greatly reduced in the Boundary Waters region by doubled CO_2 under the projections of even the conservative climate models are the following:

Mosses	feathermosses
	sphagnum
Lichens	reindeer moss
	old man's beard
Bog shrubs	labrador-tea
	leather-leaf
	bog-laurel
	bog-rosemary
	green alder
Orchids	stemless lady-slipper
	fairy slipper
	dragon's mouth
	ram's-head lady-slipper
	rose pogonia
	dwarf rattlesnake-plantain
Herbs	false Solomon's-seal
	pitcher-plant
	bunchberry
	mountain-cranberry (lingenberry)
	small cranberry
	trailing arbutus
	creeping snowberry
	one-sided pyrola
	pink pyrola

Herbs *(cont.)*	twinflower
	bluebead-lily
	bishop's-cap
	large-leaved aster

This list and the predicted losses of tree species imply major losses in species diversity for both upland and lowland ecosystems or at least major changes in species presence. It is even more difficult than for the trees to guess what new plants might replace the shrubs, herbs, grasses, sedges, mosses, and lichens that would be lost through greenhouse warming. An initial influx of native prairie and European grasses and sedges would be expected, and an increase in European weedy herbs if the large-fires scenario described earlier triggers the shift from the present vegetation to a new greenhouse vegetation. The timing of species losses and new species immigrations is even harder to foresee. If major fires trigger the demise of the boreal species, there could be a period of greatly reduced species diversity, followed by a gradual increase in diversity as new species invade. Deliberate introductions of new species by people could influence both the timing and final composition of the new vegetation. But as long as greenhouse gases continue to rise, the climate may continue to change, keeping the vegetation in constant flux. The introduction of new trees outside the wilderness reserves by foresters to restore forest productivity could also influence the timing and nature of the greenhouse vegetation.

HOW WOULD GREENHOUSE WARMING AFFECT MAMMALS AND BIRDS?

A major reorganization of the mammalian and avian fauna of the Boundary Waters region and of all of north-central North America would be triggered by the climatic and vegetational changes discussed earlier. How rapidly they would respond is difficult to say. Surely within a century or so, and for many species sooner, the boreal species would be displaced far to the north, their places perhaps assumed to some extent by northward migration of southern species.

For example, the moose would probably retreat nearly to Hudson Bay. Woodland caribou, already extirpated from all but a few enclaves in northwestern Ontario, would probably withdraw even farther northward, if they could avoid extinction. The only member of the deer family remaining in the Boundary Waters region would probably be the white-tail, and it is difficult to predict what population levels the new vegetation would support. Beaver should survive, and might even prosper, although it would need to change diets significantly. The wolf might survive if deer and beaver populations remained high enough to support it. The black bear might find its new habitat still acceptable, especially if the oaks became abundant.

Major changes in populations of the smaller mammals would surely occur. The snowshoe hare would probably retreat into Ontario in a century or less, its place perhaps assumed by the cottontail rabbit and possibly even the white-tailed jackrabbit. The forest and bog mice, voles, lemmings, shrews, and bats would face dramatically changed habitats. Several species would shift their ranges northeastward into Ontario. Prairie and deciduous-forest species might move in or increase. The red squirrel would probably become rare or disappear, its place perhaps taken by the gray squirrel. The porcupine might disappear or become rare, especially if the pines and aspen were eliminated. Muskrats would likely increase. The lynx would cease to invade the region, but the bobcat might remain. The red fox should remain, although the gray fox might also become a resident. Coyotes might become common, especially if wolves declined or disappeared. Raccoons might also become common. The pine marten would surely disappear, and the fisher probably would retreat into Canada as well. Mink and otter might remain.

These, then, are some of the changes in mammalian populations that might accompany the climatic and vegetational changes that global warming would produce in the Boundary Waters. The area would no longer be a haven for north woods and boreal forest wildlife. In fact, the north woods as it is known might cease to exist anywhere in North America.

What about the birds? Among the permanent residents, boreal species like the spruce grouse, gray jay, boreal owl, great gray owl, boreal chickadee, and northern three-toed woodpecker would disappear with the passing of the boreal conifer forests. Complex changes in natural ranges and abundance in the Boundary Waters would occur among the present migratory breeding summer residents. The disruption of normal breeding and wintering habitats, and vegetation changes along migration routes would pose major problems for many species. Large population decreases in many species and extinction for some could be expected. Neotropical migrant song birds, such as several warblers that nest primarily from the Boundary Waters region northward into the Canadian and Alaskan boreal forests and winter in the already vanishing tropical rain forests, would be especially at risk.

HOW WOULD GLOBAL WARMING AFFECT THE LAKE AND STREAM ECOSYSTEMS OF THE BOUNDARY WATERS REGION?

The temperature and precipitation changes projected for central North America by the climate models available spell major ecological changes for the lakes and streams of the Boundary Waters. The studies of the Experimental Lakes Area near Kenora, Ontario, by D. W. Schindler and his colleagues (Schindler et al. 1990) provide a well-documented foretaste of what those changes might look like. The study area is about 175 miles northwest of the BWCAW on similar Canadian Shield bedrock terrain. During the course of their studies from 1969 through 1987, the mean annual air temperature in their area increased about 2°C (3.6°F). Years with below-normal precipitation also increased. Decreased snow cover plus warmer March temperatures caused snow on lake ice surfaces to melt earlier than before. In addition, major crown fires denuded the jack pine–spruce forests on the watersheds of some of the study lakes.

These relatively modest changes in temperature and precipitation (compared to projected greenhouse effects), plus the loss of forest cover, caused significant changes in lake environments. Average and maximum lake water temperatures rose about 3.6°F, and the ice-free season increased about three weeks. Increased evaporation from the landscape and lakes and transpiration by plants along with lower precipitation caused dramatic decreases in runoff from the watersheds and lengthened water-renewal times.

Longer renewal times and increased chemical inputs from the burned watersheds concentrated chemical solutes in lake water, notably nitrogen, calcium, and sulfates. Phosphorus at first increased, then declined steeply after 1985, resulting in a doubling of the nitrogen-to-phosphorus ratio from about 25:1 to 50:1. Lake waters also became clearer. These changes caused increases in the standing crops of algae (phytoplankton). Increased lake water temperatures and greater exposure of the lakes to wind from the loss of forest cover caused thermoclines to deepen, causing a decrease in habitat for lake trout, opossum shrimp, and other cold-water species. The thermoclines of lakes with unburned watersheds also deepened, but not so much as in those with burned watersheds (Schindler et al. 1990). Warming and increased chemical concentrations in boreal fresh waters could cause the extirpation of cold-water fish and their food-web base from many waters, thus destroying some of the world's most valuable fisheries.

The lakes of the BWCAW and Quetico are particularly vulnerable to the effects of greenhouse warming because the Boundary Waters region is near the southwestern limit in North America for lakes deep enough and cold enough to support cold-water aquatic organisms, including lake trout and their prey. Many trout lakes are already only marginally deep enough and cold enough to sustain cold-water species. Such lakes might suffer a fatal shrinkage of their area and volume of deep cold waters with the deepening of thermoclines that would accompany climatic warming of even a few degrees Fahrenheit. Greenhouse warming to the extent projected by the climate models cited in tables 16.1 and 16.2 would cause the elimination of such cold-water species as the lake trout, northern cisco, lake whitefish, burbot, and many of their food organisms from most Boundary Waters lakes. Fish adapted to warmer and more fertile waters, such as bass, sunfish, crappie, and probably walleye and northern pike, might still find most of the larger lakes acceptable habitat. But the region would lose a significant element of its aquatic ecosystem diversity.

Such warming would also greatly reduce runoff from the region's watersheds, thereby lowering lake levels and water tables and greatly lowering stream flows. Many presently canoeable small streams and ponds—vital links in the

Boundary Waters labyrinth of canoe routes—would no longer be navigable except perhaps during spring snowmelt.

Managing Boundary Waters Ecosystems for Tomorrow

Here I explore realistic steps and management programs needed to restore and maintain the natural ecosystems of the BWCAW, Quetico, and Voyageurs, recognizing their global and regional contexts. The programs must be implemented mostly through public agencies at the local or regional level. We might like to believe we could restore the ecosystem to its status before European settlement by simply stopping logging of the forests (already done), limiting harvests of fish, wildlife, berries, and wild rice to levels that will not deplete those resources, and perhaps limiting visitor numbers to the carrying capacity. Restoring presettlement conditions is not an achievable goal, because of the dynamic nature of all ecosystems, past damage to the ecosystem, and the probability of some climatic change.

Programs for maintaining and restoring functioning natural ecosystems in harmony with the physical environment can be achieved. Such restored ecosystems would contain as many of the plant, animal, fish, and other species indigenous to the region as possible, at population levels in harmony with the available habitat, leaving the entire system as free as possible from manipulation by managers. Management interventions should be limited to:

- restoring species known to be missing from the system through recent human impacts and thought to be still adapted to the environment
- restoring populations of adapted indigenous species to localities where they recently were abundant but have been virtually eliminated by recent human actions
- controlling or eliminating recently introduced exotic species where this can be accomplished with minimal impact on other species and the environment
- managing visitor numbers and impacts to minimize alteration of the physical environment and populations of indigenous plants and animals
- providing fire management sufficient to protect human life, private property, structures, and forests managed

for timber production outside the wilderness, and to restore forest fire regimes matching as closely as practicable the natural regimes that would prevail in a restored ecosystem without essential fire protection.

The ecosystem resulting from the interaction of the environment with the biota, given these protective and restorative management actions, would be accepted as natural, recognizing that even the physical environment itself has been modified to some degree by human inputs. I will now describe some of the elements that management programs should include.

RESTORING NATURAL FIRE REGIMES

For the forest ecosystems of the Boundary Waters wilderness reserves, no management action is more urgent than restoring natural fire regimes. As seen in earlier chapters, the natural diversity of the patchlike mosaic of forest age classes and vegetation types on the landscape and the habitat for terrestrial wildlife were shaped by periodic fire for millennia. The near exclusion of fire over the past 80 years has tended to homogenize the vegetation of the remaining virgin areas, producing vast contiguous areas of senescent jack pine, black spruce, and aspen-birch-fir forests. Although restoring fire to a fully natural role may not be achievable for many practical reasons, we cannot claim to have accomplished much in restoring natural conditions until major progress is made toward allowing fire to play a more natural role.

Unfortunately, four complicating factors make it harder to define objectives and attain a semblance of natural conditions:

- Some climatic change in the coming century must be anticipated even if catastrophic global warming is avoided.
- Fire-management programs must provide for protecting towns, resorts, isolated homes, and timber-producing forests adjacent to the wilderness areas.
- Lightning-caused ignitions outside the wilderness that under natural conditions might eventually burn large areas within the reserves must be quickly extinguished in most cases.
- The forest vegetation mosaic and fuels complex on the

landscape have been modified by 80 years of nearly successful fire exclusion, in some cases changing probable fire size, expected ecological effects, and other factors.

The managers of all large parks and wilderness areas characterized by fire-dependent forest ecosystems must face the global-warming issue and develop flexible plans that can be changed if a climatic scenario different from that anticipated begins to unfold. Initially it will be wise to plan for modest global warming by about 2050. Particular attention should be given to assuring that excessive fuels in red and white pine stands caused by 80 years of fire exclusion do not produce crown fires that eliminate them. With only modest climatic warming, these two species might well become the best-adapted forest dominants, capable of replacing spruce, fir, jack pine, aspen, and birch on many sites. But if the scattered old stands of red and white pine now present are lost in crown fires that sweep the senescent boreal forests, the seed trees needed for their expansion might be lost. This possibility can be reduced by management-ignited underburning of red and white pine stands with heavy fuel loads in the 1990s and early twenty-first century.

An optimistic but prudent approach to potential climatic change also dictates that the present vast areas of senescent jack pine, spruce, and aspen-birch-fir forests be regenerated by fire at a pace soon approaching a 100-year natural fire rotation. It will be important to allow large areas of these boreal species to burn early in the next century, both because their natural renewal by fire has already been long delayed by fire exclusion and because the potential for large fires will increase with time due to climate warming and continuing fuel buildup. Prescribed natural lightning-ignited fires can be used to the maximum extent feasible. But we must allow for the constraint that some lightning ignitions outside the wilderness will be extinguished that otherwise might burn large areas inside the reserves. Some ignitions inside the reserves will also be suppressed, either because they occur under burning conditions exceeding even new prescriptions matching a 100-year fire rotation or because they threaten to burn areas outside the wilderness. For both ecological reasons and to reduce the likelihood of fires leaving the wilderness, the burn area lost to these constraints must be made up by strategically located management-ignited fires.

Natural adjustments in forest composition to climatic change are more likely if something approaching a natural fire regime can be restored before climatic change produces vast holocausts that cause the extirpation or even extinction of many species. However, we cannot and should not guide the plant and animal responses to renewed fire in the ecosystem. We must simply restore this potent natural environmental factor to the system and let nature dictate the responses.

RESTORING NATURAL VEGETATION TO THE LOGGED AREAS

As noted in several previous chapters, white and red pine were greatly reduced by logging and slash fires, especially in areas cut in the early big-pine logging era. They were once the principal forest dominants on some 25 percent of the land area of the BWCAW. If white and red pine are to be restored to anything approaching their former abundance, it will be necessary to seed or plant these trees in some of the larger areas from which they were eliminated. In the virgin forests these species are still reproducing after fire. Where logging decimated their populations, restoration will be essential. Such restoration work is favored provided the seed sources used come from the BWCAW itself or its immediate perimeter. Small planted patches might be scattered through some of the large early-logging areas where the pines were cut and failed to regenerate. These patches might provide a foothold that someday could lead to their return over much of the BWCAW. Such replanting would be an act of hope and faith to prevent global warming from proceeding so far that all natural vegetation is lost. From an ecological viewpoint and as a practical matter of priorities, we can do little else that might now be effective in restoring the natural forests of the logged areas.

DEALING WITH EXOTIC PLANT INVADERS

There are many Eurasian plants and other exotics that have gained a foothold in the Boundary Waters region. Most were probably introduced via one or more of three routes.

Many plants were brought into the region during the early logging era via the importation of horse and oxen feed, most probably with oats or hay. Such plants are particularly abundant near old logging camps and dray roads, but many are now widespread, especially on land logged in the early era and on recently disturbed land nearby. A second source was the seed or plants brought in either inadvertently or purposely and established at former fly-in or water-accessible private cabins and fishing resorts in the BWCAW and Voyageurs and a few sites in Quetico. A third source was the seed used by the U.S. Forest Service in the BWCAW in the 1960s and 1970s to establish grasses on eroded campsites, portage landings, and along some portages.

The Ahlgrens (1984) reported a total of 92 introduced flowering plants out of a total flora of 817 Boundary Waters species. Grasses were the most abundant exotics at 17 species. There is no possibility now of eradicating such long-established species. A few exotics mentioned by the Ahlgrens, such as lilac, occur only at old resort or cabin sites, where they had been planted by the owners and had not yet spread to nearby wild land. If these plantings have not already died out, the U.S. Forest Service should immediately eradicate them before they escape.

A general policy by managing agencies on newly arriving exotics is needed. Where feasible, such species should be eradicated when detected. If a species arrives along a wide front as part of an already established continental population, eradication is futile. But potentially aggressive new invaders that just happen to become established in small local areas can and should be eradicated before they spread across the landscape. Purple loosestrife is an example of a recently arrived exotic that may escape because action was not taken earlier in northern Minnesota.

PROTECTING AND RESTORING BIRD AND MAMMAL POPULATIONS

The mammal and bird communities of the region still contain a remarkably diverse representation of the species present when European settlement began in the 1880s. To be sure, the passenger pigeon is extinct (it apparently did not nest extensively here), and the peregrine falcon, caribou, wolverine, and cougar are at least temporarily extirpated.

With these exceptions, most species characteristic of the region's fauna before European settlement are present, including several extirpated from most of the contiguous United States, such as the wolf, pine marten, fisher, lynx, loon, and bald eagle. Few invaders have established persistent new populations, an exception being the white-tailed deer in some localities. Bird and mammal populations in many other wilderness areas and national parks have not fared as well.

If we look at population trends and habitat changes, the picture is not so encouraging. Especially alarming is the decline of several neotropical migrant songbirds, part of a hemispheric trend stemming from tropical deforestation and habitat fragmentation in the eastern United States, but largely unrelated to changes in the Boundary Waters. Populations of the black duck and several other waterfowl have declined steeply from earlier years, perhaps mostly from habitat destruction and overhunting elsewhere. Loons, bald eagles, ospreys, mergansers, otter, and mink are in danger from mercury poisoning, although their populations had suffered no major recent declines as of 1992.

The competitive balance between moose and white-tailed deer is tenuous and likely to remain so. Neither species is now abundant in large portions of the BWCAW and Quetico, because of the widespread maturity or senescence of vast areas of boreal jack pine, spruce, and aspen-birch-fir forests due to fire exclusion. This habitat deterioration will only worsen unless an effective program of prescribed natural fires and management-ignited fires is pursued in all three reserves. We should strive to encourage moose rather than deer because the moose was clearly a Boundary Waters native. Deer are abundant elsewhere throughout the eastern United States, whereas moose occur in significant numbers only in far northern Minnesota, on Isle Royale, and in northern New England. Obviously we should also be extremely cautious with hunter harvests in the BWCAW, where the hunting of moose has been allowed.

But the regional balance between deer and moose habitat and the habitat for many other mammals and birds will in the long run also depend on many factors other than fire-management programs, the species and age structure of Boundary Waters wilderness and park forests, and BWCAW

hunting regulations. What happens on the total regional landscape, including millions of acres in Minnesota and Ontario outside these reserves, will ultimately be crucial for many species. Habitat within the 2,400,000 acres of wilderness reserves is vital, but if the surrounding regions are converted to a markedly different vegetation complex, the reserves cannot indefinitely sustain populations of sensitive species. For example, if much of the adjacent forest in Minnesota is committed to short-rotation aspen monocultures in response to the current expansion of the chipboard, oriented-strandboard, and paper industries, there will inevitably be complex regional changes in species abundance and occurrence of mammals and birds affecting the wilderness reserves. Regional biodiversity of the forest habitat must be maintained or the mammalian and avian fauna of the Boundary Waters region will ultimately be impoverished. The unique biotic resources of the Boundary Waters reserves cannot be permanently maintained if these reserves become essentially islands in a sea of drastically altered vegetation and bird and mammal populations. It is particularly important that the forest landscapes of the Superior National Forest and adjacent state, county, and private lands be carefully managed to maintain their natural biodiversity. There must be a mix of young, mid-aged, and old forests of all native species and vegetation types, mimicking the vegetation mosaic that nature would produce without manipulation by people. Most of these forests can still be used for timber if sensitive forestry with a concern for biodiversity is practiced. It is equally important that Ontario's forests adjoining Quetico be managed under policies complementary to park objectives.

The trapping of lynx, pine marten, and perhaps fisher in the Boundary Waters region probably should be prohibited. All three are boreal species near or at the southern limit of their continental ranges here. The pine marten and fisher are exceptionally vulnerable to the trap. The lynx is a particularly marginal resident, becoming common only with occasional influxes from Canada. The populations of all rare Boundary Waters birds and mammals should be carefully monitored, especially those of boreal species living on the edge of their range. The decline or disappearance of any such species may be a signal that global warming is occurring, or that other unrecognized factors are exacting a toll on biodiversity.

Woodland caribou should be reintroduced. If substantial global warming occurs, the habitat for caribou will certainly become less favorable, and a likely expansion of deer would probably bring brain worm populations intolerable to caribou. Unless studies clearly turn up insoluble problems, a reintroduction effort is justified. If we succeed and the caribou returns to its former haunts even for only a half century, our efforts will be repaid. If we fail, we will know the ecosystem has already changed too much to allow the survival of one of its most fascinating natives.

PROTECTING AND RESTORING

AQUATIC ECOSYSTEMS

The chief threats to the lake and stream ecosystems of the Boundary Waters reserves ranked in descending order are global warming, airborne pollutants, especially mercury and acid precipitation, the introduction and spread of exotic fishes and other aquatic organisms, and overharvest of preferred game fish by visitors. The deep, clear, cold-water lakes with populations of the boreal lake trout and its prey species are most at risk from global warming because the Boundary Waters region is at the southern limit of occurrence of this lake type and of the lake trout and its cold-water prey.

The first two of these threats are international and global in origin. Little can be done at the local level. Efforts should be redoubled to stimulate action by national and international political bodies toward curbing global warming.

Nothing can be done now to alter the spread of smallmouth bass into waters once dominated by lake trout or walleye. But the changes in the structure of fish populations in such lakes should make us acutely aware of the complexity of aquatic ecosystems and the folly of tampering with that which we do not understand. Now we face the spread of smelt into more lakes, and perhaps the invasion of other exotics with adverse effects on the region's aquatic organisms. Every possible effort must be made to prevent the introduction of more exotics into the Boundary Waters, of aquatic plants as well as fish, crustaceans, mollusks, and other organisms.

The stocking of Boundary Waters lakes with hatchery-reared fish, even of native species, should be stopped at once. Many of the lakes of this region are among the very few waters left in the United States where the genetic stocks of key native fish species have not yet been substantially altered by the introduction of nonlocal strains. We are now learning that important fish traits sometimes vary genetically from one water body to another. Gene-pool values are widely touted as among the most vital resources of wilderness areas, and yet public agencies have been among the last to recognize that such values are as important in aquatic ecosystems as in the plants and animals of terrestrial ecosystems. Diluting the genetic resources of a lake by introducing nonlocal hatchery-reared fish should not occur in wilderness areas or national parks, but dozens of BWCAW lakes have been stocked, some even in recent years. This practice degrades the scientific values of wilderness and makes the gene pools of the stocked species in a lake and its connecting waters of uncertain value.

In many lakes the sportfishing take by visitors of top predator fish, chiefly walleye, lake trout, northern pike, and smallmouth bass, alters predator-prey balances, influences the size-class structure of populations, and in other ways modifies fish populations. Size limits, lower catch limits, catch-and-release programs, special seasons, and other innovative regulations can help avoid the effects of selective overfishing of key species.

MINIMIZING VISITOR IMPACTS ON THE

VEGETATION AND LANDSCAPES

Recreational users of the vegetation and landscapes of the BWCAW, Quetico, and Voyageurs pose some important threats to the integrity of the ecosystem, but their impacts are much less severe than the potential impacts of global warming, airborne pollution, and failure to restore fire to something approaching its natural role.

The BWCAW and Quetico have been managed as wilderness areas with relatively stringent limits on visitor numbers, uses, and certain kinds of direct impacts since 1979. If these visitor-use and impact limits are maintained and strengthened as needed, the direct impacts of visitor use on campsites, portages, and lakeshore vegetation and landscapes can be held to acceptable levels. The computer-based visitor distribution systems and their associated entry-point quotas, in use in the BWCAW and Quetico for many years, provide an accepted mechanism for managing many user impacts. If these mechanisms are combined with sophisticated and tested user-education programs and accompanied by minimal but sometimes necessary portage maintenance and campsite restoration work, the impacts of visitors are manageable. There are and will continue to be pressures from some commercial interests and users to increase entry-point quotas, build more campsites, portages, and entry points, and allow uses or visitor activities that would degrade the natural environment. These pressures must be resisted by managing agencies. Where necessary to protect resources or visitor experiences, entry-point quotas must even be somewhat reduced on specific routes. If these kinds of management actions are implemented conscientiously, no serious long-term effects threaten the vegetation, soils, or landscapes of the lakeshores and portages or the lake water quality.

Visitor-caused forest fires are a different story. Because visitor fires tend to occur primarily on lakeshores and islands, the incidence and seasonal timing of fires along there may be quite unnatural. As noted in chapter 15, such fires may impose unknown but probably negative influences on lakeshore and island ecosystems. For these reasons they must be aggressively extinguished as quickly as possible. We should work primarily with natural lightning ignitions along shorelines and islands. The exception here is for mature red and white pine stands with heavy accumulations of organic matter and/or dense fir-spruce-cedar understories attributable to fire exclusion. In such a stand a management-ignited prescribed fire to reduce these surface and understory fuels should be conducted before it is committed to prescribed lightning ignitions.

The Value of the Boundary Waters Ecosystem for Tomorrow's Generations

What unique aspects of the Boundary Waters ecosystem will our descendants know and appreciate 25, 50, or 100 years from now? If we meet our responsibilities by preventing catastrophic global change and caring for the Boundary Waters reserves as we should, our legacy to future generations will be of inestimable value. The BWCAW, Quetico, and Voyageurs together will be seen as a vast area where the ecosystem is primarily the result of the forces of nature. And it will still evoke the sense of awe and wonder felt by perceptive visitors today. In fact, given current rates of population increase, urbanization, and conversion of natural landscapes to intensively farmed fields, managed forests, mines, roads, and cities, its values will surely increase many-fold. The special values treasured most may change with time as they have over the twentieth century, but most of its values are likely to grow.

RECREATION AND EXISTENCE VALUES

Just what are those special values that will endure if we care for these treasures as we should? First and most obvious is the opportunity for countless individuals over the generations to experience "primitive and unconfined re-creation" in a vast wild lake-land region—and here I do mean re-creation in the therapeutic-psychological sense. There will always be those who treasure canoe-trip camping, hiking, skiing, and snowshoeing in the Boundary Waters. The physical and psychological challenges of primitive travel in vast uninhabited nature reserves, and the lure of wildlife observation and of fishing in the lakes and streams of these areas will attract more and more devotees as other wildlands of the north continue to disappear through logging, road construction, and commercial and residential development. An increasing number of visitors may also come to these reserves primarily to appreciate and understand the ecosystem. The challenge will be to give as many as possible the opportunity to benefit from these values without affecting the ecosystem or detracting excessively from the values they seek.

A second value is the intrinsic worth of a vast, relatively complete, and functioning ecosystem not directly manipulated or "managed" by humans. In the words of the American Wilderness Act, this is the value of areas "where the earth and its community of life are untrammeled by man . . . retaining its primeval character and influence . . . affected primarily by the forces of nature." Although we cannot eliminate the effects of human-caused climate change, airborne pollution, managed fire regimes, or introduced organisms, ecosystem effects from such sources should be minimized by informed societal action in the decades ahead. In the twenty-first century and beyond, people will value such areas for their own sake more than today, if for no other reason than their scarcity. The three Boundary Waters reserves together will be valued more and more as a last large remnant of the old north woods. We want to know that such areas still exist. This is the so-called existence value of wilderness.

The large international complex of adjoining reserves protecting the Boundary Waters ecosystem will also have many utilitarian values little understood by most citizens today but of growing importance in tomorrow's world. Think of the gene-pool, biodiversity, scientific, and educational values of the reserves. These kinds of values will be important whether or not we succeed in curbing global warming, transboundary air pollution, or the spread of introduced organisms.

GENE-POOL AND BIODIVERSITY VALUES

The gene-pool values of the reserves have been little used as yet, but these areas contain relatively unaltered populations of many plants and animals no longer abundant or free of genetic manipulation elsewhere. This disparity will increase as the forests and lakes of the surrounding regions are modified more and more by human actions and the genetic characteristics of organisms elsewhere are altered by geneticists or other human actions. For example, large areas of virgin forests in the BWCAW and Quetico still exist where the genetic traits of native trees, shrubs, and herbs are undiluted. Here one can find many stands of old-growth red and white pine, white spruce, and black spruce, trees rapidly becoming rare except in plantations or second-growth stands of uncertain genetic quality. Some herbs still present in these virgin forests are now rare or absent from many forest plantations, cutover areas, and second-growth forests. The genetic characteristics of many fish species in some lakes have not yet been altered by the introduction of hatchery-reared stocks or nonlocal wild stocks. There are also varied native stocks of many shrubs, grasses,

lichens, birds, reptiles, amphibians, insects, fungi, and microorganisms. Reserves such as these are a step toward preserving the biodiversity of the earth. The genetic stocks of all of these organisms also have potential practical human values. Who is to say which species or stocks will be useful, or for what purpose? But intelligent tinkerers know enough to save all the pieces, and the Boundary Waters reserves are one of few areas in the Great Lakes–boreal forest transition region where that can be accomplished. If significant global warming occurs, stocks of many uncommon species may be needed to move them northward before rapid climate change causes extinctions or serious losses of genetic traits.

SCIENTIFIC VALUES

The scientific values of the Boundary Waters reserves have only recently been utilized to any extent, but already studies have contributed to knowledge in many diverse fields. The potential for contributions to science will surely grow in the coming decades. Many of the unusual scientific opportunities offered by protected wilderness areas have not yet been extensively explored except in the BWCAW for various reasons, but that situation must not continue (Franklin 1987). More can be done to take advantage of the special characteristics of the Boundary Waters reserves as a whole.

Unique research opportunities are available for the study of large-scale ecosystem characteristics, processes, and events in areas not directly manipulated by human actions. Studies of system functioning, biodiversity, and habitat variability should be conducted in areas large enough to encompass a variety of soils and landforms and a full array of the patchy vegetation types and disturbance classes generated by centuries of large-scale events. A full spectrum of lake types is also needed for comprehensive studies of aquatic ecosystems. The Boundary Waters reserves together are the only protected area in the entire Great Lakes–boreal forest transition region large enough to offer reasonable validity for such research. The natural pre–European settlement vegetation mosaic of much of this region is known, consisting of patches of distinct plant-community types and forest age classes varying in size from a few acres to hundreds of thousands of acres. We are just beginning to understand the effects on vegetation, fauna, and lake ecosystems generated by various disturbance histories and by changes in climate and other environmental factors. Only in the Boundary Waters reserves do enough areas remain of old-growth forests of all vegetation types to help us accurately sort out the relationships of native plants and animals to the full range of forest age classes and vegetation types. Better knowledge of such matters will not only enhance our understanding of natural systems but will also enable us to make better predictions of the effects of human actions on the earth's plant and animal life and suggest steps needed to preserve biodiversity and to mitigate adverse effects on the social and economic systems.

Large protected reserves offer important advantages for studies of wide-ranging animals and of predator-prey interactions. Such mammals as the wolf, black bear, and lynx cover very large areas in their annual activity cycles, and some of their prey, such as the white-tailed deer, moose, and caribou, also move long distances under some circumstances. The Boundary Waters reserves are unique in the eastern United States in having a relatively full complement of native mammalian predators and their prey, making studies of this kind especially feasible and productive. Studies of these kinds in the BWCAW and adjacent areas have already made outstanding contributions to mammalian ecology, animal behavior, and predator-prey relations, and the future holds much promise for further increases in our understanding of these fascinating animals and their roles in the total ecosystem. The reintroduction of caribou would add new dimensions to such research.

The Boundary Waters reserves present unusual opportunities to study the potential or actual ecological effects of greenhouse warming and natural climatic change and of changes in atmospheric chemistry and other human-modified environmental factors. Extensive background data on conditions before European settlement and in preindustrial times are known, and more can be obtained through the kinds of paleoecological and paleoclimatic studies pioneered in the area by investigators cited in earlier chapters. The many and varied lakes of the region are a vast storehouse of paleoecological and paleoenvironmental data. Extensive data on the present vegetation, fauna, cli-

mate, soils, geology, topography, and lake-water chemical conditions have been obtained. These reserves comprise the only large ecosystem in the Great Lakes–boreal forest transition region where both long-term and short-term studies will not be confounded by logging, agriculture, mining, road construction, urbanization, or onsite industrial activities.

LONG-TERM RESEARCH AND MONITORING VALUES

The opportunities for long-term research of many kinds are outstanding in large protected wilderness areas such as the Boundary Waters reserves. Some kinds of ecological knowledge can only be gained through long-term documentation of events and changes in vegetation, populations, and environmental variables. Long-term research will be especially important for studies of gradual changes in the total ecosystem due to global warming, depletion of stratospheric ozone, and ground-level changes in atmospheric chemistry, carbon dioxide, and air pollution by mercury and acid rain. It is vital to the health of our planet that we detect and understand any such ecosystem effects as quickly as possible, but in developed areas long-term studies are confounded by frequent changes in land use and agricultural and forestry practices, local sources of chemical inputs, and changing urban and industrial activities.

Well-supported long-term monitoring of environmental variables and of all aspects of the vegetation, fauna, and aquatic ecosystems of the Boundary Waters reserves will help us understand the impact on the regional ecosystem and evaluate programs to curb human-caused changes in climate and atmospheric chemistry. A wilderness ecosystem inventory is a basic tool both for routine ecosystem preservation programs and to establish baselines against which to measure system changes from all sources (Franklin 1990). The BWCAW stand-origin and logging-history maps resulting from my studies provide some of the baseline data needed about forested landscapes. The Superior National Forest's 1948–54 forest-type maps also provide a historical forest baseline. However, a new high-quality vegetation map is badly needed for the BWCAW. There is also need for periodic reassessments of the vegetation, including data on landscape-level changes, perhaps best documented by high-quality color aerial photographs at both large and small scales, as well as multispectral satellite imagery. Meticulous map records of forest fires, blowdowns, and large areas of insect-killed forests should be kept in perpetuity. Pertinent data from such photographs, images, and maps can be maintained in the computerized geographic information systems being widely adopted by natural-resource agencies. These landscape-level vegetation records should be backed up by permanent vegetation plots in the full spectrum of forest communities. In the BWCAW these could perhaps build on the plots already measured in the Ohmann-Ream studies of the 1960s and 1970s. There is also need for accurate long-term records of the changing populations of mammals, birds, reptiles, amphibians, fish, and even key insect species. If new members of the fauna begin to appear (perhaps immigrating southern species), records of their arrival times and sites should be kept.

Environmental data such as temperature, precipitation, evaporation, snowfall, snow depth, major storm occurrences, first and last frost dates, freeze-up and ice-out dates for key lakes, lake-temperature profiles, thermocline dates and depths, lake water chemistry, precipitation chemistry, soil chemistry, and atmospheric chemistry must also be available either from routine agency records or special monitoring stations. Many other records and studies may be needed, but these thoughts may encourage a systematic analysis of needs and the development and funding of new long-term studies. Such a program for the Boundary Waters ecosystem should coordinate and correlate all the presently scattered studies and programs so that critical data gaps are filled. Fortunately the ecosystem is already one of the best-studied wilderness ecosystems in the world, but remaining information gaps must be filled both for routine management purposes and for long-term monitoring and research.

If major human-caused global environmental changes do not develop, the data from long-term ecological studies of the kinds described may be even more valuable. Many significant environmental events and changes are natural, yet we lack adequate data to relate such factors to ecosystem changes. For example, the following kinds of climatic trends and events can have widespread ecosystem effects: decade-long cooling and severe winters such as occurred in the 1960s and 1970s; decade-long hot, dry periods such as the 1930s; severe but shorter-term droughts (like 1976); unusual dry lightning storms associated with drought, major windstorms, snowstorms, ice storms, and floods (like 1950); and unusually late or early freezes, unusual winter thaws, and prolonged periods of winter cold (like 1936) or summer heat (like 1936). Again, the Boundary Waters reserves contain the largest protected terrestrial and aquatic ecosystems in the Great Lakes–boreal forest transition region, including the only truly large areas of protected virgin forest, thousands of lakes of many types and depths, and a full spectrum of native mammals, birds, fish, and plant communities. Therefore, the opportunities to study the ecosystem-wide effects of such natural environmental changes and events are almost limitless. A fresh landscape and systemwide perspective in long-term studies could produce many new insights.

What special functions can the Boundary Waters reserves serve, and what values will they still have if major global warming does occur and the vegetation and fauna of the reserves begin to exhibit rapid and dramatic changes? Suppose our worst fears come true: tree species begin to die out, the reserves are swept by vast forest fires with unprecedented effects, major vegetation changes begin to appear, and significant changes in the fauna and lake ecosystems develop. Even then the reserves will be important sources of information if adequate environmental monitoring systems have been established and maintained. Perhaps most important, the information on emerging ecosystem changes could be an early warning that drastic action is needed to curb the causes of global change. If a network of similar monitored nature reserves exists around the globe, the need for such action might be sufficiently compelling to force action by reluctant world leaders. But if major systemwide changes do occur in the terrestrial vegetation, fauna, and aquatic ecosystems, future generations will at least have a baseline record of what the system was like before global change overwhelmed it, and a detailed chronology of system changes in relation to measured and mapped changes in the environmental variables that caused the ecosystem effects. These and similar nature reserves around the world should be maintained and studied far into the future, regardless of what ecological changes and disasters befall them, because how else will humanity ever fully document its impact on the planet? If disaster strikes, we can attempt to mitigate its effects outside the reserves by moving plants and animals about and introducing new species, possibly even some "engineered" by biotechnology. We should leave the nature reserves to the whims of nature, whatever that might mean in a world where nature as we have known it will no longer exist. How else will future generations ever know what we have done to their planet?

EDUCATIONAL VALUES

To return to a more optimistic assessment of the practical values of the Boundary Waters ecosystem, let me end this discussion by emphasizing the outstanding educational opportunities available now and in the foreseeable future in the BWCAW, Quetico, and Voyageurs. For at least four decades, a succession of graduate students in the biological and earth sciences, and even in the social sciences, has found stimulation, inspiration, and unparalleled natural resources in this region for the studies that led to their master's or doctoral degrees. For many years the Quetico-Superior Wilderness Research Center near Ely, under the sponsorship of Frank Hubachek, aided students working in the BWCAW and Quetico. Later Hubachek helped the Associated Colleges of the Midwest establish a program of summer undergraduate courses based on fieldwork in the Boundary Waters. As of 1992 this program was still active, based at the association's field station on the edge of the BWCAW. Beginning in the 1960s, the Limnological Research Center at the University of Minnesota, under the leadership of H. E. Wright Jr., sponsored a succession of graduate studies in paleoecology and limnology

in the BWCAW. Several important graduate studies in wildlife ecology have been based in part in the BWCAW and Quetico, beginning with the early wolf studies of Sigurd Olson and Milton Stenlund, the later wolf research by students of L. David Mech, and including the moose research of James Peek, the deer studies of M. E. Nelson, the bear research of Lynn Rogers, and several others. The reserves have also seen growing use as sites for studies by many graduate and undergraduate students working out of distant colleges, universities, and national laboratories. Faculty members have used the BWCAW and Quetico as temporary laboratories for short field-teaching experiences, taking students on working field trips for a few days. All of these formal educational uses of the wilderness ecosystem have aided in the training and inspiration of many bright young minds, dozens of people who have gone on to pursue productive careers in their chosen fields.

The Boundary Waters reserves are often used in both formal and informal adult education through field short courses, Elderhostel programs, and field seminars given by college and secondary schools, environmental learning centers, camps, and other qualified groups. Thousands of elementary and secondary school students are exposed to less formal educational efforts every summer on wilderness canoe trips led by teachers, church personnel, camp naturalists, and other leaders, who often share their ecological knowledge with their eager young charges. The interest in using the Boundary Waters reserves for all these kinds of educational purposes has been growing as the years pass and will surely increase still more in the future. This use is one of the greatest long-term values of wilderness, and the BWCAW and Quetico have been in the forefront in demonstrating the reality of the educational values of wilderness. The importance of these educational experiences to tomorrow's bright young minds will multiply as the gravity of the environmental problems facing the earth becomes more apparent.

Epilogue

I want to end this book on a theme not fully developed. There is another and less tangible value of the Boundary Waters. It is what has really motivated me to spend my life studying the forests and bogs of the Boundary Waters and to write this book. Perhaps it is what motivates many others who have studied or written about wilderness or painted or photographed its moods and scenes. Some of us can never get enough of nature. We do what we do because we love wild places and the mystery that will always exist in lakes, forests, deserts, mountains, and oceans.

I have asked myself many times how I came to spend my last 30 years trying to understand the natural role of fire in the Boundary Waters ecosystem. Perhaps the quest began when I stood on a high hill west of Rose Island on Quetico's Kawnipi Lake in 1939 and stared in awe at the endless pink granite ridges and blackened snags that marked the vast 1936 Kawnipi burn. I found the trail again in 1940 when I picked blueberries on another sector of that burn. The first answers may have come in the late 1940s and 1950s when I read of research on the special reproductive adaptations of jack pine and black spruce to fire, and when I revisited Kawnipi Lake and saw a vigorous new forest stretching as far as one could see from the same ridge I had climbed in 1939. Then came years of research in the great Lake Agassiz bogs along Minnesota's border with Ontario. I frequently encountered charcoal beneath many feet of peat just beneath the living layers of sphagnum and feather-

mosses of spruce forests. Once I found jack pine cones and charcoal beneath about 18 inches of peat in a spruce bog where jack pines no longer grew. In the late 1950s and early 1960s, I saw great burns and regenerating young forests in the boreal forests of Alaska, northern Manitoba, and Saskatchewan. Also in the early 1960s, I helped my colleague Bob Buckman burn some of his research plots in red pine on the Cutfoot Sioux Experimental Forest northwest of Grand Rapids, Minnesota, and I began prescribed burning experiments in black spruce south of International Falls.

My chance to study the virgin forests of the BWCAW came in 1966. I knew of Sidney Frissell's ongoing studies of the fire history of the virgin pine forests in Itasca Park. In 1967 we shared findings and field methods in the BWCAW. Most of my questions were by then formed in my mind, but what remained was the necessity of exploring all the virgin forests in the wilderness. As it happened, there was no other place in the United States east of the Missouri River where I could have discovered and understood the natural role of fire in controlling the patchlike mosaic of forest communities and age classes and the biodiversity of the ecosystem at a genuine landscape scale. Furthermore, the tree-ring record of past fires and the opportunity to recognize and map the limits of past burns were fast disappearing through logging and the senescence of many stands. That record could still be read, and with the help of several able colleagues and a sharing of records with the

Superior National Forest, the scale of past fires back into the 1600s became evident. Since 1966, I have struggled to understand the full meaning for the total ecosystem of what we found. That story is part of what I have tried to convey in this book.

As I look back, I am struck by an incredibly fortuitous set of circumstances. I had an opportunity that is fast fading from this earth. I was able to read a page from the earth's history that I had opened almost by accident, only to find the book itself crumbling to dust. I might well be the last person to be able to read those pages of history before their message becomes undecipherable. Not for centuries, if ever again, will wildfires roam unchecked through virgin pine, spruce-fir, and aspen-birch forests in what is now northeastern Minnesota, leaving their fire-year dates clearly recorded in fire scars on old pines, and their paths clearly marked by distinct age classes of forests. That record is now fading rapidly through the senescence of the trees that recorded it, and fire control that has virtually stopped the renewal process for 80 years. Even if we now allow many lightning fires to burn, as is already being done on a small scale, many valid reasons prevent full restoration of the old patterns. Even if fires could be allowed to roam freely again, it would require centuries to produce a forest whose vegetation and age-class patterns were in some sort of new dynamic balance with fire.

Our wilderness areas and large national and provincial parks, if properly protected, are libraries of genetic and ecosystem information that we will call on again and again to help us answer new questions about the way the earth's ecosystem functions. This is so even if some questions we would like to ask can never be answered because of the changes our civilization has already wrought. They will harbor plants and animals that we may find of great value as the years pass. Perhaps their greatest value is in the stimulation they can provide to eager young minds, and in the refuge they offer to the tired minds and bodies of a world growing weary of the sameness we are creating in our cities, on our farms, and in our "managed" forests.

Sigurd Olson (1957, 5–6) caught the essence of the appeal of the Boundary Waters in the first paragraph of his book *The Singing Wilderness* when he said, "The singing wilderness has to do with the calling of loons, northern lights, and the great silences of a land lying northwest of Lake Superior . . . I have heard the singing in many places, but I seem to hear it best in the wilderness lake country of the Quetico-Superior, where travel is still by pack and canoe over the ancient trails of the Indians and voyageurs."

Of course, Sig did not literally mean music but the sounds and images that come back to us again and again, even when we are far from this remarkable remnant of the Boundary Waters and the old north woods. It is the restiveness in the calls of chickadees, ravens, and gray jays as a March thaw thins the great white snow blanket that has covered their northern home since November. It is the first tiny flowers of the trailing arbutus among the last snow patches of a northern spring. It is the mysterious drumming of a male ruffed grouse coming from the lime greenery of a patch of young aspens on a warm May morning. It is the calling of loons echoing among the islands and bays of a wilderness lake on a moonlit summer night. It is a glimpse of a dark boreal forest of jack pine and black spruce marching out to the edge of a high granite ridge. It is the gray mystery of ancient white pines, mingled with the towering salmon-pink columns of giant red pines, still guarding the portages and campsites used long ago by native peoples. It is the soft carpet of feathermosses beneath a jack pine–black spruce forest, and great cushions of sphagnum mosses in a spruce bog. It is the starkness of fire-killed snags contrasting with the pink of freshly exposed granite and the bright new greenery of millions of tiny jack pine, black spruce, and aspen seedlings on a vast northern burn. It is the incredible pale blue depths of Argo, Clearwater, Mountain, and many other trout lakes best left unnamed. It is the dark green of spruce, balsam, and pine, contrasting with the golds of aspen, birch, and tamarack, the reds of maples, and the deep blue of sky and water on a brisk September day. It is the lonesome howl of timber wolves on a far-off ridge. It is the lusty bellow of a bull moose on a late September morning. It is the distant calling of geese, riding the chill and snow squalls of a biting north wind on an October day. It is the rending and cracking of newly formed lake ice on November's first subzero night. It is the overpowering silence and whiteness of a great winter-bound northern lake, surrounded by endless dark spruce and pine ridges, every tree festooned with dazzling snow pillows, framed against the deep blue of a thirty-below-zero January sky.

I have heard this "wilderness music" in the Boundary Waters. Voices in this land call us back until our last breath is drawn. Once you have heard the music of the Boundary Waters you will yearn for it until you can yearn no more!

Why, then, did I write this book? The answer is to know that tomorrow's generations will hear the music too. Some perhaps will find new questions to ask about the workings of natural ecosystems, and here find some of the answers. I do not want to leave life believing that the Boundary Waters ecosystem and all the other beautiful natural places will be devastated by our ignorance, greed, and lack of caring. Thoughtful people worldwide will lead us to see the necessity of living in harmony with the earth before it is too late. If readers are convinced that they must work actively to preserve the integrity of the Boundary Waters ecosystem, and indeed of planet Earth's total ecosystem, then one of my principal goals in writing this book will be fulfilled.

Aldo Leopold (1949, 224–25) said it all in *A Sand County Almanac* in his famous one-paragraph summation of what he meant by a land ethic: "The key log which must be moved to release the evolutionary process for an ethic is simply this: quit thinking about decent land use as solely an economic problem. Examine each question in terms of what is ethically and esthetically right, as well as what is economically expedient. A thing is right when it tends to preserve the integrity, stability and beauty of the biotic community. It is wrong when it tends otherwise."

Today we desperately need a global ecosystem ethic. Perhaps a slight rephrasing of Leopold's words might help bring their relevance to our global situation into sharper focus. We must quit thinking about decent care of the global ecosystem as a set of economic and technical problems that each nation can define in relation to its own short-term interests. We must examine each question in terms of what is ethically and esthetically right and ecologically sound for the whole planet instead of what is economically expedient. A thing is right when it tends to preserve the integrity, stability, and beauty of the earth's living ecosystems. It is wrong when it tends otherwise.

APPENDIXES

Chronology of Administrative, Legislative, and Judicial Actions to Protect the Boundary Waters Wilderness Region

America and Canada experienced a new conservation consciousness in the last decades of the nineteenth century, largely in reaction to the excesses of big-tree logging and to the decimation of buffalo, elk, moose, caribou, and other game animals and birds. In Minnesota this new concern resulted in the creation of Itasca State Park in 1891 at the headwaters of the Mississippi River to preserve a small remnant of the virgin forests of the northwestern timber region. Farther east the first conservation move, also in 1891, was an abortive drive to create a national park along the international boundary in the area that eventually became Voyageurs National Park (Treuer 1979). Then, just after the turn of the century, General Christopher C. Andrews, a retired army officer, became Minnesota's first forestry commissioner. Andrews was an energetic and politically astute crusader for many conservation causes, among them the remaining virgin forests and the moose herd in the Boundary Waters. Thus began the continuing saga of efforts to protect the Boundary Waters region. Much of the early conservation history of the region that follows has already been the subject of books such as *Saving Quetico-Superior* (Searle 1977), but the series of events since 1964 is based on my records and recollections.

1902–08
General Andrews Obtains Federal Land Withdrawals.
In 1902, Andrews persuaded the commissioner of the U.S. General Land Office to withdraw 500,000 acres of public domain land in northeastern Minnesota from entry under the land-disposal laws. Much of that land is now part of the BWCAW. Additional withdrawals of 659,700 acres came between 1905 and 1908 after Andrews, by then in his late seventies, took a canoe trip in the Lac La Croix area and redoubled his efforts to save the scenic beauty and wildlife of the region (Searle 1977).

1909
President Roosevelt Establishes Superior National Forest.
On February 13, 1909, President Theodore Roosevelt created the Superior National Forest from some 1,000,000 acres of the withdrawn public domain lands, largely in response to the urgings of Andrews and others. The new forest included much of the present BWCAW, but several large areas, such as the Basswood Lake, Knife Lake, and Big Trout Lake regions, were already in the hands of the timber companies and being logged (Searle 1977).

1909

Ontario Establishes Quetico Forest and Game Reserve.
At the urging of Canadian conservationists W. A. Preston, a
Rainy River District Member of Parliament, Arthur Hawkes
of the Canadian Northern Railway, and others, the government of Ontario created the Quetico Provincial Forest and
Game Reserve just a few weeks after the Superior Forest
was established. Again the concern was the killing of moose
and caribou near logging and mining camps and the prospect
of wholesale logging and mining (Walshe 1984; Ontario
Ministry of Natural Resources 1992).

1909

Minnesota Establishes Superior Game Refuge.
Later in 1909 the Minnesota legislature created the 1,200,000-
acre statutory Superior Game Refuge, which coincided
with the new national forest over most of its area, also including much of the present bwcaw. This action was aimed
primarily at saving the last Minnesota moose and caribou.

1913

Ontario Designates Quetico Provincial Park.
Continuing concern for protecting wildlife, plus other
factors, resulted in a government Order in Council creating
Quetico Provincial Park from the earlier forest and game
reserve in 1913. Provincial parks were closed to hunting,
a status Quetico has kept ever since. Quetico was placed
under the jurisdiction of the Ontario Ministry of Lands
and Forests (Ontario Ministry of Natural Resources 1992).

1919–22

**Carhart Proposes Canoeing Area
for Superior National Forest.**
After World War I, recreational use of the Boundary Waters
region grew. The U.S. Forest Service hired landscape architect Arthur H. Carhart to prepare a recreation plan for the
Superior National Forest. After three years of study and
canoe travel throughout the area, Carhart submitted a plan
that emphasized canoeing and enjoyment of the wilderness qualities of the area. It included restrictions on road
building, lakeshore cottages, and commercial resort development but allowed timber cutting away from scenic shore-

lines. The plan was not implemented, and Carhart left the
Forest Service. But his plan stands as perhaps the first proposal in the world for a wilderness area (Carhart 1922).

1923–26
**Road-Building Controversy Brews
on Superior National Forest.**
As automobiles improved after World War I, local business-
men, county officials, and the U.S. Forest Service developed
plans for an extensive road system in the new national
forest. Major new roads were projected from Ely northwest
to Buyck and from Ely east to the Gunflint Trail via Fernberg (near Snowbank Lake). In addition, the Gunflint Trail
(which then ended just west of Gunflint Lake) would be
extended to Sea Gull Lake, and spur roads would be built
from the Ely-Buyck road to Lac La Croix and Big Trout
Lake. Local business people envisioned summer cottages
and resorts on dozens of newly accessible lakes. But these
plans met with deep concern by those who treasured the
Boundary Waters. The opposition was galvanized by Paul
B. Riis, an Illinois landscape architect and friend of Carhart,
by Will H. Dilg, a founder of the new Izaak Walton League
of America, and by George Selover, president of the league's
Minnesota division.

1926
Road-Building Compromise—The Jardine Policy.
After two conferences, one in 1923 and a second in 1926,
a compromise road plan was finally worked out by the U.S.
Forest Service with Aldo Leopold, then active in the Wisconsin Izaak Walton League, and Seth Gordon, the league's
national conservation director, serving as liaison with the
conservation groups. On September 17, 1926, U.S. Secretary
of Agriculture W. M. Jardine signed a memorandum spelling
out a new roadless area wilderness policy. The Ely-Buyck
road, the Gunflint extension to Sea Gull Lake, and the Ely
to Fernberg roads would be built to facilitate fire control, but the connection from Fernberg to the Gunflint
was dropped, as were the spurs to Lac La Croix and Trout
Lake off the Ely-Buyck road (now called the Echo Trail).
The memo contained the following explicit policy statements (Jardine 1926, 1–2):

The Department of Agriculture recognizes the exceptional value of large portions of the Superior National Forest, containing its principal lakes and waterways . . . It will be the policy of the Department to retain as much as possible of the land which has recreational opportunities of this nature as a wilderness . . . Not less than one thousand square miles containing the best of the lakes and waterways will be kept as wilderness recreation areas.

The memo spelled out which roads would be built and which dropped. It pointed out the need for more fire protection roads but then stated, "the utmost contemplated in this direction . . . will leave not less than 1,000 square miles of the best canoe country in the Superior without roads of any character" (Jardine 1926, 4).

These roadless "wilderness areas" were identified on maps. Their boundaries were similar to the present BWCAW, except that several large areas including part of the international boundary were not included because they were still in the hands of the timber companies. This policy statement was the first official identification of wilderness units. Then, as now, there were three separate units: the main Superior unit, the southwestern Little Indian Sioux unit south of the projected Ely-Buyck road, and the Caribou unit east of the Gunflint Trail.

1925–34
Backus Power Dams Controversy.
In 1925 Edward W. Backus, owner-manager of the Backus and Brooks Lumber Company, the Minnesota and Ontario Paper Company, the Koochiching Falls dam at the outlet of Rainy Lake, and several other businesses at International Falls, Minnesota and Fort Frances, Ontario, began his formal participation in the "Rainy Lake Reference" to the International Joint Commission. The question before the commission involved approval or denial of a Backus plan to dam the international boundary chain of lakes all the way from Rainy Lake to Saganaga Lake. The dam at International Falls would be increased 3 feet in height, and new dams would raise Little Vermilion Lake 80 feet, Lac La Croix 16 feet, Loon Lake 33 feet, and Saganaga and Crooked lakes 15 feet. This massive plan was proposed simply to supply additional power and timber for the Backus enterprises. Backus was opposed by a group of conservation allies headed by Ernest C. Oberholtzer, who lived on Rainy Lake, and including Sewell Tyng (a New York attorney), Frank B. Hubachek and Charles S. Kelly (Minneapolis and later Chicago attorneys), and Frederick S. Winston (a Twin Cities attorney) (Searle 1977). Oberholtzer's plan soon involved a double strategy: they would fight the Backus proposal by all possible means and also push their own alternative plan for the Rainy Lake watershed. Oberholtzer's dream was for an International Peace Memorial Forest on both sides of the border, encompassing the entire Quetico-Superior region. The Izaak Walton League, the American Legion, and many other groups cooperated in these efforts. Finally, in 1928, an umbrella action group called the Quetico-Superior Council was formed, with Oberholtzer as its president.

1930
The Shipstead-Newton-Nolan Act.
The first major tactic of the Quetico-Superior Council was to block the Backus proposal with an act of the U.S. Congress. After a long fight, Oberholtzer and his group persuaded the Congress to pass the Shipstead-Newton-Nolan Act (U.S. Public Law 71-539, July 10, 1930). This law prohibits logging on federal land within 400 feet of recreational waterways and forbids any further alteration of natural water levels affecting federal land within a large area that encompassed the entire Superior National Forest at the time, plus the boundary water lakes westward to Black Bay of Rainy Lake. It also withdrew all federal land within the same area from entry under the U.S. land laws.

1934
International Joint Commission
Recommends against Backus Proposal.
In July 1934, the final report of the International Joint Commission was published. It commented that "nothing should be done that might mar the beauty or disturb the wildlife of this last great wilderness" (International Joint Commission 1934, 48), and it advocated the status quo with respect to dams and water levels. By then the Great Depression was at its depths, and the Backus companies

were in receivership. On October 29, 1934, Edward Backus died while in New York still trying to raise funds to save his enterprises (Searle 1977).

1934
Minnesota Legislature Passes "Little Shipstead-Nolan Act."
In 1934 the Minnesota legislature passed an act applying to state land within the area defined by the Shipstead-Newton-Nolan Act, providing essentially the same protections against logging and water-level alterations as the federal law.

1934
President Roosevelt Appoints Quetico-Superior Committee.
In 1934 President Franklin D. Roosevelt was persuaded to appoint the President's Quetico-Superior Committee to advise appropriate executive agencies on matters concerning the Quetico-Superior program. This committee served for more than 40 years. It was terminated by President Jimmy Carter, who abolished many advisory committees in 1977.

1930–41
Forest Service Acquires Land within the Wilderness.
As the depression came on, much cutover timberland and some other properties within the Superior National Forest came onto the market because the owners were delinquent in their taxes. The U.S. Forest Service purchased much land within the present BWCAW during this era, especially in the Basswood-Knife lakes and Big Trout Lake regions. Mineral rights were often not acquired. The boundaries of the forest were officially expanded in 1936 to include several new purchase units.

1938
Minnesota Opens Superior Game Refuge to Deer Hunting.
By 1938, the deer population had increased to the point of damaging its own range within parts of the Superior Game Refuge, and the state began opening certain areas to deer hunting. Eventually the refuge was abandoned entirely.

1938
U.S. Forest Service Establishes Superior Roadless Primitive Areas.
In 1938 the Superior National Forest, with the help of Robert Marshall, then in charge of recreation in the Washington office of the Forest Service, drew up plans for three Superior Roadless Primitive Areas. The boundaries of these revised areas were similar to those of the old "wilderness" areas set up in 1926. Now the areas included the recently acquired lands in the Basswood to Saganaga international boundary area, as well as the Big Trout Lake area. They were also similar to the present BWCAW but included some areas near Silver Island Lake, Lake Isabella, and elsewhere that were later deleted (in 1948) and never restored. Marshall is said to have selected the name. (He was a founder of The Wilderness Society and one of the first champions of the wilderness movement.) Apparently the Plan of Management for the new roadless areas was approved July 25, 1939, by the Acting Chief under authority of Regulation L-20 (U.S. Forest Service 1948). Timber cutting and motorboats were allowed. Marshall died in 1939.

1942
U.S. Forest Service Establishes Lac La Croix Research Natural Area.
In 1942 the Lake States Forest Experiment Station and Superior National Forest established the Lac La Croix Research Natural Area encompassing the extensive stands of old red and white pine between the Boulder River and Boulder Bay and Lady Boot Bay of Lac La Croix. This action, which required approval by the chief of the Forest Service, effectively protected these stands from logging.

1941
U.S. Forest Service Establishes First No-Cutting Areas.
As World War II developed, timber markets on the Superior became active again, prompting concern over logging in the wilderness. The Superior National Forest administratively established a 362,000-acre belt of no-cutting areas along the international boundary.

1943
Izaak Walton League Begins Purchase
of Private Resorts in Wilderness.

In 1943 the Izaak Walton League set up an endowment fund to finance the purchase of private inholdings within the wilderness, particularly parcels having resorts or cabins that seriously affected the wilderness. The plan was to resell these properties to the government as federal funds became available. By 1948, this fund, administered by Paul Clement, had purchased 11 tracts and 6 resorts and turned them over to the government at a net loss to the league.

1945
Forest Service Makes "Tomahawk Sale"
of Large Timber Block in Roadless Area.

During World War II and thereafter, the demand for jack pine and spruce pulpwood and for rough pine and aspen lumber increased dramatically. On December 19, 1945, the Superior National Forest sold a block of timber involving some 130 square miles of land and water north of Lake Isabella to the Tomahawk Timber Company of Wisconsin. By 1948, a railroad had been built to a yarding area just south of Lake Isabella, and a small logging "town" called Forest Center was established there. A network of year-round gravel roads soon fanned out into the "roadless area."

1948
U.S. Forest Service Revises Roadless Areas
Management Plan, Shrinks Boundaries.

Late in 1947 and early in 1948, the Superior National Forest revised its management plan for the roadless areas and reclassified them under the secretary of agriculture's Regulation U-3. There were also significant deletions of areas south of Lake Isabella and near Kawishiwi Lake to accommodate the Forest Center town site and railroad landing and projected logging roads, and perhaps also to placate local officials. One of the largest deletions included about a township of land (36 square miles) in the Silver Island Lake area. The plan's (U.S. Forest Service 1948) stated purpose was "without unnecessary restrictions on other uses including that of timber, to maintain the primitive character of the areas, particularly in the vicinity of lakes, streams, and portages, and to prevent as far as possible the further intrusion of roads, aircraft, motorboats and other developments inharmonious with that aim." (Some of this language was to reappear verbatim in the 1964 Wilderness Act.) The plan was signed by the secretary of agriculture on February 13, 1948.

1948
U.S. Congress Passes Thye-Blatnik Act
to Acquire Resorts in the Wilderness.

Immediately after World War II, there was a dramatic increase in floatplane fishing traffic in the roadless areas. Dozens of new fly-in resorts and scores of private cabins were built on scattered inholdings. Conservationists were alarmed and mounted a drive for federal funds and authorization to acquire all inholdings. The effort was headed by Sigurd Olson, Frank Hubachek, Charles Kelly, Chester S. Wilson, and the Izaak Walton League. Olson was hired by the league as its wilderness ecologist and acted as a consultant to the the President's Quetico-Superior Committee and to the Wilderness Society (Searle 1977). After a two-year fight, the Thye-Blatnik Act was passed and became law June 22, 1948 (U.S Public Law 80-733). It directed the secretary of agriculture to acquire by purchase, exchange, or condemnation "any lands . . . and improvements thereto that impair or threaten to impair the unique qualities and natural features of the remaining wilderness canoe country." The power of condemnation was limited initially, however, and important areas were excluded. The act also provided for the compensation of St. Louis, Lake, and Cook counties in lieu of taxes on federal land within the roadless areas. Eventually the act was broadened to provide for condemnation wherever necessary throughout the wilderness, and additional funds were appropriated to acquire all inholdings within the roadless areas (Public Law 84-607, 1956; Public Law 87-351, 1961; Public Law 94-384, 1976). In the end $9,000,000 was spent to acquire some 45 resorts and 115 cabins under these Thye-Blatnik appropriations.

1949

President Truman Establishes Airspace Reservation over Wilderness.

The Thye-Blatnik Act was a long-range solution to much of the fly-in traffic over the Boundary Waters, but an immediate crisis existed, and some of the floatplane activity was independent of inholdings. Conservationists and the Forest Service conceived the idea of a presidential order establishing an airspace reservation that would prohibit flights over the roadless areas. The conservationists collaborated with officials of the Superior National Forest in this effort. Among the conservationists were Sigurd Olson; Frank Hubachek; William N. Rom Sr., an Ely canoe outfitter; Wesley Libbey, an Izaak Walton League activist from Grand Rapids; William H. Magie, an engineer from Duluth who had once worked for the International Joint Commission; and Frank Robertson, Side Lake, Minnesota. Magie and Robertson formed an umbrella support group called Friends of the Wilderness to coordinate local support in northern Minnesota for an aircraft ban. The two Forest Service officials who were most active in the effort were Forest Supervisor Galen W. Pike and Ely Ranger J. William (Bill) Trygg. Chester S. Wilson, Minnesota's conservation commissioner, also was helpful. Opposition came from Ely Chamber of Commerce leaders John A. Smrekar, William E. Gustason, and Stanley Pechaver; Ray A. Glumac, a pilot from Virginia, Minnesota; fly-in resort operators William Zupancich, Martin Skala, and Joseph Perko, all from Ely; and Elwyn West, a pilot from Ely who serviced the latter three men's resorts. The effort to obtain an airspace order became bitter, drawn out, and legally complex. Finally, on December 17, 1949, President Harry S. Truman signed an order prohibiting flights over the roadless areas below an altitude of 4,000 feet above sea level after January 1, 1951, but allowing direct flights to and from private lands until January 1, 1952, where such flights were a customary means of travel to such properties (Searle 1977). Landing of aircraft was also prohibited in Quetico shortly thereafter (Littlejohn 1965).

1952–56

Air Ban Violations and Court Tests.

On January 2, 1952, pilot Elwyn West deliberately violated the airspace order and flew his ski plane to Zupancich's resort at Curtain Falls and on to Perko's on Friday Bay of Crooked Lake. On March 20, 1952, the United States filed suits against Perko, Skala, West, and later Zupancich. Skala's resort was near Lady Boot Bay of Lac La Croix. The case was decided against these men in both the district court of Judge Gunner Nordbye and the Eighth Circuit Court of Appeals. Nordbye forbid further flights in September 1952. He allowed flights to these resorts only for the purpose of preserving their properties until their appeal was decided. The appeals court did not rule until May 25, 1953. On Memorial Day weekend in 1953 West flew at least 50 flights to the three resorts, carrying 110 passengers. The violations continued. On July 2, 1953, U.S. marshalls seized West's aircraft and the FBI gathered evidence. West pled guilty to violating the air ban and was fined on July 13, 1953. Even these actions did not put an end to the matter. An appeal to the U.S. Supreme Court failed in October 1953. Thereafter Zupancich and Perko attempted to transport guests to their Crooked Lake resorts by truck and an amphibious vehicle (a "weasel") over the old Gun Lake railroad grade and across a chain of small lakes and portages to Friday Bay of Crooked Lake. Their use of the Gun Lake grade was said to be illegal by the Forest Service, but in the fall of 1954 Zupancich and Perko even used a small bulldozer to make a rough trail from Gun Lake to Crooked Lake. In 1955 Perko and Zupancich sued the Forest Service and the Northwest Paper Company, owners of the grade, for an injunction requiring the Gun Lake grade to be opened as a public road. Meanwhile, they continued to trespass. Finally, on May 31, 1956, District Judge Dennis F. Donovan held that Perko and Zupancich had no right of access other than by the traditional means of boat, canoe, and portage. He reaffirmed an earlier decision by Judge Nordbye that no public roads and no private rights to roads existed within the roadless areas (Searle 1977). Many precedents in wilderness law were set by this long series of court cases.

1958

Forest Service Changes Name of Roadless Areas to Boundary Waters Canoe Area.

In 1958 the U.S. Forest Service renamed the roadless areas the Boundary Waters Canoe Area (BWCA), apparently because the name better characterized the area and was more realistic because of the growing presence of logging roads. Conservationists suspected the name change signaled a retreat from the 1926 Jardine policy of no roads.

1957–63

Motorboat, Snowmobile, and Logging Conflicts Grow.

During the fifties and early sixties recreational use of the BWCA grew dramatically. Canoe-trip outfitting became big business in Ely and Grand Marais and on the Gunflint Trail. Motorboat use also increased greatly, and lightweight motors and aluminum boats made it possible for motorized fishermen to cross portages and penetrate far into the backcountry. Truck portages into Basswood Lake, Lac La Croix, and Big Trout Lake made for easy access to these lakes and their connecting waters by large, high-speed motorboats. In the late fifties a new threat to the solitude of the winter wilderness also appeared—the snowmobile. By 1963 there were hundreds of machines, some pushing far back into the most remote lakes to take lake trout. Wilderness-seeking canoeists and a few hardy snowshoers, skiers, and winter campers saw their opportunities for solitude disappearing. Conflicts between motorized and non-motorized users increased. Litter at campsites grew. Simultaneously, new logging roads on the Tomahawk Sale and on new pulpwood sales, such as the Finn Lake Sale off the Gunflint Trail, were pushing into the backcountry. Main haul roads were often graveled and ditched, culverts or bridges were installed to cross streams, some of which were canoe routes, and many portages were crossed by logging roads. Chain saws and bulldozers were heard on such remote lakes as Insula, Nina Moose, Ramshead, Polly, Malberg, and Maniwaki. All was not well in the Boundary Waters.

1964–65

The Selke Committee and Freeman Directive.

By 1964 concern over logging, motorboats, and snowmobiles in the BWCA boiled up into a public controversy. A Twin Cities–based group called Conservation Affiliates, sparked by Dr. Clayton G. Rudd, president of the Natural History Society, and Glen Ross, an Izaak Walton League activist, sought help from Secretary of Agriculture Orville Freeman, a former Minnesota governor. Freeman responded by appointing George A. Selke, a noted educator and former Minnesota conservation commissioner, to head a five-member fact-finding and policy-recommending committee.

The Selke committee held hearings in the north and in the Twin Cities and made field investigations. Conservationists pressed for a new wilderness policy that would ban all logging and eliminate motorboats and snowmobiles. Their voices were not unanimous, however.

At a Quetico-Superior Foundation forum at the University of Minnesota, it became clear that two old stalwarts, Frank Hubachek and Charles Kelly, did not favor a logging ban. Timber harvest, properly conducted, had always been a part of Oberholtzer's International Peace Memorial Forest plan. Hubachek and Kelly could not see a need for change and were backed by Frank Kaufert, dean of the University of Minnesota College of Forestry. Oberholtzer was too feeble to participate, and Winston had died. Sigurd Olson also spoke at this symposium. It was a watershed for him. Obviously under great strain, he broke with his compatriots who had fought the good fight with him for almost four decades and came out solidly for full wilderness status for his beloved "singing wilderness." The rift was never totally healed, but thereafter Olson became the most eloquent spokesperson for new wilderness policies in the BWCA. His mighty pen continued to spell out the human values of wilderness to the end of his years.

The Selke committee was perceptive and sensed a need for change. In December 1964, the committee submitted its recommendations in a detailed report. Freeman implemented most of its proposed new policies in a directive issued December 15, 1965. He increased the no-cutting zones by 150,000 acres immediately and designated another 100,000 acres to be added by 1975 as existing logging contracts were completed. This brought the total area closed to logging up to 511,000 acres in 1965 and to 612,000 acres by 1975. Unfortunately, many areas of remaining virgin forest were left in the so-called portal zone still subject to logging. Motorboats and snowmobiles were for the first time limited to certain designated routes. Freeman also identified several areas adjoining the BWCA that he asked the Forest Service to administer "like the BWCA" itself. Visitor registration for the area was initiated.

1964
Congress Includes BWCA in National Wilderness Act.

On September 3, 1964, while the Selke committee was considering BWCA policies, the Wilderness Act became law (Public Law 88-577). The BWCA was included in the new National Wilderness System as one of the "instant wildernesses" under the act. But unlike any other area, the BWCA was singled out as a special case with ambiguous language with respect to logging and motorboat use, language soon to become the source of more controversy. Paragraph 4(d)(5) of the act reads in part:

> Other provisions of this Act to the contrary notwithstanding, the management of the Boundary Waters Canoe Area . . . shall be in accordance with regulations established by the Secretary of Agriculture in accordance with the general principle of maintaining, without unnecessary restrictions on other uses, including that of timber, the primitive character of the area, particularly in the vicinity of lakes, streams and portages: *Provided*, that nothing in this Act shall preclude the continuance within the area of any already established use of motorboats.

These provisions were inserted by Senator (later Vice President) Hubert Humphrey, who was a strong and early sponsor of the Wilderness Act. He insisted on this language to avoid introducing the volatile BWCA issues into congressional debates on the act.

1969–73
Copper-Nickel Mining Threat in BWCA Blocked by Lawsuits.

Between about 1952 and 1968, exploratory drilling for copper-nickel sulfide ores began just outside the BWCA near the South Kawishiwi River. This activity was concentrated along the northern edge of the massive Duluth Gabbro formation, and the International Nickel Company was one of the most active firms. Then, in 1969, businessman George St. Clair hired a prospecting crew to explore a site deep within the BWCA near Howard Lake. He claimed to own or control more than 100,000 acres of subsurface drilling rights in the BWCA, even though the surface was owned by the federal government, or in some cases by Lake or Cook counties. In December he notified the Forest Service of his plans to enter the BWCA with drilling rigs. The Izaak Walton League sued St. Clair in federal district court to block exploration and mining. The U.S. Forest Service was a codefendant, but the state of Minnesota joined the league's side. The league argued that since the BWCA was zoned as wilderness by many acts of Congress and court decisions, St. Clair could not exercise his mineral rights. Their attorney was Raymond Haik. Judge Phillip Neville ruled for the league and the state in 1973, although his injunction was later lifted by the Eighth Circuit Court of Appeals on procedural grounds. The substance of his decision still stands. St. Clair died, and no drilling within the BWCA occurred.

1969–77
Quetico Logging Controversy Leads to Wilderness Park Status.

About 1969 a controversy over logging in Quetico heated up on the Ontario side of the border. Large timber licenses had been granted in the northwestern and northeastern sections of the Quetico. Clear-cut areas, roads, and logging debris were changing the pristine landscape in vast areas. A bridge even spanned the historic French River. A Quetico Advisory Committee, appointed in 1970, held hearings and accepted briefs. In 1971 a moratorium on logging was imposed by the Ministry of Natural Resources, and in 1973

Quetico became Ontario's first real wilderness park. Quetico was formally reclassified, all logging was permanently stopped, snowmobiles were banned, and a motorboat phase-out was begun. In 1977 a new park master plan was implemented. Motorboats were eliminated from all of Quetico after 1978 except for seven lakes on the western edge, where licensed guides from the Lac La Croix Indian Band were permitted to use motors; cans and bottles were banned; a visitor distribution program was initiated; and visitor group size was limited to nine persons. A precedent had been set for the United States to follow.

1971

Minnesota Initiates State BWCA Protective Measures.

In 1971 Jarle Lierfallom, Minnesota's commissioner of natural resources, issued a new regulation (NR 1000) establishing state protective measures in the BWCA. This regulation was needed because the state owned some 103,000 acres of land within the BWCA and claimed jurisdiction over most of the waters and lake beds within the entire area. A hearing was held in St. Paul to get public input, and the order was then issued. Lierfallom was a canoeist and BWCA devotee himself and knew the problems well. Among the most important points in his order was the prohibition of boat caches on state land and of the mooring of unattended boats on state waters. Cached-boat storage on interior wilderness lakes had become a common means of facilitating motor use within the BWCA, and when this practice was banned on federal land, some resort owners and local citizens moved their boats onto the nearest state land or moored them in the water just offshore. The order also closed several lakes to motorboat use where the state controlled key portages or waters. The regulations closely paralleled federal rules and authorized joint cooperative agreements with the U.S. Forest Service for management and enforcement.

1971

U.S. Congress Creates Voyageurs National Park.

While the BWCA and Quetico debates intensified, just to the west a new national park was in the making. The effort to establish Voyageurs had been long, but finally in 1971 the Congress moved the legislation. On January 8, 1971, President Nixon signed Public Law 91-661, and Voyageurs became a reality. Ernest Oberholtzer's lifetime dream of an International Peace Memorial Forest encompassing the entire Rainy Lake watershed may have faded, but with the creation of Voyageurs National Park, the Quetico-Superior region now had nearly 2.5 million acres of contiguous landscape with some sort of special legal status. Protection was increasing on both sides of the border. Oberholtzer's vision was soon to become more than a dream.

1972–1977

BWCA Virgin Forest Logging Brings Court Challenges.

By the fall of 1972 the massive scale of modern mechanized pulpwood logging operations in the BWCA brought the logging issue to a boil again. There were 13 active federal timber sales in virgin forest. Hundreds of miles of logging roads had been built since World War II, and several were graveled and still in use. Signs at portage crossings claimed that such roads were only "temporary" and would be "obliterated" when logging was completed, yet some had been used for 10 to 20 years. Late in 1972 the Minnesota Public Interest Research Group (MPIRG) brought suit against the Superior National Forest and Secretary of Agriculture Earl Butz under the National Environmental Policy Act (NEPA), charging that BWCA logging was "major federal action" under NEPA. MPIRG's attorney was Charles K. Dayton, a BWCA devotee who knew the area well. He sought an injunction to stop the renewal of a timber sale until the Forest Service prepared an environmental impact statement (EIS). Trial began under U.S. District Judge Miles Lord in Minneapolis in January 1973. On April 16, 1973, Judge Lord issued a detailed opinion, finding for MPIRG and ordering an EIS. On June 28, 1974, the Forest Service filed its EIS and a new BWCA management plan. The plan allowed logging to proceed on all seven timber sales, although the cutting plans were modified.

Environmental attorney Dayton, representing the Sierra Club as well as MPIRG, advised a new lawsuit to test the legality under the Wilderness Act of logging the remaining virgin forests of the Boundary Waters. The suit was filed, and a second trial in Judge Lord's courtroom took place in the fall of 1974. On August 13, 1975, Judge Lord again ruled for the plaintiffs, MPIRG and the Sierra Club. The six remaining timber sales were permanently enjoined, as was all further logging within large contiguous tracts of virgin forest in the entire BWCA. The Forest Service and the timber companies immediately appealed to the Eighth Circuit Court of Appeals. In 1976 the appeals court reversed Judge Lord's decision, and in 1977 an appeal by MPIRG to the U.S. Supreme Court failed, but by then the BWCA logging issue was before the U.S. Congress.

1975–76
Secretary of Agriculture Butz Bans Snowmobiles in BWCA.

Concurrent with these lawsuits, the Sierra Club, with Dayton as counsel, lodged a package of administrative appeals of other BWCA issues with the secretary of agriculture. The only appeal that bore fruit was a request for a snowmobile ban. Secretary Earl Butz responded with a ban that was to take effect in the 1975–76 winter. When snowmobilers brought suit, however, the ban was delayed for one year. MINNTOUR and the U.S. Ski Association countered with a second suit. On January 18, 1977, U.S. District Judge Donald Alsop ruled that the matter was discretionary with the secretary, and the 1976–77 ban stood.

1976
Minnesota Legislature Passes BWCA Mining Ban.

In 1975 and 1976 an effort was made to prohibit mining, peat harvesting, and logging on the 102,555 acres of state-owned land in the BWCA. The legislative campaign became a personal effort by Lieutenant Governor (later Governor) Rudy Perpich. Perpich toured the state on behalf of the bill, making impassioned speeches at numerous colleges and civic gatherings. Timber industry lobbyists succeeded in stripping the logging prohibition from the bill in the 1976 legislative session, but the mining and peat-harvesting ban passed (Minn. Statutes 84.523). It prohibits mining and peat harvesting on state land within the (1975) BWCA boundaries, and the leasing of any state natural resources for such purposes within that area. There is a (strict) national emergency exception.

1976–79
U.S. Congress Enacts BWCA Wilderness Act.

The Minnesota environmental community was well aware that the real solution to all of the BWCA problems was new federal legislation. An abortive last-minute amendment to the Eastern Wilderness Areas Act had already been tried in November 1974. Then on October 14, 1975, James Oberstar, U.S. representative for the Eighth District in Minnesota (northeastern Minnesota) unveiled a bill to "resolve" the BWCA issues. His first bill (H.R. 10247) would have given full wilderness status (no logging, no motors, etc.) to 600,000 acres of the BWCA, but it also would have removed some 400,000 acres from the National Wilderness System and turned those regions into a National Recreation Area with less protection than the BWCA already had. In May 1976 the environmental groups formed a group called Friends of the Boundary Waters Wilderness, with M.L. Heinselman as chair. In June 1976 the group persuaded U.S. Representative Donald Fraser of Minneapolis to sponsor a new full wilderness bill for the BWCA (H.R. 14576). Thus began an incredible three-year political fight to achieve full wilderness status for the BWCA.

The field hearing of the House Subcommittee on National Parks and Insular Affairs in Ely in July 1977 was filled with social tension. Trucks loaded with motorboats, snowmobiles, and logs were parked in front of the high school where the hearings were held. Sig Olson and I found our names on a crumpled dummy hung in effigy from the winch of a pulpwood truck. Olson was booed when he attempted to testify. U.S. Representative Bruce Vento, St. Paul, who chaired the session, was only able to restore order by threatening to stop the hearing.

The political consequences of the effort to pass the Fraser-Vento-Anderson Act, as Public Law 95-495 is sometimes called, were considerable. The Eighth Congressional District in Minnesota was pivotal in the elections of 1978. Congressman Fraser's and Senator Wendell Anderson's roles in the BWCA fight probably contributed to their defeat in their bids for U.S. Senate seats. DFL Governor Rudy Perpich was also defeated. Congressman Vento survived. The Friends of the Boundary Waters organization was probably successful in achieving new legislation primarily because it mobilized support from literally thousands of BWCA users from throughout the nation. Hundreds of these devotees came to Washington to lobby their own representatives and senators. Thus Congress saw the legislation as a national issue.

The key role of U.S. Representative Phillip Burton (California), chairman of the House Subcommittee on National Parks and Insular Affairs, in perfecting this legislation and in managing its way through the House can hardly be overstated. He insisted on learning the details of every issue, personally examined the maps showing all proposed boundary changes, and approved or disapproved of each change after hearing the arguments for and against each one. I know, because I had to make the case for most such changes and explain every issue. Many late hours were spent in Burton's office going over such details in 1977 and 1978.

In the end there were many compromises, but logging was banned entirely, snowmobiles were to be eliminated after a five-year phaseout period, and a strong mining provision was included. The final bill (H.R. 12250) embodied a compromise on motorized use hammered out in a marathon negotiating session in Washington in August 1978 by Friends of the Boundary Waters attorney Charles Dayton and Ronald Walls, attorney for the Boundary Waters Conservation Alliance (the Ely-based opponents of BWCA wilderness). Motorboat use in the wilderness was reduced from routes encompassing 62 percent of the water area to 24 percent of the water area (after the final phaseouts of 1999). Some 50,000 acres were added to the BWCAW. The final conference report bill passed the House of Representatives on the last morning of the Ninety-fifth Congress by a vote margin of 248 to 111. The Senate passed the bill on a consent vote just hours before adjournment. President Jimmy Carter signed the measure on October 21, 1978.

1979–82
Alliance and State Challenge Public Law 95-495, Courts Uphold Act.

The ink was hardly dry on President Carter's signature before opponents of the new Boundary Waters Wilderness Act were talking of legal challenges. On July 17, 1979, Texas attorney Ben A. Wallis Jr., representing the Boundary

Waters Conservation Alliance and an organization called the National Association of Property Owners, argued in the Washington, D.C. federal court of Judge Harold Greene for a temporary restraining order (T.R.O.) that would have blocked implementation of Public Law 95-495. Judge Greene denied the T.R.O. The Alliance then refiled its request for a T.R.O. in the Duluth court of U.S. Magistrate Patrick McNulty, who heard the arguments and again denied the T.R.O. On December 27, 1979, the state of Minnesota filed a companion suit against the United States, challenging, among other things, the constitutionality of section 15 of Public Law 95-495 dealing with jurisdiction over the waters of the BWCAW. The state was represented by attorney Wayne Olson, former commissioner of natural resources, and a member of the Selke committee. The Friends of the Boundary Waters Wilderness, the Sierra Club, and other environmental organizations intervened on the side of the United States, represented by Minneapolis attorneys Brian B. O'Neill and Charles Dayton, and several other volunteer attorneys. The case was transferred to the court of Chief U.S. District Judge Miles Lord, who heard the arguments in April and May 1980. Judge Lord consolidated the Alliance case and the state's case, and on July 24, 1980, he ruled in favor of the United States on all issues. In his opinion Judge Lord noted:

> The new Act does not divest the state of jurisdiction over the surface waters within the Wilderness. The only extent to which the state's jurisdiction is restricted by the new Act concerns the situation where Minnesota would wish to open more surface water for motorized use—this the state cannot do. The state, however, could issue regulations restricting motorized uses which are more stringent than the federal restrictions; under the Act, the state could close all the surface waters of the Wilderness to motorboats and snowmobiles . . . This Court reads (Sections) 15 and 16 as stating that Minnesota retains its jurisdiction to control mining in the Wilderness. Nothing in the Act divests the state of its authority to regulate mining in the BWCAW. In fact, since the Act specifically states that Minnesota retains jurisdiction over its waters and may issue even more stringent regulations, it could there-

by restrict the use of the waters in such a fashion as would close the area to mining altogether.

In October 1980 the state and the Alliance appealed Judge Lord's decision to the Eighth Circuit Court of Appeals. The Sierra Club and the Friends of the Boundary Waters Wilderness again intervened on the side of the United States. On June 18, 1981, the case was argued in St. Paul before Circuit Judges Lay, Bright, and Stephenson. On September 30, 1981, the U.S. Court of Appeals upheld Judge Lord's decision on all counts. In a 40-page ruling, the court made these key points:

> The motor use restrictions form only a small part of an elaborate system of regulation considered necessary to preserve the BWCAW as a wilderness. The United States owns close to ninety percent of the land surrounding the waters at issue. Congress concluded that motorized vehicles significantly interfere with the use of the wilderness by canoeists, hikers, and skiers and that restricted motorized use would enhance and preserve the wilderness values of the area. From the evidence presented, Congress could rationally reach these conclusions. We hold, therefore, that Congress acted within its power under the constitution to pass needful regulations respecting public lands . . . Congress, through the Act, has brought the regulation of the BWCAW in line with that of other wilderness areas, thus recognizing that historically the use of motor vehicles could not be reconciled with retaining a primitive wilderness area . . . The restrictions on the use of motorboats and snowmobiles regulate only private conduct, and not the state itself. The state retains broad jurisdiction over conduct occurring on state lands and waterways. We conclude, therefore, that the tenth amendment presents no bar to these restrictions.

The state was still not satisfied, however, and in December 1981 Minnesota filed a petition for writ of certiorari (review) with the U.S. Supreme Court. On March 8, 1982, the day of William H. Magie's funeral in Duluth, the Supreme Court voted eight to one not to review the appellate court decision.

Chronology of the Fur Trade, 1620 to 1890

1620–41

French explorer Étienne Brulé traded on Lake Superior, and Jean Nicolet traded on lakes Huron and Michigan. A mission was established at Sault Sainte Marie. Montreal became a fur-trading center.

1659–60

Two more Frenchmen, Médard Chouart, sieur des Groseilliers and Pierre Radisson, not properly licensed by their government, explored the north shore of Lake Superior, possibly landed at the Pigeon River, and returned to Montreal with many canoe loads of furs.

1668–83

Groseilliers and Radisson turned to England after being rebuffed by France. After Groseilliers and Radisson made a successful trip to Hudson Bay in 1668, the English formed Hudson's Bay Company in 1670, licensed to trade in all of northern North America. The company established trading posts on Hudson Bay at the mouths of the Moose (Moose Factory), Albany (Fort Albany), and eventually Hayes (York Factory) and Severn (Fort Severn) rivers. Trade began with Cree Indians.

1671

The Lake Superior region, including Minnesota, was annexed by France as the French lay claim to all of interior North America, with ceremonies at Sault Sainte Marie conducted by Sieur de St. Lusson.

1679–83

Daniel Greysolon, sieur Du Lhut (Duluth), a Frenchman, explored the north shore of Lake Superior, built forts at the mouths of the Nipigon and Kaministikwia rivers to prevent Native Americans from trading with Hudson's Bay Company, and built trading posts along the Nipigon-Albany canoe routes to Hudson Bay.

1688–89

Jacques de Noyon, perhaps an employee of Du Lhut, with Crees explored the Kaministikwia River canoe route upstream from the present site of Thunder Bay, via Dog River, Lac des Mille Lacs, and through the present Quetico Provincial Park via French, Pickerel, and Sturgeon lakes, the Maligne River, and Lac La Croix to Namakan and Rainy lakes in present Voyageurs National Park.

1696–1713

French fur markets were depressed with furs; Louis xiv revoked fur licenses in 1696, leaving the field open to Hudson's Bay Company. By the 1713 Treaty of Utrecht, France surrendered many of its North American claims to England, including the Hudson Bay region.

1731

Pierre Gaultier de Varennes, sieur de la Vérendrye, born in Three Rivers, Quebec, and his sons arrived at Grand Portage. Using a map drawn by Indian Auchagah, Vérendrye's sons traveled the Boundary Waters canoe route to Rainy Lake via Grand Portage, Pigeon River, Saganaga, Basswood, La Croix, and Namakan lakes and built a post at the outlet of Rainy Lake, the first of many at this site. Vérendrye overwintered at the mouth of the Kaministikwia River.

1732

Vérendrye and his party built Fort St. Charles on Lake of the Woods (at Northwest Angle) and posts on Lake Winnipeg and elsewhere.

1732–56

Many French fur traders used the Boundary Waters canoe route. Posts were established at Moose, Saganaga, and Basswood lakes. Bourassa built a fort on Little Vermilion Lake in 1736 to defend the site from warring Dakota. Vérendrye and his sons explored the Saskatchewan River and other routes westward in search of the Northwest Passage.

1735–36

Ojibwa began to occupy the Rainy Lake region. One of Vérendrye's sons, 19 voyageurs, and the missionary Jean-Pierre Aulneau were massacred by Dakota on Massacre Island in Lake of the Woods in 1736.

1760

The first English fur traders were in the Boundary Waters region.

1763

Northeastern Minnesota became British by the Treaty of Paris between Britain and France as the British took over all of Canada at the end of the French and Indian War, in which the Ojibwa sided with France.

1768

John Askin (or Erskine) built a crude post at or near Grand Portage.

1774

Hudson's Bay Company built Cumberland House on the North Saskatchewan River, the company's first inland post. Northeastern Minnesota became part of Province of Quebec.

1775

Alexander Henry, the elder, from the colony of New Jersey, trading along the Boundary Waters route, described the Ojibwa on Saganaga: "there was formerly a large village of the Chippeways here, now destroyed by the (Sioux). I found only three lodges filled with poor, dirty and almost naked inhabitants, of whom I bought fish, and wild rice, which latter they had in great abundance" (as quoted in Nute 1941, 24).

1778

British soldiers were briefly at Grand Portage, marking the only involvement of the region in the American Revolution.

1778

Peter Pond located Methye Portage linking the Boundary Waters canoe routes and the Churchill River route with the vast fur-rich regions tributary to Lake Athabasca.

1779

The North West Company was organized by British traders with headquarters in Montreal. The company built a great depot at the Lake Superior end of the 9-mile-long Grand Portage and an ancillary post at Fort Charlotte on the Pigeon River end. A new fort was built at the outlet of Rainy Lake. Way stations and wintering posts were built along the route at Moose, Knife, Basswood, and Little Vermilion lakes. Thus began the heyday of fur trade along the present international boundary.

The fur trade logistics of the North West Company were a significant factor in the chronology at this point. Between 1779 and 1803, the Boundary Waters route from Rainy Lake to Grand Portage became a key link in far-flung operations that brought furs from as far away as the Athabasca region to Grand Portage for transshipment to Montreal and the European markets. The total distance from Fort Chipewyan on Lake Athabasca to Montreal, about 3,000 miles, was simply too far for an annual round trip by canoe of 6,000 miles in the five months between spring ice-out and fall freeze-up at Athabasca. The solution was to split the operation into segments, with different crews of French voyageurs moving trade goods and furs simultaneously in opposite directions. Grand Portage became the rendezvous point for these canoe brigades.

The trapping was done in late fall and winter largely by Native Americans along the remote lakes from north of Lake Superior northwestward about 1,500 miles to Athabasca and beyond. Furs were traded for the usual trade goods at remote posts throughout the region. Most of the trading was done at the remote posts by overwintering French-speaking voyageurs, who learned the ways of the Native Americans and often took Native American wives. With the spring breakup, brigades of North Canoes (the Athabasca brigades) laden with furs departed from as far as Athabasca for the long trip to the southeast, while simultaneously brigades of Montreal Canoes moved northwestward from Lachine at Montreal loaded with trade goods. These brigades or their replacements held their annual rendezvous at Grand Portage in mid-July. The Athabasca brigades dared not risk the full trip to Grand Portage for fear of being caught by the fall freeze-up before reaching their posts on the return. The solution was to bring their furs only as far as the Rainy Lake depot, where they were exchanged for trade goods in early July, in time to begin the return with a margin for safety. Replacement canoe groups then moved the furs to Grand Portage, storing their canoes at Fort Charlotte before packing the furs the last 9 miles to the depot on Lake Superior. After a week or two of trading and revelry at Grand Portage, the Montreal brigades departed eastward with their furs, down Lake Superior, across northern Lake Huron to the French River, up the French to Lake Nipissing, through the Mattawa, and down the Ottawa to Montreal at Lachine. The voyageurs from less remote overwintering posts headed back westward with new trade goods for the Rainy Lake depot and for the Native American families that supplied the furs from within their own operating areas.

The Montreal brigades, faced with crossing Lakes Huron and Superior and only 36 portages between Montreal-Lachine and Grand Portage, used the big Montreal Canoe, about 36 feet long, capable of carrying 3 tons. This craft was paddled by 12 to 14 voyageurs and required several men to portage—bottom side up. In contrast, the overwintering Athabasca brigades, and even the wintering voyageurs making shorter trading trips to Grand Portage, faced many difficult and long portages, and the need to navigate miles of small streams, rocky rapids, and shallow ponds, as well as large lakes and great rivers. The canoe of choice for this purpose was the North Canoe, about 25 feet long, paddled by 8 to 10 men, capable of carrying a ton and a half, and light enough for two men to portage. Both types of canoes were built largely by Native American crews using cedar frames and birch-bark skins sewn with spruce roots and sealed with spruce gum, following time-tested methods. There were 36 portages from Grand Portage to Rainy Lake and 26 more to Lake Winnipeg. For the Athabasca brigades there were countless additional portages and wild rapids along such great rivers of the north as the Saskatchewan, Sturgeon-Weir, Churchill, Clearwater, and Athabasca.

1780

The great smallpox epidemic caused many Native American deaths.

1783

By the treaty ending the Revolutionary War, Britain ceded the area south of the Boundary Waters canoe route to the fledgling United States, but retained de facto control until after the War of 1812.

1787

The United States set up the government for the American side of the border under the Northwest Territories Ordinance.

1789

Alexander Mackenzie traveled the Boundary Waters en route to the far northwest, where he "discovered" the Mackenzie River. His diary commented on the scarcity of game and on how few Native Americans were present in the Basswood Lake region after wars with the Dakota and the smallpox epidemic, a population that was formerly "very numerous" (Nute 1941).

1793

Hudson's Bay Company established a post at the outlet of Rainy Lake, the company's first post in the region, and soon also posts on Rainy River. But by 1798 they were gone. Hundreds of traders traveled the Boundary Waters canoe route each year.

1797

David Thompson joined North West Company and visited the Boundary Waters region. An astronomer and map-maker, he produced the first good maps of the region.

1798

The XY Company was formed by dissident partners of North West Company. This new competing company built posts at Grand Portage and Fort Charlotte.

1800

Northeastern Minnesota became part of the Indiana Territory. John Tanner identified a great beaver die-off in the Boundary Waters region about this time. Nute (1941, 61) ascribes the die-off to "the great forest fires of 1803–04" and to "certain obscure diseases."

1800

Alexander Henry, the younger, reported Native Americans making canoes on Saganaga, Basswood, La Croix, and Namakan lakes and described modern Prairie Portage, where on July 26 he met three canoes eastbound from the Athabasca region. Heading westward again after waiting on Basswood Lake for the Native Americans to make a canoe for his brigade, he described Basswood River portages and reported meeting a brigade of nine canoes "loaded with Athabasca packs" at the Pictured Rocks on Crooked Lake and meeting many canoes en route (Nute 1941).

1803

This was the last year of significant use by the North West Company of the international boundary canoe route from Lac La Croix to Grand Portage. The heyday of the voyageurs was from 1778 to 1803. The United States began to enforce customs charges at Grand Portage.

1804

North West Company abandoned the Boundary Waters route to Grand Portage to avoid customs and controls. It shifted operations to the Kamanistikwia River route from Lake Superior to Lac La Croix via the Kam-Dog rivers, Lac des Mille Lacs, Pickerel and Sturgeon lakes, and the Maligne River and built Fort William at the mouth of the Kam, the present site of Thunder Bay. XY Company united with North West Company. Use of the Boundary Waters route from Lac La Croix to Grand Portage diminished to a trickle.

1807

Dr. John McLoughlin, a trader at Little Vermilion Lake, described the Native American population, fish, and wild-life of the region. The population comprised 107 men, 118 women, and 230 children (455 total). The area covered by this enumeration was not specified. The fish caught were sturgeon, (northern) pike, pickerel (Canadian name for walleyed pike), (lake) trout, and sucker. The mammals described were moose, caribou, wolf, wolverine, fisher, lynx, marten, bear, fox, (snowshoe) hare, beaver, muskrat, and mink. Marten and muskrat were the furbearers he traded in; beaver were said to be "diminishing for these several years past. . . ." Caribou and moose, while present were so scarce that the Native Americans could not obtain enough to "supply themselves with leather for their Mogosins and snow Shoes" (as quoted in Nute 1941, 62).

1808

John Jacob Astor formed the American Fur Company in New York.

1809

Northeastern Minnesota became part of the Illinois Territory.

1812

Lord Selkirk, chief Hudson's Bay Company stockholder, established Red River settlements at Fort Garry and St. Boniface (present Winnipeg)—the first permanent white settlements in the region—partly to complicate the North West Company's use of the Lake Winnipeg route to the Athabasca region.

1814–16

After the War of 1812, the United States prohibited foreigners from trading furs on the U.S. side of the border. David Thompson became cartographer for the British International Boundary Commission.

1816

Hudson's Bay Company men under Lord Selkirk attacked North West Company posts at Rainy Lake and Fort William.

1818

Hudson's Bay Company rebuilt the post at the outlet of Rainy Lake (site of Fort Frances) and built subsidiary posts on Basswood, Crane, and Moose lakes. Minnesota became part of the Michigan Territory.

1821

Hudson's Bay Company took over North West Company. Fort William and the Kaministikwia route were abandoned. Trade with Montreal via Lake Superior ended. The Montreal brigades and the voyageurs era came to a close. The movement of furs from the Boundary Waters region was redirected primarily toward York Factory on Hudson Bay via Rainy River, Lake of the Woods, and Lake Winnipeg.

1822

A Hudson's Bay Company wintering post was built on Basswood Lake. David Thompson's map of 1823 showed it on a small peninsula on the Canadian side of the narrows between Bayley Bay and Inlet Bay. Thirty or 40 years later the post may have been moved to Ottawa Island near the former site of a Quetico Park Ranger station (Nute 1941).

1822

A George Johnston had a post on the U.S. side of Crane Lake and attempted unsuccessfully to take over a Hudson's Bay Company post there; instead he was driven out.

1822–24

The U.S.–British Boundary Commission explored canoe routes to determine the international boundary. David Thompson mapped the "usual canoe route and portages" from Grand Portage to Lake of the Woods, which was to become the boundary.

1823–33

The American Fur Company monopolized fur trade on the U.S. border and built a post on Rainy Lake at the site of present International Falls in 1823 and posts at Grand Marais, Grand Portage, and Moose, Basswood, Little Vermilion, and Vermilion lakes.

1830

Fort Frances, at the outlet of Rainy Lake, was named for the bride of Hudson's Bay Company governor George Simpson.

1833–42

American Fur Company agreed to eliminate competition with Hudson's Bay Company in the Boundary Waters region for annual payments of 300 pounds sterling.

1836

Northeastern Minnesota became part of the Wisconsin Territory.

1842

The Webster-Ashburton Treaty between the United States and Britain settled boundary disputes.

1847

American Fur Company failed, a victim of a financial panic in 1842 plus trade wars with Hudson's Bay Company and independent American traders.

1847

Frederick Graham met a large encampment of Saulteux (Ojibwa) Indians (evidently about a hundred) fishing sturgeon at Tar Point on the Canadian side of Namakan Lake where the Namakan River enters the lake. They were living in bark lodges at the site (Bolz 1960).

1849

The Minnesota Territory included the Boundary Waters region.

1849
Hudson's Bay Company posts were still in operation on the Canadian side of Little Vermilion and Moose lakes, but competition with independent traders was bitter.

1857
Henry Hind, geologist, and Simon Dawson, engineer, began exploration of the "Dawson Trail" along the old Kaministikwia canoe route as a possible route for settlers to Fort Garry and the Canadian prairies.

1858
Minnesota became a state.

1865
The Vermilion Gold Rush attracted a flurry of activity to the Lake Vermilion region. No gold was found.

1867–69
The Vermilion Trail, a wagon road from Duluth to Lake Vermilion, was built.

1868–69
Construction of the "Dawson Road" began at Fort Garry on the west end and from Port Arthur (now Thunder Bay) 50 miles west to Lake Shebandowan.

1870
Lois Riel led a rebellion of métis at the Red River settlements to preserve squatters rights.

1870
Colonel Garnet Wolseley led an expedition of 1,500 men from Port Arthur to Fort Garry to quell the Riel rebellion and completed the Dawson Road by clearing the remaining roadway and all portages along the old Kaministikwia

canoe route, plus the Dawson Portage from Lac La Croix to Sand Point Lake.

1870–80
Many Canadian settlers and traders traveled from Port Arthur to the Red River region via the Dawson Road route through present QuetiCompany Steamboats were used on Sturgeon, La Croix, and Rainy lakes. York boats, canoes, carts, and stagecoaches were used for much of route. The road was never a success because of difficult travel.

1880
The Canadian Pacific Railroad was completed through Ontario connecting eastern Canada with Fort Garry, eliminating use of the Dawson Road.

1884
The Duluth and Iron Range Railroad was completed from Two Harbors to Tower, Minnesota. The first iron ore was shipped the from Vermilion Range.

1890
Iron ore was discovered on the Mesabi Range.

1895
Big-pine logging began in the present BWCAW.

1902
The last Hudson's Bay Company post in Fort Frances burned down. One or more posts had occupied this general area continuously from 1688, when Noyon built the first post. This last post had stood from 1816 to 1902. Civilization was now encircling the Boundary Waters, but the lakes, land, and forests that are now the BWCAW, Quetico, and Voyageurs were still little changed by those first two centuries of European exploitation.

Plants and Animals of the Boundary Waters Region

TREES	
ash	
—black	*Fraxinus nigra*
—green	*Fraxinus pennsylvanica*
aspen	
—large-toothed or bigtooth	*Populus grandidentata*
—quaking or trembling	*Populus tremuloides*
balsam fir	*Abies balsamea*
balsam poplar	*Populus balsamifera*
basswood	*Tilia americana*
beech	*Fagus grandifolia*
birch	
—paper	*Betula papyrifera*
—yellow	*Betula lutea*
box elder	*Acer negundo*
cedar	
—northern white	*Thuja occidentalis*
elm (American)	*Ulmus americana*
hemlock, eastern	*Tsuga canadensis*
maple	
—Manitoba	*Acer negundo*
—red	*Acer rubrum*
—silver	*Acer saccharinum*
—sugar	*Acer saccharum*
oak	
—bur	*Quercus macrocarpa*
—northern pin	*Quercus ellipsoidalis*
—red	*Quercus borealis*
pine	
—jack	*Pinus banksiana*

TREES *(cont.)*	
—red, Norway	*Pinus resinosa*
—white	*Pinus strobus*
spruce	
—black	*Picea mariana*
—white	*Picea glauca*
tamarack	*Larix laricina*

LICHENS	
hairy tree	*Bryoria*
liverworts	
old man's beard	*Usnea*
red-capped British soldiers	
reindeer moss	*Cladonia alpestris*
reindeer moss	*Cladonia rangiferina*

MOSSES	
	Ceratodon purpureus
	Dicranum spp.
	Funaria hygrometrica
	Pohlia nutans
hylocomium splendens	*Hylocomium splendens*
hair-cap moss	*Polytrichum commune*
plume moss	*Hypnum crista-castrensis*
ribbed bog	*Mnium* and *Thuidium* spp.
Schreber's feathermoss	*Pleurozium schreberi*
sphagnum moss	*Sphagnum* spp.

CLUBMOSSES	
bristly clubmoss	*Lycopodium annotinum*
ground-pine	*Lycopodium obscurum*
running clubmoss	*Lycopodium clavatum*
horsetails	*Equisetum* spp.

FERNS	
bracken	*Pteridium aquilinum*
cinnamon-fern	*Osmunda cinnamomea*
interrupted fern	*Osmunda claytoniana*
lady-fern	*Athyrium filix-femina*
rattlesnake-fern	*Botrychium virginianum*
royal fern	*Osmunda regalis*
sensitive fern	*Onoclea sensibilis*

WOODY TALL SHRUBS	
alder, green	*Alnus crispa*
alder, speckled	*Alnus rugosa*
bog-birch, dwarf birch	*Betula glandulosa*
choke-cherry	*Prunus virginiana*
cranberry, high-bush	*Viburnum opulus*
dogwood, pagoda-	*Cornus alternifolia*
dogwood, red osier	*Cornus stolonifera*
dogwood, round-leaved	*Cornus rugosa*
downy arrow-wood	*Viburnum rafinesquianum*
elder, red-berried	*Sambucus pubens*
hazelnut, beaked	*Corylus cornuta*
honeysuckle, fly-	*Lonicera canadensis*

WOODY TALL SHRUBS *(cont.)*

juneberry, northern	*Amelanchier bartramiana*
juneberry, red-twig	*Amelanchier sanguinea*
juneberry, smooth	*Amelanchier laevis*
meadow-sweet	*Spiraea alba*
mountain-ash, American	*Sorbus americana*
mountain-ash, showy	*Sorbus decora*
mountain-maple	*Acer spicatum*
pin-cherry	*Prunus pensylvanica*
raspberry, red	*Rubus strigosus*
sweet fern	*Myrica asplenifolia*
willow	*Salix* spp.
yew, American	*Taxus canadensis*

LOW SHRUBS

alder, dwarf-	*Rhamnus alnifolia*
bearberry	*Arctostaphylos uva-ursi*
blackberry, arundel	*Rubus arundelanus*
blueberry, lowbush	*Vaccinium angustifolium*
blueberry, velvet-leaf	*Vaccinium myrtilloides*
bog-laurel	*Kalmia polifolia*
bog-rosemary	*Andromeda glaucophylla*
buffalo-berry	*Shepherdia argentea*
cranberry, large	*Vaccinium macrocarpon*
cranberry, mountain-	*Vaccinium vitis-idaea*
cranberry, small	*Vaccinium oxycoccus*
creeping snowberry	*Gaultheria hispidula*
currants	*Ribes* spp.
dewberry, common eastern	*Rubus flagellaris*
gooseberry, northern	*Ribes oxyacanthoides*
honeysuckle, bush-	*Diervilla lonicera*
juneberry, low	*Amelanchier spicata*
juniper, common	*Juniperus communis*
Labrador-tea	*Ledum groenlandicum*
leather-leaf	*Chamaedaphne calyculata*
pipsissewa	*Chimaphila umbellata*
poison ivy	*Rhus radicans*

LOW SHRUBS *(cont.)*

soapberry	*Shepherdia canadensis*
sweet gale	*Myrica gale*
thimbleberry	*Rubus parviflorus*
wild rose, prickly	*Rosa acicularis*
wild rose, smooth	*Rosa blanda*
winterberry	*Ilex verticillata*
wintergreen	*Gaultheria procumbens*

AQUATIC HERBS

arrowheads	*Sagittaria* spp.
bladderworts	*Utricularia* spp.
bur-reeds	*Sparganium* spp.
cattails	*Typha* spp.
duckweed, greater	*Spirodela polyrhiza*
duckweed, lesser	*Lemna minor*
naiad, slender	*Najas flexilis*
pipewort	*Eriocaulon septangulare*
pondweeds	*Potamogeton* spp.
reed grass	*Phragmites communis*
tapegrass	*Vallisneria americana*
water-lilies, white	*Nymphaea* spp.
water-lilies, yellow	*Nuphar* spp.
water-milfoils	*Myriophyllum* spp.
water-shield	*Brasenia schreberi*
water-smartweed	*Polygonum natans*
waterweed, common	*Elodea canadensis*

GRASSES (AQUATIC AND TERRESTRIAL)

big bluestem	*Andropogon gerardii*
blue-joint grass	*Calamagrostis canadensis*
wild rice	*Zizania palustris*

SEDGES (AQUATIC AND TERRESTRIAL)

bulrushes	*Scirpus* spp.
cotton-grasses	*Eriophorum* spp.
sedges	*Carex* spp.
spike-rushes	*Eleocharis* spp.

TERRESTRIAL HERBS

anemone, wood	*Anemone quinquefolia*
asters	*Aster* spp.
bedstraws	*Galium* spp.
Bicknell's geranium	*Geranium bicknelli*
bishop's-cap	*Mitella nuda*

TERRESTRIAL HERBS *(cont.)*

blue flag	*Iris versicolor*
bluebead-lily	*Clintonia borealis*
bluebell (harebell)	*Campanula rotundifolia*
bog false Solomon's-seal	*Smilacina trifolia*
bristly crowfoot	*Ranunculus pensylvanicus*
bristly sarsaparilla	*Aralia hispida*
bugle-weed	*Lycopus uniflorus*
bunchberry	*Cornus canadensis*
clovers	*Trifolium* spp.
cinquefoils	*Potentilla* spp.
cow-wheat	*Melampyrum lineare*
dodder	*Cuscuta gronovii*
evening-primrose (sundrops)	*Oenothera perennis*
everlasting	*Antennaria neglecta*
false Solomon's-seal	*Smilacina racemosa*
field-mint	*Mentha arvensis*
fireweed	*Epilobium angustifolium*
fringed bindweed	*Polygonum cilinode*
goldenrods	*Solidago* spp.
goldthread	*Coptis trifolia*
houstonia, common	*Houstonia longifolia*
Indian pipe	*Monotropa uniflora*
Joe-Pye weed	*Eupatorium maculatum*
lungwort, tall	*Mertensia paniculata*
marsh-marigold	*Caltha palustris*
orchids	
—blunt-leaf	*Habenaria obtusata*
—club-spur	*Habenaria clavellata*
—dragon's-mouth	*Arethusa bulbosa*
—dwarf rattlesnake-plantain	*Goodyera repens*
—fairy slipper	*Calypso bulbosa*
—grass-pink	*Calopogon pulchellus*
—greater rattlesnake-plantain	*Goodyera tesselata*
—purple fringed	*Habenaria psycodes*
—ram's-head lady-slipper	*Cypripedium arietinum*
—rose pogonia	*Pogonia ophioglossoides*
—stemless lady-slipper	*Cypripedium acaule*

TERRESTRIAL HERBS *(cont.)*	
pale corydalis	*Corydalis sempervirens*
pale pea	*Lathyrus ochroleucus*
pearly everlasting	*Anaphalis margaritacea*
pitcher-plant	*Sarracenia purpurea*
pyrola	
—nodding	*Pyrola virens*
—one-flowered	*Moneses uniflora*
—one-sided	*Pyrola secunda*
—pink	*Pyrola asarifolia*
—shinleaf	*Pyrola elliptica*
ragwort, northern	*Senecio pauperculus*
red baneberry	*Actaea rubra*
skullcap, common	*Scutellaria galericulata*
skullcap, mad-dog	*Scutellaria lateriflora*
spearwort	*Ranunculus flammula*
spreading dogbane	*Apocynum androsaemifolium*
starflower	*Trientalis borealis*
strawberry, meadow	*Fragaria virginiana*
strawberry, woodland	*Fragaria vesca*
sundew, round-leaved	*Drosera rotundifolia*
sundew, spatula-leaved	*Drosera intermedia*
swamp-loosestrife	*Lysimachia terrestris*
sweet coltsfoot	*Petasites sagittatus*
sweet coltsfoot, early	*Petasites frigidus*
thoroughwort	*Eupatorium perfoliatum*
touch-me-not, jewelweed	*Impatiens biflora*
trailing arbutus	*Epigaea repens*
trillium, nodding	*Trillium cernuum*
twinflower	*Linnaea borealis*
twisted-stalk	*Streptopus roseus*
violet, blue marsh	*Viola cucullata*
violets	*Viola* spp.
Virginia creeper	*Parthenocissus vitacea*
water-hemlock, spotted	*Cicuta maculata*
wild lily-of-the-valley	*Maianthemum canadense*
wild sarsaparilla	*Aralia nudicaulis*

MAMMALS	
bat	
—big brown	*Eptesicus fuscus*
—eastern long-eared	*Myotis keenii*
—hoary	*Lasiurus cinereus*
—little brown	*Myotis lucifugus*
—red	*Lasiurus borealis*
—silver-haired	*Lasionycteris noctivagans*
bear	*Ursus americanus*
beaver	*Castor canadensis*
bobcat	*Lynx rufus*
caribou, woodland	*Rangifer tarandus*
chipmunk	
—eastern	*Tamias striatus*
—least	*Eutamius minimus*
coyote	*Canis latrans*
deer, white-tailed	*Odocoileus virginianus*
fisher	*Martes pennanti*
fox, red	*Vulpes vulpes*
lemming, southern bog	*Synaptomys cooperi*
lynx	*Lynx canadensis*
marten, pine	*Martes americana*
mink	*Mustela vison*
mole, star-nosed	*Condylura cristata*
moose	*Alces alces*
mouse	
—meadow jumping	*Zapus hudsonius*
—woodland deer	*Peromyscus maniculatus gracilis*
—woodland jumping	*Napaeozapus insignis*
muskrat	*Ondatra zibethicus*
otter, river	*Lutra canadensis*
porcupine	*Erethizon dorsatum*
shrew	
—arctic	*Sorex arcticus*
—masked	*Sorex cinereus*
—water	*Sorex palustris*
—pygmy	*Microsorex hoyi*
—short-tailed	*Blarina brevicauda*
skunk, striped	*Mephitis mephitis*
snowshoe hare	*Lepus americanus*
squirrel	
—northern flying	*Glaucomys sabrinus*
—red	*Tamiasciurus hudsonicus*

MAMMALS *(cont.)*	
vole	
—meadow	*Microtus pennsylvanicus*
—red-backed, southern	*Clethrionomys gapperi*
—rock, yellownosed	*Microtus chrotorrhinus*
weasel	
—least	*Mustela nivalis*
—long-tailed	*Mustela frenata*
—short-tailed	*Mustela erminea*
wolf, gray (timber)	*Canis lupus*
wolverine	*Gulo gulo*
woodchuck	*Marmota monax*

BIRDS	
American bittern	*Botaurus lentiginosus*
American woodcock	*Scolopax minor*
bald eagle	*Haliaeetus leucocephalus*
belted kingfisher	*Ceryle alcyon*
black-billed cuckoo	*Coccyzus erythropthalmus*
blackbird	
—red-winged	*Agelaius phoeniceus*
—rusty	*Euphagus carolinus*
black tern	*Childonias niger*
brown creeper	*Certhia americana*
brown thrasher	*Toxostoma rufum*
cedar waxwing	*Bombycilla cedrorum*
chickadee	
—black-capped	*Parus atricapillus*
—boreal	*Parus hudsonicus*
crossbill	
—red	*Loxia curvirostra*
—white-winged	*Loxia leucoptera*
crow, American	*Corvus brachyrhynchos*
duck	
—American wigeon	*Anas americana*
—black	*Anas rubripes*
—blue-winged teal	*Anas discors*
—common goldeneye	*Bucephala clangula*
—mallard	*Anas platyrhynchos*
—ring-necked	*Aythya collaris*
—wood	*Aix sponsa*
eastern kingbird	*Tyrannus tyrannus*
eastern phoebe	*Sayornis nigricans*
eastern wood-pewee	*Contopus virens*

BIRDS *(cont.)*	
falcon	
—American Kestrel	*Falco sparverius*
—merlin	*Falco columbarius*
—peregrine	*Falco peregrinus*
finch	
—American goldfinch	*Carduelis tristis*
—purple	*Carpodacus purpureus*
—pine siskin	*Carduelis pinus*
flycatcher	
—alder	*Empidonax alnorum*
—least	*Empidonax minimus*
—olive-sided	*Contopus borealis*
—yellow-bellied	*Empidonax flaviventris*
goose	
—Canada	*Branta canadensis*
—snow	*Chen caerulescens*
grackle, common	*Quiscalus quiscula*
gray catbird	*Dumetella carolinensis*
great blue heron	*Ardea herodias*
grosbeak	
—evening	*Coccothraustes vespertinus*
—pine	*Pinicola enucleator*
—rose-breasted	*Pheucticus ludovicianus*
grouse	
—ruffed	*Bonasa umbellus*
—spruce	*Dendragapus canadensis*
hawk	
—goshawk	*Accipiter gentilis*
—broad-winged	*Buteo platypterus*
—northern harrier (marsh hawk)	*Circus cyaneus*
—red-tailed	*Buteo jamaicensis*
—sharp-shinned	*Accipiter striatus*
herring gull	*Larus argentatus*
indigo bunting	*Passerina cyanea*
jay	
—blue	*Cyanocitta cristata*
—gray (Canada)	*Perisoreus canadensis*
killdeer	*Charadrius vociferus*
kinglet	
—golden-crowned	*Regulus satrapa*
—ruby-crowned	*Regulus calendula*
loon, common	*Gavia immer*

BIRDS *(cont.)*	
merganser	
—common	*Mergus merganser*
—hooded	*Lophodytes cucullatus*
nighthawk, common	*Chordeiles minor*
northern flicker	*Colaptes auratus*
nuthatch	
—red-breasted	*Sitta canadensis*
—white-breasted	*Sitta carolinensis*
osprey	*Pandion haliaetus*
owl	
—barred	*Strix varia*
—boreal	*Aegolius funereus*
—great gray	*Strix nebulosa*
—great horned	*Bubo virginianus*
—long-eared	*Asio otus*
—saw-whet	*Aegolius acadicus*
pied-billed grebe	*Podilymbus podiceps*
raven, common	*Corvus corax*
redpoll, common	*Carduelis flammea*
ruby-throated hummingbird	*Archilochus colubris*
scarlet tanager	*Piranga olivacea*
snipe, common	*Gallinago gallinago*
sparrow	
—chipping	*Spizella passerina*
—clay-colored	*Spizella pallida*
—dark-eyed junco	*Junco hyemalis*
—Le Conte's	*Ammodramus leconteii*
—Lincoln's	*Melospiza lincolnii*
—song	*Melospiza melodia*
—swamp	*Melospiza georgiana*
—white-throated	*Zonotrichia albicollis*
spotted sandpiper	*Actitis macularia*
starling	*Sturnus vulgaris*
swallow	
—barn	*Hirundo rustica*
—tree	*Tachycineta bicolor*
thrush	
—hermit	*Catharus guttatus*
—robin	*Turdus migratorius*
—Swainson's	*Catharus ustulatus*
—veery	*Catharus fuscescens*
turkey vulture	*Cathartes aura*
vireo	
—Philadelphia	*Vireo philadelphicus*

BIRDS *(cont.)*	
—red-eyed	*Vireo olivaceus*
—solitary	*Vireo solitarius*
warbler	
—American redstart	*Setophaga ruticilla*
—bay-breasted	*Dendroica castanea*
—black-and-white	*Mniotilta varia*
—blackburnian	*Dendroica fusca*
—black-throated blue	*Dendroica caerulescens*
—black-throated green	*Dendroica virens*
—Canada	*Wilsonia canadensis*
—Cape May	*Dendroica tigrina*
—chestnut-sided	*Dendroica pensylvanica*
—common yellowthroat	*Geothlypis trichas*
—Connecticut	*Oporornis agilis*
—golden-winged	*Vermivora chrysoptera*
—magnolia	*Dendroica magnolia*
—mourning	*Oporornis philadelphia*
—Nashville	*Vermivora ruficapilla*
—northern parula	*Parula americana*
—northern waterthrush	*Seiurus noveboracensis*
—ovenbird	*Seiurus aurocapillus*
—palm	*Dendroica palmarum*
—pine	*Dendroica pinus*
—Tennessee	*Vermivora peregrina*
—Wilson's	*Wilsonia pusilla*
—yellow	*Dendroica petechia*
—yellow-rumped	*Dendroica coronata*
whip-poor-will	*Caprimulgus vociferus*
woodpecker	
—black-backed	*Picoides arcticus*
—black-backed three-toed	*Picoides arcticus*
—common flicker	*Colaptes auratus*
—downy	*Picoides pubescens*
—hairy	*Picoides villosus*
—pileated	*Dryocopus pileatus*
—three-toed	*Picoides tridactylus*
—yellow-bellied sapsucker	*Sphyrapicus varius*
wren	
—house	*Troglodytes aedon*
—sedge	*Cistothorus platensis*
—winter	*Troglodytes troglodytes*

FISH	
bass	
—largemouth	*Micropterus salmoides*
—smallmouth	*Micropterus dolomieui*
—rock	*Ambloplites rupestris*
black crappie	*Pomoxis nigromaculatus*
burbot	*Lota lota*
cisco	*Coregonus artedi*
lake sturgeon	*Acipenser fulvescens*
lake trout	*Salvelinus namaycush*
lake whitefish	*Coregonus clupeaformis*
longnose sucker	*Catostomus catostomus*
northern pike	*Esox lucius*
rainbow smelt	*Osmerus mordax*
rusty crayfish	*Orconectes rusticus*
sauger	*Stizostedion canadense*
silver lamprey	*Ichthyomyzon unicuspis*
sunfish	*Lepomis* spp.
tadpole madtom	*Noturus gyrinus*
walleye	*Stizostedion vitreum*
white sucker	*Catostomus commersoni*
yellow perch	*Perca flavescens*

Stand-Origin Maps

These maps are a selection from the total of 49 stand-origin maps covering all of the virgin forest in the Boundary Waters Canoe Area Wilderness. Forests date from after the indicated fire year. Where stands consist of two or more age classes dating from separate fires, the years for each fire are given, with the earliest fire above the line.

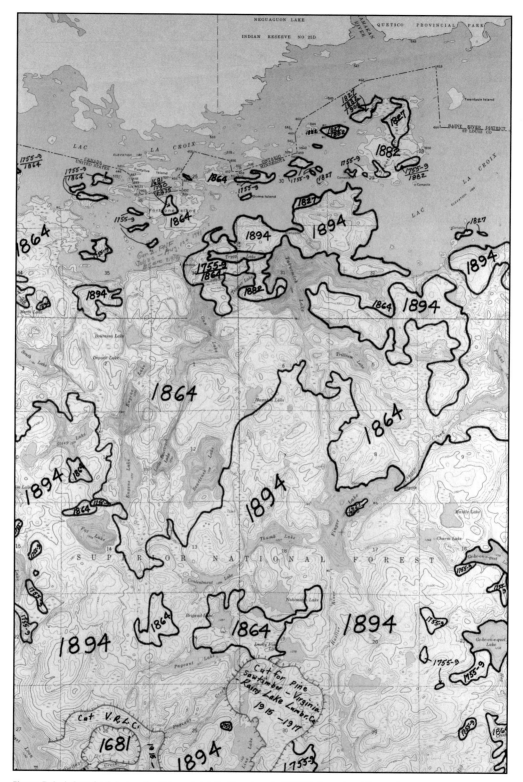

Figure D.1 / Stand origins on the Takucmich Lake Quadrangle (USGS), Boundary Waters Canoe Area, 1973

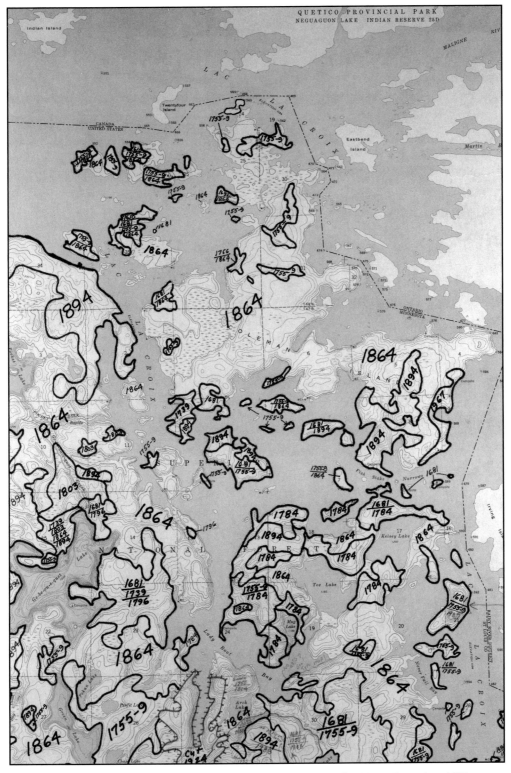

Figure D.2 / Stand origins on the Coleman Island Quadrangle (USGS), Boundary Waters Canoe Area, 1973

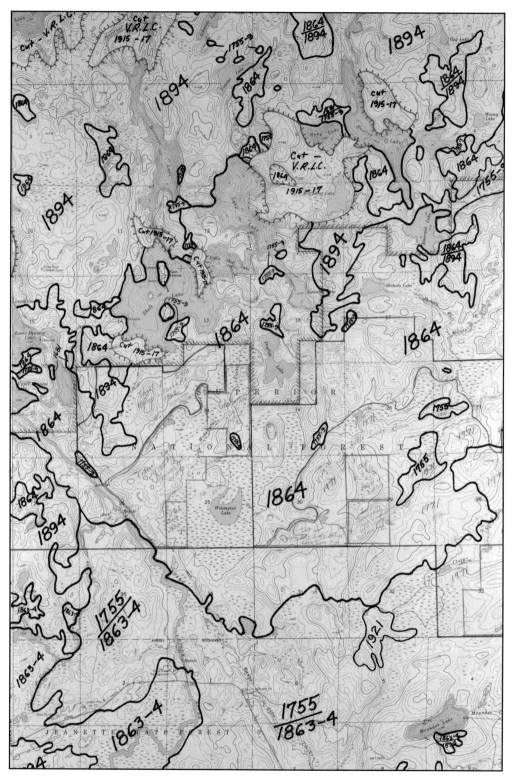

Figure D.3 / Stand origins on the Shell Lake Quadrangle (USGS), Boundary Waters Canoe Area, 1973

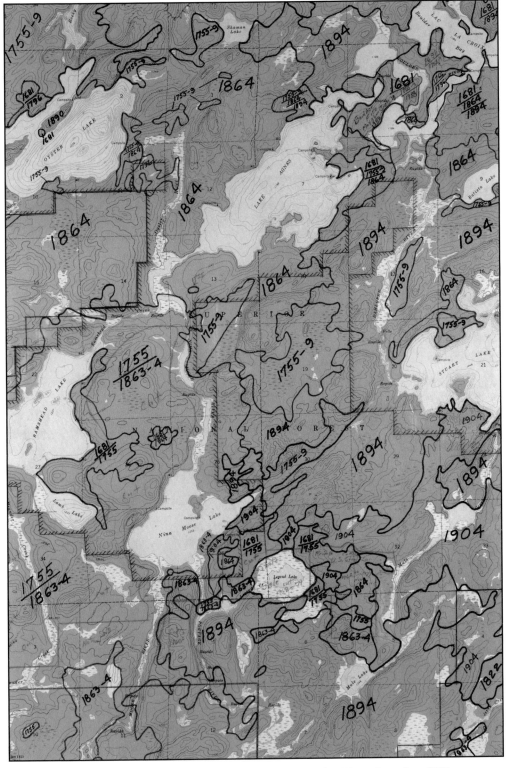

Figure D.4 / Stand origins on the Lake Agnes Quadrangle (USGS), Boundary Waters Canoe Area, 1973

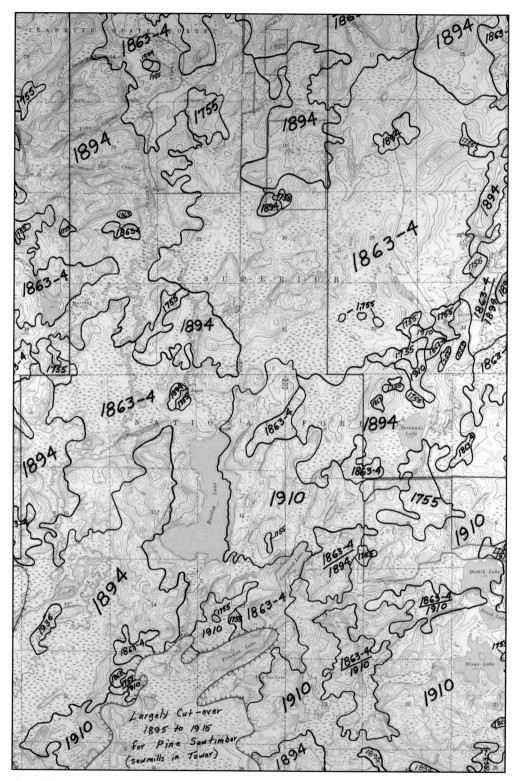

Figure D.5 / Stand origins on the Bootleg Lake Quadrangle (USGS), Boundary Waters Canoe Area, 1973

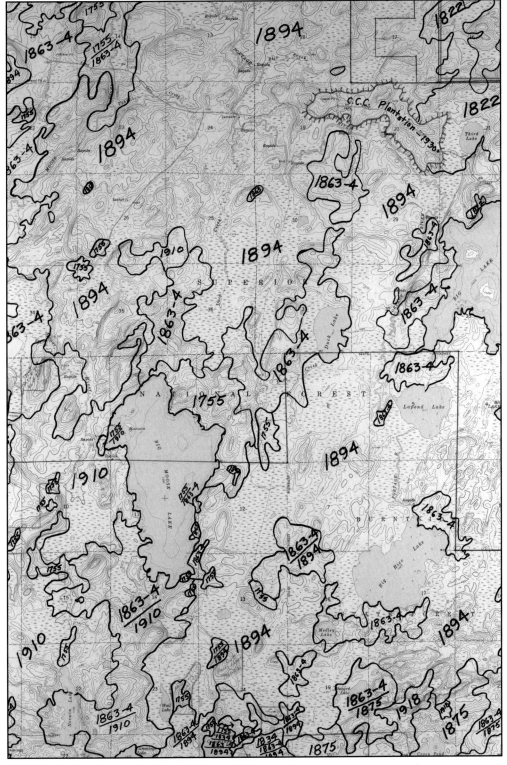

Figure D.6 / Stand origins on the Lapond Lake Quadrangle (USGS), Boundary Waters Canoe Area, 1973

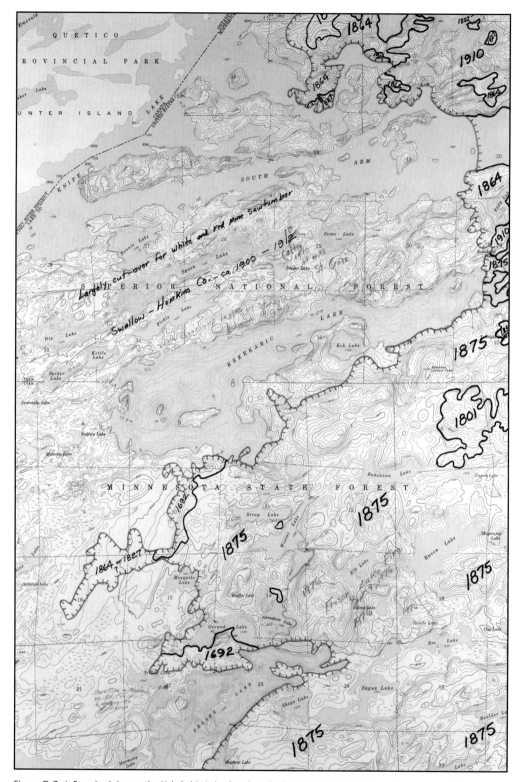

Figure D.7 / Stand origins on the Kekekabic Lake Quadrangle (USGS), Boundary Waters Canoe Area, 1973

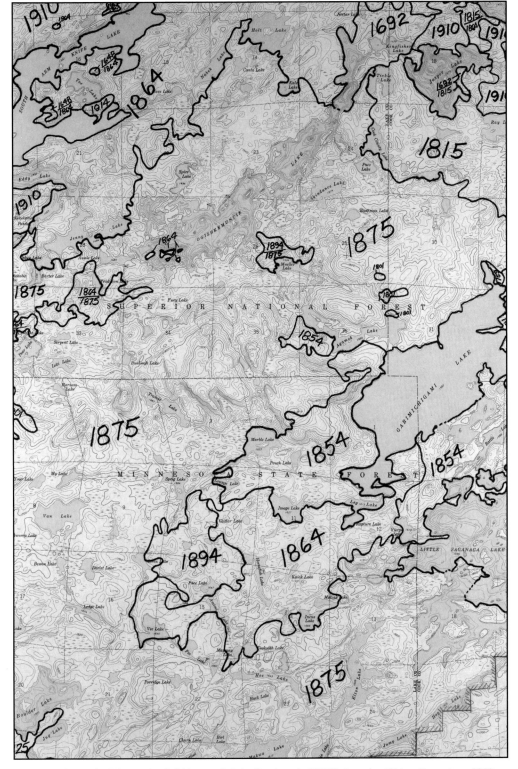

Figure D.8 / Stand origins on the Ogishkemuncie Lake Quadrangle (USGS), Boundary Waters Canoe Area, 1973

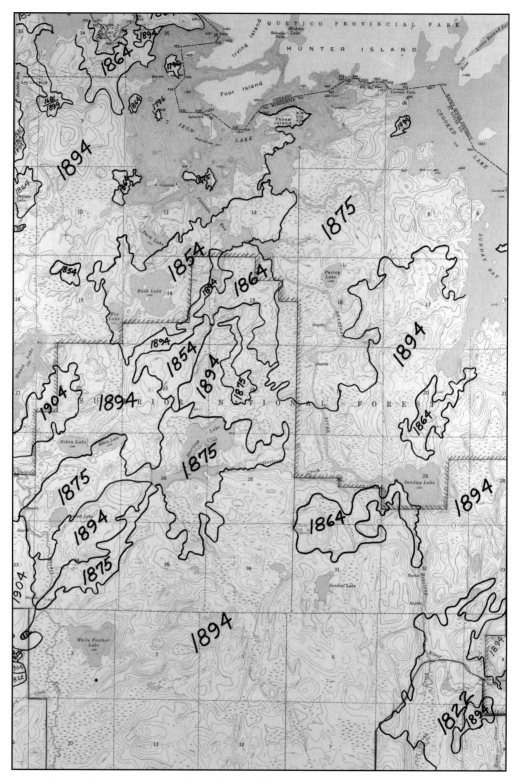

Figure D.9 / Stand origins on the Iron Lake Quadrangle (USGS), Boundary Waters Canoe Area, 1973

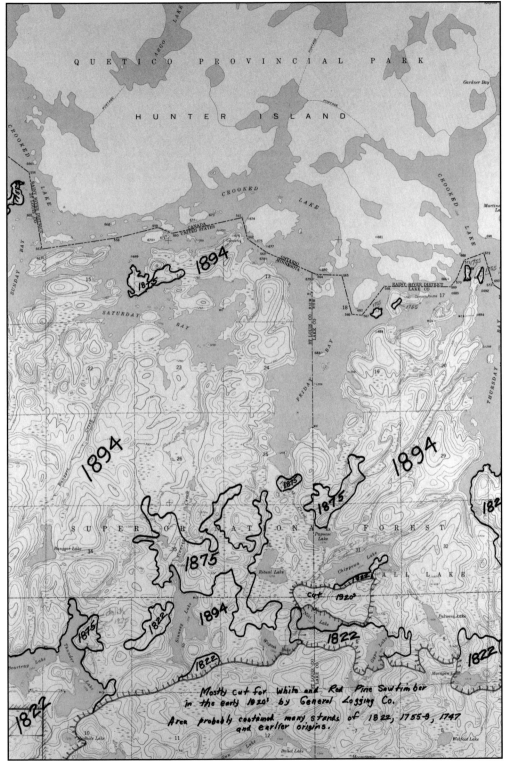

Figure D.10 / Stand origins on the Friday Bay Quadrangle (USGS), Boundary Waters Canoe Area, 1973

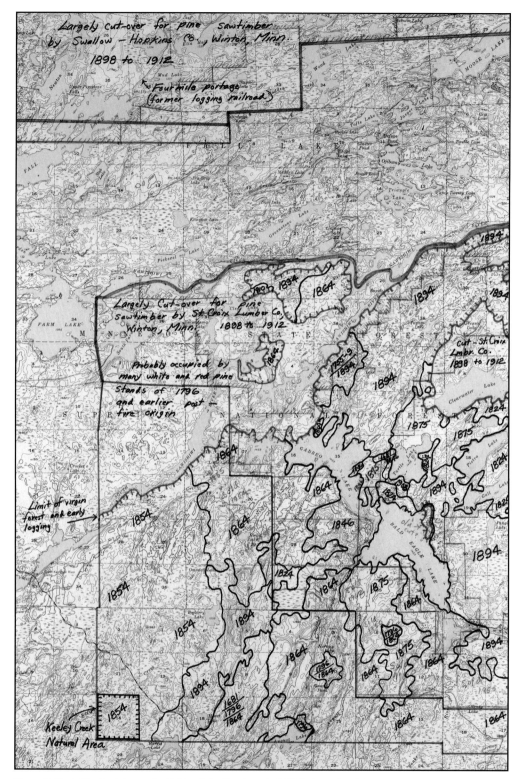

Figure D.11 / Stand origins on the Gabbro Lake Quadrangle (USGS), Boundary Waters Canoe Area, 1973

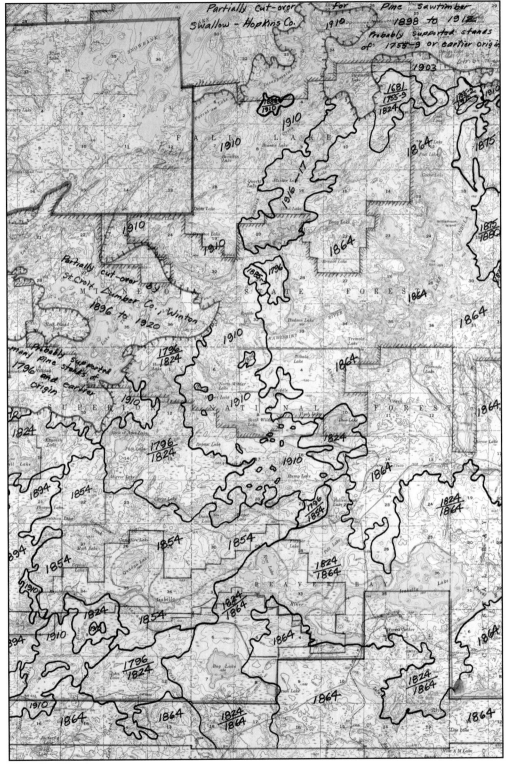

Figure D.12 / Stand origins on the Forest Center Quadrangle (USGS), Boundary Waters Canoe Area, 1973

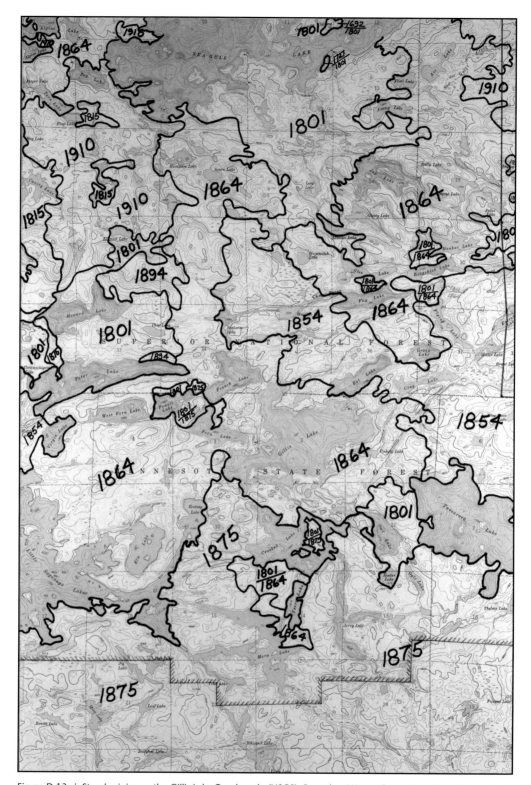

Figure D.13 / Stand origins on the Gillis Lake Quadrangle (USGS), Boundary Waters Canoe Area, 1973. (From M. L. Hein-selman1973, copyright 1973 by University of Washington. Reprinted by permission of the Ecological Society of America.)

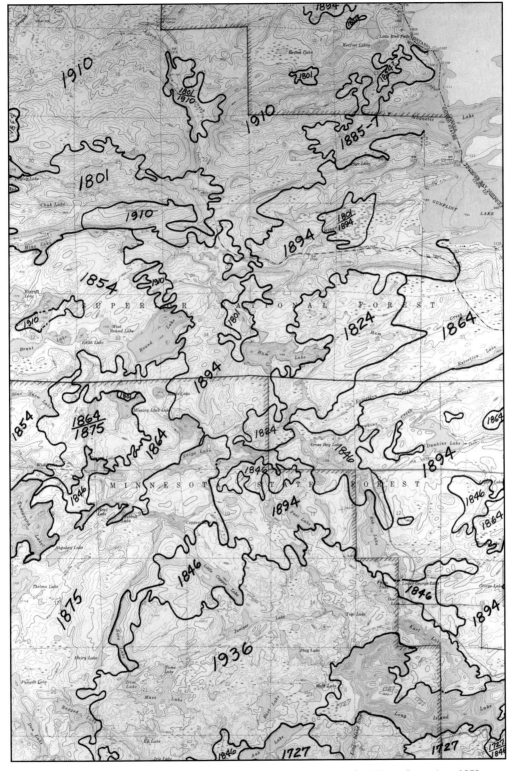

Figure D.14 / Stand origins on the Long Island Lake Quadrangle (USGS), Boundary Waters Canoe Area, 1973

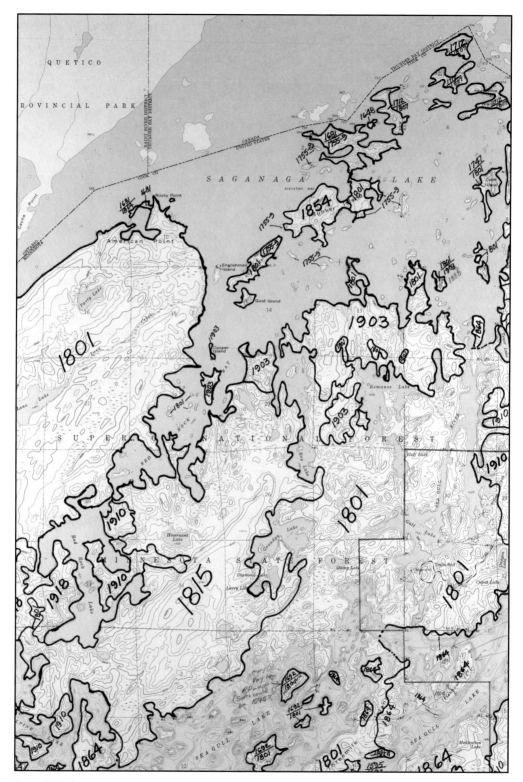

Figure D.15 / Stand origins on the Munker Island Quadrangle (USGS), Boundary Waters Canoe Area, 1973

Notes

1   Interviews with L. R. Beatty, Duluth, Minnesota; J. A. Bolz, Grand Rapids, Minnesota; G. A. Limstrom, Duluth; W. H. Magie, Duluth; E. C. Oberholtzer, Ranier, Minnesota; S. F. Olson, Ely, Minnesota; J. W. Trygg, Ely; J. W. White, Duluth; J. F. Wolff, Duluth.

2   Most of this history of St. Croix Lumber Company operations is based on an interview with J. W. Trygg, Ely, Minnesota, 1967, by the author, and an interview with E. M. Heinselman, Aug. 27, 1966, by the author. Location of cutting areas is based partially on a map prepared by J. W. Trygg, a copy of which is in files of the author. Many cutting area limits and locations of dams and sluiceways are based on fieldwork by the author.

3   Description of these railroad portages is based on an interview with J. W. Trygg, Ely, 1967; short reproduced typescript articles by J. W. Trygg, purchased from him in 1967; an interview with Leslie Beatty, 1967; an interview with W. H. Magie, 1967; articles in the *Ely Miner* by Lee Brownelle; and personal inspections on the ground. Trygg obtained his information in 1952 from G. H. Good, former superintendent of the Swallow and Hopkins mill. His interview with Good is contained in an illustrated typescript article.

4   Samuel A. Graham's description of this logging and his speculations about the origin of the regeneration are contained in correspondence with the Superior National Forest in 1965, copies of which are in the files of the author.

5   For more information on the Oliver Iron Mining Company operations in the Burntside Lake area, see Stenlund (1986).

6   These generalized cutting areas are based in part on a map by J. W. Trygg, a copy of which is in the files of the author.

7   This account of the Brule Lake or Camp 3 and Camp 8 fires is based on reports in the files of the Superior National Forest, Duluth, originally designated Fire, Superior, Camp 3 Fire, August 10, 1929. A popular account of the fire based on these records is available in Wolff (1958).

8   John J. Allison, former professor of forest economics at the University of Minnesota, gave a detailed account of this problem in a course in forest economics about 1948.

Literature Cited

Adelman, B. J., T. A. Heberlein, and T. M. Bonnicksen. 1982. Social psychological explanations for the persistence of a conflict between paddling canoeists and motorcraft users in the Boundary Waters Canoe Area. *Leisure Sciences* 5(1):45–62.

Ahlgren, C. E. 1959. Some effects of fire on forest reproduction in northeastern Minnesota. *J. Forestry* 57:194–200.

———. 1960. Some effects of fire on reproduction and growth of vegetation in northeastern Minnesota. *Ecology* 41:431–45.

———. 1966. Small mammals and reforestation following prescribed burning. *J. Forestry* 64:614–17.

———. 1969. *Eighteen years of weather in the Boundary Waters Canoe Area.* Univ. of Minnesota, Agricultural Experiment Station Miscellaneous Report 88.

———. 1970. *Some effects of prescribed burning on jack pine reproduction in northeastern Minnesota.* Univ. of Minnesota Agric. Expt. Sta. Misc. Rept. 94, Forestry Series 5-1970.

———. 1976. Regeneration of red pine and white pine following wildfire and logging in northeastern Minnesota. *J. Forestry* 74:135–40.

Ahlgren, C. E., and I. Ahlgren. 1984. *Lob trees in the wilderness.* Univ. of Minnesota Press, Minneapolis.

Ahlgren, I. F., and C. E. Ahlgren. 1960. Ecological effects of forest fires. *Bot. Review* 26:483–533.

Akcakaya, H. R. 1992. Population cycles of mammals: Evidence for a ratio-dependent predation hypothesis. *Ecol. Monogr.* 62:119–42.

Amundson, D. C., and H. E. Wright Jr. 1979. Forest changes in Minnesota at the end of the Pleistocene. *Ecol. Monogr.* 49:1–16.

Anderson, C. G., and D. W. Lime. 1984. Boundary Water Canoe Area-Quetico Provincial Park: An international partnership. *Western Wildlands* 10(2):13–19.

Anderson, D. H. 1980. Long-time Boundary Waters visitors change use patterns. *Naturalist* 31(4):2–5.

———. 1981. The effect of user experience on displacement. Pages 272–79 in J. W. Frazier and B. J. Epstein, eds., Proc. Applied Geography Confer., Oct 22–24, Tempe, Ariz., vol. 4.

Anderson, R. C. 1972. The ecological relationships of meningeal worm and native cervids in North America. *J. Wildl. Disease,* 8:304–10.

Anderson, R. L., and F. H. Kaufert. 1959. Brooming response of black spruce to dwarf mistletoe. *Forest Sci.* 5:356–64.

Anfinson, S. F. 1990. Archaeological regions in Minnesota and the Woodland Period. Pages 135–66 in G. E. Gibbon, ed., *The Woodland Tradition in the western Great Lakes: Papers presented to Elden Johnson.* Univ. of Minnesota Publications in Anthropology, no. 4.

Apfelbaum, S. I., and A. Haney. 1981. Bird populations before and after wildfire in a Great Lakes pine forest. *Condor* 83:347–54.

———. 1986. Changes in bird populations during succession following fire in the northern Great Lakes wilderness. Pages 10–16 in R. C. Lucas, compiler, Proc. National Wilderness Research Conference, 1985: Current research, July 23–26, Ft. Collins, Colo.; USDA, Forest Service Gen. Tech. Rept. INT-212, Ogden, Utah.

Arimond, S. R. 1979. Fruit production in black bear habitat of northeastern Minnesota. M.S. thesis. Univ. of Minnesota, Duluth.

———. 1980. Black bears of northeast Minnesota: Ecology and management. Pages 67–69 in Mammalian ecology and habitat management in Minnesota., Proc. of symposium, Bald Eagle Outdoor Learning Center, Cass Lake, Minn., March 7–9, 1980.

Arno, S. F., and J. K. Brown. 1989. Managing fire in our forests: Time for a new initiative. *J. Forestry* 87(12):44–46.

Audubon. 1990. Special issue on the last wetlands. July 1990, vol. 92. no. 4. National Audubon Society, New York.

Ayres, H. B. 1899. Timber conditions of the pine region of Minnesota: Part I. Forest reserves. U.S. Geol. Survey, 21st Annual Report, with map.

Baker, D. G., D. A. Haines, and J. H. Strub Jr. 1967. *Precipitation facts, normals, and extremes.* Climate of Minnesota, Part V, Univ. of Minnesota Agric. Expt. Sta. Tech. Bull. 254.

Baker, D. G., and E. L. Kuehnast. 1978. *Precipitation normals for Minnesota: 1941–1970.* Climate of Minnesota, Part X, Univ. of Minnesota Agric. Expt. Sta. Tech. Bull. 314.

Baker, D. G., E. L. Kuehnast, and J. A. Zandlo. 1985. *Normal temperatures (1951–1980) and their application.* Climate of Minnesota, Part XV, Univ. of Minnesota Agricultural Experiment Station AD-SB-2777.

Baker, D. G., W. W. Nelson, and E. L. Kuehnast. 1979. *The hydrologic cycle and soil water.* Climate of Minnesota, Part XII, Univ. of Minnesota Agric. Expt. Sta. Tech. Bull. 322.

Baker, D. G., and J. H. Strub Jr. 1965. *Temperature and its application.* Climate of Minnesota, Part III, Univ. of Minnesota Agric. Expt. Sta. Tech. Bull. 248.

Baker, W. L. 1989a. Effect of scale and spatial heterogeneity on fire-interval distributions. *Can. J. For. Res.* 19:700–706.

———. 1989b. Landscape ecology and nature reserve design in the Boundary Waters Canoe Area, Minnesota. *Ecology* 70:23–35.

Barney, R. J. 1971. Wildfires in Alaska: Some historical and projected effects and aspects. Pages 51–59 in Proc. of Fire in the northern environment: A symposium, Fairbanks, Ala., 1971.

Beamish, R. J. 1976. Acidification of lakes in Canada by acid precipitation and the resulting effects on fishes. *Water, Air, Soil Pollut.* 6:501–14.

Beamish, R. J., and H. H. Harvey. 1972. Acidification of the LaCloche Mountain lakes. *J. Fish. Res. Board Can.* 29:1131–43.

Beamish, R. J., W. L. Lockhart, J. C. Van Loon, and H. H. Harvey. 1975. Long-term acidification of a lake and resulting effects on fishes. *Ambio* 4:98–102.

Beaufait, W. R. 1960. Some effects of high temperatures on the cones and seeds of jack pine. *Forest Sci.* 6:194–99.

Beer, J. R., R. B. Brander, and C. T. Cushwa. 1973. Small mammal populations. Part III, pages 27–30 in L. F. Ohmann et al., *Wilderness Ecology: The upland plant communities, woody browse production, and small mammals of two adjacent 33-year-old wildfire areas in northeastern Minnesota.* USDA, Forest Service Gen. Tech. Rept. NC-7.

Beer, J. R., P. W. Lukens, and D. Olson. 1954. Small mammal populations on the islands of Basswood Lake, Minnesota. *Ecology* 35:437–45.

Benyus, J. M. 1989. *Northwoods wildlife: A watchers guide to habitats.* NorthWord Press, Minocqua, Wis.

Berg, B. 1987. Northern predators and furbearers. Part 1: The Mustelids. *Minnesota Forests*, spring 1987:8–9.

Bergeron, Y. 1991. The influence of island and mainland landscapes on boreal forest fire regimes. *Ecology* 72:1980–92.

Bergeron, Y., and J. Brisson. 1990. Fire regime in red pine stands at the northern limit of the species range. *Ecology* 71:1352–64.

Bergerud, A. T. 1971. The population dynamics of Newfoundland caribou. The Wildl. Soc., *Wildl. Monogr.* 25.

———. 1985. Antipredator strategies of caribou: Dispersion along shorelines. *Can. J. Zool.* 63:1324–29.

Bergerud, A. T., and W. E. Mercer. 1989. Caribou introductions in eastern North America. *Wildl. Soc. Bull.* 17:111–20.

Bergman, H. F., and Stallard, H. 1916. The development of climax formations in northern Minnesota. *Minn. Bot. Studies* 4:333–78.

Bergstedt, B., and G. J. Niemi. 1974. A comparison of two breeding bird censuses following the Little Sioux forest fire. *The Loon*, spring 1974:28–32.

Birney, E. C. 1974. Twentieth-century records of wolverine in Minnesota. *The Loon* 46:78–81.

Blais, J. R. 1983. Predicting tree mortality induced by spruce budworm: A discussion. *Forestry-Chronicle* 59 (6):294–97.

Bolz, J. A. 1960. *Portage into the past.* Univ. of Minnesota Press, Minneapolis.

Books, D. J. 1972. Little Sioux burn: Year 2. *Naturalist* (J. of Minn. Nat. Hist. Soc.) 23 (autumn and winter):2–7.

Bormann, F. H., and G. E. Likens. 1979. *Pattern and process in a forested ecosystem.* Springer-Verlag, New York.

Botkin, D. B., R. A. Nisbet, and T. E. Reynales. 1989. Effects of climate change on the forests of the Great Lakes states. Pages 2–1 to 2–31 in J. B. Smith and D. A. Tirpak, eds., *The potential effects of global climate change on the United States.* EPA-203-05-89-054, U.S. Environmental Protection Agency, Washington, D.C.

Botkin, D. B., and R. A. Nisbet. 1992. Forest response to climatic change: Effects of parameter estimation and choice of weather patterns on the reliability of projections. *Climatic Change* 20:87–111.

Braekke, F. H., ed. 1976. Impact of acid precipitation on forest and freshwater ecosystems in Norway. Summary report, Phase 1, Norwegian SNSF Project, Oslo.

Brandner, T. A., R. O. Peterson, and K. L. Risenhoover. 1990. Balsam fir on Isle Royale: Effects of moose herbivory and population density. *Ecology* 71:155–64.

Braniff, E. A. 1903. The proposed Lake Superior Forest Reserve, Lake and Cook Counties, Minnesota. Official report in files of Superior National Forest, Duluth, Minn.

Breining, G. A., and J. A. Bolz. 1987. *Voyageurs National Park.* Lake States Interpretive Assn., International Falls, Minn.

Bright, A., and M. Manfredo. 1989. *A model for evaluating the effects of a recreation information campaign and an evaluation of BWCAW 1988 wilderness communication efforts.* Technical report to the Forest Service. Colorado State Univ., Dept of Recreation Resources and Landscape Architecture.

Brownelle, L. 1982. Article in *Ely Miner.* Sept. 8, 1982.

Bryson, R. A., W. M. Wendland, J. D. Ives, and J. T. Andrews. 1969. Radiocarbon isochrones on the disintegration of the Laurentide ice sheet. *Arctic and Alpine Research* 1:1–14.

Buckman, R. E. 1964a. Silvicultural use of prescribed burning in the Lake States. Pages 38–40 in Proc. Soc. Amer. Foresters, Denver, Colo.

———. 1964b. Effects of prescribed burning on hazel in Minnesota. *Ecology* 45:626–29.

Buech, R. R., K. P. Siderits, R. E. Radtke, H. L. Sheldon, and D. Elsing. 1977. Small mammal populations after a wildfire in northeast Minnesota. USDA, Forest Service Research Paper NC-151.

Buell, M. F., and W. A. Niering. 1957. Fir-spruce-birch forest in northern Minnesota. *Ecology* 38:602–10.

Carhart, A. 1922. Recreation plan: Superior National Forest. In 2320 Arthur Carhart folder, Superior National Forest records.

Chapin, F. S. III, and K. Van Cleve. 1981. Plant nutrient absorption and retention under different fire regimes. Pages 301–21 in H. A. Mooney, T. M. Bonnicksen, N. L. Christensen, J. E. Lotan, and W. A. Reiners, coordinators, *Fire regimes and ecosystem properties.* Proc. of conference, Honolulu, Hawaii. 1978. USDA, Forest Service Gen. Tech. Rept. WO-26.

Clark, J. S. 1988. Effect of climate change on fire regimes in northwestern Minnesota. *Nature* 334:233–35.

———. 1989. Ecological disturbance as a renewal process: Theory and application to fire history. *Oikos* 56:17–30.

———. 1990a. Fire and climate change during the last 750 yr. in northwestern Minnesota. *Ecol. Monogr.* 60:135–59.

———. 1990b. Twentieth-century climate change, fire suppression, and forest production and decomposition in northwestern Minnesota. *Can. J. For. Res.* 20:219–32.

Clements, F. E. 1910. *The life history of lodgepole burn forests.* U.S. Forest Service Bull. 79.

————. 1916. *Plant succession: An analysis of the development of vegetation*. Carnegie Inst. Pub. 242, Washington, D.C.

Coffin, B. A. 1988. The natural vegetation of Minnesota at the time of the Public Land Survey: 1847–1907. Biological Report No. 1, Minn. Department of Natural Resources, St. Paul.

Coffin, B., and L. Pfannmuller, 1988. *Minnesota's endangered flora and fauna*. Univ. of Minnesota Press, Minneapolis.

Cohn, J. P. 1990. Endangered wolf population increases. *Bioscience* 40:628–32.

Cole, D. N. 1987. Research on soil and vegetation in wilderness: A state of knowledge review. Pages 135–77 in R. C. Lucas, ed., Proc. of National Wilderness research conference: Issues, state-of-knowledge, future directions. USDA, Forest Service Gen. Tech. Rept. INT-220.

————. 1990a. Ecological impacts of wilderness recreation and their management. Pages 425–66 in J. C. Hendee, G. H. Stankey, and R. C. Lucas, eds., *Wilderness management*. North American Press, Golden Colo.

————. 1990b. Some principles to guide wilderness campsite management. Pages 181–87 in D. W. Lime, ed., *Managing America's wilderness resource*. Proc. of the conference, Minneapolis, Minn. Sept. 11–17, 1989. Extension Service and Minn. Agricultural Experimental Station, Univ. of Minnesota, St. Paul.

Cooper, W. S. 1913. The climax forest of Isle Royle, Lake Superior, and its development. *Bot. Gaz.* 15:1–44, 115–40, 189–235.

Craig, A. J. 1972. Pollen influx to laminated sediments: A pollen diagram from northeastern Minnesota. *Ecology* 53:46–57.

Crossman, E. J. 1976. *Quetico fishes*. Royal Ontario Museum, Toronto.

Crowley, K., and M. Link. 1987. *Love of loons*. Voyageur Press, Stillwater, Minn.

Cwynar, L. C. 1977. The recent fire history of Barron Township, Algonquin Park. *Can. J. Bot.* 55:1524–38.

————. 1978. Recent history of fire and vegetation from laminated sediment of Greenleaf Lake, Algonquin Park, Ontario. *Can. J. Bot.* 56:10–21.

Darby, W. R., H. R. Timmerman, J. B. Snider, K. F. Abraham, R. A. Stefanski, and C. A. Johnson. 1989. *Woodland caribou in Ontario, background to a policy*. Ontario Ministry of Natural Resources, unnumbered report.

Davis, M. B. 1981. Quaternary history and the stability of forest communities. Pages 132–53 in D. C. West, H. H. Shugart, and D. B. Botkin, eds., *Forest succession, concepts and application*. Springer-Verlag, New York.

————. 1989a. Insights from paleoecology on global change. *Ecol. Society of Amer. Bull.* 70:222–28.

————. 1989b. Lags in vegetation response to greenhouse warming. *Climatic Change* 15:75–82.

————. 1990. Climatic change and survival of forest species. Pages 99–110 in G. M. Woodwell, ed., *The earth in transition: Patterns and processes of biotic impoverishment*. Cambridge Univ. Press, Cambridge.

Davis, M. B., and C. Zabinski. 1992. Changes in geographical ranges resulting from greenhouse warming-effects on biodiversity in forests. In R. Peters and T. Lovejoy, eds., *Consequences of greenhouse warming to biodiversity*. Yale Univ. Press, New Haven, Conn.

Dawson, D. K. 1979. Bird communities associated with succession and management of lowland conifer forests. Pages 120–31 in M. DeGraaf and K. E. Evans, *Management of north central and northeastern forests for nongame birds*. Workshop Proc., Jan 23–25, Minneapolis, Minn., USDA, Forest Service Gen. Tech. Rept. NC-51.

Day, R. J. 1990. The dynamic nature of Ontario's forests from postglacial times to the present day. Pages 63–122 in Old Growth Forests . . . What are they, How do they work? Proc. of Conference on Old Growth Forests. Faculty of Forestry, Univ. of Toronto, eds., Canadian Scholar's Press, Toronto.

Dean, J. L. 1971. Wetland forest communities of the eastern Boundary Waters Canoe Area. M.S. thesis, Univ. of Minnesota.

DelGiudice, G. D., L. D. Mech, and U. S. Seal. 1991. Gray wolf density and its association with weights and hematology of pups from 1970 to 1988. *J. Wildlife Diseases*, 27:630–36.

DelGiudice, G. D., M. E. Nelson, and L. D. Mech. 1991. *Winter nutrition and population ecology of white-tailed deer in the central Superior National Forest*. USDA, Forest Service Gen. Tech. Rept. NC-147.

Dewdney, S., and K. E. Kidd. 1967. *Indian rock paintings of the Great Lakes*. Univ. of Toronto Press, Toronto.

EIFAC Working Party on Water Quality Criteria for European Fresh-Water Fish. 1969. Water quality criteria for European fresh-water fish: Extreme pH values and inland fisheries. *Water Res.* 3:593–611.

Ely Echo. 1988. *Ely, since 1988*. Ely Echo.

Erickson, A. B., V. E. Gunvalson, M. H. Stenlund, D. W. Burcalow, and L. H. Blankenship. 1961. *The white-tailed deer of Minnesota*. Minn. Dept. of Conservation Tech. Bull. 5.

Fair, J., and L. Rogers. 1990. *The great American bear*. NorthWord Press, Minocqua Wis.

Farrand, J. Jr., ed. 1983. *The Audubon Society master guide to birding*, vol. 3, *Warblers to sparrows*. Alfred Knopf, New York.

Fashingbauer, B. A. 1965. The woodland caribou in Minnesota. Pages 133–66 in *Big game in Minnesota*. Minn. Dept. of Conservation Tech. Bull. 9.

Foster, D. R. 1983. The history and pattern of fire in the boreal forest of southeastern Labrador. *Can. J. Bot.* 61:2459–71.

Fowells, H. A. 1965. *Silvics of forest trees of the United States*. USDA, Forest Service, Agric. Handbook 271.

Franklin, J. F. 1987. Scientific uses of wilderness. Pages 42–46 in R. C. Lucas, ed., Proc. of National Wilderness research conference: Issues, state-of-knowledge, future directions, July 1985, Ft. Collins, Colo. U.S. Forest Service Gen. Tech. Rep. INT-220.

————. 1990. Wilderness ecosystems. Pages 240–61 in J. C. Hendee, G. H. Stankey, and R. C. Lucas, eds., *Wilderness Management*. North American Press, Golden, Colo.

Friends of Quetico Park. 1989. Fire management planning in Quetico. *Touchstone* (newsletter), Aug. 1989, Atikokan, Ont.

Fries, M. 1962. Pollen profiles of late Pleistocene and recent sediments from Weber Lake, Minnesota. *Ecology* 43:295–308.

Frissell, S. S. 1973. The importance of fire as a natural ecological factor in Itasca State Park, Minnesota. *Quaternary Research* 3:397–407.

Frissell, S. S., and D. P. Duncan. 1965. Campsite preference and deterioration in the Quetico-Superior Canoe Country. *J. Forestry* 63:256–60.

Gilbert, G. C., G. L. Peterson, and D. W. Lime. 1972. Toward a model of travel behavior in the Boundary Waters Canoe Area. *Environment and Behavior* 4(2):131–57.

Gilbert, G. C., G. L. Peterson, and J. L. Schofer. 1972. Markov renewal model of linked trip travel behavior. *Transportation Engineering Jour.* ASCE. 98(TE3):691–704.

318

Gilman, C., 1982. *Where two worlds meet: The Great Lakes fur trade.* Minn. Historical Society, St. Paul.

Glass, G. E., and O. L. Loucks, eds. 1980. *Impacts of airborne pollutants on wilderness areas along the Minnesota-Ontario border.* U.S. Envir. Protection Agency, Envir. Research Lab., Duluth, Minn. EPA-600/3-80-044.

Gogan, P. J., P. A. Jordan, and J. L. Nelson. 1990. Planning to reintroduce woodland caribou to Minnesota. *Trans. No. Amer. Wildlife and Natural Resource Conference* 55:599–608.

Goldman, C. R., and A. J. Horne. 1983. *Limnology.* McGraw-Hill, New York.

Goodman, B. 1991. Keeping anglers happy has a price. *Bioscience* 41(5):294–300.

Graham, R. L., M. G. Turner, and V. Dale. 1990. How increasing CO_2 and climate change affect forests. *Bioscience* 40:575–87.

Grange, W. B. 1949. *The way to game abundance.* Chas. Scribner's, New York.

———. 1965. Fire and tree growth relationships to snowshoe rabbits. Pages 110–25 in Proc. of Fourth Annual Tall Timbers Fire Ecology Conference, Tallahassee, Fla., 1965.

Green, J. C. 1991. A landscape classification for breeding birds in Minnesota: An approach to describing regional biodiversity. *The Loon* 63:80–91.

Green, J. C., and G. J. Niemi. 1980. *Birds of the Superior National Forest.* Superior National Forest, Forest Service, U.S. Department of Agric.

Green, J. C., G. J. Niemi, and K. P. Siderits. 1978. *Birds of the Superior National Forest.* Eastern Region, U.S. Forest Service.

Grigal, D. F., and L. F. Ohmann. 1975. Classification, description, and dynamics of upland plant communities within a Minnesota wilderness area. *Ecol. Monogr.* 45:389–407.

Gullion, G. 1989. *The ruffed grouse.* NorthWord Press, Minocqua, Wis.

Gunderson, H. L., and J. R. Beer. 1953. *The mammals of Minnesota.* Univ. of Minnesota Press, Minneapolis.

Haines, D. A., and R. W. Sando. 1969. *Climatic conditions preceding historically great fires in the north central region.* U.S. Forest Service Research Paper NC-34.

Hardy, Y. M. Mainville, and D. M. Schmitt. 1986. *An atlas of spruce budworm defoliation in eastern North America, 1938–80.* USDA, Forest Service Misc. Publ. 1449.

Harrington, F. H., and L. D. Mech. 1979. Wolf howling and its role in territory maintenance. *Behaviour* 68:207–49.

Harrison, C. 1978. *A field guide to the nests, eggs, and nestlings of North American birds.* Collins, Cleveland, Ohio.

Harrison, H. H. 1975. *A field guide to birds nests in the United States east of the Mississippi River.* Houghton Mifflin, Boston.

Hazard, E. B. 1982. *The mammals of Minnesota.* Univ. of Minnesota Press, Minneapolis.

Heinselman, M. L. 1961. Black spruce on the peatlands of former Glacial Lake Agassiz and adjacent areas in Minnesota: A study of forest sites, bog processes, and bog types. Ph.D. thesis, Univ. of Minnesota.

———. 1963. Forest sites, bog processes, and peatland types in the Glacial Lake Agassiz region of Minnesota. *Ecol. Monogr.* 33:327–74.

———. 1970. Landscape evolution, peatland types, and the environment in the Lake Agassiz Peatlands Natural Area, Minnesota. *Ecol. Monogr.* 40:235–61.

———. 1973. Fire in the virgin forests of the Boundary Waters Canoe Area, Minnesota. *Quaternary Research* 3:329–82.

———. 1974. Interpretation of Francis J. Marschner's map of the original vegetation of Minnesota. Text on back of Marschner's map, "The original vegetation of Minnesota." U.S. Forest Service, North Central Forest Expt. Sta., St. Paul.

———. 1978. Fire in wilderness ecosystems. Pages 249–78 in J. C. Hendee, G. H. Stankey, and R. C. Lucas, eds. *Wilderness Management.* USDA, Forest Service Misc. Pub. 1365, U.S. Gov. Printing Office, Washington, D.C.

———. 1981a. Fire and succession in the conifer forests of northern North America. Pages 374–405 in D. C. West, H. H. Shugart, and D. B. Botkin, eds., *Forest succession, concepts and application.* Springer-Verlag, New York.

———. 1981b. Fire intensity and frequency as factors in the distribution and structure of northern ecosystems. Pages 7–57 in H. A. Mooney, T. M. Bonnicksen, N. L. Christensen, J. E. Lotan, and W. A. Reiners, coordinators, *Fire regimes and ecosystem properties.* Proc. of conference, Honolulu, Hawaii, 1978. USDA, Forest Service Gen. Tech. Rept. WO-26.

———. 1985. Fire regimes and management options in ecosystems with large high-intensity fires. Pages 101–9 in J. T. Lotan, B. M. Kilgore, W. C. Fischer, and R. W. Mutch, coordinators, Proc. of symposium and workshop on wilderness fire, Missoula, Mont., Nov. 1983, USDA, Forest Service Gen. Tech. Rept. INT-182.

Heiskary, S. A., and R. D. Payer. 1983. *Acid deposition: A study on the impact of snowmelt on the surface water quality of northeastern Minnesota.* Minn. Pollution Control Agency and Minn. Dept. of Natural Resources, St. Paul.

Helwig, D. D., and S. A. Heiskary. 1985. Acid rain: Intensive study lakes program, status report for the study lakes (1981–1984). Minn. Pollution Control Agency. Division of Water Quality, St. Paul.

Hendee, J. C. 1990. Principles of wilderness management. Pages 180–93 in J. C. Hendee, G. H. Stankey, and R. C. Lucas, *Wilderness management.* North American Press, Golden, Colo.

Hendee, J. C., and G. H. Stankey. 1973. Biocentricity in wilderness management. *Bioscience* 23:535–38.

Hendee, J. C., G. H. Stankey, and R. C. Lucas. 1990. *Wilderness management.* 2d ed. North American Press, Golden, Colo.

Hendee, J. C., and R. von Koch. 1990. Wilderness management planning. Pages 194–213 in J. C. Hendee, G. H. Stankey, and R. C. Lucas, *Wilderness management.* North American Press, Golden, Colo.

Higgins, J. F. 1977. A visitor distribution program for the Boundary Waters Canoe Area. *Naturalist* 28(4):22–29.

Higgins, S. M. 1908. Additional area to the proposed Lake Superior National Forest, Minnesota. Unpublished report in historical files of Superior National Forest, Duluth, Minn., U.S. Forest Service.

Hobbs, H. C., and J. E. Goebel. 1982. Geologic map of Minnesota, quaternary geology. Minnesota Geological Survey, Univ. of Minnesota.

Horton, K. W., and G. H. D. Bedell. 1960. *White and red pine ecology, silviculture, and management.* Canada Dept. North. Affairs and Natl. Resources, Forestry Branch Bull. 124.

Hoskinson, R. L., and L. D. Mech. 1976. White-tailed deer migration and its role in wolf predation. *J. Wildl. Mgt.* 40:429–41.

Hulbert, J. H., and J. F. Higgins. 1977. BWCA Visitor Distribution System. *J. Forestry* 75:338–40.

International Joint Commission. 1934. *Final report of the International Joint Commission on the Rainy Lake reference.* J. O. Patenaude, Ottawa.

Irving, F. D., and D. W. French. 1971. Control by fire of dwarf mistletoe in black spruce. *J. Forestry* 69:28–30.

Irwin, L. L. 1974. Relationships between deer and moose on a burn in northeastern Minnesota. M.S. thesis, Univ. of Idaho.

Jacobson, G. L. Jr. 1979. The paleoecology of white pine (*Pinus strobus*) in Minnesota. *J. of Ecol.* 67:697–726.

Jacobson, G. L. Jr., T. Webb III, and E. C. Grimm. 1987. Patterns and rates of vegetation change during the deglaciation of eastern North America. Chap. 13 in W. F. Ruddiman and H. E. Wright Jr., eds., *North America and adjacent oceans during the last deglaciation.* The Geology of North America, vol. K-3. Geol. Soc. of America.

Janssen, C. R. 1968. Myrtle Lake: A late and post-glacial pollen diagram from northern Minnesota. *Can. J. Bot.* 46:1397–1408.

Janssen, R. B. 1987. *Birds in Minnesota.* Univ. of Minnesota Press, Minneapolis.

Janssens, J. A. 1992. Bryophytes. Pages 44–57 in H. E. Wright, B. A. Coffin, and N. E. Aaseng, eds., *The patterned peatlands of Minnesota.* Univ. of Minnesota Press, Minneapolis.

Jardine, W. M. 1926. The policy of the Department of Agriculture in relation to road building and recreational use of the Superior National Forest. Office of the Secretary, USDA, Washington, D.C. (copy in author's files).

Johnson, E. 1988. *The prehistoric peoples of Minnesota.* Minn. Prehistoric Archaeology Series, no. 3, Minn. Historical Society Press, St. Paul.

Johnson, E. A., and J. S. Rowe. 1975. Fire in the subarctic wintering ground of the Beverley caribou herd. *Amer. Midl. Nat.* 94:1–14.

Johnson, F. H., and J. G. Hale. 1977. Interrelations between walleye and smallmouth bass in four northeastern Minnesota lakes, 1948–69. *J. Fish. Res. Board Can.* 34:1626–32.

Johnson, M. G., J. H. Leach, C. K. Minns, and C. H. Olver. 1977. Limnological characteristics of Ontario lakes in relation to associations of walleye, northern pike, lake trout, and smallmouth bass. *J. Fish. Res. Board Can.* 34:1592–1601.

Johnston, W. F. 1971. Broadcast burning slash favors black spruce reproduction on organic soil in Minnesota. *Forestry Chronicle* 47(1):33–35.

Jones, P. E. 1987. An evaluation of the "BWCAW User Education Program": A cognitive and behavioral analysis. Ph.D. diss., Univ. of Minnesota.

Jones, P. E., and L. H. McAvoy. 1987. An evaluation of a wilderness users education program: A cognitive and behavioral analysis. Pages 56–63 in L. Brochu, and M. Legg, eds., Proc. of the symposium: National interpreters workshop, Nov. 1–5, St. Louis, Mo. Assn. of Interpretive Naturalists and Western Interpreters Assn.

Jordan, P. A. 1987. Aquatic foraging and sodium ecology of moose: A review. *Swedish Wildlife Research Supplement* 1(1):119–37.

Jordan, P. A., D. B. Botkin, A. Dominski, H. Lowendorf, and G. E. Belovsky. 1973. Sodium as a critical nutrient for the moose of Isle Royale. *Trans. N. Amer. Moose Workshop:* 13–42.

Jordan, P. A., and W. Pitt. 1989. A survey for *Parelaphostrongylus tenuis* in the proposed caribou reintroduction site, Little Saganaga Lake area of the BWCAW, Minnesota. Final Rept. to the North Central Caribou Corp., Duluth. Dept. of Fisheries and Wildlife, Univ. of Minnesota.

Karl, T. R., R. R. Heim Jr., and R. G. Quayle. 1991. The greenhouse effect in central North America: If not now, when? *Science* 251:1058–61.

Karns, P. D. 1967a. The moose in northeastern Minnesota. *J. of Minn. Acad. of Science,* 34:(2)114–16.

———. 1967b. *Pneumostrongylus tenuis* in the white-tailed deer in Minnesota and its implications to moose. *J. Wildl. Mgt.,* 31:299–303.

Keith, L. B., and D. C. Surrendi. 1971. Effects of fire on a snowshoe hare population. *J. Wildl. Mgt.* 35:16–26.

Keith, L. B., and L. A. Windberg. 1978. A demographic analysis of the snowshoe hare cycle. *Wildl. Monogr.* 58:6–70.

Kilgore, B. M. 1987. The role of fire in wilderness: A state-of-knowledge review. Pages 70–103 in R. C. Lucas, compiler, Proc. of National Wilderness research conference: Issues, state-of-knowledge, future directions, July 1985, Ft. Collins, Colo. USDA, Forest Service Gen. Tech. Rept. INT-220.

Kilgore, B. M., and M. L. Heinselman. 1990. Fire in wilderness ecosystems. Pages 297–335 in J. C. Hendee, G. H. Stankey, and R. C. Lucas. *Wilderness management.* North American Press, Golden, Colo.

King, J. G. 1971. The effects of recreational use on water quality in the vicinity of campsites in the Boundary Waters Canoe Area. Master's thesis, School of Forestry, Univ. of Minnesota, St. Paul.

King, J. G., and A. C. Mace. 1974. Effects of recreation on water quality. *J. Water Pollution Control* 46:2453–59.

Kortright, F. H. 1943. *The ducks, geese and swans of North America.* American Wildlife Institute, Washington, D.C.

Krefting, L. W., and C. E. Ahlgren. 1974. Small mammals and vegetation changes after fire in a mixed conifer-hardwood forest. *Ecology* 55:1391–98.

Kuchler, A. W. 1966. Potential natural vegetation of the United States, including Alaska and Hawaii. Pages 89–92 in U.S. Dept. Interior, Geol. Survey, *National atlas of the U.S.,* color map, republ., 1978, by USDA, Forest Service, Washington, D.C.

Kuehnast, E. L., D. G. Baker, and J. A. Zandlo. 1982. *Duration and depth of snowcover.* Climate of Minnesota, Part XIII, Univ. of Minnesota Agric. Expt. Sta. Tech. Bull. 333.

Kurmis, V., H. L. Hansen, J. J. Olson, and A. R. Aho. 1978. *Vegetation types, species and areas of concern and forest resources utilization of northern Minnesota peatlands.* Minn. Dept. of Natural Resources. St. Paul, Minn.

Kurmis, V., L. C. Merriam, M. Grafstrom, and J. Kirwan. 1978. Primary plant communities of Voyageurs National Park, Rept. No. 1, Univ. of Minnesota, College of Forestry, Contract CX 6000-7-R020.

Lasko, R. 1991. Wilderness fire. *Boundary Waters Journal,* winter 1991: 15–17.

LeBarron, R. K. 1939. The role of forest fires in the reproduction of black spruce. *Proc. of Minn. Acad. of Science* 7:10–14.

———. 1944. Influence of controllable environmental conditions on regeneration of jack pine and black spruce. *Jour. of Agric. Res.* 68:97–119.

Lehman, N., A. Eisenhawer, K. Hansen, L. D. Mech, R. O. Peterson, P. Gogan, and R. K. Wayne. 1991. Introgression of coyote mitochondrial DNA into sympatric North American gray wolf populations. *Evolution* 45:104–19.

Lenius, B. J., and D. M. Olinyk. 1990. The Rainy River Composite: Revisions to Late Woodland taxonomy. Pages 77–112 in

G. E. Gibbon, ed., *The Woodland Tradition in the western Great Lakes: Papers presented to Elden Johnson.* Univ. of Minnesota Publications in Anthropology, no. 4.

Leopold, A. 1949. *A Sand County Almanac.* Oxford Univ. Press, New York.

Lewis, M. S. 1993. An exploration of backcountry encounter norms in the Boundary Waters Canoe Area Wilderness semiprimitive nonmotorized management zone. M.S. thesis, Univ. of Minnesota, Dept. of Forest Resources, St. Paul, Minn.

Lime, D. W. 1972. Large groups in the Boundary Waters Canoe Area: Their numbers, characteristics, and impact. U.S. Forest Service, North Central Forest Exp. Sta., Research Note NC-142.

———. 1975. Sources of congestion and visitor dissatisfaction in the Boundary Waters Canoe Area. Pages 68–82 in Proc., Quetico-Superior Foundation, Institute on the Boundary Waters Canoe Area, May 9, Duluth, Minn. Quetico-Superior Foundation, Minneapolis.

———. 1977. When the wilderness gets crowded . . . ? *Naturalist* 28(4):2–7.

———. 1990. *The 1988 visitor use study, Boundary Waters Canoe Area Wilderness, Superior National Forest, Minn.* Final Report, Univ. of Minnesota, College of Natural Resources.

———. 1991. *Procedures to monitor social conditions in the Boundary Waters Canoe Area Wilderness following the Limits of Acceptable Change (LAC) planning framework.* Technical Report to the USDA Forest Service, Superior National Forest. Univ. of Minnesota, Dept. of Forest Resources, St. Paul, Minn.

Lime, D. W., and M. S. Lewis. 1992. *Characteristics, use patterns perceptions and preferences of campers visiting the Boundary Waters Canoe Area Wilderness: Selected findings of a 1991 study.* Technical report to the Superior National Forest. Univ. of Minnesota, Dept. of Forest Resources, St. Paul, Minn.

Lime, D. W., and R. C. Lucas. 1977. Good information improves the wilderness experience. *Naturalist* 28(4):18–21.

Lime, D., C. Dybiec, J. Blaming, and D. Phelps. 1990. *1989 visitor use study: Boundary Waters Canoe Area Wilderness, Superior National Forest, Minnesota.* Univ. of Minnesota, Department of Forest Resources, St. Paul. Tech. Report for the Superior National Forest.

Lindeman, R. L. 1942. The trophic-dynamic aspect of ecology. *Ecology* 23:399–418.

Littlejohn, B. M. 1965. Quetico country. *Naturalist* 16(4):19–31.

Liu, Kam-bin. 1990. Holocene paleoecology of the boreal forest and Great Lakes–St. Lawrence forest in northern Ontario. *Ecol. Monogr.* 60:179–212.

Lodge, D. M., A. L. Beckel, and J. J. Magnuson. 1985. Lake-bottom tyrant. *Nature*, July 1985:33–36.

Longley, W. H., and J. B. Moyle. 1963. *The beaver in Minnesota.* Minn. Dept. of Conservation Tech. Bull. 6.

Loucks, O. L. 1970. Evolution of diversity, efficiency, and community stability. *Amer. Zoologist* 10:17–25.

Lucas, R. C. 1962. The Quetico-Superior area: Recreational use in relation to capacity. Ph.D. diss., Univ. of Minnesota.

———. 1964a. *The recreational use of the Quetico-Superior area.* Lake States Forest Exp. Sta., U.S. Forest Service, St. Paul, Minn., Res. Paper LS-8.

———. 1964b. *The recreational capacity of the Quetico-Superior area.* Lake States Forest Exp. Sta., U.S. Forest Service, St. Paul, Minn., Res. Paper LS-15.

———. 1964c. Wilderness perception and use: The example of the Boundary Waters Canoe Area. *Natural Resources Jour.* 3:394–411.

———. 1981. Redistributing wilderness use through information supplied to visitors. USDA, Forest Service Research Paper INT-277.

Lukens, P. W. 1963. Some ethnozoological implications of mammalian faunas from Minnesota archaeological sites. Ph.D. thesis, Univ. of Minnesota.

———. 1973. The vertebrate fauna from Pike Bay Mound, Smith Mound 4, and McKinstry Mound. Pages 37–45 in J. B. Stoltman, ed., *The Laurel Culture in Minnesota.* Minn. Prehistoric Archaeology Series no. 8, Minn. Historical Society, St. Paul.

MacLean, D. A., S. J. Woodley, M. G. Weber, and R. W. Wein. 1983. Fire and nutrient cycling. Pages 111–32 in R. W. Wein and D. A. MacLean, eds., *The role of fire in northern circumpolar ecosystems.* SCOPE. John Wiley, New York.

McAndrews, J. H. 1966. Postglacial history of prairie, savanna, and forest in northwestern Minnesota. *Memoirs of the Torry Botanical Club* 22(2):1–72.

McAvoy, L. H., C. Schatz, and D. W. Lime. 1991. Cooperation in resource management: A model planning process for promoting partnership between resource managers and private sector providers. *Journal of Park and Recreation Administration* 9(4):42–58.

McColl, J. G., and D. F. Grigal. 1975. Forest fire: Effects on phosphorus movement to lakes. *Science* 188:1109–11.

———. 1977. Nutrient changes following a forest wildfire in northeastern Minnesota: Effects in watersheds with differing soils. *Oikos* 28:105–12.

McCool, S. F., L. C. Merriam, and C. T. Cushwa. 1969. The condition of wilderness campsites in the Boundary Waters Canoe Area. Univ. of Minnesota School of Forestry, St. Paul, Forestry Res. Note 202.

McIntosh, R. P. 1981. Succession and ecological theory. Pages 10–23 in D. C. West, H. H. Shugart, and D. B. Botkin. *Forest succession, concepts and application.* Springer-Verlag, New York.

McIntyre, J. W. 1988. *The common loon, spirit of northern lakes.* Univ. of Minnesota Press, Minneapolis.

Marion, J. L. 1984. Ecological changes resulting from recreational use: A study of backcountry campsites in the Boundary Waters Canoe Area Wilderness, Minnesota. Ph.D. diss., Univ. of Minnesota, St. Paul.

———. 1991. *Results from the application of a campsite inventory and impact monitoring system in eleven Wilderness Areas of the Jefferson National Forest.* Final Report, U.S. Forest Service, Jefferson National Forest, and U.S. National Park Service.

Marion, J., D. Cole, and D. Reynolds. 1985. Limits of Acceptable Change: A frame work for assessing carrying capacity. *Park Science* 6(1):9–11.

Marion, J. L., and L. C. Merriam. 1985a. *Recreational impacts on well-established campsites in the Boundary Waters Canoe Area Wilderness.* Univ. of Minnesota Agric. Expt. Sta. Bull. AD-SB-2502.

———. 1985b. Predictability of recreational impact on soils. *Soil Science Society of America Journal* 49(3):751–53.

Marion, J. L., and T. Sober. 1987. Environmental impact management in a Wilderness Area. *Northern J. Applied Forestry* 4(1):7–10.

Marschner, F. J. [1930] 1974. The original vegetation of Minnesota (large-scale map in full color). U.S. Forest Service, North Central Forest Expt. Sta., St. Paul, Minn.

Martin, R. J., ed. 1934a. *Climatic summary of the United States, Section 46-Southeastern Minnesota.* USDA, Weather Bureau.

———. 1934b. *Climatic summary of the United States, Section 44-Northern Minnesota.* USDA, Weather Bureau.

Mech, L. D. 1966. *The wolves of Isle Royale.* U.S. National Park Service, Fauna of the National Parks Series 7, Washington, D.C.

———. 1970. *The wolf: The ecology and behavior of an endangered species.* Doubleday, New York.

———. 1973. *Wolf numbers in the Superior National Forest of Minnesota.* USDA, Forest Service Res. Paper NC-97.

———. 1977a. Wolf pack buffer zones as prey reservoirs. *Science* 198:320–21.

———. 1977b. Productivity, mortality, and population trends of wolves in northeastern Minnesota. *J. Mammalogy* 58:559–74.

———. 1977c. Record movement of a Canadian lynx. *J. Mammal.* 58:676–77.

———. 1980. Age, sex, reproduction, and spatial organization of lynxes colonizing northeastern Minnesota. *J. Mammal.* 61: 261–67.

———. 1986. *Wolf population in the central Superior National Forest, 1967–1985.* USDA, Forest Service Res. Paper NC-270.

———. 1987. Age, season, distance, direction, and social aspects of wolf dispersal from a Minnesota pack. Pages 55–74 in B. D. Chepko-Sade and Z. Halpin, eds., *Mammalian dispersal patterns.* Univ. of Chicago Press, Chicago.

———. 1991. *The way of the wolf.* Voyageur Press, Stillwater, Minn.

Mech, L. D., and P. D. Karns. 1977. *Role of the wolf in a deer decline in the Superior National Forest.* USDA, Forest Service Res. Pap. NC-148.

Mech, L. D., R. E. McRoberts, R. O. Peterson, and R. E. Page. 1987. Relationship of deer and moose populations to previous winters' snow. *J. Animal Ecology* 56:615–27.

Mech, L. D., and M. E. Nelson. 1990a. Non-family, *Canis lupus,* wolf packs. *Can. Field Naturalist.* 104:482–83.

———. 1990b. Evidence of prey-caused mortality in three wolves. *Amer. Midland Nat.* 123:207–8.

Mech, L. D., M. E. Nelson, and H. F. Drabik. 1982. Reoccurrence of caribou in Minnesota. *Amer. Midland Nat.* 108(1):206–8.

Mech, L. D., and L. L. Rogers. 1977. *Status, distribution, and movements of martens in northeastern Minnesota.* USDA, Forest Service Res. Paper NC-143.

Merriam, L. C., and C. K. Smith. 1974. Visitor impact on newly developed campsites in the Boundary Waters Canoe Area. *J. Forestry* 72:627–30.

Merriam, L. C., C. K. Smith, D. E. Miller, C. T. Huang, J. C. Tappeiner, K. Goeckermann, J. A. Bloemendal, and T. M. Costello. 1973. *Newly developed campsites in the Boundary Waters Canoe Area, a study of 5 years use.* Univ. of Minnesota Agric. Exp. Sta. Bull. 511, Forestry Series 14.

Minnesota Department of Health. n.d. Giardiasis in a tri-county area, 1982–1989. Table, acute disease epidemiology section of the Minn. Department of Health.

Minnesota Dept. of Health. 1989. *Minnesota fish consumption advisory.* Minn. Dept. of Health, Minneapolis.

Minnesota Department of Natural Resources. 1990. *Fishing guide to the lakes and streams of Lake County.* Minn. Dept. of Natural Resources and Lake Co. Recreation Board.

Minnesota Pollution Control Agency. 1985. Statement of need and reasonableness, re Proposed Acid Deposition Control Plan (SONAR). Minn. Pollution Control Agency, St. Paul.

Mooney, H. A., B. G. Drake, R. J. Luxmoore, W. C. Oechel, and L. F. Pitelka. 1991. Predicting ecosystem responses to elevated CO_2 concentrations. *Bioscience* 41:96–104.

Moore, J. M., and R. W. Wein. 1977. Viable seed populations by soil depth and potential site recolonization after disturbance. *Can. J. Bot.* 55:2408–12.

Morey, G. B. 1969. *The geology of the middle Precambrian Rove Formation in northeastern Minnesota.* University of Minnesota, Minneapolis.

Morse, E. W. 1962. Canoe routes of the voyageurs: The geography and logistics of the Canadian fur trade. Quetico Foundation and Minn. Historical Society, Toronto and St. Paul.

Mutch, R. W. 1970. Wildland fires and ecosystems: A hypothesis. *Ecology* 51:1046–51.

Naiman, R. J., J. M. Melillo, and J. E. Hobbie. 1986. Ecosystem alteration of boreal forest streams by beaver (*Castor canadensis*). *Ecology* 67:1254–69.

National Fish and Wildlife Foundation. 1991. The neotropical bird conservation program: Partners in Flight. 1st report, vol. 1, no. 1.

Nelson, D. 1989. Sponges of the BWCAW. *Boundary Waters Journal* 3(2):56–61.

Nelson, M. E. 1990. Gene flow, effective population size, and genetic population structure in white-tailed deer (*Odocoileus virginianus*) in northeastern Minnesota. Ph.D. diss., Univ. of Minnesota.

Nelson, M. E., and L. D. Mech. 1981. Deer social organization and wolf predation in northeastern Minnesota. *Wildlife Monogr.* no. 77.

———. 1985. Observation of a wolf killed by a deer. *J. Mammal.* 66:187–88.

———. 1986a. Mortality of white-tailed deer in northeastern Minnesota. *J. Wildl. Mgt.* 50:691–98.

———. 1986b. *Deer population in the central Superior National Forest, 1967–1985.* USDA, Forest Service Res. Paper NC-271.

———. 1987. Demes within a northeastern Minnesota deer population. Pages 27–40 in B. D. Cepko-Sade and Z. Halpin, eds., *Mammalian dispersal patterns.* Univ. of Chicago Press, Chicago.

———. 1991. Wolf predation risk associated with white-tailed deer movements. *Can. J. Zool.* 69(10):2696–99.

Nicholls, T. H. 1990. *Habitat requirements of migratory birds.* Study plan summary, North Central For. Expt. Sta., U.S. Forest Service, Study FS-NC-4202 90-01.

Nicholls, T. H., and M. R. Fuller. 1987. Territorial aspects of Barred Owl home range and behavior in Minnesota. Pages 121–28 in R. W. Nero et al., Proc. of Symposium, *Biology and conservation of northern forest owls,* Feb. 3–7, 1987, Winnipeg, Man. USDA, Forest Service Gen. Tech. Rept. RM-142.

Niemi, G.J. 1978. Breeding birds of burned and unburned areas in northern Minnesota. *The Loon,* summer 1978: 73–83.

Niemi, G. J., J. M. Hanowski, T. H. Nicholls, and M. Fuller. 1991. *Monitoring bird populations on National Forest lands.* Study plan summary, North Central For. Expt. Sta., U.S. Forest Service, Study FS-NC-4202 91-02, Coop. Aid. 23-91-16.

Noble, I. R., and R. O. Slatyer. 1977. Post fire succession of plants in Mediterranean ecosystems. Pages 27–36 in H. A. Mooney and C. E. Conrad, eds., Proc. of symposium on the environmental consequences of fire and fuel management in Mediterranean ecosystems. USDA, Forest Service Gen. Tech. Rept. WO-3.

Nute, G. L. 1941. *The Voyageur's Highway.* Minn. Historical Society, St. Paul.

————. 1955. *The voyageur*. Minn. Historical Society, St. Paul.

Odum, E. P. 1971. *Fundamentals of ecology*. 3d ed. Saunders, Philadelphia, Penn.

Ohmann, L. F., and D. F. Grigal. 1979. Early revegetation and nutrient dynamics following the 1971 Little Sioux forest fire in northeastern Minnesota. *Forest Science Monograph* 21.

————. 1985. *Plant species biomass estimates for 13 upland community types of northeastern Minnesota*. USDA, Forest Service Resource Bull. NC-88.

Ohmann, L. F., and R. R. Ream. 1971. Wilderness ecology: Virgin plant communities of the Boundary Waters Canoe Area. U.S. Forest Service Res. Paper NC-63.

Ojakangas, R. W., and C. L. Matsch. 1982. *Minnesota's geology*. Univ. of Minnesota Press, Minneapolis.

Olson, S. F. 1938a. Organization and range of the pack. *Ecology* 19: 168–70.

————. 1938b. A study in predatory relationship with particular reference to the wolf. *Sci. Monthly* 46:323–36.

————. 1957. *The singing wilderness*. Alfred Knopf, New York.

————. 1961. *The lonely land*. Alfred Knopf, New York.

Olson, S. T., and W. H. Marshall. 1952. *The Common Loon in Minnesota*. Minn. Museum of Nat. Hist. Occas. Paper 5. Univ. of Minnesota Press, Minneapolis.

Ontario Ministry of Natural Resources. 1977. Surficial geology. Pages 7–11 in Quetico Provincial Park Master Plan.

————. 1992. Quetico Provincial Park Lac La Croix amendment proposal. Ontario Ministry of Natural Resources.

Ostry, M. E., T. H. Nicholls, and D. W. French. 1983. Animal vectors of eastern dwarf mistletoe of black spruce. USDA, Forest Service Research Paper NC-232.

Overpeck, J. T., P. J. Bartlein, and T. Webb III. 1991. Potential magnitudes of future vegetation change in eastern North America: Comparisons with the past. *Science* 254:692–95.

Pastor, J., and W. M. Post. 1988. Response of northern forests to CO_2-induced climate change. *Nature* 334:55–58.

Peek, J. M. 1971. Moose habitat selection and relationships to forest management in northeastern Minnesota. Ph.D. thesis, Univ. of Minnesota.

————. 1974. Initial response of moose to a forest fire in northern Minnesota. *Amer. Midland Nat.* 91:435–38.

Peterson, G. L. 1977. The computer takes a canoe trip. *Naturalist* 28(4):9–11.

Peterson, R. T. 1980. *A field guide to the birds*. Houghton Mifflin, Boston.

Phillips, G. L., W. D. Schmid, and J. C. Underhill. 1982. *Fishes of the Minnesota region*. Univ. of Minnesota Press.

Pickett, S. T. A., and P. S. White, eds. 1985. *The ecology of natural disturbance and patch dynamics*. Academic Press, Orlando, Fla.

Pitt, W. C., and P. A. Jordan. 1991. A survey for *Parelaphostrongylus tenuis* in the region of a proposed caribou reintroduction site. Final Report for 1990 to the North Central Caribou Corp., Dept. of Fisheries and Wildlife, Univ. of Minnesota.

Place, I. C. M. 1955. *The influence of seedbed conditions in the regeneration of spruce and balsam fir*. Canada Dept. North. Affairs and Nat. Resources, Forestry Branch Bull. 117.

Powell, R. A. 1972. A comparison of populations of boreal red-backed vole (*Clethrionomys gapperi*) in tornado blowdown and standing forest. *Can. Field-Nat.* 86:377–79.

————. 1982. *The fisher: Life history, ecology, and behavior*. Univ. of Minnesota Press, Minneapolis.

Rapp, G. Jr., J. D. Allert, and G. R. Peters. 1990. The origins of copper in three northern Minnesota sites: Pauley, River Point, and Big Rice. Pages 233–38 in G. E. Gibbon, ed., *The Woodland Tradition in the western Great Lakes: Papers presented to Elden Johnson*. Univ. of Minnesota Publications in Anthropology, no. 4.

Ramanathan, V. 1988. The greenhouse theory of climate change: A test by an inadvertent global experiment. *Science* 240:293–99.

Robbins, C. S., B. Bruun, and H. S. Zim. 1966. *Birds of North America: A guide to field identification*. Golden Press, New York.

Robbins, C. S., J. R. Sauer, R. S. Greenberg, and S. Droege. 1989. Population declines in North American birds that migrate to the neotropics. *Proc. Natl. Acad. Sci.* 86:7658–62.

Roberts, M. K. 1988. Acid rain regulation: Federal failure and state success. *Virginia Jour. of Natural Resources Law* 8(1):1–74.

Rogers, L. L. 1976. Effects of mast and berry crop failures on survival, growth, and reproductive success of black bears. *Trans. 41st North Amer. Wildl. and Natural Res. Confer.*:431–38.

————. 1977a. The ubiquitous American black bear. Pages 28–33 in W. H. Nesbitt and J. S. Parker, eds., *North American Big Game*. The Boone and Crockett Club and National Rifle Assn., Washington, D.C.

————. 1977b. Social relationships, movements, and population dynamics of black bears in northeastern Minnesota. Ph.D. thesis, Univ. of Minnesota.

————. 1978. Effects of food supply, predation, cannibalism, parasites, and other health problems on black bear populations. Pages 194–211 in Proc. of symposium on natural regulation of wildlife populations, Vancouver, B.C., March 10, 1978.

————. 1980. Inheritance of coat color and changes in pelage coloration in black bears in northern Minnesota. *J. Mammal.* 61:324–27.

————. 1981. A bear in its lair. *Natural History* 90:64–70.

————. 1987. Boundary Waters bears. BWCA *Wilderness News* (newsletter of Friends of the Boundary Waters Wilderness) spring/summer:10–11.

————. 1991. Are white pines too valuable to cut? *Minnesota Volunteer* Sept./Oct.:8–21.

Rogers, L. L., L. D. Mech, D. K. Dawson, J. M. Peek, and M. Korb. 1980. Deer distribution in relation to wolf pack territory edges. *J. Wildl. Mgt.* 44:253–58.

Romme, W. H. 1982. Fire and landscape diversity in subalpine forests of Yellowstone National Park. *Ecol. Monogr.* 52:199–221.

Romme, W. H., and D. G. Despain. 1989. Historical perspectives on the Yellowstone fires of 1988. *Bioscience* 39:695–99.

Roussopoulos, P. J. 1978. A decision aid for wilderness fire prescriptions in the Boundary Waters Canoe Area. Pages 52–58 in Proc., Fifth joint conference on fire and forest meteorology, Amer. Meteorological Society, Boston.

Rowe, J. S. 1972. *Forest regions of Canada*. Can. Dept. of Environment, Can. Forest Service Publ. 1300.

————. 1983. Concepts of fire effects on plant species and individuals. Pages 135–54 in R. W. Wein and D. A. MacLean, eds., *The role of fire in northern circumpolar ecosystems*. SCOPE, John Wiley, New York.

Russell, E. B. 1983. Indian-set fires in the forests of the northeastern United States. *Ecology* 64:78–88.

Rusterholz, K. A. 1973. Island bird communities on Burntside Lake, Minnesota. M.S. thesis, Univ. of Minnesota.

Sando, R. J. 1969. *Prescribed burning weather in Minnesota*. USDA, Forest Service Research Paper NC-28.

Sando, R. J., and D. A. Haines. 1972. *Fire weather and behavior of the Little Sioux fire.* USDA, Forest Service Res. Paper. NC-76.

Sando, R. J., and C. H. Wick. 1972. *A method of evaluating crown fuels in forest stands.* USDA, Forest Service Res. Paper NC-84.

Schindler, D. W., K. G. Beaty, E. J. Fee, D. R. Cruikshank, E. R. DeBruyn, D. L. Findlay, G. A. Linsey, J. A. Shearer, M. P. Stainton, and M. A. Turner. 1990. Effects of climatic warming on lakes of the central boreal forest. *Science* 250:967–70.

Schindler, D. W., K. H. Mills, D. F. Malley, D. L. Findlay, J. A. Schearer, I. J. Davies, M. A. Turner, G. A. Linsey, and D. R. Cruikshank. 1985. Long-term effects of years of experimental acidification on a small lake. *Science* 228:1395–1401.

Schofield, C. F. 1976. Effects of acid precipitation on fish. *Ambio* 5:228–30.

Schomaker, P. J. 1990. Off-site visitor education in the Boundary Waters Canoe Area Wilderness: The BWCAW user education program. Pages 142–47 in D. W. Lime, ed., *Managing America's wilderness resource,* Proc. of the conference, Minneapolis, Minn., Sept. 11–17, Minn. Extension Service, and Minn. Agric. Expt. Sta., Univ. of Minnesota, St. Paul.

Scott, W. B., and E. J. Crossman. 1973. *Freshwater fishes of Canada.* Fisheries Res. Board of Canada Bull. 184.

Searle, R. N. 1977. *Saving Quetico-Superior: A land set apart.* Minn. Historical Society, St Paul.

Shay, C. T. 1971. *The Itasca bison kill site: An ecological analysis.* Minn. Historical Society, St. Paul.

———. 1990. Perspectives on the late prehistory of the northeastern plains. Pages 113–33 in G. E. Gibbon, ed., *The Woodland Tradition in the western Great Lakes: Papers presented to Elden Johnson.* Univ. of Minnesota Publications in Anthropology, no. 4.

Shugart, H. H., and D. C. West. 1981. Long-term dynamics of forest ecosystems. *Am. Sci.* 69:647–52.

Siderits, K. P. 1981. *Mammals of the Superior National Forest.* U.S. Forest Service, Superior National Forest, Duluth, Minn.

Soderberg, B. A. 1987. Canoes, computers, and cooperation, or high tech tranquility in Minnesota's Boundary Waters Canoe Area Wilderness. Paper presented to the World Wilderness Conference, Sept. 12–18, 1987, Estes Park, Colo.

Southwick, D. L., and P. W. Weiblen. 1971. Geologic history of the Boundary Waters Canoe Area. *Naturalist* 22(4):24–32.

Spofford, W. O. Jr. 1986. Giardiasis: A return of waterbourne disease? *Resources* (Resources for the Future), spring 1986:5–9.

Stankey, G. H. 1973. Visitor perception of wilderness recreation carrying capacity. U.S. Forest Service Research Paper INT 142.

Stankey, G. H., D. N. Cole, R. C. Lucas, M. E. Petersen, and S. S. Frissell. 1985. The Limits of Acceptable Change (LAC) system for wilderness planning. U.S. Forest Service Gen. Tech. Rept. INT-176.

Stankey, G. H., S. F. McCool, and G. L. Stokes. 1990. Managing for appropriate wilderness conditions: The carrying capacity issue. Pages 214–39 in J. C. Hendee, G. H. Stankey, and R. C. Lucas, *Wilderness management.* North American Press, Golden, Colo.

Steinbring, J. 1974. The preceramic archaeology of northern Minnesota. Pages 64–73 in E. Johnson, ed., *Aspects of Upper Great Lakes anthropology.* Minn. Prehistoric Archaeology Series no. 11. Minn. Historical Society, St. Paul.

Stenlund, M. 1986. Burntside Lake—The early years 1880–1920. Ely-Winton Historical Society, Ely, Minn.

Stenlund, M. H. 1955. *A field study of the timber wolf (Canis lupus) on the Superior National Forest, Minnesota.* Minn. Dept. of Conservation Tech. Bull. 4.

Stocks, B. J. 1975. The 1974 wildfire situation in northwestern Ontario. Can. Forest Service, Great Lakes Forest Research Centre, Sault Ste. Marie, Ont., Rept. O-X-232.

———. 1987a. Fire behavior in immature jack pine. *Can. J. For. Res.* 17:80–86.

———. 1987b. Fire potential in the spruce budworm-damaged forests of Ontario. *Forestry Chronicle* 73:8–14.

———. 1989. Fire behavior in mature jack pine. *Can. J. For. Res.* 19:783–90.

Stoltman, J. B. 1973. *The Laurel Culture in Minnesota.* Minn. Prehistoric Archaeology Series no. 8, Minn. Historical Society, St. Paul.

Stuiver, M. 1971. Evidence for the variation of atmospheric C-14 content in the Late Quaternary. Pages 57–70 in K. K. Turekian, ed., *Late Cenozoic Glacial Ages.* Yale Univ. Press, New Haven, Conn.

———. 1975. Climate versus changes in C-14 content of the organic component of lake sediments during the Late Quaternary. *Quaternary Research* 5:251–62.

Swain, A. M. 1973. A history of fire and vegetation in northeastern Minnesota as recorded in lake sediments. *Quaternary Research* 3:383–96.

Swain, E. B. 1989. *Assessment of mercury contamination in selected Minnesota lakes and streams.* Executive summary, Report to the Legislative Commission on Minn. Resources, Minn. Pollution Control Agency, St. Paul.

Swain, E. B., and D. D. Helwig. 1989. Mercury in fish from northeastern Minnesota lakes: Historical trends, environmental correlates, and potential sources. *J. of Minn. Acad. Sci.* 55(1):103–9.

Telfer, E. S., and J. P. Kelsall. 1984. Adaptation of some large North American mammals for survival in snow. *Ecology* 65:1828–34.

Terborgh, J. 1989. *Where have all the birds gone?* Princeton Univ. Press, Princeton, N.J.

Terres, J. K. 1980. *The Audubon Society encyclopedia of North American Birds.* Alfred Knopf, New York.

Thornton, J. D., R. D. Payer, and J. Matta. 1982. *Acid precipitation in Minnesota.* Report to the Legislative Commission on Minnesota Resources, Minn. Pollution Control Agency, Minn. Dept. of Natural Resources, and Minn. Dept. of Health, St. Paul.

Timber Producers Association. 1971. End is near for Lake Superior rafts. *Timber Producers Association Bulletin* 26:8–10.

Titus, J., and L. Van Druff. 1981. Response of the Common Loon to recreational pressure in the Boundary Waters Canoe Area, northeastern Minnesota. *Wildlife Monogr.* 79.

Treuer, R. 1979. *Voyageur country: A park in the wilderness.* Univ. of Minnesota Press, Minneapolis.

Trippel, E. A., and F. W. Beamish. 1989. Lake trout growth potential predicted from cisco population structure and conductivity. *Can. J. Fish. Aquat. Sci.* 46:1531–38.

Trygg, J. W., comp. 1966. General description and other comments. Abstracts from U.S. land surveyors' original field notes in northeastern Minnesota.

Turner, M. G. 1989. Landscape ecology: The effect of pattern on process. *Ann. Review of Ecol. and Systematics.* 20:171–97.

Turner, M. G., and W. H. Romme. 1994. Landscape dynamics in crown fire ecosystems. *Landscape Ecology* 19(1):59–77.

324

Urban, D. L., R. V. O'Neill, and H. H. Shugart. 1987. Landscape ecology. *Bioscience* 37:119–27.

U.S. Dept. of Agriculture. 1941. *Climate and man*. U.S. Dept. of Agriculture Yearbook. U.S. Government Printing Office, Washington, D.C.

U.S. Forest Service. 1948. *Plan of management: Superior Roadless Areas*. Superior National Forest, Duluth, Minn.

———. 1969. *BWCA management handbook*. Superior National Forest, U.S. Department of Agriculture Eastern Region.

———. 1974. *Boundary Waters Canoe Area Management Plan and Environmental Statement*. Superior National Forest, Duluth, Minn.

———. 1991a. *Fire management action plan*. Superior National Forest, Duluth, Minn.

———. 1991b. *1990 monitoring and evaluation report*. Superior National Forest, Duluth, Minn.

U.S. Public Law 80-733, 80th Congress, June 22, 1948. *Thye-Blatnik Act*.

U.S. Public Law 88-577, 88th Congress, Sept. 3, 1964. *Wilderness Act*.

U.S. Public Law 95-495, 95th Congress, Oct. 15, 1978. *BWCA Wilderness Act*.

Van Cleve, K., and L. A. Viereck. 1981. Forest succession in relation to nutrient cycling in the boreal forest of Alaska. Pages 185–211 in D. C. West, H. H. Shugart, and D. B. Botkin, eds., *Forest succession, concepts and application*. Springer-Verlag, New York.

Van Wagner, C. E. 1977. Conditions for the start and spread of crown fires. *Can. J. For. Res.* 7:23–34.

———. 1978. Age class distribution and the forest fire cycle. *Can. J. For. Res.* 8:220–27.

———. 1983. Fire behavior in northern conifer forests and shrublands. Pages 65–80 in R. W. Wein and D. A. MacLean, eds., *The role of fire in northern circumpolar ecosystems*. SCOPE, John Wiley, New York.

———. 1987. *Development and structure of the Canadian Forest Fire Weather Index System*. Can. Forest Service For. Tech. Rep. No. 35.

Viereck, L. A. 1983. The effects of fire in black spruce ecosystems of Alaska and northern Canada. Pages 201–20 in R. W. Wein and D. A. MacLean, eds., *The role of fire in northern circumpolar ecosystems*. SCOPE, John Wiley, New York.

Voyageurs National Park. 1989. *Wildland fire management plan*. U.S. Dept. of Interior, Voyageurs National Park, International Falls, Minn.

Walshe, S. 1980. *Plants of Quetico and the Ontario Shield*. Univ. of Toronto Press, Toronto.

———. 1984. *Saga of the Quetico Superior wilderness—1909–1984: 75 years of international cooperation*. S. Walshe assisted by S. Peraniak. Ontario Ministry of Natural Resources.

Waters, T. F. 1987. *The Superior North Shore*. Univ. of Minnesota Press, Minneapolis.

Watson, B. F. 1974. *Minnesota weather almanac*. Bolger Press, Minneapolis.

West, F. H. 1983. The antiquity of man in America. Pages 364–82 in S. C. Porter, ed., *Late-Quaternary environments of the United States*, vol. 1, *The Late Pleistocene*, Univ. of Minnesota Press, Minneapolis.

Wheeler, R. C., W. A. Kenyon, A. R. Woolworth, and D. A. Birk. 1975. *Voices from the rapids: An underwater search for fur trade artifacts, 1960–1973*. Minn. Historical Society, St. Paul.

White, J. W., comp. 1974. *Historical sketches of the Quetico-Superior*. vol. XI.

Wiens, J. A. 1975. Avian communities, energetics, and functions in coniferous forest habitats. In D. Smith, ed., Proc. of symposium on management of forest and range habitats for nongame birds. USDA, Forest Service Gen. Tech. Rept. WO-1.

Wilcove, D. 1990. Empty skies. *Nature Conservancy* 40(1):4–13.

Williams, G. 1983. The Hudson's Bay Company and the fur trade: 1670–1870. *The Beaver*, special issue, autumn 1983.

Wilson, F. 1977. Quetico Provincial Park. *Naturalist* 28(4):12–15.

Wilton, W. C. 1963. Black spruce seedfall immediately following fire. *Forestry Chronicle* 39:477–78.

Wolfe, R. R., R. A. Nelson, M. H. Wolfe, and L. L. Rogers. 1982. Nitrogen cycling in hibernating bears. *Proc. Amer. Soc. Mass Spectroscopy* 30:426.

Wolff, J., Jr. 1958. Forest fires of the Sawbill country. Typed manuscript in the author's files.

Woods, G. T., and R. J. Day. 1977. *A summary of the fire ecology study of Quetico Provincial Park*. Ontario Ministry of Natural Resources, Atikokan District, Fire Ecology Study, Report no. 8.

Wright, H. E. Jr. 1972. Quaternary history of Minnesota. Pages 515–47 in P.K. Sims and G. B. Morey, eds., *Geology of Minnesota: A Centennial Volume*. Minn. Geol. Survey, St. Paul.

———. 1974. Landscape development, forest fires, and wilderness management. *Science* 186:487–95.

———. 1976. Ice retreat and revegetation in the western Great Lakes area. Pages 119–32 in W. C. Mahney, ed., *Quaternary stratigraphy of North America*. Dowden, Hutchinson, and Ross, Stroudsburg, Penn.

———. 1981. The role of fire in land/water interactions. Pages 421–44 in H. A. Mooney, T. M. Bonnicksen, N. L. Christensen, J. E. Lotan, and W. A. Reiners, coordinators, *Fire regimes and ecosystem properties*. Proc. of conference, Honolulu, Hawaii, 1978. USDA, Forest Service Gen. Tech. Rept. WO-26.

———. 1989. The amphi-Atlantic distribution of the Younger Dryas paleoclimatic oscillation. *Quaternary Science Reviews* 8:295–306.

Wright, R. F. 1976. The impact of forest fire on the nutrient influxes to small lakes in northeastern Minnesota. *Ecology* 57:649–63.

Zasada, J. C. 1971. Natural regeneration of interior Alaska forests: Seedbed and vegetative reproduction considerations. Pages 231–46 in Proc., *Fire in the northern environment: A symposium*, Fairbanks, Ala. USDA, Forest Service, Pacific NW Forest Exper. Sta., Portland, Oreg.

Zoltai, S. C. 1961. Glacial history of part of northwestern Ontario. *Proc. Geol. Assoc. Can.* 13: 61.

Zoltai, S. C. 1965. Glacial features of the Quetico-Nipigon area. *Can. J. Earth Sciences* 2:247–69.

Zumberge, J. H. 1952. *The lakes of Minnesota, their origin and classification*. Univ. of Minnesota Press, Minneapolis.

Index

Compiled by Doug Easton

DR. MIRON HEINSELMAN (1920–93) was born in Duluth, Minnesota. He received the bachelor of arts from the University of Minnesota in 1942. After serving in the U.S. Army during World War II, he returned to the University of Minnesota to obtain the bachelor of science in forestry in 1948 and the master of science in forestry in 1951. His career as a research scientist in forest ecology with the U.S. Forest Service began in Rhinelander, Wisconsin, in 1948 at the Lake States Forest Experiment Station (now the North Central Forest Experiment Station). In 1951 he transferred to the Grand Rapids, Minnesota, field station, where he conducted silvicultural studies in the management of quaking aspen, pine, and peatland black spruce. Research into the factors determining forest site quality on peatlands and in basic peatland ecology, begun in 1954, became the subject of his doctoral dissertation. He received the Ph.D. degree from the University of Minnesota in 1961. While at Grand Rapids, Dr. Heinselman also initiated studies in the use of prescribed fire in the natural regeneration of black spruce on peatland sites. In 1966 he transferred to the North Central Forest Experiment Station in St. Paul as principal plant ecologist. From 1966 through 1974, his research involved the location and mapping of the remaining virgin forests of the million-acre Boundary Waters Canoe Area, work that demonstrated that virtually all existing virgin stands owe their origin to past forest fires, and that led to his mapping of the present mosaic of postfire stands by fire years. In 1974 Dr. Heinselman retired from the U.S. Forest Service. He was also an adjunct professor in the Department of Ecology and Behavioral Biology at the University of Minnesota until his retirement in 1974. He continued his research and writing in forest ecology after his retirement.

From 1960 Dr. Heinselman was active in local and national environmental work, particularly in the conservation of scientific and natural areas, wilderness areas, national parks, and similar ecological reserves. From 1976 to 1978, he was chair of the Friends of the Boundary Waters Wilderness, a coalition of national and local environmental organizations formed to obtain federal legislation, passed in 1978, to protect the Boundary Waters Canoe Area from logging, mining, and mechanized recreational activities. Dr. Heinselman later served as chair emeritus of the Friends of the Boundary Waters Wilderness.

In 1977 Dr. Heinselman received the National Academy of Science's Cottrell Award for Research Contributions in Environmental Quality, the American Motors Conservation Award, and a distinguished conservationist award from the Minnesota division of the Izaak Walton League of America. In 1978 he received the Minneapolis Jaycees Dr. Robert G. Green Conservation Award and several additional environmental awards.

Dr. Heinselman married Frances Ruth Brown in 1942. Frances frequently assisted him in field research and also served as his secretary. They have a son, Russell, and a daughter, Ann Heinselman Stolee, both graduates of the University of Minnesota, and two grandchildren.

H. E. WRIGHT JR. is Regents' Professor Emeritus of Geology, Ecology, and Botany and past director of the Limnological Research Center at the University of Minnesota.

The Boundary Waters Wilderness Ecosystem

Typefaces	Adobe Garamond
	Stone Sans
Design & composition	The Art Dept.
	Manhattan, Montana
Paper	Sterling Satin
Printing & binding	Edwards Brothers
	Ann Arbor, Michigan

COLOR SECTION

Separations & prepress	Pettit Network
	Afton, Minnesota
Paper	Warren Lustro Gloss
Printing	Litho Technical Services
	Bloomington, Minnesota